Nationality Matters
Statelessness under International Law

To Mark

SCHOOL OF HUMAN RIGHTS RESEARCH SERIES, Volume 29

The titles published in this series are listed at the end of this volume.

Nationality Matters
Statelessness under International Law

Laura van Waas

intersentia

Antwerp – Oxford – Portland

Cover: Picture by Sarah Hayward

Laura van Waas
Nationality Matters. Statelessness under International Law

ISBN 978-90-5095-854-7
D/2008/7849/95
NUR 828

ACKNOWLEDGEMENTS

I am writing this on the day that I acquire Dutch nationality. It wasn't planned that way, but it is a thought-provoking coincidence. After I attend the "naturalisation ceremony" this afternoon (i.e. share cheese and wine with a local civil servant and the other aspirant-Dutchies), I will be a dual national. British and Dutch. And I cannot deny that this moment has gained added significance thanks to the understanding that I now have of the value of citizenship. As you can see, the PhD manuscript to which I have just put the finishing touches is on statelessness. An entire study devoted to those who have not two nationalities, not even one, but none.

Statelessness is a fascinating anomoly - the idea that a person can be denied membership of every one of the world's states, cast into an officially-sanctioned, legal limbo is somehow incredible. It is a phenomenon that readily captures both the imagination and the heart. My own first encounter with statelessness certainly raised many questions, like how does statelessness come about, how does it impact people's lives and what are we doing to tackle it? It is a good thing that I found (and still find) the topic so compelling because it meant that these and other questions kept me very happily occupied for the last four years.

I feel very privileged to have had the opportunity to devote so much time to what really began as a personal interest. This would not have been possible without my supervisor, Willem van Genugten, putting his faith in my ability to turn my personal interest into a worthy academic study. His unrelinquishing encouragement helped me to keep up the momentum in my research and gave me the confidence to take on all sorts of other activities alongside working on my manuscript. I would also like to thank my second supervisor, Helen Oosterom, for her enthusiasm for my research and her continuing willingness to discuss trouble spots and comment on draft texts. I am indebted to the further members of the reading committee, Cees Flinterman, Pieter Boeles and Anton van Kalmthout, for taking the time to read and assess this sturdy document. And I would like to thank my sister, Sarah Hayward, for crafting the perfect cover illustration to accompany my manuscript.

The last four years were made all the more enjoyable by two things: the fact that I was able to participate in several practical projects to satisfy my idealistic drive and all of the fun that I have had with both colleagues and friends. I owe a real debt of gratitude to Philippe Leclerc and Mark Manly of UNHCR, as well as Simon Heap of Plan International, for allowing me to get involved in the "real world" of statelessness. This offered me insights that I would not have gained purely within the academic setting and gave me great satisfaction. Then to all the kind and committed people who I have had the privilege to work with through Books 4 Life over the years – thank you, you have been a true inspiration. Please keep up the fabulous work.

So I come to those colleagues with whom I have shared so many cups of tea, slices of cake, beers and laughs with. There is nothing that boosts your morale quite like "melige woensdag" or a spontaneous trip to the Efteling. Jeroen, Christophe, Vera, Tamara, Nicola, Conny and Femke – you have kept me sane in this otherwise oh-so-lonely profession, thanks. Thank yous also to those friends outside of work who have added so much colour to my life; to my parents, for many things, among which their winning decision to ensure that English is my mother tongue - it has been a real help; and of course Mark, who makes me smile and laugh most of all and with whom I cannot wait to embark on the next adventure.

Laura van Waas
20 August 2008

TABLE OF CONTENTS

Acknowledgements v

Table of contents vii

PART 1 WHY STATELESSNESS?

CHAPTER I
NATIONALITY MATTERS: AN INTRODUCTION **3**

1 Research questions 4
2 Research approach 4

CHAPTER II
THE STATELESSNESS PHENOMONON AND A FIRST ENCOUNTER WITH THE INTERNATIONAL RESPONSE **7**

1 Discovering statelessness 7
2 The worldwide severity of statelessness: magnitude and consequences 9
3 The international response to statelessness 15
4 A first concrete dilemma: defining statelessness 19
5 Conclusion: why statelessness? 27

PART 2 PREVENTING STATELESSNESS

CHAPTER III
BACKGROUND TO PREVENTING STATELESSNESS **31**

1 The attribution of nationality: doctrines and competences 31
2 International law and the attribution of nationality 36
3 The 1961 Convention on the Reduction of Statelessness 40
4 Purpose and method of part 2 47

CHAPTER IV
ADDRESSING THE TECHNICAL CAUSES OF STATELESSNESS **49**

1 Jus sanguinis versus jus soli 50
 1.1 1961 Convention
 1.2 International human rights law
2 Abandoned and orphaned children 68

2.1 1961 Convention
2.2 International human rights law
3 Marriage (or divorce) and adoption 71
3.1 1961 Convention
3.2 International human rights law
4 Loss, deprivation or renunciation of nationality 78
4.1 1961 Convention
4.2 International human rights law
5 Conclusion 88

CHAPTER V
ADDRESSING STATELESSNESS RESULTING FROM THE ARBITRARY DEPRIVATION OF NATIONALITY **93**

1 Discriminatory deprivation of nationality and "denial of citizenship" 95
1.1 1961 Convention
1.2 International human rights law
2 Illegal deprivation of nationality and the lack of due process 113
2.1 1961 Convention
2.2 International human rights law
3 Conclusion 118

CHAPTER VI
ADDRESSING STATELESSNESS IN THE CONTEXT OF STATE SUCCESSION **121**

1 State succession and the nationality of persons affected 123
2 1961 Convention 130
3 International (human rights) law 134
4 Conclusion 145

CHAPTER VII
ADDRESSING THE "NEW" CAUSES OF STATELESSNESS **151**

1 Birth and marriage registration 153
1.1 Connecting statelessness to (deficient) birth and marriage registration
1.2 International human rights law
2 Migration 163
2.1 Irregular migration
2.1.1 Connecting statelessness to irregular migration
2.1.2 International human rights law
2.2 Trafficking in human beings and refugee situations
2.2.1 Connecting statelessness to trafficking and refugee situations
2.2.2 International human rights law
3 Conclusion 187

CHAPTER VIII
INTERNATIONAL LAW AND THE PREVENTION OF STATELESSNESS **193**

1 The value of the 1961 Convention on the Reduction of Statelessness in the prevention of statelessness 194
2 The role of international (human rights) law in the prevention of statelessness 198
3 Normative gaps in the prevention of statelessness under international law and suggested remedies 201
4 Prospects for the implementation and enforcement of norms for the prevention of statelessness 205
5 Conclusion 212

PART 3 PROTECTING STATELESS PERSONS

CHAPTER IX
BACKGROUND TO PROTECTING STATELESS PERSONS **217**

1 The substance of nationality: rights and duties 217
2 International law and the substance of nationality 220
3 The 1954 Convention relating to the Status of Stateless Persons 225
4 Purpose and method of part 3 233

CHAPTER X
PROTECTING THE CIVIL AND POLITICAL RIGHTS OF STATELESS PERSONS **235**

1 Non-nationals, non-discrimination and the enjoyment of civil and political rights 236
2 Freedom of movement 240
2.1 Internal freedom of movement
2.1.1 1954 Convention
2.1.2 International human rights law
2.2 International freedom of movement
2.2.1 1954 Convention
2.2.2 International human rights law
3 Right to legal personhood 262
3.1 1954 Convention
3.2 International human rights law
4 Access to courts 265
4.1 1954 Convention
4.2 International human rights law
5 Freedom of religion 275
5.1 1954 Convention
5.2 International human rights law
6 Right to property 280
6.1 1954 Convention
6.2 International human rights law

7 Civil and political rights absent from the 1954 Statelessness Convention 285
7.1 Freedom from arbitrary detention
7.2 Freedom of opinion, expression and (political) assembly
7.3 Right to participate in government
7.4 Minority rights
8 Conclusion 297

CHAPTER XI
PROTECTING THE ECONOMIC, SOCIAL AND CULTURAL RIGHTS OF THE STATELESS **301**

1 Non-nationals, non-discrimination and the enjoyment of economic, social and cultural rights 302
2 Right to work and labour-related rights 307
2.1 1954 Convention
2.2 International human rights law
3 Freedom of association 317
3.1 1954 Convention
3.2 International human rights law
4 Right to social security 323
4.1 1954 Convention
4.2 International human rights law
5 Right to an adequate standard of living 332
5.1 1954 Convention
5.2 International human rights law
6 Right to education 340
6.1 1954 Convention
6.2 International human rights law
7 Right to intellectual property 346
7.1 1954 Convention
7.2 International human rights law
8 Economic, social and cultural rights absent from the 1954 Statelessness Convention 353
9 Conclusion 356

CHAPTER XII
PROTECTING THE SPECIAL NEEDS OF THE STATELESS **359**

1 Naturalisation 360
1.1 1954 Convention
1.2 International (human rights) law
2 Documentation 370
2.1 1954 Convention
2.2 International (human rights) law
3 Special needs absent from the 1954 Statelessness Convention 380
4 Conclusion 385

CHAPTER XIII
INTERNATIONAL LAW AND THE PROTECTION OF STATELESS PERSONS **389**

1 The value of the 1954 Convention relating to the Status of Stateless Persons in the protection of stateless persons 390
2 The role of international (human rights) law in the protection of stateless persons 395
3 Normative gaps in the protection of stateless persons under international law 398
4 Prospects for the implementation and enforcement of norms for the protection of stateless persons 402
5 Conclusion 407

PART 4 WHAT FUTURE FOR THE STATELESSNESS CONVENTIONS?

CHAPTER XIV
FINAL OBSERVATIONS **413**

1 Nationality and statelessness in the 21st century 414
2 Prevention, protection and more 418
3 Meeting the challenge of identification 423
4 What future for the Statelessness Conventions? 432

ANNEX 1
The 1961 Convention on the Reduction of Statelessness 437

ANNEX 2
The 1954 Convention relating to the Status of Stateless Persons 445

ANNEX 3
Schematic overview of the 1954 Statelessness Convention 455

Summary 457

Samenvatting (Dutch summary) 463

Bibliography 469

Index 493

Curriculum Vitae 499

School of Human Rights Research Series 501

PART 1

WHY STATELESSNESS?

CHAPTER I

NATIONALITY MATTERS: AN INTRODUCTION

"Nationality matters" seems a curious title for an academic study. The phrase is vague and ambiguous; indeed it carries a double meaning. This is in contradiction to the usual nature of scholarly work that strives for clarity and precision. Yet it is for precisely this ambiguity that the words were carefully chosen to lead this text. The reader is (hopefully) intrigued as to whether this work discusses *nationality* matters by focussing on issues, problems and perspectives relating to nationality law and practice. Or, the reader may ponder, perhaps the main argument defended here is that nationality *matters*: that the legal bond of nationality is of real significance to the state and the individual involved. In fact, as alluded-to above, these questions that the title conjures in the mind of the reader are both equally valid and indeed both addressed in this book.

The two dimensions of the phrase "nationality matters" reflect the dual aspects of the problem of statelessness. On the one hand, an investigation into the issue of statelessness necessitates an analysis of matters relating to *nationality* - its acquisition and loss – whereby circumstances may arise through which an individual is left stateless. In order to prevent or resolve cases of statelessness, a full understanding is required of what constitutes the link between the individual and a state that results (or should result) in the legal bond of nationality. On the other hand, the statelessness phenomenon obliges us to discover to what extent nationality *matters* in today's world. By discerning whether nationality is relevant for the enjoyment of certain fundamental rights and thereby whether a stateless person is rendered at a disadvantage because of his lack of any nationality, then we can determine if and where international law is required to fill this protection gap.

These dual aspects can be traced in the international community's response to the worldwide problem of statelessness. There are two separate, yet complimentary, conventions aimed at addressing statelessness: the 1961 Convention on the Reduction of Statelessness and the 1954 Convention relating to the Status of Stateless Persons.[1] The first addresses matters relating to *nationality* and aims to limit the number of cases of statelessness occurring. The second offers stateless persons a corresponding legal status and a number of rights, thus aspiring to fill any protection gap that statelessness creates in areas of the law where nationality

[1] Referred to collectively hereinafter as the Statelessness Conventions. The full text of these instruments has been included as Annex 1 (1961 Convention) and Annex 2 (1954 Convention).

matters. As will be explained, this dual nature is also reflected in the approach taken to the study of statelessness in this book.

1 Research Questions

In the following work I intend to discover whether the international community has reacted adequately to address the complex issue of statelessness. The aforementioned Statelessness Conventions are taken as the point of departure because they are specifically designed to be *the* legal regime dealing with statelessness at the international level and together they address the two dimensions of the statelessness question. These will be set off against other sources of international obligations relevant to the problem of statelessness, in particular those found in the area of human rights law. In essence, the overall research question posed in this work is the following:

How can the way in which international law deals with the issue of statelessness be improved so as to ensure optimal protection of the individual and his rights?

Once again, the dual aspects of the issue of statelessness must be reflected, which necessitates splitting this research question in two:

1) **How can the way in which international law deals with the *prevention of statelessness* be improved so as to ensure optimal protection against statelessness for the individual (i.e. the realisation of the right to a nationality)?**

2) **How can the way in which international law deals with the *legal status and entitlements of stateless persons* be improved so as to ensure optimal protection of the individual's rights in the absence of nationality?**

The separation of these questions facilitates the approach taken, namely that of using the existing Statelessness Conventions as a point of departure in the search for optimal legal solutions. An assessment will be made as to whether the conventions are relevant and effective in meeting the goal of protection of individuals or, then again, whether they have become superfluous in view of more recent developments in international (human rights) law. This will provide a basis for recommending improvements, whether this involves the further promotion, implementation and supervision of the existing Statelessness Conventions or the use of alternative or creation of new instruments.

2 Research Approach

In conjunction with the title of this Part of the book - "Why statelessness?" - it is important to first discuss the extent to which the world is blighted by statelessness and determine whether it is indeed a problem worthy of detailed research. This brief investigation will be guided by such questions as: What is statelessness? How severe is the global problem of statelessness? Why is it an issue deserving of international attention? And what reason is there to question the international community's response to the issue? Chapter II is devoted to answering these basic questions as well as providing a brief introduction to the two Statelessness Conventions that are centre-stage in this study.

Part 2 then takes a closer look at the 1961 Convention on the Reduction of Statelessness, while Part 3 analyses the 1954 Convention relating to the Status of Stateless Persons.[2] The investigation is guided by the research questions presented above. Therefore, Part 2 will identify the various causes of statelessness before advising on the effectiveness of instruments designed to prevent its occurrence and ensure that everyone enjoys the right to a nationality. Similarly, Part 3 will first uncover to what extent a protection gap is created by statelessness before proceeding with the search for optimal solutions. In each case, the content and scope of the Statelessness Conventions themselves are investigated, before attention is turned to alternative sources of norms that offer similar or perhaps broader protection. Once the totality of international legal sources which address statelessness has been uncovered, it becomes possible to determine whether statelessness is dealt with effectively; what additional measures – if any – are needed; and what the position of the Statelessness Conventions is within this picture. In line with this approach, a conclusion to the first research question is presented in chapter VIII and an answer to the second is given in chapter XIII.

Thereafter, in Part 4 the findings of this research will be drawn together and final observations will be made on the suitability and effectiveness of the international response to the issue of statelessness to date. Guided by the question "What future for the Statelessness Conventions?" the conclusions from the previous sections will be reviewed in order to determine what role the 1961 Convention on the Reduction of Statelessness and the 1954 Convention relating to the Status of Stateless Persons can play in the protection of individuals worldwide. Lastly, some more general reflections will be offered on how to tackle the challenges that remain in the field of statelessness.

[2] Please note that, rather than considering the instruments in chronological order, the 1961 Convention on the Reduction of Statelessness will be dealt with first because the primary aim of the international community is the avoidance of statelessness and this is the universal instrument that was devised to that effect. A secondary question – and one that only becomes relevant when the avoidance of statelessness cannot be guaranteed – is that of the protection of stateless persons, as provided for by the 1954 Convention relating to the Status of Stateless Persons.

CHAPTER II

THE STATELESSNESS PHENOMENON AND A FIRST ENCOUNTER WITH THE INTERNATIONAL RESPONSE

Immediately embarking on the quest to answer the research questions that were put forward in the previous chapter would be overly hasty as it would disregard the vital query which heads this part of the book: *why statelessness?* For if statelessness is not in fact a "problem" at all, then no matter how interestingly or creatively this work tries to present "solutions", it would not be worth its weight in paper let alone the time and energy spent in producing it. This second introductory chapter therefore considers a series of basic questions: What is statelessness? How many people are currently affected and what impact does statelessness have on their lives? What has been the international community's response to date? And how is statelessness actually defined for the purposes of applying the relevant international standards? The answers to these questions, as presented below, offer an introduction to the statelessness phenomenon and simultaneously illustrate that it is indeed an issue that is worthy of further attention and detailed study.

1 DISCOVERING STATELESSNESS

Generally speaking, each of us has one nationality - no more, no less - and as we grow up we do not naturally question this state of affairs. For a long time, I felt that my nationality was among those characteristics that were fundamental and immutable such as my name, eye colour and gender. Yet time has since shed light on the hidden complexities of nationality and the discovery of statelessness was a particular eye-opener. So, since I feel that the best way to set the scene and to offer some sense of the phenomenon of statelessness is to put forward a concrete, real-life example, I would like to open this chapter by relating my own discovery of statelessness. This is the story of the first stateless person I knew:[1]

> *Once upon a time, in a town in the Southeast of the Netherlands, a baby boy was born. His parents were thrilled and named him Omar, seeing this extension of their family as a good sign for the future and a fresh start for them all. Omar's parents had been forced to flee their homes in the Middle East some years before, leaving everything that they had behind. They eventually won the right to settle in the Netherlands and were making the most of it. Omar's father found a job and quickly picked up the language. As soon as he was eligible, he successfully applied for the*

[1] The name has been changed and details somewhat simplified but the story is accurate.

Dutch nationality in order to affirm his new link with the country. But what he most dearly wanted was to be able to marry Omar's mother. Sadly, they did not have the documents required by Dutch law to do so. Instead, they muddled along in the hope that one day they would be able to afford to send for the right documents or pay for the replacements in order to get married.

Then Omar was born and they were overjoyed. Omar's father went straight from the hospital to the town hall to register the birth, all the while oozing the pride of a man who has newly become a father. Omar was registered: his name, date and place of birth recorded. But when the registrar logged "unknown" in the box marked "nationality", Omar's father grew worried. After all, he was Dutch and his son was born on Dutch soil, so surely Omar would also be Dutch.

Little did he know that just a few months previously a new law had come into force. This law required him to register the imminent birth of his son while his girlfriend was still pregnant. Failing to do so - and because he and Omar's mother were not married - he would not automatically be recognised as the boy's father and his son would not acquire his nationality.

Omar's father quickly made the necessary arrangements at the local court to be legally recognised as the father, but this procedure did not grant Omar the Dutch nationality. Nor could Omar acquire the nationality of his mother, as she was the national of a country that did not allow women to pass on their nationality to their children. Omar's nationality was therefore more than unknown: it was absent. He was stateless.

After they had recovered from the shock, Omar's parents began to discover the consequences of his statelessness. Omar could not obtain a passport, or be included in the passport of either of his parents, he could only apply for a foreigners' travel pass at substantial cost. Omar was also registered by the immigration service as "a foreigner who entered the country for family reunification purposes" – an interesting feat for a baby just a few days old. His parents would have to pay a sizeable fee for a residence permit for Omar, without which he could, in theory, be subject to expulsion.

Later, in order to have any hope of resolving his plight, Omar's parents would have to fight for his formal recognition as a stateless person. This may then allow Omar to benefit from provisions in the Dutch law that offer nationality to a stateless child after three year, so long as he remains within the country in that time and under the care of his Dutch father.

This initial experience of statelessness provides much food for thought and one possible answer to the question "why statelessness?" can arguably already be found in the personal struggle of this family. Statelessness presents a real, human dilemma for this one boy and his parents.

2 THE WORLDWIDE SEVERITY OF STATELESSNESS: MAGNITUDE AND CONSEQUENCES

When I "discovered" statelessness, it was in a random, individual and apparently largely isolated case - one that formed a clear exception to the norm for children born in the Netherlands (as evidenced by the public outcry in response to a similar case later the same year).[2] However, further investigation uncovers many more stories of statelessness, in many more countries, springing from many more different causes and resulting in many more troublesome consequences. This section therefore offers a brief introduction to the *severity* of statelessness while over the course of this book we will see plenty of further examples of the gravity of this phenomenon.

To begin with then, it is generally agreed that statelessness is a substantial, rather than a one-off, anomaly. Disappointingly however, when trying to gain a clearer picture of the scope of the phenomenon by assessing the magnitude of statelessness across the globe, there is a distinct absence of concrete and reliable information. The only fact about which there is any certainty is that no one really knows the full extent of the problem. There are several reasons for the varying approximations of the number of stateless persons,[3] not least of which is the ongoing discussion surrounding the definition of statelessness.[4] Continuing contention as to what qualifies an individual as stateless means that different organisations and states often still adopt their own approach – not only to the *definition* itself, but also to *procedures* for the recognition of "stateless person status"[5] and requirements surrounding the establishment of *proof* of statelessness.[6] Without a universal interpretation and application of the term "stateless", it comes as no surprise that statistics on the matter are hazy. In cases where there is an opportunity to identify a person as stateless, for example in the event of a census or where an individual statelessness-status determination procedure does exist, there is no guarantee that they will be (correctly) registered as such. To register a stateless

---

[2] See on the response to this issue in the Netherlands Één Vandaag, *IND wil baby uitzetten* [Immigration and Naturalisation Service wants to deport baby], news broadcast, 6 December 2004, http://www.tweevandaag.nl/index.php?module=PX_Story&func=view&cid=2&sid=28947.

[3] For instance, estimations by United Nations High Commissioner for Refugees (UNHCR) over the past few years have ranged from one million to nine million, seeming at one point to admit defeat and simply state that there are "millions" of stateless persons worldwide. According to UNHCR's annual *Global Appeal,* in 2002 the estimate was 8.9 million stateless persons, in 2003 and 2004 the estimate was 1 million and in 2005 it was the less-specific "millions"; UNHCR Global Appeal 2002 – 2005.

[4] As discussed in detail in section 4 below.

[5] Indeed, according to the 2004 *Final Report* on a statelessness survey performed by the UNHCR, only 51.4% of the respondent states indicated that there was even a procedure in place to identify cases of statelessness, therefore many states have no standard method of identifying stateless persons on the territory of their state; UNHCR, *Final report concerning the Questionnaire on statelessness pursuant to the Agenda for Protection,* Geneva: March 2004, page 26

[6] It can be very difficult to provide satisfactory evidence of statelessness as it requires proving a negative, proving the *absence* of a nationality. This means that agreement on the burden of proof and on the weighing of evidence are of utmost importance. See further Nehemiah Robinson, *Convention relating to the status of stateless persons - Its history and interpretation*, UNHCR, Geneva: 1955, pages 11-16

person as a person of "unknown nationality"[7] or simply as a "non-citizen"[8] is to further obscure the statistics and add to the invisibility of this group.[9] Finally there is the consideration that statelessness is often a highly politicised issue.[10] Therefore, the absence of any data in some states on the magnitude of the statelessness plight may imply that the authorities may have chosen to ignore the problem rather than publicise it.[11] Moreover, the quality and reliability of any statistical data that *is* offered by governments and institutions is by no means beyond question – it may be heavily influenced by an underlying agenda.

Although it is, therefore, unlikely that the precise figure will ever be known, all estimates point towards statelessness being an issue of global proportions and reach. In 2005, a comprehensive international report on statelessness by the non-governmental organisation *Refugees International* gave the estimate of approximately 11 million stateless persons worldwide.[12] During 2006, UNHCR made renewed efforts to identify and tally stateless populations and by the end of the year put the total global figure at 5.8 million. This number however, included only those populations about which some statistics were available and the data has been described as "provisional, incomplete, subject to change and [including] estimates".[13] In fact, the agency currently "believes the true total may be closer to 15 million"[14] – a hefty number.[15] Meanwhile, UNHCR's *Global Questionnaire on Statelessness* confirmed that statelessness is an issue that spans the world.[16] Of the countries that completed the questionnaire, 59.4% admitted to encountering problems of statelessness.[17] Therefore, more than half of the respondent states have actually identified cases of statelessness within their territory, despite the many difficulties mentioned above. The survey shows that statelessness is a truly global issue as there is no region of the world that is exempt from this problem. Statelessness has arisen in every area of the world, regardless of whether there had recently been a case of state succession and independently of the question as to

---

[7] Such was the way in which the nationality of Omar in the story described in section 1 was recorded in the municipal records in the Netherlands.

[8] For example, Latvia labels Ex-USSR nationals who fulfil certain criteria as "non-citizens", a separate category to "stateless" under Latvian law, even though these individuals are without a nationality; See both the Law on the Status of Former USSR Citizens Who Are Not Citizens of Latvia or Any Other State, May 1995 and the Law of Stateless Persons, March 2004.

[9] UNHCR, *Statistical Yearbook 2001,* Geneva, October 2002, page 23; Maureen Lynch, *Lives on hold: The human cost of statelessness,* Washington: 2005, page 7.

[10] UNHCR, *The World's Stateless - Questions and Answers,* Geneva: 2004, page 12.

[11] Hannah Arendt, "The Decline of the Nation-State and the End of the Rights of Man" in *The origins of totalitarianism*, Harcourt Brace Jovanovich, New York: 1948, page 279

[12] According to *Refugees International,* 11 million is a "low end estimate"; Maureen Lynch, *Lives on hold: The human cost of statelessness,* Washington: 2005, page 1.

[13] UNHCR, *Global Trends 2006,* Table 14 – Stateless Persons.

[14] UNHCR, "The World's Stateless People" in *Refugees Magazine,* Number 147, Issue 3, 2007.

[15] By way of comparison, UNHCR's figures on refugees at the time showed a population of just under 10 million. UNHCR, *Global Trends 2006,* Table 1 – Refugees, asylum seekers, IDPs, returnees, stateless persons and others of concern to UNHCR.

[16] The survey was undertaken in 2003 with the results published in UNHCR, *Final report concerning the Questionnaire on statelessness pursuant to the Agenda for Protection,* Geneva: March 2004.

[17] UNHCR, *Final report concerning the Questionnaire on statelessness pursuant to the Agenda for Protection,* Geneva: March 2004, page 11.

whether the *jus soli* or *jus sanguinis* nationality doctrine is the preferred method of attributing nationality at birth.[18]

Also worth mentioning at this point is the finding that statelessness is not only the plight of random individuals, but whole groups can suffer from a sort-of collective statelessness. Here are a few examples:

- in Latvia and Estonia there is a population of 393,000 and 119,000 Russian "non-citizens" respectively, persons who were rendered stateless following the independence of these Baltic states and the dissolution of the USSR;

- other former soviet republics, including the Russian Federation, Kazakhstan and Ukraine, also host tens of thousands of stateless persons;

- in Africa, Kenya is home to a stateless population of 100,000 and other states such as Zimbabwe and the Democratic Republic of Congo are also known to host large stateless groups;

- other states where statelessness is a widespread problem include Kuwait (88,000), Syrian Arab Republic (300,000), Nepal (400,000), Bangladesh (300,000) and Myanmar (670,000); and

- even in states where the problem is relatively low-key, recent estimates show that there may still be several thousands of stateless persons – for example the Netherlands (4,461) and Sweden (5,571).[19]

Again, these numbers may be unreliable due to the difficulty of definition and identification of statelessness, but they provide a general picture of the problem. In later chapters these and other examples will occasionally be drawn upon as illustrations or test cases in the discussion of specific aspect of statelessness.

For now it suffices to say that the existence of these large groups of stateless persons, as well as the global occurrence of sporadic cases, provides a strong argument for taking a closer look at the issue. Indeed, the widespread and large-scale nature of the phenomenon suggest, at the very least, that efforts to *prevent* statelessness through the adoption and implementation of international norms are not yet thoroughly effective. Therefore, through the first of my two research questions I propose to pursue an in depth study of the international community's

---

[18] State succession and the strict application of the *jus sanguinis* nationality doctrines are two well-known potential causes of statelessness. What this survey shows is that there are other factors that may also play a part in causing statelessness, heightening the universality of this problem. The causes of statelessness are discussed in depth in part 2, with an introduction to the *jus soli* and *jus sanguinis* doctrines provided in chapter III.

[19] These figures are taken from UNHCR's Global Trends 2006 and from the 2005 global report on statelessness by *Refugees International;* Maureen Lynch, *Lives on hold: The human cost of statelessness,* Washington: 2005, pages 27-46.

approach to the prevention of statelessness in order to uncover areas in which improvements can be made to optimise the avoidance of statelessness in future.[20]

Meanwhile, if we conceive that there are up to 15 million – if not more – stateless persons dispersed across the globe, the question that naturally follows is what consequences statelessness has for these individuals and their families; the communities and the states involved; and the international community as a whole. The first impression garnered from the literature on the subject, is that the impact of statelessness can be dramatic. UNHCR has described the stateless as "unclaimed" and their situation as being "outcasts from the global political system of states which has evolved in the last century".[21] Indeed, as statelessness is an exceptional phenomenon in a world where having a nationality is the norm, the stateless find themselves excluded from the normal legal regime. More than that, the stateless "outcasts" are susceptible to increased marginalisation, discrimination and insecurity, as we will see.

For individuals, statelessness can result in an inability to effectuate a range of rights and an increased vulnerability to abuse in both the public and private sphere. According to the UNHCR publication *What would life be like if you had no nationality?* if you are stateless, you may not be able to

> go to university; get a job; get medical care; own property; travel; register the birth of your children; marry and found a family; enjoy legal protection; have a sense of identity and belonging; [or] participate fully in developments in a world composed of states, in which nationality is key to membership.[22]

The stateless thus "often have minimal, if any, access to the kind of basic political and social rights that most civilians take for granted".[23] The lack of a nationality forms an enormous obstacle when it comes to even the simplest of administrative procedures. Stateless persons are generally unable to obtain travel documents or even any form of identity document.[24] This, in turn, leads to an increased risk of becoming a victim of human trafficking or other forms of exploitation – particularly for women and children. One poignant example that has been identified is the problem that stateless women may seek marriage with a national in the hope of resolving their statelessness or improving their legal status, only to become trapped in an abusive relationship:

> In the United States, prior to the 1994 Violence Against Women Act (VAWA), only a permanent US resident or citizen spouse could petition for a stateless or foreign spouse to become a resident; and the petitioner controlled if and when the residency application was filed. All too frequently, this control over if and when

---

[20] The research question was elaborated in chapter I. Part 2 is devoted to answering this question.

[21] UNHCR, *The Problem of Statelessness has Become a Live Issue Again,* 2001, accessible via http://www.unhcr.org.

[22] UNHCR, *What would life be like if you had no nationality?* Information booklet, March 1999, page 3.

[23] UNHCR, *The World's Stateless - Questions and Answers,* Geneva: 2004, page 4.

[24] Guy Goodwin Gill, "The rights of refugees and stateless persons" in Saksena (ed) *Human rights perspectives & challenges (in 1900's and beyond)*, Lancers Books, New Delhi: 1994, page 379.

the residency application was filed allowed physically abusive spouses, predominantly men, inordinate control over their non-resident spouses.[25]

Another aspect of the problem of statelessness is that the registration of births, marriages and deaths becomes much more difficult,[26] when such registration can, in fact, also be vital in the reduction or prevention of statelessness. As we will see later, for this and other reasons, "many stateless people are condemned to pass on their statelessness to their children – as if it were some sort of genetic disease".[27] Then, already excluded from the legal regime, stateless persons often find themselves excluded from society: the long-term (immigration) detention of stateless persons is a serious issue.[28] This is usually due to a lack of documentation or the inability to return the individuals to their country of origin. Such circumstances may result in "indefinite family separation",[29] as well as leading to a general and continuing uncertainty in any dealings with state authorities.[30] Finally, the rejection that statelessness implies and the dire consequences that it can have contribute to a debilitating "sense of worthlessness"[31] among the stateless and this can lead to depression, alcoholism, violence and suicide.[32]

The individual insecurity experienced by stateless persons becomes a communal, national or even international issue when it escalates into collective insecurity of a large stateless group. UNHCR has, for instance, traced a link between statelessness and mass displacement. There are many examples of stateless groups that have fled the country of former nationality or habitual residence: the Bidoons from Kuwait and the Rohingyas from Myanmar are but two such cases.[33] Incidents of mass expulsion of stateless persons from their country of habitual

[25] David Weissbrodt; Clay Collins, 'The Human Rights of Stateless Persons', in *Human Rights Quarterly,* Vol. 28, 2006, page 270. See also UN Division for the Advancement of Women, *Women, Nationality and Citizenship,* New York: 2003. On the vulnerability of stateless children to abuse and trafficking, see for instance Youth Advocate Program International, *Stateless Children - Youth Who are Without Citizenship,* Washington DC: 2002.

[26] Carol Batchelor, "The International Legal Framework Concerning Statelessness and Access for Stateless Persons", *European Union Seminar on the Content and Scope of International Protection: Panel 1 - Legal basis of international protection,* Madrid: 2002, page 4.

[27] Philippe Leclerc and Rupert Colville, "In the Shadows", in *Refugees Magazine,* No. 147, Issue 3, 2007, page 6.

[28] UNHCR, *Stateless persons: a discussion note,* EC/1992/SCP/CRP.4, Geneva: 1 April 1992; David Weissbrodt; Clay Collins, 'The Human Rights of Stateless Persons', in *Human Rights Quarterly,* Vol. 28, 2006, page 267; Refugees International, "Refugee Voices: Detained Stateless People in Kuwait", 24 September 2007; Stefanie Grant, "The Legal Protection of Stranded Migrants" in *International Migration Law,* R. Cholewinski, R. Perruchoud and E. MacDonald [Eds.], TMS Asser Press, The Hague 2007, pages 29-47.

[29] UNHCR, *Statelessness in Canadian Context – A Discussion Paper,* Ottawa, July 2003, page 3.

[30] Guy Goodwin Gill, "The rights of refugees and stateless persons" in Saksena (ed) *Human rights perspectives & challenges (in 1900's and beyond),* Lancers Books, New Delhi: 1994, page 379.

[31] Feelings expressed by a stateless woman as cited in Philippe Leclerc and Rupert Colville, "In the Shadows", in *Refugees Magazine,* No. 147, Issue 3, 2007, page 6.

[32] Advisory Board on Human Security (prepared by Constantin Sokoloff), *Denial of Citizenship: A Challenge to Human Security,* February 2005.

[33] UNHCR, "Statelessness and Citizenship" in *The State of the World's Refugees - A Humanitarian Agenda,* Oxford University Press, Oxford: 1997, page 244-245.

residence add to the numbers of stateless living in exile – think of the ethnic Nepali minority in Bhutan who were both stripped of their nationality and expelled from the country.[34] The creation of large groups that flee across international borders puts a heavy strain on the resources of the reception country as well as on the relations between the states involved. The continuing existence of statelessness can, therefore, contribute to instability in international relations.[35]

Not only has a link been traced between statelessness and forced migration, which can lead to international insecurity, but a more direct connection has been made between nationality issues and armed conflict. Indeed,

> when a community resides for many years in a State and, in practice, functions as a community but its members are not given the full right to become citizens, the outcome is a population of second-class persons. This result is unjustified, immoral and *dangerous to democracy, and has the potential for engendering uprisings and civil revolt.*[36]

With this in mind, the Advisory Board on Human Security has chosen to take a closer look at the denial of citizenship and how this relates to human (in)security. Each of the individual and societal consequences of statelessness introduced above gains a mention in the Advisory Board's 2005 report.[37] Where it goes one step further is in expounding a number of cases where nationality disputes have more or less directly contributed to internal and even international conflict.[38] While the report emphasises that this connection is very real, giving as examples the conflicts in the Great Lakes Region of Africa and in the Balkans, it admits that the links are also complex. Nevertheless, addressing nationality issues is generally recognised as an important element of conflict prevention efforts and can also be a vital aspect of post-conflict peace-building.[39]

These findings confirm that statelessness is not only a pervasive issue, but also one that warrants – even demands - international attention. From the accounts given of the experiences of stateless persons, it would seem that the international community also has some way to go in ensuring the optimal protection of the rights

---

[34] UNHCR, *Stateless persons: a discussion note,* EC/1992/SCP/CRP.4, Geneva: 1 April 1992; Maureen Lynch, *Lives on hold: The human cost of statelessness,* Washington: 2005, page 37.

[35] UNHCR, *Progress report on UNHCR activities in the field of statelessness,* EC/49/SC/CRP.15, Geneva: 4 June 1999.

[36] Emphasis added. Yaffa Zilberschats, "Chapter 3 - The Horizontal Aspect of Citizenship" in *The Human Right to Citizenship*, Transnational Publishers, Ardsley, NY: 2002, page 95.

[37] Advisory Board on Human Security (prepared by Constantin Sokoloff), *Denial of Citizenship: A Challenge to Human Security,* February 2005, pages 3-5.

[38] UNHCR has also explained that two of the motivations for states and concerned organisations to tackle statelessness are to "strengthen national solidarity and stability by providing all people with a sense of belonging and identity" and to "improve international relations and stability by resolving disputes related to nationality". UNHCR, *What would life be like if you had no nationality?* Information booklet, March 1999, page 11.

[39] Advisory Board on Human Security (prepared by Constantin Sokoloff), *Denial of Citizenship: A Challenge to Human Security,* February 2005, pages 21-23. See also Gay McDougall, *Promotion and Protection of all Human Rights, Civil, Political, Economic, Social and Cultural Rights, Including the Right to Development – Report of the Independent Expert on Minority Issues,* A/HRC/7/23, 28 February 2008, paras. 47 - 48.

of the stateless. It appears that the existing international legal framework has, as yet, failed to stave off all of the detrimental consequences of a person being left unclaimed by any state and this is causing various severe knock-on effects. Through the second of my research questions, I will therefore endeavor hope to uncover the gaps and weaknesses in the international community's approach to the protection of stateless persons in order to also recommend ways to optimise this aspect of the response to statelessness.[40]

3 THE INTERNATIONAL RESPONSE TO STATELESSNESS

The conclusion that was drawn from the foregoing comments on the severity of statelessness worldwide was that, to date, the international response to the issue has failed to fully and effectively prevent cases of statelessness or offer adequate protection to stateless persons. This is not to suggest that the international community has not been engaged in efforts to tackle statelessness. In fact, statelessness did, at one time, command the full attention of the world's governments and over the past century, numerous efforts have actually been taken to tackle this issue in one way or another. The most notable outcome of these efforts is the pair of Conventions adopted in the wake of the Second World War: the 1961 Convention on the Reduction of Statelessness and the 1954 Convention relating to the Status of Stateless Persons. These are tailor-made instruments designed, respectively, to prevent statelessness and protect stateless persons. So, as we undertake an assessment of the international response to statelessness, these Statelessness Conventions will take centre-stage - we will consider their effectiveness and determine their place and value within the broader setting of international law as it stands today. At the same time, it is important to realise early-on that these instruments are not the only source of international standards relating to statelessness. In particular, developments in the field of human rights law[41] and the promulgation of a number of instruments that address specific (sub)topics relating to the problem of statelessness[42] have contributed to an expanding set of relevant standards. By way of introduction to this overall international legal framework, what follows is a brief overview of the international community's response to statelessness to date, starting with the advent of the Statelessness Conventions. This account will offer its own insight into the question "why statelessness?"

Shortly after World War II, a study commissioned by the newly formed United Nations highlighted a number of protection issues regarding persons who had, in some way, become disconnected from their own state.[43] This group included

[40] The research question was elaborated in chapter I. Part 3 is devoted to answering this question.

[41] In particular the adoption of universal instruments such as the International Covenant on Civil and Political Rights, the International Covenant on Economic, Social and Cultural Rights and the Convention on the Rights of the Child themselves to "everyone" as well as the promulgation of numerous regional human rights conventions that take a similar approach.

[42] These include the European Convention on Nationality, the Council of Europe Convention on the avoidance of statelessness in relation to State succession, the International Law Commission's Draft Articles on Nationality of Natural Persons in relation to the Succession States and Draft Articles on Diplomatic Protection – all of which will be considered in the chapters to come.

[43] UN, *A Study of Statelessness*, E/1112, New York: August 1949.

both "stateless persons" and "refugees" – terms that were, as yet, undefined. On the basis of the study, the decision was taken to formulate a multilateral agreement to respond to the problem. And so, work began towards formulating an international convention to protect the basic rights of these "unprotected persons" – again including both stateless persons and refugees. In the end, two separate international instruments were adopted, each addressing a specific sub-category of persons in need of protection. The first was the 1951 Convention relating to the Status of Refugees.[44] The application of this convention is limited to persons who fulfil the criteria set by the definition of a "refugee" offered in article 1 of the instrument. The nationality – or lack of it – is not a crucial factor in the refugee definition. As a consequence, while some stateless persons would be able to claim protection on the basis of the Refugee Convention, others would not satisfy the criteria and would need to rely on another source for the protection of their rights.[45] In 1954, a second, similarly worded convention was agreed upon: the Convention relating to the Status of Stateless Persons.[46] Article 1, which housed the definition of a refugee in the Refugee Convention, now contained a definition of a "stateless person", which will be considered in depth in section 4 of this chapter. Having established who is a stateless person, the 1954 Statelessness Convention offers a catalogue of rights and benefits to be enjoyed by those individuals who qualify under the definition. The 1954 Statelessness Convention was thus deemed to provide for a number of improvements to the legal status and situation of stateless persons. Still, the avoidance of statelessness and the (re)instatement of nationality remained the ultimate goal.[47] To this end, another Statelessness Convention was adopted: the 1961 Convention on the Reduction of Statelessness.[48] The aim was to prevent statelessness from arising by prohibiting states from withdrawing nationality if that would result in statelessness as well as by placing a positive obligation on states to grant nationality to individuals who would otherwise be stateless. Together then, the 1954 and 1961 Statelessness Conventions were designed to offer distinct yet complimentary approaches to the statelessness phenomenon - aspiring to allocate rights directly to stateless persons and avoid statelessness respectively.

In the half-century since the adoption of the Statelessness Conventions, two important trends can be traced that corroborate the aptness and timeliness of an in depth study of statelessness today ("why statelessness?"). The first, is the long period of neglect suffered by the Statelessness Conventions after their adoption and, indeed, the virtual abandonment of any efforts to further study or respond to the phenomenon of statelessness itself. The second is the resurgence of interest in and

---

[44] The 1951 Convention relating to the Status of Refugees entered into force on the 22nd of April 1954. Hereinafter commonly referred to as the 1951 Refugee Convention. Note that a protocol to the 1951 Refugee Convention followed in 1967 and entered into force on the 4th of October of that year.

[45] Guy Goodwin Gill, "The rights of refugees and stateless persons" in Saksena (ed) *Human rights perspectives & challenges (in 1900's and beyond)*, Lancers Books, New Delhi: 1994, page 382.

[46] The 1954 Convention relating to the Status of Stateless Persons entered into force on the 6th of June 1960; hereinafter commonly referred to as the 1954 Statelessness Convention.

[47] Carol Batchelor, "The International Legal Framework Concerning Statelessness and Access for Stateless Persons", *European Union Seminar on the Content and Scope of International Protection: Panel 1 - Legal basis of international protection,* Madrid: 2002, page 6.

[48] The 1961 Convention on the Reduction of Statelessness entered into force on the 13th of December 1975; hereinafter commonly referred to as the 1961 Statelessness Convention.

debate on the problem of statelessness since the early 1990s. We will consider the significance of each in turn.

For many years following the formulation of the Statelessness Conventions, while existing cases of statelessness remained unresolved and new cases continued to surface, it was not an issue with which the international community was actively engaged. Instead, mass displacement and the battle to deal with ever-increasing numbers of refugees took priority. The Statelessness Conventions which lay in wait for ratifications attracted very few, while the number of state parties to the Refugee Convention took flight. By 1980, the Refugee Convention had 76 parties, while the 1954 and 1961 Statelessness Conventions just 31 and 9 respectively. This severely limited the geographical scope of application of the provisions of the Statelessness Conventions and was evidence of the overall lack of attention to the issue.[49] In that period, nationality was still largely regarded as a strictly sovereign matter. Statelessness was also seen as an internal – rather than an international – concern and it was therefore felt to be a delicate political issue, blocking discussion at both levels.[50] Further evidence of the disinterest in statelessness (in contrast, again, to the attention and funds devoted to refugees) can be found in the allocation of resources within the United Nations High Commissioner for Refugees. Charged with a mandate on both refugee and statelessness issues, the organisation employs over 6,000 members of staff worldwide but, even today, less than a handful of full-time staff are specifically devoted to the problem of statelessness.

The failure by states to adopt and implement the standards outlined in the Statelessness Conventions as well as the concomitant stagnation of discussion and activity on the issue has had a clear impact on the enduring enormity and harshness of the statelessness phenomenon - as illustrated by the findings in the previous section.[51] Moreover, existing literature on the subject has raised the suggestion that the international community's failure to effectively tackle statelessness is not only to be blamed on *neglect* of the Statelessness Conventions, but also on the *content* of the instruments themselves. Thus, on the one hand, the Conventions have been criticised as being "promulgated more from the view of a state's prerogatives and

[49] By the time of writing, the rate of accession to the conventions had improved slightly. The 1954 and 1961 Conventions have now drawn a total of 62 and 34 state parties respectively as compared to the 142 parties to the 1951 Refugee Convention. See further UNHCR, "Statelessness and Citizenship" in *The State of the World's Refugees - A Humanitarian Agenda*, Oxford University Press, Oxford: 1997, page 257.

[50] UNHCR, *Final report concerning the Questionnaire on statelessness pursuant to the Agenda for Protection,* Geneva: March 2004, page 12

[51] See section 2 above. Note also that in 1947, a report on *Stateless Children* by the International Union for Child Welfare warned that "one of the outstanding problems of our time is that created by the thousands of persons whom no state recognises as its nationals". International Union for Child Welfare, *Stateless Children - A Comparative Study of National Legislation and Suggested Solutions to the Problem of Statelessness of Children,* Geneva: 1947, foreword. All evidence points to an increase in the number of stateless persons since the Second World War. – a fact that has been blamed in part on "political upheavals and armed conflict"; Ruth Donner, "Chapter 3: The Imposition and Withdrawal of Nationality" in *The Regulation of Nationality in International Law*, Transnational Publishers, New York: 1994. With the global stateless population now estimated to be somewhere in the *millions* and reports describing the detrimental conditions in which stateless persons continue to live, the Statelessness Conventions have certainly not been meeting their aim.

sovereignty than an individual's rights"[52] – thereby espousing standards that were not forceful enough to fulfil their purpose. On the other hand, with few states and even less international resources committed to implementing or monitoring the terms of the Statelessness Conventions, the standards themselves have also had little opportunity to be tried, tested or further developed – again, this stands in stark contrast to other fields of international law such as human rights or refugee law that has continued to evolve over the same period. There is now a genuine concern that the norms espoused in the Statelessness Conventions have been outrun by practical and legal developments since the promulgation of these instruments. If this is the case, then even the recent spate of accessions to the two instruments offers little hope for an improvement of the situation on the ground.[53] Either way, it is arguable that an assessment of the actual content of the Statelessness Conventions is overdue - particularly since, for some reason, the instruments never really took flight while statelessness continues to present itself as a problem. By taking a careful look at the terms of the Statelessness Conventions and weighing their strengths and weaknesses, some comment can be made on their true potential and whether they present an appropriate way forward for the international response to statelessness.

The second trend that was mentioned above is the recent revival of interest in statelessness – following decades of disregard. Events of the late 1980s and early 1990s brought about new and grave situations of statelessness that alerted the world community anew to the need to address this problem. For starters there was the disintegration of a number of federal states, in particular the former USSR and Socialist Federal Republic of Yugoslavia.[54] These cases of state succession gave rise to difficult questions surrounding the nationality of those affected and problems of statelessness ensued. A related issue that drew attention to statelessness was the emergence of a new form of insecurity: inter-ethnic, communal conflicts sprung up in many regions.[55] In a number of cases, nationality became an issue or even a weapon in the dispute, with statelessness the detrimental result. A third reason for statelessness being viewed with a renewed sense of urgency is the aforementioned realisation that there is an intimate connection between statelessness and forced displacement. Still battling to cope with high numbers of refugees, the international community began to take interest in the finding that statelessness can not only lead to large scale population movements, but that the resolution of these situations also

[52] Quote by Independent Commission on International Humanitarian Issues, taken from UNHCR, "Statelessness and Citizenship" in *The State of the World's Refugees - A Humanitarian Agenda*, Oxford University Press, Oxford: 1997, page 256.

[53] Since the mid-1990s, the number of state parties to the Statelessness Conventions has steadily expanded, thanks largely to a promotional campaign by UNHCR that commenced in 1994. However, the number of accessions remains relatively low when compared to the 1951 Refugee Convention or many of the major human rights instruments. See note 49 above.

[54] UNHCR, "Statelessness and Citizenship" in *The State of the World's Refugees - A Humanitarian Agenda*, Oxford University Press, Oxford: 1997, page 229

[55] Carol Batchelor, 'Statelessness and the Problem of Resolving Nationality Status', in *International Journal of Refugee Law,* Vol. 10, 1998, page 157; UNHCR, *Information and accession package: the 1954 Convention relating to the status of stateless persons and the 1961 Convention on the reduction of statelessness,* Geneva: January 1999, page 2.

relies on providing an answer to any unresolved nationality disputes.[56] And finally, with the penetration of multi-party democracy into ever more countries, new citizenship disputes and cases of statelessness have surfaced – especially in Africa:

> Ironically, the growing number of elections being held in African states has in some cases inflamed the debate over nationality [...] some regimes find it difficult to resist the temptation to manipulate nationality issues in order to erase political opposition.[57]

These last two reasons in particular have ensured that statelessness retained its place on the international agenda as we moved into the new century.

The overall result was that, from the mid 1990s onwards, states, international organisations (including UNHCR) and human rights institutions began to pay greater attention to nationality matters and statelessness in their activities and reports. Interest in the Statelessness Conventions is on the up, with a small surge in the number of state parties and an increasing variety of actors petitioning states to accede to the instruments.[58] At the same time, the true potential of the broader human rights framework to offer protection from and in statelessness is now beginning to come to light and a number of new international instruments have also been developed with a focus on (an aspect of the problem of) statelessness.[59] This means that it is not only pertinent to consider the potential utility of the Statelessness Conventions in answering the statelessness challenge, but that this is also an opportune and appropriate moment to undertake such a study. The aim is to reappraise the value of the tailor-made Statelessness Conventions within the setting of the 21st century international legal framework as well as to discover where the framework as a whole still needs some work to ensure that statelessness receives a more effective response in the future.

4 A FIRST CONCRETE DILEMMA: DEFINING STATELESSNESS

The first critical and compelling dilemma to be dealt with, before we can even progress to consider the substantive protection offered from and in statelessness, is that of actually *defining* statelessness. As with any (international) legal concept, it is important to be clear as to the meaning of "statelessness" in order to determine which situations are covered by the expression and which fall beyond its reach. Only once the question of definition has been satisfied is the scope of application of norms specifically relating to statelessness established and can the task of identifying cases of statelessness for the purpose of applying such norms begin. Thus, in a work that resolves to undertake a thorough assessment of the way in

---

56 UNHCR, "Statelessness and Citizenship" in *The State of the World's Refugees - A Humanitarian Agenda*, Oxford University Press, Oxford: 1997, page 227

57 Cécile Pouilly, "Africa's Hidden Problem", in *Refugees Magazine,* Number 147, Issue 3, 2007, pages 29-30. See also James Goldston, 'Holes in the Rights Framework: Racial Discrimination, Citizenship, and the Rights of Noncitizens', in *Ethics and International Affairs,* Vol. 20, 2006.

58 See on the newer accessions note 47 above. Among those bodies and organisations that are now regularly calling upon states to sign up to the conventions are the UN treaty bodies, UNHCR and non-governmental organisations such as Refugees International and Open Society Justice Initiative.

59 See note 42 above.

which international law deals with statelessness, the appropriateness and adequacy of the definition employed by the international community – decisive as it is for the enjoyment of relevant legal standards – is something that must be included in the investigation. The purpose of this section is therefore to present and elucidate the definition of statelessness as elaborated under international law as well as to offer some reflection upon its aptness. And it is in undertaking this basic exercise that the first potential, concrete "problem" with the international response to statelessness is uncovered. As we will see, it appears that ongoing contention and debate surrounding the meaning of statelessness[60] – in spite of the existence of a formal, internationally acknowledged definition – may be jeopardising the implementation of norms that address the prevention of statelessness and the protection of stateless persons.

In delineating standards that are applicable to situations of statelessness, the international community has tackled the accompanying and vital task of defining this term. According to international law, in particular as expressed in article 1 of the 1954 Convention relating to the Status of Stateless Persons,

> the term "stateless person" means a person who is not considered a national by any state under the operation of its law.[61]

Whether an individual qualifies under this definition is purely dependent on a point of law – an arguably unremarkable approach since nationality is itself a *legal* connection between a person and a state. The focus is on the existence (or absence) of a formal bond of nationality, without pausing to consider the quality or effectiveness of citizenship.[62] To reflect this approach, the persons qualifying under this definition are commonly referred to as "*de jure* stateless". The definition excludes persons who may, in reality, live in very similar circumstances: those who lack protection *de facto* (in fact) as opposed to *de jure* (in law) because, although they do retain the formal bond of nationality, they are unable to rely on their country of nationality for protection. And it is on this point that the subsequent contention rests.

The international community's decision to include only *de jure* cases within the definition of statelessness was greatly influenced by the drafting history of the

---

[60] This is evidenced by the differing definitions of statelessness and descriptions of stateless cases in such sources as Paul Weis, "The United Nations Convention on the Reduction of Statelessness, 1961" in *International and Comparative Law Quarterly,* Vol. 11, No. 4, 1962, pages 1073-1096; Carol Batchelor, 'Stateless Persons: Some Gaps in International Protection', in *International Journal of Refugee Law,* Vol. 7, 1995; Carol Batchelor, 'Statelessness and the Problem of Resolving Nationality Status', in *International Journal of Refugee Law,* Vol. 10, 1998; Maureen Lynch, *Lives on hold: The human cost of statelessness,* Washington: 2005; David Weissbrodt; Clay Collins, 'The Human Rights of Stateless Persons', in *Human Rights Quarterly,* Vol. 28, 2006; and Abbas Shiblak, *Citizens, Sub-citizens and Non-citizens: Statelessness in the Arab Region,* unpublished paper

[61] See also article 1, paragraph c of the Council of Europe Convention on the avoidance of statelessness in relation to State succession (2006) as well as the Explanatory Memorandum to the European Convention on Nationality (1997), paragraph 33.

[62] Please note that the terms "nationality" and "citizenship" (as well as "national" and "citizen") will – unless specific reference to the contrary - be used interchangeably throughout this work to denote the legal bond between an individual and a state.

1954 Statelessness Convention. The fact that the instrument started life as a protocol to the Convention relating to the Status of Refugees had a particular impact. The line of thought was that, together, the Refugee Convention and Statelessness Protocol would offer protection to both categories of "unprotected" person – the *de facto* and the *de jure*.[63] Indeed, when the Refugee Convention was adopted in 1951 (without the accompanying Statelessness Protocol) the international community did establish a protection regime for those lacking protection *de facto*: the definition of a refugee, the basis for the personal scope of the Refugee Convention, relies on a question of fact rather than of law. However, the definition does not encompass *all* persons who *de facto* lack national protection, but rather only those who

> owing to well-founded fear of being persecuted for reasons of race, religion, nationality, membership of a particular social group or political opinion, is outside the country of his nationality and is unable or, owing to such fear, is unwilling to avail himself of the protection of that country.[64]

States considered a simple lack of protection to be insufficient to qualify for the benefits espoused under the 1951 Refugee Convention and determined that additional criteria must also be met. As such, this definition of a refugee reflects the extent to which the international community was willing to offer protection to those who suffered from *de facto* "unprotection".[65]

So, when it came to the ensuing discussion of the definition of *statelessness*, there was a tendency to consider the *de facto* issue as closed and concentrate on the problem of a *de jure* absence of protection – as evidenced by the definition adopted.[66] Yet, even as the definition was being debated, some representatives raised their voices in favour of expanding the definition of statelessness – and thereby the personal scope of the 1954 Statelessness Convention – to include so-called "*de facto* stateless persons".[67] The apprehension that some individuals would qualify neither for protection as a refugee nor as a "*de jure* stateless person", yet still be in a situation of concern was persistent. In the end, a non-binding recommendation was adopted in an attempt to address such cases. Thus, through the Final Act of the 1954 Convention relating to the Status of Stateless Persons,

> the Conference recommends that each Contracting State, when it recognises as valid the reasons for which a person has renounced the protection of the State of which he

[63] As recommended by the "Study of Statelessness" that was carried out in 1949 to investigate the problem of persons lacking national protection. UN, *A Study of Statelessness,* E/1112, New York: August 1949

[64] Article 1 of the Convention relating to the Status of Refugees, 1951 (read together with the 1967 Protocol).

[65] A statement to this effect was also made by the British representative in discussions surrounding the draft statelessness convention, Nehemiah Robinson, *Convention relating to the status of stateless persons - Its history and interpretation*, UNHCR, Geneva: 1955, page 12.

[66] Carol Batchelor, 'Statelessness and the Problem of Resolving Nationality Status', in *International Journal of Refugee Law,* Vol. 10, 1998, page 172.

[67] Nehemiah Robinson, *Convention relating to the status of stateless persons - Its history and interpretation*, UNHCR, Geneva: 1955, pages 11-13.

> is a national, consider sympathetically the possibility of according to that person the treatment which the Convention accords to stateless persons.[68]

This recommendation has since been seized upon as evidence of the recognition of "*de facto* statelessness". For instance, according to the joint UNHCR and IPU Handbook on statelessness, "this recommendation was included on behalf of *de facto* stateless persons who, technically, still hold a nationality but do not receive any of the benefits generally associated with nationality".[69] Yet the recommendation does not refer to *de facto* statelessness and actually clearly enunciates that those persons to whom governments choose to extend the protection of the Convention on the basis of this recommendation are *not* stateless persons.[70] The 1954 Statelessness Convention then, clearly and unambiguously, limits the definition of stateless persons to those individuals who lack protection *de jure*.

Notwithstanding these observations, debate on the problem of "*de facto* statelessness" continued as scholars and practitioners grappled with the reconciliation of the official definition of statelessness with what they perceived to be the widespread difficulties experienced in practice.[71] This, in itself, signals the potential inadequacy of the definition and thereby a potential first problem in the approach taken to the issue of statelessness under international law. In essence, the question that has fed an enduring discussion on the sidelines to this day is this: should the *de facto* lack of protection also be addressed as an issue of *statelessness*?

The concerns raised are threefold. Firstly, as mentioned above, there is the argument that a narrow focus on the *de jure* unprotected ignores the reality that *de jure* and *de facto* unprotected persons live side by side and share the same needs. Since "the crucial question [is] one of protection",[72] to address only the fact and not the quality of nationality is to create an arbitrary and unjust distinction between these two similarly situated groups. In other words, "persons with no effective

---

[68] Article 1 of the Final Act of the Convention relating to the Status of Stateless Persons, UN, 1954.

[69] UNHCR and IPU, *Nationality and statelessness. A handbook for parliamentarians*, 2005, page 25. See also UNHCR, *Information and accession package: the 1954 Convention relating to the status of stateless persons and the 1961 Convention on the reduction of statelessness,* Geneva: January 1999, page 13.

[70] Moreover, it can be questioned whether the recommendation has any added value whatsoever when placed in the proper context: when read in conjunction with both the 1954 Statelessness Convention and the 1951 Refugee Convention, it seems fair to assume that, once again, it is the "well-founded fear of persecution" to which the definition of a refugee refers that reflects the international consensus on which reasons are "valid" for refusing to avail oneself of national protection. This is in line with the aforementioned argument made by the British against expanding the protection of the Statelessness Convention to cases of *de facto* "unprotection". See note 65 above.

[71] Including in Paul Weis, "The United Nations Convention on the Reduction of Statelessness, 1961" in *International and Comparative Law Quarterly,* Vol. 11, No. 4, 1962, pages 1073-1096; Carol Batchelor, 'Stateless Persons: Some Gaps in International Protection', in *International Journal of Refugee Law,* Vol. 7, 1995; Carol Batchelor, 'Statelessness and the Problem of Resolving Nationality Status', in *International Journal of Refugee Law,* Vol. 10, 1998; Maureen Lynch, *Lives on hold: The human cost of statelessness,* Washington: 2005; David Weissbrodt; Clay Collins, 'The Human Rights of Stateless Persons', in *Human Rights Quarterly,* Vol. 28, 2006; and Abbas Shiblak, *Citizens, Sub-citizens and Non-citizens: Statelessness in the Arab Region,* unpublished paper.

[72] Carol Batchelor, 'Stateless Persons: Some Gaps in International Protection', in *International Journal of Refugee Law,* Vol. 7, 1995, page 252

nationality are, for all practical purposes, stateless, and should be labelled and treated as such".[73] A second, related concern is that, if a case of "unprotection" is considered to be resolved the moment that a bond of nationality is (re)established *de jure*, there is a severe risk of producing a shift from a *de jure* to a *de facto* lack of protection without achieving any real improvement in the status or treatment of the person concerned.[74] Finally, it was pointed out that differentiating between a *de jure* and *de facto* lack of protection may be unworkable in practice:

> There are many cases where a person's nationality status cannot be established, where it is doubtful, undetermined or unknown [...] The borderline between what is commonly called *de jure* statelessness and *de facto* statelessness is sometimes difficult to draw.[75]

With this in mind, some organisations that are engaged on the issue of statelessness have elected to adopt a pragmatic, flexible approach to the question of definition. For their protection and advocacy work, rather than attempting to distinguish exactly between *de jure* and *de facto* cases, these organisations focus more broadly on the treatment of – or problems faced by – the persons involved, using this as a means of identifying situations of concern.[76]

On the basis of these credible and ostensibly persuasive arguments, the term "*de facto* statelessness" has entered "common use and has acquired a meaning".[77] However, this has not been reflected in the international legal framework and the term has no *legal* significance.[78] How can these two facts be reconciled? I would

[73] David Weissbrodt; Clay Collins, 'The Human Rights of Stateless Persons', in *Human Rights Quarterly*, Vol. 28, 2006, page 251.

[74] Manley Hudson, *Report on Nationality, including Statelessness*, A/CN.4/50, 21 February 1952, page 49.

[75] Statement by Paul Weis to the United Nations Conference on the Elimination or Reduction of Future Statelessness, 25 August 1961, as cited in Carol Batchelor, 'Stateless Persons: Some Gaps in International Protection', in *International Journal of Refugee Law*, Vol. 7, 1995, page 252.

[76] See in particular Maureen Lynch, *Lives on hold: The human cost of statelessness*, Washington: 2005. For instance, this report mentions Afghans among the stateless persons identified in Indonesia although the actual description of the situation of these Afghans does not explain why this group is stateless or address the subject of nationality at all. It simply refers, without any further explanation, to the Afghan asylum seekers who attempted to reach Australia but were deported to Indonesia. The same report determines that "40,000 to 50,000 Roma in Bosnia and Herzegovina are exposed to abuses of civil, political, economic and social rights" before admitting that "an unknown number of them are stateless" and carrying on to describe the treatment experienced by "individuals who lack personal documents" or simply "many Roma". See also the discussion of several situations of "statelessness" in UNHCR, "Statelessness and Citizenship" in *The State of the World's Refugees - A Humanitarian Agenda*, Oxford University Press, Oxford: 1997.

[77] Statement by Paul Weis to the United Nations Conference on the Elimination or Reduction of Future Statelessness, 25 August 1961, as cited in Carol Batchelor, 'Stateless Persons: Some Gaps in International Protection', in *International Journal of Refugee Law*, Vol. 7, 1995, page 252.

[78] In spite of the arguments raised in favour of the inclusion of *de facto* cases in the concept of "statelessness", there are just two places in which this inclusive approach to statelessness receives any corroboration in the field of international law. The first is in the recommendation included in the final act of the 1961 Convention on the Reduction of Statelessness: "The Conference recommends that persons who are stateless *de facto* should as far as possible be treated as stateless *de jure* to enable them to acquire an *effective* nationality". But even here, de facto statelessness is only the subject of another

argue: perhaps more readily than may be expected. I base this conclusion on two key points. The first is that, while it may have been astute at the time that the 1954 and 1961 Statelessness Conventions were adopted to fear for a protection gap for those who could benefit from neither the guarantees offered to the *de jure* unprotected nor to *refugees,* advances in the field of human rights law have since appeased this concern. The second point relates to the fine line that exists between the question of definition, or *substance,* and the problem of identification, or *procedure.* Thus, concerns expressed about the difficulty of detecting cases of *de jure* "unprotection" and distinguishing these from the *de facto* unprotected do not necessarily warrant a new or more inclusive approach to defining statelessness, but rather a clear agreement on rules of procedure and evidence.

To illustrate these arguments, let us consider the three scenarios that are now widely considered to be encapsulated within the expression "*de facto* statelessness":

- where a person is deprived of the enjoyment of those rights that are generally attached to nationality;

- where a person's nationality is contested or disputed by one or more states; and

- where a person is unable to establish or prove his or her nationality.[79]

The first situation describes the problem of an *ineffective* nationality, whereby a certain sub-section of nationals "do not enjoy the rights of citizenship enjoyed by other non-criminal citizens of the same state".[80] Such treatment contravenes international human rights standards that delineate the rights to be enjoyed by *everyone* as well as the rights to be enjoyed by *citizens* on an equal basis.[81] There is

---

non-binding recommendation so the definition of statelessness offered under international law remains in tact. See further chapter III, section 3. The second place in which the phenomenon of *de facto* statelessness is clearly alluded to is in a 2005 ruling by the Inter-American Court of Human Rights. The court stated that the condition of statelessness "arises from the lack of a nationality, when an individual does not qualify to receive this under a State's laws, owing to arbitrary deprivation *or the granting of a nationality that, in actual fact, is not effective".* Emphasis added. Inter-American Court of Human Rights, *Case of Yean and Bosico v. Dominican Republic,* 8 September 2005, paragraph 142.

[79] See Carol Batchelor, 'Stateless Persons: Some Gaps in International Protection', in *International Journal of Refugee Law,* Vol. 7, 1995; UNHCR, "Statelessness and Citizenship" in *The State of the World's Refugees - A Humanitarian Agenda,* Oxford University Press, Oxford: 1997; Carol Batchelor, 'Statelessness and the Problem of Resolving Nationality Status', in *International Journal of Refugee Law,* Vol. 10, 1998; Maureen Lynch, *Lives on hold: The human cost of statelessness,* Washington: 2005; David Weissbrodt; Clay Collins, 'The Human Rights of Stateless Persons', in *Human Rights Quarterly,* Vol. 28, 2006; UNHCR Executive Committee, *Conclusion on Identification, Prevention and Reduction of Statelessness and Protection of Stateless Persons, No. 106,* 57th Session, Geneva, 2006.

[80] David Weissbrodt; Clay Collins, 'The Human Rights of Stateless Persons', in *Human Rights Quarterly,* Vol. 28, 2006, page 263.

[81] It is possible that where an individual's nationality has become entirely ineffective through the cumulative violation of numerous rights that are generally accorded to citizens, the violation of the right to a nationality could be added to the list of complaints because the legal status is thereby deprived of all substance. Even then though, this keeps the problem of so-called "*de facto* statelessness" within the realms of general human rights law.

no need for a special regime, based on the notion of *de facto* statelessness or otherwise, to address the plight of these individuals because their situation simply falls within the ambit of general human rights law and is subject to the regular system of implementation and supervision.[82] By contrast, the *de jure* absence of a nationality has the effect of throwing an individual into a legal vacuum because international (human rights) law accords certain functions to citizenship: as we will see in more detail later,[83] the lack of access to rights and benefits is in some instances a direct consequence of the fact that the human rights system admits certain privileges in the treatment of citizens. The absence of the legal bond of nationality with any state results in exclusion from these rights. This group is therefore reliant on additional legal measures - a specialised regime – to redress their plight.[84]

The other two scenarios of "*de facto* statelessness"– where citizenship is disputed or cannot be established – call for a (re)think about how cases of statelessness are to be *identified,* but do not require the definition itself to be revisited. The task of identification raises such questions as what type of procedure should be followed and what evidence is required to establish the nationality or, by default, the absence of a nationality of an individual? Weis addresses this question in detail, reflecting upon the practice of states and international tribunals.[85] He suggests that

> since nationality is determined by the law of the country whose nationality is claimed, evidence – usually of a documentary nature – that the person was considered as a national by an authority qualified under municipal law to determine or to certify nationality will, as a rule, be the best evidence.[86]

[82] It is true that in the resolution of cases of statelessness (*de jure*), the aim should be for the individual to acquire not just a nationality *de jure*, but one that is *effective*. To minimise the risk of acquisition of an *ineffective* nationality it can be important to promote the conferral of nationality by a state with which the individual has a real connection. However, if upon the (re)establishment of the formal bond of nationality with a state, the individual is nevertheless (still) denied the rights that are generally accorded to citizens, it falls to the broader system of human rights law to ensure that this situation is remedied. The enduring problem of an *ineffective* nationality is simply evidence of a continuing need to address the non-compliance of states with their human rights obligations.

[83] In Part 3.

[84] Just which rights need to be included in such a specialised regime – and the extent to which this need is met – is one of the matters that will be investigated in depth in Part 3 of this study. Meanwhile, the ongoing necessity of a specialised regime to deal with *refugees* can be seen in the context of the severity of their situation. If the system of human rights protection breaks down so dramatically as to allow the persecution and corresponding forced displacement of individuals, additional protections must be in place to ensure at least the non-penalisation of such persons in the event of unlawful entry into another country to seek refuge and the non-return of these persons to the state in which they fear for their lives or safety (*non-refoulement*). The 1951 Convention relating to the Status of Refugees deals with both of these matters as well as a elaborating a minimum standards of treatment for refugees in their host state.

[85] Paul Weis, *Nationality and Statelessness in International Law*, Kluwer Academic Publishers Group, Dordrecht: 1979, chapter 13 on "Proof of Nationality", pages 204-236.

[86] Paul Weis, *Nationality and Statelessness in International Law*, Kluwer Academic Publishers Group, Dordrecht: 1979, page 215.

However, such evidence may not always be readily available and proof of statelessness – the absence of a bond of nationality – is an even trickier question than proof of nationality.[87] Thus, if a state disputes the citizenship of an individual or the person is unable to produce or acquire confirmation of his status as a national from the authorities of any country with which he has some factual connection, it may be possible to put this forward as evidence of the fact that the person is "not considered a national by any state under the operation of its law" and therefore *stateless* for the purpose of international law. Similarly, the contested or ambiguous citizenship status of the parents may contribute to the determination that a child "would otherwise be stateless" for the purpose of applying the fall-back provisions of the 1961 Convention on the Reduction of Statelessness. Moreover, the problem of an *ineffective* nationality, as described above, may also contribute to the identification of cases of *de jure* "unprotection": the denial of rights that are generally accorded to citizens can be taken into account as evidence of the fact that a state does not consider a person to be its national "under the operation of its law". According to Weis, among the secondary evidence of nationality admitted by international tribunals are "certain facts from which nationality may be inferred, such as voting in elections, holding public office, etc".[88] It is conceivable that, in the reverse situation, the clear denial of such privileges without further justification could be taken as evidence of the lack of the bond of nationality – although it is important to be aware of the constraints inherent in the use of such evidence, such as the inapplicability of these particular elements of proof in cases involving children.

The central question is nevertheless how the definition of statelessness is to be applied and what factors can practicably be taken into account in proving the absence of a nationality. Rules on evidence are needed to establish to what extent the refusal to confirm an individual as a citizen (or non-citizen) or the denial of rights generally accorded to citizens carry weight in identifying statelessness. Through the application of such rules it becomes possible to determine which cases of "*de facto* statelessness" in fact fall within the scope of the internationally-recognised definition of statelessness. It will also be possible to establish, on the other hand, which persons retain the bond of nationality with a state and are owed treatment as a citizen accordingly.

In sum, once the full picture has been uncovered, *defining* statelessness is a less contentious question than an initial perusal of the literature may suggest. "Statelessness" as a concept of international law refers only to the situation in which a person lacks the legal bond of nationality – cases commonly referred to as *de jure* statelessness. In today's human rights environment, this approach - criticised on occasion for being too narrow and for failing to adequately reflect the

---

[87] Thus, *"documentary evidence from a responsible State authority certifying that the person concerned is not a national is normally a reliable form of evidence for the purposes of establishing statelessness. However, such documentary evidence will not always be available, in part precisely because States will not readily feel accountable for indicating which persons do not have a legal bond of nationality"*. Carol Batchelor The 1954 Convention relating to the Status of Stateless Persons: Implementation within the European Union Member States and Recommendations for Harmonisation 2004, pages 14-15.

[88] Paul Weis, *Nationality and Statelessness in International Law*, Kluwer Academic Publishers Group, Dordrecht: 1979, page 216.

situation on the ground[89] - can actually be deemed to pass muster. It addresses those instances in which the international legal framework itself creates a need for special measures. And, while concern continues for the problem of so-called "*de facto* statelessness", closer inspection showed that the scenarios presented under this notion do not demand specialist treatment. The "*de facto* stateless" are either the victims of (multiple) human rights violations and should be able to assert their rights under that regime or may actually qualify for protection as stateless persons (*de jure*) if the rules of evidence were clarified and implemented effectively. Indeed, the continued use of the term "*de facto* statelessness" (and alongside it the expression "*de jure* statelessness" as though it indicated a *subset* of stateless persons) may be counterproductive since it has no legal significance. Moreover, ongoing disagreement on the scope of the term "statelessness" can have a highly disruptive impact on the implementation of the relevant international standards. The continuing divergent practices in the use of this label is obscuring efforts to actually identify cases of statelessness that warrant the applicable legal protection. It would be far more fruitful to concentrate efforts on the implementation of the existing definition of statelessness – on the *identification* of statelessness – as well as on measures to ensure that states honour their human rights commitments to their nationals so as to preclude the problem of an *ineffective* nationality.[90]

As far as the approach to defining and identifying statelessness in this manuscript goes: in looking at how international law deals with "statelessness", the focus is on an assessment of the guarantees offered against – and the protection offered in the event of – the formal absence of any legal bond of nationality. As I have explained, there is in fact no good reason not to stick to the existing official definition of statelessness. However, one of the questions that will necessarily be posed in the context of this study is how the identification of statelessness has been dealt with in the context of both prevention and protection. In view of the foregoing discussion, this is an area in which the international standards may well be found wanting.

5 Conclusion: Why statelessness?

There are, in fact, many possible answers to the question "why statelessness?" one of which is that it is an issue that I have personally been drawn to and find fascinating. Another argument is that a quick perusal of (legal) publications uncovers scant and scattered attention for the subject to date, suggesting that an in depth study may well be overdue. Yet, what this chapter really has shown is that statelessness is (still) an international problem of significant magnitude and severe consequence: two facts that immediately imply that the international response to the issue is failing in some way. Moreover, a brief look at that international response confirmed that the approach to the statelessness phenomenon to date may indeed be questionable. A particular concern is that the tailor-made standards have enjoyed too little attention and support for too long so there has been no opportunity to try,

[89] As evidenced by the adoption of a wider definition by many scholars and organisations engaged on the issue of statelessness. Recall notes 73 and 77 above.

[90] This latter problem is beyond the scope of this study since it does not address issues of *statelessness* but deals more generally with the question of compliance of states with human rights law.

test and further develop them. Interestingly though, when we actually took a close look at the first concrete dilemma in tackling statelessness – the problem of definition – we came to a somewhat unexpected conclusion. Despite criticism being directed towards the definition of statelessness adopted under international law, we found that the real threat comes not from this legal framework but from the ongoing, unproductive debate on the issue of definition which may in fact be further hampering the implementation of existing legal standards by obstructing discussion on the *identification* of statelessness. It is therefore far too premature to conclude that the international framework for tackling statelessness is entirely inappropriate. Further study is plainly needed to pin-point where exactly the gaps are that are letting the system down.

What is certainly clear, to borrow a phrase from one of the few articles that has been devoted to the subject is that

> hitherto, international co-operation in improving the status of stateless persons, or in reducing or eliminating statelessness, has enjoyed limited success, often disappearing down relatively unproductive paths. The time has come for a revision of such arrangements, deconstruction of earlier analytical approaches and their substitution with practical arrangements which reflect the principles generally shared by the community of nations.[91]

With the re-emerging international interest in the question of statelessness, now is a suitable moment to conduct an in depth study into the plight of the stateless. More importantly, at a time when numerous different bodies and institutions are calling for states to accede to the Statelessness Conventions in order to take on the problem of statelessness, an assessment of the appropriateness of this legal regime is called for: is it (still) relevant and does it (still) suffice? Through the following analysis of the international legal framework, first for the prevention of statelessness (part 2) and then for the protection of stateless persons (part 3), I hope to contribute to current discussion on this subject and offer some recommendations to guide the international community towards a more comprehensive and effective overall response.

---

[91] Guy Goodwin Gill, "The rights of refugees and stateless persons" in Saksena (ed) *Human rights perspectives & challenges (in 1900's and beyond)*, Lancers Books, New Delhi: 1994, page 394

PART 2

PREVENTING STATELESSNESS

CHAPTER III

BACKGROUND TO PREVENTING STATELESSNESS

In order to kick off the consideration of the problem of prevention of statelessness it is important to look at how individuals can acquire and lose the esteemed legal status of nationality - *nationality* matters. To know how nationality is attributed is key to tracing the origins of the statelessness phenomenon and divining ways to nip it in the bud. Armed with an understanding of the causes of statelessness, it becomes possible to assess the effectiveness of the international community's reaction to the issue. Chapters three to eight, which together make up Part 2 of this work, aspire to do just that by first outlining the circumstances under which statelessness may be created and then considering whether international law prescribes an adequate remedy to ensure the prevention of statelessness in each case: both through the 1961 Convention on the Reduction of Statelessness and under broader human rights commitments. This introductory chapter therefore provides not only a background to the 1961 Convention, but also some general observations on the attribution of nationality and the role of international law in that context.[1]

1 THE ATTRIBUTION OF NATIONALITY: DOCTRINES AND COMPETENCES

A fundamental, centuries-old issue underlies the whole question of the attribution of nationality: inclusion vs. exclusion. Who can be considered a member of one's own community? Who belongs? And who is an outsider? This problem of defining who is "us" and who is "them" has been challenging societies throughout the ages, from determining who were citizens of the polis in Ancient Greece to deciding who are nationals of the modern nation-state.[2] As we will see in detail later, membership of such a political entity is not unimportant – it brings with it all manner of rights and duties.[3] The question here is, with a running total of over 190 nation-states worldwide, how do we decide who belongs where? How do we determine who is Estonian or Ethiopian, Japanese or Jamaican – what criteria are or should be used?

[1] The full text of the 1961 Convention on the Reduction of Statelessness can be found in Annex 1.

[2] Mija Zagar, "Citizenship - Nationality: A Proper Balance Between the Interests of States and those of Individuals" in *Council of Europe's First European Conference on Nationality*, Strasbourg: 1999, pages 94-95.

[3] Part 3 of this book uncovers the full significance of drawing this line of membership and the meaning or content of nationality as membership of a state.

Furthermore, who is authorised to take that decision and grant or deprive an individual of a particular nationality?

The formal acceptance of an individual as a member of a state through the bestowal of the legal bond of nationality is not a random act - it is the recognition of an existing factual link with that state. The International Court of Justice described it thus:

> Nationality is a legal bond having as its basis a social fact of attachment, a genuine connection of existence, interests and sentiments. [4]

There are many different factors that may serve as evidence of this "social fact of attachment" - the so-called *genuine link* - for the purposes of nationality attribution. Among them: place of birth, descent, residence, family ties, language and ethnicity. States employ one or more of these components of nationality in delineating the original make-up of their body of nationals and thereafter in the course of determining who is worthy of this legal status.[5] Although endless permutations and combinations are imaginable, in general states adhere to doctrines based closely on one or more of the following principles: *jus soli, jus sanguinis* and *jus domicilli.* Any additional, secondary factors that are taken into consideration serve merely to offer variations on the same theme.

The birth of a child is one of the pivotal events that nationality policy must deal with since it entails the arrival of a new human life which must be given its place in the global political system. If left "unclaimed" by any state as its national, the child will be stateless. The factors that are considered to constitute the required *genuine link* between a state and a newborn baby are place of birth and parentage. Thus the first two principles mentioned above – *jus soli* and *jus sanguinis* – govern the question of attribution of nationality at birth. Following the *jus soli* principle or "law of the soil", nationality is acquired at birth by virtue of being born on the territory of the state. Historically, its roots can be traced to the feudal era, when in Great Britain for example, all "natural-born British subjects [...] owed loyalty to the King and were entitled to his protection".[6] Thereafter, it was widely adopted by the immigration states of the New World because recent arrivals were viewed as potential citizens and the *jus soli* doctrine was a way of solidifying their bond with the state of destination: the second generation of immigrants automatically become nationals of the state in which their parents choose to settle. The rationale for this mode of nationality attribution is that

[4] International Court of Justice, *"Nottebohm Case" (Liechtenstein v. Guatamala)*, 1953, page 23.

[5] It should be noted that "to a larger extent than is the case with the territory of a State, the body of nationals – since it is in a perpetual state of flux owing to births, deaths, migration and similar factors – is in constant need of determination". This necessitates a continuous and ongoing string of decisions about who is a citizen and who is not. Haro van Panhuys, "Chapter VII: Restrictions Imposed by International Law upon the Competence of Ctates to Lay Down Nationality Rules" in *The Role of Nationality in International Law*, A.W. Sijthoff's Uitgeversmaatschappij, Leiden: 1959, page 150.

[6] Verena Stolcke, "The 'Nature' of nationality" in Bader (ed) *Citizenship and exclusion*, Macmillan Press, London: 1997, page 70; Rainer Bauböck, *Transnational Citizenship. Membership and Rights in International Migration*, Edward Elgar, Cheltenham: 2002, page 35.

> it is with the territory on which he is born that any individual is the most closely connected and that, since he grows up and lives in that territory, he assimilates the customs and habits of thought of its inhabitants and gradually merges into their community.[7]

To this day, the *jus soli* principle is particularly prevalent in states which have traditionally been countries of immigration, although it has also spread to other areas of the world.

The competing *jus sanguinis* principle, otherwise known as the "law of the blood", recognises descent or parentage as the indication of a *genuine link*. Accordingly, nationality is granted by a particular state to a child at birth if one or both of his parents are nationals of that state themselves – it is handed down from one generation to the next through the bloodline. The origin of the principle can be traced back to ancient Greece[8] and the first European nationality codes contained *jus sanguinis* provisions.[9] Initially, the determination of nationality in this way was justified on the grounds of a shared race or culture. Later, this argument was replaced with notion that *jus sanguinis* recognises the role of the family in the upbringing of the child and the importance of family unity.[10] To this day, *jus sanguinis* is the preferred doctrine of the so-called emigration states – mainly European, Asian and Arab nations – as a way of retaining the allegiance of populations that have moved abroad.[11]

These two doctrines can be traced in one shape or another – nowadays usually in a mixed form – in the policy of all states on attribution of nationality at birth.[12] However, it is also possible to acquire a (different) nationality later in life, in recognition of a more recently established *genuine link* with a state. The most important principle in this respect is that of *jus domicilli,* or the "law of residence". This principle is the most common ground for naturalisation where the nationality of the state is granted upon application to the competent authorities. *Jus domicilli* recognises the bond that an individual develops with a state after a significant period of habitual or permanent residence, often determined to be in the region of five to ten years.[13] The reasoning behind *jus domicilli* is similar to that of *jus soli* and has been expressed as follows:

---

[7] International Union for Child Welfare, *Stateless Children - A Comparative Study of National Legislation and Suggested Solutions to the Problem of Statelessness of Children,* Geneva: 1947, page 19.

[8] Rainer Bauböck, *Transnational Citizenship. Membership and Rights in International Migration,* Edward Elgar, Cheltenham: 2002, page 39.

[9] An example is the 1804 Napoleonic Code; Verena Stolcke, "The 'Nature' of nationality" in Bader (ed) *Citizenship and exclusion,* Macmillan Press, London: 1997, pages 66-67.

[10] International Union for Child Welfare, *Stateless Children - A Comparative Study of National Legislation and Suggested Solutions to the Problem of Statelessness of Children,* Geneva: 1947, page 9.

[11] Stephen Castles; Alastair Davidson, *Citizenship and Migration. Globalisation and the Politics of Belonging,* Macmillan Press, London: 2000, page 85.

[12] The two doctrines are both fully developed and are considered to be equally legitimate. Carol Batchelor, 'Statelessness and the Problem of Resolving Nationality Status', in *International Journal of Refugee Law,* Vol. 10, 1998, 1998, page 169.

[13] The exact conditions that must be met to qualify for naturalisation, such as the period of habitual residence required and additional criteria (e.g. knowledge of the national language), are set by domestic regulations and vary from state to state; See further Ruth Donner, "Chapter 2: The Principle of the

> It is the persons living in the State who take part in shaping its experiences, developing its economy, and fashioning its social life, and, accordingly, they are the ones who are primarily entitled to become full members of it.[14]

An individual can also forge a bond with a state later in life through adoption by or marriage to a national.[15] This is usually recognised as a ground for (at least facilitated) naturalisation, for access to nationality by option, registration or declaration, or even for automatic acquisition of nationality by operation of the law.

Having introduced the principles underlying the conferral of nationality, it is important to mention the possibility of loss, deprivation or renunciation of an existing nationality. In short the legal bond of nationality, once acquired, can be forfeited – there is no lifetime guarantee. An individual may voluntarily renounce his nationality, an act which is often linked to the acquisition of a new nationality by naturalisation. As to loss or deprivation of nationality, it is not always clear where the line is drawn between these two phenomena, but the essence is that it concerns the withdrawal of nationality in circumstances other than at the request of the individual himself.[16] Another term for this practice is "denationalisation" or – where the nationality had been acquired through naturalisation – "denaturalisation". A number of the reasons for the loss or deprivation of nationality are: a prolonged period of residence in a foreign state (seen as allowing the connection with the state of nationality to decay, eventually forfeiting the legal bond); deliberate (mass) denationalisation by decree (usually linked to discriminatory policies targeted towards a particular population group); denaturalisation where nationality was acquired through fraudulent means; or deprivation of nationality as a punitive measure or in reaction to acts committed by the individual that are considered disloyal to the interests of the state (for example serving in the armed forces of a foreign state). This by way of introduction - the legitimacy of such measures, particularly when resulting in statelessness - will be considered later.

Armed with a basic notion of the conditions under which nationality is conferred and withdrawn, we can move on to the question of competence: who is authorised to grant or deprive an individual of a particular nationality? Borrowing again from the words of Manley Hudson, the answer is:

"Link" in Nationality Law" in *The Regulation of Nationality in International Law*, Transnational Publishers, New York: 1994, pages 33-34.

[14] Yaffa Zilberschats, "Chapter 3 - The Horizontal Aspect of Citizenship" in *The Human Right to Citizenship*, Transnational Publishers, Ardsley, NY: 2002, page 94.

[15] The rationale here is similar to that underlying the *jus sanguinis* principle. Rainer Bauböck, *Transnational Citizenship. Membership and Rights in International Migration*, Edward Elgar, Cheltenham: 2002, page 43.

[16] One possible means of differentiation is to interpret "loss of nationality" as the automatic withdrawal of nationality, *ex lege*, while "deprivation of nationality" is at the initiative of the state party (although the conditions for this should also be set down in the law). This is suggested by the phrasing used in article 7 of the European Convention on Nationality, 1997, a provision which is said to deal with both loss and deprivation of nationality. However, the two terms are used interchangeably and with little consistency.

> In principle, questions of nationality fall within the domestic jurisdiction of each state.[17]

One of the manifestations of the sovereignty of nation-states is this right to "determine the rules governing the attribution of their own nationality in accordance with their interests".[18] Indeed the authority to confer or withdraw nationality is an essential element of a state's sovereignty for it is this act which delineates the scope of personal supremacy of that state.[19] With the arrival of democracy, "the people" became sovereign (i.e. they were no longer subjected to the rule of a supreme monarch) and the significance of being a member of a particular nation-state grew.[20] So too did the vested interest of the state to regulate its own membership as nationals gained the right to exert influence over state affairs and politics. At this stage in history – the late 19th and early 20th century – the freedom of states to determine who are and who are not their nationals was considered virtually unfettered.[21] As we will see, there have since been significant developments in the field of international (human rights) law which have impacted on this freedom. However, the authority to settle questions of membership remains at the heart of state sovereignty making it a jealously guarded competence to this day.[22] In fact, one principle of international law has even strengthened states' claims to the power to regulate matters of nationality: "the principle of self-determination, which holds that citizens of a state have the right to determine their destiny, including the right to decide the terms and conditions of membership of their community".[23] Moreover, because nationality is entwined with such issues as sovereignty, the ascription of rights and duties (among which the tools for political empowerment) and the very identity of the state, it remains a controversial topic and one that must be approached with a certain delicacy.[24] It is important to be conscious of such

[17] Manley Hudson, *Report on Nationality, including Statelessness,* A/CN.4/50, 21 February 1952, page 12. States regulate nationality attribution through the codification and implementation of nationality legislation.

[18] Ruth Donner, "Chapter 3: The Imposition and Withdrawal of Nationality" in *The Regulation of Nationality in International Law*, Transnational Publishers, New York: 1994, page 121.

[19] Just as the construction of borders between territories determines the range of the state's territorial supremacy. Paul Weis, *Nationality and Statelessness in International Law*, Kluwer Academic Publishers Group, Dordrecht: 1979, page 65.

[20] Mija Zagar, "Citizenship - Nationality: A Proper Balance Between the Interests of States and those of Individuals" in *Council of Europe's First European Conference on Nationality*, Strasbourg: 1999, page 99.

[21] Johannes Chan, 'The Right to a Nationality as a Human Right - The Current Trend Towards Recognition', in *Human Rights Law Journal,* Vol. 12, 1991, page 1; Yaffa Zilberschats, "Chapter 2 - Citizenship and International Law" in *The Human Right to Citizenship*, Transnational Publishers, Ardsley, NY: 2002, page 8.

[22] Johannes Chan, 'The Right to a Nationality as a Human Right - The Current Trend Towards Recognition', in *Human Rights Law Journal,* Vol. 12, 1991, page 1.

[23] James Goldston, 'Holes in the Rights Framework: Racial Discrimination, Citizenship, and the Rights of Noncitizens', in *Ethics and International Affairs,* Vol. 20, 2006, page 338.

[24] Verena Stolcke, "The 'Nature' of nationality" in Bader (ed) *Citizenship and exclusion*, Macmillan Press, London: 1997, page 61; UNHCR and IPU, *Nationality and statelessness. A handbook for parliamentarians*, 2005, page 8.

sensitivities when assessing the part that international law does or should play in nationality matters.

What implications do the foregoing observations have for the problem of statelessness? The answer is simple. The existence of different doctrines for the attribution of nationality – along with a multitude of variations through the introduction of secondary components – combined with the basic autonomy of states to regulate the conferral and withdrawal of their nationality opens the door to both the deliberate and inadvertent creation of statelessness.[25] The inherent mobility of people puts the compatibility of these divergent yet coexisting doctrines under added pressure. Since people may cross borders, marry nationals of other states or bare children in a state in which they are not themselves a citizen, if states do not communicate or cooperate on nationality matters then conflicts between their individual policies may leave some individuals entirely overlooked and without the nationality of any state. In addition, unless limits are placed on the freedom of states to determine who is worthy of citizenship, certain persons may be singled out and rendered stateless. Clearly then, there is a role for international law in preventing and resolving cases of statelessness - and so to the question of how international law treats the problem of nationality attribution.

2 International Law and the Attribution of Nationality

International law, as created in the main by states themselves, respects the principles of sovereignty and equality of states. Generally speaking, without the all-important "consent to be bound", a state cannot be compelled to accept new obligations under international law.[26] Nor is interference in the domestic jurisdiction of another state acceptable.[27] It therefore comes as no surprise that the initial approach to nationality under international law was not to meddle with the competence of states to regulate the attribution of this legal bond of membership. As mentioned, this was a carefully guarded sovereign privilege. However, the possibility was never ruled out that nationality matters could be the subject of international law, if states so decided. This was the gist of the most commonly cited case concerning the influence of international law on nationality: the *Tunis and Morocco Nationality Decrees case*, decided by the Permanent Court of International Justice in 1923. The court was asked to determine whether the disputed French Nationality Decrees were purely a matter of domestic jurisdiction and, as such, beyond the advisory competences of the League of Nations. [28] It decided as follows:

[25] The same factors also contribute to the existence of dual or even multiple nationality.

[26] With the important exception of the peremptory norms of international law (*jus cogens*), from whose binding character no state can escape as well as, in certain cases, customary law and general principles of international law.

[27] Ian Brownlie, *Principles of Public International Law*, Oxford University Press, Oxford: 2003, pages 18-19 and 288-289.

[28] Great Britain claimed that the French Decrees were unlawful as they imposed French citizenship on the children of British subjects, born in the French Protectorate areas of Tunis and Morocco. The Court had to advise as to the competence of the League of Nations since Article 15 (8) of the Covenant of the League of Nations decrees that the League is not competent to advise on matters that fall solely within the domestic jurisdiction of states. See further Paul Weis, *Nationality and Statelessness in International Law*, Kluwer Academic Publishers Group, Dordrecht: 1979, chapter 5.

> The question of whether a certain matter is or is not solely within the jurisdiction of a State is an essentially relative question; it depends upon the development of international relations. Thus, in the present state of international law, questions of nationality are, in the opinion of this court, in principle within this reserved domain.[29]

This case confirmed that, at the time, the attribution of nationality was a matter for each individual state to settle, but admitted that if international law were to develop along those lines, then nationality matters would no longer fall under this *domaine réservé*.[30] The question of just how free states are to determine who are their nationals, untouched by international obligations, can therefore only be answered by analysing the developments in international law in that field and the current state of play.[31] Then it becomes clear that, in the eighty-odd years since the Permanent Court of Justice considered the problem, much has changed.

To begin with, in 1930, under the auspices of the League of Nations, the Hague Convention on Certain Questions relating to the Conflict of Nationality Laws was drafted.[32] This was the first serious attempt by states to agree on a number of basic rules relating to nationality matters.[33] While reaffirming the sovereignty of states to regulate nationality attribution, the Convention does not rest there, as its purpose was to resolve some of the conflicts of laws that spore precisely from the freedom of states to determine who their nationals are - to address statelessness and dual nationality. This explains the Convention's approach as, set out in its first provision:

> It is for each State to determine under its own law who are its nationals. This law shall be recognised by other States in so far as it is consistent with international conventions, international custom, and the principles of law generally recognised with regard to nationality.[34]

This article focuses on the international effects of an individual's nationality. Rather than determining that nationality may not be attributed in contravention of

[29] Permanent Court of International Justice, *Tunis and Morocco Nationality Decrees case*, 1923, p.24.

[30] Paul Weis, *Nationality and Statelessness in International Law*, Kluwer Academic Publishers Group, Dordrecht: 1979, page 66

[31] Johannes Chan, 'The Right to a Nationality as a Human Right - The Current Trend Towards Recognition', in *Human Rights Law Journal,* Vol. 12, 1991, page 2; UNHCR, *Information and accession package: the 1954 Convention relating to the status of stateless persons and the 1961 Convention on the reduction of statelessness,* Geneva: January 1999 page 5.

[32] Hereafter the 1930 Hague Convention.

[33] Still earlier, in 1885, the Institute for International Law formulated a number of principles concerning the attribution of nationality such as "No one shall be without a nationality", "No one shall have two nationalities simultaneously" and "Everyone shall have the right to change nationality". Ruth Donner, "Chapter 2: The Principle of the "Link" in Nationality Law" in *The Regulation of Nationality in International Law*, Transnational Publishers, New York: 1994, page 44.

[34] Here it of course echoes Article 38 of the Statute of the International Court of Justice which also defines these to be the primary sources of international law. 1930 Convention on Certain Questions relating to the Conflict of Nationality Laws, Article 1.

international law, it provides that any case of attribution of nationality that is inconsistent with international law will not be recognised on the international playing field. Just in case there is any residual doubt as to the freedom of states to determine who are their nationals, for good measure Article 2 states:

> Any question as to whether a person possesses the nationality of a particular state shall be determined in accordance with the law of that state.[35]

In drafting this document, governments deliberately chose to enunciate once more the principle that it is municipal law of individual states that actually confers nationality on individuals.

Yet the 1930 Hague Convention also recognises what has been put so eloquently by Weis, that "while questions of nationality are normally determined by municipal law, this legislative competence does not amount to omnipotence".[36] Indeed state parties to the Convention commit to a number of principles that should be enshrined in domestic nationality acts. For example, that "a child whose parents are both unknown shall have the nationality of the country of birth".[37] International law thereby left its first real mark on the rules for the attribution of nationality and the adoption of the 1930 Hague Convention heralded the onset of a gradual trend towards the acceptance of limitations to the exclusive competence of states in this matter. At the time, the fabled evils were both statelessness and dual nationality. States were slowly coming to realise that such problems can only be combated effectively through cooperation and as such, "common standards should be sought at international level".[38]

In the decades that followed, as international law developed at a rapid pace in many fields, this idea of cooperating to resolve nationality conflicts resurfaced a number of times.[39] It found expression in the 1957 Convention on the Nationality of Married Women, the 1963 Convention on the reduction of cases of multiple nationality and on military obligations in cases of multiple nationality and, of course, the 1961 Convention on the Reduction of Statelessness. Provisions relating to nationality can also be found in a multitude of human rights instruments – both regional and universal - following the spirit of the Universal Declaration of Human Rights and its Article 15: "Everyone has the right to a nationality".[40] Most recently,

---

[35] 1930 Convention on Certain Questions relating to the Conflict of Nationality Laws, Article 2.

[36] Paul Weis, *Nationality and Statelessness in International Law*, Kluwer Academic Publishers Group, Dordrecht: 1979, page 241.

[37] Article 14, 1930 Convention on Certain Questions relating to the Conflict of Nationality Laws.

[38] Carol Batchelor, 'Stateless Persons: Some Gaps in International Protection', in *International Journal of Refugee Law*, Vol. 7, 1995, page 249.

[39] UNHCR, *Information and accession package: the 1954 Convention relating to the status of stateless persons and the 1961 Convention on the reduction of statelessness*, Geneva: January 1999, page 1.

[40] These include article 24 of the International Covenant on Civil and Political Rights; article 7 of the Convention on the Rights of the Child; article 29 of the International Convention on the Protection of the Rights of All Migrant Workers and Members of Their Families; article 9 of the Convention on the Elimination of All Forms of Discrimination Against Women; article 5 of the Convention on the Elimination of All Forms of Racial Discrimination; article 18 of the Convention on the Rights of Persons with Disabilities (not yet entered into force); article 6 of the African Charter on the Rights and Welfare of the Child; article 20 of the American Convention on Human Rights; article 4 of the

the adoption of two conventions that deal explicitly with nationality attribution within the Council of Europe is evidence of the progress that is now being made in this field.[41]

The "present state of international law", upon which the freedom of states to determine the attribution of nationality rests, is very different now from what it was at the time that the *Tunis and Morocco Nationality Decrees* case was brought before the Permanent Court of International Justice. In 1959, Van Panhuys already contended that "conceptions about nationality may have changed".[42] In the time that has since elapsed, there is absolutely no doubt that this is the case and it is now agreed that nationality matters no longer fall within the exclusive jurisdiction of states.[43] It is currently held that international law "favour[s] human rights over claims to State sovereignty"[44] in the question of nationality attribution.[45] Certainly, the codification and further elaboration of the right to a nationality in global and regional human rights instruments has had an enormous influence on the perception of nationality matters. In the specific context of statelessness, these developments have contributed to the progressive acceptance of an overall prohibition against statelessness.[46] There is a general onus on states to refrain from creating statelessness and take efforts to resolve cases of statelessness. Where states are called upon "to adopt and implement nationality legislation with a view to

---

European Convention on Nationality; and article 7 of the Covenant on the Rights of the Child in Islam. See also article 6 of the UN Declaration on the Rights of Indigenous Peoples; paragraph 55 of chapter VI on The Human Dimension of the *Concluding Document of Helsinki*, Conference for Security and Cooperation in Europe, 1992; and paragraph 19 of the *Charter for European Security* of the Organisation for Security and Cooperation in Europe, 1999.

[41] Although the European Convention on Nationality, 1997 (and the Council of Europe Convention on the avoidance of statelessness in relation to State succession, 2006) is a regional instrument, its influence may extend beyond the European continent: "It can encourage other regional or international organisations to take similar initiative in developing declarations or conventions, introduce new principles into international law, or influence the development of nationality law in countries around the world [...] The convention lays out basic principles of nationality law that can guide governments in their negotiations, cooperations and interactions". Norman Sabourin, "The relevance of the European Convention on Nationality for non-European states" in *Council of Europe's First Conference on Nationality*, Strasbourg: 1999, pages 114 and 123.

[42] Haro van Panhuys, "Chapter VII: Restrictions Imposed by International Law upon the Competence of Ctates to Lay Down Nationality Rules" in *The Role of Nationality in International Law*, A.W. Sijthoff's Uitgeversmaatschappij, Leiden: 1959, chapter VII, page 154.

[43] "The manner in which states regulate matters bearing on nationality cannot today be deemed within their sole jurisdiction". Inter-American Court of Human Rights, *Advisory Opinion on the Proposed Amendments to the Naturalisation provision of the Constitution of Costa Rica*, OC-4/84, 19 January 1984, para. 32; See also UNHCR, "Statelessness and Citizenship" in *The State of the World's Refugees - A Humanitarian Agenda*, Oxford University Press, Oxford: 1997, page 251.

[44] UNHCR and IPU, *Nationality and statelessness. A handbook for parliamentarians*, 2005, page 9

[45] The preamble to the 1997 Draft Articles on the Nationality of Natural Persons in Relation to the Succession of States confirms this view.

[46] Johannes Chan, 'The Right to a Nationality as a Human Right - The Current Trend Towards Recognition', in *Human Rights Law Journal*, Vol. 12, 1991, page 11; Open Society Justice Initiative, *Citizenship and Equality in Practice: Guaranteeing Non-Discriminatory Access to Nationality, Protecting the Right to be Free from Arbitrary Deprivation of Nationality and Combating Statelessness*, November 2005, pages 6-7.

preventing and reducing statelessness"[47] this clearly impacts on their freedom to attribute nationality however they deem fit.[48] It has even been suggested that wherever the nationality of an individual is withdrawn with the effect of rendering him stateless, this may amount to arbitrary deprivation of nationality which is prohibited by numerous international instruments.[49] However, this interpretation is not beyond dispute.[50] Nevertheless, states are certainly under an overall duty to promote the right to a nationality and prevent statelessness. But what concrete obligations exist to compel states to adapt their policies of nationality attribution? This question is central to the investigation in the following chapters.

3 The 1961 Convention on the Reduction of Statelessness

The most obvious and comprehensive source of concrete international agreements on the prevention of statelessness is the 1961 Convention on the Reduction of Statelessness. Since it is the utility and effectiveness of this instrument that is being evaluated against the backdrop of alternative sources of obligations under international law, some explanation of its development, scope and basic content is of value here. The 1961 Statelessness Convention is not the first international instrument to deal with the problem of statelessness. As we have seen, the 1930 Hague Convention on Certain Questions Relating to the Conflict of Nationality Laws introduced some limits on the autonomy of states in nationality matters and one of its aspirations was to ensure that everyone held a nationality.[51] However revolutionary it may have seemed at the time, the 1930 Hague Convention was not rigorous enough to seriously impact on the existence of statelessness. Nor has it

[47] UN Commission on Human Rights, *Resolution on Human rights and arbitrary deprivation of nationality,* Human Rights Resolution 2005/45.

[48] Similar considerations have been expressed by the Inter-American Court of Human Rights: "States have the obligation not to adopt practices or laws concerning the granting of nationality, the application of which fosters an increase in the number of stateless persons". Inter-American Court of Human Rights, *Case of Yean and Bosico v. Dominican Republic,* 8 September 2005, para. 142. The Human Rights Committee mentions a similar obligation upon states in the specific context of preventing statelessness at birth: "States are required to adopt every appropriate measure, both internally and in cooperation with other States, to ensure that every child has a nationality when he is born". Human Rights Committee, *General Comment No. 17 on the Rights of the Child,* 1989.

[49] Open Society Justice Initiative, *Citizenship and Equality in Practice: Guaranteeing Non-Discriminatory Access to Nationality, Protecting the Right to be Free from Arbitrary Deprivation of Nationality and Combating Statelessness,* November 2005, page 9. Ruth Donner, "Chapter 4: Human Rights Conventions and other Instruments" in *The Regulation of Nationality in International Law,* Transnational Publishers, New York: 1994 ; Johannes Chan, 'The Right to a Nationality as a Human Right - The Current Trend Towards Recognition', in *Human Rights Law Journal,* Vol. 12, 1991 ; James Goldston, 'Holes in the Rights Framework: Racial Discrimination, Citizenship, and the Rights of Noncitizens', in *Ethics and International Affairs,* Vol. 20, 2006.

[50] See Paul Weis, *Nationality and Statelessness in International Law,* Kluwer Academic Publishers Group, Dordrecht: 1979, page 125.

[51] For this reason, the 1930 Hague Convention has been dubbed the "first international attempt to provide everyone with a nationality". Carol Batchelor, 'Stateless Persons: Some Gaps in International Protection', in *International Journal of Refugee Law,* Vol. 7, 1995, page 249; UNHCR, "Statelessness and Citizenship" in *The State of the World's Refugees - A Humanitarian Agenda,* Oxford University Press, Oxford: 1997, page 25; UNHCR and IPU, *Nationality and statelessness. A handbook for parliamentarians,* 2005, page 8.

ever attracted many state parties.[52] Nevertheless, what this Convention did accomplish was to show that multilateral agreements could provide a way forward in resolving nationality problems and combating statelessness.

Thus, some thirty years later, when nationality matters were back on the international agenda, the idea of an international convention was again taken up. It was becoming abundantly clear that more assertive action was needed to address the mounting statelessness plight. There was an immediate need to improve the legal status and secure the enjoyment of basic rights for the existing stateless populations around the globe. The 1954 Convention relating to the Status of Stateless Persons was designed for this purpose.[53] However, the elimination of statelessness was considered an integral aspect of "conflict prevention, of post-conflict resolution, reduction of cases of displacement, and as part of the protection of the human rights of individuals".[54] So the ultimate aim remained the reduction and indeed eradication of statelessness itself. This required a further concretisation of the aspiration expressed in Article 15 of the Universal Declaration,[55] for this provision is not designed to be legally binding[56] and, as such, it left vital questions such as "which nationality?" unanswered.[57] The International Law Commission was invited to compile a suitable text, building upon relevant provisions and principles

---

[52] The number of state parties now stands at 20. See also Manley Hudson, *Report on Nationality, including Statelessness,* A/CN.4/50, 21 February 1952, page 32.

[53] As we will see in Part 3, the rights provided in the 1954 Convention relating to the Status of Stateless Persons were not designed to *replace* nationality. See also Carol Batchelor, "The International Legal Framework Concerning Statelessness and Access for Stateless Persons", *European Union Seminar on the Content and Scope of International Protection: Panel 1 - Legal basis of international protection,* Madrid: 2002, page 6; UNHCR and IPU, *Nationality and statelessness. A handbook for parliamentarians*, 2005, page 10.

[54] Carol Batchelor, "The International Legal Framework Concerning Statelessness and Access for Stateless Persons", *European Union Seminar on the Content and Scope of International Protection: Panel 1 - Legal basis of international protection,* Madrid: 2002, page 5.

[55] Where article 15 of the Universal Declaration of Human Rights espoused that "Everyone has the right to a nationality" it cannot be denied that it reflected the ideal of eradicating statelessness.

[56] The Universal Declaration "was meant to precede more detailed and comprehensive provisions [...] when approved or adopted, it is hortary and aspirational, recommendatory rather than, in a formal sense, binding". Henry Steiner; Philip Alston, *International Human Rights in Context. Law, Politics and Morals*, Oxford University Press, Oxford: 2000, pages 139 and 142. It should be noted that in spite of this technical limitation, the Declaration is an influential text with great moral force and some of the norms it contains are now considered to belong to customary international law or constitute general principles of law. See also Ian Brownlie, *Principles of Public International Law*, Oxford University Press, Oxford: 2003, pages 534-535.

[57] It is interesting to note that the original draft provision on the right to a nationality, as presented by Professor Lauterpacht in May 1948, contained much greater detail and actually specified concrete obligations for states: "Every person shall be entitled to the nationality of the State where his is born unless and until on attaining majority he declares for the nationality open to him by virtue of descent. No one shall be deprived of his nationality by way of punishment or deemed to have lost his nationality except concurrently with the acquisition of a new nationality. The right of emigration and expatriation shall not be denied"; Article 10 of the Rapporteur's Draft of the International Bill of the Rights of man, as found in the report of the Human Rights Committee entitled "Human Rights, the charter of the United Nations and the International Bill of the Rights of Man", prepared by Professor H. Lauterpacht, May 1948.

that had been formulated to date - including those of the 1930 Hague Convention.[58] Conscious of the delicacy of the issue, two alternative documents were drafted for consideration by state governments: the Draft Convention on the *Elimination* of Future Statelessness and the Draft Convention on the *Reduction* of Future Statelessness.[59] Substantively, the two drafts were similar, but the text on the *reduction* of future statelessness included a number of additional clauses whereby states would not be required to totally eradicate statelessness under all circumstances. Both draft instruments dealt with the issue of conflict of nationality laws (similarly to the 1930 Hague Convention) as well as broaching on other causes of statelessness such as state succession.

When government representatives convened at the 1959 Conference, the decision as to which draft to proceed in discussing was quickly taken. They found the draft on the *elimination* of future statelessness "too radical" since its provisions were formulated in very absolute terms – thus encroaching further on their sovereignty in nationality matters - so opted instead to debate the Draft Convention on the *Reduction* of Future Statelessness.[60] The debate on this text filled the time reserved for the conference without any conclusive progress. A particular sticking point, for example, was disagreement over provisions relating to the deprivation of nationality.[61] Only when the delegates reconvened for a second conference two years later did the text make it over the finishing line, to be adopted as the 1961 Convention on the Reduction of Statelessness. This was eleven years after the International Law Commission started work on drafting the document and it would take a further 12 years for the Convention to attract the six ratifications required for entry into force.[62] This in itself is proof of the fact that governments were dealing with a sensitive issue, nationality being an area in which they would not readily surrender their sovereignty. To date, the level of accession remains poor: at the time of writing, the Convention has just 34 state parties.[63]

What is perhaps the most surprising feature of the 1961 Statelessness Convention is the absence of idealistic preambles and loftily formulated general principles as was very much the rage with multilateral texts of this sort at the time. Instead, after mentioning that it is considered "desirable to reduce statelessness by international agreement",[64] the Convention opens immediately with the substantive

---

[58] Upon request of the Economic and Social Council in its resolution 319B III (XI) of the 11th of August 1950.

[59] UNHCR and IPU, *Nationality and statelessness. A handbook for parliamentarians*, 2005, page 12.

[60] Carol Batchelor, 'Stateless Persons: Some Gaps in International Protection', in *International Journal of Refugee Law,* Vol. 7, 1995, page 250; UNHCR and IPU, *Nationality and statelessness. A handbook for parliamentarians*, 2005, page 12.

[61] The Final Act of the Convention mentions the following resolution that was adopted by the first Conference in 1959: "The Conference, being unable to terminate the work entrusted to it within the time provided for its work, proposes to the competent organ of the United Nations to reconvene the Conference at the earliest possible time in order to continue and complete its work"; Paragraph 3, Final Act of the 1961 Convention on the Reduction of Statelessness; Paul Weis, *Nationality and Statelessness in International Law*, Kluwer Academic Publishers Group, Dordrecht: 1979, page 166.

[62] The sixth party to accede was Australia on the 13th of December 1973. In accordance with its article 18, the Convention on the Reduction of Statelessness then entered into force two years later.

[63] The most recent accessions were by Romania and Rwanda in 2006 and Brazil in 2007.

[64] This declaration is made in the only substantive preamble to precede the text of the Convention itself.

provision of article 1 which prescribes granting nationality under certain circumstances to a child born on state territory.[65] This is very different to the 1930 Hague Convention which clarifies its aspirations in its preambles before opening with a series of articles pertaining to general principles rather than real substance.[66] It is especially peculiar that the 1961 Statelessness Convention neglects to reiterate that "everyone has the right to a nationality" while claiming to be a concretisation of Article 15 of the Universal Declaration.[67] Of equal interest is the notable absence of the basic rule that it is for each state to determine who is considered a national.

Even so, the instrument has been described in the following terms by the "Information and Accession Package" that accompanies it:

> The 1961 Convention may be seen as consolidating principles of equality, non-discrimination, protection of ethnic minorities, rights of children, territorial integrity, the right to a nationality and the avoidance of statelessness.[68]

Rather than repeating such principles, the Convention indeed *consolidates* them: transforming idealistic notions into concrete obligations that can be implemented directly by state parties. On the basis of the description given in the "Information and Accession Package", the Convention would seem to cover a very broad spectrum of issues. However, its scope is definitively narrowed by the determination that it is only applicable to cases of statelessness. For example:

> A contracting state shall grant its nationality to a person born in its territory *who would otherwise be stateless...*[69]

Thus the Convention does not purport to prescribe a general policy of nationality attribution, but deals only with situations in which statelessness threatens.[70] It is not

---

[65] The Draft Conventions put forward for debate by the International Law Commission did include a short series of preambles which included a reference to the right to a nationality in the Universal Declaration of Human Rights. These phrases were obviously dropped during the consideration of the text by the government representatives during the codification conference. UN Yearbook 1954, page 421.

[66] Similarly, the 1954 Statelessness Convention includes a short series of preambles explaining the background to its adoption and opens with articles that provide definitions and general principles to clarify the scope of application of the Convention; 1954 Convention relating to the Status of Stateless Persons.

[67] The Draft Convention submitted by the International Law Commission for discussion did include a number of preambles, among which a reaffirmation of the right to a nationality as proclaimed by the Universal Declaration. These paragraphs obviously disappeared at some point in the course of the debate although it is unclear why.

[68] UNHCR, *Information and accession package: the 1954 Convention relating to the status of stateless persons and the 1961 Convention on the reduction of statelessness,* Geneva: January 1999, page 7.

[69] The first phrase of article 1, emphasis added; 1961 Convention on the Reduction of Statelessness

[70] Paul Weis, *Nationality and Statelessness in International Law*, Kluwer Academic Publishers Group, Dordrecht: 1979, page 253

an international law on nationality but simply what the title depicts: a Convention on the Reduction of *Statelessness*.[71]

The substantive articles of the 1961 Statelessness Convention attempt to tackle the prevention of statelessness in three specific situations: the creation of statelessness at birth where a child fails to acquire the nationality of any state; the creation of statelessness later in life where a person loses, renounces or is deprived of his nationality without gaining another; and the creation of statelessness in the specific circumstance of state succession. In approaching these situations, the Convention does not ask states to grant nationality to just any person who is (at risk of being) stateless. The obligations have been carefully formulated, taking into consideration factors like birth, descent and residence in ascertaining whether there is an appropriate link with the state upon which to base the attribution of nationality.[72] Moreover, state parties are not permitted to lodge any reservations against these articles and limit the scope of the treaty obligations regarding the attribution of nationality in the event of statelessness.[73] After a few further comments on the general approach of the 1961 Statelessness Convention here, a full discussion of its substantive provisions will be undertaken in the following chapters as we look at the way in which international law deals with each of the root causes of statelessness.

Although the Convention's norms are only applicable where there is a risk of statelessness, the instrument does not offer any further guidance on either the definition of statelessness or the identification of situations where statelessness threatens. As to definition, it is generally understood that by refraining from offering its own perspective on the question, the 1961 Statelessness Convention defers the matter back to the 1954 Convention relating to the Status of Stateless Persons:[74] "the term 'stateless person' means a person who is not considered a national by any state under operation of its law".[75] We can, however, recall from the discussion of the question of definition in chapter II, section 4, that the 1961 Statelessness Convention includes a resolution on the subject of "*de facto* statelessness" in its Final Act:

---

[71] In this respect it is narrower in application than the 1930 Hague Convention which also deals with the question of dual nationality. Yet it is also broader in scope in that it addresses situations that arise from other circumstances than a conflict of nationality laws.

[72] UNHCR, *Information and accession package: the 1954 Convention relating to the status of stateless persons and the 1961 Convention on the reduction of statelessness*, Geneva: January 1999, page 7; Carol Batchelor, 'Statelessness and the Problem of Resolving Nationality Status', in *International Journal of Refugee Law*, Vol. 10, 1998, page 162.

[73] States may only make a declaration under article 8, paragraph 3 of the Convention when they accede to the instrument, by which they specify the inclusion of one or more additional grounds for deprivation of nationality under their municipal law. Beyond this, the Convention explicitly permits reservations to Article 11 (regarding the supervisory mechanism of an international agency), Article 14 (granting jurisdiction to the ICJ for the settlement of disputes) and Article 15 (relating to territories for which the state party is responsible) and then just to be absolutely clear – expressly prohibits reservations in respect of all other articles. Article 17, paragraphs 1 and 2 of the 1961 Convention on the Reduction of Statelessness.

[74] Carol Batchelor, 'Stateless Persons: Some Gaps in International Protection', in *International Journal of Refugee Law*, Vol. 7, 1995, page 250.

[75] Article 1 of the 1954 Convention relating to the Status of Stateless Persons.

> The Conference recommends that persons who are stateless de facto should as far as possible be treated as stateless de jure to enable them to acquire an effective nationality.[76]

What is to be understood here under the expression "*de facto* stateless" is not precisely elucidated although it can be inferred from the reference to the acquisition of an effective nationality that some degree of ineffectiveness of citizenship is implied. Yet, even with this inference in mind and even if states were to take this non-binding recommendation to heart, it is not clear how it could be implemented in practice. For instance, where the Convention compels states to offer nationality *ius soli* to a child who would "otherwise be stateless", the recommendation would seem to call upon states to also confer citizenship *ius soli* to a child who would otherwise acquire an ineffective nationality. Quite how a state should go about making such a prediction is not explained. Similarly, where nationality is not to be deprived, in certain circumstances, where the individual would thereby be rendered stateless, the recommendation would appear to prohibit the deprivation of nationality from a dual national whose second nationality is ineffective. Again, exactly how this fact should be ascertained – or indeed how often such a scenario may come up in practice – is not addressed.[77]

This brings us to the wider problem of the identification of (the risk of) statelessness for the purposes of applying the guarantees housed in the 1961 Statelessness Convention. As mentioned, the text of the instrument offers no indication as to how state parties are to determine an imminent risk of statelessness – establishing the fact, for instance, that a child would "otherwise be stateless" to prevent statelessness at birth or ascertaining that a person does not possess or acquire another nationality in order to avoid statelessness upon loss, deprivation or renunciation of nationality. The Convention thus fails to address such questions as where the burden of proof lies (with the individual concerned or with the state), what types of evidence may be accepted and what weight is to be given to different forms of proof. Nor are state parties compelled to cooperate with a view to confirming the nationality – or statelessness – of an individual. The absence of clarity on how to undertake the task of identification is highly regrettable since it can seriously jeopardise the implementation of the Convention. As evidenced by the widely-publicised "baby Andrew" case in Japan, the problem of identification of situations in which the Convention's terms are applicable is a very real dilemma.[78]

---

[76] Resolution I of the Final Act of the 1961 Convention on the Reduction of Statelessness. It is likely that the inclusion of this recommendation was due in part to a final plea by the then United Nations High Commissioner for Refugees to address the plight of the "*de facto* stateless". Carol Batchelor, 'Stateless Persons: Some Gaps in International Protection', in *International Journal of Refugee Law*, Vol. 7, 1995, page 251.

[77] Recall from chapter II, section 4 that other instruments that attempt to deal with the avoidance of statelessness limit themselves to the definition of statelessness as the *de jure* absence of a nationality. See article 1, paragraph c of the Council of Europe Convention on the avoidance of statelessness in relation to State succession (2006) as well as the Explanatory Memorandum to the European Convention on Nationality (1997), paragraph 33.

[78] The "baby Andrew" case involved a dispute as to the applicability of a provision in the Japanese Nationality Act that aims to prevent statelessness at birth. The article in question determined that a child shall be a Japanese national if born in Japan when both parents are unknown or have no

So, by leaving it entirely to states parties to identify situations in which the Convention guarantees are applicable, there remains a significant threat that the effectiveness of the instrument will be undermined as states – deliberately or inadvertently – exclude individuals from the protection of the Convention through their approach to the question of proof.

With the foregoing comments in mind, the availability of an enforcement mechanism or procedure to ensure the comprehensive and correct implementation of the 1961 Statelessness Convention becomes all the more relevant. On this point, the Convention earns a somewhat mixed appraisal. To begin with, similarly to many other international treaties – including the 1954 Convention relating to the Status of Stateless Persons - the instrument grants jurisdiction to the International Court of Justice to settle any disputes arising over its interpretation or application.[79] However, to date, no such referral has been made to the Court. In fact, it seems an unlikely scenario that state parties would ever challenge each other before the Court on the basis of this Convention as stateless persons are renowned for being voiceless – having no government to espouse their claim is precisely the crux of their problem.[80] Conscious of this peculiarity of the statelessness phenomenon, when the Convention was being prepared:

> The draft of the International Law Commission had provided for the establishment within the framework of the United Nations of an agency to act on behalf of stateless persons before governments and the establishment also within this framework of a tribunal competent to decide on claims presented by the agency on behalf of individuals claiming to have been denied nationality in violation of the provisions of the Convention.[81]

When the text was eventually adopted, only the reference to an international agency remained. Thus article 11 stipulates that, as a means of monitoring the instrument's implementation by state parties, a body shall be established "to which a person claiming the benefit of this Convention may apply for the examination of his claim

---

nationality. Initially, the Ministry of Justice determined that this provision did not apply to Andrew because his mother was not unknown but was considered – by the Japanese authorities – to be a national of the Philippines. Throughout the litigation process, all the way to the Supreme Court, the interpretation of the terms of the article and the problem of the burden of proof that formed the central questions. This case is evidence of how contentious these matters can be and how crucial to the outcome of the case – and to the prevention of statelessness in practice. For a discussion of the case, see Stacey Steele, "Comments on Okuda, Statelessness and the Nationality Act of Japan: Baby Andrew Becomes a Teenager and other Changes?" *Journal of Japanese Law,* Volume 9, Number 18, 2004, pages 178-192. Similar issues arose in European Court of Human Rights, *Decision as to the admissibility of Karassev v. Finland,* Application No. 31414/96, 12 January 1999, that will be discussed in more detail later.

[79] This is provided for in article 14 of the 1961 Convention on the Reduction of Statelessness.

[80] Paul Weis, *Nationality and Statelessness in International Law*, Kluwer Academic Publishers Group, Dordrecht: 1979, page 255; Carol Batchelor, 'Stateless Persons: Some Gaps in International Protection', in *International Journal of Refugee Law,* Vol. 7, 1995, page 253; UNHCR and IPU, *Nationality and statelessness. A handbook for parliamentarians*, 2005, page 13.

[81] Paul Weis, "The United Nations Convention on the Reduction of Statelessness, 1961" in *International and Comparative Law Quarterly,* Vol. 11, No. 4, 1962, pages 1084-1085.

and for assistance in presenting it to the *appropriate authority*".[82] This approach reverts the question of the legitimacy of an individual's claim to the relevant domestic authorities. Nor has the agency mandated to exercise this advisory task on behalf of persons seeking a remedy under the 1961 Convention, the United Nations High Commissioner for Refugees, issued any concrete guidelines on the most pressing questions associated with the implementation of the Convention, such as the issues raised above.[83] Regardless of the outcome of the assessment of its substantive provisions, these limitations inherent in the approach of the 1961 Convention on the Reduction of Statelessness must be kept in mind when it comes to the evaluation of the instrument's overall value.

4 Purpose and Method of Part 2

For now, having introduced the basic doctrines involved in nationality attribution and having provided a background on the main international instrument to deal with the reduction of statelessness, it is time to commence the investigation into the origins of statelessness itself and how these are addressed under the 1961 Convention and broader international law. This study will be guided by the research question presented in chapter I:

> **How can the way in which international law deals with the *prevention of statelessness* be improved so as to ensure optimal protection against statelessness for the individual (i.e. the realisation of the right to a nationality)?**

The analysis has been broken down into four chapters each dealing with a different category of root causes of statelessness: technical causes of statelessness (chapter IV), statelessness in the context of state succession (chapter V), denial of citizenship resulting in statelessness (chapter VI) and the so-called "new" causes of statelessness (chapter VII). It will be followed by a chapter in which the findings are consolidated and compared, enabling the determination of the precise obligations states have in countering statelessness, the role is - or could be - cast for the 1961 Convention on the Reduction of Statelessness and the overall way in which international law deals with the prevention of statelessness can be improved.

[82] Emphasis added. Article 11 of the 1961 Convention on the Reduction of Statelessness.
[83] When the 1961 Convention on the Reduction of Statelessness entered into force in 1975, the UN General Assembly requested UNHCR to fulfil this task. Thereafter, the agency's statelessness mandate has been reaffirmed, clarified and expanded through subsequent General Assembly resolutions as well as thanks to the conclusions adopted by UNHCR's own Executive Committee. See UN Docs. A/Res/3274 (XXIX) 1974; A/Res/31/36 1976; A/Res/49/169 1995; A/Res/50/152 1996; and A/Res/61/137 2007.

CHAPTER IV

ADDRESSING THE TECHNICAL CAUSES OF STATELESSNESS

When asked how statelessness comes about – often the first question to come up when talking about this research – I have found that people are most fascinated by its so-called "technical causes". Indeed, the first stateless person to draw my own attention lacked a nationality due entirely to a "technicality". I refer here to the tale of Omar, who was born in the Netherlands to a Dutch father and foreign mother and failed to acquire a nationality at birth due to a conflict of nationality laws.[1] While other causes of statelessness are connected to more dramatic or exciting events, this story continues to compel. It just does not seem possible (or excusable) that a newborn child can fail to acquire a nationality simply because the countries with which he is connected have neglected to ensure that their nationality regulations are compatible. However, this is but one example. The technical causes of statelessness are many and varied, creating statelessness both from birth and later in life. They are "technical causes" because statelessness is the unintentional result of the acts of individuals or the operation of particular municipal laws or policies.

As the story of Omar demonstrates, it is possible for a baby that has just been brought into the world to remain "unclaimed" by any state due to a glitch in law or policy. It can be caused by conflicts in the application of the law of two or more states, but also by unilateral state (in)action. The result is the same: original or absolute statelessness, where a child lacks a nationality from birth. The causes of original statelessness will be dealt with under two sub-headings: "jus sanguinis versus jus soli" (section 1) and "abandoned or orphaned children" (section 2). If a child escapes all of the pitfalls that can result in statelessness from birth, he is still not necessarily home free. Over the course of a lifetime there are a number of – not particularly earth-shattering – events that can also result in an individual being rendered stateless. Similarly to original statelessness, this subsequent statelessness has a number of different technical causes. Many of these are related to conflict of laws situations where the cumulative effect of the application of the domestic

[1] A brief reminder: Although his father was Dutch and he was born on Dutch soil, Omar failed to acquire Dutch nationality at birth because his father and mother were unmarried and his father did not take the necessary steps during his partner's pregnancy to ensure that he was legally recognised as Omar's father from the very start. Meanwhile, Omar had no right to his mother's nationality as the laws of that country did not provide for the passing on of nationality from mother to child. The full story of Omar is recounted in chapter II, section 1.

nationality provisions of two or more different states is the creation of a new case of statelessness. Again, there are two main categories of problems which will be discussed in turn: "marriage (or divorce) and adoption" (section 3) and "loss, deprivation or renunciation of nationality" (section 4). Once these origins of statelessness have been traced in greater detail, the next step is to put the 1961 Convention on the Reduction of Statelessness and other international instruments to the test and see whether they copes sufficiently with each of the trouble spots.

1 *Jus sanguinis* versus *jus soli*

As a direct consequence of the autonomy of states to stipulate their own nationality regulations, statelessness may be the unintentional result of a conflict between the domestic legislation of two or more countries. In particular, the existence of two contradicting principles on which to base the attribution of nationality to a child at birth – *jus sanguinis* and *jus soli* – has inadvertently led to many cases of statelessness.[2] It can be this simple: a child who is born to parents who are nationals of a state that grants nationality *jus soli* on the territory of a state that grants nationality *jus sanguinis* fails to acquire any nationality at birth. The child cannot acquire the nationality of the parents, as this is not passed on by descent and the child was born on foreign soil. Similarly, he does not qualify for the nationality of the state in which he was born because this country only grants nationality by descent. This is a "negative" conflict of laws.[3] While the laws of the states involved may be perfectly correct and acceptable individually, when implemented together, problems nevertheless occur.[4] In the absence of a remedy in these exceptional circumstances, the child is stateless from birth.

Although it has long been recognised as a problem, the incidence of statelessness arising from this type of conflict of laws situation is growing worldwide. According to a UNHCR progress report on statelessness in 1999:

> In a world of global interaction, frequent movement across borders, mixed marriages, and increased numbers of people living outside their country of nationality, it is no longer possible for states to avoid the creation of statelessness solely through independent application of national laws.[5]

While it might once have been fair to assume that every child would be born on the territory of the state of which his parents are also nationals - discounting the possibility of a conflict of laws situation - this is certainly no longer the case. Moreover, in reaction to the increasing mobility of populations, some states have adapted their nationality laws in such a way as to actually aggravate the risk of statelessness. For example, a number of countries that grant nationality *jus*

[2] See chapter III, section 1 for an explanation of these doctrines.

[3] In the opposite circumstances, the result is a "positive" conflict of laws, creating cases of dual nationality; International Union for Child Welfare, *Stateless Children - A Comparative Study of National Legislation and Suggested Solutions to the Problem of Statelessness of Children,* Geneva: 1947, page 22.

[4] UNHCR and IPU, *Nationality and statelessness. A handbook for parliamentarians*, 2005, page 27.

[5] UNHCR, *Progress report on UNHCR activities in the field of statelessness,* EC/49/SC/CRP.15, Geneva: 4 June 1999

sanguinis at birth have amended their legislation to prevent nationality being passed down continuously, from one generation to the next, once the actual tie with the country has been severed. This is considered to be the case when the individual emigrates permanently to another state, forfeiting the genuine link in the eyes of the state of nationality. For instance, under British law the first generation of children born abroad to a British national will still automatically acquire British nationality *jus sanguinis*. However, these individuals are termed "British citizens by descent"[6] - a status which impacts on their right to pass on their British nationality *jus sanguinis*. The child of a "British citizen by descent", if born outside the United Kingdom, is not automatically entitled to British nationality. In the event that both of the child's parents are similarly situated, rendering them unable to transmit their nationality *jus sanguinis* and the state upon whose territory the child is born does not grant nationality *jus soli*, then statelessness may result. [7] Placing this type of limitation on the conferral of nationality *jus sanguinis* can thus heighten the risk of statelessness.

The example outlined above is just one of the known weaknesses of the *jus sanguinis* doctrine in countering statelessness. A major point of contention in relation to this principle is the distinction often made between legitimate and illegitimate children. The issue of attribution of nationality to children born out of wedlock was highlighted in the 1947 report on "Stateless Children" by the International Union for Child Welfare.[8] Fifty years on, this is still a problem today.[9]

---

[6] As opposed to a "British citizen otherwise than by descent", who is for example an individual born in the United Kingdom of a British parent or naturalised; Information leaflet BN4 on the British Nationality Act 1981, "Children born outside the United Kingdom", issued by the Home Office, 2002, pages 1-2.

[7] In the particular case of the British Nationality Act, if the child is born abroad to a "British citizen by descent" and is thereby rendered stateless, the child can be registered as a British national as long as certain criteria are met; Information leaflet BN4 on the British Nationality Act 1981, "Children born outside the United Kingdom", issued by the Home Office, 2002, pages 3-5.

[8] International Union for Child Welfare, *Stateless Children - A Comparative Study of National Legislation and Suggested Solutions to the Problem of Statelessness of Children,* Geneva: 1947, page 10.

[9] In fact, in Europe at least, "in many states the number of marriages is reducing and the number of children "born out of wedlock" is consequently increasing". Committee of Experts on Nationality, *Report on Conditions for the Acquisition and Loss of Nationality,* Strasbourg: 14 January 2003, page 6. Furthermore, the nationality status of children fathered by members of a foreign military engaged in a conflict or peacekeeping mission in a state is a particular and enduring cause for concern: "The children fathered by U.S. soldiers who had been sent to Korea [during the war in the 1950s and 60s] were called 'children of the dust'. They were shunned in Korean society, where interracial relationships are traditionally unaccepted. Already abandoned by their fathers who returned to the United States, most of these children were later abandoned by their mothers because of social pressure or lack of resources to care for them [...] When news of the impoverished lives of these children reached the international community, there was increased pressure from both within the United States and the Korean government for the U.S. government to recognise these children as American citizens. The resulting U.S. legislation regarding the status of Amerasian children was woefully inadequate [...] After 50 years, only a small number of those American children have been granted U.S. citizenship". Youth Advocate Program International, *Stateless Children – Children who are without citizenship,* Booklet No. 7 in a series on International Youth Issues, 2002, page 19. Today, similar issues are being raised surrounding the right to nationality of illegitimate children born ot members of UN peacekeeping troops and female nationals.

Referring once more to the story of Omar, we see that the reason that he did not gain his father's Dutch nationality is because his parents were unmarried and were, therefore, required to take additional steps to ensure the recognition from birth of the paternal bond. Having failed to do so, even the subsequent legal recognition of this bond acquired through the local court was not enough to rectify the situation as regards Omar's nationality. Where the law only allows for the bestowal of nationality *jus sanguinis* to legitimate children and prevents the father (or even both parents) from passing on their nationality to children born out of wedlock, statelessness may result.

The problem is compounded when the *jus sanguinis* principle has been laid down in gender-sensitive legislation. A number of states that adhere to the *jus sanguinis* doctrine provide only for the transmission of nationality from father to child – the mother does not hold the same right even if the child is born on the territory of the mother's state.[10] This has the effect of dramatically multiplying the risk of statelessness, for the child can rely on just one parent – the father – for the acquisition of a nationality. If the child is illegitimate, or the father unknown, stateless, deceased or unwilling to take the necessary steps to ensure that the child acquires a nationality, statelessness is inevitable unless there are special provisions in place to prevent it. The complaint that gender-sensitive nationality legislation creates a large number of stateless children every year is echoed in many reports.[11] Today, despite signs of change, the problem remains particularly prevalent in the regions of North-Africa, the Middle East and Asia.[12]

A final criticism which is often voiced about the *jus sanguinis* principle is its role in the perpetuation of statelessness. Not only can jus sanguinis nationality laws contribute to the creation of entirely new cases of statelessness, they can also – if applied strictly – be responsible for the inheritance of statelessness.[13] Just as the nationality of the child is determined according to the nationality of the parents, where the parents' nationality is lacking the child will simply inherit this status. The result, statelessness at birth, can be identical if the parents' nationality is unknown or undetermined.[14]

---

[10] UNHCR, "Statelessness and Citizenship" in *The State of the World's Refugees - A Humanitarian Agenda*, Oxford University Press, Oxford: 1997, page 226; UNHCR and IPU, *Nationality and statelessness. A handbook for parliamentarians*, 2005, page 32.

[11] These include Maureen Lynch, *Lives on hold: The human cost of statelessness*, Washington: 2005, pages 27-32; UN Division for the Advancement of Women, *Women, nationality and citizenship*, June 2003, pages 8-10; Youth Advocate Program International, *Stateless Children – Youth who are without citizenship*, Booklet No. 7 in a series on International Youth Issues, 2002, pages 9-10; and UNHCR, *UNHCR Handbook for the Protection of Women and Girls*, January 2008, page 187.

[12] Mark Manly, "Sorry, wrong gender" in *Refugees Magazine*, Number 147, Issue 3, 2007, pages 24-27.

[13] UNHCR, *Information and accession package: the 1954 Convention relating to the status of stateless persons and the 1961 Convention on the reduction of statelessness*, Geneva: January 1999, page 3; UNHCR, "Statelessness and Citizenship" in *The State of the World's Refugees - A Humanitarian Agenda*, Oxford University Press, Oxford: 1997, page 226; UNHCR, *The World's Stateless - Questions and Answers*, Geneva: , page 9.

[14] Furthermore, a child born to stateless parents *de facto* who cannot establish their nationality may then become stateless *de jure* himself. International Union for Child Welfare, *Stateless Children - A Comparative Study of National Legislation and Suggested Solutions to the Problem of Statelessness of Children*, Geneva: 1947, page 15;

The considerations outlined above with respect to the *jus sanguinis* principle have motivated a number of scholars to suggest that universal adoption of the *jus soli* doctrine would be desirable in the fight against statelessness.[15] Their argument: every child is born somewhere and this place of birth is usually relatively easy to establish.[16] The place of birth remains unaffected whether the child is legitimate or illegitimate and whether the parents are nationals, (irregular) foreigners or even stateless. The opposing argument is readily raised that birth on the territory of a state may be of a more coincidental nature and not, in fact, illustrative of any genuine link.[17] Indeed, the *jus soli* doctrine has been considered vulnerable to "abuse by expectant mothers engaged in 'forum shopping'"[18] or "birth tourism".[19] The *jus soli* doctrine also raises its own questions, for example as to the definition of territory and thus the nationality of children born aboard a ship or aircraft. Moreover, original statelessness has been identified in states whose legislation is based on the *jus soli* principle, so this is not necessarily a ready-made solution.[20] Thus, although scholars have been grappling with the idea for many decades, advocating for the adoption of just one and the same doctrine for the attribution of

---

[15] The Independent Commission on International Humanitarian Issues has reported called for the adoption of an instrument that prescribes the *jus soli* doctrine for all states; UNHCR, "Statelessness and Citizenship" in *The State of the World's Refugees - A Humanitarian Agenda*, Oxford University Press, Oxford: 1997, page 256.

[16] International Union for Child Welfare, *Stateless Children - A Comparative Study of National Legislation and Suggested Solutions to the Problem of Statelessness of Children*, Geneva: 1947

[17] Jus soli may result in the acquisition of nationality through purely incidental circumstances; Haro van Panhuys, "Chapter VII: Restrictions Imposed by International Law upon the Competence of Ctates to Lay Down Nationality Rules" in *The Role of Nationality in International Law*, A.W. Sijthoff's Uitgeversmaatschappij, Leiden: 1959

[18] Andrew Grossman, "Birthright Citizenship as Nationality of Convenience", *3rd European Conference on Nationality - Nationality and the Child*, Strasbourg: 2004, page 3.

[19] This is the situation where: "Pregnant women [enter] the territory of a state in order to give birth to their child and thereby enabled the child to acquire the nationality of that State, [possibly enabling the mother] to remain in the territory of the state when she would otherwise not have qualified to do so, and perhaps later acquire the nationality of that State along with other members of the family". Committee of Experts on Nationality, *Report on Misuse of Nationality Laws*, Strasbourg: 20 April 2004, paragraph 7. Some states have now moved away from automatic *jus soli* precisely in order to avoid the situation of the "anchor babies". Consider the case of Ireland where the law was changed in 2004 (following the *Baby Chen case* before the European Court of Justice and a national referendum) when additional criteria were introduced to supplement the *jus soli* doctrine and curtail access to birthright citizenship for children of irregular immigrants. Andrew Grossman, "Birthright Citizenship as Nationality of Convenience", *3rd European Conference on Nationality - Nationality and the Child*, Strasbourg: 2004, page 4.

[20] International Union for Child Welfare, *Stateless Children - A Comparative Study of National Legislation and Suggested Solutions to the Problem of Statelessness of Children*, Geneva: 1947, page 20; Manley Hudson, *Report on Nationality, including Statelessness*, A/CN.4/50, 21 February 1952, page 44; Ian Brownlie, *Principles of Public International Law*, Oxford University Press, Oxford: 2003, page 380. The Dominican Republic is an example of a state that adheres to the *jus soli* doctrine but where large-scale statelessness remains an issue, see Laura van Waas, *Is Permanent Illegality Inevitable? The Challenges to Ensuring Birth Registration and the Right to a Nationality for the Children of Irregular Migrants - Thailand and the Dominican Republic*, Woking: 2006.

nationality at birth by all states is neither a realistic nor a desirable solution.[21] Yet it is certainly worthwhile building an understanding of the strengths and weaknesses of the two doctrines for attributing nationality at birth in order to assess the approach taken by international law. The extent to which there is an obligation under international law to extend nationality either *jus sanguinis* or *jus soli* under certain conditions will be investigated in the next two sections.

1.1 The 1961 Convention on the Reduction of Statelessness

The 1961 Statelessness Convention is a joint production of both *jus sanguinis* and *jus soli* states, meaning that it reflects a compromise between these principles. The convention does not compel states to adopt one doctrine or the other, but seeks a balance in their application, accepting both birthplace and descent as evidence of a genuine link.[22] Thus article 1 requires states to grant nationality *jus soli* to a child born on their territory who would otherwise be stateless while article 4 prescribes the attribution of nationality *jus sanguinis* to a child born outside the territory of the state who would otherwise be stateless, if one of his parents is a national:

> *Article 1*
> A Contracting State shall grant its nationality to a person born on its territory who would otherwise be stateless.
>
> *Article 4*
> A Contracting State shall grant nationality to a person, not born in the territory of a Contracting State, who would otherwise be stateless, if the nationality of one of his parents at the time of the person's birth was that of that State.[23]

The technique chosen is therefore to prescribe legislative amendments for both *jus sanguinis* and *jus soli* countries. States that adhere to a strict *jus sanguinis* doctrine are compelled by article 1 to introduce the possibility of attributing nationality *jus soli* in the particular case of a child who would otherwise be stateless – for example a child born on the state's territory to parents who hold the nationality of a *jus soli* state. States that attribute nationality *jus soli* must add an exception clause to their nationality regulations, allowing for attribution *jus sanguinis* to a child born abroad if he would otherwise be stateless – for example if he is born on the territory of a *jus sanguinis* state.

If contracting states were simply required to adopt such additional provisions in their nationality acts, a conflict of laws may still arise. A newborn child that

---

[21] Richard Flournoy, 'International Problems in Respect to Nationality by Birth', in *American Society of International Law Proceedings,* Vol. 20, 1926; William Samore, 'Statelessness as a consequence of the conflict of nationality laws', in *American Journal of International Law,* Vol. 45, 1951; Andrew Grossman, "Birthright Citizenship as Nationality of Convenience", *3rd European Conference on Nationality - Nationality and the Child,* Strasbourg: 2004.

[22] UNHCR, "Statelessness and Citizenship" in *The State of the World's Refugees - A Humanitarian Agenda,* Oxford University Press, Oxford: 1997, page 256; Carol Batchelor, "Developments in International law: The Avoidance of Statelessness Through Positive Application of the Right to a Nationality" in *Council of Europe's First Conference on Nationality,* Strasbourg: 2001, page 56.

[23] First lines of articles 1 and 4 of 1961 Convention on the Reduction of Statelessness.

would otherwise be stateless would now most likely be claimed by at least two states through the implementation of article 1 and article 4 of the Statelessness Convention. This may herald a dispute as to which state is required to grant nationality to the child or lead to cases of dual nationality - still considered undesirable by a number of states. However, a closer reading of article 4 unearths the astuteness of the drafters in pre-empting this problem. The conferral of nationality *jus sanguinis* prescribed by this provision is made conditional on the child not being born on the territory of another contracting state. Where a newborn would otherwise be stateless, the Convention thereby gives precedence to the attribution of nationality *jus soli* since every contracting state is required to grant nationality *jus soli* in the event that the child would otherwise be stateless.

Thus far it would seem that the 1961 Convention on the Reduction of Statelessness has adopted an appropriate and effective approach to preventing original statelessness from arising due to a conflict of *jus sanguinis* and *jus soli* doctrines. However, this conclusion must be tempered because articles 1 and 4 of the Convention have a major drawback that has yet to be mentioned: the obligations are not expressed in unequivocal terms but are watered down by allowing additional criteria to be set for the attribution of nationality. Nationality shall be granted "at birth, by operation of the law" or "upon an application being lodged with the appropriate authority". In the latter case, the contracting states may make the grant of nationality "subject to one or more conditions".[24] The conditions that may be set relate to: the period during which the application for nationality may be lodged, substantiation of the genuine link with the state through a certain length of habitual residence, the criterion that the person must be free from particular criminal convictions and the requirement that the individual has always been stateless.[25] If the conditions are met, an application for nationality may not be rejected.[26] Introducing the possibility of setting such additional criteria for the attribution of nationality to persons who would otherwise be stateless was a conscious choice of state representatives when the draft convention was being discussed.[27] The absence of such escape clauses in the Draft Convention on the *Elimination* of Future Statelessness was the reason why it was not taken up for discussion by states who preferred the alternative Draft Convention on the *Reduction* of Future Statelessness.[28] The effect of these additional sub-paragraphs in articles 1 and 4 is already explained by the difference in title between the two International Law Commission's drafts: without such clauses the provisions would (if adopted by all states) *eliminate* statelessness in future,[29] while the best that can be achieved if such

[24] Article 1, paragraph 1 and article 4, paragraph 1; 1961 Convention on the Reduction of Statelessness.

[25] These conditions are housed in article 1, paragraph 2 and article 4, paragraph 2; 1961 Convention on the Reduction of Statelessness.

[26] Article 1, paragraph 1b and article 4, paragraph 1b; 1961 Convention on the Reduction of Statelessness.

[27] In particular this move was a concession to the *jus sanguinis* states. Paul Weis, *Nationality and Statelessness in International Law*, Kluwer Academic Publishers Group, Dordrecht: 1979, page 166.

[28] As explained in chapter III, section 3, the Draft Convention on the *Eradication* of Future Statelessness was simply considered too radical; Carol Batchelor, 'Stateless Persons: Some Gaps in International Protection', in *International Journal of Refugee Law*, Vol. 7, 1995, page 250; UNHCR and IPU, *Nationality and statelessness. A handbook for parliamentarians*, 2005, page 12.

[29] Statelessness that arises from the conflict of laws with respect to *jus sanguinis* and *jus soli* doctrines.

additional conditions are set is a reduction in the number of cases that will arise.[30] In fact, the text of the 1961 Convention on the Reduction of Statelessness, in the form that it was eventually adopted, allows many more conditions to be set for the attribution of nationality than the Draft Convention included.[31] At the time, states were clearly not ready to make such drastic changes to their municipal nationality acts. These limitations in the effect of the 1961 Convention reaffirm the need to look elsewhere in the international legal framework for comparable or even stronger obligations upon states to address this problem with the required clout. This will be done shortly, but first we must see how the 1961 Convention deals with the weaknesses in the unilateral application of the *jus sanguinis* and *jus soli* doctrines that may also lead to statelessness.

In section 1 above, four situations that may lead to statelessness under a *jus sanguinis* system were discussed: the restrictions posed on continuous transferral of nationality *jus sanguinis* after taking up residence abroad, the treatment of illegitimate children, gender-sensitive *jus sanguinis* regulations and the inheritance of statelessness. The first case involved the relatively recent development in a number of countries – the example given was Britain – of preventing nationality from being passed on indefinitely from one generation to the next through the *jus sanguinis* doctrine if the family has long since taken up permanent residence abroad. This practice heightens the risk of a newborn being overlooked by the nationality acts of all relevant states. The 1961 Statelessness Convention does not explicitly deal with this type of policy – it was adopted before these restrictions were imposed by Britain and others – yet the general provision of article 1 provides a remedy. If the parents are prevented from transmitting their nationality *jus sanguinis* due to this type of restriction with the result that their child would be stateless, the state upon whose territory the child is born is simply required to grant nationality. If this is not a state party, but the country of nationality of the parents is, article 4 prescribes the attribution of nationality *jus sanguinis* after all, as an exception to the restriction imposed, because the child would otherwise be stateless. The Statelessness Convention thereby offers the same level of protection against statelessness in these particular circumstances as in the case of a general conflict of nationality laws – subject to the same conditions. An identical conclusion can be drawn about the way in which the 1961 Convention works to prevent the inheritance of statelessness (the fourth of the concerns mentioned in relation to the *jus sanguinis* doctrine). No explicit reference is made to the strategy to be employed by *jus sanguinis* countries in the event of statelessness of the parents, but if the child would thereby "otherwise be stateless" then nationality must be attributed by the Contracting States according to article 1 or 4.

This leaves us with the two other *jus sanguinis* trouble spots: the distinction made in some *jus sanguinis* states between legitimate and illegitimate children and gender-sensitive nationality acts. They will be considered together as they are closely related since in both scenarios the risk of statelessness is heightened in that

[30] The child in question will also remain stateless from his birth until such a time as such requirements can be met.

[31] For example, articles 1 and 4 of the Draft Convention on the Reduction of Future Statelessness as put forward by the International Law Commission do not include a condition relating to the individual's criminal record.

a child can rely on only one parent for the acquisition of nationality through the bloodline.[32] Looking at the 1961 Statelessness Convention, we could simply refer once more to the general obligation under article 1 and 4 to grant nationality *jus soli* (and failing that *jus sanguinis*) to a child who would otherwise be stateless. However, there are a few details in these provisions that should not be overlooked. Article 1, paragraph 3 is of particular interest:

> Notwithstanding the provisions of paragraphs 1 (b) and 2 of this article, a child born in wedlock in the territory of a Contracting State, whose mother has the nationality of that State, shall acquire at birth that nationality if it otherwise would be stateless.[33]

The effect of this provision is to prescribe an absolute obligation to grant nationality *jus soli* to a legitimate child who would otherwise be stateless, if the child's mother also possesses the nationality of the state. In such cases, nationality must be attributed automatically at birth by operation of the law and no additional conditions may be set. This provision tells us two things. Firstly, in requiring that the child be born in wedlock, it copies the differentiation of treatment found in many municipal regulations between legitimate and illegitimate children. The Convention thereby accepts the legitimacy of such a distinction. Secondly, this text hints that gender-sensitive legislation may not be acceptable. It did not appear necessary to compose a provision of this sort for the case in which the father holds the nationality of the state. This is because, if the father holds the nationality, the legitimate child will almost without exception simply acquire that nationality automatically through the *jus sanguinis* doctrine. The provision is only relevant in states where the nationality act is gender sensitive and would not normally prescribe the attribution of nationality through the maternal bloodline.

An additional indication that the 1961 Convention does not approve of a gender imbalance can be traced in article 1, paragraph 4 and article 4, paragraph 1. There it states that if a child's parents do not possess the same nationality, "the question of whether the nationality of the person concerned should follow that of the father or that of the mother shall be determined by the national law of that contracting state".[34] It has moved away from the original Draft Convention as presented by the International Law Commission which determined that "the nationality of the father shall prevail over that of the mother"[35] to be more conducive of the principle of equality of men and women. All this being said, there is no outright prohibition of gender-sensitive nationality acts, so some problems

---

[32] Recall that in the case of illegitimate children, the paternal bond is often not (automatically) recognised by the state, meaning that the child must rely on the mother for inheritance of nationality. Where a state has promulgated gender-sensitive legislation, nationality can generally be transmitted through the paternal bond only, meaning that the child is reliant on the father for his nationality. In a state that combines these two policies, an illegitimate child will be unable to acquire a nationality *jus sanguinis* as the paternal bond is not formally recognised and the maternal bond is irrelevant for transferral of nationality.

[33] Article 1, paragraph 3 of the 1961 Convention on the Reduction of Statelessness.

[34] Article 1, paragraph 4 and article 4, paragraph 1 of the 1961 Convention on the Reduction of Statelessness.

[35] Article 1 paragraph 4 and article 4 of the Draft Convention on the Reduction of Future Statelessness.

may still arise. Moreover, the additional condition in article 1, paragraph 3 that the child be born in wedlock means that illegitimate children will still fall prey to gender-sensitive *jus sanguinis* legislation.

The final issue to be considered under the heading of *jus sanguinis* vs. *jus soli* is the difficulty of defining the precise territory of the state for the purposes of attribution of nationality *jus soli*. Recall that in the absence of an effective answer to this question, births in particular locations such as on board a ship or aircraft, may fall outside of the range of application of *jus soli* and produce cases of original statelessness. The 1961 Statelessness Convention affirms what has repeatedly been suggested as the most appropriate approach:

> For the purpose of determining the obligations of Contracting States under this Convention, birth on a ship or in an aircraft shall be deemed to have taken place in the territory of the State whose flag the ship flies or in the territory of the State in which the aircraft is registered, as the case may be.[36]

While this provision is only applicable to situations governed by the Convention – the Convention was formulated to prevent statelessness, not as an international code of nationality[37] - it may be informative in guiding states as to how the definition of territory for the purposes of the attribution of nationality *jus soli* should be undertaken. Furthermore, if a contracting state that grants nationality *jus soli* has not adopted this as a blanket approach, it will nevertheless be forced to do so where the child would otherwise be stateless on the basis of article 1 and this article 3 of the Convention. Overall then, the assessment of the 1961 Statelessness Convention's approach to *jus sanguinis* and *jus soli* issues has produced mixed results, dealing effectively with some of the situations, but allowing some cases of original statelessness to slip through the net. The next task is to perform a similar evaluation of international human rights instruments.

1.2 International human rights law

During the formulation of the 1966 International Covenant on Civil and Political Rights (ICCPR) – one of the instruments designed to transpose the ideals in the Universal Declaration of Human Rights into binding legal obligations – the provision relating to nationality underwent an interesting transformation. Where the Universal Declaration proclaimed a general right to a nationality, the Covenant refers only to the nationality of children: "Every child has the right to acquire a nationality".[38] It appears that nationality issues and statelessness were still considered too complex to enable states to reach a consensus on a general affirmation of the right to a nationality. States agreed, however, that every child

[36] Article 3 of the 1961 Convention on the Reduction of Statelessness.

[37] Paul Weis, *Nationality and Statelessness in International Law*, Kluwer Academic Publishers Group, Dordrecht: 1979, page 253.

[38] Article 24, paragraph 3, 1966 International Covenant on Civil and Political Rights.

should acquire an original nationality, even if no firm decision could be made on the right of an individual to be protected against statelessness later in life.[39]

Although this brief mention of the right of every child to acquire a nationality does not seem to provide enough detail for a substantive, concrete obligation on state parties, the interpretation provided by the Human Rights Committee charged with monitoring the implementation of the Covenant suggests otherwise in its General Comment 17:

> While the purpose of this provision is to prevent a child from being afforded less protection by society and the State because he is stateless, it does not necessarily make it an obligation for States to give their nationality to every child born in their territory. However, States are required to adopt every appropriate measure, both internally and in cooperation with other States, to ensure that every child has a nationality when he is born.[40]

These few lines provide us with a much better understanding of the substance of the obligation. There is indeed a very concrete obligation on states to adopt measures to prevent statelessness at birth, including mechanisms to prevent statelessness from arising from a conflict of *jus sanguinis* and *jus soli* doctrines. The most interesting segment of the text cited above is this: "it does not *necessarily* make it an obligation for States to give their nationality to every child born in their territory". While clearly, the Covenant does not prescribe universal adoption of the *jus soli* doctrine, the Human Rights Committee seems to suggest that states – if failing to secure another solution - may well be obliged to grant nationality to a child born on the territory of the state if the child would otherwise be stateless.[41] In the years since the adoption of this General Comment, the Human Rights Committee has clarified its views on the obligations of states still further in the Concluding Observations of a number of country reports. For example, in the consideration of Colombia's report in 1997, the Committee reminded the state of its duty to ensure that every child born in Colombia enjoys its right to acquire a nationality. It went on to declare that "the State party should consider conferring Colombian nationality on stateless children born in Colombia".[42] More recently, Syria was urged to provide a nationality to the Syrian-born children of stateless Kurds.[43] Clearly then, the Committee is advocating the application of *jus soli* as an exceptional measure where the child would otherwise be stateless – such as in the event of a conflict of laws - in order to substantiate the obligation laid down in article 24 of the Covenant.

---

[39] Johannes Chan, 'The Right to a Nationality as a Human Right - The Current Trend Towards Recognition', in *Human Rights Law Journal,* Vol. 12, 1991, page 4.

[40] Human Rights Committee, *CCPR General Comment No. 17: Rights of the Child (Art. 24),* Geneva: 7 April 1989, paragraph 8.

[41] Johannes Chan, 'The Right to a Nationality as a Human Right - The Current Trend Towards Recognition', in *Human Rights Law Journal,* Vol. 12, 1991, page 5.

[42] Human Rights Committee, *Concluding Observations: Colombia*, A/52/40 vol.1, Geneva: 1997, paragraph 306.

[43] Human Rights Committee, *Concluding Observations: Syrian Arab Republic,* A/60/40 vol. 1, Geneva: 2005, section 94, paragraph 19.

Almost 25 years after the adoption of the International Covenant on Civil and Political Rights, the Convention on the Rights of the Child (CRC) was settled. In its article 7 it copies the Covenant by including the right of a child to "acquire a nationality".[44] The second paragraph of this provision takes things a step further by reminding states that particular care must be taken to avoid statelessness - this being considered a worthy enough goal to receive special mention. Sadly, the Committee on the Rights of the Child has yet to issue a General Comment on this article of the Convention, so we must rely on the reading of its Concluding Observations to country reports to unearth the proper interpretation of this treaty provision.[45] While these documents provide ample references to the right of children to a nationality, there is no indication that the Committee would favour the attribution of nationality *jus soli* where the child would otherwise be stateless. In fact, the Committee does not express any preference with regards to the mechanisms to be adopted by states to prevent statelessness or deal with a conflict of nationality laws, it merely calls for "expedited" or "facilitated" procedures for the acquisition of citizenship to reduce the number of stateless children.[46]

Looking at how regional instruments have approached this question, we see that historically there has been a considerable divergence in approach which in recent years has been undergoing significant harmonisation. In 1950, the European Convention on Human Rights was established, but this instrument does not include a right to a nationality. When the Organisation of American States formulated the American Convention on Human Rights – its answer to the European Convention - in 1969, they included the most far-reaching right to a nationality in a legally binding human rights document to date. When a conflict of laws would result in original statelessness, the American Convention clearly prescribes the adoption of *jus soli* to ensure that those individuals acquire a nationality: "Every person has the right to the nationality of the state in whose territory he was born if he does not have the right to any other nationality".[47] The adoption of this radical but commendable and simple solution to the problem of statelessness at birth can be explained through the observation that *jus soli* is already the preferred method of

---

[44] It should be noted that the wording chosen for the Convention on the Rights of the Child – the right to "acquire a nationality" – deviated from the UN Declaration on the Rights of the Child which enunciated a child's entitlement from his birth to "a nationality". This choice has been explained with the reasoning that states were unwilling to accept any general obligation to implement *jus soli.* Jaap Doek, 'The CRC and the Right to Acquire and to Preserve a Nationality', in *Refugee Survey Quarterly,* Vol. 25, 2006, page 26.

[45] The Committee on the Rights of the Child has requested that states include in their periodic reports information on "measures adopted pursuant to article 7, paragraph 2, to ensure the child's right to acquire a nationality, in particular where the child would otherwise be stateless". UN Committee on the Rights of the Child, *General guidelines regarding the form and contents of periodic reports to be submitted by state parties,* CRC/C/58, 20 November 1996, para. 53.

[46] This may involve attributing nationality to children born on state territory, but need not take the form of automatic *jus soli* conferral of citizenship – it is sufficient to provide facilitated naturalisation. Committee on the Rights of the Child, *Concluding Observations: Czech Republic,* CRC/C/15/Add.201, Geneva: 18 March 2003, para. 38; *Estonia,* CRC/C/15/Add.196, Geneva: 17 March 2003, para. 29; *Kazakhstan,* CRC/C/15/Add.213, Geneva: 10 July 2003, para. 33; *Romania,* CRC/C/15/Add.199, Geneva: 18 March 2003, para. 33; *Syrian Arab Republic,* CRC/C/15/Add.212, Geneva: 10 July 2003, para. 33.

[47] Article 20, paragraph 2, American Convention on Human Rights, 1969.

nationality attribution in the Americas.[48] Meanwhile, on the African continent, another regional human rights document was composed. Adopted in 1981, the African Charter on Human and Peoples' Rights is – just like the European Convention – entirely silent on the question of nationality.[49]

However, newer European and African instruments are illustrative of a more proactive approach to the problem of statelessness at birth. The European Convention on Nationality was drafted under the auspices of the Council of Europe and opened for signature on the 6th of November 1997.[50] Although not strictly a human rights document, but rather a consolidation of developments in municipal and international law with regard to nationality,[51] it aims to ensure the respect of a number of basic human rights principles in the field of nationality.[52] Many of the Convention's provisions are therefore of importance in preventing statelessness, including statelessness at birth. In dealing with original statelessness it provides for *jus soli* attribution of nationality to children either automatically at birth or later, upon application to the appropriate authority. In the event of the latter, the European Convention also allows the state party to impose the additional conditions of "lawful and habitual residence on its territory for a period not exceeding five years immediately preceding the lodging of the application" and that the child has "remained stateless".[53] It is interesting to note that despite being inspired by the 1961 Convention on the Reduction of Statelessness, this provision in the European Convention on Nationality differs substantively from its counterpart on a number of points, not all of them positive. While the European Convention does not permit the imposition of a condition linked to criminal convictions,[54] the time limit for application for nationality is less favourable as are the residence requirements.[55] For

[48] Carol Batchelor, 'Statelessness and the Problem of Resolving Nationality Status', in *International Journal of Refugee Law*, Vol. 10, 1998, page 170.

[49] African Charter on Human and Peoples' Rights, 1981.

[50] At the time of writing, the European Convention on Nationality counted 17 Contracting States; Council of Europe Treaty Office, http://conventions.coe.int

[51] Council of Europe, *European Convention on Nationality: Explanatory report*, Strasbourg: 1997.

[52] Article 4 of the European Convention on Nationality determines that "The rules on nationality of each State Party shall be based on the following principles:

a. everyone has the right to a nationality;
b. statelessness shall be avoided;
c. no one shall be arbitrarily deprived of his or her nationality;
d. neither marriage nor the dissolution of a marriage between a national of a State Party and an alien, nor the change of nationality by one of the spouses during marriage, shall automatically affect the nationality of the other spouse."

[53] Article 6, paragraph 2 of the European Convention on Nationality, 1997. On the impact of the condition of *lawful* residence on access to nationality for irregular migrants, see chapter VII.

[54] The 1961 Statelessness Convention allows states to make the attribution of nationality conditional upon the person "neither being convicted of an offence against national security nor [...] sentenced to imprisonment for a term of five years or more on a criminal charge", see article 1, paragraph 2 c) of the 1961 Convention on the Reduction of Statelessness.

[55] The 1961 Statelessness Convention determines that in delineating the period in which applications for nationality may be lodged, this period may begin no later than when the individual reaches the age of 18 years and end no earlier than when he attains the age of 21. The applicant must moreover be assured at least one full year upon reaching the age of majority in the relevant state in which they can submit the application of their own accord. The European Convention on Nationality on the other hand determines that the application must be lodged by a child, defined elsewhere in the instrument as a

approximately half of the state parties to the European Convention on Nationality, these remarkable differences between the two texts will be of little consequence for they have also acceded to the 1961 Statelessness Convention and are obliged to offer individuals the most favourable treatment available.[56]

Turning back to Africa, we see that the concept of granting nationality *jus soli* to children who would otherwise be stateless has now also permeated that region. The 1999 African Charter on the Rights and Welfare of the Child proclaims not only a general right of every child to acquire a nationality, but also specifies that:

> State Parties to the Charter shall undertake to ensure that their Constitutional legislation recognises the principles according to which a child shall acquire the nationality of the State in the territory in which he was born if, at the time of the child's birth, he is not granted nationality by any other State in accordance with its laws.[57]

These recent developments at regional level, combined with what has already been said of the universal human rights obligations, attest to a conclusion that was already drawn well over a decade ago by a number of scholars: that there is evidence of a general obligation under international law for states to grant nationality to children born on their territory who would otherwise be stateless.[58]

---

person "below the age of 18 years unless, under the law applicable to the child, majority is attained earlier". Once the person has reached the age of majority, the window of opportunity to acquiring nationality closes. This provision means, in effect, that the stateless child be dependent on the action of his parents to acquire a nationality since it is likely that they will have to submit the application on his behalf. With regard to the residency requirements, the 1961 Statelessness Convention allows states to set a qualifying period of *habitual* residence, not exceeding 5 years immediately preceding the application for nationality or 10 years in total. By contrast, the European Convention on Nationality clearly demands *lawful* and habitual residence for a period not exceeding 5 years immediately prior to submitting an application for nationality. These conditions are harder to meet because they ignore the duration of residence accrued overall, taking into account only the period immediately prior to application and render ineligible any children who are irregularly present in the state. See for an explanation of the terms in the European Convention on Nationality Council of Europe, *European Convention on Nationality: Explanatory report,* Strasbourg: 1997, page 34. The significance of the requirement of *lawful* residence is investigated further in chapter VII, section 2.1.

[56] See article 26 of the European Convention on Nationality, 1997 and article 13 of the 1961 Convention on the Reduction of Statelessness.

[57] Article 6, paragraph 4 of the African Charter on the Rights and Welfare of the Child, 1999. Note that the phrase "*undertake* to ensure" weakens the obligation enunciated here.

[58] See for example Ruth Donner, "Chapter 4: Human Rights Conventions and other Instruments" in *The Regulation of Nationality in International Law*, Transnational Publishers, New York: 1994, page 230; Johannes Chan, 'The Right to a Nationality as a Human Right - The Current Trend Towards Recognition', in *Human Rights Law Journal,* Vol. 12, 1991, page 11; and more recently David Weissbrodt, *Final Report on Prevention of Discrimination - The Rights of Non-Citizens,* E/CN.4/Sub.2/2003/23, 26 May 2003, page 6. Recent instruments on nationality and statelessness in the context of state succession also prescribe *jus soli* attribution of nationality to children who would otherwise be stateless thanks to the effect that the succession of states had on the nationality of their parents. See chapter VI, section 3. Meanwhile the recently adopted Covenant on the Rights of the Child in Islam emphasises the importance of both *jus soli* and *jus sanguinis* measures where it calls upon states to "resolve the issue of statelessness for any child born on their territories or to any of their

While I feel that the arguments put forward in the past have not always been entirely convincing,[59] I would – particularly in view of these most recent developments – agree with their conclusion. The obligation emanating from the human rights field thereby reinforces the strategy adopted in the 1961 Convention on the Reduction of Statelessness, although no further guidance is provided on how this commitment should be implemented and whether additional conditions may be set.

Alongside a general duty to avoid creating statelessness at birth, human rights instruments and their guardians have also addressed some of the particular deficiencies of municipal laws and policies that heighten the risk of statelessness, providing in some cases strong and explicit obligations for states. As to restrictions placed on continued inheritance of nationality *jus sanguinis* after several generations of residence abroad, only the Human Rights Committee has expressed concern at this practice. It did so in its Concluding Observations on Zimbabwe's state report in 1998: "it is also of concern that children born to Zimbabweans abroad may not acquire Zimbabwean citizenship".[60] The Constitution of the Republic of Zimbabwe and the Citizenship of Zimbabwe Act provide for the attribution of two main categories of citizenship: "citizenship by descent" and

citizens outside their territory". Article 7, paragraph 2 of the Covenant on the Rights of the Child in Islam.

[59] For example, I do not agree that the near universal ratification of the Convention on the Rights of the Child is in itself enough to testify to the existence of an international norm prescribing the application of *jus soli* to the children of non-citizen parents as suggested by Weissbrodt in David Weissbrodt, *Final Report on Prevention of Discrimination - The Rights of Non-Citizens,* E/CN.4/Sub.2/2003/23, 26 May 2003. This is not laid down as such in the Convention, nor – as we have seen - has it been prescribed by the Committee on the Rights of the Child. Indeed records of the drafting process of the Convention on the Rights of the Child show that a deliberate move was made away from prescribing *jus soli* attribution of nationality to a child who would otherwise be stateless towards a more open provision that recognises the equal validity of *jus sanguinis* regimes. See Sharon Detrick, *The United Nations Convention on the Rights of the Child,* Martinus Nijhoff, Dordrecht: 1992, pages 123-131; Sharon Detrick, *A commentary on the United Nations Convention on the Rights of the Child,* Kluwer, The Hague: 1999, page 151. A General Comment would be warmly welcomed on the right to acquire a nationality under the Convention on the Rights of the Child. Rather, evidence of universal acceptance of the attribution of nationality *jus soli* to a child who would otherwise be stateless is to my mind provided by the inclusion of this principle in a number of important regional instruments and the interpretation of article 24 of the Covenant on Civil and Political Rights by the Human Rights Committee. Nor can I agree with the contention in "The Human Rights of Stateless Persons", that article 5 of the Convention on the Elimination of Racial Discrimination precludes *jus sanguinis* laws altogether as this article is simply a restatement of the right to equal enjoyment – free from discrimination – of the right to a nationality. It does not in any way give precedence to either the *jus soli* or the *jus sanguinis* doctrine. Nor can it be maintained that the adherence to *jus sanguinis* is of itself a violation of the right to a nationality, it is simply one - widely accepted and utilised – method of attributing nationality at birth by equating the genuine link with the state to the parentage of the child. David Weissbrodt; Clay Collins, 'The Human Rights of Stateless Persons', in *Human Rights Quarterly,* Vol. 28, 2006, page 256.

[60] Human Right Committee, *Concluding Observations: Zimbabwe,* A/53/40 vol. 1, Geneva: 1998, paragraph 221; Committee on the Rights of the Child, *Concluding Observations: Lithuania,* CRC/C/103, Geneva: 2001, paragraph 274.

"citizenship otherwise than by descent".[61] Similarly to the British example given earlier, citizens by descent (those already born outside the territory of Zimbabwe) are restricted in their right to pass on that citizenship to their children. The Human Rights Committee picked out this policy in the consideration of Zimbabwe's report because it may lead to statelessness. Moreover, the principle of non-discrimination between nationals in the enjoyment of rights may stand in the way of such policies.[62] As to the inheritance of statelessness, both the Human Rights Committee and the Committee on the Rights of the Child have expressed concern at any policy which allows the children of stateless parents to be deprived of a nationality of origin, hinting that nationality should then be granted *jus soli* by the state upon whose territory the child is born.[63] The Committee on the Rights of the Child even makes it clear that the residence status of the parents cannot influence the acquisition of nationality of a child in this way if the parents are stateless.[64] These statements point to a general condemnation of the practice of allowing statelessness to be inherited.[65]

Next we come to the difficulties associated with illegitimate children and gender-sensitive nationality acts. This is an area in which we saw that the 1961 Statelessness Convention was less forthcoming. Interestingly, the human rights field is very much outspoken on these issues. To begin with, the Universal Declaration on Human Rights determines that children are entitled to equal protection of their rights whether born in or out of wedlock.[66] Furthermore, the Convention on the Rights of the Child provides that the rights which it houses are to be enjoyed by all children "irrespective of the child's or *his or her parent's* or legal guardian's race, colour, sex, language, religion, political or other opinion, national, ethnic or social origin, property, disability, birth *or other status*".[67] While the marital status of the parents is not mentioned explicitly as an unlawful ground for discrimination, the enumeration of grounds is not exhaustive, so discrimination between legitimate and illegitimate children may be prohibited under the general reference to "other status". It can therefore be argued that the enjoyment of the right to acquire a nationality as proclaimed in article 7 of the convention should be protected equally for children born in and out of wedlock. The Concluding Observations of the Committee on the Rights of the Child on a number of state

[61] See articles 5 and 6 of the Constitution of the Republic of Zimbabwe, 18 April 1980 and the preliminary paragraphs of the Citizenship of Zimbabwe Act [Chapter 4:01], 1 December 1984.

[62] These policies in effect differentiate between persons who acquired citizenship by descent and those who gained nationality otherwise than by descent in the enjoyment of the ability to pass on nationality *jus sanguinis*, thus in effect creating two classes of citizenship. Discrimination between nationals should be avoided. Article 5, paragraph 2 of the European Convention on Nationality.

[63] Human Rights Committee, *Concluding Observations: Kuwait,* Geneva: 27 July 2000, paragraph 481; Committee on the Rights of the Child, *Concluding Observations:Liechtenstein,* CRC/C/103, Geneva: 2001, paragraph 89; *Lithuania*, CRC/C/103, Geneva: 2001, paragraphs 274 and 275; *Syrian Arab Republic,* CRC/C/132, Geneva: 2003, paragraph 558.

[64] CRC, *Concluding Observations: Lithuania*, CRC/C/103, Geneva: 2001, paragraph 274.

[65] Such sentiments can also be traced in, for example, article II, paragraph a of Recommendation R (1999) 18 of the Committee of Ministers to Member States on the Avoidance and Reduction of Statelessness, Council of Europe, 1999. See also the explanatory memorandum accompanying this recommendation, paragraph 65.

[66] Article 25, paragraph 2 of the Universal Declaration of Human Rights, 1948.

[67] Emphasis added; article 2, paragraph 1 of the 1989 Convention on the Rights of the Child.

party reports confirm this interpretation. The Committee has expressed concern at the discrimination between legitimate and illegitimate children in the field of nationality and in particular at the restrictions imposed on the transmission of nationality from father to child in the case of illegitimate children.[68] Thus while the 1961 Statelessness Convention itself distinguished between children born in and out of wedlock for the enjoyment of the rights promulgated, this differentiation has in recent years been interpreted as unlawful discrimination under the most widely accepted human rights instrument in existence.[69] The other UN instruments and treaty bodies and the regional human rights mechanisms have not addressed this specific problem. At the regional level, the messages are mixed. The American Convention on Human Rights prescribes equal rights for children born in and out of wedlock.[70] Meanwhile the European Convention on Nationality appears to admit to the possibility of different treatment by determining that the conferral of nationality "to children whose parenthood is established by recognition, court order or similar procedures" may be subject to the procedure set out under domestic law.[71] Further guidance is needed as to how this provision should be implemented with a view to avoiding statelessness and respecting the aforementioned concern for non-discrimination between children on the basis of the parent's marital status.[72]

Where gender-imbalanced nationality acts are concerned there is ample evidence that this amounts to prohibited discrimination on the grounds of gender. In fact, there are so many references to that effect that to mention them all would be to fill countless pages with text; therefore what follows is a carefully selected overview. Firstly, it cannot be ignored that the principle of non-discrimination, including on the grounds of gender, has become a matter of customary international law.[73] This is evidenced not only by the inclusion of this principle in the preambles and among the fundamental principles espoused by the Charter of the United Nations, but also by its affirmation in the Universal Declaration of Human Rights and every important human rights instrument adopted to date.[74] Moreover, the international community has devoted an entire Convention to the realisation of this principle: the Convention on the Elimination of All Forms of Discrimination

[68] See for example the Concluding observations on the United Kingdom where reference is made to article 2 together with article 7, in Committee on the Rights of the Child, *Concluding Observations: United Kingdom of Great Britain and Northern Ireland,* CRC/C/38, Geneva: 1995, paragraph 214 and again in CRC, *Concluding Observations: United Kingdom of Great Britain and Northern Ireland,* CRC/C/121, Geneva: 2002, paragraph 114. See also CRC, *Concluding Observations: Lebanon,* CRC/C/54, Geneva: 1996, paragraph 39; *Japan,* CRC/C/137, Geneva: 2004, paragraphs 626 and 627.

[69] The Convention on the Rights of the Child has been ratified by all by 2 of the world's states.

[70] Article 17, paragraph 5 of the American Convention.

[71] Article 6, paragraph 1(a) of the European Convention on Nationality.

[72] Committee of Experts on Nationality, *Report on Conditions for the Acquisition and Loss of Nationality,* Strasbourg: 14 January 2003, page 6.

[73] Malcolm Shaw, *International Law*, Cambridge University Press, Cambridge: 2003, page 257; Vladimir Kartashkin, *The rights of women married to foreigners,* E/CN.4/Sub.2/2003/34, 30 June 2003, page 6.

[74] The prohibition of discrimination on the grounds of sex is included in article 1 of the UN Charter; article 2 of the Universal Declaration of Human Rights; article 2 of the International Covenant on Civil and Political Rights and the International Covenant on Economic, Social and Cultural Rights; article 2 of the Convention on the Rights of the Child.

against Women.[75] States are thereby compelled to eradicate discriminatory legislation and policy, which would include such instruments as nationality regulations. In fact, this issue is considered of such great importance that the convention explicitly prohibits gender-sensitive nationality acts in article 9: "States Parties shall grant women equal rights with men with respect to the nationality of their children".[76] The Committee responsible for overseeing the implementation of the convention has been very active in pushing states to incorporate this obligation into their municipal nationality acts.[77]

As mentioned, all of the major human rights instruments adopted under the auspices of the United Nations contain a clause prohibiting gender discrimination in the enjoyment of the rights set out in that document – including, where applicable, a child's right to acquire a nationality. Clearly this prohibits discrimination between boys and girls in the attribution of nationality to a child at birth. However, it also outlaws discrimination between the mother and the father's ability to transmit their nationality where the state has adopted the *jus sanguinis* doctrine. This point has been made repeatedly in the responses to country reports by the Human Rights Committee, under article 24 and article 2 of the ICCPR[78] and the Committee on the Rights of the Child under article 7 and article 2 of the CRC.[79]

More surprising is the discovery that the Committee on Economic, Social and Cultural Rights has also taken up the cause. In response to numerous state reports over the past decade, this committee has noted any gender imbalance identified in nationality legislation. At first, these references were relatively neutral in tone, such as in the concluding observations on the report from the Republic of Korea in 1996: "Notice is also taken of such anachronistic rules as the legal inability of a woman in

[75] Aopted on the 18th of December 1979, entered into force on the 3rd of September 1981 and now boasting an impressive 180 State Parties.

[76] Article 9, paragraph 2 of the 1979 Convention on the Elimination of All Forms of Discrimination against Women. It should however be noted that, while the Convention itself has been widely ratified, this article on the equality of men and women with respect to nationality matters (both paragraphs 1 and 2) has been the subject of a substantial number of reservations and interpretative declarations by state parties. For a discussion of this phenomenon, see UN Division for the Advancement of Women, *Women, nationality and citizenship,* June 2003, pages 15-16.

[77] See the Committee on the Elimination of Discrimination Against Women, *Concluding Observations: Morocco*, A/52/38/Rev.1 part I, New York: 1997, paragraph 63; *Turkey*, A/52/38/Rev.1 part I New York: 1997, paragraph 200; *Algeria*, A/54/38/Rev.1 part I, New York: 1999, paragraph 83; *India*, A/55/38 part I, New York: 2000, paragraph 50; *Jordan*, A/55/38 part I, New York: 2000, paragraph 172; *Maldives*, A/56/38 part I, New York: 2001, paragraph 127; *Singapore*, A/56/38 part II, New York: 2001, paragraph 75; *Sri Lanka*, A/57/38 part I, New York: 2002, paragraph 275.

[78] Some examples can be found in the following reports: Human Rights Committee, *Concluding Observations: Jordan*, A/49/40 vol. I, Geneva: 1994, paragraph 232; *Libyan Arab Jamahiriya,* A/54/40 vol. I, Geneva: 1999, paragraph 137; *Monaco*, A/56/40 vol. I, Geneva: 2001, paragraph 84; *Yemen,* A/57/40 vol. I, Geneva: 2002, paragraph 83 (11); *Egypt*, A/58/40 vol. I, Geneva: 2003, paragraph 77(10); *Morocco*, A/60/40 vol. I , Geneva: 2005, paragraph 32.

[79] For example in Committee on the Rights of the Child, *Concluding Observations: Iraq,* CRC/C/80, Geneva: 1998, paragraph 76; *Kuwait,* CRC/C/80, Geneva: 1998, paragraph 138; *Egypt,* CRC/C/103 , Geneva: 2001, paragraphs 224-225; *Saudi Arabia*, CRC/C/103, Geneva: 2001, paragraph 397; *Bhutan*, CRC/C/108, Geneva: 2001, paragraph 459; *Lebanon*, CRC/C/114, Geneva: 2002, paragraph 81; *Brunei Darussalam,* CRC/C/133, Geneva: 2003, paragraphs 359-360; *Indonesia,* CRC/C/137, Geneva: 2004, paragraphs 58 and 60; *Togo,* CRC/C/146, Geneva: 2005, paragraph 547.

certain cases to vest her nationality in her child".[80] Similar terms are used in respect of Cyprus' report in 1999.[81] With the new millennium came a more stern approach by the Committee which began to "express concern" at such discriminatory nationality regulations.[82] It is not only this gradual introduction of stronger language by the Committee which is interesting, but the very reference to nationality acts at all. The legal basis in the International Covenant on Economic, Social and Cultural Rights for this step is not immediately obvious. One possibility would be an expansive reading of article 10, paragraph 1 which deals with the protection of the family, in particular in the care of dependent children.[83] This can be read in combination with article 2, paragraph 2 which contains the general prohibition of discrimination and article 3 which clearly espouses the equal right of men and women to the enjoyment of the rights contained in the Covenant. On the other hand, it is feasible that the Committee simply felt compelled to respond to the finding of discriminatory laws in any field in its role as a human rights body and in view of the fundamental nature of the prohibition of gender discrimination.

Since the consideration of universal instruments has already provided sufficient evidence of an internationally accepted prohibition of gender-discrimination, including in the formulation of nationality acts, we need only briefly look at regional documents. Unsurprisingly, we find that all relevant instruments have included a general non-discrimination clause as one of the first provisions in the text.[84] In the African context, the Protocol to the African Charter on Human and Peoples' Rights on the Rights of Women in Africa contains not only a general equality clause, but also a specific provision on the matter. This article states that "a woman and a man shall have equal rights, with respect to the nationality of their children", going on, however, to qualify this by adding "except where this is contrary to a provision in national legislation or is contrary to national security interests".[85] This last phrase is at the very least questionable for it appears to nullify

[80] Committee on Economic, Social and Cultural Rights, *Concluding Observations: Republic of Korea*, E/1996/22, New York and Geneva: 1995, paragraph 73.

[81] Committee on Economic, Social and Cultural Rights, *Concluding Observations : Cyprus*, E/1999/22 New York and Geneva: 1998, paragraph 291.

[82] In the field of UN diplomacy and human rights, "expresses concern" finds itself somewhere in the middle of the scale of language used, with "notes" being at the milder end and "condemns" at the stronger. Committee on Economic, Social and Cultural Rights, *Concluding Observations:Jordan*, E/2001/22, New Yorka and Geneva: 2000, paragraph 234; *Nepal*, E/2002/22, New York and Geneva: 2001, paragraph 533.

[83] The provision reads as follows: "State Parties to the present Covenant recognise that [...] the widest possible protection and assistance should be accorded to the family, which is the natural and fundamental group unit of society, particularly for its establishment and while it is responsible for the care and education of dependent children", article 10, paragraph 1 of the 1966 International Covenant on Economic, Social and Cultural Rights

[84] Article 1 of the American Convention on Human Rights, 1969; article 2 of the African Charter on the Rights and Welfare of the Child, 1999 and article 5 of the European Convention on Nationality, 1997.

[85] Article 6, section h of the Protocol to the African Charter on Human and Peoples' Rights on the Rights of Women in Africa, 2003. The African Charter on Human and Peoples' Rights also prescribes the "elimination of every discrimination against women" and the "protection of the rights of women and the child as stipulated in international declarations and conventions", which would include the universal human rights instruments already discussed; article 18, paragraph 3 of the African Charter on Human and Peoples' Rights, 1981.

the effect of the entire provision. After all, where else would the attribution of nationality be regulated if not in national legislation? Moreover, this clause is in contradiction with earlier agreements into which many of the state parties have entered, among which the clearly formulated article 9 of the Convention on the Elimination of All Forms of Discrimination again Women.[86] The prohibition of discrimination belongs to the group of human rights which cannot be derogated, even in an emergency, meaning that allowing national security considerations to retain precedence is equally disputable.[87] In the event of a conflict, states will nevertheless be held by the prohibition of discrimination as a principle of customary international law.[88] It has already been made clear that this principle is applicable to nationality legislation and that a gender imbalanced *jus sanguinis* act is unacceptable – whether there is a threat of ensuing statelessness or not. Here, international human rights law clearly goes a step further in the protection offered than the 1961 Convention on the Reduction of Statelessness was able to achieve.

We have come to the last problem relating to the mechanisms for attributing nationality at birth: the definition of state territory for the purposes of the *jus soli* system. According to legal doctrine on the subject, states generally equate births on board a ship or aircraft registered under their flag to births on the territory proper of a state for the purposes of applying the *jus soli* doctrine. It is even suggested that this is a principle of customary international law.[89] However, in the field of human rights this principle has not been included for codification. None of the universal or regional conventions discussed above prescribe a particular territorial application of the *jus soli* doctrine. Even the European Convention on Nationality remains entirely silent on the matter, despite being specifically designed as a consolidation of principles related to nationality. Since international law does provide for the acquisition of birth *jus soli* by a child who would otherwise be stateless, the definition of a state's territory is of utmost importance - although births on board an aircraft or ship can be deemed to be very rare. It would therefore be advisable for the Human Rights Committee or the Committee on the Rights of the Child to include this question in a general comment on the right of a child to acquire a nationality in order to clarify the application of the *jus soli* principle where a child would otherwise be stateless.

2 ABANDONED OR ORPHANED CHILDREN

A category of children that is particularly vulnerable to statelessness, right from the very start, is that of abandoned or orphaned children.[90] Children may be

---

[86] Which as cited above has been ratified by 180 states.

[87] As stated in Ruth Donner, "Chapter 4: Human Rights Conventions and other Instruments" in *The Regulation of Nationality in International Law*, Transnational Publishers, New York: 1994, page 236 and; Carmen Tiburcio, "Chapter IV. Fundamental Rights" in *The human rights of aliens under international and comparative law*, Kluwer Law International, The Hague: 2001, page 75.

[88] Malcolm Shaw, *International Law*, Cambridge University Press, Cambridge: 2003, page 257.

[89] Ian Brownlie, *Principles of Public International Law*, Oxford University Press, Oxford: 2003, page 384.

[90] Maureen Lynch, *Lives on hold: The human cost of statelessness,* Washington: 2005, page 5; UNHCR and IPU, *Nationality and statelessness. A handbook for parliamentarians*, 2005, page 32.

> Abandoned for political or economic reasons, or as a result of social practices and traditions. Examples of such situations include the following: preferences for male children, bias against interracial marriages, fear and shame of children with birth defects, and stigmas against women who are sexually active outside of marriage.[91]

Whenever a baby is found having been abandoned, perhaps in an alleyway, at a train station, medical clinic, or orphanage, a problem of establishing identity arises. How do we know where this child was born or when? Even more problematic is the question: who are the baby's parents? Without the answers to these questions, the legal status of the child remains undetermined and - in the absence of any special arrangement in the law dealing with the nationality of foundlings - he will be stateless. This is the case regardless of whether the state where the child is found attributes nationality *jus soli* or *jus sanguinis* because neither the bond by soil nor blood can be proven. With regards to orphaned children, particularly those who are orphaned at a very young age, similar problems may arise as the identity or nationality of their parents may be unknown. According to Carol Batchelor, "UNHCR has encountered thousands of stateless children in orphanages".[92] Moreover, the problem is likely become more acute in years to come because the number of orphans worldwide is on the increase as the AIDS pandemic claims more lives.[93]

2.1 The 1961 Convention on the Reduction of Statelessness

After a lengthy discussion in section 1.1 of this chapter of articles 1, 3 and 4 of the 1961 Convention on the Reduction of Statelessness, we now turn our attention to article 2, the last article to deal with original statelessness. It reads as follows:

> A foundling found in the territory of a Contracting State shall, in the absence of proof to the contrary, be considered to have been born within that territory of parents possessing the nationality of that state.[94]

Once more, the wording of this provision is evidence of the compromise reached between *jus soli* and *jus sanguinis* countries. Rather than determining that a child found abandoned on the territory of the state will automatically acquire the nationality of that state, it declares that the child will be assumed to have both the necessary *jus soli* and *jus sanguinis* links with the state: born on the territory to

---

[91] Youth Advocate Program International, *Stateless Children – Youth who are without citizenship,* Booklet No. 7 in a series on International Youth Issues, 2002, page 18.

[92] Carol Batchelor, "The International Legal Framework Concerning Statelessness and Access for Stateless Persons", *European Union Seminar on the Content and Scope of International Protection: Panel 1 - Legal basis of international protection,* Madrid: 2002, page 4.

[93] By 2003, 15 million children worldwide had been orphaned by AIDS; AVERT, *Aids Orphans,* 2006, accessible via www.avert.org/aidsorphans.htm

[94] Article 2 of the 1961 Convention on the Reduction of Statelessness. This text uses the accepted term "foundling" to refer to any child who has been abandoned and whose parents are unknown.

parents possessing the nationality of the state.[95] This means that the child will then simply acquire nationality *ex lege* under the normal operation of the state's nationality regulations - the effect being the same in both *jus soli* or *jus sanguinis* regimes. No attempt is made to further define the type of evidence that may be accepted as "proof to the contrary", this being left to the discretion of the contracting states.

2.2 International human rights law

Beyond what has already been said in section 1.2 on a general obligation of states to provide a nationality to children born on their territory who would otherwise be stateless, international human rights instruments provide little solace in dealing with abandoned or orphaned children. Neither the International Covenant on Civil and Political Rights, nor the Convention on the Rights of the Child, mention the particular situation of foundlings. However, many states have recognised the vulnerable position of foundlings and adopted specific provisions in their domestic legislation to deal with their nationality status.[96] Whether this was inspired by the poorly ratified 1961 Statelessness Convention or the older, even more poorly ratified 1930 Hague Convention is impossible to determine.[97] Either way, there is evidence of a widespread state practice, carried out over a significant period of time, of providing foundlings with the nationality of the state on which they are found by special constructions in the law of both *jus soli* and *jus sanguinis* states. The UNHCR global questionnaire provides some quantification of this general practice: 86.5% of participating states reported that they provide for a legal status or nationality for abandoned children and orphans.[98]

In order to contend that a rule of customary international law has thereby been established, we must also prove that states are legislating in this way due to the conviction that they are legally compelled to do so – the *opinio juris sive necessitatis*.[99] The codification of the obligation to grant nationality to foundlings in the 1930 Hague Convention and the 1961 Statelessness Convention cannot be taken as sufficient evidence due, mainly, to the low number of state parties to both

---

[95] This is a change from the Draft Convention put forward by the International Law Commission which simply stated that a foundling will be presumed to have been born on the territory of the state in which he is found, nationality then being granted *jus soli* under article 1 of the same draft convention if the child would otherwise be stateless. United Nations Yearbook of the United Nations 1954, page 421.

[96] Hudson for example already claimed this to be the case in his 1952 report. Manley Hudson, *Report on Nationality, including Statelessness,* A/CN.4/50, 21 February 1952, page 44. More recently, Brownlie attests to the same in Ian Brownlie, *Principles of Public International Law*, Oxford University Press, Oxford: 2003, page 383.

[97] The 1930 Hague Convention determines in article 14 that "A child whose parents are both unknown shall have the nationality of the country of birth [...] A foundling is, until the contrary is proved, presumed to have been born on the territory of the State in which it is found". League of Nations The Hague Convention on Certain Questions relating to Conflict of Nationality Laws 1930.

[98] UNHCR, *Final report concerning the Questionnaire on statelessness pursuant to the Agenda for Protection,* Geneva: March 2004, page 23.

[99] International custom is established through "evidence of a general practice accepted as law"; article 38 of the Statute of the International Court of Justice, 1945.

instruments.[100] However, it can be argued that the acceptance of a general obligation upon states to prevent statelessness, particularly of children, can be seen as the foundation for the *opinio iuris*: states feel compelled to address the situation of foundlings who would otherwise be stateless. Moreover, in the most recent international instrument dealing with nationality – albeit a regional convention – we find the following provision:

> Each State Party shall provide in its internal law for its nationality to be acquired ex lege by [...] foundlings found in its territory who would otherwise be stateless.[101]

Clearly, at least within the context of the Council of Europe, it was felt that this principle belonged among the developments in internal and international law that the Convention was designed to reflect. The specific right of foundlings to a nationality can also be found in the Covenant on the Rights of the Child in Islam, although this text does not specify which state is required to fulfil this right.[102] Overall then, it would seem safe to conclude that this treatment of foundlings has truly become a matter of international custom. Nevertheless, for the purposes of ensuring its universal application, increased accession to the 1961 Convention on the Reduction of Statelessness would be desirable and would also add to the supporting evidence of a customary international norm.

3 Marriage (or Divorce) and Adoption

The first of the technical causes of subsequent statelessness – statelessness arising in later life - that we will look at here relates to a change in civil status through marriage, divorce or adoption. Familial ties have long been recognised by states as an indication of a "genuine link". Thus, if a foreigner marries a national, this is seen as a ground for (at least facilitated) acquisition of the nationality of the spouse's state. As an elective process, these days such (facilitated) naturalisation is usually open to either spouse.[103] However, historically in the event of marriage it was the woman's legal status which was affected as her status was considered to be dependent on that of her husband's.[104] She was seen to forge a bond with her husband's state through the vows of matrimony and lose her *genuine link* with her state of original nationality. This perspective was translated by many states into laws which prescribed an automatic change of nationality of the female spouse

---

[100] It is, however, important to note that the provision on foundlings was not singled out as being particularly controversial in the debate on the 1961 Convention and is therefore likely to be one of the more widely accepted of its articles.

[101] Article 6, paragraph 1 b) of the European Convention on Nationality, 1997.

[102] Article 7, paragraph 3 of the Covenant on the Rights of the Child in Islam.

[103] For example, according to the Law on Dutch Nationality, the naturalisation procedure for the non-national spouse of a Dutch citizen is facilitated. After three years of marriage and residence under one roof with the Dutch spouse, the requirement of 5 years of habitual residence on Dutch soil prior to the application for naturalisation is waived. Article 8, paragraph 2 of the Rijkswet op de Nederlanderschap [Law on Dutch nationality], 1984.

[104] Lung-chu Chen, 'The Equal Protection of Women in Reference to Nationality and Freedom of Movement', in *American Society of International Law Proceedings,* Vol. 69, 1975, page 19.

upon marriage to a non-national.[105] Some such domestic laws are still in force today, [106] despite the - well-recognised - danger that they may be a source of statelessness.[107] Specifically, if the wife's state of nationality assumes a change of nationality following the unity of the spouses and prescribes the automatic loss of that nationality upon marriage to a non-national, while the husband's state does not in fact automatically grant nationality through marriage to a national, she is rendered stateless.[108] Women may also be at risk of statelessness in the event of a divorce. When the marriage is dissolved, the nationality acquired through her husband may be automatically lost while there is no guarantee that her original nationality will be restored.[109] This has recently been flagged as a substantial problem for "economic brides" from Vietnam: more than 3,000 Vietnamese women have ended up stateless after marrying a non-national, renouncing their Vietnamese citizenship in order to apply for the nationality of their husband and then failing to complete the naturalisation proceedings before the marriage breaks down.[110] With an increasing mobilisation of people across international borders comes a corresponding increase in the number of marriages between nationals of different states.[111] This issue is thereby likely to remain a considerable source of statelessness unless there is a change in state policy.

A negative conflict of laws leading to statelessness may arise not only in the event of marriage, but can also be brought about by the process of inter-country adoption in which the nationality of the child differs from the nationality of the prospective parents. In much the same way as marriage, adoption can affect the

---

[105] UN Division for the Advancement of Women, *Women, nationality and citizenship,* June 2003, pages 5-7.

[106] UNHCR's 2003 Global Questionnaire on Statelessness found that of the respondent states, 6.8% have laws prescribing an automatic change of nationality in the event of marriage or the dissolution of marriage. UNHCR, *Final report concerning the Questionnaire on statelessness pursuant to the Agenda for Protection,* Geneva: March 2004, page 20.

[107] Laws relating to marriage are cited as a source of statelessness in numerous recent publications, including UNHCR, "Statelessness and Citizenship" in *The State of the World's Refugees - A Humanitarian Agenda*, Oxford University Press, Oxford: 1997page 226; UNHCR, *Information and accession package: the 1954 Convention relating to the status of stateless persons and the 1961 Convention on the reduction of statelessness,* Geneva: January 1999, page 3; Vladimir Kartashkin, *The rights of women married to foreigners,* E/CN.4/Sub.2/2003/34, 30 June 2003, page 3; UN Division for the Advancement of Women, *Women, nationality and citizenship,* June 2003, page 5; Maureen Lynch, *Lives on hold: The human cost of statelessness,* Washington: 2005, page 5; Mark Manly, "Sorry, wrong gender" in *Refugees Magazine,* Number 147, Issue 3, 2007, pages 24-27; UNHCR, *UNHCR Handbook for the Protection of Women and Girls,* January 2008, pages 186-187. Of course the same laws are also a source of *dual* nationality.

[108] She will be similarly affected if she automatically loses her nationality and her husband has no nationality himself as there will be no state to provide her with a new nationality; UNHCR and IPU, *Nationality and statelessness. A handbook for parliamentarians*, 2005, page 33.

[109] UNHCR, "Statelessness and Citizenship" in *The State of the World's Refugees - A Humanitarian Agenda*, Oxford University Press, Oxford: 1997, page 226; UNHCR and IPU, *Nationality and statelessness. A handbook for parliamentarians*, 2005, page 33.

[110] UNHCR, *Divorce leaves some Vietnamese women broken-hearted and stateless,* 14 February 2007, accessible via http://www.unhcr.org; Mark Manly, "Sorry, wrong gender" in *Refugees Magazine,* Number 147, Issue 3, 2007, pages 24-27.

[111] Vladimir Kartashkin, *The rights of women married to foreigners,* E/CN.4/Sub.2/2003/34, 30 June 2003, page 11.

legal status, including the nationality, of an individual.[112] With the automatic change of nationality comes the risk of statelessness if the approach of states is not harmonised. There is currently a tendency towards automatically granting the child the nationality of the adoptive parent in the case of inter-country adoption, but this is not the case in all countries. Meanwhile a number of states provide for the automatic loss of nationality by a child who is adopted abroad.[113] Therefore adoption is also a known source of statelessness.[114]

3.1 The 1961 Convention on the Reduction of Statelessness

The effect on nationality of a change in personal status – such as marriage, divorce or adoption – is addressed in article 5 of the 1961 Convention on the Reduction of Statelessness. Its first paragraph houses a fluent and straightforward obligation for state parties:

> If the law of a Contracting State entails loss of nationality as a consequence of any change in the personal status of a person such as marriage, termination of marriage, legitimation, recognition or adoption, such loss shall be conditional upon possession or acquisition of another nationality.[115]

This provision does not judge the overall lawfulness of prescribing the loss of nationality in conjunction with a change of personal status, it is aimed solely at the prevention of statelessness in those circumstances. It covers "any change in the personal status of a person" - the list that follows provides merely examples of situations in which this provision applies.[116] Moreover, the article employs gender-

---

[112] Hudson mentions adoption, legitimation, recognision by affiliation and marriage as the different changes in civil status that can automatically effect nationality, Manley Hudson, *Report on Nationality, including Statelessness,* A/CN.4/50, 21 February 1952, page 15; See also International Union for Child Welfare, *Stateless Children - A Comparative Study of National Legislation and Suggested Solutions to the Problem of Statelessness of Children,* Geneva: 1947, pages 27-28.

[113] The example given is Korea; William Duncan, "Nationality and the Protection of Children Across Frontiers: The Case of Intercountry Adoption", *3rd European Conference on Nationality - Nationality and the Child,* Strasbourg: 2004, page 9.

[114] See for instance UNHCR and IPU, *Nationality and statelessness. A handbook for parliamentarians,* 2005, page 32.

[115] Article 5, paragraph 1 of the 1961 Convention on the Reduction of Statelessness. "Possession or acquisition" in this case should be taken to mean prior possession or assurance of acquiring another nationality; UNHCR Information and Accession Package, page 14.

[116] Paragraph 2 of the same article provides additionally for the recovery of previous nationality by a child born out of wedlock who lost that nationality due to recognition of affiliation. This paragraph appears superfluous in view of the fist paragraph in which loss of nationality in the event of recognition is already prohibited if the child would be rendered stateless. It could then be argued that paragraph 2 allows the child to opt for his original nationality or even dual nationality, however the contracting states are allowed to set additional conditions, including that the child is stateless. It is in fact worrying that states are free to lay down a number of conditions for recovery of nationality here because the person involved would have been rendered stateless in contravention of paragraph 1 of this article in the first place. It could be argued that the prohibition of the loss of nationality in the event of a change in personal status, where the person would become stateless, includes an obligation to redress the situation by allowing recovery of nationality if individuals have been allowed to fall through the net. See article

neutral terms meaning, for example, that it is equally applicable in the case of loss of nationality of the male or female spouse at the time of marriage or dissolution of marriage.[117] It also covers cases of inter-country adoption. If implemented correctly – with states running a thorough check to ensure that the individual involved has or indeed will receive another nationality before allowing the original nationality to be lost – the provision should be sufficient to prevent statelessness from arising in these circumstances.

3.2 International human rights law

Where the 1961 Statelessness Convention has – thanks to its focus on the prevention of statelessness - tucked all obligations relating to marriage, adoption or another change in personal status neatly away into one provision, the same cannot be said of international human rights instruments. In particular, we discover that most texts deal with either the problem of nationality in the event of marriage (or divorce) or the situation of adoption or recognition of a child, but few address both. We will therefore consider them separately, starting with the question of marriage since this has been dealt with most extensively under human rights law - the Universal Declaration of Human Rights taking the first step.

Article 16 of the Universal Declaration protects the right of men and women to marry and found a family. It goes on to espouse equal rights of men and women "as to marriage, during marriage and at its dissolution".[118] The International Covenant on Civil and Political Rights has adopted a similar text ensuring "equality of rights and responsibilities of spouses as to marriage, during marriage and at its dissolution".[119] It is true that this general restatement of the prohibition of discrimination does not directly preclude the creation of statelessness in the event of marriage or the dissolution of marriage. However, it does prohibit the adoption of a discriminatory nationality policy which, for example, provides for automatic loss of nationality for a woman marrying a non-national but not for a man, or facilitating access to nationality for the female non-national spouse but not for the male. It also illustrates that laws relating to changes in status, rights and duties of individuals when they marry or divorce are not free from influence by international human rights law.

Fortunately, more concrete provisions relating to marriage and nationality can be found in a number of other instruments, clarifying the obligations of states with regard to this particular question. In fact, a separate document exists to deal with

5, paragraph 2 read together with article 1, paragraph 2 of the 1961 Convention on the Reduction of Statelessness.

[117] Although in practice only the female spouse has been reported to be adversely affected by an automatic change of nationality in the event of marriage or dissolution of marriage, gender-neutral provisions are to be welcomed as a general recognition of the principle of non-discrimination. However, the unbiased nature of this provision could in fact be explained by its broad scope, which includes not only marriage, but also adoption or recognition in the events to which it is applicable – hence the unspecific reference to "a person".

[118] Article 16, paragraph 1 of the Universal Declaration of Human Rights.

[119] Article 23, paragraph 4 of the 1966 International Covenant on Civil and Political Rights. The American Convention on Human Rights copies these universal instruments in its article 17, paragraph 4.

precisely this issue: the Convention on the Nationality of Married Women. Adopted in 1957 – thereby predating the 1961 Convention on the Reduction of Statelessness – this Convention has been reasonably well-received with 70 contracting parties to date.[120] Article 1 of this convention has the following to say about the effect of marriage on nationality:

> Each Contracting State agrees that neither the celebration nor the dissolution of a marriage between one of its nationals and an alien [...] shall automatically affect the nationality of the wife.[121]

This means that the simple act of marriage or divorce may not – in and of itself – render a woman stateless. States are prohibited from prescribing the automatic loss of nationality for a woman who marries a non-national or divorces a national. The younger and more widely ratified Convention on the Elimination of All Discrimination Against Women also prohibits the automatic change of nationality of the wife in the event of marriage, adding expressly that marriage to an alien shall not "render her stateless".[122] These two instruments are designed to ensure at the very least that statelessness is not an automatic result – *ex lege* - of marriage due to a conflict of nationality laws. However, it seems that states may allow for voluntary loss of original nationality or voluntary acquisition of the nationality of the spouse. It is therefore conceivable that such acts – if uncoordinated - may still lead to isolated cases of statelessness. From the sole point of view of the prevention of statelessness, the approach taken in the 1961 Statelessness Convention therefore seems more appropriate in this case: making loss of nationality (whether automatic or voluntary) in the event of marriage or dissolution of marriage conditional upon the possession or acquisition of another.

The European Convention on Nationality takes the same approach as these two universal instruments. One of the four basic principles espoused in article 4 of the Convention is the prohibition of automatic change of nationality by marriage or the dissolution of marriage.[123] Gender is not specified and the principle is equally valid for the male and female spouse – a deliberate move away from the formulation in the Convention on the Nationality of Married Women in order to recognise the principle of gender equality.[124] The Convention also prescribes facilitated acquisition of nationality for the non-national spouse of one of the Contracting States' nationals.[125] The American Convention on Human Rights states simply the basic principle of equality of the rights of spouses "as to marriage, during marriage

---

[120] UN Treaty Collection, Status of ratifications, reservations and declarations as of 2 February 2002.

[121] Article 1 of the Convention on the Nationality of Married Women, 1957. Together with article 2, this article forms the core of the obligations on states under this Convention, as evidenced by the non-acceptance of reservations to these two provisions.

[122] Article 9, paragraph 1 of the 1979 Convention on the Elimination of All Forms of Discrimination against Women.

[123] Article 4, section d) of the European Convention on Nationality, 1997.

[124] Explanatory Memorandum of the European Convention on Nationality, page 32. Substantively this makes little difference for traditionally it is the status of the wife that is effected but the use of gender neutral terminology send an important message on overall intolerance of gender discrimination.

[125] Article 6, paragraph 4 a) of the European Convention on Nationality, 1997.

and in the event of its dissolution".[126] While this compels states to outlaw gender discrimination in the context of any effect that marriage may have on the nationality of the spouses, it does not prescribe or prohibit any particular measures relating to a change of nationality in the event of marriage.[127] The Protocol to the African Charter on Human and Peoples' Rights on women's rights takes things a step further: it states that "a woman shall have the right to retain her nationality or to acquire the nationality of her husband".[128] At first glance this appears to be an excellent provision. It makes clear that if the woman has no right to acquire the nationality of her husband, she must be able to hold onto her original nationality, thereby preventing her from becoming stateless. This seems very straightforward indeed. However, upon further consideration we see that the wording used will actually make the article difficult to implement and statelessness may not always be successfully avoided. The Protocol presents a choice: either the woman has the right to keep her original nationality *or* she has the right to acquire the nationality of her husband, she does not necessarily have both. States are therefore free to provide for the loss of nationality of the wife upon marriage to a non-national so long as the state of nationality of the husband provides a right to acquire that nationality. But, the difference between having a *right to acquire* a nationality and acquiring a nationality can be great. The phrase employed is therefore unfortunate, for a state which provides for the loss of nationality of the woman could argue that she has the right to acquire the nationality of the husband, even if actual conferral of that nationality is not guaranteed: for example where the wife of a national has facilitated access to naturalisation or even where the wife may automatically be eligible for the nationality of the husband but this is perhaps subject to national security considerations. She may have the *right to acquire* the nationality of the husband yet still be rendered stateless if she is unable to effectuate this right. Here again, the approach of the 1961 Statelessness Convention is preferable as it permits loss of nationality only where there is prior possession or the guarantee of acquisition of an alternative nationality. Moreover, the African Protocol does not elaborate on the effect of the dissolution of marriage on nationality, while the provision in the 1961 Statelessness Convention is applicable to any change in personal status.

Moving on to the subject of adoption and its influence on the nationality of the adopted child, we turn our attention once more to the Convention on the Rights of

---

[126] Article 17, paragraph 4 of the American Convention on Human Rights, 1969.

[127] In its case law, the Inter-American Court of Human Rights was called upon to consider the compatibility with the American Convention of a naturalisation policy that would allow a spouse who was rendered stateless through the loss of nationality by act of marriage (by the laws of another state), to remain stateless for at least a period of two years, if not indefinitely. Although there are signs of criticism for this policy, the Court did not find in it a violation of article 20 (right to a nationality) of the Convention. However, the Court hinted that it *would* find fault with the policy which entailed the loss of nationality through the act of marriage, resulting in statelessness. In this it referred to the Convention on the Nationality of Married Women and the Convention on the Elimination of all Forms of Discrimination Against Women. Inter-American Court of Human Rights, *Advisory Opinion on the Proposed Amendments to the Naturalisation provision of the Constitution of Costa Rica,* OC-4/84, 19 January 1984, paras. 46-51.

[128] Article 6, section g) of the Protocol to the African Charter on Human and Peoples' Rights on the Rights of Women in Africa, 2003.

the Child and its monitoring Committee. We have already looked at article 7 on the acquisition of a nationality in some detail. In this section we will consider article 8 through which "State Parties undertake to respect the right of the child to preserve his or her identity, including nationality".[129] The point of departure in nationality matters for a child who has been adopted by a non-national (couple) must therefore be the retention of original nationality as a form of preservation of the identity of the child. To find out more about the duties of states in relation to the attribution of nationality to a child who has been adopted, we browse the convention for additional clauses relevant to the adoption process. Article 21 of the CRC covers the rights of the child in the context of an adoption procedure, but is silent on the topic of nationality. The only provision in this article that may have some application to nationality questions can be found in section c where state parties proclaim to "ensure that the child concerned by inter-country adoption enjoys safeguards and standards equivalent to those existing in the case of national adoption".[130] Seeing as a child would not be rendered stateless in the context of a purely national adoption procedure, it could be argued that states are hereby required to prevent a child who is involved in inter-country adoption from becoming stateless. The Committee on the Rights of the Child has considered the issue of nationality of children involved in inter-country adoption a number of times and has recognised the danger that such adoption procedures may lead to statelessness. The Committee's approach to these cases is to encourage the acquisition of the nationality of the adoptive parents.[131] No mention is made of the need to prevent the loss of the nationality of origin. It should also be noted that the Convention on Protection of Children and Co-operation in Respect of Intercountry Adoption is entirely silent on the question of the effect that such adoption has on the nationality of the child.[132]

Instruments that have been adopted within the Council of Europe are more specific in their delineation of the duties of states in the context of inter-country adoption. In 1967, the European Convention on the Adoption of Children was formulated to regulate all aspects of international adoption procedures.[133] Article 11 deals with the impact of adoption on the nationality of the child. It prescribes facilitated acquisition by the child of the nationality of the adoptive parent(s), but – more importantly – also makes any loss of nationality resulting from adoption "conditional upon possession or acquisition of another nationality".[134] According to the explanatory report on the convention, this provision was designed to ensure the avoidance of statelessness which it considered not only to be reflective of a general

[129] Article 8 of the Convention on the Rights of the Child, 1989.

[130] Article 21, section c) of the Convention on the Rights of the Child, 1989.

[131] This problem has been discussed in Committee on the Rights of the Child, *Concluding Observations: Palau*, CRC/C/103, Geneva: 2001, paragraph 458; *Switzerland*, CRC/C/118, Geneva: 2002, paragraphs 340-341; *Canada*, CRC/C/133, Geneva: 2003, paragraphs 76-77.

[132] The Convention on Protection of Children and Co-operation in Respect of Intercountry Adoption entered into force on the 1st of May 2005 and is designed to regulate the procedure for intercountry adoption with a view to protecting the best interests of the child.

[133] The European Convention on the Adoption of Children entered into force on the 26th of April, 1968 and had 18 state parties on the 28th of February 2006.

[134] Article 11, paragraphs 1 and 2 of the European Convention on the Adoption of Children, 1967.

principle but also in the best interests of the child.[135] The European Convention on Nationality copies this dual approach: prescribing facilitated access to nationality for children adopted by a national of the state and prohibiting loss of nationality in the adoption of a child if the child would thereby be rendered stateless.[136] In this way, these two European instruments back up the 1961 Convention on the Reduction of Statelessness in its approach to the prevention of statelessness in the adoption process. They also incorporate what is considered to be the best interests of the child affected by inter-country adoption – access to the nationality of the adoptive parents, reflecting the link with the new state which is formed through adoption and helping to promote family unity.[137]

4 LOSS, DEPRIVATION AND RENUNCIATION OF NATIONALITY

When municipal legislation prescribes the automatic loss of nationality for an individual who marries a foreigner, it is a reflection of the idea that by the act of marriage the genuine link with the original state is eroded and a bond of allegiance with a new state formed. Using an identical motivation, some states prescribe the automatic loss of nationality for individuals who emigrate and take up long-term residence on foreign soil.[138] In chapter III, section 1 we discovered that *jus domicilli,* or the law of residence, is a recognised ground for the attribution of nationality. The most common legal basis for naturalisation is therefore a certain period of permanent residence on the territory of a state. The automatic loss of nationality due to long-term residence abroad is the inverse situation. Thus numerous states have adopted provisions in their domestic legislation enabling them to revoke the nationality of persons who leave the country to reside abroad. This has also been described as "giving effect to the national's desire for expatriation"[139] and is indeed seen by some countries as a form of voluntary renunciation of nationality rather than the withdrawal of citizenship at the initiative of the state. Such practices are not limited to any particular region of the world: examples of states that currently provide for the loss of nationality in this way are Haiti, Malawi, Sudan and India.[140]

---

[135] Explanatory Report on the European Convention on the Adoption of Children, accessible via http://conventions.coe.int/Treaty/en/Reports/Html/058.htm.

[136] Article 6, paragraph 4d) and article 7 paragraphs 1g) and 3 of the European Convention on Nationality, 1997.

[137] This is considered to be important for "the integration of the child into the adoptive family" and there is now "a clear trend in favour of according automatically to the adopted child the nationality of the receiving state"; William Duncan, Nationality and the Protection of Children across Frontiers, 2004, pages 8-9.

[138] This is similar to automatic loss of nationality by an individual who naturalises abroad which is prescribed in the laws of many countries, for example in China, under article 9 of the Nationality Law of the People's Republic of China 1980. However, automatic loss of the original nationality once a person has been naturalised abroad does not lead to statelessness as the old nationality is simply traded in for a new one.

[139] Manley Hudson, *Report on Nationality, including Statelessness,* A/CN.4/50, 21 February 1952, page 45.

[140] Haiti, under article 13 of the Constitution of the Republic of Haiti 1987; Malawi, under article 25 of the Citizenship Act 1966; Sudan, under article 13 of the Citizenship Act 1957; and India, under article 10 of the Citizenship Act 1955.

In some instances, this loss of nationality can be prevented by regular registration of the intention to remain a national at the embassy of the state of nationality. However, individuals are not always properly informed of this option and such procedural protections are not in place in all countries – particularly to the benefit of those who gained their nationality by naturalisation.[141] There are also some circumstances in which the use of such procedural guarantees is hampered, such as in the case of refugee populations.[142] Meanwhile, the state in which the individual has taken up residence is free to determine the criteria under which a person can be naturalised. This will often include a significant period of permanent and lawful residence (whereas loss of nationality may be prescribed within just a few months of departure)[143] and additional conditions such as knowledge of the national language and culture. The revocation of nationality for those taking up residence abroad therefore in no way coincides with conferral of the nationality of the new state of residence. Statelessness may be the direct consequence of legislative provisions prescribing automatic loss of nationality in this way.[144]

Closely related to loss of nationality – to the extent that differentiation is not always possible – is individual deprivation of nationality.[145] Here, again, nationality is withdrawn when an individual has behaved in a particular way. The most common grounds for such deprivation of nationality are: a change of allegiance which may be evidenced by the pledging of a formal oath of allegiance to a foreign state[146] or voluntary service in the armed forces or government of a foreign state;[147] committing acts which are in contravention with the vital interests of the state;[148] a prison sentence within a certain period after naturalisation in the country of

[141] Procedural protection against "denaturalisation" (withdrawal of nationality acquired by naturalisation) is usually weaker than against "denationalisation" (withdrawal of nationality acquired at birth); International Union for Child Welfare, *Stateless Children - A Comparative Study of National Legislation and Suggested Solutions to the Problem of Statelessness of Children,* Geneva: 1947, page 29; see also UNHCR and IPU, *Nationality and statelessness. A handbook for parliamentarians*, 2005, page 33.

[142] In the event that an individual has been forced to flee persecution in the state of nationality, compelling him to contact the state authorities in order to declare his intention to remain a national is a particularly difficult or indeed dangerous condition to meet.

[143] UNHCR and IPU, *Nationality and statelessness. A handbook for parliamentarians*, 2005, page 33.

[144] UNHCR, *Information and accession package: the 1954 Convention relating to the status of stateless persons and the 1961 Convention on the reduction of statelessness,* Geneva: January 1999, page 3; UNHCR, "Statelessness and Citizenship" in *The State of the World's Refugees - A Humanitarian Agenda*, Oxford University Press, Oxford: 1997, page 226; Carol Batchelor The 1954 Convention relating to the Status of Stateless Persons: Implementation within the European Union Member States and Recommendations for Harmonisation 2004, page 11; UNHCR and IPU, *Nationality and statelessness. A handbook for parliamentarians*, 2005, page 33.

[145] This is a separate question to collective deprivation of nationality which is usually linked to discriminatory policies and will be dealt with in Chapter V under the title "Arbitrary deprivation of nationality".

[146] This is for example the case in Belize where it is prescribed in article 22, paragraph 1f) of the Belizean Nationality Act 1981.

[147] For example, Haitian nationality is lost by "Holding a political post in the service of a foreign country"; article 13, subsection c of the Constitution of the Republic of Haiti, 1987.

[148] Examples can be found in: Section 19, paragraph 3 of the Thai Nationality Act, 2508; article 25, paragraph 2, subsection a of the Citizenship Act of Malawi, 1966; and article 10, paragraph 2, subsection b or c of the Citizenship Act of India, 1955.

nationality;[149] and acquisition of nationality by misrepresentation or fraud (for example during the naturalisation procedure).[150] In this sense, deprivation of nationality may be employed as a punitive measure by the state, perhaps alongside criminal or civil proceedings against the individual.[151] Again, persons who have obtained their nationality by naturalisation are generally more vulnerable to deprivation of nationality.

Not only can an individuals lose or be deprived of their nationality without necessarily acquiring another, some countries also grant people the freedom to renounce their nationality, without any safeguards against statelessness. The ability to renounce one's nationality is a vital element of the right to change allegiance and adopt the nationality of another state. It is certainly not uncommon for people who take up residence in a different country to consolidate their newly formed bond with that state by applying for naturalisation. Often, naturalisation is granted on the condition of renunciation of the original nationality, in order to avoid dual nationality, therefore an individual must be free to do so. The ideal scenario is one whereby the renunciation of nationality either coincides with or follows shortly after naturalisation. However, not all states require the prior acquisition of a new nationality before allowing the individual to be released from his original nationality.[152] He may renounce his nationality before applying for naturalisation, resulting in temporary statelessness that becomes a permanent state of affairs if the naturalisation procedure is not successfully completed.[153] Even though it is clear that the renunciation of nationality prior to the acquisition of another is a source of statelessness, some states nevertheless make the prior renunciation of one's original nationality a requirement for entering an application for naturalisation.[154] The

[149] Examples can be found in: article 13, paragraph 1, subsection c of the Sudanese Nationality Act, 1957; article 10, paragraph 1, subsection d of the Citizenship Act of India, 1955; and article 33, paragraph 4 of the Tunisian Nationality Act, 1963.

[150] Examples can be found in: article 37 of the Tunisian Nationality Act, 1963; article 10 of the Canadian Citizenship Act, 1985; article 17, paragraph 2 of the Citizenship Act of New Zealand, 1977; and article 13, paragraph 1, subsection a of the Sudanese Nationality Act, 1957.

[151] Throughout history, exile has been used as a penalty for criminal acts. This is closely related to the concept of deprivation of nationality as a punitive measure for both enable the state to exclude the "undesired" individual. See for example Ruth Donner, "Chapter 3: The Imposition and Withdrawal of Nationality" in *The Regulation of Nationality in International Law*, Transnational Publishers, New York: 1994, pages 152-153.

[152] For example, China allows its citizens to renounce their nationality if "they are near relatives of foreign nationals, they have settled abroad or they have other legitimate reasons"; articles 10 and 11 of the Nationality Law of the People's Republic of China, 1980.

[153] The applicant may be considered to fall short of the further criteria for naturalisation - for example due to an insufficient knowledge of the local language. Alternatively, the naturalisation procedure itself may be unduly stringent, requiring excessive fees or documentation, or prescribing unrealistic deadlines. This contributes to the likelihood of an application failing, or perhaps not even being lodged, even though the individual may be perfectly eligible - increasingly the likelihood that the individual will fail to complete the change of nationality to which he has aspired. UNHCR and IPU, *Nationality and statelessness. A handbook for parliamentarians*, 2005, pages 28 and 32; UNHCR, "Statelessness and Citizenship" in *The State of the World's Refugees - A Humanitarian Agenda*, Oxford University Press, Oxford: 1997, page 226; Maureen Lynch, *Lives on hold: The human cost of statelessness*, Washington: 2005, page 5.

[154] UNHCR and IPU, *Nationality and statelessness. A handbook for parliamentarians*, 2005, page 28.

incongruity of being able or even *required* to lose or renounce your nationality without the guarantee of acquiring an alternative nationality thereby causes statelessness.[155] This is a fact that may even be taken advantage of by those who desire access to facilitated naturalisation procedures that may exist for stateless persons and therefore deliberately renounce their only nationality.[156] Of the respondent states to the 2003 UNHCR Questionnaire on statelessness, 16.2% admitted to the absence of safeguards in their municipal legislation to combat this source of statelessness.[157] Furthermore, where a nationality is lost, deprived or renounced by an individual, this action may automatically affect the person's spouse or children, whose own nationality may also be withdrawn.[158]

4.1 The 1961 Convention on the Reduction of Statelessness

So far we have looked at articles 1 to 5 of the 1961 Statelessness Convention - half of the substantive articles housed in the document. In this section we will be assessing articles 6, 7 and 8 which deal collectively with loss, deprivation and renunciation of nationality. We will also conduct a preliminary reading of article 9 on arbitrary deprivation of nationality, although this issue is the subject of the next chapter. As the provisions of the 1961 Convention are rather disorganised, we will take the individual issues in the order that they were introduced above, starting with the problem of loss of nationality *ex lege* as a result of long-term residence on foreign soil.

The general principle is that loss of nationality shall not be effectuated "unless the person concerned possesses or acquires another nationality".[159] Where loss of nationality is prescribed due merely to residence rather than naturalisation abroad, the individual would not possess or acquire another nationality, therefore such action would be prohibited.[160] However, the 1961 Convention differentiates in its approach to this question between naturalised persons and persons who have acquired their nationality other than by naturalisation.[161] As far as naturalised persons are concerned an exception is made to the general rule:

---

[155] See also Betty de Hart; Kees Groenendijk, "Multiple Nationality: The Practice of Germany and the Netherlands" in R. Cholewinski (ed) *International Migration Law*, TMC Asser Press, The Hague: 2007, pages 96-100. Here the example is given of a case that presented itself in the Netherlands "of an Egyptian national who had not renounced his nationality, although the IND [Immigration and Naturalisation Service] had urged him to do so several times. After a third letter requesting renunciation remained unanswered, the IND withdrew his Dutch nationality. They did so despite the fact that by then the applicant had provided proof of his renunciation of Egyptian nationality. The IND claimed it was too late. The applicant had now lost both nationalities and had become stateless".

[156] Committee of Experts on Nationality, *Report on Misuse of Nationality Laws,* Strasbourg: 20 April 2004, paragraphs 10 and 24.

[157] UNHCR, *Final report concerning the Questionnaire on statelessness pursuant to the Agenda for Protection,* Geneva: March 2004, page 16.

[158] For example, in Belize, the nationality of the minor children or spouse of a naturalised individual whose nationality has been lost or deprived under the nationality act may also be lost or deprived at the discretion of the minister; article 22, paragraph 3 of the Belizean Nationality Act 1981.

[159] Article 7, paragraph 1a) of the 1961 Convention on the Reduction of Statelessness.

[160] This is also contained in an express prohibition in paragraph 3 of article 7 of the 1961 Convention.

[161] According to the Information and Accession Package to the Convention, the concept of a "naturalised person" simply means an individual "who has acquired nationality upon an application

> A naturalised person may lose his nationality on account of residence abroad for a period, not less than seven consecutive years, specified by the law of the Contracting State concerned if he fails to declare to the appropriate authority his intention to retain his nationality.[162]

It is therefore possible, under the 1961 Convention, to prescribe the loss of nationality in the simple event of long-term residence abroad, but only if a number of cumulative conditions are met. The person must have acquired nationality by naturalisation, must have lived abroad for at least 7 years (no shorter term may be set by the municipal law of the state concerned) and he must have neglected to re-register in order to retain his nationality.[163] This provision goes at least some way to limiting the freedom of states to provide for the loss of nationality *ex lege* when a person has chosen to move abroad but does not entirely pre-empt the creation of statelessness.[164] Paragraph 5 of the same article contains another exception to the general rule: where a child is born outside the territory of the state it is possible for him to lose that nationality when he reaches adulthood if he has not taken up residence in that state or registered his desire to retain his nationality with the appropriate authority. The final paragraph of the same article repeats the prohibition of loss of nationality where the person would be rendered stateless other than in the circumstances expressly provided for – these are therefore the only permitted exceptions.[165]

Article 8 of the 1961 Statelessness Convention adopts the same approach: prohibiting deprivation of nationality that would result in statelessness except in a handful of circumstances which are explicitly laid down in the text.[166] The first situation in which deprivation is still permissible is in fact identical to that for which loss of nationality is permitted: reference is simply made to article 7, paragraphs 4 and 5.[167] The Convention thereby allows states the option to choose

---

which the Contracting State concerned, in its discretion, could have refused". It does not include persons who have acquired nationality *ex lege* later in life. See UNHCR, *Information and accession package: the 1954 Convention relating to the status of stateless persons and the 1961 Convention on the reduction of statelessness*, Geneva: January 1999, page 14.

[162] Article 7, paragraph 4 of the 1961 Convention on the Reduction of Statelessness.

[163] The Final Act of the Convention defines a naturalised person for the purposes of the application of the instrument as "a person who has acquired nationality upon an application which the contracting State concerned may in its discretion refuse". Resolution 2 of the Final Act of the 1961 Convention on the Reduction of Statelessness. Meanwhile, Resolution 3 of the Final Act recommends "Contracting States making the retention of nationality by their nationals abroad subject to a declaration or registration to take all possible steps to ensure that such persons are informed in time of the formalities and time-limits to be observed if they are to retain their nationality".

[164] The fact that – under the 1961 Statelessness Convention - a refugee would be subjected to the same requirements in order to retain his nationality when resident abroad is highly unsatisfactory in view of the precarious situation of refugees.

[165] Article 7, paragraph 6 of the 1961 Convention on the Reduction of Statelessness.

[166] Article 8 opens by determining that "a Contracting State shall not deprive a person of his nationality if such deprivation would render him stateless", a statement which is followed in paragraph 2 by the introduction of a number of exceptions. 1961 Convention on the Reduction of Statelessness.

[167] Which covered loss of nationality for naturalised persons who take up residence abroad and loss of nationality for children born abroad upon attaining majority.

whether nationality is lost *ex lege* in such circumstances or whether it requires an act on the part of the state authority to take effect in the individual case.[168] The second situation in which states may deprive a person of their nationality is "where the nationality has been obtained by misrepresentation or fraud".[169] The most obvious case to spring to mind would be where a person has provided false information in support of their application for naturalisation and has thereby acquired nationality under false pretences. Interestingly, this provision does not specify that it is applicable to "naturalised persons" as we saw in the event of loss of nationality due to long-term residence abroad. There remains therefore, the possibility of providing for the deprivation of a nationality that has been obtained otherwise than by naturalisation. Consider the theoretical situation whereby an individual produces a forged marriage licence or contracts a so-called "marriage of convenience" in order to claim nationality *ex lege* in a state where this is provided for through marriage to a national. Another conceivable case would be where parents ensure the conferral of nationality on their child by producing documents establishing a false place of birth or misrepresenting their own nationality or residence status. In any of these situations, the state would retain the right to withdraw the nationality which had been obtained in a fraudulent manner.

The 1961 Statelessness Convention goes on to introduce various additional exceptions to the general rule which forbids deprivation of nationality resulting in statelessness. Specifically, it allows states that have already prescribed a number of other grounds for deprivation of nationality in their municipal legislation to retain those provisions as long as they make a declaration to that effect when they become Contracting States to the Convention.[170] There are thus three further acceptable grounds for deprivation of nationality, even where this would lead to statelessness, namely where the person:

> Inconsistently with his duty of loyalty to the Contracting State [...] has, in disregard of an express prohibition by the Contracting State rendered or continued to render services to, or received or continued to receive emoluments from, another State; or has conducted himself in a manner seriously prejudicial to the vital interests of the State; [or] has taken an oath, or made a formal declaration, of allegiance to another State, or given definite evidence of his determination to repudiate his allegiance with the Contracting State.[171]

This list is also limitative, although it leaves some room for manoeuvre in the interpretation of what is "seriously prejudicial to the vital interests of states". Other grounds for deprivation of nationality are forbidden. This is made very clear in the phrasing of the provision and is confirmed by the reactions of a number of state parties to the declaration made by Tunisia at the time of accession to the instrument in 2000. The Tunisian declaration included a long list of grounds which it would continue to uphold in its municipal legislation for the deprivation of nationality.

[168] The presumed difference between "loss" and "deprivation".
[169] Article 8, paragraph 2b) of the 1961 Convention on the Reduction of Statelessness.
[170] An option that Austria, France, Ireland, the United Kingdom and Tunisia all took advantage of.
[171] Article 8, paragraph 3 of the 1961 Convention on the Reduction of Statelessness.

Among them, for example, the possibility of depriving a person of his nationality "if he is convicted in Tunisia or abroad for an act held to be a crime under Tunisian law and carrying a sentence of at least five years' imprisonment" or "if he is convicted of evading his obligations under the law regarding recruitment into the armed services".[172] Other contracting states found this declaration to be unacceptable and incompatible with the object and purpose of the Convention, confirming that the list of grounds in article 8, paragraph 3 is indeed limitative.[173]

Therefore, with regards to depriving an individual of his nationality, the 1961 Statelessness Convention clearly sets out a general prohibition of statelessness followed by a number of permissible exceptions. The fact that Contracting States were presented with the option of retaining some of their domestic provisions on deprivation of nationality appears to be evidence of yet another compromise reached during the drafting process of the instrument. The Draft Convention on the Elimination of Future Statelessness – considered too radical by state parties – did not permit any exceptions and the Draft Convention on the Reduction of Future Statelessness which formed the basis for discussion by governments included fewer permissible grounds for deprivation that would lead to statelessness.[174] Article 8 of the 1961 Convention closes with a provision that is designed to ensure proper application of the exception clauses. It determines that deprivation of nationality on one of these grounds may only be effectuated in accordance with the law and accompanied by procedural guarantees like the right to a fair hearing by a court or independent body.[175]

Finally, on the subject of deprivation of nationality, article 9 declares that there may be no deprivation of nationality – individually or collectively – on racial, ethnic, religious or political grounds. This is the only provision in the convention that is not directly aimed towards the prevention of statelessness, but is an expression of a more general nationality principle: the prohibition of arbitrary deprivation of nationality. It is irrelevant whether such deprivation leads to statelessness, it is an outright prohibition and any such act of the state is unlawful under the Convention. The application of this principle is relevant to cases which involve a policy of discrimination on the part of the state, something that will be covered in chapter V.

At this stage it is appropriate to also take a brief look at article 6 of the 1961 Convention since it deals with the effect of the loss or deprivation of nationality on the nationality of a person's spouse and children. This article provides, unconditionally, that "if the law of a Contracting State provides for loss of its nationality by a person's spouse or children as a consequence of that person losing or being deprived of that nationality, such loss shall be conditional upon their possession or acquisition of another nationality".[176] Under no circumstances is it therefore acceptable that statelessness results from the automatic withdrawal of

[172] Extracts from the declaration by the state of Tunisia upon accession to the 1961 Convention on the Reduction of Statelessness on the 12th of May 2000.
[173] Objections were raised by Germany on the 15th of May 2001, Norway and Sweden on the 23rd of May 2001 and The Netherlands on the 6th of June 2001.
[174] UN Yearbook 1954, pages 420 and 422.
[175] Article 8, paragraph 4 of the 1961 Convention on the Reduction of Statelessness.
[176] Article 6 of the 1961 Convention on the Reduction of Statelessness.

citizenship from the dependents of someone who has lost or been deprived of his nationality.

This brings us to the final issue in this section: the freedom to renounce one's nationality. Article 7 of the Convention is unequivocal on this matter, determining that renunciation of nationality may not be allowed to take effect unless the person possesses or is assured of acquiring another nationality.[177] Moreover, the Convention does not permit states to prescribe the loss of nationality merely on the grounds of him having submitted an application for naturalisation in a foreign state.[178] From this it can also be deduced that, where the conditions for naturalisation are concerned, it would incompatible with the object and purpose of the Convention for states to require an individual to renounce his nationality before entering an application for naturalisation. After all, this is a feat that – on the basis of this Convention – he would be unable to perform. The instrument is clearly attempting to ensure that no individual is rendered stateless in the process of attempting to change his nationality.

Generally then, the way in which the 1961 Convention on the Reduction of Statelessness deals with the creation of statelessness from loss, deprivation or renunciation of nationality, is illustrative of the compromises that had to be reached between states involved in the drafting process. Where the "radical" Draft Convention on the *Elimination* of Future Statelessness did not allow states to create statelessness under any circumstances, the text that was eventually adopted permits a range of carefully delineated exceptions whereby new cases of statelessness will continue to arise. It is time to look at alternative obligations under international human rights law to see if there has since been any change in the attitude of states towards this question.

4.2 International human rights law

After the expansive way in which the 1961 Statelessness Convention has dealt with the subject, human rights instruments appear deafeningly silent with regard to the permissibility of municipal nationality acts that allow for loss, deprivation or renunciation of nationality even where the individual would be rendered stateless. There is certainly no overall prohibition of the loss of nationality in later life – in fact this is part of the right to change one's nationality, recognised in a number of instruments.[179] Nevertheless, there is one important norm that has great bearing on this question: the prohibition of arbitrary deprivation of nationality.[180] Explicit references to this rule can be found in the Universal Declaration of Human Rights as well the American and European Conventions on human rights, but it is also considered to be an implicit counterpart to the right to a nationality. As mentioned

---

177 Article 7, paragraph 1a) of the 1961 Convention on the Reduction of Statelessness. See also UNHCR, *Information and accession package: the 1954 Convention relating to the status of stateless persons and the 1961 Convention on the reduction of statelessness,* Geneva: January 1999, page 14.

178 He must first acquire either the new nationality itself or an assurance that his application will be honoured. Article 7, paragraph 2 of the 1961 Convention on the Reduction of Statelessness.

179 For example in article 15 of the Universal Declaration of Human Rights, article 9 of the Convention on the Elimination of All Forms of Discrimination Against Women and article 20 of the American Convention on Human Rights.

180 This norm will be discussed in full in chapter V.

in the previous chapter,[181] an increasingly feasible interpretation of this norm, in combination with the general principle of the avoidance of statelessness, is that any withdrawal of an existing nationality that would result in statelessness for the individual is by definition arbitrary and therefore prohibited.[182] This would mean that a person may not lose, be deprived of or renounce his nationality unless he already holds (or is guaranteed of acquiring) the citizenship of another state. However, there is insufficient evidence as yet to establish this position as an absolute and irrefutable interpretation of the international norm.

There are two further provisions in universal conventions that may be relevant here. Firstly, article 8 of the Convention on the Rights of the Child provides – as we have already seen – for the right of a child to preserve his identity, including nationality. It has been argued that where a child's parents lose, renounce or are deprived of their nationality, this provision is relevant for the effect that such loss, renunciation or deprivation will have on the nationality of the child. Indeed this article stands in the way of the automatic loss of nationality by that child,[183] particularly when read in conjunction with the more general obligation to take measures against the statelessness of children under article 7, paragraph 2 of the same Convention. Secondly, article 9 of the Convention on the Elimination of All Forms of Discrimination Against Women provides that the change of nationality by the husband during a marriage will not automatically affect the nationality of the wife nor render her stateless.[184] If a man loses, renounces or is deprived of his nationality (i.e. there is a change in his nationality status), this must not result in the statelessness of his wife.

Yet these provisions are only applicable in relation to the dependents of a person who has lost, renounced or been deprived of their nationality, they do not judge the validity of the act itself. The only instrument to do so is the 1997 European Convention on Nationality. This text determines under precisely which circumstances a state party may provide for nationality to be lost or deprived. There are a total of 7 scenarios in which loss or deprivation of nationality may be prescribed by law, listed in article 7 of the Convention. These include loss of nationality in the event of "voluntary acquisition of another nationality" or where there is a "lack of a genuine link between the State Party and a national habitually

[181] See chapter III, section 2.

[182] See for example Johannes Chan, 'The Right to a Nationality as a Human Right - The Current Trend Towards Recognition', in *Human Rights Law Journal,* Vol. 12, 1991; Ruth Donner, "Chapter 4: Human Rights Conventions and other Instruments" in *The Regulation of Nationality in International Law,* Transnational Publishers, New York: 1994; Open Society Justice Initiative, *Citizenship and Equality in Practice: Guaranteeing Non-Discriminatory Access to Nationality, Protecting the Right to be Free from Arbitrary Deprivation of Nationality and Combating Statelessness,* November 2005, page 9; James Goldston, 'Holes in the Rights Framework: Racial Discrimination, Citizenship, and the Rights of Noncitizens', in *Ethics and International Affairs,* Vol. 20, 2006.

[183] Jaap Doek, 'The CRC and the Right to Acquire and to Preserve a Nationality', in *Refugee Survey Quarterly,* Vol. 25, 2006, page 30.

[184] Article 9, paragraph 1 of 1979 Convention on the Elimination of All Forms of Discrimination against Women. Similar obligations can be found in articles 1 and 2 of the 1957 Convention on the Nationality of Married Women and article 4, section d) of the 1997 European Convention on Nationality.

residing abroad".[185] Deprivation of nationality may be prescribed when nationality has been acquired by fraud or where the individual serves in a foreign military force or acts to jeopardise of the vital interests of the state.[186] The Convention also accepts the possibility of loss of nationality by the child of a person whose nationality has been lost or deprived.[187] However, paragraph 3 of this article is the most important in the context of the prevention of statelessness. It prohibits the loss or deprivation of nationality – even on the grounds which are listed as permissible – if the person concerned would thereby be rendered stateless. There is but one exception to this anti-statelessness clause: where nationality has been acquired through "fraudulent conduct, false information or concealment of any relevant fact attributable to the applicant".[188] Moreover, the principle of non-discrimination between nationals stands in the way of such policies that are allowed by the 1961 Statelessness Convention whereby a naturalised citizen is more vulnerable to loss of nationality.[189] As to renunciation of nationality, this is outlawed under article 8 of the Convention where the individual would become stateless – also implying a lack of tolerance for laws that would require an individual to undertake this act prior to submitting an application for naturalisation. Indeed, if an individual has renounced his nationality but subsequently fails to acquire another nationality (despite a guarantee to that effect), the state should declare the act of renunciation void.[190]

In sum then, the European Convention on Nationality outlaws any loss, deprivation or renunciation of nationality that would result in statelessness, with the sole exception of the deprivation of a nationality acquired by fraud. And where fraudulent conduct has been ascertained, "the gravity of the facts, as well as other relevant circumstances, such as the genuine and effective link of these persons with the state concerned, should be taken into account".[191] Thus the retention of nationality may nevertheless be justified. Moreover, all efforts should be made to avoid the interpretation of "fraud" so expansively as to effectively re-introduce other grounds for the deprivation of nationality through this back-door.[192] In this strict stance to the withdrawal of nationality, the European Convention on

---

[185] The simple fact of residence abroad may not be enough, there must also be evidence of erosion of the *genuine link.* Article 7, paragraph 1, sections a, e, f and g determine the circumstances in which nationality may be lost; 1997 European Convention on Nationality.

[186] Article 7, paragraph 1, sections b, c and d of the 1997 European Convention on Nationality.

[187] With the exception of when that nationality was deprived for voluntary service in a foreign military force or acts against the vital interests of the state; article 7, paragraph 2 of the European Convention on Nationality.

[188] Article 7, paragraph 3 read together with paragraph 1 b) of the European Convention on Nationality. According to the Explanatory Memorandum to the Convention, statelessness will also be tolerated for the children of such persons who lose their nationality along with their parents.

[189] Article 5, paragraph 2 of the European Convention on Nationality provides that discrimination between nationals should be avoided.

[190] Section II, article C, paragraph a of the Council of Europe, *Recommendation of the Committee of Ministers to Member States on the Avoidance and Reduction of Statelessness,* No. R (1999) 18, Strasbourg, 15 September 1999.

[191] Section II, article C, paragraph c of the Council of Europe, *Recommendation of the Committee of Ministers to Member States on the Avoidance and Reduction of Statelessness,* No. R (1999) 18, Strasbourg, 15 September 1999.

[192] Ruth Donner, "Chapter 3: The Imposition and Withdrawal of Nationality" in *The Regulation of Nationality in International Law*, Transnational Publishers, New York: 1994, page 151.

Nationality clearly takes one step further towards the ideal of the eradication of statelessness than the 1961 Convention on the Reduction of Statelessness was able to. If international law is indeed progressing in the direction of an almost outright ban of withdrawal of nationality resulting in statelessness – as has been argued by numerous scholars[193] - then the 1961 Statelessness Convention is in need of an update. Clarification of this matter at the global level would certainly be of great benefit.

5 Conclusion

An attempt has been made in this chapter to deal with each of the technical causes of statelessness and uncover how the 1961 Convention on the Reduction of Statelessness and international human rights instruments address these problems. This objective has resulted in a voluminous treatise from which it is difficult to draw a singular conclusion. Instead, a number of findings must be commented upon and their greater relevance exposed. Firstly, it has become clear that the bulk of the provisions in the 1961 Convention on the Reduction of Statelessness were designed to tackle technical causes of statelessness. We are left with just two substantive provisions to discuss in the upcoming chapters on statelessness resulting from arbitrary deprivation of nationality and state succession – one each.[194] This can be explained by both the variety and complexity of the technical causes of statelessness and the need that states obviously felt to address these problems in detail. The compromises that evidently had to be reached between *jus sanguinis* and *jus soli* states coupled with a notable lack of real decisiveness further contributed to the quantity of provisions needed to deal with these issues. Thanks to the apparent volume and detail of relevant provisions, expectations based solely on first-sight of the Convention were high.

However, these very compromises and lack of strength of decision are responsible for introducing a number of substantial weaknesses into the Convention in its dealings with the technical causes of statelessness. In particular, we have discovered a selection of additional conditions and exception clauses that water down the strength of the general rules expounded in the document. For example, although articles 1 and 4 provide for the attribution of nationality at birth to a child who would otherwise be stateless, this conferral may be realised only later, upon application to the competent authorities and a number of conditions may be set.[195] Original statelessness is thereby reduced, but not eradicated. Similarly, the Convention determines that no-one shall lose or be deprived of their nationality unless they hold or acquire another nationality. Thereafter, several exceptional circumstances are outlined in which a person may after all be rendered stateless by loss or deprivation of nationality – for example in the case of a naturalised person who has resided abroad for over 7 years and failed to register his intention of retaining his nationality. In sum, "both the grant and the loss of citizenship may be

[193] See note 182 above.

[194] Thereafter, chapter VII which deals with the "new" causes of statelessness, addresses issues that have not been dealt with in the 1961 Convention on the Reduction of Statelessness.

[195] Although we also saw that these conditions were to some extent less stringent than those that were later laid down in the European Convention on Nationality.

made conditional on the person concerned meeting certain basic criteria, hence, the drafters of the Convention recognised that there may be isolated and exceptional instances in which a person will be stateless".[196] Moreover, it is necessary to recall the observation made in chapter III, that the Convention does not prescribe measures or procedures for the identification of cases of (potential) statelessness. No guidance is given to state parties as to how to deal with the problem of evidence of nationality or of the absence of nationality for the purposes of applying the guarantees espoused in the text and successfully ensuring the avoidance of statelessness.[197]

This was sufficient reason to spur on the search for alternative obligations under international human rights law - a search that also yielded mixed results. As to the prevention of statelessness at birth, we found evidence of a growing consensus among states that nationality should be granted *jus soli* to a child who would otherwise be stateless. This conclusion is particularly reinforced by recent developments on the African and European continents which are joining step behind the American Convention on Human Rights in providing for *jus soli* attribution of nationality to avoid original statelessness. The 1961 Statelessness Convention appears to be becoming superfluous on this point. With regards to statelessness resulting from loss, renunciation or deprivation of nationality, international human rights law does no better job than the 1961 Statelessness Convention. The only instrument to take one step closer to eradicating statelessness from these sources is the 1997 European Convention on Nationality which accepts withdrawal of nationality resulting in statelessness only when that nationality was originally obtained under false pretences. This is not necessarily illustrative of an international consensus on the subject, however a number of scholars claim that

> although a general right to a nationality has not become part of customary international law, the current trend of development in international law suggests a strong presumption in favour of the elimination of statelessness *in any change of nationality*. While there may be no positive duty on a state to confer its nationality on an alien, *there is a negative duty not to create statelessness.*[198]

It is certainly true that to permit the loss or deprivation of nationality in the knowledge that this will lead to statelessness is becoming increasingly unacceptable and is deemed by some to amount to (prohibited) arbitrary deprivation of nationality.[199] However, until an international convention, treaty body or court

---

[196] Carol Batchelor, "The International Legal Framework Concerning Statelessness and Access for Stateless Persons", *European Union Seminar on the Content and Scope of International Protection: Panel 1 - Legal basis of international protection,* Madrid: 2002, page 7

[197] See chapter III, section 3.

[198] Emphasis added; Johannes Chan, 'The Right to a Nationality as a Human Right - The Current Trend Towards Recognition', in *Human Rights Law Journal,* Vol. 12, 1991, page 11. Recall also chapter III, section 2.

[199] Open Society Justice Initiative, *Citizenship and Equality in Practice: Guaranteeing Non-Discriminatory Access to Nationality, Protecting the Right to be Free from Arbitrary Deprivation of Nationality and Combating Statelessness,* November 2005, page 9. Ruth Donner, "Chapter 4: Human Rights Conventions and other Instruments" in *The Regulation of Nationality in International Law,*

explicitly address this question, it will remain unclear in which exact circumstances the creation of statelessness in this manner is or is not permissible. For now it would seem that the 1961 Statelessness Convention retains its use in this matter, even if its approach is flawed.

The 1961 Convention on the Reduction of Statelessness also has a number of clear strengths. It unequivocally obliges state parties to confer their nationality upon foundlings, whether they adhere to *jus sanguinis* or *jus soli*. There is evidence that such an obligation has become part of customary international law, but this fact could still be debated. The 1961 Convention is a useful tool to consolidate this obligation. Furthermore, the 1961 Convention does not allow an individual's renunciation of nationality to take effect unless they already hold or are guaranteed of acquiring another nationality. This again, is not generally prescribed under international human rights law, although it is reflected in the European Convention on Nationality. Finally the 1961 Statelessness Convention prohibits the loss of nationality as a consequence of any change in personal status – marriage, dissolution of marriage or adoption – unless the individual possesses or is guaranteed to acquire another nationality. It also outlaws the withdrawal of nationality from the dependents (spouse or minor children) of an individual who has lost or been deprived of his own nationality if this were to lead to their statelessness. From the point of view of these clear and unambiguous protections against statelessness, the Convention is an effective tool in these particular circumstances, more so than relying purely on states' obligations under general international human rights law.

Despite the above-mentioned notes of optimism concerning the 1961 Convention on the Reduction of Statelessness, the investigation undertaken in this chapter also leads us to conclude that this instrument is behind the times and may no longer be an appropriate tool for effectively dealing with the prevention of statelessness. In particular we have revealed that under international human rights law there is now a patent obligation on states to withdraw any differentiations made in their nationality acts with regard to the conferral of nationality on legitimate and illegitimate children. Gender-sensitive nationality regulations are also outlawed. These are two areas in which general human rights law is now a step ahead of the almost 50-year old Statelessness Convention.

Finally, an interesting lesson learnt in this chapter is the opportunity provided by international human rights law to introduce alternative supervisory mechanisms to deal with statelessness. The human rights treaty bodies have clearly taken an interest in preventing statelessness and are calling upon states to make changes in their legislation. We will see this pattern continue in coming chapters. It is also noteworthy to see that they are also encouraging states to become a party to the 1961 Statelessness Convention (as well as the 1954 Statelessness Convention), so they obviously see the protection offered by these conventions as an integral part of the overall human rights framework.

Transnational Publishers, New York: 1994 ; Johannes Chan, 'The Right to a Nationality as a Human Right - The Current Trend Towards Recognition', in *Human Rights Law Journal,* Vol. 12, 1991 ; James Goldston, 'Holes in the Rights Framework: Racial Discrimination, Citizenship, and the Rights of Noncitizens', in *Ethics and International Affairs,* Vol. 20, 2006.

On the basis of the evaluation of the 1961 Convention's response to the technical causes of statelessness, it seems fair to conclude that this convention is worthy of its title: the Convention on the *Reduction* of Statelessness. A number of its provisions, if properly implemented, should reduce the number of newly emerging cases of statelessness. What it does not do, at least not with regard to statelessness which results from these technical sources, is to eradicate future statelessness. In some areas it seems that its provisions do not go any further than what has already been accepted by many states under human rights instruments. From this point of view it could be argued that ratification of the 1961 Convention should not be objectionable – it would be in line with commitments that states have already made. However, if human rights law covers many of the situations for which the Convention provides (and it does), as well as moving with the times to incorporate newly developed principles and rights, the question remains as to whether promoting ratification of this instrument is really worthwhile. In this chapter we uncovered only three situations for which increased ratification of the Convention may be helpful in that it would clarify the obligations of states in those cases.[200] In the chapters to come, the assessment of the utility of the 1961 Statelessness Convention continues as we look at the other main causes of statelessness.

[200] These are the cases of prevention of statelessness among foundlings, the definition of state territory under *jus soli* to include births on board a ship or aircraft registered in that country and the prohibition of loss, renunciation or deprivation of nationality if the person would be rendered stateless (albeit still permitted under the Convention in certain circumstances).

CHAPTER V

ADDRESSING STATELESSNESS RESULTING FROM ARBITRARY DEPRIVATION OF NATIONALITY

The words "arbitrary deprivation of nationality" denote by far the most complex and sensitive origin of statelessness. The modern-day caseloads that fall into this category are among the most grave and volatile, as well as the most protracted, of all stateless situations worldwide. Moreover, the problem of arbitrary deprivation of nationality often rears its head in circumstances where nationality policy is already under pressure and there is an increased risk of statelessness, such as state succession or (forced) migration, making difficult matters worse.[1] Meanwhile historically, the statelessness cases that first commanded the attention of the international community were also those created by what we now call arbitrary deprivation of nationality. The mass denationalisation campaigns which surrounded the first and second World Wars are forceful examples of the "dangers inherent in the power of nation-states to define their own rules of exit".[2] This experience contributed to the motivation of states to include the prohibition of arbitrary deprivation of nationality in the Universal Declaration of Human Rights and to gradually introduce limits on state sovereignty in the matter of nationality attribution.[3] In preceding chapters, the phrase "arbitrary deprivation of nationality" already popped up a number of times and we alluded to the fact that – thanks also to

---

[1] These specific issues will be dealt with in detail in chapters VI (on statelessness in cases of state succession) and VII (on "new" sources of statelessness).

[2] In the 1920's, the former Soviet Union issued a series of denationalisation decrees, which retracted the Russian nationality of some 2 million people. Rainer Bauböck, *Transnational Citizenship. Membership and Rights in International Migration*, Edward Elgar, Cheltenham: 2002, page 128. A similar policy of issuing denationalisation decrees was employed by the Nazi regime in Germany as a tool of persecution: *"Before the emergence of international human rights law, citizenship or nationality was sometimes arbitrarily withdrawn, even on the grounds of race or ethnicity. One of the worst examples is Nazi Germany's 'German Reich Citizenship Law' of 1935, one of the so-called Nuremberg Laws, by which German citizenship was limited to 'persons of German or cognate blood', which was one of the first steps in the process leading to the Holocaust affecting Jews, Romanis and others"*. Asbjorn Eide, "Citizenship and the minority rights of non-citizens", Working Paper prepared for the UN Sub-Commission on Prevention of Discrimination and Protection of Minorities, E/CN.4/Sub.2/AC.5/1999/WP.3, 15 April 1999, paragraph 19.

[3] Ruth Donner, "Chapter 3: The Imposition and Withdrawal of Nationality" in *The Regulation of Nationality in International Law*, Transnational Publishers, New York: 1994, pages 154-156; Open Society Justice Intitiative, *Citizenship and equality in practice: guaranteeing non-discriminatory access to nationality, protecting the right to be free from arbitrary deprivation of nationality and combating statelessness*, November 2005, page 7.

the Universal Declaration – it is generally considered impermissible under international law. However, we have yet to fully reflect on the scope and content of this expression or on the related international norms. That is the purpose of this chapter. It should thereby be noted from the outset that, until now, we have spoken only of deprivation of nationality in the sense of denationalisation at the initiative of the state.[4] However, in the context of this chapter, the word "deprivation" should be interpreted in the broadest possible sense. As we will discover, the prohibition of arbitrary deprivation of nationality may impact not only on states' powers of denationalisation but also on their decisions relating to the conferral of nationality at birth and even naturalisation.[5]

Arbitrariness is a recurring notion in the context of international law, particularly in the field of human rights.[6] According to its dictionary definition, "arbitrary" can mean: discretionary, dependent upon will or pleasure, derived from mere opinion or preference, capricious and even tyrannical. At the very least, for an act of state not to be considered arbitrary – or tyrannical – it must be in conformity with the relevant law.[7] To avoid an allegation of arbitrariness, citizenship may only be deprived as prescribed by law. Thus the first situation that the phrase "arbitrary deprivation of nationality" describes is the *unlawful* or *illegal* deprivation of nationality. However, the scope of arbitrariness is clearly broader than illegal, suggesting rather an abuse of power that is either outside the law or is indeed achieved through the law, where the law itself is arbitrary.[8] On this basis, scholars

[4] See chapter III, section 1 and chapter IV, section 4.

[5] As an initial example, consider the case of Yean and Bosico v. Dominican Republic, where the Inter-American Court on Human Rights found that "the State failed to grant nationality to the children, which constituted an arbitrary deprivation of their nationality". Inter-American Court on Human Rights, *Case of Yean and Bosico v. Dominican Republic,* Series C, Case 130, 8 September 2005, para. 174.

[6] Consider the prohibitions of arbitrary arrest or detention (article 9 ICCPR) and of arbitrary interference in a person's private or family life (article 17 ICCPR).

[7] Nehemiah Robinson, *The Universal Declaration of Human Rights. Its Origin, Significance, Application and Interpretation*, Institute of Jewish Affairs, New York: 1958; Albert Verdoodt, *Naissance et Signification de la Déclaration Universelle des Droits de l'Homme*, E. Warny, Louvain: 1964; Open Society Justice Initiative, *Racial Discrimination and the Rights of Non-Citizens. Submission to the UN Committee on the Elimination of Racial Discrimination on the occasion of its 64th Session,* New York: 2004.

[8] This interpretation follows from the traveaux preparatoires of the prohibition of arbitrary deprivation of nationality in the Universal Declaration of Human Rights, Nehemiah Robinson, *The Universal Declaration of Human Rights. Its Origin, Significance, Application and Interpretation*, Institute of Jewish Affairs, New York: 1958; Albert Verdoodt, *Naissance et Signification de la Déclaration Universelle des Droits de l'Homme*, E. Warny, Louvain: 1964. The Human Rights Committee also elaborated on the notion of arbitrariness in the context of the prohibition of arbitrary interference with an individual's private and family life: "The introduction of the concept of arbitrariness is intended to guarantee that even interference provided for by the law should be in accordance with the provisions, aims and objectives of the covenant and should be, in any event, reasonable in the particular circumstances". Human Rights Committee, *General Comment 16: The right to respect of privacy, family, home and correspondence, and protection of honour and reputation,*Geneva: 8 April 1988, para. 4. The jurisprudence of the Human Rights Committee on the subject arbitrary detention also sheds light on the interpretation of arbitrariness: "'arbitrariness' is not to be equated with 'against the law', but must be interpreted more broadly to include elements of inappropriateness, injustice, lack of predictability and due process of law". Human Rights Committee, *Case of Van Alphen v. The Netherlands,* Comm. No. 305/1988, Geneva: 23 July 1990, paragraph 5.8.

have therefore identified two further circumstances in which the deprivation of nationality shall be considered arbitrary. Thus, the second manifestation of arbitrary deprivation of nationality is where such deprivation is *discriminatory*. As will be revealed, this refers to situations that are now commonly described as "denial of citizenship". The third is where the deprivation of nationality is not accompanied by "due procedural process, including review or appeal".[9] In the following sections, these three variants of *arbitrary* deprivation of nationality will be dealt with, considering the role that they play in rendering individuals stateless and the reaction that international law prescribes in each case.[10] We will consider the *discriminatory* deprivation of citizenship first (section 1) - and in greatest detail - because this is the most severe form and tends to be the core issue in all cases of arbitrary deprivation of nationality, whereby unlawfulness of decisions and the lack of due process are secondary accompaniments. Thereafter, unlawful deprivation of nationality and the absence of due process will be dealt with together (section 2), forming, as such, the procedural guarantees encapsulated in the prohibition of arbitrary deprivation of nationality.

1 Discriminatory Deprivation of Nationality and "Denial of Citizenship"

Discriminatory deprivation of nationality fundamentally describes the situation where a state withholds or withdraws the nationality of an individual on the basis of a distinction that is deemed unreasonable and untenable, such as on the grounds of some immutable characteristic like skin colour. Exactly what type of distinction is considered to amount to discrimination under international law - in the specific context of nationality attribution – will be investigated in the upcoming two

[9] Open Society Justice Initiative, *Racial Discrimination and the Rights of Non-Citizens. Submission to the UN Committee on the Elimination of Racial Discrimination on the occasion of its 64th Session*, New York: 2004.

[10] To complete this initial introduction to the concept of arbitrary deprivation of nationality, two further remarks should be made. The first relates to the submission made by numerous scholars that any deprivation of nationality resulting in statelessness must be considered arbitrary, although deprivation appears to be used in this context in its narrower sense as denationalisation: loss or withdrawal of an existing nationality. This would add a fourth variant to the list of "arbitrary" measures outlined above. As we have already noted in previous chapters, while international law is certainly developing towards a stronger condemnation of the creation of statelessness and a firmer obligation on states to prevent statelessness, there is insufficient evidence that the deprivation of nationality resulting in statelessness *per se* qualifies as arbitrary deprivation of nationality. However, where this work identifies concrete obligations on states to refrain from denationalising a certain person and rendering them stateless, it is arguable that to nevertheless do so – in breach of international law – could also amount to arbitrary deprivation of nationality. The second comment relates to the issue of collective denationalisation. Large-scale withdrawal of citizenship must be considered arbitrary – whether technically prescribed by law or not - both because it (usually) involves identifying a particular population group for deprivation of citizenship on discriminatory grounds and because the condition of procedural due process cannot be met with *en masse* decision-making. Therefore, it is important to note that the expression arbitrary deprivation of nationality automatically covers situations of collective denationalisation, such as the historical examples provided above (in note 2), which have proven to be a significant source of statelessness. There is no need to discuss this matter separately; the evaluation of applicable international norms that is contained in this chapter is also relevant to this dire phenomenon.

subsections. However, I would like to first call attention to a closely related issue: the development of the newest catchphrase relating to nationality matters to emerge into the international arena, namely "denial of citizenship". It has been taken up by – among others – the UNHCR in its Handbook on nationality and statelessness, the Committee on the Elimination of Racial Discrimination in a General Recommendation and NGOs in their reports on citizenship issues.[11] In spite of the increasingly frequent usage of this phrase, no actual definition has been provided to date. Nor can the phrase as such be found in international legal instruments. Nevertheless, its meaning can be inferred from writings on the subject whereby it becomes clear that "denial of citizenship" has become the popular term used in describing situations of *discriminatory* deprivation of nationality (amounting to arbitrary deprivation of nationality). The recognition of the equivalence of these phrases is of vital importance since it provides content to the otherwise hollow expression "denial of citizenship" that has become so commonplace. It also establishes the link to international norms that apply to cases of denial of citizenship with the result that to label a situation as such is no longer vague and trivial but is in fact an appraisal which is loaded with (legal) consequence.

In view of the significance of equating denial of citizenship to discriminatory deprivation of nationality, let us explore how this conclusion was reached. One report that came close to ascribing a tangible meaning to the denial of citizenship is "Denial of citizenship: A challenge to human security" compiled for the Advisory Board on Human Security. In a footnote to the main text it suggests that denial of citizenship may stand for:

> An individual's inability to obtain participative membership in a given State despite that individual's meeting the citizenship requirements generally identified under international standards.[12]

---

[11] UNHCR and IPU, *Nationality and statelessness. A handbook for parliamentarians*, 2005, page 39; CERD General Recommendation 30: Discrimination against Non-Citizens 2004, paragraph 15; Open Society Justice Initiative, *Racial Discrimination and the Rights of Non-Citizens. Submission to the UN Committee on the Elimination of Racial Discrimination on the occasion of its 64th Session,* New York: 2004; Human Rights Watch report on Malaysia, "The Rohingya's citizenship: the root of the problem", 2000; The term can be found in the working paper prepared by Fernand de Varennes for the UN Working Group on Minorities in 1998 entitled "Towards effective political participation and representation of minorities". The phrase has also been employed by former UNHCR Legal Advisor on Statelessness, Carol Batchelor in her publications, such as Carol Batchelor, 'Statelessness and the Problem of Resolving Nationality Status', in *International Journal of Refugee Law,* Vol. 10, 1998.

[12] Advisory Board on Human Security (prepared by Constantin Sokoloff), *Denial of Citizenship: A Challenge to Human Security,* February 2005, page 6. It is of interest to note the reference to "participatory membership". In choosing this term instead of simply referring to nationality or *legal* membership, it would appear that consideration should be given not just to the fact of nationality, but also to its quality. Where an individual is a *de jure* national but is prevented from exercising his rights of citizenship, for example he is unable to vote or re-enter state territory, this could be qualified as denial of citizenship because he lacks *participatory* membership – an *effective* nationality. This take on the issue may provide the opportunity to tackle the problem of ineffective citizenship under international norms relating to the arbitrary deprivation of nationality. Although this does not concern a problem of statelessness (see chapter II, section 4) and is therefore beyond the scope of this study, it is important to note that the potential existence of means for ensuring that people are able to exercise the rights accorded to them through the bond of nationality is an important component of the overall regime

Note that denial of citizenship would result in statelessness where the words "a given State" can be replaced with "any State" or simply deleted.[13] However, this prospective definition has one undeniable weakness. This weakness lies in its closing words: "despite that individual's meeting the *citizenship requirements generally identified under international law*".[14] There are two problems with this segment of the text. First of all, the conditions that must be met for an individual to acquire the nationality of a particular state are set by the municipal law of that state. International law does not espouse a clear set of citizenship requirements to be enacted by all states, it merely prescribes certain limits on the freedom of states to lay down their own conditions for nationality attribution. It is therefore not immediately obvious how you would determine whether there has been a denial of citizenship under this definition. Secondly, if we were to proceed by assuming that the lack of attribution of nationality in violation of *any* international standard were to amount to a denial of citizenship, then the phrase itself would lose all defining value. This approach would result in the inclusion of technical causes of statelessness and statelessness as a consequence of state succession – in fact any case where citizenship is deprived or refused in breach of international law. Not only would this render the expression "denial of citizenship" useless in the context of this chapter – in identifying a specific, distinct source of statelessness – but this does not seem to be the correct use of the phrase as understood from writings on the topic.

The prospective definition introduced above is therefore not entirely satisfactory. More precisely, it fails to identify *which* international standards on the attribution of nationality are violated in the context of denial of citizenship. To do so, let us consider the caseloads put forward in the Advisory Board's report as examples of the phenomenon. These include – among others – the Rohingyas in Myanmar, the Banyarwanda in the Democratic Republic of Congo and the Lhotshampas in Bhutan. It is clear that the situations covered by the phrase "denial of citizenship" are manifold and diverse. However, you need only briefly scan the description of the plight of each of these groups to realise that there are a number of recurring buzz-words such as *deliberate, marginalisation, exclusion, disenfranchisement* and *ethnicity*. There is therefore one uniting element: *discrimination.* Denial of citizenship is about unequal access to nationality and the lack of justification for such bias. As the UNHCR Guidelines on statelessness suggest:

---

for the protection of individual rights. On the other hand, since the prospective definition goes on to discuss the fact of the individual meeting "citizenship requirements", the phrase "participative membership" could equally be construed as synonymous with nationality.

[13] For the sake of clarity, the term nationality should also be substituted for the phrase "participative membership" in view of the comments made in the previous footnote. Note that in reality, denial of citizenship will more often than not result in statelessness for it is usually the state with which an individual is most closely connected that effects the denial of citizenship. Only where another state with which the individual has a *genuine link* intervenes to grant legal membership (or in cases of dual nationality), will such denial of citizenship not create a new case of statelessness.

[14] Emphasis added.

> All nationality laws have distinctions and not all persons will be equally connected with all States. Nevertheless, in some cases persons are unable to acquire nationality in any State despite very strong ties which are sufficient for the grant of nationality to other equally-situated persons. There may be either overt discrimination or discrimination created inadvertently in the laws or through their implementation.[15]

This interpretation of denial of citizenship is backed in another international report which explains the idea of "exclusion of minorities from the political process through the denial of citizenship" as follows:

> Historically, some governments have limited political participation and representation to certain categories of individuals by making it more difficult for members of certain minority groups to become citizens.[16]

Thus denial of citizenship distinguishes itself through the element of discrimination and the notion that it targets particular population groups. Or put simply: denial of citizenship *is* the discriminatory deprivation of nationality.

On the basis of the foregoing it is clear that we are not looking at lack of access to nationality in contravention of *any* international standard, but, more particularly, in violation of the principle of equal treatment and the complimentary prohibition of discrimination. If we translate these findings into a working definition of denial of citizenship – and thereby also of discriminatory deprivation of nationality – we can present a fully revised version of the problematic description presented above:

> An individual's inability to obtain or retain nationality in a given State in contravention of international standards on non-discrimination.[17]

---

[15] UNHCR, *Guidelines: Field Office Activities Concerning Statelessness,* Field-Office Memorandum No.70/98, 28 September 1998, page 6.

[16] Working paper by Fernand de Varennes, "Towards effective participation and representation of minorities", prepared for the Sub-Commission on Prevention of Discrimination and Protection of Minorities of the UN Commission on Human Rights, May 1998, E/CN.4/Sub.2/AC5/1998/WP4. See also Gay McDougall, *Promotion and Protection of all Human Rights, Civil, Political, Economic, Social and Cultural Rights, Including the Right to Development – Report of the Independent Expert on Minority Issues,* A/HRC/7/23, 28 February 2008, paras. 13-15.

[17] Note that "nationality" was substituted for "participative membership" to avoid ambiguity. Furthermore, the words "or retain" were added in order to reflect the understanding that denial of citizenship and discriminatory deprivation of nationality may refer equally to situations where a person has been unable to acquire the nationality of a state and where a person has been denationalised. This is in line with the previous assertion that "deprivation" in the context of arbitrary deprivation of nationality should currently be interpreted in the broadest possible sense. In fact cases of denial of citizenship often demonstrate both the discriminatory loss or deprivation of citizenship from a particular generation in combination with the discriminatory refusal to bestow nationality upon successive generations. Consider for example the Lhotshampas (ethnic Nepalese Hindus) of Bhutan, many of whom saw their citizenship revoked by the 1985 Citizenship Act when it (retroactively) required both parents to be citizens of Bhutan for eligibility to Bhutanese nationality by birth or proof of permanent residence on Bhutanese soil since before 31 December 1958 for eligibility to Bhutanese nationality by registration. These amendments also made it impossible for successive generations to acquire Bhutanese citizenship. Denial of citizenship affected many more after large numbers of

This definition covers both the situation where citizenship requirements set by the state are of themselves discriminatory and cases of discriminatory (non- or incorrect) application of the municipal rules on the attribution of nationality.[18]

Again it should be noted that where denial of citizenship results in statelessness the words "a given State" must either be replaced with "any State" or simply omitted. Thus, since this work focuses on the problem of statelessness, we are particularly interested in the denial of citizenship in the following two contexts: where a person is denationalised in contravention of international standards on non-discrimination and where a (potentially) stateless person is denied access to nationality in contravention of those same standards. Before investigating the exact scope of the relevant international norms, let us take a brief look at two statelessness situations that provide a case in point for these variants of denial of citizenship as identified by the international community. The situation of the Kurds in the Syrian Arab Republic is an example of the first – withdrawal of citizenship resulting in statelessness. In 1962, the government issued Decree No. 93, providing for a population census that affected the withdrawal of citizenship from some 120,000 Syrian Kurds. In the decades that followed, the number of lives that were impacted by this decree rose and in January 2006 it was estimated that as many as 300,000 Kurds had been denied citizenship and rendered stateless.[19] Officially, the census required people to prove that they had been resident in Syria since before 1945 in order to retain their citizenship. Yet reportedly, the implementation of this policy resulted in the discriminatory denationalisation of Kurds, even those who were able to produce proof of residence.[20] Whether discriminatory in intent or not, the implementation of the government policy was undeniably discriminatory in effect, specifically targeting the Kurdish population.[21] Their statelessness remains a serious concern to the international community.[22]

Lhotshampa fled to neighbouring Nepal and Bhutan contended that they had willingly forfeited their citizenship by voluntarily emigrating (a ground for loss of citizenship under the 1977 Citizenship Act). Advisory Board on Human Security (prepared by Constantin Sokoloff), *Denial of Citizenship: A Challenge to Human Security,* February 2005, page 10; Hiram Ruiz and Michelle Berg, *Unending limbo: Warehousing Bhutanese Refugees in Nepal,* UNHCR World Refugee Survey 2004, pages 98-105; Michael Hutt, *Unbecoming Citizens. Culture, Nationhood, and the Flight of Refugees from Bhutan.*, Oxford University Press, New Delhi: 2005, pages 147-149 and 221.

[18] It thereby reflects the notion that "arbitrariness" under international law goes beyond mere "illegality" to also consider the quality of the law which is being implemented.

[19] Many of these are not only labelled as foreigners (Anjanib) but are entirely undocumented and invisible – Maktoumeen.

[20] Human Rights Watch, *Syria – The silenced Kurds,* Vol. 8, No. 4, October 1996; Maureen Lynch and Perveen Ali, *Buried Alive. Stateless Kurds in Syria,* Report for Refugees International, January 2006.

[21] Such requirements as proof of long-term residence (over several generations) or lineage may be non-discriminatory or neutral on the face of it but result in indirect discrimination of particular population groups because when applied, even without any intent to discriminate, it has an "exclusive or disproportionate adverse effect on a certain category of persons". See Human Rights Committee, *Case of Derksen v. the Netherlands,* CCPR/C/80/D/976/2001, 15 June 2004, paragraph 9.3. Alternatively, discrimination may be direct and explicit in the legislation or policy, such as in the case of the Rohingyas in Myanmar whose denial of citizenship resulted from the introduction of the 1982 Citizenship Act. This law allowed only certain ethnic groups – 135 "national races"- access to full citizenship. The Rohingyas were not among them. Advisory Board on Human Security (prepared by

As to statelessness created through the second variant of denial of citizenship – discriminatory refusal of access to nationality – the situation of the Dominican-born children of (supposed) Haitian descent is a current example. Although the Dominican Republic subscribes to the *jus soli* doctrine of nationality attribution at birth, large numbers of children born on Dominican soil are refused birthright citizenship. The constitutional exception clause which renders the Dominican-born children of parents who are "in transit" ineligible for Dominican citizenship has been the subject of a severely controversial, expansive interpretation: all children of irregular migrants are excluded from *jus soli* acquisition of nationality.[23] Moreover, the implementation of this policy is steeped in racial discrimination as the "irregular migrant" is equated with the "Haitian" and this, in turn, is interpreted on the basis of (perceived) ethnic traits. In practice, the decision as to which children's claim to *jus soli* citizenship will be accepted and which rejected, is often based on the parents skin colour, language ability and surname.[24] This instance of denial of citizenship is estimated to have caused anywhere upwards of 200,000 individual cases of statelessness.[25] In the event of either discriminatory refusal of access to nationality and discriminatory denationalisation, the outcome is the same: the creation of a new

---

Constantin Sokoloff), *Denial of Citizenship: A Challenge to Human Security,* February 2005, page 7; Open Society Justice Initiative, *Written Comments on the Case of Dilcea Yean and Violeta Bosico v. Dominican Republic,* New York: April 2005, page 35; Bill Frelick, *Statelessness: The Denial of a Fundamental Human Right,* 19 April 2005, pages 11-12; Doudou Diène, *Report by the Special Rapporteur on contemporary forms of racism, racial discrimination, xenophobia and related intolerance, Addendum – Summary of cases transmitted to Governments and replies received,* A/HRC/4/19/Add.1, 5 June 2007, paragraph 126.

[22] Committee on the Rights of the Child, *Concluding Observations: Syrian Arab Republic,* A/53/41, Geneva: 1998, para. 624; Committee on the Elimination of All Forms of Racial Discrimination, *Concluding observations: Syrian Arab Republic,* A/54/18, New York: 1999, paras. 17-176 and 180; Human Rights Committee, *Concluding Observations: Syrian Arab Republic,* CCPR/CO84/SYR, Geneva: 2005, para. 19

[23] Article 11 of the Dominican Constitution states "Dominicans are: All persons who were born on the territory of the Republic, with the exception of the legitimate children of foreign diplomats resident in the country or those who are transiting through it". The interpretation of "transient" to be synonymous with irregular migrant has received much criticism from the international and NGO community. See for example Inter-American Commission on Human Rights, "Chapter IX: Situation of Haitian migrant workers and their families in the Dominican Republic, in *Report on the situation of human rights in the Dominican Republic,* OEA/Ser.L/V/II.104, 7 October 1999, para. 363; Human Rights Committee, *Concluding Observations: Dominican Republic,* UN Doc. CCPR/CO/71/DOM, Geneva: 26 April 2001, para. 18.

[24] With the result that not all those excluded are children of irregular immigrants or even of foreign nationals. Movement of Haitian and Dominico-Haitian Women (MUDHA), *Solidarity. With the struggle of the Dominican minority of Haitian descent for citizenship and justice,* Santo Domingo, August 2001; Human Rights Watch, *"Illegal People": Haitians and Dominico-Haitians in the Dominican Republic,* Vol. 14, Number 1, April 2002; Bridget Wooding and Richard Mosely-Williams, *Needed but unwanted,* Catholic Institute for International Relations, London 2004; Inter-American Court on Human Rights, *Case of Yean and Bosico v. Dominican Republic,* Series C, Case 130, 8 September 2005.

[25] For a full analysis of the situation in the Dominican Republic, see Laura van Waas, *Is Permanent Illegality Inevitable? The Challenges to Ensuring Birth Registration and the Right to a Nationality for the Children of Irregular Migrants - Thailand and the Dominican Republic,* Woking: 2006

(and often large) stateless population thanks to denial of citizenship.[26] These two examples will be relied upon where appropriate as we turn to the question as to what extent international law stands in the way of such policies.

1.1 The 1961 Convention on the Reduction of Statelessness

In the introduction to the 1961 Statelessness Convention, provided in chapter III, we noted the unusual absence of any preambles or general principles. This is where we might otherwise have expected to find at least a preliminary reference to the principle of equality of treatment, a rendition of the prohibition of discrimination or indeed a proclamation of the prohibition of arbitrary deprivation of nationality.[27] Instead, the important matter of denial of citizenship is first dealt with in the Convention's substantive provisions. Article 9 decrees:

> A Contracting State may not deprive any person or group of persons of their nationality on racial, ethnic, religious or political grounds.[28]

Just four prohibited grounds are listed: race, ethnicity, religion and political affiliation. The way that the provision is formulated implies that this is a finite list: the words "or other status" which are commonly included at the end of such an inventory of prohibited grounds of discrimination are absent here. Nor does the "Information and Accession package" that accompanies the convention mention the possibility of other grounds of discrimination being read into this article. Moreover, the position of this provision in the Convention impies that "deprivation" is used here in its narrower sense, thus to prohibit only the *withdrawal* of nationality on the enumerated grounds.[29] There is no broader reference to non-discrimination in the Convention's text or any proclamation that in the implementation of its provisions the principle of equality is to be respected to counter this conclusion.

With these points in mind, it must be conceded that this provision will not cover all conceivable instances of denial of citizenship. Granted, it does prohibit denationalisation on racial or ethnic grounds which would have stood in the way of

---

[26] Denial of citizenship need not necessarily occur on such a large scale, it may also be evident in strictly individual decisions. Consider the denial of citizenship where parliamentary or presidential candidates are the target. One example is the reciprocal campaign by opposing parties in Zambia to prove that the other's leader was not a citizen. In the end, the political opponents of Kenneth Kaunda, the country's former president, were successful in forcing a High Court Ruling that revoked Mr Kaunda of his Zambian citizenship, rendering him stateless. Donald McNeil, "Founder of Zambia is declared stateless in high court ruling" *New York Times,* New York: 1999. See also Cécile Pouilly, "Africa's Hidden Problem" and Jack Redden, "Suddenly, you are nobody" in *Refugees Magazine,* Number 147, Issue 3, 2007, pages 28-31.

[27] Nor is there any mention of "denial of citizenship" as an issue.

[28] This is the only substantive article in the 1961 Convention on the Reduction of Statelessness that is not strictly focused on the prevention of statelessness but concerns itself with a broader principle in the field of nationality attribution. Under the operation of this instrument, deprivation of nationality on these grounds is prohibited whether it leads to statelessness or not.

[29] Article 9 follows an article that clearly deals with deprivation of citizenship in the sense of loss or withdrawal of an existing nationality rather than perhaps at the beginning of the convention as a more general principle. The *traveaux preparatoires* of the convention do not provide any clarification on this point.

Syria's treatment of its Kurdish population had it been a state party.[30] And the deprivation of nationality on political grounds, as has been reported in several young multi-party democracies, would also be outlawed. However, even if the four prohibited grounds were interpreted expansively,[31] they will undoubtedly leave some gaps because it is simply not feasible to read entirely new or different grounds into this finite list of terms. For example, the failure to prohibit deprivation of nationality on the grounds of gender is one obvious concern that cannot simply be overcome.[32] Moreover, in order to ensure that the four prohibited grounds of discrimination that are listed are interpreted in line with developments in international law, a competent monitoring body must be in place to lead the way. As hinted in chapter III, the supervisory mechanism provided for by the 1961 Statelessness Convention is unlikely to be able to fulfil this task. Perhaps even more severe is the gap that this Convention leaves in preventing discrimination in access to nationality. This may equally result in statelessness - as we have seen in the Dominican Republic where children of (presumed) irregular Haitian immigrants are rendered stateless due to discriminatory denial of access to *jus soli* Dominican citizenship. Let us now consider alternative sources of protection against denial of citizenship.

1.2 International human rights law

The prohibition of arbitrary deprivation of nationality is considered to be a fundamental norm of international law, the infringement of which amounts to a violation of basic human rights and fundamental freedoms.[33] It has been promulgated in a number of human rights instruments and should be considered as the counterpart to the right to a nationality which is included in many more.[34] The

[30] The Syrian Arab Republic is not a party to either of the Statelessness Conventions.

[31] For example, racial or ethnic grounds also cover discrimination on the basis of colour and descent . Plus, where apparently objective distinctions are used (e.g. language) with the effect of discriminating on one of these grounds, this can also be interpreted as prohibited discrimination.

[32] Tang Lay Lee, *Statelessness, human rights and gender: irregular migrant workers from Burma in Thailand*, Martinus Nijhoff Publishers, 2005, page 40. In chapter IV we saw the impact that policies discriminating on the grounds of gender can have on access to nationality and the risk of statelessness.

[33] UNHCR Executive Committee, *Conclusion on the Prevention and Reduction of Statelessness and the Protection of Stateless Persons,* No. 78, 1995; UN General Assembly, *Resolution on the Office of the United Nations High Commissioner for Refugees,* A/RES/50/152, 9 February 1996, para. 16; UN Human Rights Commission, *Resolutions on Human rights and arbitrary deprivation of nationality,* 1997/36, 11 April 1997; 1998/48, 17 April 1998; 1999/28, 26 April 1999 and 2005/45, 19 April 2005; Asian-African Legal Consultative Organisation Resolution on Legal Identity and Statelessness 2006. See also Paul Weis, *Nationality and Statelessness in International Law*, Kluwer Academic Publishers Group, Dordrecht: 1979, page 248; Johannes Chan, 'The Right to a Nationality as a Human Right - The Current Trend Towards Recognition', in *Human Rights Law Journal,* Vol. 12, 1991; Lisa Stratton, 'The Right to Have Rights: Gender Discrimination in Nationality Laws', in *Minnesota Law Review,* Vol. 77, 1992; Open Society Justice Initiative, *Written Comments on the Case of Dilcea Yean and Violeta Bosico v. Dominican Republic,* New York: April 2005.

[34] The prohibition of arbitrary deprivation of nationality is explicitly included in the Universal Declaration of Human Rights and the American Convention on Human Rights. It can also be found in article 4 of the European Convention on Nationality; Articles 15 and 16 of the ILC *Draft Articles on Nationality of Natural Persons in relation to the Succession of States*; Paragraph 55 of chapter VI on

renditions of this prohibition do not elaborate on the scope of the rule. It is however agreed that a major element of the prohibition of arbitrary deprivation of nationality is the prohibition of *discriminatory* deprivation of nationality, i.e. the denial of citizenship.[35] What we need to discover is what kind of differentiation is considered legitimate and what is deemed to amount to discrimination in this context. We must therefore look to rules on non-discrimination for further guidance on the content of this norm.

The general principle of non-discrimination enjoys such widespread recognition that it has become a matter of customary international law.[36] Moreover, the prohibition of *racial* discrimination is one of the most fundamental of international norms and has joined the ranks of *jus cogens.*[37] The principle can also be traced in the UN Charter and in every major human rights instrument adopted to date. The term "racial discrimination" covers distinctions based on "race, colour, descent, or national or ethnic origin".[38] This general prohibition clearly restricts the freedom of states to legislate on nationality matters by demanding that such regulations must not differentiate between individuals on the basis of any of these qualities, either in purpose or in effect. Neither access to, nor withdrawal of, nationality may be ascribed on these prohibited grounds.[39]

The *jus cogens* norm prohibiting racial discrimination therefore goes some way to delineating the scope of the denial of citizenship by providing initial content to the "international standards on non-discrimination" that were alluded to above.[40] The specific non-discrimination clauses of many human rights instruments prohibit discrimination on a number of additional grounds. The UN Charter itself decrees

The Human Dimension of the *Concluding Document of Helsinki*, Conference for Security and Cooperation in Europe, 1992; Paragraph 19 of the *Charter for European Security* of the Organisation for Security and Cooperation in Europe, 1999.

[35] Ruth Donner, *The Regulation of Nationality in International Law*, Transnational Publishers, New York: 1994; Johannes Chan, 'The Right to a Nationality as a Human Right - The Current Trend Towards Recognition', in *Human Rights Law Journal,* Vol. 12, 1991.

[36] See the discussion in chapter IV, section 1.2 on the subject of gender-sensitive nationality acts.

[37] Very few rules and principles have acquired the status of *jus cogens* - peremptory international norms. Alongside the prohibition of racial discrimination we find other fundamental matters such as the prohibitions of slavery and of genocide. Such rules can "be modified only by a subsequent norm of general international law having the same character". Article 53 of the Vienna Convention on the Law of Treaties. See also Ian Brownlie, *Principles of Public International Law*, Oxford University Press, Oxford: 2003, pages 488-489; James Crawford, *The International Law Commission's Articles on State Responsibility*, Cambridge University Press, Cambridge: 2002, pages 245-246.

[38] Article 1 of the Convention on the Elimination of All Forms of Racial Discrimination.

[39] The Convention on the Elimination of Racial Discrimination explicitly reminds us that the prohibition of racial discrimination is applicable to the enjoyment of the right to a nationality. Article 5 of the Convention on the Elimination of All Forms of Racial Discrimination, 1965. The Committee on the Elimination of Racial Discrimination has also stated that "deprivation of citizenship on the basis of race, colour, descent, or national or ethnic origin is a breach of States parties' obligations to ensure non-discriminatory enjoyment of the right to nationality". UN Committee on the Elimination of Racial Discrimination, *General Recommendation 30: Discrimination against non-citizens,* 1 October 2004, para. 14.

[40] Put another way, "the realm of State discretion in the field of nationality has an outer limit – the prohibition of racial discrimination". Open Society Justice Initiative, *Written Comments on the Case of Dilcea Yean and Violeta Bosico v. Dominican Republic,* Amicus brief to the Inter-American Court on Human Rights, April 2005, page 24.

that human rights shall be respected and observed "without distinction as to race, sex, language or religion".[41] To this list, the Universal Declaration of Human Rights and the International Covenants add a number of additional qualities, bringing the complete list to:

> Race, colour, sex, language, religion, political or other opinion, national or social origin, property, birth or other status.[42]

The enjoyment of all of the rights that are promulgated in these texts is thereby guaranteed to all "on an equal basis and in their totality".[43] Where the document includes the right to a nationality, the effect is to prescribe non-discriminatory enjoyment of this right.[44] On the face of it then, under the operation of these agreements the protection against denial of citizenship is broader in scope than under the 1961 Convention on the Reduction of Statelessness. At least three additional prohibited grounds of discrimination are introduced: sex, language and property.[45] Moreover, there is the prospect of ruling out further unjust distinctions

---

[41] Article 55 of the Charter of the United Nations. It should be noted that where the discriminatory deprivation of nationality on the grounds of gender is concerned, the comments made in the previous chapter (IV) on gender imbalance in *jus sanguinis* citizenship legislation and the discriminatory position of women in relation to nationality in the event of marriage are also relevant here.

[42] Article 2, paragraph 1 of the International Covenant on Civil and Political Rights, 1966; Article 2, paragraph 2 of the International Covenant on Economic, Social and Cultural Rights, 1966. Such a clause can also be found in article 1 of the International Convention on the Protection of the Rights of All Migrant Workers and Members of their Families. The Convention on the Rights of the Child maintains a similar list but with the added element that discrimination is prohibited on these grounds whether both in respect of the child and his parents. Article 2, paragraph 1 of the Convention on the Rights of the Child, 1989. It should be noted that some of these terms overlap since "racial discrimination" is already considered to include distinctions based on colour or national origin. Meanwhile, the Convention on the Elimination of All Forms of Discrimination Against Women focuses on outlawing gender discrimination in a similar context. All of the major regional human rights instruments render (their own version of) the same list: Article 14 of the European Convention on Human Rights; Article 1 of the American Convention on Human Rights; Article 2 of the African Charter on Human and Peoples' Rights; Article 3 of the African Charter on the Rights and Welfare of the Child; and Article 5 of the Covenant on the Rights of the Child in Islam. There are subtle variations, for example the term "property" is replaced in the African Charters with the word "fortune" and the European Convention on Human Rights includes an additional ground, namely "association with a national minority". However these differences are negligible.

[43] Human Rights Committee, *General Comment 28: Equality of rights between men and women,* 29 March 2000, para. 2.

[44] As we have seen, the right to a nationality or the right of a child to acquire a nationality is included in the International Covenant on Civil and Political Rights, the Convention on the Rights of the Child, the Convention on the Elimination of All Forms of Discrimination Against Women, the American Convention on Human Rights, the International Convention on the Protection of the Rights of All Migrant Workers and Members of their Families, the American Convention on Human Rights, the African Charter on the Rights and Welfare of the Child and the Covenant on the Rights of the Child in Islam.

[45] Colour and national origin are both encapsulated in the term "race". It could be argued that the grounds "social origin" and "birth" are first introduced in these international and regional human rights instruments. However, the content of the term "social origin" as distinct from national or ethnic origin or from property is ambiguous. Additionally, "birth" may be considered to fall within the broader term "racial discrimination" which includes distinctions on the grounds of "descent", although it also

under the category "other status" – an option that is not available under the 1961 Statelessness Convention. This opportunity has been seized, upon occasion, to denounce distinctions on grounds such as migratory status[46] or discrimination against persons who are affected by HIV/AIDS.[47]

It is tempting to conclude that the provisions on the right to a nationality and the prohibition of discrimination work in conjunction to forbid distinctions on any of the grounds listed in all domestic rules and practice on the attribution of nationality. This position is reinforced by provisions such as article 26 of the International Covenant on Civil and Political Rights which provides for equality (thereby prohibiting discrimination) before the law.[48] The impact of this norm was outlined in a general comment by the UN Human Rights Committee: "It prohibits discrimination in law or in fact in any field regulated and protected by public authorities".[49] The attribution of nationality is per definition such a field. Nevertheless, the matter is not that straightforward. The "application of the non-discrimination principle of equal access to rights does not mean identical treatment"[50] so we must look more carefully to see how the principle of non-discrimination is interpreted and applied in the specific context of nationality attribution. At present, beyond the absolute prohibition of racial discrimination as a *jus cogens* norm,[51] international human rights law is not altogether clear on this point. There are two issues that have yet to be fully crystallised. The first is to what extent *differentiation* on each of the grounds enumerated above is considered to amount to *discrimination* in the specific context of nationality attribution. The second is the problem of whether such discrimination is prohibited in all questions of nationality attribution or only in reference to, for example, denationalisation.

---

prohibits distinctions between legitimate and illegitimate children. See European Court of Human Rights, *Case of Marckx vs. Belgium*, No. 6833/74, 13 June 1979, para. 31.

[46] Inter-American Court on Human Rights, *Case of Yean and Bosico v. Dominican Republic,* Series C, Case 130, 8 September 2005, paras. 155 – 156.

[47] CERD, *Concluding Observations: Lithuania,* A/57/18, New York: 2002, para. 171.

[48] Similar guarantees can be found in article 24 of the American Convention on Human Rights; Article 3 of the African Convention on Human and Peoples' Rights; and Article 1 of Protocol No. 12 to the European Convention on Human Rights.

[49] Human Rights Committee, *General Comment 18: Non-discrimination,* Geneva: 10 November 1989, para. 12. The Inter-American Court of Human Rights used similar terms to describe the norm: "recognising equality before the law [...] prohibits all discriminatory treatment originating in a legal prescription". Inter-American Court on Human Rights, *Advisory Opinion on the Proposed Amendments to the Naturalisation Provision of the Constitution of Costa Rica,* OC-4/84, 19 January 1984, para. 54.

[50] Committee on the Rights of the Child, *General Comment 5: General Measures of Implementation of the Convention on the Rights of the Child,* Geneva: 27 November 2003. Also with regards to article 26 on equality before the law in the International Covenant on Civil and Political Rights: "a differentiation which is compatible with the provisions of the Covenant and is based on reasonable grounds does not amount to prohibited discrimination within the meaning of article 26". Human Rights Committee, *Kulomin v. Hungary,* case no. 521/1992, A/51/40 vol. II, 22 March 1996, para. 12.4.

[51] The special status of the prohibition of racial discrimination in international law is further evidenced by the ruling of the European Court of Human Rights in the case of *Cyprus v. Turkey.* There it was determined that "differential treatment on the basis of race might, in certain circumstances, constitute a special affront to human dignity" (para. 207). As such, racial discrimination may amount to inhuman and degrading punishment as prohibited under article 3 of the European Convention on Human Rights. ECHR, *Cyprus v. Turkey,* Judgement of 10 May 2001, No. 25781/94.

Some initial clues to answering the first question are provided by the resolutions on "Human rights and arbitrary deprivation of nationality" that were adopted by the UN Commission on Human Rights.[52] Four such texts have been approved by the Commission in recent years. Each contains an operative paragraph on arbitrary deprivation of nationality that includes a list of prohibited grounds of discrimination in that particular context. A comparison of these clauses reveals the interesting finding that they are not identical. In the first resolution, adopted in 1997, the list refers to "racial, national, ethnic or religious grounds".[53] By the following year, deprivation of nationality on the grounds of gender was also included under the term arbitrary deprivation of nationality.[54] In the last resolution to be passed in the UN Human Rights Commission, in 2005, there was a further expansion of the prohibited grounds for discrimination in this context: "political grounds" was also included.[55] These observations illustrate two things. Firstly they are evidence of the shifting nature of the international norm that deals with denial of citizenship. What was understood to amount to discrimination 50 years ago under the phrase discriminatory deprivation of nationality may be very different to what it means today and what it will mean in the future. This type of natural progression is common in the field of human rights. The rules certainly appear to be getting stricter rather than more lax, with the introduction of additional grounds upon which differentiation is forbidden.[56] Secondly, the fact that differences were traced over such a short period of time also hints at a pervading lack of consistency or uniformity in the interpretation of discriminatory (thus arbitrary) deprivation of nationality today. This question appears to still be hotly-debated, making it simply very difficult to ascertain what type of distinction is generally considered reasonable and what kind is essentially unacceptable.

Turning to another source of information on the scope of arbitrary deprivation of nationality, the European Convention on Nationality, we find that the picture becomes yet more complicated. This text includes the prohibition of arbitrary deprivation of nationality among the basic principles upon which "the

---

[52] The resolutions of bodies such as the UN Commission on Human Rights can be important sources of information on the prevailing understanding of international norms at the time. It should be noted that the Commission on Human Rights is now obsolete – it was replaced in 2006 by the Human Rights Council. Although the Council has retained the question of arbitrary deprivation of nationality on its agenda, at the time of writing it has yet to adopt a resolution on the substance of the matter.

[53] UN Human Rights Commission, *Resolution on Human rights and arbitrary deprivation of nationality,* 1997/36, 11 April 1997, operative paragraph. 2.

[54] UN Human Rights Commission, *Resolution on Human rights and arbitrary deprivation of nationality,* 1998/48, 17 April 1998, operative paragraph 2. The year after, the same list (including gender) was repeated in Resolution 1999/28, 26 April 1999, operative paragraph 2.

[55] UN Human Rights Commission, *Resolution on Human rights and arbitrary deprivation of nationality,* 2005/45, 19 April 2005, operative paragraph 2.

[56] This is also suggested by the commentary to the Draft Articles on Nationality of Natural Persons in relation to the Succession of States of the International Law Commission. Article 15 prohibits discrimination on *any grounds* in access to nationality in the context of state succession. In the commentary, the ILC explains that they decided against including an illustrative list of grounds because this may not be sufficiently inclusive, there being possible "still other grounds for discrimination in relation to a succession of states". International Law Commission, 'Draft Articles on Nationality of Natural Persons in Relation to the Succession of States - With Commentaries', in *Yearbook of the International Law Commission,* Vol. II, 1999.

rules on nationality of each State Party shall be based".[57] Thereafter follows a separate article entirely devoted to non-discrimination:

> The rules of a State Party on nationality shall not contain distinctions or include any practice which amount to discrimination on the grounds of sex, religion, race, colour or national or ethnic origin.[58]

Although similar, this list is slightly different again to that espoused in the most recent resolution of the UN Commission on Human Rights – political grounds are missing here. Moreover, as compared to the European Convention on Human Rights, several other elements of discrimination have been left out.[59] The Explanatory Memorandum to the European Convention on Nationality elucidates this choice by noting that the European Convention on Human Rights does not deal with matters of citizenship.[60] It goes on to explain that the grounds that were not transcribed from the human rights convention to the article quoted above were "considered as not amounting to discrimination in the field of nationality".[61] This may in fact explain the absence of the qualities of "language" and "property" from provisions specifically relating to non-discrimination in the attribution of nationality, not only in the European Convention on Nationality, but also in the aforementioned resolutions of the Human Rights Commission.[62]

What is certain is that different sources currently produce different answers to the question of what types of distinction are acceptable in the matter of nationality attribution and, conversely, what amounts to discriminatory deprivation of nationality.[63] There is still one other nuance to the story which may explain (some

---

[57] These are set out in article 4 of the European Convention on Nationality, 1997.

[58] Article 5, paragraph 1 of the European Convention on Nationality, 1997.

[59] The European Convention on Human Rights prohibits discrimination on the grounds of "sex, race, colour, language, religion, political or other opinion, national or social origin, association with a national minority, property, birth or other status". Article 14 of the 1950 European Convention for the Protection of Human Rights and Fundamental Freedoms.

[60] The right to a nationality is absent from the provisions of the European Convention on Human Rights, but the court has considered questions relating to citizenship regulations – in particular the alleged arbitrary denial of citizenship - through article 8 on right to respect for private and family life. See for instance European Court of Human Rights, *Decision as to the admissibility of Karassev v. Finland,* Application No. 31414/96, 12 January 1999.

[61] This was the reason given for the absence of the various grounds in the non-discrimination clause, apart from "social origin" which was simply considered to be too imprecise a term. Council of Europe, *Explanatory Memorandum of the European Convention on Nationality,* Strasbourg: 1997, pages 32 – 33.

[62] Interestingly, the non-discrimination clause of the European Convention on the Avoidance of Statelessness in relation to State Succession does reproduce the full list of prohibited grounds that are found in article 14 of the European Convention of Human Rights. This suggests that the approach taken in the European Convention on Nationality may not be set in stone. Article 4 of the 2006 European Convention on the avoidance of statelessness in relation to State Succession.

[63] The contributions of scholars have in some instances added to the haziness of this matter. For example, Weis expresses the view that discrimination on each of the grounds that are promulgated in the UN Charter is forbidden. This list includes language, which is not to be found in either the European Convention on Nationality or the resolutions of the UN Commission on Human Rights on the arbitrary deprivation of nationality. Paul Weis, *Nationality and Statelessness in International Law*, Kluwer Academic Publishers Group, Dordrecht: 1979, page 125.

of) the ambiguity. This brings us to the second issue raised above: which elements of nationality attribution are influenced by the principle of non-discrimination? As we have seen, rules on the attribution of nationality basically deal with three main situations. The first is the conferral of nationality at birth, the second is the acquisition of nationality later in life and the third is the loss of nationality. It is reasonable to expect the principle of non-discrimination to be equally applicable to the regulation of all three matters, but this is not the case. Although arbitrary deprivation of nationality can be established with respect to either conferral or withdrawal of nationality, the demands made by international law are different in each case. The rules on acceptance as a national and withdrawal of that status have been described as "morally asymmetric":

> Depriving somebody of her citizenship is a grave intrusion into a basic human right, whereas not granting naturalisation in a discriminatory procedure is in most cases not.[64]

This citation illustrates the underlying philosophy that explains why international law deals differently with the different modes of nationality attribution. States are typically granted greater freedom in questions of naturalisation and are faced with much more stringent control when it comes to denationalisation. As to the attribution of nationality to a child at birth – this falls somewhere between the two.

Deprivation of nationality in the sense of withdrawal, loss or revocation of nationality (i.e. denationalisation) severs the legal bond between a person and his state. As we will see in Part 3, this can have grave consequences for his enjoyment of rights. It is therefore arguable that the non-discriminatory enjoyment of the right to a nationality demands that, once held, this esteemed legal status is not interfered with on any of the grounds listed in the non-discrimination clause of human rights instruments that also promulgate the right to a nationality. This is the most exhaustive list which includes, for example, language and property as prohibited distinctions. Thus any denationalisation that is based on one of these qualities - or indeed "any other status" that is not reasonable and objective - would be in violation of the respective treaty obligations on non-discriminatory enjoyment of rights, equality before the law, the right to a nationality and the prohibition of arbitrary deprivation of nationality. The example provided above of the denationalisation of Syrian Kurds would amount to a violation in this way, which explains the reactions by the UN treaty bodies to the plight of the stateless Kurds.[65] So too would denationalisation on political grounds – a concerning phenomenon that is becoming increasingly widespread in up-and-coming multiparty

---

[64] Note that deprive is used here in the narrower sense of denationalisation. Rainer Bauböck, *Transnational Citizenship. Membership and Rights in International Migration*, Edward Elgar, Cheltenham: 2002, page 135. See also James Goldston, 'Holes in the Rights Framework: Racial Discrimination, Citizenship, and the Rights of Noncitizens', in *Ethics and International Affairs*, Vol. 20, 2006, page 333.

[65] The UN Human Rights Committee and the Committees on the Elimination of Racial Discrimination and the Rights of the Child have all commented on the denationalisation and continued statelessness of the Kurds in Syria. It is a violation of Syria's treaty obligations in each of the respective instruments. See note 22.

democracies.[66] When withdrawal of nationality in this manner is combined with expulsion from state territory, the violation of international law becomes yet more severe.[67] Not only may this breach further human rights obligations to which the state has agreed, such as the duty not to act to destroy an individual's enjoyment of fundamental rights, but it may also amount to a breach of the territorial integrity of another state by forcing it to accept these newly-stateless persons.[68]

As to the rules on the attribution of nationality at birth, there is an ever-growing awareness of the importance of obtaining a nationality at birth – an original nationality – particularly in the context of the fight against statelessness. Similarly to denationalisation, the inability to acquire an original nationality has a dire impact on the enjoyment of fundamental rights. This is why the right of every child to acquire a nationality at birth was explicitly included in such instruments as the International Covenant on Civil and Political Rights and the Convention on the Rights of the Child. Arguably then, the combined effect of this right of every child to acquire a nationality at birth and the corresponding provisions on non-discrimination is to outlaw discrimination in access to an original nationality with equal stringency as the prohibition of discriminatory denationalisation.[69] The full list of forbidden distinctions that was valid for loss or withdrawal of citizenship must also be applicable here: no differentiation may be made on any of those grounds, in relation to either the child or his parents, so as to impact on the child's access to citizenship. Unlike the 1961 Convention on the Reduction of Statelessness which did not deal with discriminatory deprivation of *access* to nationality (at birth or otherwise), international human rights law prohibits such distinctions as were put into practice in the Dominican Republic in determining eligibility to birthright citizenship.

Indeed, when tasked with ruling on the conformity of the Dominican Republic's citizenship policy with its human rights obligations, the Inter-American Court of Human Rights confirmed this interpretation. The case in question was brought before the court on behalf of two children, Dilcia Yean and Violeta Bosico, to whom the Dominican authorities refused to grant *jus soli* citizenship on the

---

[66] James Goldston, 'Holes in the Rights Framework: Racial Discrimination, Citizenship, and the Rights of Noncitizens', in *Ethics and International Affairs,* Vol. 20, 2006, page 326; Maureen Lynch, *Lives on hold: The human cost of statelessness,* Washington: 2005, page 29 on Swaziland; Open Society Justice Initiative, *Africa Citizenship and Discrimination Audit,* New York: 2004, page 1. Consider also the withdrawal of citizenship from former Zambian President, Kenneth Kaunda (note 26 above).

[67] According to the UNHCR, expulsion often follows discriminatory denationalisation of an individual. UNHCR and IPU, *Nationality and statelessness. A handbook for parliamentarians,* 2005, page 39.

[68] Although the European Convention on Human Rights does not contain the right to a nationality, the European Commission on Human Rights recognised that to denationalise and expel a citizen may amount to a breach of article 17 of the Convention which forbids any act aimed at destroying the rights and freedoms contained in the document. Ruth Donner, "Chapter 4: Human Rights Conventions and other Instruments" in *The Regulation of Nationality in International Law,* Transnational Publishers, New York: 1994, pages 227-228.

[69] The Committee on the Rights of the Child has expressed concern at cases of discrimination on the grounds of race, language (i.e. belonging to a linguistic minority), sex and (parents') political opinion in access to nationality at birth. Committee on the Rights of the Child, *Concluding Observations: Cambodia,* CRC/C/97, Geneva: 2000, paras. 361 – 362; *Democratic Republic of Congo,* CRC/C/108, Geneva: 2001, paras. 177-178; *Estonia,* CRC/C/124, Geneva: 2003, paras. 45-46; *Cyprus,* CRC/C/132, Geneva: 2003, para. 116.

grounds that their parents were irregular Haitian immigrants. The court decided in favour of the girls and established numerous violations of the American Convention on Human Rights by the Dominican state. Two considerations expressed by the court are of particular relevance here. Firstly, when the court determined that the Dominican Republic had violated the girls' right to a nationality, it read article 20 of the American Convention (on the right to a nationality) in conjunction with article 24 (on the right to equal protection). Thus the court did not merely establish an infringement of the girls' right to a nationality as such – as contained in article 20, paragraph 1 – but it further qualified the violation as an "arbitrary deprivation of their nationality".[70] This added element was introduced because the two girls had been refused access to Dominican citizenship at birth for "discriminatory reasons".[71] Discrimination in access to nationality can therefore be qualified as arbitrary *deprivation* of nationality under international human rights law.[72] The second point of interest in this decision by the Inter-American Court can be found in a consideration which precedes the aforementioned conclusion:

> The obligation to respect and ensure the principle of the right to equal protection and non-discrimination is irrespective of a person's migratory status in a State [...] The migratory status of a person cannot be a condition for the State to grant nationality, because migratory status can never constitute a justification for depriving a person of the right to nationality or the enjoyment and exercise of his rights.[73]

Here the court determines that differentiating between persons on the basis of migratory status for the purposes of nationality attribution is an unreasonable distinction and amounts to discrimination. It thereby introduces a new prohibited ground for discrimination in relation to the right to a nationality. Although it is questionable whether this assertion reflects the present state of international law,[74] this finding by the court does illustrate the versatility of human rights law in countering any unreasonable distinctions, even if they are not explicitly outlined in a treaty text. This increases the scope for protection against discriminatory deprivation of nationality and thereby against statelessness. The 1961 Convention

[70] Thereby also in contravention of article 20, paragraph 3 of the American Convention on Human Rights. Inter-American Court on Human Rights, *Case of Yean and Bosico v. Dominican Republic,* Series C, Case 130, 8 September 2005, para. 174.

[71] Inter-American Court on Human Rights, *Case of Yean and Bosico v. Dominican Republic,* Series C, Case 130, 8 September 2005, para. 174. Of interest is the finding later in this same paragraph that rendering the two children stateless in this way also had a detrimental impact on their enjoyment of article 1, paragraph 1 and article 19 of the American Convention: the right to enjoy the rights set forth in the Convention without discrimination and the right to special measures of protection as a child.

[72] These findings by the court mark a clear progression in its case law on nationality towards a broader interpretation of the norms espoused in article 20 of the American Convention on Human Rights. Twenty years previously, the same court determined that article 20, paragraph 1 (right to a nationality) could not be deemed to be violated if no loss of nationality took place. Inter-American Court on Human Rights, *Advisory Opinion on the Proposed Amendments to the Naturalisation Provision of the Constitution of Costa Rica,* OC-4/84, 19 January 1984, para. 42.

[73] Inter-American Court on Human Rights, *Case of Yean and Bosico v. Dominican Republic,* Series C, Case 130, 8 September 2005, paras. 155 - 156.

[74] See chapter VII.

on the Reduction of Statelessness lacks this capacity due to the absence of a general provision on non-discrimination, a limitative list of prohibited grounds for denationalisation and the absence of any mechanism to further develop the norms espoused in the text, i.e. through case law.

Finally we come to the question of denial of citizenship in the context of conferral of nationality later in life through naturalisation. This was undoubtedly the furthest concern from the minds of government representatives at the time that the text "no one shall be arbitrarily deprived of his nationality" was approved for article 15 of the Universal Declaration of Human Rights.[75] However, even the rules on voluntary acquisition of nationality are not beyond influence from international law:

> *As long as such rules do not conflict with superior norms*, it is the state conferring nationality which is best able to judge what conditions to impose to ensure that an effective link exists between the applicant for naturalisation and the systems of values and interests of the society with which he seeks to associate himself.[76]

The prohibition of racial discrimination indisputably belongs to the realms of the "superior norms" alluded to here, thus the conditions set for naturalisation may not differentiate on the grounds of race, colour, descent, or national or ethnic origin.[77] More generally, a state may not raise "unreasonable impediments" to the acquisition of nationality by naturalisation.[78] As to the other distinctions that are thereby considered impermissible in the context of naturalisation, we see that the list necessarily differs from the exhaustive catalogue that applies to denationalisation and access to nationality at birth. For example, applicants for naturalisation are commonly tested on language ability. Sufficient knowledge of the national language is viewed as a legitimate requirement for eligibility for naturalisation, whereas we saw that denationalisation on the grounds of "language" will be considered unreasonable and discriminatory.[79] This observation serves also to better explain the choice made in the European Convention on Nationality as to

[75] As we have noted, they were confronted with large-scale denationalisation.

[76] Emphasis added. Inter-American Court on Human Rights, *Advisory Opinion on the Proposed Amendments to the Naturalisation Provision of the Constitution of Costa Rica,* OC-4/84, 19 January 1984, para. 36.

[77] The UN Committee on the Elimination of Racial Discrimination has expressed its concern at instances of racial discrimination in laws and regulations on naturalisation and their implementation. CERD, *Concluding Observations: Croatia,* A/50/18, New York: 1995, paras. 173 and 175; *Republic of Korea,* A/51/18, New York: 1996, para. 328; *Switzerland,* A/57/18, New York: 2002, para. 251. So too has the Special Rapporteur on contemporary forms of racism, racial discrimination, xenophobia and related intolerance. See for example Doudou Diène, *Report by the Special Rapporteur on contemporary forms of racism, racial discrimination, xenophobia and related intolerance, Addendum – Summary of cases transmitted to Governments and replies received,* A/HRC/4/19/Add.1, 5 June 2007, paragraphs 65-67 and Doudou Diène, *Report by the Special Rapporteur on contemporary forms of racism, racial discrimination, xenophobia and related intolerance, Addendum – Mission to the Russian Federation,* A/HRC/4/19/Add.3, 30 May 2007.

[78] Human Rights Committee, *Individual complaint of Capena v. Canada,* case number 558/1993, A/52/40, vol. II, Geneva: 3 April 1997, para. 11.3.

[79] See Inter-American Court on Human Rights, *Advisory Opinion on the Proposed Amendments to the Naturalisation Provision of the Constitution of Costa Rica,* OC-4/84, 19 January 1984, paragraph 63.

which grounds to include in the provision on non-discrimination. Where elements such as language and property were left out with the argument that such differentiation does not amount to discrimination in the field of nationality, it is important to note that the article in question applies to all domestic rules on nationality, including those on naturalisation.[80]

We should, therefore, consider the more concise and finite list of grounds espoused in the European Convention on Nationality to be a good reflection of the present scope of denial of citizenship in the specific context of naturalisation procedures.[81] Meanwhile it is important to remember that non-prohibited grounds such as language requirements and the like "should exclusively be used and regarded as an element of integrating non-nationals and should not be used as a discriminatory means for a state to select its nationals".[82] Beyond these grounds, it is also understood that discrimination against a *particular* nationality in access to naturalisation is an unreasonable distinction.[83] In sum, it is possible for a state to commit arbitrary deprivation of nationality by enforcing discriminatory conditions for naturalisation. Although this may not appear immediately relevant in the context of the prevention of statelessness, be reminded that the inability to access naturalisation procedures does contribute to the creation and prolongation of instances of statelessness. The suggestion that it is possible to "arbitrarily deprive [a stateless person] of the right to acquire the nationality of the country of residence",[84] i.e. the ability to gain naturalisation, is a major and important advance

[80] As previously cited, article 5 of the European Convention on Nationality reads: "The rules of a State Party on nationality shall not contain distinctions or include any practice which amount to discrimination on the grounds of sex, religion, colour or national or ethnic origin". Note again, however, that the Council of Europe Convention on the avoidance of statelessness in relation to State Succession reproduces the full list of prohibited grounds of discrimination espoused in the European Convention on Human Rights. This implies that where access to naturalisation is used as a tool for the prevention or reduction of statelessness – at least in the specific context of state succession – there is a reduced level of tolerance for any form of distinction that may impede the avoidance of statelessness.

[81] Alongside references to racial discrimination in the acquisition of nationality by naturalisation, the Committee on the Elimination of Racial Discrimination has also expressed concern at religious distinctions and the Human Rights Committee has expressed concern at gender discrimination. CERD, *Concluding Observations: Yemen,* A/57/18, New York: 2002, para. 464. Human Rights Committee, *Concluding Observations: Jordan,* A/49/40 vol.1, Geneva: 1994, para. 232; *Libyan Arab Jamahiriya,* A/54/40 vol. 1, Geneva: 1999, para. 137. In addition, the Inter-American Court on Human Rights has clearly denounced distinctions on the grounds of gender in the context of access to nationality. See Inter-American Court on Human Rights, *Advisory Opinion on the Proposed Amendments to the Naturalisation Provision of the Constitution of Costa Rica,* OC-4/84, 19 January 1984, paragraphs 64-67.

[82] Committee of Experts on Nationality, *Report on Conditions for the Acquisition and Loss of Nationality,* Strasbourg: 14 January 2003, page 12. Similarly, in assessing the compliance with international law of the Czech Republic's rules on naturalisation, Human Rights Watch has convincingly argued that other conditions, such as the requirement of a clean criminal record, may also amount to indirect discrimination if implemented in such a way as to unreasonably and disproportionately target a particular group – in this case the Roma. See Human Rights Watch, *Roma in the Czech Republic – Foreigners in Their Own Land,* 1 June 1996.

[83] Article 1, paragraph 3 of the Convention on the Elimination of all Forms of Racial Discrimination; CERD General Recommendation 30: Discrimination against Non-Citizens, New York: 2004, para. 13.

[84] Human Rights Committee, *Individual complaint of Stewart v. Canada,* case number 538/1993, A/52/40, vol. II, Geneva: 1 November 1996, para. 12.4.

in the field of international law with consequences reaching far beyond the obligations of states under the 1961 Statelessness Convention.

2 Illegal deprivation of nationality and the lack of due process

The lengthy discussion of discriminatory deprivation of nationality has provided an insight into the substantive limits set by the prohibition of arbitrary deprivation of nationality. Existing alongside the question of what a state may and may not prescribe in the field of nationality before it is considered to amount to arbitrary deprivation of nationality is the more technical question: in what way must the attribution of nationality be regulated so as not to be branded as arbitrary? In the introduction to this chapter we saw that the most basic formality or procedural condition to be met for a decision not to be deemed arbitrary is that it must conform to the law in force. This is an important criterion because it helps to ensure that the decisions of the authority are foreseeable and not slapdash. Thus the deprivation of nationality must be prescribed by law.[85] Again, deprivation is to be read here in the broadest possible sense, as referring to denationalisation but also denial of access to a nationality. If the state authorities go beyond the terms of the law in withdrawing or refusing citizenship, this will amount to arbitrary deprivation of nationality. New cases of statelessness may thereby be created (or existing plights prolonged) in situations where perhaps no fault can be found with the relevant domestic law. This contributes to the invisibleness of stateless populations because at first sight, from a perusal of the domestic law alone, the problems may not be apparent.

The second procedural safeguard against arbitrariness is the requirement that the deprivation of nationality be accompanied by further guarantees of due process. More specifically, there should be opportunity to apply for a review of the decision to withdraw or withhold nationality. This has also been described as the need to provide a "*meaningful* opportunity for individuals to go before an independent tribunal".[86] This obligation may include aspects such as ensuring that the decision to revoke or refuse nationality is provided in writing and that the underlying motivation is also disclosed. The necessity of an effective review mechanism as a tool for fighting statelessness requires little explanation. It provides an opportunity for overturning unlawful, unreasonable or discriminatory decisions, but also for reconsidering the position of the individual in view of the threat of statelessness.[87] Moreover, a review mechanism is an aid in the fight against

---

[85] In relation to nationality attribution, the role of the law is paramount since nationality is the *legal* bond that an individual enjoys with a state. The definition of a stateless person reminds us of this fact where it declares that a stateless person is "a person who is not considered as a national by any state *under operation of its law*".

[86] Emphasis added. Open Society Justice Initiative, *Citizenship and Equality in Practice: Guaranteeing Non-Discriminatory Access to Nationality, Protecting the Right to be Free from Arbitrary Deprivation of Nationality, and Combating Statelessness,* New York: November 2005, page 8.

[87] In the Netherlands, for instance, a case arose where a man was rendered stateless through the withdrawal of his Dutch nationality, after he had renounced his prior Egyptian citizenship. When the case was subjected to review, the domestic court found that the withdrawal of nationality had been unlawful because of the resultant statelessness and this decision ensured that his Dutch nationality was

corruption and where the decision-making authority on nationality attribution has been decentralised it furthermore enables such powers to be kept in check - helping to secure compliance with standards of domestic and international law. As a decision with serious consequences for the rights and duties of an individual, the possibility of appeal is a practical and important safeguard.

2.1 The 1961 Convention on the Reduction of Statelessness

We have already seen that the 1961 Statelessness Convention lacks any general prohibition of the arbitrary deprivation of nationality under which these formal protections against arbitrary decision-making would be afforded. However, tucked away in article 8, paragraph 4 of the document is a provision that may offer some solace:

> A Contracting State shall not exercise a power of deprivation permitted by paragraphs 2 or 3 of this article except in accordance with law, which shall provide for the persons concerned the right to a fair hearing by a court or other independent body.[88]

This paragraph covers the two major procedural elements that must be present in the decision-making process to prevent it from being deemed arbitrary: the decision must be taken in accordance with the law and there must be an appeals process in place. Importantly, the provision requires review by a "court or other independent body" and is not content if the decision is only sent back to the same authority for renewed consideration. This increases the value of such an appeal – particularly, as suggested above, where corruption may be an issue or where competence in nationality matters has been decentralised. However, there is a serious drawback to this article, namely that it is not applicable to all cases but deals with revocation of nationality only. There is no suggestion that these safeguards should equally be in place where, for example, the claim to nationality at birth has been refused. Thus on the basis of this instrument alone, there is no procedural protection in place against arbitrary deprivation of nationality beyond the context of denationalisation.

2.2 International human rights law

As we have already noted, the arbitrary deprivation of nationality is generally considered to be forbidden under international law. This overall prohibition covers the elements of unlawfulness of decisions on the attribution of nationality and lack of a meaningful review mechanism. But international law also offers us the more general notions of due process and of an effective remedy, which are prescribed in a number of instruments. On the one hand, there is the guarantee of an effective remedy in cases where an individual's fundamental rights have been violated. Thus the International Covenant on Civil and Political Rights, following suit with the Universal Declaration, obliges state parties to "ensure that any person whose rights

---

reinstated. Betty de Hart; Kees Groenendijk, "Multiple Nationality: The Practice of Germany and the Netherlands" in R. Cholewinski (ed) *International Migration Law*, TMC Asser Press, The Hague: 2007.

[88] Emphasis added. Article 8, paragraph 4 of the 1961 Convention on the Reduction of Statelessness.

or freedoms as herein recognised are violated shall have an effective remedy".[89] A person who feels that their right to (acquire a) nationality has been violated must therefore be able to lodge a complaint.[90]

On the other hand there are the elaborations of the right to a – fair and public – hearing, in the context of both criminal and civil suits: "In the determination of any criminal charge against him, or of his rights and obligations in a suit at law, everyone shall be entitled to a fair and public hearing by the competent, independent and impartial tribunal established by law".[91] However, the difficulty here is whether cases involving the determination of nationality could be regarded as *civil* suits for the purposes of such provisions. The Human Rights Committee has yet to deal with the question of the applicability of this right to a fair hearing to nationality disputes and generally defers interpretation of "rights and obligations in a suit at law" to each state party's domestic law.[92] Meanwhile, the European Court of Human Rights has been called upon to rule on this matter. In the case of X. v. Austria, the Court explained that

> the applicant complains that he was deprived of his Austrian citizenship without even a fair hearing. He alleges a violation of article 6(1) of the Convention [...] The provisions or this Article, however, apply exclusively to proceedings which deal with "the determination of... civil rights and obligations or of any criminal charge". Accordingly, they do not apply to the above proceedings instituted by the applicant since they clearly did not determine a criminal charge brought against him and his civil rights and obligations were not involved as it is the prerogative of the State to regulate citizenship and the relevant rules constitute public law. The proceedings in question, therefore, were of a public law nature.[93]

---

[89] Article 2, paragraph 3 of the International Covenant on Civil and Political Rights. Article 8 of the Universal Declaration of Human Rights states: "Everyone has the right to an effective remedy by the competent national tribunals for acts violating fundamental rights granted him by the constitution or the law". A similar provision is included in article 25 of the American Convention on Human Rights.

[90] The Human Rights Committee "attaches importance to States Parties' establishing appropriate judicial and administrative mechanisms for addressing claims of rights violations under domestic law". See Human Rights Committee, *General Comment No. 31: Nature of the General Legal Obligations Imposed on States Parties to the covenant,* CCPR/C/21/Rev.1/Add.13, Geneva: 26 May 2004, paragraph 15.

[91] Article 14 of the International Covenant on Civil and Political Rights. A similar guarantee can be found in article 8 of the American Convention on Human Rights and article 6 of the European Convention on Human Rights. See also article 7 of the African Charter on Human and Peoples' Rights.

[92] The Committee has however found that the protection offered under article 14 of the ICCPR "does not apply to extradition, expulsion and deportation procedures" – arguably a similar field to nationality decisions being an area of public law involving the determination of legal status. UN Human Rights Committee, *General Comment 32 on Article 14: Right to equality before courts and tribunals and to a fair trial,* CCPR/C/GC/32, Geneva: 23 August 2007, para. 17 (Replacing *General Comment 13 on Article 14: Equality before the courts and the Right to a Fair and Public Hearing by an Independent Court Established by Law,* A/39/40, 13 April 1984).

[93] European Court of Human Rights, *Case of X. v. Austria,* Application No. 5212/71, Decision on Admissability, 5 October 1972. Moreover, in relation to the applicability of the same provision to questions regarding immigration law, this Court also determined that "decisions regarding the entry, stay and deportation of aliens do not concern the determination of an applicant's civil rights or

Within the European regional context then, decisions relating to nationality are not subject to the guarantees encapsulated in the right to a fair hearing. When the Inter-American *Commission* on Human Rights was presented with the same question in the context of the case of *Yean and Bosico v. Dominican Republic,* it sided with the claimants by determining that the Dominican state had violated articles 8 and 25 of the American Convention – the right to a fair trial and the right to judicial protection – by failing to ensure access to an effective appeals procedure in relation to the decision on nationality attribution.[94] Regrettably, the Inter-American Court failed to rule on the substance of this particular allegation due to a procedural technicality in the case - not because the charge necessarily lacked merit.[95] An opportunity was thereby lost to clarify the scope of application of this type of fair trial provision. It therefore remains unclear what the value of these particular provisions is in relation to nationality matters.

It is certainly disappointing that human rights instruments are not any more specific in their enunciation of the procedural obligations of states in the particular context of nationality attribution. While this may seem like an unnecessary and unlikely level of detail to expect of human rights provisions, it is interesting to note that the International Covenant on Civil and Political Rights *does* provide a greatly detailed account of the duties of states to offer procedural guarantees in the event of the expulsion of a non-national:

> An alien lawfully in the territory of a State Party to the present Covenant may be expelled therefrom only in pursuance of a decision reached in accordance with law and shall, except where compelling reasons of national security otherwise require, be allowed to submit the reasons against his expulsion and have the case reviewed by, and be represented for the purpose before, the competent authority or a person or persons especially designated by the competent authority.[96]

This article is designed to protect aliens against arbitrary expulsion. Not only may there be no collective expulsions or discriminatory decisions on expulsion,[97] but the decision must be in accordance with the law and there must be due process. In this, it shows very many parallels with the way in which the prohibition of arbitrary deprivation of nationality is commonly understood. What is different about this provision is that the content of the duty to provide due process in this context is further elaborated: there must be an opportunity to request a review of the decision, the complainant must be able to submit reasons against the decision and he may organise representation in pleading his case. Although the meaning that is thereby

obligations or of a criminal charge against him". European Court of Human Rights, *Case of Maaouia v. France,* No. 39652/98, 5 October 2000, para. 40.

[94] Inter-American Court on Human Rights, *Case of Yean and Bosico v. Dominican Republic,* Series C, Case 130, 8 September 2005, para. 198.

[95] Inter-American Court on Human Rights, *Case of Yean and Bosico v. Dominican Republic,* Series C, Case 130, 8 September 2005, para. 201.

[96] Article 13 of the International Covenant on Civil and Political Rights.

[97] Human Rights Committee, *General Comment 15: The position of aliens under the Covenant,* A/41/40, Geneva: 1986, para. 10.

given to the due process guarantee may provide inspiration for decisions relating to nationality attribution, the lack of an equivalent to this provision in relation to the denationalisation of citizens or the arbitrary deprivation of nationality in any international human rights instrument illustrates a missed opportunity to deal more decisively with this important question.

Only the European Convention on Nationality is more specific in its demands of states in the area of due process in nationality attribution.[98] The reference in its article on the competence of states in nationality matters, and thereafter throughout the text, to the need to regulate the attribution of nationality (in a certain way) in domestic law is evidence of the non-acceptance of illegal deprivation of nationality.[99] This is also an element of the principle prohibiting arbitrary deprivation of nationality which is included separately in the Convention.[100] Then, in chapter IV on "Procedures relating to nationality" a number of additional due process conditions are set. Each state party is to ensure that applications or decisions relating to the attribution of nationality will:

- be processed within a reasonable time *(article 10)*
- contain reasons in writing *(article 11)*
- be subject to reasonable fees *(article 13, paragraph 1)*
- be open to an administrative or judicial review *(article 12)*, the fee for which may not be an obstacle for applicants *(article 13, paragraph 2)*

As an instrument that concentrates solely on nationality matters, the European Convention on Nationality hereby provides strict, concrete guidelines to states in guaranteeing due process in relation to nationality attribution. While this treaty binds only state parties, the rendition of the content of "due process" does provide a valuable insight into what may be understood under the procedural demands of the principle on arbitrary deprivation of nationality.[101]

Another matter that comes to light in the perusal of the European Convention on Nationality is that international law is not just concerned with preventing unlawful denationalisation or ensuring the existence of an effective remedy in cases of withdrawal of nationality: the importance of such formalities in the decision-making process is also recognised in relation to the conferral of nationality, either at birth or through naturalisation. The procedural obligations of states under the

[98] Article 17 of the International Law Commission Draft Articles on Nationality of Natural Persons in relation to the Succession of States includes "procedures relating to nationality issues", specifying that applications are to be processed without due delay and that relevant decisions shall be issued in writing and be open to effective review. The European Convention on the avoidance of statelessness in relation to State Succession also details procedural guarantees. However, neither of these instruments has entered into force.

[99] Article 3, paragraph 1 and thereafter, European Convention on Nationality.

[100] Article 4, paragraph c, European Convention of Nationality.

[101] Note that the same detailed procedural requirements are repeated in article 12 of the Council of Europe, *Council of Europe Convention on the avoidance of statelessness in relation to State succession - Explanatory Report,* Strasbourg: 2006.

European Convention on Nationality are valid for decisions relating to the "acquisition, retention, loss, recovery or certification" of citizenship.[102] Universal and regional human rights instruments seemingly take a similar approach. Due process is to be ensured in relation to any decisions on nationality attribution, also those where attribution of nationality at birth is at stake[103] and even in the context of naturalisation proceedings:

> The Committee is [...] concerned that according to legislation still in force decisions taken in accordance with [naturalisation] procedures are not subject to legal review. The Committee is of the view that the right to appeal against decisions, in particular arbitrary or discriminatory ones, in matters relating to naturalisation has to be made an integral part of the policy on naturalisation.[104]

In this regard, the procedural protections offered by international (human rights) law are superior to those contained within the 1961 Convention on the Reduction of Statelessness which provides such guarantees only in the context of denationalisation.

3 Conclusion

"Arbitrary deprivation of nationality" is a phrase that covers a number of distinct problems. It deals with situations of denationalisation but also of refusal of access to nationality, for example at birth or through naturalisation. It refers to cases where the deprivation of nationality is the result of discrimination, so-called "denial of citizenship",[105] but also where it is unlawful or unaccompanied by adequate procedural safeguards. It is a source of statelessness where an individual is revoked of his only existing bond of nationality or where he is refused access to the citizenship of any state.[106] As such, the arbitrary deprivation of nationality is of serious concern to the international community and a legitimate subject for this chapter, the second to deal with the origins of statelessness. This time, the assessment of the 1961 Convention on the Reduction of Statelessness yielded less positive findings.

In tackling the grave issue of denial of citizenship, the 1961 Statelessness Convention demonstrated a number of serious shortcomings. To begin with, it listed only four grounds on which deprivation of nationality is considered *discriminatory* and thereby prohibited. The most notable shortfall is the failure to include gender in

[102] See articles 10 to 13 of the European Convention on Nationality.

[103] Inter-American Court on Human Rights, *Case of Yean and Bosico v. Dominican Republic,* Series C, Case 130, 8 September 2005.

[104] CERD, *Concluding Observations: Switzerland,* A/57/18, New York: 2002, para. 251.

[105] The illumination of the equivalence of the phrase "denial of citizenship" with "discriminatory deprivation of nationality" was of itself an important conclusion because, in consequence, to label a situation as denial of citizenship is to determine that it is in violation of the international norm prohibiting arbitrary deprivation of nationality.

[106] This will typically consist of the rejection of a claim to nationality at birth or – where already stateless - through the refusal of an application for naturalisation from the only state with which the person has a genuine link.

this list when this has clearly become a forbidden ground for differentiation in relation to nationality attribution under international human rights law.[107] Secondly, from the formulation and positioning of the article on denial of citizenship in the 1961 Convention, it is apparent that the provision only addresses discriminatory *denationalisation.* Of the two large stateless caseloads resulting from the denial of citizenship that were introduced in this chapter – the Kurds in Syria and the children of (presumed) Haitian descent in the Dominican Republic – the 1961 Statelessness Convention thereby addresses only the first. In contrast, the human rights field admits that denial of citizenship may equally result from discriminatory refusal of access to citizenship at birth or later in life, thus allowing situations such as that of the Dominican-born children of Haitian descent to also be dealt with.

A further considerable weakness of the 1961 Statelessness Convention is the lack of scope for expanding the protection against discriminatory deprivation of nationality, for example by developing the norm over time to reflect any changes in the position of states. This problem stems from three main factors. Firstly, there is no general prohibition of discrimination in the document nor an overall prohibition of arbitrary deprivation of nationality that could be interpreted according to the prevailing international law. Secondly, the list of prohibited grounds of discrimination in article 9 of the 1961 Convention is limitative, offering no room to read additional elements into the text. And finally, the instrument lacks a genuine supervisory mechanism with the ability to interpret and further develop the convention's norms. Where the human rights field shows the progressive development of the understanding of *discriminatory* deprivation of nationality over time, towards greater protection of the individual, the 1961 Statelessness Convention has stood still. Thus overall, international human rights law offers broader protection against denial of citizenship: with regard to discriminatory denationalisation, many more grounds for differentiation are outlawed and discrimination in access to nationality is also prohibited.

On a more positive note, discriminatory deprivation of nationality on "political grounds" *is* prohibited under the 1961 Statelessness Convention whereas this element was overlooked in the European Convention on Nationality and was only introduced into the UN Human Rights Commission's resolution on the arbitrary deprivation of nationality in 2005. Seeing as denationalisation on political grounds is a genuine issue in young, multiparty democracies, the clear prohibition of such action by the 1961 Convention is obviously beneficial in the prevention of statelessness. Moreover, the prohibition of discriminatory deprivation of nationality as included in the 1961 Statelessness Convention forbids discriminatory deprivation of nationality whether provided for by law or not. This allows cases of statelessness deriving from abusive law-making to be addressed, such as the situation of the Rohingyas of Myanmar.[108] It must, however, be admitted that international human rights law also covers cases of denial of citizenship where it is effected by discriminatory municipal laws, thus the 1961 Convention merely reflects the general scope of international law in this respect.

[107] In chapter IV we saw how gender discrimination in nationality law may contribute to the creation of statelessness.
[108] See note 21.

Lastly in this chapter we considered the approach of the 1961 Convention on the Reduction of Statelessness to the other dimensions of arbitrary deprivation of nationality that may play a part in the creation of statelessness: the unlawful deprivation of nationality and the absence of effective procedural safeguards such as a review mechanism. Here again, it was discovered that the 1961 Convention deals only with these matters in the specific context of denationalisation. This stands in stark contrast to sources of human rights law which prohibit any unlawful decisions on nationality attribution under the overall prohibition of arbitrary deprivation of nationality and provide for the right to an effective remedy where a violation of fundamental rights – including the right to a nationality – is at stake. Moreover, the right to a fair hearing in the context of decisions that effect a persons rights and duties under the law may also offer an avenue for ensuring an effective remedy in the context of nationality disputes.[109] Thus under international human rights law, the protections against all elements of arbitrary deprivation of nationality are generally strong and well developed while the 1961 Convention on the Reduction of Statelessness leaves several serious gaps that will undoubtedly allow new cases of statelessness to be created. Yet in spite of this largely positive conclusion as to the state of international law, populations around the world continue to be rendered stateless through arbitrary deprivation of nationality in one manifestation or another. This fact points to a severe problem of enforcement, an issue that we will come back to in detail once the evaluation of the content of international obligations towards the prevention of statelessness is complete.[110]

[109] It should be noted that for the concretisation of these procedural guarantees, much could be learnt from the detailed prohibition of arbitrary expulsion of aliens under article 13 of the International Covenant on Civil and Political Rights as well as from Chapter IV on "Procedures relating to nationality" of the European Convention on Nationality.
[110] In chapter VIII, section 4.

CHAPTER VI

ADDRESSING STATELESSNESS IN THE CONTEXT OF STATE SUCCESSION

For an existing state with a fixed territory, regulating the acquisition and loss of nationality is relatively straightforward. There is already a body of nationals, so the state need only define the criteria for the attribution of nationality to new arrivals (both immigrants and newborns) and perhaps provide for the possibility of loss, deprivation or renunciation of nationality under certain circumstances. These minor additions and subtractions do not have a drastic impact on the overall composition of the body of citizens. However, a new state must define itself, mould its own identity and delineate its territory and population – deliberate about who belongs and who does not.[1] When sovereignty over a territory enters new hands, the actual population occupying the land need not change,[2] raising the question: what happens to the inhabitants of the territory which undergoes the change in sovereignty?[3] This is considered to be among the most difficult issues raised by the succession of states.[4] It is also one of the most important, particularly when a new state is born, because, through the enjoyment and exercise of citizenship, "all persons concerned by State succession should be able to participate in the building up of these States and in the crucial period of setting up new State structures".[5] However, in determining who is and who is not a national in the context of state succession,

[1] In the context of state succession, the decision as to who is "us" and who is "them" is particularly symbolic and issues an important message as to the identity of the state. Kees Groenendijk, 'Nationality, Minorities and Statelessness. The Case of the Baltic States', in *Helsinki Monitor,* Vol. 4, 1993, page 16.
[2] Ruth Donner, "Chapter 5: Nationality and State Succession" in *The Regulation of Nationality in International Law*, Transnational Publishers, New York: 1994, page 248.
[3] Jeffrey Blackman, 'State Succession and Statelessness: The Emerging Right to an Effective Nationality under International Law', in *Michigan Journal of International law,* Vol. 19, 1998, page 1145; Ian Brownlie, *Principles of Public International Law*, Oxford University Press, Oxford: 2003, page 908.
[4] There are difficulties in the determination of the "manner in which change of nationality may be brought about [...] which categories of person are susceptible of having their nationality affected by change of sovereignty [and] the question whether or not the inhabitants of absorbed territory may avoid a change of nationality". D.P. O'Connell, *State succession in municipal and international law*, Cambridge University Press, Cambridge: 1967, page 497.
[5] Roland Schärer, *Statelessness in Relation to State Succession. Feasibility Study: The Necessity of an Additional Instrument to the European Convention on Nationality,* Council of Europe Committee of Experts on Nationality, Strasbourg, 12 October 2001, page 4.

there is a "particularly high potential"[6] that the decision taken will lead to large-scale statelessness as certain areas of the affected population may be overlooked.

In fact, the redrawing of international borders has proven to be a considerable source of statelessness historically. One of the oldest known groups of stateless persons was the "Heimatlosen" – literally *homeless* or *rootless* – whose statelessness resulted from the dissolution of Austria-Hungary and the settlement of the 1919 Peace Treaties.[7] Statelessness was produced not only in the reshuffling of territories in the aftermath of the First and Second World Wars, but also as a result of the decolonisation process in the 1950s and 1960s and more recently in the disintegration of a number of federal states. Since the end of World War II, more than one hundred new independent states have been formed[8] and many of the large groups of stateless persons found in the world today can trace the origin of their plight to some form of territorial transfer. The Estate Tamils in Sri Lanka, the Tatars in the Ukraine, the Bihari in Bangladesh and the ex-Russians in Latvia and Estonia are but a few examples. Indeed, the numerous sudden cases of state succession in the early 1990s and the ensuing nationality disputes were a major factor in the revival of interest in statelessness by the international community.[9] Moreover,

> throughout history the death and birth of states has been a bloody process, usually fuelled by ethnic hatred and often entailing the commission of mass atrocities against vulnerable minority groups.[10]

This has meant that discrimination, marginalisation and the playing out of old vendettas has often accompanied such events, compounding the problem of nationality attribution and leading to many instances of denial of citizenship in the context of state succession.[11] Fortunately, like the current attitude to the creation of statelessness generally, there is a "growing awareness among States of the compelling need to fight the plight of statelessness [...] in relation to the succession of states".[12] Thus, after elaborating on the nature of state succession and the impact

---

[6] Roland Schärer, 'The Council of Europe and the Reduction of Statelessness', in *Refugee Survey Quarterly,* Vol. 25, 2006, page 33.

[7] Hannah Arendt, "The Decline of the Nation-State and the End of the Rights of Man" in *The origins of totalitarianism*, Harcourt Brace Jovanovich, New York: 1948; C. Luella Gettys, 'The Effect of Changes of Sovereignty on Nationality', in *American Journal of International Law,* Vol. 21, 1927; Manley Hudson, *Report on Nationality, including Statelessness,* A/CN.4/50, 21 February 1952, pages 18-19.

[8] Malcolm Shaw, *International Law*, Cambridge University Press, Cambridge: 2003, page 861.

[9] Consider the collapse of the USSR and the Socialist Federal Republic of Yugoslavia. UNHCR, "Statelessness and Citizenship" in *The State of the World's Refugees - A Humanitarian Agenda*, Oxford University Press, Oxford: 1997, page 227.

[10] Jeffrey Blackman, 'State Succession and Statelessness: The Emerging Right to an Effective Nationality under International Law', in *Michigan Journal of International law,* Vol. 19, 1998, page 1141.

[11] Numerous recent examples testify to the overlapping issues of state succession and arbitrary deprivation of nationality, including the aforementioned Bihari in Bangladesh and former Russians in Latvia and Estonia.

[12] Václav Mikulka, *Third report on Nationality in relation to the Succession of States,* A/CN.4/480, Geneva: 27 February 1997, page 42.

that it has on matters of nationality, we will turn to the response of international law to the problem of statelessness in this context.

1 State succession and the nationality of persons affected

State succession is the official term used to describe the transfer of territory or sovereignty and has been defined as: "the replacement of one State by another in the responsibility for the international relations of territory".[13] The phrase covers four main situations, namely the unification or dissolution of a state, the transfer of territory from one state to another and the separation of part of a state.[14] Sovereignty over a particular patch of land is transferred from a "predecessor state" to a "successor state". In principle citizenship matters in the context of state succession, as otherwise, must be settled by the nationality laws of the states concerned.[15] If the issue is not comprehensively addressed or if the policies adopted by the respective states are not harmonised (for example by treaty), there is a risk that some individuals will be overlooked. In essence, statelessness then arises from a negative conflict of laws situation that has been created in the process of the transfer of territory or sovereignty and the concurrent adoption of new nationality regulations.[16] Additionally, as we have already noted, the exclusion of particular population groups from citizenship in the context of state succession may be down to discriminatory deprivation of nationality.[17] Therefore, much that has already been said about the technical causes of statelessness as well as statelessness arising from arbitrary deprivation of nationality is equally relevant to the problem of statelessness in the context of the succession of states. Nevertheless, the circumstance of succession is not altogether irrelevant since – as we will discover - it generates specific obligations for the states concerned under international law.

While each case of state succession is unique thanks to the specific historical and political circumstances, for the purposes of the nationality question it is sufficient to distinguish between two broad categories: universal succession and partial succession.[18] In the event of universal succession, the predecessor state has been entirely deposed and actually ceases to exist. A modern-day example is the disintegration of the USSR, a federation that was extinguished to make way for the

---

[13] This is the definition of state succession as found in international instruments on the subject, such as in Article 2 of the Vienna Convention on Succession of States in Respect of Treaties, 1978; Article 2 of the 1999 Draft Articles on Nationality of Natural Persons in Relation to the Succession of States; and Article 1 of the 2006 European Convention on the avoidance of statelessness in relation to State Succession.

[14] The distinction between these types of state succession can also be found in the Vienna Convention on Succession of States in Respect of Treaties, 1978 and the 1999 Draft Articles on Nationality of Natural Persons in Relation to the Succession of States.

[15] Malcolm Shaw, *International Law*, Cambridge University Press, Cambridge: 2003, page 908.

[16] Affecting both the persons immediately concerned and successive generations thereafter. Manley Hudson, *Report on Nationality, including Statelessness*, A/CN.4/50, 21 February 1952, page 46.

[17] Note the overlap in cases cited in the context of this chapter with those included in the report on denial of citizenship by the Advisory Board on Human Security which was discussed in chapter V.

[18] Paul Weis, *Nationality and Statelessness in International Law*, Kluwer Academic Publishers Group, Dordrecht: 1979, page 136; Ruth Donner, "Chapter 5: Nationality and State Succession" in *The Regulation of Nationality in International Law*, Transnational Publishers, New York: 1994, page 249.

emergence of 15 independent republics in the early 1990s.[19] With the extinction of the state, its nationality becomes obsolete. All individuals who were once nationals of the predecessor state are dependent on the successor state(s) or third countries with which they may have a genuine link to acquire a replacement nationality. After December 1991, it was simply no longer possible to hold the nationality of the former Soviet Union, leaving 287 million people with a new nationality or with the determination of their citizenship pending.[20] In such situations the risk of statelessness is obviously greatest.

The other basic class of state succession, partial succession, is precisely what its name denotes: part of the territory of a state undergoes a change in sovereignty through acquisition by another state or the formation of a new state. In this case, the predecessor state continues to exist. The classic example of partial succession is the decolonisation process that changed the face of the globe during the latter half of the 20th century. The colonising powers withdrew or were forcibly ousted, leaving sovereignty over the territory in the hands of a newly independent state. For example, while the British Empire crumbled, the state of Great Britain subsisted and with it the British nationality. Meanwhile, the newly independent states needed a population of their own and compiled nationality acts to determine who belonged to their body of citizens. With partial succession, there are therefore at least two nationalities involved: those of the predecessor and successor state(s). Not only is the question raised as to when an individual is to acquire the nationality of the successor state, but also as to when the nationality of the predecessor state is to be lost.[21] Here, the possibility arises of a negative conflict of laws or an inter-state dispute over nationality, resulting in statelessness.

In the past, the general practice traced with regard to the question of the nationality of persons affected by state succession reveals that

> as a rule, successor States have adopted specific legislation conferring their nationality on former nationals of the predecessor State who continued to have their habitual residence in the transferred territory.[22]

Most commonly then, the nationality of the people has followed the change of sovereignty over the land.[23] A closer look at the treaties settled between states and

[19] These are the twelve states that went on to join the Commonwealth of Independent States (CIS) and the Baltic states of Estonia, Latvia and Lithuania.

[20] UNHCR, "Statelessness and Citizenship" in *The State of the World's Refugees - A Humanitarian Agenda*, Oxford University Press, Oxford: 1997, page 233.

[21] Paul Weis, *Nationality and Statelessness in International Law*, Kluwer Academic Publishers Group, Dordrecht: 1979, page 145.

[22] European Commission for Democracy through Law, *Consequences of state succession for nationality*, Strasbourg: 10 February 1997, para. 8.

[23] This assessment of the usual practice of states can be traced in much of the literature on the subject. See for example Ian Brownlie, 'The Relations of Nationality in Public International Law', in *British Yearbook of International Law*, Vol. 39, 1963, page 320; D.P. O'Connell, *State succession in municipal and international law*, Cambridge University Press, Cambridge: 1967, page 499; Jeffrey Blackman, 'State Succession and Statelessness: The Emerging Right to an Effective Nationality under International Law', in *Michigan Journal of International law*, Vol. 19, 1998, pages 1161-1163; and more recently in Nida M. Gelazis, 'The European Union and the Statelessness Problem in the Baltic States', in *European*

the laws adopted to regulate the nationality of persons affected by succession actually exposes several mechanisms used to identify exactly which people's citizenship will undergo such a change.[24] Breaking these down, we see that the determination of nationality tends to be based on one or more of the following: previous nationality, territorial jurisdiction and ethnicity. This has resulted in three basic models for the initial attribution of nationality by the successor state, after which time, the regular mix of *jus soli, jus sanguinis* and *jus domicilli* principles return to further regulate the future conferral of nationality to newborns and newcomers.

The strategy that involves conferring nationality of the successor state on the basis of previous nationality is known as the "restored citizenship model". This is often favoured by states that have regained independence after a period of (perceived) occupation or incorporation by another state.[25] Simply put, everyone who possessed the nationality of the state before it was occupied is entitled to that nationality once more, now that the country is once again independent.[26] So too are the descendents of such persons. This was the model adopted by Latvia and Estonia upon partition from the Soviet Union in 1991. All three of the Baltic States – Latvia, Estonia and Lithuania – enjoyed a brief period of independence after the First World War, before being annexed and incorporated into the Soviet Union in 1940.[27] As noted above, the dissolution of the USSR in 1991 meant that Soviet citizenship ceased to exist. The decision by Latvia and Estonia to attribute nationality only to those persons who were citizens before the occupation of 1940 and their descendents meant that many people resident on Latvian or Estonian territory in 1991 were excluded from the citizenship of these successor states. During the period of Soviet incorporation, many thousands of Russians emigrated to these territories and they were the ones who were now overlooked by the new nationality laws. Having lost their Soviet citizenship, if they wanted to gain Latvian or Estonian nationality they were forced to resort to applying for it under the strict and complex naturalisation procedures that were put in place.[28] As former USSR-citizens, they could alternatively apply for nationality of the Russian Federation, however, this also involved meeting various conditions and proved to be an

Journal of Migration and Law, Vol. 6, 2004, page 236. However, this practice is not considered to reflect an international legal norm. Paul Weis, *Nationality and Statelessness in International Law*, Kluwer Academic Publishers Group, Dordrecht: 1979, pages 143-144.

[24] The peace treaties that were settled after the First World War provided the first evidence of additional considerations in regulating the nationality of persons affected by state succession. C. Luella Gettys, 'The Effect of Changes of Sovereignty on Nationality', in *American Journal of International Law,* Vol. 21, 1927.

[25] Peter van Krieken, 'Disintegration and statelessness', in *Netherlands Quarterly of Human Rights,* Vol. 12, 1994, page 26; Nida M. Gelazis, 'The European Union and the Statelessness Problem in the Baltic States', in *European Journal of Migration and Law,* Vol. 6, 2004, page 228.

[26] This model may also be used in the dissolution of federal states where prior to state succession individuals held both citizenship of the federation and nationality of one of its constituent units or republics. The previous nationality that is used as a basis for the bestowal of citizenship after state succession is this bond with the constituent unit that is now part of the territory of the successor state.

[27] UNHCR, "Statelessness and Citizenship" in *The State of the World's Refugees - A Humanitarian Agenda*, Oxford University Press, Oxford: 1997, page 238.

[28] UNHCR, "Statelessness and Citizenship" in *The State of the World's Refugees - A Humanitarian Agenda*, Oxford University Press, Oxford: 1997, page 238.

unpopular choice.[29] The overall result: large-scale statelessness in both territories.[30] In 2007, UNHCR estimated the residual number of stateless cases in Latvia and Estonia to be approximately 420,000 and 136,000 respectively, all tracing the origin of their plight to the succession of states that occurred over a decade before.[31]

When attributing nationality according to territorial jurisdiction, the basic rule that is reflected in the legislation of successor states is as follows:

> Everyone who at the time of independence is legally residing in the country concerned is entitled to its citizenship.[32]

This model is called "zero-option" and was adopted by many African states when they gained independence as part of the decolonisation process as well as by the 12 countries to emerge from the former Soviet Union alongside the three Baltic States.[33] It coincides with the feudal concept of territorial sovereignty where "ownership" of population and property follows ownership of the land. Like the previous model, this strategy for attribution of nationality to an initial body of citizens is not without its problems, particularly in the event of universal succession

---

[29] Russian Federation citizenship could be denied for reasons such as previous criminal convictions or party affiliation. In 1993 it was reported that of the 600,000 persons of non-Estonian origin residing in Estonia, the number of persons that planned to apply for Russian nationality was only 30,000. Moreover, "independent observers have confirmed the impression that the large majority of the Russian-speaking population of the Baltic states for various reasons prefer to live in their country of residence and to acquire its nationality". Kees Groenendijk, 'Nationality, Minorities and Statelessness. The Case of the Baltic States', in *Helsinki Monitor,* Vol. 4, 1993, pages 18-19.

[30] Lithuania, the third Baltic State, adopted instead a model that combined aspects of the restored citizenship model with a system of attributing nationality based on residence, thereby limiting the incidence of statelessness on its own territory. Peter van Krieken, 'Disintegration and statelessness', in *Netherlands Quarterly of Human Rights,* Vol. 12, 1994, page 26. This difference in approach has been explained as reflecting the difference in extent of "russification" of the three territories. Due to in and out migration in the Soviet era, the population in Estonia and Latvia changed its face dramatically. For example, 75.5% of the population of Latvia was ethnic Latvian in 1935 and by 1995 this had dropped to just 55.1%. Meanwhile, in Lithuania, the demographic makeup changed relatively little over the same period. Thus, "the fact that Lithuanians felt that they could accommodate a sizeable proportion of non-Lithuanians (around 20 percent) without sacrificing their democratic ambitions, sovereignty or native language and culture, was decisive in their decision to adopt a relatively liberal policy on naturalising Soviet-era migrants". Nida M. Gelazis, 'The European Union and the Statelessness Problem in the Baltic States', in *European Journal of Migration and Law,* Vol. 6, 2004, page 228.

[31] UNHCR, *Global Trends 2006*, 15 June 2007, table 14. A detailed study of the citizenship issues to arise following the independence of the Baltic states can be found in Ineta Ziemele, *State Continuity and Nationality: The Baltic States and Russia. Past, Present and Future as Defined by International Law,* Martinus Nijhoff Publishers, Leiden: 2005; and Nida Gelazis, "An Evaluation of International Instruments that Address the Condition of Statelessness: A Case Study of Estonia and Latvia" in R. Cholewinski (ed) *International Migration Law*, T.M.C. Asser Press, The Hague: 2007.

[32] Peter van Krieken, 'Disintegration and statelessness', in *Netherlands Quarterly of Human Rights,* Vol. 12, 1994, page 26. Usually, nationality is only extended to persons who were nationals of the predecessor state and are resident on the territory of the successor state, leaving the citizenship of nationals from third countries unaffected.

[33] UNHCR, "Statelessness and Citizenship" in *The State of the World's Refugees - A Humanitarian Agenda*, Oxford University Press, Oxford: 1997, page 236; Peter van Krieken, 'Disintegration and statelessness', in *Netherlands Quarterly of Human Rights,* Vol. 12, 1994, page 26.

where the predecessor state (and its nationality) ceases to exist. This was evidenced in the experience of the Ukraine.

Upon gaining independence, the Ukraine adopted a "Declaration on State Sovereignty" in which it determined that its initial body of citizens shall be comprised of former Soviet nationals who had their permanent residence on Ukrainian soil on the date of independence (24th of August, 1991).[34] This "zero option" approach to citizenship does not deal with persons who at the time reside outside the territory over which sovereignty is transferred but are, nevertheless, affected by the succession of states. It is indeed highly unlikely that all nationals of the predecessor state actually live on its soil at the moment of transfer of territory. While this issue may only affect small numbers of emigrants, in the example of the Ukraine there was a large population group that was thereby exposed to the risk of statelessness: the so-called "Formerly Deported Persons" (FDPs). This group, composed mainly of Crimean Tatars, consists of those who were deported from the Crimea (now a region in the Ukraine) very abruptly in May 1944 upon being accused of "siding with the Nazis".[35] Around the time that the Ukraine gained independence, these FDPs and their descendents started returning to the Crimea. Those who managed to settle and register in the area before the promulgation of the Ukrainian citizenship act were automatically entitled to nationality. However, over 100,000 FDPs returned to the Ukraine after the nationality legislation entered into force. Of these, some 25,000 also missed out on the opportunity to acquire citizenship of one of the other newly independent states through this move and were rendered stateless.[36] Thanks to bilateral and multilateral efforts, as well as technical support from UNHCR, the statelessness of many of the FDPs who have (re)settled in the Ukraine was resolved by the end of the 1990s.[37] Yet to this day, many Formerly Deported Persons continue to return to the region, testing the aptness of the newly amended and simplified Ukrainian naturalisation law in overcoming any issues of statelessness to the full. On the one hand, this example therefore shows that zero-option citizenship models can also produce statelessness in the context of

[34] The citizenship legislation that was consequently adopted put this policy into effect by automatically granting such persons citizenship unless they already held another nationality or objected to the acquisition of Ukrainian citizenship. UNHCR, *Overview of UNHCR's Citizenship Campaign in Crimea,* Simferopol: December 2000, pages 5-6.

[35] UNHCR, *Crimean Tatars Receive Help from UNHCR to Return Home*, 9 June 2005, accessible via http://www.unhcr.org.

[36] Many had fallen through the gap between the Ukrainian and Uzbek citizenship acts, both of which adopted the zero-option strategy. Uzbek citizenship was granted to residents of the territory on the 28th of July 1992.

[37] For a full discussion of the campaign for the resolution of the statelessness of Ukraine's Formerly Deported Persons, see UNHCR, *Overview of UNHCR's Citizenship Campaign in Crimea,* Simferopol: December 2000; and Hans Schodder, "Assisting the integration of formerly deported people in Crimea: ten years of UNHCR experiences" in *Beyond Borders,* Bulletin of UNHCR in Ukraine, 2005. It should, however, be noted that the legal status of the Crimean Tatars in the Ukraine remains disputed: the discussion has moved from one of citizenship status to one of national minority or indigenous person status and related rights. Oxana Shevel, "Crimean Tatars and the Ukrainian state: the challenge of politics, the use of law, and the meaning of rhetoric", paper delivered the Association for the Study of the Nationalities (ASN) Fifth Annual World Convention "Identity and the State: Nationalism And Sovereignty in a Changing World," Columbia University, New York, NY, April 13-15, 2000.

state succession, but it also illustrates the possibilities for addressing such situations by adopting tailor-made solutions to prevent or eliminate statelessness.

The third and final factor upon which nationality attribution has been based in the context of state succession is ethnicity. In the process of decolonisation, according to Weis:

> Ethnic considerations normally played a role in the determination of the criteria for the conferment of nationality although they are explicitly mentioned in the legislation of a few States only.[38]

He goes on to mention a number of twentieth century examples where this was the case, including Burma, Chad, Indonesia and Sierra Leone. Indeed an element of discrimination (be it often implicit or indirect) can be traced in the nationality acts adopted by many states that have been involved in state succession. The Latvian nationality law was criticised because it "seems to single out the ethnic Russian population as unsuitable to gain citizenship".[39] The citizenship policy of newly independent Sri Lanka (upon partition from India) and Bangladesh (upon separation from Pakistan) also indirectly targeted particular population groups. In Sri Lanka, the Ceylon Citizenship Act of 1948 required proof of birth in the country going back two generations which effectively ensured that the Estate Tamils were excluded from acquiring nationality.[40] Thereafter, the citizenship of this group remained a subject of dispute between India and Sri Lanka, only to be resolved in 2003 with a new legislative act granting the majority of these persons the nationality of Sri Lanka. In Bangladesh, citizenship was attributed at independence from West Pakistan according to territorial jurisdiction. However, the resident Bihari population, targeted as "Pakistani collaborators", saw their claim to Bangladeshi nationality rejected which rendered them stateless.[41] These last two examples serve also to illustrate that the risk of statelessness is equally real in the context of partial succession - whereby two or more nationalities are theoretically on offer – as a consequence of bilateral disputes between the states concerned.

As we move on to assess the approach of international law to this issue, these many different dimensions and variations of the problem of statelessness

[38] Paul Weis, *Nationality and Statelessness in International Law*, Kluwer Academic Publishers Group, Dordrecht: 1979, page 155.

[39] Nida M. Gelazis, 'The European Union and the Statelessness Problem in the Baltic States', in *European Journal of Migration and Law,* Vol. 6, 2004, page 233.

[40] The "estate Tamils" are persons of Indian origin who were brought to Sri Lanka by the British colonisers as labourers for the tea plantations. They and their descendents (numbering upwards of half a million persons in 2004) were rendered stateless in the partition of Sri Lanka from India. The requirement to establish birth in Sri Lanka going back two generations "essentially discriminated against Hill Tamils, many of whom returned to Tamil Nadu to give birth and most of whom could not produce documents to prove two generations of family born in Sri Lanka". UNHCR, *Sri Lanka makes citizens out of stateless tea pickers,* 2004, accessible via www.unhcr.ch; Katja Kerdel, *Stateless persons of Indian origin in Sri Lanka - an overview,* Colombo: 9 June 2004.

[41] To this day, the citizenship status of upwards of a quarter of a million "stranded Biharis" remains unclear with neither Pakistan nor Bangladesh accepting full responsibility for this group. Eric Paulsen, 'The citizenship status of the Urdu-speakers / Biharis in Bangladesh', in *Refugee Survey Quarterly,* Vol. 25, 2006; Maureen Lynch; Thatcher Cook, *Citizens of nowhere. The stateless Biharis of Bangladesh,* Washington: 2005.

resulting from the succession of states must be kept in mind. Before progressing to the discussion of international law there are two additional considerations that must be noted. The first relates to the question of a right of option for persons whose nationality is affected by state succession. This is a much discussed issue in literature on the impact of state succession on nationality. In essence it is suggested that where the citizenship of two or more states becomes available to an individual as a consequence of the succession of states, he should be entitled to opt for the nationality that he himself places the most value on or deems most appropriate.[42] While this may seem to be a "rich man's dilemma", as it concerns situations where multiple nationalities are on offer, it is not irrelevant to the problem of statelessness. The granting of the right of option has led to statelessness in the past where

> options have [...] been held invalid on the grounds of expiration of time limits or non-compliance with formalities prescribed for the exercise of the right of option or when the right was granted to particular groups only (racial, linguistic or religious minorities) because the optant was held not to belong to the eligible group.[43]

In addition, any policy which enables an individual to opt out of the citizenship of a country involved in state succession must be exercised diligently so as not to introduce the risk of statelessness – for example by allowing a person to repudiate the nationality offered by one successor state before ascertaining whether the citizenship of the predecessor state or another successor state is truly assured.[44] When we turn to the relevant international legal norms we will therefore also be looking at how they deal with the right of option.

The second residual issue that should briefly be noted here is the question to what extent international law – in particular international *treaty* law – is actually applicable to successor states. It has been suggested that even if there was an international convention dealing specifically with the nationality of persons affected by state succession,

---

[42] The practice of permitting the right of option has a long history. Initially it grew from the notion that a person should be able to opt out or refuse the nationality of a state which is being involuntarily imposed on them through automatic naturalisation in the context of state succession. Later, however, the value of the right of option came to be seen in the opportunity it provides to ensure that an individual holds the nationality of the state with which he has the closest genuine link. D.P. O'Connell, *State succession in municipal and international law*, Cambridge University Press, Cambridge: 1967, page 529; Paul Weis, *Nationality and Statelessness in International Law*, Kluwer Academic Publishers Group, Dordrecht: 1979, page 156 and further; Jeffrey Blackman, 'State Succession and Statelessness: The Emerging Right to an Effective Nationality under International Law', in *Michigan Journal of International law*, Vol. 19, 1998, page 1169; UNHCR and IPU, *Nationality and statelessness. A handbook for parliamentarians*, 2005, page 34.

[43] Manley Hudson, *Report on Nationality, including Statelessness*, A/CN.4/50, 21 February 1952.

[44] It is also worth noting that the availability of a right of option may be a useful tool in countering the problem of an ineffective nationality since it helps to promote the attribution of nationality according to a real and genuine link with a state and thereby increases the likelihood that the citizenship acquired will be an effective one.

> [it] would not be binding on successor states, which as newly-created subjects of international law are not signatories to [...] international instruments. Rather, new states are bound initially only by those norms that form part of customary international law.[45]

According to this line of reasoning, only international norms on nationality attribution in relation to the succession of states that have attained the status of customary international law would have any real impact. If this were the case, to devise a treaty that lays down obligations on both predecessor and successor states would be a futile exercise since successor states are by definition not a party to such instruments at the time of state succession. However, the effect of state succession on treaty commitments is still a hazy area of international law. The Vienna Convention on Succession of States in Respect of Treaties determines that in some cases the successor state will be bound by the treaty commitments of the predecessor state.[46] It depends very much on the kind of state succession as well as the type of treaty that is in question. In particular, it has been persuasively argued that the succession of states "does not effect obligations arising from human rights treaties".[47] Thus, in the context of this chapter, where human rights documents and other international instruments that are a clear concretisation of human rights norms are under the microscope, there is certainly scope for proposing that these commitments will be of real – rather than purely theoretical – relevance to the responsibilities of successor states as well as predecessor states in the circumstance of state succession. Moreover, the adoption of multiple provisions and even entire instruments devoted to tackling problems relating to nationality in the context of state succession is evidence of the conviction that successor states can be held to such international commitments.

2 The 1961 Convention on the Reduction of Statelessness

The discussion of statelessness arising in the context of state succession brings us to the final substantive article in the 1961 Statelessness Convention. Article 10 of the 1961 Convention on the Reduction of Statelessness reads:

> 1. Every treaty between Contracting States providing for the transfer of territory shall include provisions designed to secure that no person shall become stateless as a result of the transfer. A Contracting State shall use its best endeavours to secure that any such treaty made by it with a State which is not a Party to this Convention includes such provisions.

---

[45] Jeffrey Blackman, 'State Succession and Statelessness: The Emerging Right to an Effective Nationality under International Law', in *Michigan Journal of International law,* Vol. 19, 1998, page 1142.

[46] Vienna Convention on Succession of States in Respect of Treaties, 1978. Entered into force on the 6th of November 1996. As of 1 December 2006, the Convention has attracted just 21 state parties.

[47] This submission is based on an analysis of both recent state practice and the opinions expressed by such bodies as the International Labour Organisation, the International Committee of the Red Cross, the UN Commission on Human Rights and various United Nations Treaty Bodies. Menno Kamminga, 'State Succession in Respect of Human Rights Treaties', in *European Journal of International Law,* Vol. 7, 1996, page 484.

> 2. In the absence of such provisions a Contracting State to which territory is transferred or which otherwise acquires territory shall confer its nationality on such persons as would otherwise become stateless as a result of the transfer or acquisition.

Where UNHCR has explained the content of this article – as it has in various publications – it has basically summarised the obligation as meaning that "treaties shall ensure that statelessness does not occur as a result of a transfer of territory [and] where no treaty is signed, the State shall confer its nationality on those who would otherwise be stateless".[48] While this is the essence of the article, it is a somewhat oversimplified rendition of the rules housed in the text.

To begin with, the commitment to ensuring that any treaty in which the succession of states is organised will prevent statelessness from arising is actually formulated in less resolute terms. Paragraph 1, as cited above, determines merely that provisions "designed to secure" the avoidance of statelessness should be included in succession treaties. No words are spared on what sort of content could or should be given to such provisions, how stringent the implementation and monitoring of these arrangements should be or what action should be undertaken should the provisions fail to live up to their design. These shortcomings are particularly conspicuous in view of the norm elaborated in the second paragraph: where no arrangements have been made by treaty, a contracting state is obliged to actually grant citizenship to certain persons in order to prevent statelessness. What is striking here is that if states fail to ensure that the question of nationality is settled by treaty (put forward as the most desirable course of action under this article), the protection offered against statelessness may actually be greater.[49] Moreover, if the treaty provisions which are "designed to secure" that no-one is rendered stateless are ineffective, there is no further consequence because the existence of such provisions is of itself enough to meet the commitment under the 1961 Statelessness Convention.

By comparison then, the second paragraph of article 10 is much more satisfactory as it contains a concrete norm. It is clear about what action is to be taken: to avert statelessness, citizenship must be conferred on persons who would otherwise be left without a nationality due to the succession of states. It also pinpoints which state is thus obliged: the state "to which territory is transferred or which otherwise acquires territory". It thus falls upon the successor state to bestow nationality upon persons who would otherwise be stateless - a reflection of the notion that the population follows the territory in the change of sovereignty. Moreover, it does not limit the scope of application to only those persons who are,

[48] UNHCR, *Information and accession package: the 1954 Convention relating to the status of stateless persons and the 1961 Convention on the reduction of statelessness*, Geneva: January 1999, page 15. See also UNHCR and IPU, *Nationality and statelessness. A handbook for parliamentarians*, 2005, page 34.

[49] The International Law Commission explains the priority given to treaty arrangements as a reflection of the understanding that inter-state agreements to ensure the prevention of statelessness are generally likely to be more effective than individual domestic measures adopted independently and without coordination. International Law Commission, 'Draft Articles on Nationality of Natural Persons in Relation to the Succession of States - With Commentaries', in *Yearbook of the International Law Commission,* Vol. II, 1999, page 28.

at the time, resident on the territory in question. Since this rule is applicable to all "such persons as would otherwise become stateless", it assures that even those who live abroad will be protected against statelessness in the event of loss of nationality of the predecessor state.

Nevertheless, this second paragraph also produces some difficulties of interpretation and implementation. Firstly, in referring to the state "to which territory is transferred" rather than using the term "successor state", there is some doubt as to whether this provision deals with all cases of state succession. As it reads, it appears to focus on instances in which there is a redefinition of an existing border, thus where an area of land is transferred from the sovereignty of one country to another - already existing - state. It is unclear whether the norm would also apply to the situation in which one or more newly independent states are formed – the circumstance of most of the cases of state succession of the latter 20th century.[50] This brings us to the second problem. If we are to assume that it is the intention of this article to cover all situations of state succession, then the question arises whether a newly independent state would ever be bound by this norm being as it is only applicable through this treaty to state parties. As mentioned in the introduction to the problem of statelessness in state succession, the issue of whether a successor state is bound to the treaty obligations of the predecessor state is a matter of great contention and little consensus. The practice of states that have emerged from state succession with regard to the 1951 Refugee Convention and the 1954 Statelessness Convention has been to succeed to these documents, including – where appropriate – reaffirming or redrafting the declarations and reservations that were made to these texts by the predecessor state at the time of accession.[51] It must thereby be assumed that these instruments remained in force in the relevant territories throughout. As to the 1961 Statelessness Convention itself, Kiribati is the sole state to have succeeded to the instrument,[52] but the relevant circumstances have only presented themselves in this one instance. Therefore, on the basis of the overall treatment of the refugee and statelessness protection regimes and the intent and purpose of this article in the 1961 Convention on the Reduction of Statelessness, it seems fair to assume that a successor state should be considered bound by these norms if the predecessor state has committed itself to the text. Nevertheless, in the absence of any real state practice, it remains to be seen whether this point is refuted by newly independent states.

The third setback with this provision is the lack of attention for the role of the predecessor state. It falls upon the successor state to attribute nationality to those who would otherwise be rendered stateless by the succession of states. However, the predecessor state is not required to play any role in the prevention of statelessness. There is no duty, for example, to refrain from withdrawing nationality until such time as the acquisition by the individual of the citizenship of the

[50] The Draft Convention on the Reduction of Future Statelessness, as submitted for consideration by the International Law Commission, also referred in paragraph 2 of article 10 to "a new State formed on territory previously belonging to another State or States". This suggests that the text as finally adopted deliberately excludes from its scope of application any newly independent states.

[51] Information on state parties, reservations and declarations to the 1951 Convention relating to the Status of Refugees and the 1954 Convention relating to the status of Stateless Persons is available via http://www.unhcr.org.

[52] Upon independence from the United Kingdom.

successor state has been realised. In view of the ambiguity surrounding the application of this provision to newly independent states, an opportunity may have thereby been missed to further narrow the risk of (even temporary) statelessness. Finally, while admirable for the reasons cited above, the broad reference to "such persons as would otherwise become stateless" may also lead to problems of implementation. Not only may a state be unwilling to accept responsibility for certain persons that are rendered stateless by the policy of the predecessor state (which is not subject to any restrictions under this article), but what happens if there is more than one successor state? Consider the situation in which a federal state has dissolved to make way for a number of successor states, as was the case with the break up of the Soviet Union. The nationality of the predecessor state is no longer available, so all citizens of that state "would otherwise become stateless", but which of the various successor states must confer nationality to which individuals? This vagueness may allow states to enter into an unending dispute as to who must grant nationality to a particular population group.[53] The 1961 Statelessness Convention does not offer any guidance as to how such matters should be settled. In particular, it does not mention the possibility or obligation of allowing the individual in question a right of option for the most appropriate nationality.[54]

In interpreting and applying this article of the 1961 Statelessness Convention, the aforementioned difficulties may never arise. If the spirit rather than the letter of the text is followed, then the result should indeed be as UNHCR suggested: that states "either conclude treaties or confer nationality to ensure statelessness will not occur as a result of a transfer of territory".[55] However, it cannot be denied that the wording of the provision leaves ample room for contention and dispute. Once again, an effective supervisory mechanism is an important asset to ensuring interpretation and application of the text in accordance with its purpose – the avoidance of statelessness.[56] Most likely, it simply proved too ambitious of the 1961 Convention on the Reduction of Statelessness to attempt to deal with the complex issue of statelessness arising from state succession in just one provision, featured – almost as an afterthought - at the end of the series of substantive provisions and in a much watered down form than originally put forward by the International Law Commission for consideration.[57] In contrast, as

[53] The original Draft Convention on the Reduction of Future Statelessness required states to deal only with the potential statelessness of inhabitants of their territory. This had the advantage of forestalling nationality disputes to some extent but the disadvantage of negating what has been said above about this provision dealing with *all* persons who would otherwise be stateless.

[54] In fact the instrument does not deal with the right of option at all, nor the risk of statelessness that such a mechanism may introduce. Again, the Draft Convention on the Reduction of Future Statelessness that was put forward by the International Law Commission did mention the right of option, but this wording was lost before the acceptance of the final text by government representatives in 1961.

[55] See note 48.

[56] The problem of enforcement of the 1961 Statelessness Convention was broached in chapter III, section 3. We will return to this question in chapter VIII.

[57] In comparison to the number and volume of the provisions of the 1961 Statelessness Convention that deal with statelessness arising from regular conflict of laws situations, it is unsurprising that the brevity with which the problem of statelessness in state succession – an equally complex issue - is dealt with leaves something to be desired.

we turn to the alternative sources of obligations in this field, we will see how the concretisation of the right to a nationality in the context of state succession has lead to entire, detailed instruments being elaborated to deal with this matter.

3 International (Human Rights) Law

International human rights instruments do not deal with the specific issue of statelessness resulting from the succession of states. Nevertheless, the general norms on the right to a nationality and the prohibition of arbitrary deprivation of nationality are equally applicable in the context of state succession and must therefore be taken into account. This has provided treaty bodies with the opportunity to comment on policies relating to the attribution of nationality to persons affected by state succession. Thus, in a perhaps surprising number of concluding observations on state party reports, the various committees have commented on the enjoyment of the right to a nationality (explicitly or implicitly) in the context of the succession of states. For example, in reference to the Russian Federation the UN Committee on Economic, Social and Cultural Rights had this to say:

> The Committee notes the statement of the State party's delegation that any former citizen of the Soviet Union living in the country can exchange their old Soviet passports for new Russian Federation ones without any difficulty. However, the Committee is concerned about reports that registration and recognition of citizenship have been denied to some groups, particularly the Meskhetians living in Krasnador Krai.[58]

The other treaty bodies have dealt with similar concerns - or expressed praise at positive developments – in particular on the situation in Latvia, Estonia, Sri Lanka, Slovenia, Croatia and Ukraine.[59]

---

[58] UN Committee on Economic, Social and Cultural Rights, *Concluding Observations: Russian Federation,* E/2004/22, New York and Geneva: 2003, para 455. Similar concerns were expressed by the UN Committee on the Elimination of Racial Discrimination in *Concluding Observations: Russian Federation,* A/58/18, New York: 2003, paras 180 and 183. Elsewhere, the statelessness of the Meskhetians in the aftermath of the break-up of the Soviet Union has also been reported on. UNHCR, "Statelessness and Citizenship" in *The State of the World's Refugees - A Humanitarian Agenda,* Oxford University Press, Oxford: 1997, page 235; Maureen Lynch, *Lives on hold: The human cost of statelessness,* Washington: 2005, page 43.

[59] CERD, *Concluding Observations: Croatia,* A/50/18, New York: 1995, paras. 173 and 175; *Croatia,* A/553/18, New York: 1998, para 316; *Latvia,* A/54/18, New York: 1999, para 395; *Sri Lanka,* A/56/18, New York: 2001, para 334; *Ukraine,* A/56/18, New York: 2001, para 374; *Estonia,* A/57/18, New York: 2002, para 353; *Slovenia,* A/58/18, New York, 2003, paras 232 and 240. Human Rights Committee, *Concluding Observations: Ukraine,* A/50/40, vol.1, Geneva: 1995, para 322; *Latvia,* A/50/40, vol.1, Geneva: 1995, para. 350; *Estonia,* A/51/40, vol.1, Geneva: 1996, para 110; *Estonia,* A/58/40, vol.1, Geneva: 2003, para 79(14). Committee on Economic, Social and Cultural Rights, *Concluding Observations: Sri Lanka,* E/1999/22, New York and Geneva: 1998, para 82; *Croatia,* E/2002/22, New York and Geneva: 2001, para 894. Committee on the Rights of the Child, *Concluding Observations: Latvia,* CRC/C/103, Geneva: 2001, para. 52; *Estonia,* CRC/C/124, Geneva: 2003, paras 45-46. Also in reference to the United Kingdom in the context of the transfer of sovereignty over Hong Kong to China in CERD, *Concluding Observations: United Kingdom of Great Britain and Northern*

The UN Committee on the Elimination of Racial Discrimination has clearly been most active in this regard. In response to the country report of Lithuania in 2002, the Committee even went so far as to note with satisfaction the choice of "zero option" as the mechanism for the attribution of nationality upon state succession as this "enabled the majority of the population to obtain Lithuanian citizenship [and] has led to the construction of a more stable society".[60] The Committee has thereby taken one step beyond expressing concern at discriminatory policies of nationality attribution in the context of state succession by appearing to voice a preference for a particular mechanism in order to protect the right to a nationality. This development is supported by the reference in the General Recommendation on *Discrimination against non-citizens* that was promulgated by the Committee in 2004. In paragraph 17 it recommends that states adopt measures to:

> Regularise the status of former citizens of predecessor States who now reside within the jurisdiction of the State Party.[61]

The Committee on the Elimination of Racial Discrimination thus seems to favour the attribution of citizenship by territorial jurisdiction to persons affected by state succession. Perhaps most interestingly, this recommendation does not refer to successor states, only to the state of residence of former nationals of a predecessor state, which may, in fact, be a third country that was not directly involved in the state succession.[62] The important point here is that this is a clear illustration of the way in which the right to a nationality is encroaching upon the issue of state succession even in the absence of explicit human rights treaty provisions to that effect.

Meanwhile, inspired by developments in the human rights field and a desire to limit the occurrence of statelessness and in the knowledge of the particular difficulties raised by state succession for the enjoyment of nationality, the international community has been growing increasingly active on this issue.[63] In fact, thanks to the elaboration of more comprehensive norms to deal with the

---

Ireland, A/51/18, New York: 1996, paras 238 and 254; and in reference to the territory of Macau in Human Rights Committee, *Concluding Observations: Portugal,* A/55/40, vol.1, Geneva: 2000, para. 175.

[60] CERD, *Concluding Observations: Lithuania,* A/57/18, 2002, para 163.

[61] CERD General Recommendation 30: Discrimination against Non-Citizens, Geneva: 2004, para. 17.

[62] It should also be noted that states are asked to "regularise" the status of former citizens of the predecessor state, rather than confer nationality upon such individuals. This may, in fact, be interpreted narrowly to mean the legalisation of immigration status only. However, thanks to its placing among the paragraphs that house recommendations on the right to a nationality and the avoidance of statelessness it can be inferred that the establishment of citizenship is the desired solution.

[63] The numerous cases of sudden state succession towards the end of the 20th Century provided an additional impetus to the international community to begin to tackle the issues of state succession and nationality jointly, rather than as separate problems which had previously been the approach. Zdzislaw Galicki, "State Succession and Nationality" in *Council of Europe's First Conference on Nationality*, Strasbourg: 1999. Not only through the UN human rights system and UNHCR has attention grown for this predicament, but even in the work of organisations such as the Organisation for Security and Cooperation in Europe. OSCE, *Ottawa Declaration of the OSCE Parliamentary Assembly,* Ottawa, July 1995, paras 33 and 34.

attribution of nationality to persons affected by state succession, it is now the area in which the right to a nationality has received its most thorough and detailed concretisation. There are two instruments that are designed to deal specifically and explicitly with the problem of the nationality in the context of state succession.[64] The first is the *Draft Articles on Nationality of Natural Persons in relation to the Succession of States*[65] that was prepared by the International Law Commission at the request of the UN General Assembly.[66] At the time of writing, the General Assembly was still considering whether these norms should be adopted in the form of a Declaration or perhaps even a Convention.[67] Nevertheless, the articles reflect a certain consensus on how international law currently stands on the issue. The second is the *Council of Europe Convention on the avoidance of statelessness in relation to State succession*,[68] opened for signature in May 2006 and yet to enter into force.[69] This Convention

> builds upon Chapter VI of the European Convention on Nationality by developing more detailed rules to be applied by States in the context of State succession with a view to preventing, or at least as far as possible reducing, cases of statelessness arising from such situations.[70]

By tracing common standards in these two instruments, it is possible to draw some conclusions about the direction in which international law has been developing since the adoption of the 1961 Statelessness Convention.

---

[64] As instruments specifically designed to deal with the succession of states it is to be assumed that where the predecessor state was a party to these texts, the successor state(s) would also be bound to implement the rules contained therein, otherwise the instruments would lose all value.

[65] Hereinafter the ILC Draft Articles.

[66] The Draft Articles are annexed to the text of UN General Assembly, *Resolution on Nationality of natural persons in relation to the succession of States,* A/RES/55/153, 30 January 2001. They can also be found, with accompanying commentary in ILC Yearbook. International Law Commission, 'Draft Articles on Nationality of Natural Persons in Relation to the Succession of States - With Commentaries', in *Yearbook of the International Law Commission,* Vol. II, 1999

[67] UN General Assembly, *Resolution on Nationality of natural persons in relation to the succession of States,* A/RES/59/34, 16 December 2004; see also background documents such as the comments and observations received from governments, UN General Assembly, *Note by the secretariat on Nationality of natural persons in relation to the succession of States,* A/59/180, 26 July 2004 and A/59/180/Add.1, 26 August 2004; UN General Assembly, *Report of the Sixth Committee on Nationality of natural persons in relation to the succession of States,* A/59/504, 19 November 2004.

[68] Hereinafter the Council of Europe Convention.

[69] Since being opened for signature, the Council of Europe Convention has been ratified by 2 states (Moldova and Norway) and has been signed – but not ratified – by two further states (Ukraine and Montenegro). The ratification of 3 states is needed for the entry into force of the instrument. The Convention on Nationality that was also adopted within the framework of the Council of Europe and had the same conditions for entry into force attracted the required number of ratifications within three years of it being opened for signature.

[70] Council of Europe, *Council of Europe Convention on the avoidance of statelessness in relation to State succession - Explanatory Report,* Strasbourg: 2006. The chapter of the European Convention on Nationality referred to will not be considered because it has received further concretisation in the Council of Europe Convention on the avoidance of statelessness in relation to State succession that is being discussed here.

After an elaborate preamble, both the ILC Draft Articles and the Council of Europe Convention open with a restatement of the right to a nationality for the specific context of the succession of states.[71] While the scope of the two instruments is limited to the *continuing* enjoyment of the right to a nationality for persons who held the nationality of the predecessor state prior to state succession, precisely because of this very specific focus it becomes possible to identify which state is obliged to fulfil this right for the individuals concerned by providing for the conferral or retention of citizenship.[72] Moreover, although the ILC Draft Articles are concerned with all aspects of nationality attribution in relation to state succession - not just with the avoidance of statelessness like the Council of Europe Convention – the right to a nationality is the "main principle from which other draft articles are derived".[73] Both documents therefore have a clear focus on avoiding the creation of new cases of statelessness in the process of the transfer of territory. Indeed, for good measure, both texts go on to explicitly assert the principle of the prevention of statelessness, again in relation to persons who prior to state succession possessed the nationality of the predecessor state.[74]

The wording of these provisions is of great interest. In spite of the ideal that they clearly strive towards, a first reading of the text is disappointing. The state(s) concerned are required to "take all appropriate measures" to prevent statelessness from arising among the nationals of the predecessor state.[75] This choice of phrase results in an "obligation of conduct" rather than an "obligation of result".[76] Where there are several concerned states, statelessness may nevertheless crop up even where appropriate measures have been taken, because these have

[71] The ILC Draft Articles assert the right to a nationality in article 1, followed by a provision which contains the definition of terms used in the text. The Council of Europe Convention elaborates on the definition of terms first, then article 2 proclaims the right to a nationality.

[72] International Law Commission, 'Draft Articles on Nationality of Natural Persons in Relation to the Succession of States - With Commentaries', in *Yearbook of the International Law Commission,* Vol. II, 1999, page 25. Jeffrey Blackman, 'State Succession and Statelessness: The Emerging Right to an Effective Nationality under International Law', in *Michigan Journal of International law,* Vol. 19, 1998, page 1173.

[73] International Law Commission, 'Draft Articles on Nationality of Natural Persons in Relation to the Succession of States - With Commentaries', in *Yearbook of the International Law Commission,* Vol. II, 1999, page 25. Similarly, the Special Rapporteur remarked that "the assumption that States concerned should be under the obligation to prevent statelessness was one of the basic premises on which the Working Group based its deliberations and received clear support in the Commission". Václav Mikulka, *Third report on Nationality in relation to the Succession of States,* A/CN.4/480, Geneva: 27 February 1997, page 43.

[74] Article 4 of the ILC Draft Articles; Article 3 of the Council of Europe Convention. States are free to redress the statelessness of residents of their territory who were already stateless prior to the succession of states or to extend the protection offered against statelessness to *de facto* stateless persons, but these measures are not required by the instruments. International Law Commission, 'Draft Articles on Nationality of Natural Persons in Relation to the Succession of States - With Commentaries', in *Yearbook of the International Law Commission,* Vol. II, 1999, page 28; COE Explanatory Report, para 16.

[75] The wording of article 4 of the ILC Draft Articles and Article 3 of the Council of Europe Convention is virtually identical.

[76] International Law Commission, 'Draft Articles on Nationality of Natural Persons in Relation to the Succession of States - With Commentaries', in *Yearbook of the International Law Commission,* Vol. II, 1999, page 28.

proven inadequate. This approach has been sternly criticised as "a tepid affirmation of the duty to prevent statelessness, [...] an obligation without teeth".[77] A similar critique was voiced in the previous section with regard to article 10, paragraph 1 of the 1961 Statelessness Convention whereby states commit to settling a treaty which includes "provisions *designed to secure* that no person shall become stateless". However, there is a significant difference between these instruments. While the 1961 Statelessness Convention does not go on to specify what could be deemed as provisions designed to secure the prevention of statelessness, the ILC Draft Articles and the Council of Europe Convention both (largely) dedicate the remainder of their provisions to delineating what are considered "appropriate measures":

> The principle stated in Article 3 [of the Council of Europe Convention] indicates the general framework upon which other, more specific obligations are based. The elimination of statelessness is the outcome to be achieved by application of the set of principles and rules contained in the Convention.[78]

To evaluate the effectiveness of the ILC Draft Articles and the Council of Europe Convention in preventing statelessness in relation to state succession on the basis of this statement of principle alone is therefore severely premature. Instead, we must consider the concrete, substantive norms contained in these instruments.

Where the 1961 Convention on the reduction of statelessness was insufficiently clear and unambiguous to guarantee trouble-free implementation, the ILC Draft Articles and the Council of Europe Convention are much more detailed. These instruments also concentrate mainly on the role of the successor state in conferring nationality and preventing statelessness, but they are more specific in determining which individuals must be granted citizenship by which successor state. Although the ILC Draft Articles prescribe separate measures of nationality attribution for each of the four main types of state succession[79] and the Council of Europe Convention covers all situations in just one article, substantively the norms are incredibly similar.[80] If an individual would otherwise be rendered stateless by

---

[77] Jeffrey Blackman, 'State Succession and Statelessness: The Emerging Right to an Effective Nationality under International Law', in *Michigan Journal of International law,* Vol. 19, 1998, page 1181. It should be noted that Blackman was referring to a previous draft by the ILC in which states were obliged to take all *reasonable* measures to prevent statelessness in relation to state succession. Nevertheless, his comments are equally relevant to the text of the ILC Draft Articles as approved in 1999.

[78] Council of Europe, *Council of Europe Convention on the avoidance of statelessness in relation to State succession - Explanatory Report,* Strasbourg: 2006, para 15; Explanation of article 4 of the ILC Draft Articles is almost identical, word for word. International Law Commission, 'Draft Articles on Nationality of Natural Persons in Relation to the Succession of States - With Commentaries', in *Yearbook of the International Law Commission,* Vol. II, 1999, page 28.

[79] Transfer of territory from one state to another, unification of states, dissolution of states and separation of part of a state.

[80] Please be reminded that each of these norms relates only to those persons who prior to the succession of states held the nationality of the predecessor state. Once again, note that the ILC Draft Articles prescribe general measures for nationality attribution in cases of state succession whereas the Council of Europe Convention only obliges states to confer nationality along these lines where the individual would otherwise be stateless. Since we are only interested here in what is prescribed where a person

the transfer of territory, then, in order to determine which state has a duty to confer citizenship, it must first be ascertained in which state the person is habitually resident. If the state of habitual residence is (one of) the successor state(s) then, in reflection of general state practice by which the change of citizenship follows the change of sovereignty, that state must grant nationality.[81] As to persons at risk of statelessness due to state succession who are not habitually resident on the territory of (any of) the successor state(s) at the time of transfer: they will nevertheless be entitled to the nationality of such a state if there is an "appropriate connection".[82] An appropriate connection may consist of a legal bond to a territorial unit of the predecessor state that now belongs to the successor states' territory (for example "citizenship" of one of the republics that constituted a federation in the predecessor state); birth on the territory that has been transferred; or last habitual residence on the territory that has been transferred.[83]

By dealing with the risk of statelessness of those who are resident on the territory that undergoes a change of sovereignty, as well as those who are living abroad at the time of state succession *and* by clearly delineating simple factors that account for an appropriate connection,[84] the protection offered against statelessness is maximised. In fact, in many cases this approach is likely to lead to eligibility for the nationality of more than one successor state. Without taking a stance on the appropriateness of dual nationality,[85] the two instruments have foreseen the difficulties that may arise from this situation and taken measures to forestall

---

would otherwise be stateless, it is not immediately relevant that the rules prescribed by the ILC Draft Articles are also applicable to nationality in relation to state succession generally.

[81] Articles 20, 22 (a) and 24 (a) of the ILC Draft Articles; Article 5, paragraph 1(a) of the Council of Europe Convention. Only with regard to the unification of states is the basic rule any different – in that case, the ILC Draft Articles determine that nationality shall be attributed by the successor state to *all* nationals of the predecessor states, regardless of other factors.

[82] The ILC Draft Articles even allow the attribution of nationality by successor states to non-permanent residents with an appropriate connection *against their will* if they would otherwise be stateless. In ordinary circumstances, where there is no risk of statelessness, a successor state may only bestow nationality upon non-residents if they agree to the conferral. This exception is therefore another admission of the special importance of preventing statelessness. Article 8, paragraph 2 of the ILC Draft Articles.

[83] Article 22 (b) and article 24 (b) of the ILC Draft Articles; Article 5, paragraphs 1(b) and 2 of the Council of Europe Convention. Both instruments admit that there may be other factors that constitute an appropriate connection for the conferral of nationality, but these are the only three upon which the states concerned are obliged to attribute nationality. In the commentary to the ILC Draft Articles it is suggested that family ties may be another indication of an appropriate connection. International Law Commission, 'Draft Articles on Nationality of Natural Persons in Relation to the Succession of States - With Commentaries', in *Yearbook of the International Law Commission,* Vol. II, 1999, page 45. In relation to the Council of Europe Convention, "long-term previous residence in their territory or descent from a person originating from it" are mentioned as alternative evidence of an appropriate connection with the state concerned. Roland Schärer, 'The Council of Europe and the Reduction of Statelessness', in *Refugee Survey Quarterly,* Vol. 25, 2006, page 36.

[84] As well as allowing other factors to be taken into account where necessary by devising a non-limitative list.

[85] The Council of Europe Convention concerns itself only with the problem of statelessness and the ILC Draft Articles are "completely neutral" on the question of dual or multiple nationality. International Law Commission, 'Draft Articles on Nationality of Natural Persons in Relation to the Succession of States - With Commentaries', in *Yearbook of the International Law Commission,* Vol. II, 1999, page 25.

disputes that might otherwise lead to a prolonged situation of uncertainty or statelessness for the individuals involved. Where the person in question resides on the territory of a successor state, it is that state which is responsible for fulfilling his right to a nationality. Therefore, as mentioned, only where the individual is *not* habitually resident on the soil of any successor state must another "appropriate connection" be sought.[86] If the person is found to have an appropriate connection with more than one successor state (for example, birth on the soil of one successor state but last habitual residence on the territory of another), a dispute is still conceivable. This problem has been resolved by leaving the choice to the individual: a right of option must be offered where more than one nationality is available.[87] There must be a real opportunity to exercise such a right of option and states may not pre-empt that choice:

> A successor state shall not refuse to grant its nationality under Article 5, paragraph 1, sub-paragraph b [on the basis of an appropriate connection], where such nationality reflects the expressed will of the persons concerned, on the grounds that such a person can acquire the nationality of another State concerned on the basis of an appropriate connection with that state.[88]

Any dispute that may arise between states as to which nationality a person should acquire is therefore to be resolved by the individual himself and the relevant states are required to respect that decision. Only once the individual in question has actually acquired the nationality for which he has opted are the other states absolved of their duty to offer citizenship or can they give effect to any expressed desire to "opt out" of the nationality that they have offered.[89] Again this is a useful tool in the prevention of statelessness.

While the rules discussed so far may be the most progressive and remarkable of the provisions included in the ILC Draft Articles and the Council of Europe Convention - because they clearly identify which state is obliged to fulfil which persons' right to a nationality - there are other norms that also deal with the problem of statelessness in relation to state succession. The first of these addresses the role of the predecessor state. Both instruments determine that the predecessor state (if still in existence after the succession of states) may not withdraw its citizenship until the nationality of a successor state is actually acquired, be it automatically or through voluntary act.[90] This obligation on the predecessor state does not detract from the duty of successor states to offer citizenship to the categories of persons

---

[86] Articles 22 and 24 read together with article 8 of the ILC Draft Articles; Article 5, paragraph 2 of the Council of Europe Convention. Moreover, the ILC Draft Articles give second priority, after habitual residence, to a legal connection with a constituent unit of the predecessor state that has become part of the successor state. Only where this is lacking must the search for an appropriate connection continue to consider such aspects as place of birth and place of last habitual residence.

[87] Articles 23 and 26 of the ILC Draft Articles; Article 7 of the Council of Europe Convention.

[88] Article 7 of the Council of Europe Convention. Article 11 of the ILC Draft Articles provides a similar safeguard against the shirking of responsibility by any state with which an individual has an appropriate connection and against the risk of (temporary) statelessness in the exercise of the right of option.

[89] See also articles 9 and 10 of the ILC Draft Articles.

[90] Articles 20 and 25 of the ILC Draft Articles; Article 6 of the Council of Europe Convention.

outlined above.[91] It is, however, a key fallback clause to avert temporary statelessness[92] and even permanent statelessness in exceptional cases. Thus the role of the predecessor state is central to the prevention of statelessness wherever it subsists after the transfer of territory.[93]

Another important norm that has been included in the ILC Draft Articles and the Council of Europe Convention is the prohibition of discrimination in the enjoyment of the right to a nationality and its application to the context of state succession. There may be no discrimination in decisions regarding the retention of nationality of the predecessor state, the conferral of nationality by a successor state or the grant of the right of option.[94] The Council of Europe Convention lists the following grounds upon which discrimination is prohibited in relation to the attribution of nationality upon transfer of territory: "sex, race, colour, language, religion, political or other opinion, national or social origin, association with a national minority, property, birth or other status".[95] The same article admits that discrimination on other grounds may also be unacceptable. Meanwhile the International Law Commission deliberately chose to prohibit discrimination "on any ground" and omitted any such illustrative list. The reasoning behind this choice was that in the specific context of state succession, there "may still be other grounds for discrimination in nationality matters" which it could not necessarily predict from the outset but which may be equally intolerable.[96] Thus substantial protection

---

[91] The ILC Draft Articles delineate the cases in which the predecessor state incurs the duty to maintain the bond of citizenship with its nationals in article 25 (for example nationality will not be withdrawn from habitual residents of the territory that remains part of the predecessor state). Where this is the case and the nationality of a successor state is also available to such individuals, they must again be granted an effective right of option including the additional safeguards against statelessness (article 26 of the ILC Draft Articles).

[92] Another tool used to prevent temporary statelessness has been included in the ILC Draft Articles. Article 7 determines that the attribution of nationality in the context of state succession (whether automatic or by exercise of a right of option) shall "take effect on the date of such succession, if persons concerned would otherwise be stateless during the period between the date of the succession of States and such attribution or acquisition of nationality". This exception to the general principle of non-retroactivity of law in order to counter the effects of (even temporary) statelessness is a further illustration of the importance attributed to the prevention of statelessness by the international community. See also International Law Commission, 'Draft Articles on Nationality of Natural Persons in Relation to the Succession of States - With Commentaries', in *Yearbook of the International Law Commission,* Vol. II, 1999, page 30.

[93] Roland Schärer, 'The Council of Europe and the Reduction of Statelessness', in *Refugee Survey Quarterly,* Vol. 25, 2006, page 36.

[94] Article 15 of the ILC Draft Articles; Article 4 of the Council of Europe Convention. The ILC Draft Articles explicitly prohibit discrimination with regards to these three issues while the Council of Europe Convention simply decrees that states shall not discriminate in the application of any of the norms in the convention.

[95] This list is based on article 14 of the European Convention on Human Rights and (as discussed in chapter V) is much more extensive than that offered by the European Convention on Nationality. This suggests that in the context of the concrete obligations of states that have been formulated for the avoidance of statelessness in state succession, a much broader protection against discrimination is appropriate.

[96] The example given was the application of the requirement of a clean criminal record for conferral of nationality by way of option. International Law Commission, 'Draft Articles on Nationality of Natural

is offered against discrimination in the attribution of nationality in state succession with the result that such examples as were given by Weis of the delineation of a successor state's body of citizens on the basis of ethnicity would be decisively outlawed,[97] as would many other types of distinction.

Accompanying the norms which delineate *who* is to be attributed nationality in the context of state succession are rules on *how* this is to be achieved. In particular, there are a number of procedural guarantees that also form an important defence against the creation of statelessness. States must:

- provide sufficient information on rules and procedures to persons concerned,[98]
- process relevant applications without delay,[99]
- provide decisions, including reasons, in writing,[100]
- provide an effective administrative or judicial review for decisions,[101]
- ensure that relevant fees are reasonable and not an obstacle for applicants.[102]

The aim is to "ensure that the procedure followed with regard to nationality matters in cases of succession of states is orderly, given its possible large-scale impact".[103] This will, in turn, contribute to the proper implementation of the substantive norms and help to lower the risk of statelessness.

This delineation of procedural safeguards constitutes a simple translation of existing international norms in the field of nationality to the specific context of state succession.[104] However, the Council of Europe Convention also introduces an important novelty in its article 8 that deals with "rules of proof". The provision acknowledges the turbulence that tends to characterise the period of state succession and the difficulties that this may raise for establishing certain facts:

Persons in Relation to the Succession of States - With Commentaries', in *Yearbook of the International Law Commission,* Vol. II, 1999, page 37.

[97] Note that such distinctions on the basis of ethnicity are also prohibited under the *jus cogens* norm on racial discrimination. See note 38 above.

[98] Article 6 of the ILC Draft Articles; Article 11 of the Council of Europe Convention.

[99] Article 17 of the ILC Draft Articles; Article 12, paragraph a of the Council of Europe Convention.

[100] Article 17 of the ILC Draft Articles; Article 12, paragraph b of the Council of Europe Convention.

[101] Article 17 of the ILC Draft Articles; Article 12, paragraph b of the Council of Europe Convention.

[102] Article 12, paragraph c of the Council of Europe Convention. The International Law Commission considers that in principle the attribution of nationality in the context of state succession should not be subject to any fee. International Law Commission, 'Draft Articles on Nationality of Natural Persons in Relation to the Succession of States - With Commentaries', in *Yearbook of the International Law Commission,* Vol. II, 1999, page 38.

[103] Here, the International Law Commission refers to a warning from the UNHCR of the dire consequences of statelessness and the inability to establish one's nationality. International Law Commission, 'Draft Articles on Nationality of Natural Persons in Relation to the Succession of States - With Commentaries', in *Yearbook of the International Law Commission,* Vol. II, 1999, page 38.

[104] See chapter V, section 2.2.

> It might in some cases be impossible for a person to provide full documentary proof of his or her descent if, for instance, the civil registry archives have been destroyed, or it may be impossible to provide documentary proof of place of residence in cases where this was not registered. The provision includes the situation where it might objectively be feasible for a person to provide proof but where it would be unreasonable to demand for instance an action by a person which might put his or her life or health in danger.[105]

Thus the requirements of proof that must be met in order to establish eligibility for citizenship are deliberately lowered by determining that a successor state "shall not insist on its standard requirements of proof necessary for the granting of its nationality" if the individual would otherwise be stateless or if this amounted to an unreasonable burden.[106] This is the first time that we have come across any provision relating to the question of evidence in relation to nationality matters.[107] Although this article does not delineate what rules are to be followed by state parties in establishing eligibility for nationality (or indeed the threat of statelessness) – leaving this question to states - the rule should nevertheless go some way to ensuring that problems of evidence do not stand in the way of the application of the Convention and, in particular, do not form an obstacle to the resolution of statelessness.

Similarly "new" in nationality matters under international law is the obligation, within the context of state succession, to cooperate internationally to resolve nationality disputes and prevent statelessness. Since state succession is by definition an international event, involving more than one country, such a duty is more than logical. We already saw that the 1961 Convention on the Reduction of Statelessness called upon states to deal with nationality issues by treaty in this context. Now the ILC Draft Articles and the Council of Europe Convention add another dimension to this duty to cooperate. Not only may the states concerned be asked to tackle nationality disputes and statelessness by attempting to settle international agreements as appropriate,[108] but with the same objective they are also required to exchange information and engage in consultations.[109] In particular, it may be necessary to communicate on the operation of domestic nationality regulations in order to investigate the need for coordination of policy. The Council of Europe Convention even prescribes cooperation with UNHCR and, "where appropriate", with third states and other international organisations.[110] This

---

[105] Council of Europe, *Council of Europe Convention on the avoidance of statelessness in relation to State succession - Explanatory Report,* Strasbourg: 2006, para 33.

[106] Article 8, paragraph 1 of the Council of Europe Convention. Under paragraph 2 of the same article, a successor state shall further "not require proof of non-acquisition of another nationality before granting its nationality to persons who were habitually resident on its territory at the time of the State succession and who have or would become stateless as a result of the State succession".

[107] Recall the discussion of the problem of identification of (potential) statelessness in chapter II, section 2 and chapter III, section 3.

[108] Article 18, paragraph 2 of the ILC Draft Norms; Article 13 of the Council of Europe Convention.

[109] Article 18, paragraph 1 of the ILC Draft Norms; Article 14 of the Council of Europe Convention.

[110] Article 14, paragraph 2 of the Council of Europe Convention. "The question of which international organisations to include will depend on the particular situation" and "states concerned are free to extend

provision recognises the intrinsic value of the consultative role that is often already played by UNHCR and other actors in devising solutions to the problem of statelessness in the context of state succession and aspires to extend the use of such important mechanisms.[111]

Finally, it must be noted that if all of the above-mentioned safeguards against statelessness fail and some persons are nevertheless left without a nationality, the ILC Draft Articles and the Council of Europe Convention do not rest there. In particular, article 9 of the Council of Europe Convention is

> intended to fill any gaps after the application of Articles 5 and 6, either as a result of the predecessor State not being a party to the Convention or because of its disappearance as a result of which all persons who possessed its nationality automatically become stateless. If these persons subsequently fail to fulfil the conditions for the acquisition of nationality of a successor State they will remain stateless.[112]

Thus the provision in question obliges whichever of the concerned states (predecessor or successor) upon which the person is lawfully and habitually resident to facilitate the acquisition of its nationality by persons who have become stateless.[113] In contrast, the ILC Draft Norms do not prescribe facilitated access to nationality by those who were rendered stateless in the succession of states. Instead, it determines that where the states concerned fail to live up to their obligations in attributing nationality to certain persons in relation to state succession, leaving them

---

this co-operation to non-governmental organisations as well". Council of Europe, *Council of Europe Convention on the avoidance of statelessness in relation to State succession - Explanatory Report,* Strasbourg: 2006, para 55.

[111] For example, UNHCR and the Council of Europe engaged in dialogue with Bosnia and Herzegovina in order to avoid statelessness resulting from state succession. In all, UNHCR has consulted with and provided advice to over 40 states in relation to nationality laws both in the context of state succession and simply in the adoption of new legislation. UNHCR, *UNHCR's activities in the field of statelessness: Progress Report,* EC/55/SC/CRP.13/Rev.1, Geneva: 30 June 2005, page 3. Another example is Ukraine where, following state succession, UNHCR, the Organisation for Security and Cooperation in Europe and the Council of Europe were all involved in the promotion of solutions for statelessness. See "Good Practices: Ukraine" in UNHCR and IPU, *Nationality and statelessness. A handbook for parliamentarians*, 2005, pages 29-31.

[112] Council of Europe, *Council of Europe Convention on the avoidance of statelessness in relation to State succession - Explanatory Report,* Strasbourg: 2006, para 38. It is interesting to note the reference to the situation where the predecessor state is not a party to this Convention. Were this the case, then – apart from in a simple transfer of territory – the successor state(s) would also not be bound by this instrument. Only if the successor state(s) were to become a party to the Council of Europe Convention and declare by notification its retroactive application to the state succession would any of the rules actually be binding.

[113] Whereas in the allocation of responsibility for conferral of nationality in relation to state succession, the rules discussed above required only "habitual residence" as a matter of fact, this provision will benefit only persons who are also lawfully present on the state's territory. In practice this may result in the exclusion of many individuals who, upon being rendered stateless, face further difficulties with their legal status under (new) immigration laws. It should be noted that the ILC Draft Articles (article 14) provide that persons who were habitual residents on the territory prior to state succession shall retain their status after the transfer of territory. The Council of Europe Convention does not contain such a provision.

stateless, other states are free to treat such persons as though they nevertheless acquired or retained the citizenship in question.[114] This approach may only be invoked to the *benefit* of the individuals involved, for example to extend to these persons some form of favourable treatment that is also offered to the nationals of the state in question..[115] The two instruments then concur on the undesirability of nationality disputes resulting from state succession impacting upon the second generation – children born after the transfer of territory.[116] Rationalising the inclusion of these provisions on the norm espoused in article 7 of the UN Convention on the Rights of the Child, both texts advocate *jus soli* attribution of citizenship to a child who (thanks to the effect of the succession of states on his parents nationality) would otherwise be stateless.[117] In view of such forward-thinking provisions and all of the foregoing comments, the ILC Draft Articles and the Council of Europe Convention prove to be full and comprehensive instruments that are paving the way for a new approach to the attribution of nationality and the prevention of statelessness in relation to state succession under international law.

4 Conclusion

The succession of states is inevitably a source of great upheaval, both for the states concerned and for the wider international community. Through numerous international agreements, efforts have been made to regulate various aspects of state succession.[118] In recent years, there has been particular interest in the position of the individuals affected by the transfer of territory. Motivated by human rights norms, including the right to nationality, developments in international law reflect the understanding that

> of paramount importance in the case of the succession of states is the need to ensure that everyone who had a nationality prior to the succession has

---

[114] Article 19 of the ILC Draft Articles.

[115] In contrast, "they may not, for example, deport such persons to that State as they could do with its actual nationals". International Law Commission, 'Draft Articles on Nationality of Natural Persons in Relation to the Succession of States - With Commentaries', in *Yearbook of the International Law Commission,* Vol. II, 1999, page 40.

[116] Article 13 of the ILC Draft Articles; Article 10 of the Council of Europe Convention.

[117] International Law Commission, 'Draft Articles on Nationality of Natural Persons in Relation to the Succession of States - With Commentaries', in *Yearbook of the International Law Commission,* Vol. II, 1999, page 36; Council of Europe, *Council of Europe Convention on the avoidance of statelessness in relation to State succession - Explanatory Report,* Strasbourg: 2006, para 42. There is a subtle difference between the provisions in the two instruments. The ILC Draft Articles provides the children in question with only the "right to the nationality" of the concerned state in which he was born whereas the Council of Europe Convention states plainly that such a state "shall grant its nationality at birth". The latter obligation is the more forceful of the two as it obliges attribution of citizenship *ex lege* to the children in question, going further than even the European Convention on Nationality prescribes for children who would otherwise be stateless at birth. Roland Schärer, 'The Council of Europe and the Reduction of Statelessness', in *Refugee Survey Quarterly,* Vol. 25, 2006, page 37.

[118] Consider the Vienna Convention on Succession of States in Respect of Treaties, 1978 and the Vienna Convention on Succession of States in Respect of State Property, Archives and Debts, 1983.

> one following. Statelessness should not result from this change in circumstances well beyond the control of the individuals involved.[119]

It seems strange to single out the succession of states for special treatment in this way because so far virtually all of the causes of statelessness that we have covered in this section of the book are arguably "beyond the control of the individuals involved".[120] Nevertheless, this idea that the transfer of territory is an exceptional case that warrants every effort in protecting the persons concerned from any detrimental effects has clearly influenced the thinking of the international community on this issue. The rules and standards that have been developed and codified to deal with the avoidance of statelessness in relation to state succession clearly constitute the most progressive and detailed concretisation to date of the right to a nationality and the principle of the avoidance of statelessness.

These new standards can be found in the International Law Commission's *Draft Articles on Nationality of Natural Persons in relation to the Succession of States* and the *Council of Europe Convention on the avoidance of statelessness in relation to State succession.*[121] The two texts build upon existing norms such as the right to a nationality as espoused in numerous instruments and interpreted by various human rights bodies, the European Convention on Nationality and, indeed, the 1961 Convention on the Reduction of Statelessness.[122] A further elaboration was needed because each of these pre-existing instruments

> contains [...] only general principles and not specific rules with regard to statelessness in cases of State succession. Past experience has demonstrated that this is not sufficient because an effective prevention of statelessness can be achieved only if States concerned by State succession are bound by clearly defined obligations to that effect.[123]

Thus while the 1961 Statelessness Convention makes an admirable attempt to deal with statelessness in the context of state succession - even though its main focus is the resolution of conflict of laws cases - the provision elaborated simply falls short of the required depth and detail to address the problem decisively. The discussion of the ILC Draft Articles and the Council of Europe Convention make clear from the outset that great progress has been made since the formulation of the 1961

---

[119] Carol Batchelor, 'Transforming International Legal Principles into National Law: The Right to a Nationality and the Avoidance of Statelessness', in *Refugee Survey Quarterly,* Vol. 25, 2006, page 18.

[120] With the exception perhaps of the deprivation of nationality as a punitive measure or in response to fraudulent conduct in acquiring citizenship, resulting in statelessness.

[121] As previously noted, the form in which the ILC Draft Articles will be adopted is as yet uncertain and the Council of Europe Convention has yet to enter into force. Nevertheless, the value of these instruments for tracing the direction in which international law is developing in this field should not be underestimated.

[122] See the preambular paragraphs of the ILC Draft Articles and the Council of Europe Convention.

[123] Schärer is referring to the European Convention on Nationality in the context of the elaboration of the Council of Europe Convention on the avoidance of statelessness in relation to State succession, however the observation is equally valid for the relevant human rights instruments and the 1961 Statelessness Convention. Roland Schärer, 'The Council of Europe and the Reduction of Statelessness', in *Refugee Survey Quarterly,* Vol. 25, 2006, pages 33-34.

Statelessness Convention in delineating precise rules and determining the exact role to be played by each of the states concerned in preventing statelessness.

Among the innovations and improvements in the protection against statelessness in relation to state succession that have been traced in the ILC Draft Articles and the Council of Europe Convention is a clear and precise determination of which (successor) state is obliged to confer nationality upon the transfer of territory to persons who would otherwise be rendered stateless. The instruments stick close to state practice by giving the greatest weight to the person's place of habitual residence in identifying the state which must bestow citizenship. The enunciation of additional, objective factors that - if present - also compel the attribution of nationality to persons who would otherwise be stateless ensures that no individual will be overlooked. Moreover, if states' concern at the risk of multiple nationalities for the people thus affected threatens to induce endless uncertainty and nationality disputes, the instruments present the solution of the right of option: it is for the individual to decide which nationality to accept and for the states concerned to respect that decision. This precise delineation of the role of the successor states is much less likely to lead to disputes or difficulties in implementation and is, thereby, much more readily enforceable than the vague norm espoused in article 10, paragraph 2 of the 1961 Statelessness Convention.[124]

Moreover, the ILC Draft Articles and the Council of Europe Convention contain a crucial fall-back clause for the absolute prevention of statelessness in cases of partial succession of states – where the predecessor state remains in existence after the transfer of territory. The very simple, yet effective, rule is that the predecessor state may not withdraw its nationality from any person affected by the succession of states unless they have already acquired another. The absence of such a norm in the 1961 Statelessness Convention leaves a serious gap in the protection offered. A similar lapse in protection was unearthed in relation to the right of option in the context of state succession: while the ILC Draft Articles and the Council of Europe Convention guarantee an effective right of option - the exercise of which may not lead to statelessness - as a tool for resolving nationality disputes between states, the 1961 Statelessness Convention does not consider this matter at all. Nor does the 1961 Statelessness Convention prescribe non-discrimination in the elaboration and application of rules on nationality attribution in the context of the transfer of territory. This principle is central to the ILC Draft Articles and the Council of Europe Convention, where in fact the protection offered against discrimination in nationality attribution in relation to the succession of states is broader than what is offered against discriminatory deprivation of nationality generally under international law. These same instruments provide numerous procedural guarantees designed to aid in the prevention of statelessness, such as the right to an effective review of nationality decisions. In contrast, the due process rules that are found in the 1961 Statelessness Convention are not applicable

[124] Article 10, paragraph 2 reads "In the absence of [treaty provisions designed to secure that no person shall become stateless] a Contracting State to which territory is transferred or which otherwise acquires territory shall confer its nationality on such persons as would otherwise become stateless as a result of the transfer of territory". 1961 Convention on the Reduction of Statelessness.

to the situation of state succession.[125] A final significant advance made by both the ILC Draft Articles and the Council of Europe Convention over the 1961 Statelessness Convention is the admission that, despite the best of intentions, some cases of statelessness arising from the succession of states may slip through the net. Where that is the case, the ILC Draft Articles and the Council of Europe Convention make an effort to limit the fallout, for example by suggesting facilitated access to the nationality of the state of habitual residence and by including safeguards against statelessness for the second generation.

It became clear early on in this chapter that the 1961 Convention on the Reduction of Statelessness has been somewhat left behind by the developments in international law in relation to the specific question of the prevention of statelessness arising from state succession. Indeed, the very elaboration by the International Law Commission of a detailed list of Draft Articles on Nationality of Natural Persons in Relation to the Succession of States, with as one of the principle objectives the avoidance of statelessness, is evidence of the conviction that the 1961 Statelessness Convention falls short in this matter.[126] In 1961, the time was clearly not yet ripe for a resolute text that would deal more decisively with the prevention of statelessness in relation to state succession.[127] Now though, the necessity of dealing with the dire problem of statelessness arising from state succession is beginning to outweigh the initial objections to elaborating international agreements in this field and the possibility of adopting a new instrument to deal with this matter seems very real.[128]

It then becomes important to ask what form such an instrument should take. In formulating the Draft Articles, the International Law Commission chose to consider the full question of (the change of) nationality in relation to state succession, rather than limiting the scope of its work to the problem of statelessness. This approach has its advantages. For example, the ILC was able to devise rules that will help to ensure the attribution of the most appropriate nationality – including the right of option – thereby, in fact, helping to protect individuals against the affliction of an *ineffective* nationality.[129] However, there is also an obvious disadvantage: by pre-determining how states should attribute nationality generally in the event of the transfer of territory, rather than dealing only with the limited category of "persons who would otherwise be stateless", the Draft Articles may be trying to take on too much. States are likely to be less willing to accept the text if it pre-empts all decisions relating to the composition of the body of nationals upon state

[125] The due process guarantees are found in article 8, paragraph 4 and are expressly applicable only to the revocation of nationality on the grounds espoused in that same article. See chapter V, section 2.1.

[126] The 1961 Convention on the Reduction of Statelessness was itself prepared by the International Law Commission back in the 1950s.

[127] This fact is also evidenced by the substantial differences between the text of the Draft Convention on the Reduction of Future Statelessness, as put forward by the International Law Commission, and the text that was finally approved as the 1961 Convention on the Reduction of Statelessness.

[128] As previously noted, this development in the mindset towards the position of individuals in the succession of states was particularly spurred on by the experiences with cases of state succession in the early 1990s. See note 9.

[129] Sometimes described as "*de facto* statelessness".

succession.[130] As to the form that the Draft Articles may eventually take, the International Law Commission has suggested their adoption as a declaration, but the possibility of a convention is also on the table.[131] Either way, it is clear that the new instrument will be established entirely independently from the 1961 Statelessness Convention.[132] This is a logical choice in view of the difference in scope as discussed above. By presenting the text in this way, it may also allow the instrument to attract broader support, including from among the (many) states that have not yet been coaxed into ratifying the 1961 Statelessness Convention. However, this approach will undoubtedly do nothing to diminish the obscurity of the 1961 Convention on the Reduction of Statelessness and will, if anything, make the status of its provisions all the more ambiguous.

While the Council of Europe Convention obviously cannot be a substitute to the ILC Draft Articles because it is a regional rather than a universal instrument, it does offer some idea of what an alternative text might look like. Thanks to its narrow focus on the avoidance of statelessness, it is able to offer even greater protection against this plight than the ILC Draft Articles provide.[133] Such thoroughness would better befit a new instrument or optional protocol to the 1961 Statelessness Convention to deal with the specific problem of statelessness arising from state succession. Until such time as the ILC Draft Articles have been formally adopted in one form or another and their impact can be assessed, it will fall upon such institutions as the human rights treaty bodies to continue to advocate for the prevention of statelessness in relation to state succession. The standards elaborated in the ILC Draft Articles and the Council of Europe Convention will at least provide helpful guidance in advising states on how to deal with this difficult issue and states remain free to take the UN General Assembly up on its standing invitation to "take into account, as appropriate, the provisions of [the ILC Draft Articles] in dealing with issues of nationality of natural persons in relation to the succession of states".[134]

---

[130] As has been evident throughout this part of the book, the regulation of nationality is a delicate issue for states and unless a specific, widely accepted purpose (such as the avoidance of statelessness) is served by the dictation of how a state should attribute its citizenship, such rules are likely to meet with forceful resistance.

[131] It should be noted that the advantage of a convention over a declaration lies in the enforcement of the norms: a convention may provide for a supervisory mechanism, while a declaration cannot. A declaration may be favoured where it is felt that a convention would not attract many ratifications, but it should not be ignored that a controversial declaration that is adopted with a weak majority may have even less value than a convention that is at least binding on its state parties.

[132] Rather than as a protocol.

[133] Consider, for example, the innovation in the area of requirements of proof for the eligibility for nationality in its article 8.

[134] UN General Assembly, *Resolution on Nationality of natural persons in relation to the succession of States,* A/RES/55/153, 30 January 2001, para 3; UN General Assembly, *Resolution on Nationality of natural persons in relation to the succession of States,* A/RES/59/34, 16 December 2004, para 1.

CHAPTER VII

ADDRESSING THE "NEW" CAUSES OF STATELESSNESS

Every international agreement that is settled, every treaty or convention that is concluded, is not only contrived for a particular purpose, its details are also influenced by the circumstances of its conception and existing notions of the problem that it is designed to address. So too was the 1961 Convention on the Reduction of Statelessness. Although it was intended as an instrument to prevent statelessness, in the foregoing chapters we already uncovered a number of circumstances in which the protection offered against this plight is less than optimal. This was explained as a consequence of the level of development of international law in relation to nationality matters at the time as well as the (lack of) preparedness of states to pursue more radical measures. It is arguable that where progress in the field of human rights has since overtaken the protection offered by the 1961 Statelessness Convention, its provisions could be interpreted in the light of and consistent with such developments. The 1961 Convention would then retain its use as a tailor-made instrument for addressing the prevention of statelessness and, by taking the lessons learned from the study of the broader international legal framework, the current viewpoint of the international community to these long-established problems could simply be added to the equation.[1] This, however, would not solve a more troubling issue, namely the role of the 1961 Statelessness Convention in relation to sources of statelessness that were entirely overlooked in this document because they had yet to be identified as such.

While for years this ultimately remained a hypothetical concern, over the course of the past decade or so it has gained immediate, practical importance with the acknowledgement of several "new" sources of statelessness. The first of these is a deficient civil registration system, in particular with regard to the registration of births and marriages. References to birth registration as a cause of statelessness started to crop up in the late 1990's, more than thirty years after the 1961 Statelessness Convention was opened for signature.[2] UNHCR named birth registration as a source of statelessness for the first time in the 1997 publication

---

[1] How this approach might take shape is discussed in chapter VIII.

[2] Weis does not include the issue of registration practices in his 1979 work on statelessness, nor does Donner in discussing statelessness in her 1994 work on nationality. Paul Weis, *Nationality and Statelessness in International Law*, Kluwer Academic Publishers Group, Dordrecht: 1979. Ruth Donner, *The Regulation of Nationality in International Law*, Transnational Publishers, New York: 1994.

"The State of the World's Refugees".[3] From that moment on, faulty birth registration practices have been included in every summary of the origins of statelessness and the issue is attracting increasing attention from many actors.[4] In addition, generally deficient civil registration practices, in particular the non-registration of marriages, have also been identified as a cause of statelessness.

The other "new" sources of statelessness that have been identified in recent years relate to one broad issue: migration. The movement of persons, including *forced* displacement, across international frontiers has given rise to a host of problems relating to documentation, legal status and citizenship:[5]

> In a world of nation-states, in which the population of the globe is theoretically divided up into mutually exclusive bodies of citizens, international migration is an anomaly with which the state system has some awkwardness coping.[6]

The persons involved in three specific migratory phenomena are proving to be especially vulnerable to nationality disputes and statelessness. These are irregular migrants, the victims of human trafficking and refugees. The link between such forms of displacement and statelessness is only just beginning to be discussed and further elucidated through studies and reports. However, it is considered a very real and likely lasting problem because the number of persons involved is not expected to decrease in years to come.[7]

Since the 1961 Statelessness Convention did not foresee any of these problems and is therefore silent on what I have dubbed the "new" causes of statelessness - that being, in essence, what makes them "new" - this chapter takes a slightly different shape from its predecessors. The simple comment that relevant provisions are absent is enough to lay bare the (lack of) effectiveness of the 1961 Convention in relation to these matters. The conclusion that in this respect the 1961 Convention has become outdated is quickly made, so we can immediately proceed to consider how the issues are addressed under international human rights law. What follows is therefore an assessment of the extent to which the human rights field provides a viable alternative in addressing the risk of statelessness arising from

[3] UNHCR, "Statelessness and Citizenship" in *The State of the World's Refugees - A Humanitarian Agenda*, Oxford University Press, Oxford: 1997, page 226.

[4] It also reappears in numerous Conclusions of UNHCR's Executive Committee, including UNHCR Executive Committee, *General Conclusion on International Protection, No. 90,* 52nd Session, Geneva, 2001, para. (r); UNHCR Executive Committee, *General Conclusion on International Protection, No. 95,* 54th Session, Geneva, 2003, para. (x); UNHCR Executive Committee, *Conclusion on Identification, Prevention and Reduction of Statelessness and Protection of Stateless Persons, No. 106,* 57th Session, Geneva, 2006, para. (h).

[5] There is a particularly close link between statelessness and forced displacement. Not only can forced displacement lead to new cases of statelessness but, vice versa, stateless persons often find that they must flee their homes. Additionally, the fact of statelessness can block repatriation efforts. UNHCR, "Statelessness and Citizenship" in *The State of the World's Refugees - A Humanitarian Agenda*, Oxford University Press, Oxford: 1997, page 244.

[6] John Torpey, *The Invention of the Passport. Surveillance, Citizenship and the State*, Cambridge University Press, Cambridge: 2000, page 123.

[7] IOM, *World Migration 2003: Managing Migration - Challenges and Responses for People on the Move,* Geneva: 2003, page 27.

poor birth registration, irregular migration, trafficking in human beings and refugee situations.[8] The question to be born in mind throughout this chapter is whether there is the need and indeed the scope to update the protection system offered by the 1961 Statelessness Convention to include these "new" sources of statelessness.

1 Birth and Marriage Registration

One of the most tragic and, until recently, most underestimated sources of statelessness is a deficient birth registration system. I say most tragic, because a child could be born to the "right" parents, on the territory of the "right" state yet *still* be stateless from birth. Why? Because he was not registered or given a birth certificate elaborating all the details needed to prove these fortunate circumstances. Birth registration is

> the process by which a child's birth is recorded in the civil register by the applicable government authority. It provides the first legal recognition and is generally required for the child to obtain a birth certificate. [...] It is important that the registered child receives a birth certificate, since it is this that provides permanent, official and visible evidence of a state's legal recognition of his or her existence as a member of society.[9]

Unless a child is registered at birth, he remains without the all-important official, legal proof of existence. The same observation applies to the registration of marriages, for this ensures formal recognition by the state of the newly formed familial bond – and as we have already seen, contracting marriage can have an impact on the nationality of both the spouses and any children subsequently born from the union.[10] Thus, the non-registration of these important milestones in a person's life has come to be recognised in recent years as a source of statelessness.

1.1 Connecting statelessness to (deficient) birth and marriage registration

Lack of access to birth registration affects some 50 million newborns annually.[11] The level of registration varies from one country and one region to another. The poorest registration rates can be found in Sub-Saharan Africa, where on average 70% of births are not recorded each year. In South Asia, the majority of births also go unregistered (63%), while other regions are able to register between 70 and 90% of all births. Yet even in industrialised countries, where on average 98% of births are registered, there is still room for thousands of births to go unrecorded every year

---

[8] Note that this chapter does not presume – or aspire – to offer an exhaustive discussion of nor provide comprehensive solutions for tackling each of these individual issues for this would go beyond the scope of this study. Instead, the investigation is guided at all times by the research question that underlies this section of the book: how to provide optimal guarantees for the avoidance of *statelessness*.

[9] Plan International, *Universal Birth Registration - A Universal Responsibility,* Woking: 2005, page 11.

[10] See chapter IV, including section 1 on the difference in treatment between legitimate and illegitimate children and section 3 on the impact of marriage or divorce on nationality.

[11] Or 41% of all births, statistics from the year 2000; UNICEF, *Birth Registration: Right from the Start,* Florence: March 2002, page 7.

– proof of the worldwide severity of this issue.[12] In addition, within a country's borders registration rates can vary enormously. Registration coverage in urban centres is generally much better than in rural areas: "rural children are 1.7 times more likely to be unregistered than their urban peers".[13] Moreover, certain population groups tend to be more vulnerable to non-registration than others. Generally speaking, the registration of births of those belonging to a national minority or indigenous group, as well as members of a migrant or displaced community has proven to be the most troublesome.[14]

The underlying reasons for non-registration also vary between countries and population groups and may be cumulative, but generally they belong to one of two broad categories: "governmental practices or parental inaction".[15] Thus, perhaps the most basic hindrance is the failure by the family and the state in question to understand or recognise the importance of birth registration with the result that it is simply not prioritised as it should be.[16] The parents may be put off by the costs of registration, the distance that must be travelled to the registry office, the complexity and bureaucracy of procedures or an overall distrust of the civil authorities.[17] The government, on its part, may be failing to allocate enough financial resources to ensure a properly functioning civil registration system, leading to insufficient registration bureaus and equipment, inadequate storage facilities for documents and poorly trained and supervised registry officials. This also leaves the door wide open for corruption.[18] Moreover, the legal framework and administrative set-up of the birth registration procedure may be riddled with

[12] All statistics for the year 2000, found in UNICEF, *Birth Registration: Right from the Start,* Florence: March 2002, page 8. Interestingly, of the 74 states to respond to the UNHCR Questionnaire on statelessness, four did not reply to the question as to whether the state operated a system for the registration of births and two admitted that there was no such system in place (both European states). UNHCR, *Final report concerning the Questionnaire on statelessness pursuant to the Agenda for Protection,* Geneva: March 2004, page 23.

[13] For example, in the world's Least Developed Countries, the percentage of births registered over the 1999-2004 period was 44% in urban centres but just 28% in rural areas. A similar pattern can be seen in statistics across the board. UNICEF, *The State of the World's Children. Excluded and Invisible,* New York: 2006, pages 37-38.

[14] Michael Miller, "Birth Registration: Statelessness and other repercussions for unregistered children", *3rd European Conference on Nationality - Nationality and the Child,* Strasbourg: 2004, page 6. The particular link between (irregular) migration and poor birth registration rates will be investigated further in the relevant upcoming sections.

[15] Youth Advocate Program International, *Stateless Children – Children who are without citizenship,* Booklet No. 7 in a series on International Youth Issues, 2002, page 8.

[16] UNICEF, *Birth Registration: Right from the Start,* Florence: March 2002, page 12; UNICEF, *The State of the World's Children. Excluded and Invisible,* New York: 2006, page 37.

[17] As to the question of costs - even in countries where the registration of a birth and issuance of a birth certificate is free of charge there are many hidden costs such as those incurred in travelling to the registry office as well as in missing work in order to make the journey. It is also possible that registration is officially offered free of charge but corruption nevertheless leads to divergent practices. In areas with a high infant mortality rate, parents are even less likely to drum up the costs for birth registration until the child has reached a surviving age, by which time the registration process has often become more complicated, costly or even impossible. Plan International, *Universal Birth Registration - A Universal Responsibility,* Woking: 2005, pages 27 – 30.

[18] UNICEF, *Birth Registration: Right from the Start,* Florence: March 2002, page 14; Plan International, *Universal Birth Registration - A Universal Responsibility,* Woking: 2005, pages 30-31.

obstacles that – perhaps quite unintentionally - hinder the registration of births. There may, for example, be unrealistic deadlines or documentary requirements and the opportunities for so-called "late registration" (after any initial deadline) tend to be subject to additional costs and conditions. It is also possible that barriers are deliberately constructed in the law or administrative procedure to block access to birth registration for particular groups of children.[19]

There are thus a great many aspects to the problem of non-registration which collectively account for the aforementioned 50 million newborns every year whose arrival into the world is not officially recorded.[20] While the number of stateless cases produced by this predicament cannot be equated to the number of unregistered births, the lack of birth registration significantly increases the risk of the child remaining unclaimed by any state. In order to establish the child's nationality, other forms of evidence must be relied upon such as a declaration from the medical facility where the child was born (unavailable if the child was born at home), the testimony of witnesses or DNA testing. Such methods for proving the bond that a child has with a state are often prohibitively expensive and are certainly much less reliable than a birth certificate which is already proof that the child's existence, place of birth and parentage are recognised by the state. Furthermore, the process of birth registration provides a crucial point of contact between the newborn and the state. With appropriate procedures in place, such as for the exchange of information from one country to another on domestic citizenship laws or for the verification of information such as the nationality or birthplace of the child's parents, the state can take advantage of this moment to ensure that the child will acquire a nationality. Using the details provided in the birth registration process, the government authorities can identify cases of disputed nationality or statelessness of newborns and take the necessary measures to address the situation immediately.[21] Birth registration can thereby be critical to implementing such policies as the granting of nationality *jus soli* to children born on state territory or indeed *jus sanguinis* to a child born abroad who would "otherwise be stateless".[22]

Where government policy is to purposely deny certain persons access to birth registration, we see just how much overlap there can be between the issue of non-registration and the problem of statelessness. Indeed, in the Dominican Republic - where nationality is transmitted *jus soli* and the process of birth registration is *the* means of establishing a child's Dominican citizenship – the exclusion of particular children from birth registration became the mechanism for ensuring that those same children are excluded from Dominican nationality.[23] This type of careful control of access to birth registration in order to block access to

[19] UNICEF, *Birth Registration: Right from the Start,* Florence: March 2002, pages 12 – 14; Plan International, *Universal Birth Registration - A Universal Responsibility,* Woking: 2005, pages 30 – 31.
[20] See note 11.
[21] UNHCR and IPU, *Nationality and statelessness. A handbook for parliamentarians*, 2005, page 31.
[22] See chapter IV, sections 1 and 2.
[23] Inter-American Court on Human Rights, *Case of Yean and Bosico v. Dominican Republic,* Series C, Case 130, 8 September 2005, para. 147 of the case. See also Laura van Waas, *Is Permanent Illegality Inevitable? The Challenges to Ensuring Birth Registration and the Right to a Nationality for the Children of Irregular Migrants - Thailand and the Dominican Republic,* Woking: 2006.

citizenship for specific population groups is not an isolated incident.[24] The deliberate manipulation of birth registration systems in this manner is thus a further illustration of the link between registration and access to nationality. Moreover, many of the circumstances in which the risk of statelessness is heightened will also produce an increased risk of under-registration of births. I have already mentioned the particular vulnerability of migrants' children to non-registration and later in this chapter we will see how this and other problems contribute to the exposure of particular groups of displaced persons to statelessness. Another example of how these issues can merge is the fact that deficiencies with birth registration systems are more likely to arise during a period of state succession, since this is often characterised by turmoil, mass population displacement and even violent conflict. The government authorities of the states involved (predecessor and successor) may for a time be unable to perform the duties of birth registration due to the immediate situation on the ground. Or the civil registries may be destroyed in armed conflict, as was the case in Bosnia and Croatia.[25] At a time when nationality policies are being redefined and the persons affected will likely need to prove their entitlement to acquire or retain the citizenship of one of the states concerned, a deficient birth registration system will undoubtedly impede the establishment of such evidence and substantially increase the likelihood of statelessness arising.

The foregoing considerations illustrate why, in the context of the prevention of statelessness, it has become so important to consider how international law deals with the issue of birth registration. But before looking at the relevant international norms, a final comment is appropriate here. Having seen that the registration of births is vital for the protection against statelessness, it should be mentioned that the proper registration of marriages may be equally so.[26] If a marriage goes unrecorded, there is no proof that any child resulting from the union is indeed legitimate and problems may arise for the acquisition of nationality by the child as outlined in chapter IV.[27] Moreover, the non-registration of a marriage may contribute to the non-registration of subsequent births as the mother becomes less likely to be willing or able to take the necessary steps – for example, because she is reluctant to approach the authorities since the child will be considered illegitimate or because the evidentiary requirements for unmarried mothers may be harder to meet or may require the cooperation of the child's (illegitimate) father. In this way, the improper documentation of events such as births and marriages is seen as

---

[24] UNICEF, *Birth Registration: Right from the Start,* Florence: March 2002, page 13; Plan International, *Universal Birth Registration - A Universal Responsibility,* Woking: 2005, page 30.

[25] UNHCR, "Statelessness and Citizenship" in *The State of the World's Refugees - A Humanitarian Agenda*, Oxford University Press, Oxford: 1997, page 239. The disruption caused by war to civil registration systems may outlast the end of the actual conflict by many years as was shown in the case of Cambodia and others. UNICEF, *Birth Registration: Right from the Start,* Florence: March 2002, page 16.

[26] UNHCR Executive Committee, *General Conclusion on International Protection, No. 90,* 52nd session, Geneva, 2001, paragraph (r); UNHCR Executive Committee, *General Conclusion on International Protection, No. 95,* 54th Session, Geneva, 2003, para. (x); Carol Batchelor The 1954 Convention relating to the Status of Stateless Persons: Implementation within the European Union Member States and Recommendations for Harmonisation 2004, page 10; UNHCR, *UNHCR Handbook for the Protection of Women and Girls,* January 2008, pages 123-124.

[27] See in particular chapter IV, section 1.

"interconnected and self-perpetuating"[28] as is the increased risk of statelessness that results. Moreover, the registration of marriage can be key to the protection of stateless persons and the reduction of statelessness since "for stateless persons, a marriage certificate [...] may be used at a later date to prove residence or for the purpose of naturalisation".[29] In response to the UNHCR Questionnaire on statelessness, 10.8% of participating states admitted that not all marriages were recorded.[30] Sadly though, in contrast to the growing availability of statistical information concerning birth registration, no information exists on the number of marriages that actually go unrecorded every year worldwide. This means that the scale of the problem is as yet uncharted. Nevertheless, in the context of the fight against under-age marriages, there has been some attention for the problem of non-registration of marriages[31]. In the following section we will see whether this has been translated into obligations under international human rights law.

1.2 International human rights law

Human rights law recognises the right of every child to be registered at birth. It is interesting to note, however, that its promulgation was initially based on an entirely different rationale than the prevention of statelessness. The International Covenant on Civil and Political Rights does house the right to birth registration and the right to nationality as two consecutive paragraphs of the same article,[32] but this should not be taken as evidence that the two rights were necessarily linked in that way. Instead, it can be explained from the perspective that the entire provision aims to ensure special protective measures for a child in view of his vulnerable position as a minor.[33] The overall role of birth registration has since been elaborated upon by the Human Rights Committee in its General Comment 17 on child rights:

> The main purpose of the obligation to register children after birth is to reduce the danger of abduction, sale of or traffic in children, or of other types of treatment that are incompatible with the enjoyment of rights provided for in the covenant.[34]

---

[28] Carol Batchelor, "The International Legal Framework Concerning Statelessness and Access for Stateless Persons", *European Union Seminar on the Content and Scope of International Protection: Panel 1 - Legal basis of international protection,* Madrid: 2002, page 5.

[29] UNHCR, *UNHCR Handbook for the Protection of Women and Girls,* January 2008, page 123.

[30] UNHCR, *Final report concerning the Questionnaire on statelessness pursuant to the Agenda for Protection,* Geneva: March 2004, page 21.

[31] Consider, for example, the country report on Bangladesh prepared by the UN Development Programme (UNDP) in 2000, where a section is devoted to the registration of marriages with particular focus on the problem of underage marriage. UNDP Regional Bureau for Asia and the Pacific, *Common Country Assessment on Bangladesh,* 2000, section 6.4.2.

[32] Article 24 of the 1966 International Covenant on Civil and Political Rights.

[33] As suggested by the first paragraph of the same article: "Every child shall have [...] the right to such measures of protection as are required by his status as a minor, on the part of his family, society and the State".

[34] Human Rights Committee, *CCPR General Comment No. 17: Rights of the Child (Art. 24),* Geneva: 7 April 1989, paragraph 7.

While the right to acquire a nationality would certainly fall under "the enjoyment of rights provided for in the covenant" since it is the very next right to be included, it is clear that this is not the main inspiration behind the imposition of the duty of registration upon states. Nevertheless, in recent years, the Committee has illustrated its awareness of the importance of birth registration in the context of the prevention of statelessness in the Concluding Observations to several of the periodic reports of state parties to the ICCPR.[35] The Committee has even suggested that the moment of registration should be utilised to ensure that the child acquires a nationality.[36]

The Convention on the Rights of the Child adopts a virtually identical approach to the ICCPR, including a child's right to be registered at birth in the same article as the right to acquire a nationality. Almost in one breath in fact, it states: "the child shall be registered immediately after birth and shall have [...] the right to acquire a nationality".[37] The duty of state parties to register all births within their jurisdiction – children born on state territory as well as children born abroad to nationals of the state[38] - is a subject to which the Committee on the Rights of the Child has devoted substantial attention in the consideration of dozens of reports by state parties over the years. In most of these, birth registration has been addressed as an independent issue.[39] However, in a number of concluding observations, the link with the right to acquire a nationality has also been made apparent by the Committee. In some cases, the Committee has even explicitly identified the role that non-registration has played in the creation of statelessness in the state party. For example, in 2004 the Committee expressed its concern that in Japan

---

[35] For example with regards to in Human Rights Committee, *Concluding Observations: Ecuador*, A/53/40 vol. I, Geneva: 1998, paragraph 291; *Thailand*, A/60/40 vol. I, Geneva: 2005, paragraph 95 (22).

[36] In the Concluding Observation on Slovenia, the Committee states that "while recognising that registration is distinct from conferral of nationality, [it] is also concerned that some children are registered at birth without a nationality"; in Human Rights Committee, *Concluding Observations: Slovenia*, A/60/40 vol. I, Geneva: 2005, paragraph 93 (15). Regrettably, the Committee has not delineated the precise action that it envisages states to take in these circumstances.

[37] Article 7, Convention on the Rights of the Child.

[38] See Committee on the Rights of the Child, *Concluding Observations: Bosnia and Herzegovina*, CRC/C/15/Add.259, Geneva: 2005, paragraph 33.

[39] A small selection of such reports through the years is: Committee on the Rights of the Child, *Concluding Observations: Ethiopia,* CRC/C/15/Add.67, Geneva: 1997, paragraph 29; *Fiji,* CRC/C/15/Add.89, Geneva: 1998, paragraphs 15 and 35; *Belize,* CRC/C/15/Add.99, Geneva: 1999, paragraph 18; *Honduras,* CRC/C/15/Add.105, Geneva: 1999, paragraph 21; *Sierra Leone,* CRC/C/15/Add.116, Geneva: 2000, paragraphs 42-43; *Kyrgyzstan,* CRC/C/15/Add.127, Geneva: 2000, paragraphs 29-30; *Dominican Republic,* CRC/C/15/Add.150, Geneva: 2001, paragraphs 26-27; *Turkey,* CRC/C/15/Add.152, Geneva: 2001, paragraphs 35-36; *Bhutan,* CRC/C/15/Add.157, Geneva: 2001, paragraphs 34-35; *Sudan,* CRC/C/15/Add.190, Geneva: 2002, paragraphs 33-34; *Jamaica,* CRC/C15/Add.120, Geneva: 2003, paragraphs 30-31; *Pakistan,* CRC/C/15/Add.217, Geneva: 2003, paragraphs 38-39; *Brazil,* CRC/C/15/Add.241, Geneva: 2004, paragraphs 38-39; *Botswana,* CRC/C/15/Add.242, Geneva: 2004, paragraphs 34-35; *Togo,* CRC/C/15/Add.255, Geneva: 2005, paragraph 37; *Yemen,* CRC/C/15/Add.266, Geneva: 2005, paragraphs 39-40.

> undocumented migrants are unable to register the birth of their children, and that this has also resulted in cases of statelessness.[40]

In another report the Committee recalled that

> official birth registration is a fundamental first step towards securing the rights of a child to a name and nationality.[41]

In yet others, the Committee has chosen to encourage ratification of the 1954 and 1961 Statelessness Conventions in the same paragraphs in which the issue of birth registration is dealt with – implicitly reaffirming the close connection between these matters.[42]

The Concluding Observations of the Committee on the Rights of the Child on the subject of birth registration confirm that lack of access to birth registration tends to disproportionately affect particular vulnerable groups. Most commonly identified in this context are children born to indigenous persons, refugees or asylum seekers, (undocumented or illegal) migrant workers and – in Europe – Roma. The Committee has made clear that the right to be registered immediately after birth is a right that *all* children enjoy, "including asylum-seeking, refugee or migrant children – irrespective of their nationality, immigration status or statelessness".[43] Furthermore, while the child will not necessarily have a claim to the nationality of the country that is obliged to provide them with birth certification, coupled to the birth registration process there must be a system in place that is designed to "fulfil his or her right to acquire [...] a nationality".[44] Within the UN human rights system then, there is full recognition of the right of every child to be registered at birth and the importance of this right in the prevention of statelessness.

Moving to regional instruments, we see that both the African Charter on the Rights and Welfare of the Child and the Covenant on the Rights of the Child in Islam expound a right to birth registration, where it is housed alongside the right of a child to a name and a nationality.[45] In contrast, the European and American human rights conventions remain silent on this issue. This has not, however, stopped both the European Court of Human Rights and the Inter-American Court of

---

[40] Committe on the Rights of the Child, *Concluding Observations: Japan*, CRC/C/15/Add.231, Geneva: 2004, paragraph 31. Other examples of this phenomenon are the reports on the *Islamic Republic of Iran*, CRC/C/15/Add.254, Geneva: 2005, paragraphs 35-36 and *Philippines*, CRC/C/15/Add.258, Geneva: 2005, paragraph 36.

[41] Committee on the Rights of the Child, *Concluding Observations: The Former Yugoslav Republic of Macedonia* RC CRC/C/15/Add.118, Geneva: 2000, paragraph 21.

[42] For example in Committee on the Rights of the Child, *Concluding Observations: Djibouti*, CRC/C/15Add.131, Geneva: 2000, paragraph 32; *Niger*, CRC/C/15/Add.179, Geneva: 2002, paragraph 61; *Canada*, CRC/C/15/Add.215, Geneva: 2003, paragraph 27; *Kazakhstan*, CRC/C/15/Add.213, Geneva: 2003, paragraphs 32-33.

[43] Committee on the Rights of the Child, *General Comment No. 6: Treatment of unaccompanied and separated children outside their country of origin*, 2005, at paragraph 12.

[44] UN General Assembly Resolution, "A world fit for children", Twenty-Seventh Special Session of the GA, 11 October 2002, at paragraph 44 (1).

[45] Article 6, paragraph 2 of the African Charter on the Rights and Welfare of the Child; Article 7, paragraph 1 of the Covenant on the Rights of the Child in Islam.

Human Rights from dealing with the question of access to birth registration under the auspices of related provisions from the respective conventions. The European Court has read the right to birth registration into article 8 of the European Convention on Human Rights which deals with the right to respect for family life.[46] Meanwhile, the Inter-American Court addressed the matter of birth registration in depth in the case of *Yean and Bosico v. Dominican Republic* that was discussed in chapter V. The court interpreted article 18 of the American Convention on Human Rights concerning the right to a name as follows:

> Under article 18 of the Convention, States are obliged not only to protect the right to a name, but also to provide the necessary measures to facilitate the registration of an individual, immediately after birth.[47]

Indeed, both the European and Inter-American human rights courts clearly concur with the Committee on the Rights of the Child that the right to birth registration is unconditional and no (groups of) children should be excluded.[48]

In sum then, the universal and regional human rights systems together provide abundant evidence of a global consensus on the fundamental right of every child to be registered at birth. In the concluding observations to country reports of such bodies as the UN Committee on the Rights of the Child it is even possible to trace a series of suggestions as to how universal birth registration coverage is to be achieved.[49] State parties have, for example, been reminded that registration should be made compulsory for all births on state territory.[50] Where states have introduced

[46] European Court of Human Rights, *Case of Marckx vs. Belgium*, No. 6833/74, 13 June 1979; See also the case before the European Commission on Human Rights, *Case of Kalderas Gipsies v. the Federal Republic of Germany and the Netherlands*, No. 7823/77-7824/77, 6 July 1977; As cited in Geraldine van Bueren, *The International Law on the Rights of the Child*, Martinus Nijhoff, Dordrecht: 1995, page 118..

[47] Inter-American Court on Human Rights, *Case of Yean and Bosico v. Dominican Republic*, Series C, Case 130, 8 September 2005, para. 183.

[48] In particular, the European Court of Human Rights found that conditions impeding the registration of illegitimate children were intolerable. European Court of Human Rights, *Case of Marckx vs. Belgium*, No. 6833/74, 13 June 1979 as cited in Geraldine van Bueren, *The International Law on the Rights of the Child*, Martinus Nijhoff, Dordrecht: 1995, page 118. The Inter-American Court determined that the parents migratory status is irrelevant for access to birth registration. Inter-American Court on Human Rights, *Case of Yean and Bosico v. Dominican Republic*, Series C, Case 130, 8 September 2005.

[49] Similar references can be found in some instances in the concluding observations of other UN treaty bodies such as the Committee on the Elimination or Discrimination Against Women. However, the main body of work on this issue can be found in the reports of the Committee on the Rights of the Child. This Committee indeed requests that certain information relating to birth registration practices be included in country reports in order to facilitate the monitoring of this treaty obligation. Information should be provided on: "Steps taken to prevent the non-registration of children immediately after birth, including in view of possible social or cultural obstacles [...] measures taken to sensitize and mobilize public opinion on the need for birth registration of children, and to provide adequate training to registry personnel [and] information on the elements of the child's identity included in the birth registration and the measures adopted to prevent any kind of stigmatization or discrimination of the child". Committee on the Rights of the Child, *General guidelines for periodic reports*, CRC/C/58, Geneva: 20 November 1996, paras. 49-51.

[50] See for example Committee on the Rights of the Child, *Concluding observations: Malawi*, CRC/C/114, Geneva: 2002, paras. 410-411.

deadlines for registration as an incentive to ensure that the birth is recorded "immediately"[51], the Committee has nevertheless called for leniency – more particularly for the extending of initial time periods for registration, for every effort to be made to ensure late birth registration and for the abolition of sanctions such as fines for late registration as these have a severely deterrent effect.[52] Concerning the more general question of imposing a fee for birth registration, the concluding observations provide a somewhat mixed message: calling for free issuance of a birth certificate as part of the registration process,[53] asking that costs for birth registration be kept low[54] or determining that birth registration should, in fact, simply be free of charge.[55] The Committee has also called for improved access to registration procedures through the decentralisation of birth registration and where necessary the deployment of mobile registration units to the most isolated areas of the country.[56] Meanwhile, to promote the use of procedures that have been put in place, the Committee has recommended awareness raising activities on the importance of birth registration, aimed not only at parents, but also at "government officers, midwives, community and religious leaders".[57] Thus the Committee on the Rights of the Child has taken the lead in delineating the form that birth registration procedures should take in order to address many of the practical obstacles mentioned in the introduction above and to ensure that the right to birth registration is enjoyed by all children, everywhere.

Finally in this section, we must consider the registration of marriages. It can be established from the outset that international human rights instruments and bodies are less forthcoming about this issue than on the matter of birth registration. However, the Convention on the Elimination of Discrimination Against Women

---

[51] As prescribed by, among others, article 7 of the Convention on the Rights of the Child.

[52] On the extension of time limits and the overall promotion of late registration, see Committee on the Rights of the Child, *Concluding observations: Mozambique,* CRC/C/114, Geneva: 2002, para. 284; *Jamaica,* CRC/C/132 Geneva: 2003, para. 425. On the abolition of fines or fees for late birth registration see Committee on the Rights of the Child, *Concluding observations: Guinea-Bissau,* CRC/C/118, Geneva: 2002, paras. 58-59; *Zambia,* CRC/C/132, Geneva: 2003, para. 180.

[53] Committee on the Rights of the Child, *Concluding observations: Gambia,* CRC/C/111, Geneva: 2001, para. 429.

[54] "The Committee [...] recommends that the State party makes the birth registration procedure *less costly* and more accessible". Committee on the Rights of the Child, *Concluding observations: Kenya,* CRC/C/111, Geneva: 2001, para. 113; "The Committee recommends that the State party [...] make the birth registration procedure accessible free *or at a low cost".* Committee on the Rights of the Child, *Concluding observations: Malawi,* CRC/C/114, Geneva: 2002, para. 411.

[55] Committee on the Rights of the Child, *Concluding observations: Central African Republic,* CRC/C/100, Geneva: 2000, para. 434; *Kyrgyzstan,* CRC/C/97, Geneva: 2000, paras. 296-297; *Haiti,* CRC/C/124, Geneva: 2003, para. 425; *Georgia,* CRC/C/133, Geneva: 2003, para. 541.

[56] On the decentralisation of birth registration, see for example, Committee on the Rights of the Child, *Concluding observations: Greece,* CRC/C/114, Geneva: 2002, para. 132; *Haiti,* CRC/C/124, Geneva: 2003, para. 425; *Zambia,* CRC/C/132, Geneva: 2003, para. 180. On the use of mobile registration units, see for example Committee on the Rights of the Child, *Concluding observations: Cameroon,* CRC/C/111, Geneva: 2001, para. 358; *Guinea-Bissau,* CRC/C/118, Geneva: 2002, para. 59; *Eritrea,* CRC/C/132, Geneva: 2003, para. 52; *Jamaica,* CRC/C/132, Geneva: 2003, para. 424.

[57] Committee on the Rights of the Child, *Concluding observations: Kenya,* CRC/C/111, Geneva: 2001, para 113; *Gambia,* CRC/C/111, Geneva: 2001, para 429; *Malawi,* CRC/C/114, Geneva: 2002, para. 411.

does address the question of registration in its article 16, which deals mainly with discrimination against women in the context of marriage. The second paragraph of this provision prescribes the taking of "all necessary action, including legislation [...] to make the registration of marriages in an official registry compulsory".[58] In 1994, the UN treaty body mandated to monitor the implementation of this convention issued a General Recommendation on "Equality in marriage and family relations". This included the following statement:

> States parties should also require the registration of all marriages whether contracted civilly or according to custom or religious law. The State can thereby ensure compliance with the Convention and establish equality between partners, a minimum age for marriage, prohibition of bigamy and polygamy and the protection of the rights of children.[59]

The registration of marriages is thereby deemed to serve a number of purposes, including the protection of the rights of children – this being a broad reference that may arguably include protection against statelessness. Regrettably, the Committee on the Elimination of Discrimination Against Women has not been very active in pursuing the question of the registration of marriages in its consideration of state party reports.[60] Meanwhile, the only other documents to explicitly prescribe the registration of all marriages by a competent authority are the Convention on consent to marriage, minimum age for marriage and registration of marriages[61] and the Protocol to the African Charter on Human and Peoples' Rights on the Rights of Women in Africa.[62] The former is a little-known instrument dating from 1962 which has attracted just 49 state parties to date, while the latter is a very young document that has so far been ratified by less than half of the African states.[63] The impact of these two instruments is therefore limited. So although there is some understanding of the importance of the registration of marriages, the issue has yet to attract a substantial response from the international community comparable with the way in which birth registration is being addressed.

---

[58] The rest of the paragraph addresses the problem of under-age marriage. Article 16, paragraph 2 of the 1979 Convention on the Elimination of All Forms of Discrimination against Women.

[59] Committee on the Elimination of Discrimination Against Women, *General Recommendation 21: Equality in marriage and family relations*, A/49/38, New York: 1994, para. 39.

[60] Just two references to the registration of marriages can be found. Committee on the Elimination of Discrimination Against Women, *Concluding Observations: Namibia,* A/52/38/Rev.1 Part II, New York: 1997, paras. 110 and 125; *India,* A/55/38 part I, New York: 2000, para. 62. While this may also be construed as a sign that the failure to register marriages is not a widespread problem, there is no evidence to support such a conclusion. It is equally likely that the problem has not yet been thoroughly mapped.

[61] The duty to register all marriages is included in its article 3.

[62] The registration of marriages is prescribed in article 6, section d), Protocol to the African Charter on Human and Peoples' Rights on the Rights of Women in Africa, 2003.

[63] The Protocol to the African Charter on Human and Peoples' Rights on the Rights of Women in Africa has attracted 20 state parties, while the African Charter on Human and Peoples' Rights itself has been ratified by all 53 African states.

2 Migration

The second "new" cause of statelessness that has come to the fore is migration. Throughout history, migration has been a natural human impulse.[64] Homes are uprooted as people move on in search of land, food or hope - or to escape war, poverty or despair. The world today paints no different picture. In fact, international migrants now make up roughly 3% of the global population - 191 million people reside outside the country in which they were born.[65] Moreover, "migration has never been as pervasive, or as socio-economically and politically significant, as it is today".[66] No region has been left untouched.[67] These simple facts have heralded the emergence of new questions about the attribution of nationality and the coordination of citizenship policies:[68]

> The growing international mobility of people questions the basis for belonging to the nation-state. [...] The idea of the citizen who spent most of his or her life in one country and shared a common national identity is losing ground.[69]

The result is that many of the concerns raised in previous chapters are growing ever more prevalent. To begin with, there will be an increasing incidence of conflict of laws situations – of marriages between nationals of different states; of children born in a state that their parents do not hold citizenship of; and of an incongruity between the laws of the country of origin on loss of nationality and the naturalisation law of the host country. All of these situations were identified as potential "technical" sources of statelessness in chapter IV. Furthermore, where migration has preceded or accompanied the transfer of territory, we saw that the displaced population was at significantly greater risk of exposure to statelessness.[70] With present-day migration also traversing ever wider divides, not just in a geographical sense, but also religiously, linguistically, culturally and economically,[71] it brings new concerns

---

[64] Note that throughout this section the terms "migration" and "migrant" are used in a general sense to refer to any form of displacement – or person displaced – across international borders.

[65] The number of migrants is also growing, and it is growing at a more rapid pace: the growth rate was 1.4% from 1990-1995 but was up to 1.9% from 2000-2004. UN, *International migration and development,* Report of the Secretary General, UN Doc. A/60/971, 18 May 2006, pages 12 and 28. See also the section *Facts and Figures: Global estimates and trends* on the website of the International Organisation for Migration, accessible via http://www.iom.int.

[66] Stephen Castles; Mark Miller, *The Age of Migration*, The Guildford Press, London: 2003, page 278.

[67] United Nations Department of Economic and Social Affairs, *International Migration 2006 Wall Chart,* Population Division, New York, March 2006; See also Stephen Castles; Alastair Davidson, *Citizenship and Migration. Globalisation and the Politics of Belonging*, Macmillan Press, London: 2000, page 9.

[68] It has also encouraged renewed thinking on the content of nationality as a legal status upon which certain rights and duties rest – evidenced, for example, by the emergence of various forms of "quasi-citizenship" and "denizen" status, as we well see in Part 3.

[69] Stephen Castles; Alastair Davidson, *Citizenship and Migration. Globalisation and the Politics of Belonging*, Macmillan Press, London: 2000, pages vii - viii (preface).

[70] See chapter VI, including the example of the Formerly Deported Persons in the Ukraine.

[71] Stephen Castles; Alastair Davidson, *Citizenship and Migration. Globalisation and the Politics of Belonging*, Macmillan Press, London: 2000, page 9; Stephen Castles; Mark Miller, *The Age of*

to the citizenship debate with policy makers forced to consider the effect that the newcomers have in altering the social fabric of their host country and challenging the (perceived) national identity.[72] "Racism towards certain groups is to be found in virtually all immigration countries"[73] and with it come new opportunities for discrimination and denial of citizenship which may translate into statelessness.[74] In addition, cultural or linguistic barriers may prevent migrants from accessing and utilising mechanisms that can play a vital role in preventing statelessness, such as birth registration procedures or appeals procedures in the event of a nationality dispute.[75]

Fundamentally then, simply by causing a greater intermingling of people across the boundaries that formally separate nation-states, modern migration patterns precipitate and exacerbate many of the causes of statelessness that have already been identified and dealt with in preceding pages and chapters. To avoid repetition, the following paragraphs will focus rather on specific problems and corresponding international norms relating to three – variously overlapping[76] – categories of migrant or displaced person who are acutely vulnerable to statelessness: irregular migrants, victims of trafficking persons and refugees. What these groups have in common is that they defy regulation and thereby confront states with newcomers whose presence is unpredicted, uninvited and – more often than not – unwanted. In the current age of "migration management" this type of displacement raises serious policy questions in dealing with (access to) legal status and nationality. In the following sections we will consider how each of these groups can become susceptible to statelessness and to what extent international law has intervened to stave off such a troublesome result. Before doing so, it is helpful to

---

Migration, The Guildford Press, London: 2003, pages 278 and 281. For example, according to UN statistics, one third of all migrants have moved from a developing country to a developed country – implying at least that a large economic and cultural divide has been crossed. UN Report, *International migration and development,* Report of the Secretary General, UN Doc. A/60/971, 18 May 2006, page 12.

[72] Douglas Klusmeyer; Alexander Aleinikoff, *From Migrants to Citizens: Membership in a Changing World*, Carnegie Endowment for International Peace, Washington, DC: 2000, page 1; Aristide Zolberg, "Modes of Incorporation: Toward a Comparative Framework" in Bader (ed) *Citizenship and Exclusion*, Macmillan Press, London: 1997, page 141.

[73] Stephen Castles; Mark Miller, *The Age of Migration*, The Guildford Press, London: 2003, page 35.

[74] The UN warns of "rising cultural and religious tensions" in its report, *International migration and development,* Report of the Secretary General, UN Doc. A/60/971, 18 May 2006, page 7. This may significantly impact citizenship policy. See chapter V for the discussion of denial of citizenship and arbitrary deprivation of nationality. If denial of citizenship subsists and the newly formed immigrant minority remains marginalised, then there is a danger that the rising tensions will eventually be manifested in violence, destabilisation, conflict and even (a call for) the break-up of the state. In this extreme example, migration will have contributed to state succession that, in turn, introduces new risks of statelessness (see chapter VI). For a discussion of the potential of (states' reactions to) migration leading to conflict, see Stephen Castles; Alastair Davidson, *Citizenship and Migration. Globalisation and the Politics of Belonging*, Macmillan Press, London: 2000, chapter 3; Stephen Castles; Mark Miller, *The Age of Migration*, The Guildford Press, London: 2003, pages 287-288.

[75] See section 1 above and chapter V, section 2.

[76] Note that because the determination of a person's status as an irregular migrant, a victim of trafficking or a refugee is based on different criteria, these categories may overlap. An individual may be a victim of trafficking, hold an irregular immigration status and qualify under the definition of a refugee – all at once. The categories are therefore not mutually exclusive.

note that what distinguishes the groups from one another is their treatment under international law: the fact of being a victim of trafficking or a refugee has consequences for the international protection offered. In fact, the position of irregular migrants forms the baseline or minimum standard of treatment to be guaranteed to *all* persons, in an irregular status or otherwise, so this will be looked at first. Thereafter, we will also consider the additional rights ascribed to victims of trafficking and refugees to the extent that these are relevant in the fight against statelessness.

2.1 Irregular migration

Ever since the emergence of nation-states, and most notably over the course of the last hundred years or so, the question of how to regulate the movement of people across borders has been a constant preoccupation for the powers that be. States gradually assumed the authority to control migration - a process that was facilitated by institutionalising the use of identity papers and passports.[77] Today, every effort is made to regulate or *manage* migration through detailed immigration policies and border control. States can now hold what is, in effect, a selection process for prospective immigrants by pre-determining the conditions that must be met for eligibility to enter the country. This can be seen as a sort of initial qualifying round for access to citizenship: those who are approved and admitted are granted the opportunity to build up a bond with the host state that may, one day, lead to a *jus domicilli* claim to nationality (for instance through naturalisation) or indeed a *jus soli* entitlement to citizenship for future offspring.[78] It is not unsurprising then that, over the last half-century at least, efforts to carefully manage migration have been joined by measures that focus on the newcomer as a potential citizen and are devised to "integrate immigrants [and] regulate community relations"[79] in order to smoothen the transition from outsider to member of the polity.[80] It is certainly true that recent amendments to nationality acts in many countries admit that international migration must now be carefully factored into citizenship policy.[81] For example, "most *jus sanguinis* countries have realised that the exclusion [of immigrants and their children] from citizenship is problematic, leading to social marginalisation, political exclusion, conflict and racism" and have adapted their

[77] John Torpey, *The Invention of the Passport. Surveillance, Citizenship and the State*, Cambridge University Press, Cambridge: 2000, page 9.

[78] It has been argued that "the acquisition of nationality by immigrants is [...] increasingly understood as a point on a continuum of legal status ranging from "aliens" to "denizens" and then to "full citizens". Douglas Klusmeyer; Alexander Aleinikoff, *From Migrants to Citizens: Membership in a Changing World*, Carnegie Endowment for International Peace, Washington, DC: 2000, page 436.

[79] Stephen Castles; Alastair Davidson, *Citizenship and Migration. Globalisation and the Politics of Belonging*, Macmillan Press, London: 2000, page 60.

[80] Aleinikoff and Klusmeyer have persuasively argued that the basic premise behind nationality policy in the age of migration should be that "it is desirable that immigrants and their descendents become citizens and have the right to become citizens". Alexander Aleinikoff; Douglas Klusmeyer, *Citizenship Policies for an Age of Migration*, Carnegie Empowerment for International Peace, Washington D.C.: 2002.

[81] Stephen Castles; Mark Miller, *The Age of Migration*, The Guildford Press, London: 2003, page 46.

policy accordingly.[82] However, any relaxation of citizenship policy tends to benefit only those immigrants (and their children) who have correctly and successfully navigated the systems of migration management.

Meanwhile the notion that migration can be meticulously managed has proven to be flawed, as evidenced by the enduring process of irregular migration. Every year, thousands upon thousands of people defy existing systems of migration management and move to or settle in a country without authorisation under its immigration laws. This includes

> immigrants who entered the host country clandestinely, asylum-seekers who have been denied refugee status, immigrants who find themselves in a situation of *de facto* illegality, and those whose residence permits have expired.[83]

Whatever the circumstances, such persons have become *irregular* migrants: "person[s] whose presence in the territory of a state violates the domestic immigration laws".[84] They are also known as *undocumented* migrants or "illegal immigrants"[85] and they form a new, extremely vulnerable group in international relations. The International Organisation for Migration estimates there to be 30-40 million irregular migrants worldwide (or 15-20% of the globe's total migrant stock)[86] and numbers are on the rise.[87]

---

[82] Stephen Castles; Alastair Davidson, *Citizenship and Migration. Globalisation and the Politics of Belonging*, Macmillan Press, London: 2000, page 94. The prevalence of the "double *jus soli*" rule is increasing, whereby the third generation immigrant is automatically awarded citizenship at birth: double *jus soli* confers nationality at birth on the basis of birth on state soil to a child, (one of) whose parent(s) was also born on state territory. There is also "a clear trend towards increasing naturalisation of foreign residents". Stephen Castles; Mark Miller, *The Age of Migration*, The Guildford Press, London: 2003, page 243.

[83] Jorge Bustamante, *Report of the Special Rapporteur on the human rights of migrants*, E/CN.4/2006/73, 30 December 2005, page 11. It is, for instance, reported that "up to 90% of asylum applications are rejected – yet many asylum seekers cannot be deported", so they remain, indefinitely and irregularly, in the receiving state. Stephen Castles; Mark Miller, *The Age of Migration*, The Guildford Press, London: 2003, page 104.

[84] Adapted from Beth Lyon, *New International Human Rights Standards on Unauthorised Immigrant Workers Rights: Seizing an Opportunity to Pull Governments Out of the Shadows,* in A. Bayefsky (Ed.), "Human Rights and Refugees, Internally Displaced Persons and Migrant Workers", Koninklijke Brill, Leiden 2006, page 553.

[85] The latter term is often that favoured by the media and by politicians at national level while the more neutrally toned expressions *irregular migrant* and *undocumented migrant* are the approved terms of international law. See for example the International Convention on the Rights of All Migrant Workers and Members of Their Families, 18 December 1990.

[86] *Facts and Figures: Global estimates and trends* on the website of the International Organisation for Migration, www.iom.int. The United States alone is considered to host somewhere in the region of 11 million irregular immigrants and there are also an estimated 3 million US-born children whose parents are irregular immigrants in the country. Stephen Camarota, *Immigrants at mid-decade. A snapshot of America's foreign-born population in 2005,* Centre for Immigration Studies, December 2005. It should be noted, however, that irregular migration by nature "eludes registration and statistical coverage" thus such estimates are an imprecise result of a combination of empirical evidence, assumptions and guess-work. Citation from a report comparing approaches to compiling statistics on irregular migration in various states across Europe and beyond; Charles Pinkerton, Gail McLaughlan and John Salt, *Sizing the*

The composition and characteristics of the irregular migrant population vary from one host country to the next, influenced by the content of *domestic* immigration laws. This means that it is impossible to generalise about the profile of irregular migrants: the underlying motives for migration, the method of entry into the receiving state, the deportability, living conditions and other details differ from one person to another and between states.[88] Nevertheless, irregular migrants share two further characteristics, besides their unlawful status, that are relevant here. Firstly, many have become a (semi-)permanent feature of their receiving state because host states are reluctant or unable to enforce their immigration laws too strictly: there may be humanitarian objections to sending irregular migrants home (the prohibition of *non-refoulement*)[89] or the state may be conceding to the national economy's demand for 3I labour (inexpensive, imported and irregular).[90] And secondly, despite their factual, long-term presence on the territory of the host state, a great many of these migrants will never have their status regularised.[91] These basic observations are key to understanding the link between irregular migration and statelessness.

2.1.1 Connecting statelessness to irregular migration

Holding an irregular immigration status can have a detrimental impact on an individual's enjoyment of many rights, including their right to a nationality. We have already seen how migrants may lose their citizenship, for example through revocation of nationality due to long-term residence abroad or as a result of state succession which took place in their absence. The crucial difference in the position

---

illegally resident population in the UK, United Kingdom Home Office Online Report 58/04, Migration Research Unit, University College London, page 1. Elsewhere described as irregular migration's "opaqueness to measurement and scrutiny". Stephen Castles; Mark Miller, *The Age of Migration*, The Guildford Press, London: 2003, page 95.

[87] Stephen Castles; Mark Miller, *The Age of Migration*, The Guildford Press, London: 2003, pages 94 and 283

[88] Thailand makes an interesting case in point as it is home to at least 17 different categories of persons whose presence in the state is officially illegal. This includes "persons fleeing fighting" (refugees from neighbouring Myanmar who are currently warehoused in border camps), irregular migrant workers from Lao DPR, Cambodia and Myanmar, as well as numerous ethnic minority groups whose long-term presence in the country means that the term irregular *migrant* no longer really suffices. International Rescue Committee, *Basic Information on Rights of Migrant Workers in Thailand*, ICR Bangkok, 2006, p. 3.

[89] Consider situations of so-called "warehousing" of refugee populations, where the situation becomes protracted as their continuing presence is tolerated but their situation is not regularised, preventing them from accessing a range of rights. At the end of 2003, UNHCR put the number of protracted refugee situations worldwide at 38 and concluded that "the average duration of refugee situations, protracted or not, has increased: from 9 years in 1993 to 17 years in 2003". UNHCR, *Protracted refugee situations*, EC/54/SC/CRP.14, Geneva: 10 June 2004.

[90] Stephen Castles; Alastair Davidson, *Citizenship and migration. Globalisation and the politics of belonging*, Macmillan Press, London: 2000, p. 73.

[91] Amnesty programmes are still exceptional and selective, regularising the stay of certain categories of irregular migrants and often providing only short-term residence permits, whereby the individual returns to irregularity again after the permit expires. Charles Pinkerton, Gail McLaughlan and John Salt, *Sizing the illegally resident population in the UK*, United Kingdom Home Office Online Report 58/04, Migration Research Unit, University College London.

of the *irregular* migrant lies in the lack of opportunity to access an alternative nationality. Whatever the additional criteria for naturalisation in the host country, an absolute requirement in all countries is a minimum period of *lawful* residence, thereby excluding irregular migrants from the outset.[92] If an irregular migrant loses his only nationality, or is already stateless prior to displacement,[93] he is very likely to remain stateless indefinitely – particularly since the status of irregularity so often proves to be a protracted, even indefinite one.

To illustrate this scenario, let us take as an example the irregular migrants from Myanmar (Burma)[94] who have settled in Thailand. Up to 2 million persons from Myanmar are now irregularly on Thai soil – a consequence of the enduring situation in Myanmar, characterised by human rights abuses, economic collapse and persecution of minority groups.[95] Some 140,000 of those who have come to Thailand have been allowed to settle in refugee camps with the status of "persons fleeing fighting" while others (many similarly situated) are cast as "illegal migrant workers" or "unregistered illegal immigrants".[96] All are in an irregular situation under Thai immigration law. Meanwhile, it has been reported that in leaving Myanmar without permission from the government authorities, these migrants are deemed to have left the country permanently and thereby forfeited their Burmese citizenship.[97] Burmese citizenship may be withdrawn "if there is evidence of complete uprooting even if one were forced to leave and has been absent from Burma for less than a year".[98] Moreover, once Burmese nationality is lost in this manner, it cannot be recovered.[99] At the same time, the irregular status of these

---

[92] Stephen Castles; Alastair Davidson, *Citizenship and migration. Globalisation and the politics of belonging*, Macmillan Press, London: 2000, p. 86.

[93] A common problem where forced displacement and refugees are concerned. See UNHCR, "Statelessness and Citizenship" in *The State of the World's Refugees - A Humanitarian Agenda*, Oxford University Press, Oxford: 1997, page 244

[94] There is some contention surrounding the official name of Myanmar/Burma. The UN has recognised the name change from Burma to Myanmar but some governments continue to dispute the legitimacy of this change.

[95] See the successive reports of the Special Rapporteur on the situation of human rights in Myanmar, Paulo Sérgio Pinheiro, including most recently E/CN.4/2006/34, 7 February 2006; A/HRC/4/14, 12 February 2007 and A/HRC/7/24, 7 March 2008.

[96] The dire human rights situation and ongoing civil conflict in Myanmar since the 1980s has caused a mass exodus of persons seeking safety and protection. Thailand is not a party to the 1951 Refugee Convention and does not have an asylum policy so all unauthorised immigrants from neighbouring Myanmar are treated as irregular migrants, whatever other label they are given. Veronika Martin, *Myanmarese Refugees in Thailand: No Freedom, No Choices,* US Committee for Refugees, World Refugee Survey 2004, page 82.

[97] Article 16 of the Burma Citizenship Law of 1982 declares that "a citizen who leaves the state permanently [...] ceases to be a citizen". See further Nyo Nyo, "Burmese Children in Thailand: Legal Aspects", in *Legal Issues on Burma Journal,* Burma Lawyers Council, No. 10, December 2001; Human Rights Yearbook Burma 2003-2004, *Chapter 15. The Situation of Migrant Workers,* Human Rights Documentation Unit, National Coalition Government of Burma, 2002; Refugees International, *Stolen Futures: The Stateless Children of Burmese Asylum Seekers,* 25 June 2004.

[98] Tang Lay Lee, "Statelessness, Human Rights and Gender. Irregular migrant workers from Burma in Thailand", Martinus Nijhoff Publishers, Leiden 2005, page 158.

[99] Article 22 of the Burma Citizenship Law of 1982 states that "a person whose citizenship has ceased or has been revoked shall have no right to apply again for citizenship".

migrants in Thailand is an absolute bar to applying for naturalisation there. The combined effect is the enduring statelessness of many members of this group.[100]

Children born to irregular migrants on the territory of the receiving state also run a substantially increased risk of statelessness. To begin with, if their parents have been rendered stateless and they are born on the territory of a state that grants nationality *jus sanguinis,* without a back-up clause offering *jus soli* citizenship to prevent statelessness, then the plight of the parent becomes the plight of the child. It is true that this problem may affect children of all stateless migrants alike. Again, what really brings the vulnerability of the situation of the irregular migrant to light is the fact that the irregularity of the parents' migratory status often forms an additional and quite unassailable obstacle to the acquisition of a nationality by the child. Just as irregular migrants are ineligible to apply for naturalisation, the children of irregular migrants may be ineligible for *jus soli* citizenship even where it is generally on offer. Numerous countries that employ (or have partially introduced) the *jus soli* doctrine for nationality attribution have set additional conditions that must be met in order for birthright nationality to be assured. The principle group excluded in this manner is the children of irregular migrants because a particular (immigration) status is required of the parents if their children are to be granted nationality *jus soli.*[101] Instead of gaining citizenship, these children may inherit their parents' immigration status with the somewhat bizarre result of them being labelled "irregular immigrants" themselves, despite being born on the territory.[102] Excluded from nationality *jus soli*, the children of irregular migrants become definitively reliant on the country of nationality of their parents to grant citizenship *jus sanguinis*. This is a problem where the parents are themselves stateless or where

[100] See for an in depth discussion of the situation of irregular migrants in Thailand, Laura van Waas, *Is Permanent Illegality Inevitable? The Challenges to Ensuring Birth Registration and the Right to a Nationality for the Children of Irregular Migrants - Thailand and the Dominican Republic,* Woking: 2006.

[101] For example, under the Australian Citizenship Act, 1948, a child will acquire nationality *jus soli* only where one of his parents is an Australian citizen or a *permanent resident.* Children born to irregular migrants are therefore excluded from birthright citizenship. They may, however, apply for nationality on their tenth birthday if they have been resident on Australian soil since their birth. David Martin, *Citizenship in countries of immigration – Introduction,* in Alexander Aleinikoff; Douglas Klusmeyer (Eds.), "From Migrants to Citizens. Membership in a changing world", Brookings Institution Press, Washington D.C. 2000, p. 43. Such policies are intended to avoid a situation in which, thanks to the child's acquisition of citizenship of the country of birth, not only the child but also the parents become undeportable (protection of family life), thus creating a back-door for irregular migrants to settle in the state. This problem is sometimes referred to as the phenomenon of "anchor babies".

[102] The United States is a major exception here as it continues to uphold birthright citizenship as a blanket policy: "although customary exceptions to the *jus soli* rule exist (e.g. children born on foreign vessels, children of diplomatic personnel), birthright citizenship has been understood to extend to the native-born children of aliens who are in the country illegally or on a non-immigrant visa". Peter Schuck, *Immigration, refugee and citizenship law in the United States*, in Donald Horowitz and Gerard Noiriel (Eds.), "Immigrants in two democracies. French and American Experience", New York University Press, New York 1992, p. 348. See also Alexander Aleinikoff, *Between Principles and Politics: U.S. Citizenship Policy,* in Alexander Aleinikoff and Douglas Klusmeyer (Eds.), "From Migrants to Citizens. Membership in a changing world", Brookings Institution Press, Washington D.C. 2000, p. 123-128.

there are other limitations on the transmission of nationality through the bloodline such as a gender imbalance in the law or restrictions in the passing on of citizenship to successive generations born abroad.[103]

In practice, what proves to be a greater obstacle than this heightened risk of a conflict of nationality laws is the inability of irregular migrants to register the birth of their child in the host state. Taking Thailand as an example once more, we see that although Thai law provides for the registration of every birth on state territory, an official instruction to the competent registrars in fact interprets the law in such a way as to prevent the registration of children born to anyone with an irregular status.[104] Considering the aforementioned population of irregular migrants in the country (up to 2 million), this instruction means that a substantial proportion of births on Thai soil are going unrecorded. Even in the absence of direct legal or policy constraints on access to birth registration, irregular migrants across the globe are prevented from recording the birth of their child for a whole host of reasons. As mentioned above,[105] they may face a cultural or language barrier and where irregular migrants are concerned, the likelihood of the authorities investing time and resources in assisting these migrants to navigate the procedures or promoting the importance of birth registration within the immigrant community is greatly diminished.[106] Then there is the simple fact that irregular migrants are less likely to (be in a position to) give birth at a medical facility, often missing out on crucial information or evidence that can significantly facilitate the birth registration process.[107] Another enormous challenge that migrants face is discrimination. Exposure of foreigners to discrimination is nothing new and attitudes towards "illegal immigrants" tend to be particularly severe. In some states, deep-rooted discrimination towards a specific immigrant group may be the most influential factor in the non-registration of births. This is for example the major stumbling block in the Dominican Republic for anyone construed by the relevant official – in some cases arbitrarily on the basis of skin colour or surname - to be an irregular migrant.[108]

---

[103] These issues were introduced and discussed in chapter IV, section 1.

[104] Letter (MorTor 0310.1/Wor 8) of the 26th of March 2002 issued by the Bureau of Registration Administration, Ministry of Interior regarding the Act for Registration of Inhabitants for Aliens, addressed to all Provincial and Bangkok Registrars.

[105] At note 75.

[106] Moreover, there is no incentive for the government to do so since the irregular migrant population is not part of the voting constituency and cannot hold the authorities in any way politically accountable for their action or inaction.

[107] For example, in the Netherlands, attitudes and perceptions in relation to the "Linkage Law" - introduced in 1998 to couple an individual's right to various welfare services with his immigration status – have prevented many irregular migrants from seeking medical assistance with childbirth and have also reportedly led to the refusal by hospital staff to provide such a service. Petra Snelders, Sabine Kraus and Marjan Wijers, *Commentaar inzake de specifieke effecten van de Koppelingswet op de situatie van vrouwen t.b.v. de Tussentijdse Evaluatie Koppelingswet* [A commentary on the specific effects of the Linkage Law on the situation of women in aid of the mid-term evaluation of the Linkage Law] Komitee Zelfstandig Verblijfsrecht Migrantenvrouwen, E-Quality and Clara Wichmann Instituut, Amsterdam, 7 February 2000.

[108] Laura van Waas, *Is Permanent Illegality Inevitable? The Challenges to Ensuring Birth Registration and the Right to a Nationality for the Children of Irregular Migrants - Thailand and the Dominican Republic,* Woking: 2006.

Finally, the greatest practical and conceptual obstacle to birth registration for children of irregular migrants relates to the fact that it is by definition an act of a government authority. The importance of birth registration hinges on the very fact that it is the *official* recognition of the circumstances surrounding the child's birth and thereby existence. At the same time, one of the other tasks of the state authorities is to monitor and enforce immigration laws. Are these two jobs compatible or will the birth registration process necessarily uncover the parents immigration status and lead to their arrest and deportation? This is certainly the fear that prevents many irregular migrants from approaching the authorities to register the birth of their child. For example,

> the births of children born in Ecuador to undocumented refugees are frequently not registered due to the parents' fear of deportation. This situation prevents the children from claiming Ecuadorian nationality, to which any child born in Ecuador is entitled under Ecuadorian Law.[109]

Time now to turn to the question of what international law has to say about these issues that are affecting the enjoyment of the right to a nationality by irregular migrants and their children the world over.[110] Recall that this investigation will uncover the baseline standard set for all (irregular migrants) and later we will look at the specific issues facing – and protection offered to - victims of trafficking and refugees.

2.1.2 International (human rights) law

In discussing the situation of irregular migrants and their children we came across three main problems that may contribute to (protracted) statelessness among this particular group: absolute lack of access to naturalisation for all persons in an irregular situation and lack of access to *jus soli* citizenship as well as problems accessing birth registration for children born to irregular migrants. In principle, the mere fact that a person or his parent(s) holds an irregular immigration status does not excuse the host state from providing a basic level of protection - "basic human rights are not conditional upon the circumstances of residence".[111] Thus, where the aforementioned policies threaten an individual's enjoyment of his right to a nationality or right to birth registration, they may be found to violate human rights norms.

However, the right to a nationality does not include a right to naturalisation. We have already seen that naturalisation is a discretionary procedure and that states

---

[109] Human Rights Committee, *Concluding Observations: Ecuador*, A/53/40 Vol. 1, Geneva: 1998, para. 291.

[110] For a further elaboration on the connection between irregular migration, birth registration and statelessness, see Laura van Waas, 'The Children of Irregular Migrants: A Stateless Generation?' in *Netherlands Quarterly of Human Rights*, Vol. 25, 2007.

[111] Guy Goodwin-Gill, 'International Law and Human Rights: Trends Concerning International Migrants and Refugees', in *International Migration Review*, Vol. 23, 1989, page 535. See also the preliminary articles of many major international human rights instruments where it is clearly enunciated that a state is to extend protection to "all individuals within its territory". For instance, article 2, paragraph 1 of the International Covenant on Civil and Political Rights.

are generally free to set the conditions for it, so long as they do not discriminate on the basis of race, gender, religion or against any particular nationality.[112] International law does not oppose the precondition of a minimum period of lawful residence for an application for naturalisation - distinguishing between persons on the grounds of immigration status is not considered inappropriate. In fact, the European Convention on Nationality – the only instrument to set out concrete demands for naturalisation policy – admits that "*lawful* and habitual residence" is a key and legitimate requirement.[113] According to the same instrument, *lawful* and habitual residence also appears to be a justifiable condition for (facilitated) access to nationality for a number of different groups, including stateless persons, and for the recovery of nationality by persons who have lost it.[114] Until their status is regularised, irregular migrants are thus unable to benefit from such international protection and host states are free to maintain that the factual presence of the irregular migrant on state territory is irrelevant and inadequate for the accumulation of an *jus domicilli* connection that may provide access to citizenship.[115] The circumstance of an augmented risk of (prolonged) statelessness does not affect this conclusion.

International law offers a somewhat more complex picture in relation to the problems associated with the children of irregular migrants. To begin with, human rights instruments clearly prescribe the universal enjoyment of both the right to acquire a nationality and the right to be registered at birth. As we saw earlier in this chapter, the UN Committee on the Rights of the Child has confirmed that birth registration must be "available to all children – including asylum-seeking, refugee and migrant children – irrespective of their nationality, *immigration status* or statelessness".[116] The International Convention on the Protection of the Rights of All Migrant Workers and Members of Their Families also helps to remove any doubt that children of irregular migrants are entitled to both birth registration and the acquisition of a nationality.[117] Its article 29 states that "Each child of a migrant

---

[112] See chapter V, section 1.2.

[113] "Each State Party shall provide in its internal law for the possibility of naturalisation of persons *lawfully* and habitually resident on its territory". Article 6, paragraph 3 of the European Convention on Nationality, 1997.

[114] Article 6, paragraphs 4 (e), (f), and (g) as well as Article 9 of the European Convention on Nationality, 1997. The Council of Europe Convention on the avoidance of statelessness in relation to State succession similarly prescribes facilitated naturalisation for persons who are rendered stateless in the context of the succession of states only if they are *lawfully* and habitually residing on state territory.

[115] For the purposes of naturalisation, in accordance with the European Convention on Nationality, the irregular migrant only begins to accrue a relevant period of residence after the regularisation of his status.

[116] Emphasis added. Committee on the Rights of the Child, Committee on the Rights of the Child, *General Comment No. 6: Treatment of unaccompanied and separated children outside their country of origin*, 2005, at para 12; It has also made this position clear through its jurisprudence in reaction to country reports as cited in note 40.

[117] The rights ascribed to irregular migrants are not new, but the Convention does help to remove any ambiguity on their application. Doug Cassel, "Equal Labor Rights for Undocumented Migrant Workers" in Bayefsky (ed) *Human Rights and Refugees, Internally Displaced Persons and Migrant Workers*, Martinus Nijhoff, Leiden: 2006, page 495. The Convention thereby represents "the United Nations' first effort to ascribe binding rights specifically to the unauthorised". Beth Lyon, "New International Human Rights Standards on Unauthorized Immigrant Worker Rights: Seizing an

worker shall have the right to a name, to registration of birth and to a nationality". This provision is located in the general section where the rights of all – regular and irregular – migrant workers are espoused and is therefore applicable to all children of migrant workers, regardless of the immigration status of their parents.[118] Similarly, a report issued under the auspices of the Council of Europe on the human rights of irregular migrants includes the rights to a nationality and to birth registration among the *minimum rights* to which irregular migrants' children are entitled.[119] And the Inter-American Court on Human Rights has also ruled that the children of irregular migrants enjoy the right to a nationality, just the same as any other children:

> The migratory status of a person cannot be a condition for the State to grant nationality, because migratory status can never constitute a justification for depriving a person of his right to nationality or the enjoyment and exercise of his rights.[120]

So, it would certainly appear that international law calls for the enjoyment of the right to acquire a nationality and the right to be registered at birth, by *all* children, including those born to irregular migrants.[121]

Opportunity to Pull Governments Out of the Shadows" in Bayefsky (ed) *Human Rights and Refugees, Internally Displaced Persons and Migrant Workers*, Martinus Nijhoff, Leiden: 2006, page 558.

[118] The Convention also includes a series of rights which only regular migrant workers can claim. These are promulgated in articles 36-56. It should be noted that the International Convention on the Rights of All Migrant Workers and Members of Their Families has been ratified by just 34 states to date and that the majority of these are major sending rather than receiving countries of (irregular) migrants. Moreover, the Convention excludes stateless persons (and refugees) from its personal scope of application with the result that the children of *stateless* irregular migrants cannot benefit from its provisions – even if the *stateless* migrant in question meets the definition of a migrant worker that is set out in the convention. Article 3, paragraph (d) of the International Convention on the Protection of the Rights of All Migrant Workers and Members of Their Families, 1990. Nevertheless, the deliberate separation of the rights of migrant workers into two categories – those applicable to all and those applicable only to regular migrant workers - and the position of the right to birth registration and a nationality in the first group, is illustrative of the international consensus already laid down in the ICCPR and CRC.

[119] Ed van Thijn, *Human rights of irregular migrants*, Committee on Migration, Refugees and Population of the Parliamentary Assembly of the Council of Europe, Document 10924, 4 May 2006, paragraphs 26 and 107. It should be noted that these rights were not included in the Resolution that was subsequently adopted by the Parliamentary Assembly of the Council of Europe, *Resolution 1509 on Human Rights of Irregular Migrants,* Strasbourg, 27 June 2006. This issue is currently under revue by various bodies of the Council of Europe and further developments can be expected in the near future.

[120] Inter-American Court on Human Rights, *Case of Yean and Bosico v. Dominican Republic,* Series C, Case 130, 8 September 2005, para. 156. The Court refers back to its own Advisory Opinion on the Juridical Condition and Rights of Undocumented Migrants, where it ruled that "the migratory status of a person can never be a justification for depriving him of the enjoyment and exercise of his human rights". In the Advisory Opinion, this statement was made in the context of employment-related rights. Inter-American Court of Human Rights, *Advisory Opinion on Juridical Condition and Rights of Undocumented Migrants,* Requested by the United Mexican States, OC-18/03, 17 September 2003, para. 134.

[121] See also the recommendation by the UN Independent Expert on Minority Issues in her 2008 report, where she calls on states to "grant nationality to children born on their territory if the child would

On the other hand, f we look again to the European Convention on Nationality, we see that the developing international norm prescribing *jus soli* attribution where a child would otherwise be stateless may actually be qualified by the immigration status of the parents. As remarked in chapter IV, in its elaboration of this norm, the European Convention on Nationality allows states to choose between automatic attribution of citizenship at birth and subsequent conferral of nationality upon application. Thereafter, it declares that "such application may be made subject to the *lawful* and habitual residence on its territory for a period not exceeding five years immediately preceding the lodging of the application".[122] The commentary to the text explains that the residence of the child must therefore be "effective and in compliance with the provisions concerning the stay of foreigners in the State".[123] Where the child in question has inherited the irregular status of his parents in accordance with domestic law,[124] he will be unable to meet this condition even if he does manage to stay on the territory of the host state for the prescribed period. It is also quite conceivable that the child will be expelled from the territory due to his irregular status - or that of his parents - before he can meet the minimum term for application. So the protection offered to children of irregular migrants in respect of their right to acquire a nationality at birth is not as straightforward as it first appears and, within the European context at least, it would seem that there may be some gaps in protection offered against statelessness at birth. In this respect, the 1961 Convention on the Reduction of Statelessness could, in fact, have opened an avenue for more comprehensive protection: where it offers states the opportunity to set additional requirements for the attribution of nationality *jus soli* upon application later in life, one of the conditions that may be set is a certain period of "habitual residence", without the specification that such residence must also be *lawful*.[125] This does not remove the concern that the child of an irregular migrant may not, in practice, have the chance to remain habitually resident in the host state for the required period due to his own or his parents' migratory status – a concern that is very real considering the absence from the Convention of any provision for regularisation of the child's status in the intervening years. Nevertheless, the somewhat contradicting messages issuing from different sources of international law, and the comments that have just been made on the 1961 Statelessness

otherwise be stateless [and] in this case, the immigration status of the parents should be irrelevant". Gay McDougall, *Promotion and Protection of all Human Rights, Civil, Political, Economic, Social and Cultural Rights, Including the Right to Development – Report of the Independent Expert on Minority Issues,* A/HRC/7/23, 28 February 2008, para. 85.

[122] Emphasis added. Article 6, paragraph 2 (b) of the European Convention on Nationality, 1997.

[123] Council of Europe, *European Convention on Nationality: Explanatory report,* Strasbourg: 1997, page 34.

[124] This is, for example, the case in Thailand, under article 7 bis, paragraph 3 of the Nationality Act B.E. 2508 (1965).

[125] Tang Lay Lee, "Statelessness, Human Rights and Gender. Irregular migrant workers from Burma in Thailand", Martinus Nijhoff Publishers, Leiden 2005, page 47. The traveaux preparatoires of the Convention are ambiguous on the matter of the scope of "habitual residence". By reference to other international provisions it can, arguably, be inferred that the term "habitual residence" does not, of itself, imply lawful residence: other documents, including the European Convention on Nationality and the Draft Articles on Diplomatic Protection prepared by the International Law Commission. Moreover, in the Council of Europe Convention on the avoidance of statelessness in relation to State Succession (article 1), "habitual residence" is defined as "a stable *factual* residence".

Convention, show that the statelessness instrument may yet have an important role to play in respect of this "new" source of statelessness.

The same ambiguity does not exist with regard to the right to birth registration – this is a clearly enunciated right of all children, regardless of the status of their parents. But how far does international law go in providing special measures or guidance to ensure that the children of irregular immigrants are able to enjoy this right? In the introduction to this issue we found that the migratory status of the parents seriously jeopardises the chances of the child's birth being registered - one of the most serious obstacles being the (fear of) repercussions in approaching the authorities to ask for the birth of the child to be recorded. So far, this is not an issue that international instruments have dealt with, nor has it been the subject of any international jurisprudence to date. However, in its consideration of the human rights of irregular migrants, the Council of Europe Parliamentary Assembly did pause to give this substantial practical problem some thought. In its resolution of 27 of June 2006, the Assembly invited governments

> to assure that irregular migrants are able to enjoy their minimum rights in practice, including by [...] dispensing with the duty of certain authorities (for example school authorities, doctors and medical authorities) to inform on the illegal status of migrants so as to avoid the situation where irregular migrants do not claim their rights through fear of identification as irregular migrants and fear of expulsion.[126]

There are examples of cases where authorities have been able to separate their tasks of provider of rights and services and of enforcer of immigration laws.[127] Alternatively, such issues could be circumvented by exploring and expanding the role of the sending state. It has already been mentioned in passing that the UN Committee on the Rights of the Child has suggested that the duty to ensure a child's right to birth registration falls equally on the state of nationality of the parents as on the host state. In reference to the worrisome non-registration of children born to overseas Filipino workers, the Committee recommended that the Philippines "encourage and facilitate parents, irrespective of their residence status, to register their children born abroad".[128] With this recommendation, the Committee has hit upon one feasible solution to the problem of under-registration of children born to irregular migrants due to the fear of repercussions in approaching the authorities of

---

[126] Parliamentary Assembly of the Council of Europe, *Resolution 1509 on Human Rights of Irregular Migrants*, Strasbourg, 27 June 2006, para. 16.

[127] An initiative in the south-eastern USA state of Tenessee at the beginning of the 21st century is a prime example. There a campaign "fought successfully for access to a state-issued driver's licence for people who could not produce proof of lawful residence in the USA [and] within days, throngs of Latinas and Latinos descended on licensing stations". Lessons can be learned from this type of initiative about the opportunities and methods for circumventing the supposed clash between a state authority's immigration duties and the provision of vital services – among which birth registration. Fran Ansley, "Constructing Citizenship Without a Licence: The Struggle of Undocumented Immigrants in the USA for Livelihoods and Recognition" in Kabeer (ed) *Inclusive Citizenship Meanings and Expressions*, Zed Books, London: 2005, pages 199-213.

[128] UN Committee on the Rights of the Child, *Concluding observations: Philippines*, CRC/C/15/Add.258, Geneva: 2005, paras 36 and 37. See also note 38 above.

the *host* state for registration and documentation. However, where the sheer distance to the diplomatic representation of their country of nationality in the host state is an unsurpassable obstacle[129] or where the irregular migrants concerned are in fact refugees or stateless themselves, this option of reverting to the authorities of the country of nationality for the registration of births ceases to be an appropriate or workable alternative. Consider, in this respect, the example raised above of irregular migrants and refugees from Myanmar that live in many of the remote, border areas of Thailand.[130]

What has become clear from the foregoing observations is that not only the content, but also the means to successfully implement the rights of irregular migrants (and their children) requires further crystallisation. Where this has already begun in relation to, for instance, the employment-related rights of irregular migrants,[131] other areas of human rights law including the right to a nationality and the right to birth registration are currently lagging behind in the discussion. However, organisations such as the Council of Europe and mechanisms like the UN Special Rapporteur on the Human Rights of Migrants and the UN Committee on Migrant Workers charged with monitoring the implementation of the Migrant Workers Convention remain seized by this "priority issue".[132] There are therefore numerous opportunities for the – much needed - further elaboration and development of norms relating to the rights of irregular migrants and their children, whereby the prevention of statelessness and non-registration of births should be placed high on the agenda.

2.2 Human trafficking and refugee situations

Now we come to two very particular manifestations of (irregular) migration that warrant a closer look because the situation of the migrants involved calls for special

[129] The diplomatic presence of a foreign state is likely to be far less decentralised – and thereby less easily accessible – than a state's own civil registration system. There may be just one embassy or consulate in the state capital and it may be necessary for the parents to register the child there in person.

[130] See section 2.1.1 of the present chapter.

[131] Consider, for example, the work of the International Labour Organisation in elaborating standards in this regard; Beth Lyon, "New International Human Rights Standards on Unauthorized Immigrant Worker Rights: Seizing an Opportunity to Pull Governments Out of the Shadows" in Bayefsky (ed) *Human Rights and Refugees, Internally Displaced Persons and Migrant Workers*, Martinus Nijhoff, Leiden: 2006, pages 554-558. See also more generally Doug Cassel, "Equal Labor Rights for Undocumented Migrant Workers" in Bayefsky (ed) *Human Rights and Refugees, Internally Displaced Persons and Migrant Workers*, Martinus Nijhoff, Leiden: 2006, pages 478-516. See also chapter XI, section 2.2.

[132] Jorge Bustamante, *Report of the Special Rapporteur on the human rights of migrants,* E/CN.6/2006/73, 30 December 2005, page 16. The mandate of the UN Special Rapporteur was first created in 1999 and was extended for a further three years in 2005. Part of this mandate is "to examine ways and means to overcome the obstacles existing to the full and effective protection of the human rights of [migrants], including obstacles and difficulties for the return of migrants who are *non-documented or in an irregular situation*". The UN Committee on Migrant Workers held its first session in March 2004 and although it has considered some number of country reports it has yet to build up any substantial jurisprudence or formulate any General Comments on the content of the Convention. See also Parliamentary Assembly of the Council of Europe, *Resolution 1509 on Human Rights of Irregular Migrants,* Strasbourg.

treatment and international law has elaborated norms to that effect that may be relevant to the task of preventing statelessness. Thus, one specific way in which the "paper walls" that have been erected between countries by way of immigration policies and border control are circumvented is through human trafficking.[133] Trafficking is defined as:

> The recruitment, transportation, transfer, harbouring or receipt of persons, by means of the threat or use of force or other forms of coercion, of abduction, of fraud, of deception, of the abuse of power or of a position of vulnerability or of the giving and receiving of payments or benefits to achieve the consent of a person having control over another person, for the purpose of exploitation.[134]

It has many different manifestations and can affect men, women and children, but "most notoriously [...] it entails the sale of women and children to work in the sex trade without their consent".[135] As a migratory phenomenon, trafficking is on the rise and has boomed into an incredibly lucrative business.[136] It has been estimated that as many as 600,000 to 800,000 people are trafficked across international borders every year – generating an estimated US$ 9.5 billion.[137] In response, the international community has unanimously espoused the opinion that trafficking is a crime that must be suppressed and punished.[138] Thus, numerous instruments have been put in place to criminalize and prevent trafficking.[139] In addition, in

[133] References to "paper walls" found in John Torpey, *The Invention of the Passport. Surveillance, Citizenship and the State*, Cambridge University Press, Cambridge: 2000, page 139.

[134] Article 3, section a of the Protocol to Prevent, Suppress and Punish Trafficking in Persons, especially women and children, supplementing the United Nations Convention Against Transnational Organised Crime ("Palermo Protocol"), UN, 2000.

[135] Ryszard Piotrowicz, 'Victims of trafficking and de facto statelessness', in *Refugee Survey Quarterly*, Vol. 21, 2002, page 50.

[136] Trafficking is just one branch of a vast and expanding "migration industry" of which people smuggling is another major sector and within which people from travel agents to interpreters are making a living. Stephen Castles; Mark Miller, *The Age of Migration*, The Guildford Press, London: 2003, page 114.

[137] Millions more fall victim to trafficking within their own state borders. IOM, *World Migration 2003: Managing Migration - Challenges and Responses for People on the Move,* Geneva: 2003, page 27. As cited in US Department of State, *Trafficking in persons report 2006,* Washington: 2006, pages 7 and 13.

[138] Trafficking in human beings is often even described as one of the contemporary forms of slavery and the prohibition of slavery is one of the oldest *jus cogens* norms. Ian Brownlie, *Principles of Public International Law*, Oxford University Press, Oxford: 2003, pages 489 and 537.

[139] The Convention on the Elimination of All Forms of Discrimination Against Women is one example: article 6 determines that "State Parties shall take all appropriate measures, including legislation, to suppress all forms of traffic in women". The Convention on the Rights of the Child (article 35) similarly induces contracting states to "take all appropriate national, bilateral and multilateral measures to prevent the abduction of, the sale of or traffic in children". Following on from this, an Optional Protocol to the Convention on the Rights of the Child was opened for signature in 2000 on "The sale of children, child prostitution and child pornography", elaborating on how states should implement – among others – the aforementioned article of the CRC. Several regional human rights documents also house a prohibition of trafficking in persons, including in article 6 of the American Convention on Human Rights; article 29 of the African Convention on the Rights and Welfare of the Child; and article

recognition of their position as the victims of a grievous human rights violation, persons who have been trafficked are offered certain protection and rights under international law. It is among these standards that we will attempt to trace any relevant norms for the prevention of statelessness.

Meanwhile, another substantial group of migrants whose (forced) displacement across international borders challenges systems of migration management is comprised of refugees. At the end of 2006, there were an estimated 9.9 million refugees globally.[140] There were also an estimated 744,000 asylum seekers or "aspirant refugees".[141] A refugee is a person who has been displaced across an international border and whose situation meets the definition espoused in article 1 of the 1951 Convention relating to the Status of Refugees. The decisive element is that the individual holds a "well-founded fear of being persecuted for reasons of race, religion, nationality, membership of a particular social group or political opinion".[142] And it is this vulnerability and extreme dearth of protection that inspired the establishment of a special international status and the elaboration of a catalogue of accompanying rights, the most central of which is the right not to be expelled or returned to the country in which persecution threatens.[143] Once more, the question to be considered here is in what way do refugees become exposed to statelessness and whether the applicable international standards have anticipated and addressed this problem.

2.2.1 Connecting statelessness to human trafficking and refugee situations

In many cases, the victims of trafficking and even recognised refugees share the same fate as irregular migrants. This is because although some states will officially pardon the unlawful entry of victims of trafficking and/or recognised refugees, thus (temporarily or permanently) extracting them from the irregular migrant group, in other states no such provision has been made. For instance, in countries without an asylum law, all persons who seek protection as refugees will be treated in the eyes of the law as irregular immigrants, although their continuing unlawful presence on state territory may be tolerated on humanitarian grounds.[144] For the victims of

4, section g of the Protocol to the African Charter on Human and Peoples' Rights on the Rights of Women in Africa.

[140] UNHCR, *Statistical Yearbook 2006 – Trends in Displacement, Protection and Solutions,* Geneva, December 2007, page 23. An asylum seeker is a person who has crossed an international border to seek protection but whose claim to refugee status has yet to be decided.

[141] UNHCR, *Statistical Yearbook 2006 – Trends in Displacement, Protection and Solutions,* Geneva, December 2007, page 23.

[142] See also chapter II, section 4 on the development of the definition of a refugee.

[143] The prohibition of *non-refoulement,* housed in article 33 of the 1951 Convention relating to the Status of Refugees as well as being implicit in numerous human rights instruments.

[144] This is the situation in a number of Asian and Middle Eastern countries that are not party to the 1951 Refugee Convention, such as India, Pakistan, Thailand, Indonesia, Syrian Arab Republic, Saudi Arabia, Kuwait and Bahrain. These countries tolerate the presence of refugees so long as the international community provides the necessary humanitarian assistance and only until such time as repatriation or resettlement can be realised. Nor is asylum law uniformly implemented in the event of mass influxes of refugees, their status remaining irregular. See for the latest information on these – and other – states' treatment of refugees the relevant UNHCR *Country Operations Plans*, accessible through http://www.unhcr.org. Moreover, "Many of Africa's protracted refugee situations do not have a clearly

trafficking there is even less certainty of regularisation of stay. As a result, when treated simply as irregular migrants, refugees and victims of trafficking are exposed to statelessness in the same way as has already been described above. Concurrently, their children also run the same risks.[145]

Moreover, even if the individual's stay is regularised on account of being a trafficking victim or refugee, the status acquired may not be commensurate to accruing eligibility for acquisition of nationality in the host state. Whereas once, "permanent asylum and local integration were widely practiced in asylum countries in the West", today there is a clear worldwide preference for temporary protection.[146] A variety of temporary statuses has emerged - for asylum seekers awaiting a decision on their application for refugee status but also for victims of trafficking while they cooperate with procedures to prosecute the perpetrators, for recognised refugees and in response to mass influxes of persons displaced by conflict.[147] Thus, although technically lawfully resident, these persons may hold an immigration status that is "inadequate or incompatible with the residency requirements for naturalisation".[148] It may be similarly inadequate or incompatible with the conditions for access to *jus soli* citizenship for their children. In the case of refugees in particular, it may also be impossible to comply with other requirements for the acquisition of a nationality such as obtaining proof of loss of prior nationality, if required, because "for obvious reasons many refugees hesitate to approach their embassy to start procedures to give up citizenship, and for equally obvious reasons some states make problems for political opponents who apply to be released from citizenship".[149]

In addition, the risk of statelessness for both the displaced persons themselves and any children they subsequently bear can be exacerbated by problems relating to

---

defined legal status, do not have residence rights, and have no prospect of seeking naturalisation in their country of asylum". Jeff Crisp, *No solutions in sight: the problem of protracted refugee situations in Africa,* UNHCR Working Paper No. 75, January 2003, pages 11-12. See also Yante Ismail, "Is Toleration Enough?" in *Refugees Magazine,* Number 148, Issue 4, 2007, page 31.

145 Refugees often have particular difficulty securing birth registration for their children: the problems described above may be compounded by a specific state policy of not registering refugee births, often common to those countries where the child may stake a claim to citizenship *jus soli.* Youth Advocate Program International, *Stateless Children – Children who are without citizenship,* Booklet No. 7 in a series on International Youth Issues, 2002, pages 10-16. An example given was the refusal by the Honduran authorities during the 1970s and 1980s to register children born to Salvadoran refugees living in camps in the state: "Although these authorities were legally obliged to register all children born on Honduran territory, in practice, the refugee camps were treated as if they had extraterritorial status. In other instances, the problem is not one of status, but of access to procedures, especially where refugees are confined to camps.

146 Karen Jacobsen, *The forgotten solution: local integration for refugees in developing countries,* UNHCR Working Paper No. 45, July 2001, page 2.

147 Alex Schmid, "Whither Refugee? The Refugee Crisis: Problems and Solutions", PIOOM, Leiden: 1996, pages 158-159 and 167.

148 Rosa da Costa, *Rights of Refugees in the Context of Integration: Legal Standards and Recommendations,* Geneva: June 2006, page 187. See also Karen Jacobsen, *The forgotten solution: local integration for refugees in developing countries,* No. 45, Geneva: July 2001, page 2.

149 Alex Schmid, "Whither Refugee? The Refugee Crisis: Problems and Solutions", PIOOM, Leiden: 1996, page 177.

documentation.[150] Victims of trafficking and refugees suffer from an acute threat of loss of personal documentation.[151] Trafficked persons "may have their documents stolen or destroyed either on arrival in a third country or prior to transfer, often making it impossible to prove their status".[152] And refugees may similarly lose or leave behind their identity or travel documents – if they ever held any.[153] Moreover, in the event of massive refugee flows,

> the general state of upheaval, paperwork disorder, and mass confusion typical of refugee situations often overwhelm authorities in both the refugees' original country as well as the host country. Adults and children become officially lost – not accounted for by any government system.[154]

As explained in the context of discussing birth registration above, being undocumented cannot be directly equated with being stateless.[155] However, the lack of official papers to prove nationality, identity or even any other basic personal facts does heighten the risk of statelessness. It may still be difficult for the individual to firmly establish that he is not considered a national by any state and therefore stateless, but the absence of documents may equally prevent any country with which he enjoys a link from tracing or acknowledging that connection.[156] It may also become impossible for the individual to successfully claim nationality *jus sanguinis* for their offspring – or, vice versa, to establish entitlement to nationality *jus soli* for a child who would otherwise be stateless because this fact also becomes harder to establish.[157] What is more, the fact of international displacement puts the individual in a state other than his state of origin or nationality and commonly a

---

150 UNHCR, *The World's Stateless - Questions and Answers,* Geneva: 2004, page 13; David Weissbrodt; Clay Collins, 'The Human Rights of Stateless Persons', in *Human Rights Quarterly,* Vol. 28, 2006, page 263.

151 Other migrants, including irregular migrants and especially persons who have been smuggled may face similar difficulties but the problem has particularly been reported in the context of trafficking and refugee situations.

152 Carol Batchelor, "The International Legal Framework Concerning Statelessness and Access for Stateless Persons", *European Union Seminar on the Content and Scope of International Protection: Panel 1 - Legal basis of international protection,* Madrid: 2002, page 4; see also UNHCR, *UNHCR Handbook for the Protection of Women and Girls,* January 2008, page 220.

153 "Due to the circumstances in which they are sometimes forced to leave their home country, refugees are perhaps more likely than other aliens to find themselves without identity documents. Moreover, while other aliens can turn to the authorities of their country of origin for help in obtaining documents, refugees do not have this option". UNHCR, *Identity documents for refugees,* Note on International Protection, Geneva: 20 July 1984.

154 Youth Advocate Program International, *Stateless Children – Children who are without citizenship,* Booklet No. 7 in a series on International Youth Issues, 2002, page 13.

155 See section 1.1.

156 Note that the inability to establish nationality is often referred to as a problem of "*de facto* statelessness". However, recall the discussion in chapter II, section 2 of the difficulty of the *identification* versus *definition* of statelessness. This is exemplified by both this situation of undocumentation and the issue of the lack of birth registration as discussed above.

157 Recall the "baby Andrew" case that was fought all the way to the Supreme Court in Japan where the enjoyment by baby Andrew of special provisions offering Japanese nationality to a child who would otherwise be stateless hinged on the determination of the nationality of his undocumented mother. See chapter III, section 3 at note 78.

long way from home where it may otherwise have been a relatively straight-forward matter to secure secondary proof of citizenship such as witness testimony or indirect supporting documentation. This difficulty becomes more acute as time lapses and any evidence of a connection has faded still further. These problems have, for example, been reported in a number of cases of trafficking, such as among Polish women trafficked to Western Europe and among Thai women victims of trafficking.[158] Yet, when surveyed by UNHCR in 2003, only half of the participating states responded positively to having a mechanism in place to assist trafficking victims in establishing their identity and nationality.[159] In the sections to come we will see whether international law offers trafficked persons or refugees a suitable avenue for relieving this problem and what commitments states have taken on in this context.

2.2.2 International (human rights) law

We have already seen that international law offers little recourse to irregular migrants who are (threatened with) stateless(ness) and seek to acquire the nationality of their host state. *Lawful* residence is generally deemed to be an appropriate condition for naturalisation and possibly also for the acquisition of a nationality in other circumstances, even where the failure to do so leads to statelessness. The question is whether the international legal framework that deals specifically with victims of trafficking and refugees offers recourse from the same plight. Disappointingly, we find that the mere fact of being a victim of trafficking or a refugee does not affect the aforementioned conclusion with regard to the freedom of states to impose the condition of *lawful* residence for access to nationality.

However, where victims of trafficking are concerned, the international legal regime may offer indirect assistance by encouraging states to regularise their status. The Palermo Protocol on trafficking asks states to consider

> adopting legislative or other appropriate measures that permit victims of trafficking in persons to remain in its territory, temporarily or permanently, in appropriate cases [giving] appropriate consideration to humanitarian and compassionate factors.[160]

---

[158] The related problem of establishing the nationality of any children born to trafficking victims has also been reported. International Law Association, *Final Report on Women's Equality and Nationality in International Law,* Committee on Feminism and International Law, London Conference, 2000, page 5. Some research projects are now underway to investigate more closely the link between nationality disputes and trafficking, for example in the Asia-Pacific region under the auspices of the Office of the United Nations High Commissioner for Human Rights.

[159] 52.7% of states answered this question in the affirmative. UNHCR, *Final report concerning the Questionnaire on statelessness pursuant to the Agenda for Protection,* Geneva: March 2004, page 24.

[160] Article 7 of the Protocol to Prevent, Suppress and Punish Trafficking in Persons, especially women and children. Note that no such recommendation can be found in the equivalent instrument dealing with the problem of smuggling - the Protocol against the Smuggling of Migrants by Land, Sea and Air. Together. This difference in treatment of persons who have been smuggled and victims of human trafficking reflects the differences between these two phenomena. In particular, it takes into account the notion that "In trafficking, there is a clear human victim – it is a crime against the person [...] In smuggling there is only a State victim – it is a crime against public order". Brian Iselin and Melanie

Even so, the state concerned is under no concrete obligation to implement such measures. Moreover, a temporary status – which would also satisfy this plea for compassion with victims of trafficking - may not actually be adequate to comply with the residence requirements set under a particular state's naturalisation law. On the European continent, the Council of Europe Convention on Action Against Trafficking in Human Beings does at least oblige states to issue residence permits to victims of trafficking if "the competent authority considers that their stay is necessary owing to their personal situation" and/or "the competent authority considers that their stay is necessary for the purpose of their co-operation with the competent authorities in investigation or criminal proceedings".[161] Nevertheless, the article describes simply a "renewable residence permit" and there is no suggestion that the status provided must be either permanent or such that it allows for the eventual possibility of naturalisation.

The position of refugees is similarly ambiguous. While international standards remain weak and indirect on this point, there is some evidence that both the country of origin of the refugee and the receiving state – or even a third country - would be compelled to address any problems of statelessness in the context of attaining a durable solution, be it voluntary repatriation, local integration or resettlement.[162] Indeed, a number of the clauses for cessation of refugee status under the 1951 Convention relating to the Status of Refugees hinge on the (re)acquisition of a nationality where this has been lost.[163] Thus, according to (non-binding) international guidelines, in the context of *voluntary repatriation*,

> where refugees have lost their nationality, the country of origin should arrange for its restoration as well as for its granting to children born outside the territory and, as appropriate, to non-national spouses.[164]

Adams, *Distinguishing between Human Trafficking and People Smuggling,* UN Office on Drugs and Crime, 2003, page 3. Thus states must "clearly distinguish between trafficking in persons and other forms of irregular migration" for the victims of trafficking enjoy special protection and assistance that accompany that fact. United Nations Office on Drugs and Crime (UNODC), *Trafficking in Persons: Global Patterns,* Vienna: April 2006, pages 12-13.

[161] Article 14, paragraph 1 of the Council of Europe Convention on Action Against Trafficking in Human Beings. This instrument entered into force on the 1st of February 2008. It has been ratified by 17 states and a further 22 countries have signed the convention.

[162] These are the three main durable solutions recognised by the international community, as reflected in – among others – successive conclusions of UNHCR's Executive Committee. Voluntary repatriation is clearly put forward as the preferred durable solution. See, among others, UNHCR Executive Committee Conclusions No. 29 (1983); No. 50 (1988); No. 79 (1996); No. 85 (1998); and No. 95 (2003).

[163] See article 1, paragraph C of the 1951 Convention relating to the Status of Refugees.

[164] UNHCR, *Handbook on Voluntary Repatriation: International Protection*, Geneva: 1996, section 2.6. In addition, the Handbook determines that "assurances of [...] access to official documentation and citizenship including for children born abroad" are "core protection elements" to be included in any repatriation agreement with a state. See section 3.6 of the Handbook. The idea that citizenship must be available upon repatriation to children born to refugees while in exile suggests that *jus sanguinis* attribution of nationality is being prescribed even if the state usually adheres to the *jus soli* doctrine. However, this would be an over-simplification. Instead, this policy derives from the notion that, where refugee situations are concerned, the fact that the child was not born on state territory is not a matter of individual choice. Had the parents not been threatened with persecution and forced to flee, the child

Meanwhile, although there is no clear obligation upon the receiving state to offer recognised refugees a particular immigration status,[165] where local integration is pursued, the opportunity to eventually acquire nationality must be present.[166] It would seem incompatible with the overall purpose of the protection regime to never offer refugees a status that is conducive with naturalisation and thereby obstruct opportunities for local integration.[167] Additionally, by asking state parties to facilitate the naturalisation of refugees, the 1951 Convention relating to the Status of Refugees provides a possible legal basis for challenging further naturalisation requirements that refugees find difficult or impossible to meet, such as delivering proof of loss or renunciation of former nationality.[168] Lastly, in the context of resettlement, the status provided by the receiving state should "carry with it the

---

would have been born within the state and it is therefore appropriate to take this as the point of departure for the attribution of nationality. So where children are threatened with statelessness in the receiving state due to restrictions on the attribution of nationality to refugee children or those whose parents have an irregular or temporary status, it would seem that the onus is on the state of origin of the parents to confer citizenship. However, for the residual caseload – those who remain behind after large-scale repatriation – other avenues will have to be sought to avoid the (enduring) statelessness of these children. See also the conclusions of UNHCR's Executive Committee, in particular No. 18 on Voluntary Repatriation, 1980. Numerous examples of repatriation agreements providing for reacquisition of nationality for refugees who had lost their citizenship, as well as for conferral of nationality on refugee children born in exile, can be found in Amnesty International, *Bhutan: Nationality, expulsion, statelessness and the right to return,* September 2000, section 4.

[165] The 1951 Convention relating to the Status of Refugees does provide for the non-penalisation of refugees in the event of unlawful entry (article 31) – as well as, of course, the principle of non-refoulement prohibiting expulsion or return (article 33) - but it does not clearly delineate what immigration status is to be offered to refugees.

[166] The 1951 Convention relating to the Status of Refugees encourages states to facilitate naturalisation of refugees in its article 34. Local integration involves "a process of legal, economic, social and cultural incorporation of refugees, culminating in the offer of citizenship". Karen Jacobsen, *The forgotten solution: local integration for refugees in developing countries,* UNHCR Working Paper No. 45, July 2001, page 1. In its 2005 Conclusion on local integration, UNHCR's Executive Committee "welcomes the practice in States with developed asylum systems of allowing refugees to integrate locally; and calls on these States to continue supporting refugees' ability to attain this durable solution through the timely grant of a secure legal status and residency rights; and/or to facilitate naturalisation". UNHCR Executive Committee, *Conclusion on Local Integration,* No. 104, Geneva: 2005.

[167] "Best practice standards grant refugees permanent residence or an equivalent durable residence status which is compatible with naturalisation requirements and is granted automatically upon recognition, thereby permitting them to naturalise at the earliest possible opportunity". Rosa da Costa, *Rights of Refugees in the Context of Integration: Legal Standards and Recommendations,* Geneva: June 2006, page 187. Nevertheless, this is no firm international legal basis for obliging states to adopt such practices or indeed to pursue local integration as a solution. Moreover, in the current climate of temporary protection measures and warehousing of refugee populations, prospects for local integration may be minimal. Karen Jacobsen, *The forgotten solution: local integration for refugees in developing countries,* UNHCR Working Paper No. 45, July 2001; Jeff Crisp, *The local integration and local settlement of refugees: a conceptual and historical analysis,* UNHCR Working Paper No. 102, April 2004; UNHCR Standing Committee, *Protracted Refugee Situations,* 30th Meeting, EC/54/SC/CRP.14, Geneva, 10 June 2004.

[168] Article 16 of the European Convention on Nationality may also be relevant: "A State Party shall not make the renunciation or loss of another nationality a condition for the acquisition or retention of its nationality where such renunciation or loss is not possible or *cannot reasonably be acquired*".

opportunity to eventually become a naturalised citizen of the resettlement country".[169] So the principle of the avoidance of statelessness has clearly permeated international policy on the response to refugees as developed under the auspices of the United Nations High Commissioner for Refugees, even if this is not laid down in binding standards specifically applicable to refugees.

Overall, it is fair to say that access to a new or replacement nationality for victims of trafficking and refugees therefore remains a somewhat ambiguous area of international law. Does the international legal framework perhaps provide more concrete obligations where the verification of nationality and (re)issuance of personal documents is concerned? In the context of trafficking, this would appear to be the case. One aspect of the protection that may be offered under the Palermo Protocol on trafficking is the clarification and verification of the victim's identity and nationality as well as the provision of travel documents or authorisation for the victim's return to his or her country of nationality or of previous lawful permanent residence.[170] These measures should go some way to ensuring that the victim is not left in a situation of limbo or indeed statelessness. However, the Protocol has been criticised in respect of the latter provisions for being "as much about the convenience of states as the protection of the trafficked".[171] This critique refers to the problem that the duty to verify the nationality of a trafficking victim and assist in his or her repatriation is only prescribed where the receiving state has made a request to that effect. Such protection is not a right attributed to the trafficking victim directly so he or she is unable to demand the cooperation of the states involved but is reliant instead on their initiative. Moreover, the Palermo Protocol is silent on the procedure to be followed to verify nationality as well as on the question of what to do should the nationality or state of origin of the trafficked person remain undetermined or appear to be absent. For example, nowhere does the text prescribe or advise facilitated access to nationality for victims whose citizenship could not be verified or provide the opportunity for the victim to appeal the refusal by his or her presumed state of nationality to recognise and verify this bond. Thus statelessness is by no means precluded entirely. Meanwhile, the content of the Council of Europe Convention on Action Against Trafficking in Human Beings on this point is very comparable to the Palermo Protocol in that it has

---

[169] UNHCR, *Resettlement Handbook*, Geneva 2004, page 2. Note that, according also to the Handbook, resettlement "involves the selection and transfer of refugees from a State in which they have sought protection to a third State that has agreed to admit them – as refugees – with permanent residence status". The process by which a refugee enters a state for resettlement is therefore very different to the circumstances in which he arrives, unannounced, in the state of first asylum. The resettlement state has, entirely voluntarily, invited the refugee to reside within its territory and offered permanent residence for that purpose. It follows logically from this fact that the status offered should be commensurate to eventually applying for nationality – this is unobjectionable since the initial pre-selection of suitability for citizenship has been carried out within the approval process for resettlement.

[170] These obligations are housed in article 8, paragraphs 3 and 4 of the Palermo Protocol on trafficking. The Palermo Protocol on smuggling prescribes similar measures in its article 18 as part of efforts to ensure the return of smuggled migrants. UNHCR's Executive Committee encourages states to implement these obligations as part of efforts to prevent statelessness. UNHCR Executive Committee, *Conclusion No. 106 on Identification, Prevention and Reduction of Statelessness and Protection of Stateless Persons,* 57th session, Geneva, 2006, paragraph (m).

[171] Ryszard Piotrowicz, 'Victims of trafficking and de facto statelessness', in *Refugee Survey Quarterly,* Vol. 21, 2002, page 54.

adopted the same style of provision to guarantee cooperation in the verification of the victim's nationality and the facilitation of repatriation "at the request of the receiving state".[172] Only in cases where the victim is an unaccompanied child is the state party directly obliged to "take the necessary steps to establish his/her identity and nationality".[173] Moreover, similarly to the Palermo Protocol, this Council of Europe Convention does not offer any further instruction with a view to the identification or avoidance of statelessness.

One additional international norm that may prove valuable in this context is that espoused in article 8 of the Convention on the Rights of the Child. This provision deals with the right of every child to *preserve* his identity, of which nationality is one aspect. Its second paragraph determines that

> where a child is illegally deprived of some or all of the elements of his or her identity, State Parties shall provide appropriate assistance and protection, with a view to re-establishing speedily his or her identity.[174]

Although this article was drafted with the particular situation of the enforced disappearance of children in mind - as experienced in Argentina between 1975 and 1983 – it is conceivable that it could, by extension, be invoked in the context of trafficking in children.[175] In fact, the Committee on the Rights of the Child has elaborated its views on the importance of the right to preservation of identity for all separated or unaccompanied children – be they a victim of trafficking or otherwise – who find themselves displaced across an international border.[176] Moreover, with regards to *any* action concerning such children, the state is required to take into account the best interests of the child and, for those purposes, must conduct "a clear and comprehensive assessment of the child's identity, including his or her nationality".[177] This provides another avenue for ensuring that the nationality or (risk of) statelessness of the child is established and that the child is supplied with documentation enabling the preservation of its identity.[178]

[172] Article 16, paragraphs 3 and 4 of the Council of Europe Convention on Action Against Trafficking in Human Beings.

[173] Article 10, paragraph 4(b) of the Council of Europe Convention on Action Against Trafficking in Human Beings.

[174] Article 8, paragraph 2 of the Convention on the Rights of the Child.

[175] Geraldine van Bueren, *The International Law on the Rights of the Child*, Martinus Nijhoff, Dordrecht: 1995, pages 119-120. Jaap Doek, 'The CRC and the Right to Acquire and to Preserve a Nationality', in *Refugee Survey Quarterly*, Vol. 25, 2006. Trafficking is clearly an illegal, even severely criminal, act – even if the state is not complicit. Arguably the state will have a duty to ensure that the child victim is not left with problems of establishing or preserving his identity as a result of being trafficked.

[176] This should be taken into account when seeking any durable solution to the situation of the child. See Committee on the Rights of the Child, *General Comment No. 6: Treatment of unaccompanied and separated children outside their country of origin*, CRC/GC/2006/6, 1 September 2005, paragraphs 84 and 93.

[177] Committee on the Rights of the Child, *General Comment No. 6: Treatment of unaccompanied and separated children outside their country of origin*, CRC/GC/2006/6, 1 September 2005, paragraphs 19-20. This consideration is also based on article 3 of the Convention on the Rights of the Child.

[178] Thus, when confronted with separated or unaccompanied children the assessment of protection concerns should include "prompt registration by means of an interview [...] to ascertain the identity of

The scenario for refugees is necessarily more complicated because it may not be possible or advisable to immediately invoke the cooperation of the state of origin of the refugee in verifying or documenting his nationality. Instead, the regime for refugee protection concentrates on the establishment and documentation of refugee status by the receiving state.[179] Nevertheless, the process of refugee status determination necessitates an appraisal of nationality status since "an applicant's well-founded fear of persecution must be in relation to the country of his nationality".[180] It may be that the applicant is found to be stateless (in which case the assessment of his refugee claim will be based on his relationship with his country of former habitual residence).[181] This means that situations of statelessness may be uncovered within the context of procedures for Refugee Status Determination.[182] The nationality status of the person should subsequently be included in the personal documentation issued to the refugee. For instance, UNHCR's own Refugee Certificates include "the name by which the refugee is registered with UNHCR and other core bio-data including the date and place of birth, and nationality".[183]

Yet, having identified cases of statelessness – and perhaps situations where a person's nationality is not clear or documented – in this manner, the international refugee framework does not provide for any immediate further action on this point. The individual simply enjoys various rights on the basis of his refugee status, leaving the issue of nationality to resurface when the possibility of a durable solution is tabled. In those circumstances, states are clearly urged – if not compelled – to address problems of statelessness as part of whichever durable solution is envisaged, as described above. At that stage, the documentation issued to the refugee can play a crucial role. For example, in the context of the repatriation of Guatemalan refugees in the early 1990s – most of whom were undocumented at the time they fled – the Guatemalan government

---

the child, including, wherever possible, identity of both parents, other siblings, as well as the citizenship of the child, the siblings and the parents" and the children should subsequently "be provided with their own personal identity documentation as soon as possible". Committee on the Rights of the Child, *General Comment No. 6: Treatment of unaccompanied and separated children outside their country of origin,* CRC/GC/2006/6, 2005, paragraphs 31 (ii) and (iv).

[179] Articles 27 and 28 of the 1951 Convention relating to the Status of Refugees provide, respectively, for the issuance of identity papers and travel documents to refugees.

[180] UNHCR, *Handbook on Procedures and Criteria for Determining Refugee Status under the 1951 Convention and the 1967 Protocol relating to the Status of Refugees,* HCR/IP/Eng/Rev.1, Reedited January 1992, paragraph 90. Very little guidance is provided on how to establish a person's nationality beyond the statement that the possession of a passport at least creates "a prima facie presumption that the holder is a national of the country of issue". There is no explanation of how nationality is to be determined in the absence of any passport. See paragraph 93 of the same Handbook.

[181] See the definition of a refugee in article 1 of the 1951 Convention relating to the Status of Refugees.

[182] Approximately half of the states that responded to UNHCR's global questionnaire on statelessness indicated that they had a mechanism in place for identifying stateless asylum seekers within the context of refugee status determination. Indeed, some states admitted that this is the only tool in place for identifying cases of statelessness, despite the fact that not all stateless persons will apply for asylum. See UNHCR, *Final report concerning the Questionnaire on statelessness pursuant to the Agenda for Protection,* Geneva: March 2004, page 27.

[183] UNHCR, *Procedural Standards for Refugee Status Determination under UNHCR's Mandate,* Geneva: 2005, section 8.2.1.

> never contested that those who were registered as refugees in Mexico had indeed come from Guatemala and accepted the registration undertaken by the Mexican Government or by UNHCR as sufficient evidence of their identity and right to return.[184]

In a roundabout way then, the question of statelessness is being addressed in the international community's response to refugee situations. Nevertheless, explicit and binding standards on the avoidance of statelessness in this particular context have yet to develop.

3 Conclusion

This chapter covered a diverse yet interrelated selection of topics that are increasingly perceived to be contributing to the creation of statelessness. These were collectively described as "new" causes of statelessness to reflect their absence from discussions at the time that the 1961 Convention on the Reduction of Statelessness was drafted (and from the text of this instrument as adopted). The consideration of these issues went some way to uncovering the complexity of relationships between questions of statelessness and of lack of documentation generally as well as between immigration status and access to nationality. In this context, the acute difficulties involved in the *identification* of statelessness truly come to the fore. For instance, while there is growing recognition that the difficulty in establishing a nationality - due to the non-registration of births or loss of documents by migrants – may lead to statelessness, this acknowledgement has so far failed to result in the development of any further guidelines on how states or institutions are to determine where a person is simply undocumented and where an individual is (at risk of becoming) stateless for the purposes of applying the relevant international regime. This general concern was raised earlier, but it is particularly delicate in the context of these "new" causes of statelessness. In the following chapter we will give some consideration to how to move forward and address this issue. The task that remains here is to draw some conclusions as to the effectiveness with which international human rights law addresses the "new" causes of statelessness and to what extent additional instruments or measures are required to fill any potential gaps – including the question as to the role of the 1961 Statelessness Convention in this respect.

With regard to birth registration we discovered that despite a clear and unambiguous enunciation of the right of every child to be registered at birth, in practice vast numbers of children do not have their birth officially recorded. This suggests that there is room for improvement in the international community's response to the issue to date. Indeed, although some efforts have been made to address several of the practical obstacles that contribute to the under-registration of births, it would certainly be beneficial to elaborate further guidelines on appropriate procedures, including suitable measures with a view to tackling statelessness within this context. Such guidelines should bring together, clarify and build upon the

[184] Amnesty International, *Bhutan: Nationality, expulsion, statelessness and the right to return,* September 2000, section 4.4.4.

suggestions made by – amongst others – the UN Committee on the Rights of the Child in its response to individual state party reports, but also take into account the recommendations of organisations such as UNICEF and Plan International that have been undertaking numerous activities to promote universal birth registration. Thus, the guidelines should provide for: the compulsory registration of all births; improvement of the reach of registration systems through decentralisation and the use of mobile registration units to reach isolated populations; awareness raising on the importance of birth registration among all relevant actors and the facilitation of late birth registration. It should also clarify that birth registration must be free of charge, thus ending any ambiguity on this question resulting from the statements of the Committee on the Rights of the Child. In addition, the formulation of such guidelines would provide an opportunity to set standards on the transparency and simplification of all registration procedures; the opportunity to appeal against a decision whereby birth registration is refused; and the proper storage of records so as to avoid loss or damage (for example due to conflict). Where two countries may have jurisdiction over the persons in question, the role of the state of nationality of the parents as a compliment to or an alternative for the registration procedures of the host state should also be clarified – a matter that is of particular value in the circumstance of irregular migration. With the added complexity of the situation of such groups as irregular migrants and refugees – where contact with one or other of the states involved is particularly difficult – every effort should be made to elucidate feasible responsibilities and procedures for these particular circumstances, based on a careful study of best practices in this regard. Moreover, norms should be set concerning the information that should be recorded, taking into account the inappropriateness and deterrent effect of requiring information about race or religion and, in contrast, the absolute necessity of establishing and recording certain information in order to facilitate the prevention and reduction of statelessness. The latter may include details such as the nationality, birthplace and country of habitual residence of the parents (and possibly also the grandparents). Finally, such a guiding document should also elaborate on the link between birth registration and the right to acquire a nationality. In particular, it must establish the need for – and details of - procedures to be put in place for identifying and remedying cases of statelessness as an integral part of the birth registration process. A similar project of developing detailed guidelines could also be envisioned in relation to the full and proper registration of marriages - a matter that has so far attracted less attention.

At this stage, with the head-start that the Committee on the Rights of the Child has in detailing the measures to be adopted to promote birth registration, the most effective route may be for any guidelines on the correct registration of births to be drafted as a General Comment to article 7 of the Convention on the Rights of the Child by this treaty body. Alternatively, the task could be taken on by the Human Rights Committee as a General Comment to article 24 of the International Covenant on Civil and Political Rights. Similarly, the elaboration of standards on the registration of marriages could be dealt with under the auspices of a General Recommendation by the Committee on the Elimination of Discrimination Against Women. As opposed to the creation of a specialised convention, these options have the advantage of both speed and simplicity. It would also be a way of avoiding any critique surrounding the over-proliferation and fragmentation of human rights documents.[185] After all, the right of a child to be registered at birth is already clearly delineated in binding instruments, all that remains is to clarify how this right should be effectuated - arguably a job for the supervisory apparatus attached to these instruments. Yet the weakness of such an approach is evidenced in the title of the document produced: it would be a "General Comment" or a "General Recommendation" and lack full binding authority. Alternatively, all of the above issues could be dealt with jointly in a new UN convention on civil registration procedures or indeed a protocol to the 1961 Convention on the Reduction of Statelessness that addresses nationality issues in the context of civil registration. Although the process of hammering out a binding international instrument is a lengthy and complicated one, the contribution of such an exercise towards reaching some kind of consensus on the organisation of civil registration is a valuable reward. It would also provide states with the opportunity to fully debate such crucial matters as the exchange of information within the context of maintaining a civil register with a view to avoiding (prolonged) non-documentation and statelessness.

The question of statelessness arising from various forms of international migration was found to be a more complex one with less clear direction being provided by international law. It is certainly true that "large-scale settlement inevitably leads to debate on citizenship"[186] and with regards to immigrants generally, nationality policies have largely been influenced by a growing acknowledgement of the fact that

> if political participation is denied through refusal of citizenship and failure to provide channels of representation, immigrant politics is likely to take on militant forms. This applies particularly to the children of immigrants born in the countries of immigration. If they are excluded from political life through non-citizenship, social marginalisation or racism, they are likely to present a major challenge to existing political structures in the future.[187]

Nevertheless, in spite of the reality that *irregular* migrants remain increasingly indefinitely in their host state and may eventually grow dissatisfied with their vulnerable position,[188] in the debate on citizenship it appears that the position of these migrants is suffering from neglect and that they are commonly excluded from the benefits of any relaxation of nationality policy. Their unlawful immigration status influences not only their own (indefinite lack of) access to citizenship in the host state, but also renders their children especially vulnerable to lack of birth

---

[185] Carmen Tiburcio, "Conclusion" in *The human rights of aliens under international and comparative law*, Kluwer Law International, The Hague: 2001, pages 268-269.

[186] Stephen Castles; Mark Miller, *The Age of Migration*, The Guildford Press, London: 2003, page 43.

[187] Stephen Castles; Mark Miller, *The Age of Migration*, The Guildford Press, London: 2003 page 277 (see also pages 253 and 287-288).

[188] In May 2006, the United States' irregular immigrant population turned out in their masses on the streets of cities across the country to protest against their protracted powerless situation. "Today we protest and tomorrow we vote" was their non-violent plea for recognition of the inevitable – that they are there to stay and want to participate. It is possible that one day such non-violent form of protest will be dropped in favour of more militant action. BBC News, *LA feels migrant day of action,* 2 May 2006, accessible via http://news.bbc.co.uk.

registration and statelessness.[189] As the irregular migrant's overall enjoyment of rights presents itself as an ever more pressing agenda item for the international community, questions relating to their right to a nationality must be addressed to prevent a degeneration of a situation of dissatisfaction into one of instability. The UN Special Rapporteur on the Rights of Migrants and the UN Committee on Migrant Workers should take the lead in cultivating and directing this debate. These efforts should focus on minimising any risk of statelessness, for example by promoting cooperation between states, wherever feasible, to resolve problems of documentation. By reaffirming and working to ensure the avoidance of statelessness, the need to reconsider the question of access to nationality for irregular migrants in the host state can be allayed without compelling states to necessarily adapt their immigration or naturalisation policy. Nevertheless, where states are faced with stateless, *irregular* migrants, the possibility of regularisation or of waiving some of the conditions for naturalisation may have to be considered. This question, however, goes beyond the issue of *prevention* of statelessness and will naturally come up in Part 3 as we look more closely at the rights of stateless persons, including the right of solution, i.e. acquisition of nationality.

The situation of the children of irregular migrants is particularly troubling, for although international law clearly promulgates the right of every child to acquire a nationality at birth, there are certain details in instruments such as the European Convention on Nationality that call this right into question. This has led to the conclusion that "illegal immigration status has emerged as a bar to acquisition of nationality even though it would render children *de jure* stateless".[190] In view of the otherwise unambiguous statements of the child's right to acquire a nationality, this would seem to be a regressive and unacceptable development. This led to the rather surprising discovery that the 1961 Convention on the Reduction of Statelessness actually appears to offer broader protection to children of irregular migrants by allowing only the condition of a period of "habitual" - rather than "*lawful* and habitual" - residence to be set. However, the traveaux preparatoires are ambiguous on this point and the Convention does not offer any suggestions as to how *habitual* residence is to be established – particularly where it is unlawful and therefore proof of the fact of residence may be less readily available.[191] In order to settle this point of contention, it would be advisable for the Council of Europe to clarify its position, ensuring that it is guided by the principle of the avoidance of statelessness and indeed falling in step at least with the protection offered in the 1961 Statelessness Convention. Moreover, it would be helpful if one or more of the human rights treaty bodies were to offer their guidance on the implementation of a child's right to a

---

[189] Any argument that irregular immigrants have brought such problems on themselves and have by way of their disregard for immigration law essentially committed a kind of fraud for which international law accepts statelessness as a penalty is untenable considering the diverse make-up of the irregular migrant population. This includes persons who are the victims of the heinous international crime of trafficking and forced migrants such refugees.

[190] Tang Lay Lee, "Statelessness, Human Rights and Gender. Irregular migrant workers from Burma in Thailand", Martinus Nijhoff Publishers, Leiden 2005, page 47.

[191] Irregular migrants are unlikely to appear in any official state register and will, subsequently, be unable to prove the duration of their factual presence in the state. They will have to rely, instead, wholly on secondary evidence such as witness testimony or relevant supporting documentation (for example, an electricity bill or school attendance record).

nationality where the child is indeed threatened with statelessness and, in doing so, address the question whether particular residence requirements can be set and how to establish when these conditions are satisfied. Ideally, the most fail-safe policy for the prevention of statelessness at birth would be prescribed: automatic and unconditional attribution of nationality at birth where the child would otherwise be stateless. With the right guidance as to how to establish the threat of statelessness, such a policy could be implemented as part of the birth registration procedure to great effect.

Lastly we saw that the especially vulnerable position of victims of trafficking and refugees has been acknowledged and that the international community has taken numerous measures to afford protection to such individuals. As far as protection against statelessness in the context of trafficking is concerned, the measures prescribed by international instruments were found to be conditional upon the stance and initiative of the receiving state rather than securing an unequivocal right of the victim to the clarification and verification of his or her nationality status. Furthermore, the same instruments do not prescribe any additional steps that should be taken should the victim's citizenship remain undetermined. The scope for preserving or re-establishing the nationality of child victims of trafficking is greater thanks to the guarantees offered by the Convention on the Rights of the Child. Moreover, the instruments that have been tailored to tackle trafficking and offer protection to its victims are very young and there are a number of institutions that are currently involved in the promotion of such standards. One of the tasks to be tackled is the elaboration of guidelines for the prevention of statelessness and recovery of nationality and documentation in the context of trafficking. For refugees, there was a similarly mixed picture. The avoidance of statelessness is a core value that is reflected in a number of ways throughout the overall refugee protection regime. However, the prevention or resolution of statelessness is likely to be tackled only once a solution is in sight for the refugee situation as such – i.e. in the context of voluntary repatriation, local integration or resettlement. And even then, the obligatory nature of efforts to tackle statelessness is doubtful and there is no assurance that everyone will benefit from the measures envisaged.

The overall impression is that the international community has already begun to take up the fight against the newly-identified sources of statelessness, be it in a conscious effort to resolve nationality issues or as a bi-product of measures to tackle underlying issues such as human trafficking and the under-registration of births. Yes, the 1961 Convention on the Reduction of Statelessness is substantially outdated where these particular sources of statelessness are concerned - although with respect to the risk of statelessness among the children of irregular migrants it appears to retain some value as a standard-setting instrument.[192] Nevertheless, it seems feasible that each of the "new" sources of statelessness can, in fact, be addressed through an elaboration on existing mechanisms, expanded involvement of such institutions as the UN treaty bodies and a more resolute focus on the specific problem of the prevention of statelessness. To attempt to combine the

[192] We saw that the 1961 Statelessness Convention allows states to require a certain period of "habitual residence" in providing access to nationality for children who would otherwise be stateless, whereas the 1997 European Convention on Nationality adds the condition of that such residence be lawful.

diverse and complicated issues into one instrument or supplement the 1961 Statelessness Convention with a protocol addressing all of these "new" sources of statelessness would, I feel, be both unattainable and counter-productive. The international community's energy is better spent in tracing, developing and better utilising existing remedies while the broader concern of *identifying* statelessness is perhaps tabled as an issue to be (newly) investigated by an appropriate body, such as the International Law Commission. This issue of the identification of cases where statelessness threatens, and the related problem of enforcement of existing remedies, will be looked at again as we move into the next chapter where overall conclusions must be drawn about the current state of international law in the fight against statelessness.

CHAPTER VIII

INTERNATIONAL LAW AND THE PREVENTION OF STATELESSNESS

For the best part of a century, states have sought ways to tackle the undesirable anomaly that is statelessness by way of international agreements that delineate basic rules on how nationality should be attributed so as to ensure that no-one is left unclaimed. First the 1930 Hague Convention on Certain Questions relating to the Conflict of Nationality Laws, then the 1961 Convention on the Reduction of Statelessness and now a plethora of human rights instruments. The developments are such that basic conceptions on nationality matters have changed dramatically:

> Although nationality is essentially governed by national legislation, the competence of states in this field may be exercised only within the limits set by international law [...] As a result of this evolution in the field of human rights, the traditional approach based on the predominance of the interests of States over the interests of individuals has subsided.[1]

So, today international law sets out a host of measures and obligations aimed to protect "the interests of individuals" – to protect people against statelessness.

Yet statelessness still rears its head in substantial measure across the globe. UNHCR explains that people are rendered stateless "through a bewildering series of sovereign, political, legal, technical or administrative directives or oversights".[2] This is no exaggeration: even after dividing the origins of statelessness into four main categories in order to deal with them more systematically, there proved to be many sub-categories, nuances and further intricacies that had to be taken into account. The foregoing chapters therefore sought to expose the ways in which statelessness is being created in order to assess whether the international community's response corresponds to this reality. In particular, we asked how effective the 1961 Convention on the Reduction of Statelessness is in thwarting statelessness (or would be if it were universally ratified and implemented) and to what extent human rights law now compliments or even negates the protection offered by this tailor-made instrument. This investigation was guided by the following specific research question:

---

[1] International Law Commission, 'Draft Articles on Nationality of Natural Persons in Relation to the Succession of States - With Commentaries', in *Yearbook of the International Law Commission,* Vol. II, 1999, page 24.

[2] UNHCR, *The World's Stateless - Questions and Answers,* Geneva: , page 8.

How can the way in which international law deals with the *prevention of statelessness* be improved so as to ensure optimal protection against statelessness for the individual (i.e. the realisation of the right to a nationality)?

This chapter will draw together the findings of the preceding chapters and provide an overall assessment of the value of the 1961 Statelessness Convention, the role of human rights law in preventing statelessness, discuss the gaps must still be attended to and consider the potential for the implementation and enforcement of all of the relevant norms.

1 The value of the 1961 Convention on the Reduction of Statelessness in the prevention of statelessness

Designed primarily with conflict of laws situations in mind, the 1961 Convention on the Reduction of Statelessness is most at home dealing with the "technical causes" of statelessness that were uncovered in chapter IV. Eight out of the ten substantive provisions in the Convention address statelessness arising from a legal or administrative technicality. This is pursued through clear yet cautious direction. Clear, because the Convention explicitly details certain policies that states either must or must not follow in their nationality law and because, where statelessness threatens, it identifies which state is responsible for attributing nationality. In this lies the instrument's strength: determining not only what must be done – avoid statelessness – but also how this is to be achieved. For example, in respect of foundlings, the Convention determines that the state upon which the child is found must grant nationality, be it a *jus soli* or *jus sanguinis* regime. Other decisive provisions can be found in relation to the definition of territory for the purpose of *jus soli* conferral of nationality; the prohibition of automatic loss of nationality resulting in statelessness as a consequence of any change in personal status (marriage, adoption, divorce, etc); the prohibition of automatic withdrawal of nationality from the dependents of a person whose citizenship is lost or deprived; and the non-acceptance of an act of renunciation of nationality where it would lead to statelessness. In fact the Convention carefully instructs states upon how to deal with every situation where statelessness threatens from a conflict of laws or similar technicality, both at birth and later in life. The Convention offers a level of detail and clarity that is often lacking under international (human rights) law generally, thereby providing helpful guidance on how to resolve these situations.

Nevertheless, the 1961 Statelessness Convention errs on the side of caution by failing to provide *unequivocally* for the bestowal or retention of nationality wherever statelessness threatens. In this sense, the text reflects the sticking points of the debate that preceded it. Thus the Convention provides for the attribution of nationality either *jus soli* or *jus sanguinis* at birth to a child who would otherwise be stateless, but allows states to choose to delay the conferral of citizenship until late childhood or even early adulthood and set a number of additional conditions to be met.[3] Similarly, the Convention prohibits the loss or deprivation of nationality

[3] Article 1 and Article 4 of the 1961 Convention on the Reduction of Statelessness. These conditions include, among others, certain residence requirements. See chapter IV, section 1.1.

where an individual does not hold an alternative citizenship, but goes on to delineate a number of exceptional circumstances in which statelessness is nevertheless an approved consequence.[4] Thanks to such clauses, the Convention will only ever achieve a *reduction* in the instance of statelessness arising from these technical causes in future. However, the Convention does not promise to do any more than that and does therefore live up to its name.[5] Moreover, by seeking careful compromises and finding a balance between the interests of *jus soli* and *jus sanguinis* states, the Convention was thought more likely to achieve widespread support than if it had ignored the qualms of many governments and adopted a rigid and uncompromising approach that encroached much further upon the freedom of states in nationality matters. From this point of view, the enduring low number of state parties to the instrument remains something of a mystery.

A more troublesome finding in respect of its treatment of the technical causes of statelessness is that the Convention fails to denounce certain distinctions that are now considered inappropriate and untenable under international law. In the first place, the Convention actually employs the distinction between legitimate and illegitimate children in one of its articles[6] – a ground that is prohibited under the Universal Declaration of Human Rights, the Convention on the Rights of the Child and the American Convention on Human Rights. Secondly, although not explicitly approving of a gender-imbalance in nationality regulations, the Convention does not include an outright prohibition of gender-sensitive nationality acts. Gender is even left out of the list of grounds enunciated in article 9 where the discriminatory deprivation of nationality is outlawed. The Convention has thereby neglected a most fundamental international norm: gender discrimination is expressly forbidden in every major human rights instrument adopted to date.[7] In practice these shortcomings may be written off as simply untidy, since state parties will nevertheless be held to respect such standards of non-discrimination under their overall human rights commitments. However, in urging states to ratify and implement the Convention in its present form, these shortcomings send an unfortunate - if not dangerous - and regressive message.

As we turned our attention to other sources of statelessness in chapters IV, V and VI, the weaknesses of the Convention began to outweigh its strengths. Thus, in dealing with the question of arbitrary deprivation of nationality: yes, the Convention outlaws discriminatory deprivation whether this is realised outside of the law or through discriminatory lawmaking, certain procedural safeguards are introduced and discrimination on "political grounds" is also outlawed (where this is a less clear prohibition under international human rights law). But, the article leaves out other grounds, such as gender, and provides no opportunity to expand the list so as to take into account the developments in the perspective of states on this matter. More problematic still is the discovery that the prohibition of arbitrary deprivation

[4] For example, citizenship may be withdrawn due to long-term residence abroad, even if it results in statelessness, where the individual acquired nationality by naturalisation, has resided abroad for at least 7 years and has neglected to register his intent to retain his nationality. Article 7, paragraph 4. Similar exception clauses can be found in article 8 of 1961 Convention on the Reduction of Statelessness.

[5] States elected for a convention on the *reduction* rather than the *elimination* of future statelessness early on in the drafting process.

[6] Article 1, paragraph 3 of the 1961 Convention on the Reduction of Statelessness.

[7] See, for instance, chapter IV, section 1.2 at note 74.

of nationality, as elaborated in the Convention, only appears to be applicable to situations of discriminatory *denationalisation*. While this is a major issue and historical examples of the mass denationalisation of population groups on ethnic or racial grounds undoubtedly shaped the approach taken, it has become apparent that the denial of citizenship can also occur in the context of the conferral of nationality. Consider the situation of the children of (suspected) Haitian descent who are refused access to birthright citizenship in the Dominican Republic. This is an example of arbitrary deprivation of nationality that would not be covered by the 1961 Statelessness Convention but is nonetheless a very real, present-day source of statelessness.

The Convention then makes an admirable attempt to address statelessness arising from state succession, but this issue seems to have been taken up as an afterthought and the assessment of the sole provision that is devoted to it led to a perhaps inevitable conclusion: it lacks the depth and the detail to effectively prevent statelessness in the context of state succession. For example, while the article proposes to avoid statelessness by specific international agreement between the states concerned,[8] there is no fall-back clause in case such an agreement fails to meet its aim. Meanwhile, if the question of nationality is not settled by treaty, the Convention calls upon the state to which territory is transferred to grant citizenship to anyone who would otherwise be rendered stateless due to the succession of states.[9] On the face of it, this approach is straightforward and incontrovertible, but its application may nevertheless present some difficulties. Newly independent states may not be bound by this provision and where there is more than one successor state a dispute may arise as to which state is obliged to grant nationality to which persons who are at risk of statelessness. There is no mention of a right of option for the individual involved – a method that has been adopted elsewhere to stave off such nationality disputes and promote the conferral of the most appropriate nationality. Moreover, there is no effort to limit the freedom of the predecessor state (if still in existence) to withdraw its nationality and render the individuals stateless to begin with. Thus unless the states concerned do agree and implement an effective bilateral solution to nationality questions - for the modalities of which the Convention provides no suggestions – the solution offered by the Convention to statelessness in the context of state succession is unlikely to be adequate.

Finally, we found that since the adoption of the 1961 Statelessness Convention, much more has been learnt about the statelessness phenomenon and its underlying causes. In particular, a number of "new" sources of statelessness have been identified which the Convention had not foreseen: deficiencies in birth registration systems (and the registration of marriages) and problems connected to the status of irregular migrants and the position of victims of human trafficking and refugees. The Convention has little to offer in answer to these newfound issues, further diminishing its overall effectiveness as *the* instrument for the prevention of statelessness. Part of the difficulty here is that some of these "new" issues present an even greater challenge for the identification of concrete cases of – the threat of – statelessness. One critical point is where to draw the line between the simple lack of documentation and a case of statelessness. And since the 1961 Statelessness

[8] Article 10, paragraph 1 of the 1961 Convention on the Reduction of Statelessness.
[9] Article 10, paragraph 2 of the 1961 Convention on the Reduction of Statelessness.

Convention does not offer any guidance as to how a person's nationality or lack of nationality is to be established, dealing with these "new" problems will require a substantial rethink of this difficult question.

So what is the value of the 1961 Convention on the Reduction of Statelessness today? It is not easy to offer one, all-encompassing answer to this question. It simply cannot be denied that in many ways the Convention is proving to be seriously inadequate to address the "bewildering" diversity of ways in which an individual may be rendered stateless. It is particularly difficult to ignore the fact that the newly emerging sources of statelessness are not touched upon at all by this text. As to the problem of nationality and statelessness in the context of state succession, since this has pushed itself to the fore and is now being taken up in a separate, universal instrument – the ILC Draft Articles on Nationality of Natural Persons in relation to the Succession of States – the 1961 Statelessness Convention can be excused for its flaws there. In effect, if and once the ILC Draft Articles are formally adopted as a declaration or convention, article 10 of the 1961 Statelessness Convention will become more or less obsolete. With respect to the question of arbitrary deprivation of nationality however, the Convention's approach is not only inadequate to deal with situations on the ground, it is also severely outdated now that international human rights law has developed a much broader norm. Arguably, this article has, therefore, already become obsolete and state parties should simply consider themselves bound by the more expansive standard to which they are committed through their accession to human rights instruments.[10] This leaves the eight detailed provisions that address the technical causes of statelessness to rescue the fate of the Convention. And in this, in my opinion, they succeed. There is certainly room for improvement in the details of the measures prescribed – a matter that will be considered more closely when we come to address the gaps that remain in international law's approach to the prevention of statelessness. Nevertheless, the 1961 Statelessness Convention is the only *universal* instrument on offer that provides clear and detailed obligations with a view to reducing the incidence of statelessness in the future.[11] By consolidating numerous questions into one text it focuses states' attention on the goal of the prevention of statelessness and if the instrument were widely ratified and implemented it would certainly go some way to achieving that aim. And by doing so in such deliberate detail, the text sets out unambiguous measures that can be readily implemented and enforced.[12] Herein lies the enduring value of the 1961 Statelessness Convention. It should not be viewed as *the* solution to the perpetuation of statelessness, but seen rather as one valid and

[10] See also article 13 of the 1961 Convention on the Reduction of Statelessness which determines that the instrument's terms will be "shall not be construed as affecting any provisions more conducive to the reduction of statelessness" in either a states domestic or international legal commitments.

[11] The European Convention on Nationality has developed some of the norms of the 1961 Statelessness Convention much further, but it is important to recall that this is a *regional* instrument and therefore of limited geographical application. Meanwhile, under human rights law there is evidence of the development of universal norms such as the bestowal of nationality *jus soli* to a child who would otherwise be stateless, but these remain somewhat vague – for example, should this be granted *ex lege* at birth or later in life and what additional conditions may be set - and may be disputed.

[12] Leaving aside for a moment the fact that the actual prospects for implementation and enforcement are both hampered by other considerations as we will see below.

important contribution to the reduction and eventual eradication of this terrible plight.

2 The role of international (human rights) law in the prevention of statelessness

Although ending on a more positive note, the above assessment of the 1961 Convention on the Reduction of Statelessness raised serious concerns about the protection offered against statelessness under international law. But the Convention is not the only source of norms on the prevention of statelessness. There are many other instruments, particularly in the human rights field, that have an impact on - the freedom of states to establish - nationality policy and play a role in the prevention of statelessness today. Just as "human rights standards can be used to help refugees by reinforcing and supplementing refugee law",[13] so too can human rights standards assist in tackling statelessness. Indeed we have seen that in relation to all four categories of causes of statelessness, international (human rights) law has something to say. In many areas, these alternative sources of international legal obligations actually compliment the 1961 Statelessness Convention, reinforcing or even raising the overall level of protection against statelessness on offer.

The most fundamental contribution of human rights law to the prevention of statelessness is the enunciation of an individual's right to a nationality. From this basic norm, two important standards have been distilled. The first is the avoidance of statelessness at birth, to which end there is a growing consensus - evidenced also by the recent reiterations of this norm at the regional level[14] and in instruments that deal with nationality in relation to state succession[15] – that states should attribute nationality *jus soli* to a child born on their territory who would otherwise be stateless. Where foundlings are concerned, this same norm is further substantiated by a widespread state practice. The second standard that is taken from the overall right to a nationality is the mounting intolerance for any loss of nationality that would result in statelessness – whereby retraction of citizenship gained under false pretences remains an agreed exception.[16] Yet a shadow of uncertainty still hangs over these two important norms as they have yet to be consolidated in a binding, universal text. Indeed the only instrument to translate these standards into such concrete legal obligations remains the 1961 Convention on the Reduction of Statelessness. At this stage, developments in human rights law simply reaffirm the approach taken in this Convention.

Where human rights norms first take a step beyond the terms of the 1961 Convention is in relation to the principle of equality of treatment and non-

---

[13] Leonardo Franco, "Protection of Refugees and Solutions to the Refugee Problem: A Human Rights Perspective" in Schmid (ed) *Whither Refugee? The Refugee Crisis: Problems and Solutions*, PIOOM, Leiden: 1996, page 203.

[14] Article 6 of the European Convention on Nationality and article 6 of the African Charter on the Rights and Welfare of the Child – both following suit with the American Convention on Human Rights. See further chapter IV, section 1.2.

[15] Article 13 of the ILC Draft Articles on Nationality of Natural Persons in relation to the Succession or States and article 10 of the Council of Europe Convention on the avoidance of statelessness in relation to State succession. See further chapter VI, section 3.

[16] See in particular article 7 of the 1997 European Convention on Nationality.

discrimination. According to these standards, there should be no distinction between legitimate and illegitimate children in access to nationality at birth.[17] Also relevant in relation to the technical causes of statelessness, is that gender discrimination in nationality acts is outlawed – important for both *jus sanguinis* laws and policy relating to citizenship in the event of marriage.[18] In addition, human rights law proscribes the arbitrary deprivation of nationality which includes policies of denationalisation *and* refusal of access to nationality on a considerable range of prohibited grounds.[19] Such policy is outlawed whether it is achieved through or outside of the law. This norm provides vital protection against denial of citizenship, although there is some need for clarification of the scope of the standard of non-discrimination in relation to the different aspects of nationality attribution. Similarly, human rights law introduces a crucial defence against improper or arbitrary decision-making in the form of various guarantees relating to an effective remedy and due process[20] - although, except in the European Convention on Nationality,[21] no special provision has been made for the specific context of nationality disputes.

Recently, international law has been pulling out all the stops and developing detailed, progressive, innovative and thorough agreements on the proper attribution of nationality and the prevention of statelessness in the context of the succession of states. At the time of writing, these agreements had yet to enter into force, housed as they are in a brand-new Council of Europe Convention that must first achieve the ratification of 3 states and a series of Draft Articles devised by the International Law Commission whose future status is still uncertain. Nevertheless, the potential that these instruments hold is enormous and they reflect a huge achievement in the negotiation of practical, rights-oriented solutions to difficult nationality questions in relation to state succession. Where the 1961 Statelessness Convention dealt only with the role of the "state to which territory is transferred" and concentrates on international cooperation as the primary remedy, these texts diligently set out detailed obligations for the successor state(s) *and* the predecessor state. A solution is also offered to any emerging dispute over which state is responsible for conferring nationality when more than one genuine link is identified - the individual must be given an effective opportunity to opt for one of the available citizenships. Furthermore, the instruments offer:

- elaborate procedural guarantees;
- an expansive non-discrimination clause;
- an avenue for preventing statelessness for affected persons habitually resident in the states concerned *and* abroad;

[17] See chapter IV, section 1.2.
[18] See chapter IV, sections 1.2 and 3.2.
[19] See the detailed discussion of the scope of the phrase "arbitrary deprivation of nationality" in chapter V.
[20] See in particular chapter V, section 2.2.
[21] In chapter IV of the European Convention on Nationality concerning "Procedures relating to nationality".

- a more elaborate obligation to engage in international cooperation with a view to resolving nationality questions; and

- a fall-back provision limiting the long-term damage for those persons who nevertheless are rendered stateless and their offspring.[22]

In addition, the Council of Europe Convention includes the absolute innovation of lowering the standard of proof for the attribution of nationality to persons who are at risk to statelessness due to the succession of states.[23] Once these agreements have attained a definite legal status, they will provide an impressive tool in the prevention of statelessness arising from future state successions. Already they serve as an excellent reference point for best practices in this field that can be referred to by states and international (human rights) bodies alike when seeking an appropriate response to nationality concerns in the event of state succession.

In respect of the "new" causes of statelessness, human rights law goes some way to offering the answers that the 1961 Statelessness Convention could not. The right of every child to be registered at birth is recognised at both universal and regional levels.[24] The UN treaty bodies, in particular the Committee on the Rights of the Child, have even begun to advise states in some detail on how to improve birth registration coverage and use the procedure to ensure that each child enjoys his right to acquire a nationality. There is also an understanding of the importance of – and right to – the registration of marriage, although this has yet to attract the same level of attention as birth registration matters. It is possible to conceive of measures to further consolidate these developments, with a greater focus on the many practical and conceptual obstacles to be overcome and on the link between civil registration and nationality questions, but the basic tools are undoubtedly in place. International (human rights) law has, so far, provided less direction in dealing with the exposure of irregular migrants, the victims of human trafficking and refugees to statelessness. For the former, the protection against statelessness is just one of the many questions that the international community faces in respect of this increasingly prevalent and extremely vulnerable group – general affirmations of the right to birth registration and to a nationality will not suffice. For the latter two categories, a start has been made in delineating various steps that could be taken in order to stave off problems of statelessness. These include the verification and documentation of nationality for victims of trafficking (with a view to repatriation) and establishing a commitment to resolving residual nationality questions in the context of securing durable solutions for refugees. However, these standards are in their infancy and in many instances, the success of prevention is still conditional upon the goodwill or initiative of the state(s) involved.

---

[22] See chapter VI, section 3.

[23] Article 8 of the European Convention on the avoidance of statelessness in relation to State succession.

[24] For example in article 7 of the Convention on the Rights of the Child, article 6 of the African Convention on the Rights and Welfare of the Child and in the jurisprudence of both the European and Inter-American human rights courts.

International human rights law – in the broadest sense of the term – therefore closes several of the gaps that are left open by the 1961 Statelessness Convention in responding to the many and varied sources of statelessness. An added benefit of the growing attention to nationality matters under human rights law is that it allows the UN treaty bodies and courts such as the European Court on Human Rights and the Inter-American Court on Human Rights to play a part in the development and enforcement of these norms – albeit in some instances as a knock-on effect of the attention paid to other human rights concerns, such as birth registration. Nevertheless, there are some areas in which additional standard-setting is advisable and in the following section I will bring together and elaborate on a number of suggestions for ways to improve the protection offered against statelessness by building upon the foundations of existing legal norms. Thereafter we will also give closer consideration to questions relating to the actual implementation and the enforcement of international standards relating to the avoidance of statelessness.

3 Normative gaps in the prevention of statelessness under international law and suggested remedies

Even operating in conjunction, the 1961 Statelessness Convention and international human rights law are inadequate to stave off the creation of statelessness from all of its sources. With this in mind, over the course of preceding chapters, some ideas have already been tabled as to how to improve upon existing standards for the prevention of statelessness. Time now to review these suggestions and add some overall thoughts on the course to be taken by the international community in order to more effectively address the problem of statelessness. I submit that there are four main avenues that could (should) be pursued:

- consolidation and clarification of certain existing international human rights norms and their application in the context of the prevention of statelessness;

- further substantive standard-setting measures in those fields where international (human rights) norms are un(der)developed;

- revisiting the 1961 Convention on the Reduction of Statelessness with a view to updating and improving the text and promoting increased ratification; and

- elaborating additional norms with a specific focus on the prevention (and eradication) of statelessness, whereby lessons are taken from the standard-setting already accomplished in relation to nationality in the succession of states.

These options are not mutually exclusive, but rather a set of tools that should be explored and carefully coordinated so that, together, they may address all of the remaining gaps in the prevention of statelessness under international law.

The need to consolidate and clarify existing international human rights norms that impact upon the prevention of statelessness can – at this stage – best be answered by the human rights institutions charged with advising on and monitoring the implementation of those norms. In particular, the UN treaty bodies are well-placed to take on this task. The most appropriate route would then be the adoption of a General Comment by either the Human Rights Committee, based on article 24 of the International Covenant on Civil and Political Rights, or the Committee on the Rights of the Child based on article 7 of the Convention on the Rights of the Child. Or, better still, the Committees could work together to create a joint general comment on the issue since it is one that clearly straddles the two conventions.[25] Whichever the preferred option, the document should address both birth registration and the right to a nationality, with an underlying focus on the avoidance of statelessness. It should clarify whether nationality should indeed be prescribed *jus soli* to a child who would otherwise be stateless – with particular attention to the position of foundlings – and delineate the method to be employed and the conditions that may be set in implementing this policy. As submitted in chapter VII, the General Comment should consolidate the work of the Committee on the Rights of the Child in promoting universal birth registration by elaborating clear guidelines on how this can be achieved. The text should also incorporate some comment on the prohibition of arbitrary deprivation of nationality: the scope of the non-discrimination norm, the applicability of procedural remedies to nationality disputes and to what extent the withdrawal or refusal of nationality is permitted under this norm where it leads to statelessness. Although this route would not result in a binding legal instrument, it is a goal that should be relatively readily attainable in the short-term and it would help to remove the current ambiguities surrounding the interpretation of the relevant international norms. Alternatively, an independent General Comment focusing solely on the right to a nationality could be envisaged while the creation of a separate instrument devising comprehensive guidelines for civil registration is put on the agenda of an institution such as the International Law Commission.

In relation to those areas where international law is currently less expressive on the measures to be taken in order to prevent statelessness – such as in the context of irregular migration, trafficking in persons and refugee situations – there is a need for more substantive standard setting. The fundamental first step is to ensure that

[25] This may be a good opportunity for the treaty bodies to seek to collaborate in issuing an interpretation of the content of international norms that can be found in more than one universal human rights convention. In the context of investigations into the reform of the UN human rights monitoring system, such substantive cooperation is increasingly considered to be a desirable direction for the treaty bodies to go in. If there were to be a joint general comment on the right to birth registration and to a nationality – or at least some form of inter-committee cooperation in the drafting process – this could involve not only the Human Rights Committee and the Committee on the Rights of the Child, but also profit from the input of the Committee on the Elimination of Racial Discrimination (added perspective on the scope of the non-discrimination norm in relation to nationality matters), the Committee on the Elimination of Discrimination Against Women (input on gender issues in relation to nationality policy) and the Committee on Migrant Workers (consideration for the particular position of migrants, particularly irregular migrants, and their families). See on the question of reform of the treaty bodies the *Report of the working group on harmonisation of the working methods of treaty bodies,* HRI/MC/2007/2, 9 January 2007.

the relevant bodies and organisations begin to consider the dimension of statelessness in their work on these issues. Thus the UN Committee on Migrant Workers and the Special Rapporteur on the Rights of Migrants should instigate an investigation into and a discussion on the access of irregular migrants – and their children – to birth registration and a nationality. Similarly, the UN Special Rapporteur on trafficking in persons could draw greater attention to the problem of avoiding statelessness among trafficking victims in order to cultivate further debate on this issue and promote a more rights-oriented rather than state-oriented solution. Where statelessness rears its head in the context of refugee situations, UNHCR has already taken the lead in reminding states of the need to address this concern at the moment that a durable solution to the case at hand is in sight. Nevertheless, a further investigation into the nexus between statelessness and refugee situations would help to ensure that the right action is being prescribed at the right moment in order to have maximum effect for the prevention of statelessness. Guidelines could then be developed on how to deal with this specific issue on the basis of the outcome of the study. Although these tasks are inevitably complex and time-consuming, in view of its growing interest in migration-related issues generally, this is an opportune moment for raising the international community's consciousness of this important problem and starting to debate what should be done.

While the human rights norms that can play a part in the prevention of statelessness are undergoing further elaboration and concretisation, it is important not to forget the tailor-made instrument devised specifically with the aim of reducing future instances of statelessness. In view of what we have learned about the 1961 Convention on the Reduction of Statelessness over the course of the past few chapters, it may be worthwhile revisiting this text to consider how it could be updated or improved so as to not only boost its effectiveness, but also promote further accession to and implementation of the instrument. It was interesting to discover that despite developments in the field of human rights to a large extent reinforcing the norms of the 1961 Statelessness Convention, the number of state parties remains disappointingly low. This may be explained by the overall low-profile that the Convention enjoyed until the mid 1990s when UNHCR began to actively promote accession to the instrument[26] or the enduring reluctance of states to forfeit any of their (remaining) freedom in delineating nationality policy. Yet there may be another reason for its poor acceptance. If we look to the refugee regime,

> the refrain among states not party to the international refugee instruments [is] that the Refugee Convention and its Protocol is outdated, Eurocentric, and of limited relevance in dealing with refugee problems in less-developed countries [...] there is little value in becoming party to the international refugee instruments.[27]

[26] There has been a relative spate of accessions since then, with 17 states acceding to the convention since 1995, doubling the total number of state parties.

[27] Brian Gorlick, "(Mis)perception of Refugees, State Sovereignty, and the Continuing Challenge of International Protection" in Bayefsky (ed) *Human Rights and Refugees, Internally Displaced Persons and Migrant Workers*, Martinus Nijhoff, Leiden: 2006, page 69.

Perhaps states sustain similar objections to acceding to the 1961 Statelessness Convention. Thus by devising ways in which to make the instrument more attuned to the reality on the ground and more relevant in the fight against statelessness it may be possible to raise the profile of the Convention and make it more attractive to non-state parties to sign up. One way to achieve this would be to draft a protocol to the Convention that – taking into account developments in the human rights field – moderates the scope and application of a number of the Convention's existing provisions.[28] For example, it could extend the application of the procedural guarantees elaborated in the context of the withdrawal of nationality to all decisions on nationality attribution.[29] It could also introduce an overall prohibition of arbitrary deprivation of nationality or expand the scope of the current article 9 of the Convention on discriminatory deprivation of nationality. Furthermore, it could offer states the opportunity to move beyond the commitment to *reduce* future statelessness to a commitment to *eliminate* future statelessness (a step that was premature at the time that the Convention was drafted).[30] While a noble goal, it is however doubtful that this last measure would lead to a more widespread acceptance of the Convention.

Finally, and to make full use of the detailed discussion of each of the causes of – and techniques to prevent – statelessness that has been undertaken in this work, we must consider the possibility of elaborating a number of new norms that are specifically focussed on more effectively preventing statelessness. These could be taken up in the process of revisiting the 1961 Statelessness Convention and included in the suggested protocol, thereby contributing significantly to its currency and relevance. The most important source of inspiration for such standards is the progress that has been achieved in relation to the avoidance of statelessness in the context of state succession:

> If the Commission [ILC] has been able to develop techniques for identifying which of several states in a succession has the obligation to give effect to an individual's right to a nationality, then no logical reason exists as to why the same techniques cannot be extended to states generally [...] *Nationality in relation to state succession* is becoming legally indistinguishable from nationality issues generally [...] This distinction is becoming increasingly difficult to maintain as nationality issues come to be regulated by international human rights norms, which do not easily admit

[28] The International Law Commission could prepare the draft protocol using the understanding of the statelessness phenomenon gained from work on the Draft Articles on Nationality of Natural Persons in relation to the Succession of States and indeed the 1961 Convention on the Reduction of Statelessness itself.

[29] Article 8, paragraph 4 of the 1961 Convention on the Reduction of Statelessness.

[30] This can be accomplished by retracting the possibility to set conditions and exclusion clauses that allow some instances of statelessness at birth and from withdrawal of nationality later in life to slip through the net. These changes could either be introduced as binding or as facultative for those state parties that wish to move closer to the ideal of the eradication of statelessness and are seeking guidance in how best to do so.

distinction: stateless people are stateless regardless of the fact of a state succession.[31]

We must therefore ask: what exactly can we learn from the measures envisaged to prevent statelessness in relation to state succession? In short, an awful lot.

There are two particular innovations that could be adapted to tackle statelessness beyond the context of the succession of states.[32] Firstly, there is a greatly elaborated set of procedural guarantees that could easily be transposed to decisions on nationality attribution generally. These include the following considerations: the provision of sufficient information on nationality regulations, the timely processing of nationality applications, the detailing (in writing) of the decision on nationality attribution including its motivation, the insurance of an effective opportunity for review and the reasonableness of fees for nationality procedures. The second is the introduction of the right of option as a tool to prevent (ongoing) nationality disputes from leaving an individual in a protracted situation of statelessness or uncertainty. Where a person has a genuine link with more than one state and any one of them could feasibly be called upon to protect him from statelessness, he should be allowed (an effective opportunity) to opt for one or other of the nationalities "on offer". This way states cannot (continue to) defer the responsibility of allowing a person to obtain or retain citizenship where he would otherwise be stateless by pointing to another state with which the individual also has some connection.

4 Prospects for the Implementation and Enforcement of Norms for the Prevention of Statelessness

Whatever the strengths or weaknesses inherent in the current approach to the prevention of statelessness under international law, the success of the regime in actually securing the avoidance of statelessness will still be heavily dependent on the implementation and enforcement of those standards. This is a question that has largely been bypassed in the foregoing chapters, where the aim was to establish the potential of the existing substantive framework. Nevertheless, here and there problems were flagged in relation to the (lack of) clarity about how the various guarantees against statelessness should be implemented and the (in)adequacy of supervisory apparatus. Such concerns must be factored into the overall assessment of the effectiveness of the legal regime in preventing statelessness and will therefore be considered in more detail in the following paragraphs.

There are two main worries. The first relates to the problem of establishing when the relevant norms can be invoked. In order to determine whether the loss, deprivation or renunciation of nationality would result in statelessness – and should therefore be avoided in many cases – the authorities concerned need to ascertain whether the individual already possesses or is assured of acquiring an alternative nationality. Similarly, before a child can benefit from special measures to ensure

[31] Jeffrey Blackman, 'State Succession and Statelessness: The Emerging Right to an Effective Nationality under International Law', in *Michigan Journal of International law*, Vol. 19, 1998, pages 1175 and 1193.
[32] See chapter VI, section.3.

that he acquires a nationality at birth, the state must be satisfied that the child would "otherwise be stateless". These circumstances can only be established through the determination of such facts as the nationality (or statelessness) of the parents and the content, interpretation and application of all relevant citizenship regulations in the case at hand. And the list of examples goes on. In every case, the identification of the threat of statelessness is critical to the satisfactory implementation of fall-back clauses to avoid this plight.[33] Thus, in pursuit of the full and correct implementation of the various substantive standards, some agreement must be reached on the procedure and evidentiary requirements for the identification of instances where these special guarantees against statelessness should be applied. The difficulty is that, as we have seen, very little guidance has been issued on this question of identification for the purposes of the avoidance of statelessness, let alone any agreed, concrete procedures or principles for states to follow.

The 1961 Convention on the Reduction of Statelessness does not elaborate on how states are to establish whether its substantive provisions are applicable. Nor has any human rights instrument or body tackled the general question of how to actually implement the right to a nationality in practice - how to weigh the threat of statelessness. However, there is a growing awareness of the need to address this aspect of the problem. In the context of the developing international framework for the prevention of statelessness in relation to state succession we traced a few basic standards that may be relevant. There we saw international cooperation prescribed, including through exchanging information and conducting consultations, to establish the content, interpretation and effects of domestic nationality laws.[34] In fact, the European Convention on Nationality provides for similar measures in a pair of articles that we have yet to look at: article 23 on "Co-operation between the States Parties" and article 24 on "Exchange of information". State parties to the Convention are thereby required to share information on the parameters of their domestic citizenship laws, both through the apparatus of the Council of Europe and directly with one another upon request.[35] This cooperation should be geared towards dealing with "all relevant problems",[36] a broad reference which would certainly cover the aspiration of preventing statelessness.[37] The Council of Europe system for addressing nationality questions, does therefore provide at least one basic example of how the difficulty of identifying situations which call for the application of special measures for the prevention of statelessness could be appeased. Nevertheless, there is still no clear indication of how or when a state that is confronted with this question is to consider the presence or absence of an alternative nationality to be conclusively established. And although the newer

[33] Recall the "Baby Andrew" case, discussed in chapter III, section 3.

[34] See chapter VI, section 3.

[35] The Council of Europe has compiled a central record of information on municipal nationality acts at its European Documentation Centre on Nationality (EURODOC), and has published summaries of such laws through its *European Bulletin on Nationality* (last updated in 2004). Note that the Organisation for Security and Cooperation in Europe also collects domestic citizenship – and other – legislation, as does the Office of the United Nations High Commissioner for Human Rights. These can be accessed at www.legislationonline.org and www.refworld.org respectively.

[36] See article 23, paragraph 2 of the European Convention on Nationality.

[37] Recall that the avoidance of statelessness is also included as a general principle in the European Convention on Nationality, in its article 4.

Council of Europe Convention on the avoidance of statelessness in relation to State succession calls for the standard of proof to be *lowered* in order to facilitate the granting of citizenship with a view to preventing statelessness,[38] it does not explain what is generally considered to be an appropriate standard of proof or in what way this burden should be reduced.[39] Meanwhile, a call has gone out from civil society for the development of standards specifically relating to the right to a nationality on the African continent – perhaps in the form of a Protocol to the African Charter on Human and Peoples' Rights on Citizenship. Among other things, this Protocol should "place the burden of proof on the state in situations of disputed citizenship and establish the standard of proof".[40] But that is currently the full extent of the proposal and it has yet to be taken up by the African Union.

So identification remains a challenge for which, it seems, domestic authorities and courts must find their own approach in their attempts to ensure compliance with international standards for the avoidance of statelessness. The danger in this lack of universal agreement on questions relating to the burden of proof and procedures to be followed is that states may, more easily, allow themselves to be swayed by other considerations and not just the aspiration of preventing statelessness. On the other hand, the dilemma of identification goes beyond the circumstances of the *prevention* of statelessness in that it is also extremely relevant to the *protection* of stateless persons. The application of a special protection regime for stateless persons necessarily begins with the determination of whether a person is indeed stateless. Thus perhaps in that context there has been a greater effort to agree international rules on procedures and proof of statelessness.[41] Since the protection of stateless persons is the topic of part 3 of this book, we will soon discover whether this is indeed the case. If so, these standards could arguably be applied, by extension, to situations involving the prevention of statelessness. And if not, we will be forced to reconsider this point and undertake a renewed and broader search for plausible answers to this identification dilemma.

The second major concern to arise with respect to the effective implementation of norms for the prevention of statelessness, which in fact reinforces the first, is this: where the applicability or interpretation of the various guarantees against statelessness is indeed disputed, the types of enforcement procedures and mechanisms that would help to settle the matter and protect the interests of the individual may be lacking. It is true that international law demands some form of review to be made available at the domestic level to allow individuals to assert their rights.[42] However, when it comes to a subsequent international review – of particular utility in the context of preventing statelessness where more than one

[38] Article 8 of the Council of Europe Convention on the avoidance of statelessness in relation to State succession.

[39] See further chapter VI, section 3.

[40] Open Society Justice Initiative, *The Face of Statelessness: A Call for African Norms on the Right to Citizenship*, February 2007, page 10. See also www.citizenshiprightsinafrica.org.

[41] In chapter III, section 3 we saw how the 1961 Statelessness Convention is generally considered to have deferred the question of the *definition* of statelessness to the 1954 Statelessness Convention. It is feasible that this issue of *identification* of problems of statelessness has been similarly deferred.

[42] Obviously though, it is equally unclear on what basis the court or review board charged with re-examining the case is to decide on questions relating to the burden of proof and how the evidence submitted by either party – the individual or the state – is to be weighed

state may be, directly or indirectly, involved in the dispute – the opportunities are less evident. That little international case law was presented or discussed over the course of the preceding chapters is a reflection of the simple fact that there is a distinct shortage of such case law to draw from.

As mentioned in the introduction to the 1961 Convention on the Reduction of Statelessness, no dispute has ever been brought before the International Court of Justice on the interpretation or application of the instrument's provisions.[43] In addition, we saw that the idea of establishing a tribunal to decide upon individual claims brought on the basis of the document was thrown out during the document's drafting process.[44] So it falls to UNHCR, mandated with the task of helping individuals to claim their rights under the 1961 Statelessness Convention, to attempt to promote the – correct and full – implementation of its provisions[45]. But the

[43] A possibility provided for in article 14 of the 1961 Convention on the Reduction of Statelessness.

[44] Recall from chapter III, section 3, that the initial draft of the 1961 Convention by the ILC provided for "the establishment within the framework of the United Nations of an agency to act on behalf of stateless persons before governments and the establishment also within this framework of a tribunal competent to decide upon claims presented by the agency on behalf of individuals claiming to have been denied nationality in violation of the provisions of the Convention". Paul Weis, *Nationality and Statelessness in International Law*, Kluwer Academic Publishers Group, Dordrecht: 1979, page 255; Carol Batchelor, 'Stateless Persons: Some Gaps in International Protection', in *International Journal of Refugee Law,* Vol. 7, 1995, page 253; UNHCR and IPU, *Nationality and statelessness. A handbook for parliamentarians*, 2005, page 13. Again, the Council of Europe came perhaps closer to establishing a specialised, international body to settle nationality questions, this time on the basis of the European Convention on Nationality. The *Committee of Experts on Nationality* had a mandate to, among others, "encourage States, where necessary by providing them with appropriate assistance, to implement the principles and rules of the European Convention on Nationality in their internal legislation and practices and to implement other relevant international instruments in this field [and] follow up the steps taken by States to implement the European Convention on Nationality". See the *Specific Terms of Reference of the Committee of Experts on Nationality,* 2001, paragraph 4 (c). However, this group has not met since 2005. The last plenary meeting of the Committee of Experts on Nationality took place in October 2004. Since then, the European Committee on Legal Co-operation (CDCJ) approved an Action Plan making nationality one of its main priorities. See the *Action Plan of the CDCJ*, 17 October 2007. Thereafter, the Bureau of the CDCJ approved new draft terms of reference for a Group of Specialists on Nationality which were adopted by the Committee of Ministers. The Group of Specialists held its first meeting in April 2008, concentrating in particular on the further analysis of issues affecting the nationality of children – including the problem of stateless children. Despite these initiatives, it is certainly regrettable that the European Court of Human Rights, or a special chamber thereof, has not been tasked with the supervision of the already existing European Convention on Nationality. The availability of such an advanced international remedy to promote compliance with the instrument would have been highly beneficial. The Council of Europe Convention on the avoidance of statelessness in relation to State Succession has similarly separated itself from the supervisory machinery of the European Court of Human Rights and instead determines that "any dispute concerning the interpretation or application of this Convention shall primarily be settled through negotiation" (article 17).

[45] Recall that when the 1961 Convention on the Reduction of Statelessness entered into force in 1975, the UN General Assembly requested UNHCR to fulfil this task (UN Docs. A/Res/3274 (XXIX) 1974; A/Res/31/36 1976; A/Res/49/169 1995; A/Res/50/152 1996; and A/Res/61/137 2007). See also chapter III, section 3.

agency has no power to preside over cases regarding the application of the Convention in the sense of a judicial organ.[46] Moreover, it has been suggested that

> while UNHCR does have the responsibility of assisting States and individuals and has been requested by the General Assembly to assist States in avoiding statelessness, neither UNHCR, other international or regional organisations, nor third States can pronounce authoritatively on nationality in one or other State. The State concerned must indicate whether the individuals in question do or do not have its nationality, for it is that State which has both the privilege and the obligation to determine who are its citizens, according to international law. While organisations and other States may promote the recognition of a genuine and effective link and encourage recognition of these links wherever they exist, only the State concerned can indicate whether it acknowledges these links.[47]

This perspective on the matter of nationality attribution questions the very suitability of the issue for international adjudication. However, while there is a core truth to this statement in the sense that only a state can formally acknowledge the bond of nationality with an individual, there is nothing to suggest that the state cannot be found in violation of its international commitments with regard to the prevention of statelessness in the same way as it can be found to violate other international (human rights) norms which it has a responsibility to uphold.

Indeed there are some examples from the overall human rights field in which courts and various quasi-judicial institutions, such as the UN treaty bodies, have been able to provide an authoritative opinion on the interpretation and application of the international legal standards relating to the avoidance of statelessness. The Inter-American Court on Human Rights is an excellent case in point and two of its decisions have been discussed in the preceding chapters.[48] In 1984, the Inter-American Court issued an Advisory Opinion on "the proposed amendments to the naturalisation provisions of the Constitution of Costa Rica", where it had the opportunity to consider the issue of the prevention of statelessness. In the end, the decision of the Court was disappointing for it found that although

> one consequence of the amendment as drafted is that foreigners who lose their nationality upon marriage to a Costa Rican would have to remain stateless for at least two years because they cannot comply with one of the obligatory

[46] Instead, what UNHCR *can* do is work with governments, through advocacy efforts and the offering of technical and advisory services, to try to ensure that the various guarantees are reflected in the relevant domestic legislation and that these protections are implemented properly. And in fact the agency has a growing track record of successes based on exactly this approach For instance, "between 2003 and 2005, UNHCR worked with more than 40 States to help enact new nationality laws and to revise older legislation". UNHCR and IPU, *Nationality and statelessness. A handbook for parliamentarians*, 2005, page 44. Examples of these and other activities can also be found in UNHCR, *UNHCR's activities in the field of statelessness: Progress report,* EC/55/SC/CRP.13/Rev.1, 30 June 2005.

[47] Carol Batchelor, 'Statelessness and the Problem of Resolving Nationality Status', in *International Journal of Refugee Law,* Vol. 10, 1998, 1998.

[48] See chapter IV, section 3.2; chapter V, section 1.2; and chapter VII, section 1.2.

> requirements for naturalisation unless they have been married for that period of time [*and*] it should also be noted that it is by no means certain that statelessness would be limited to a period of two years only [...the amendment] would not as such create statelessness. This status would in fact be brought about by the laws of the country whose nationals, upon marrying a Costa Rican, lose their nationality. It follows that this amendment cannot therefore be deemed to be directly violative of Article 20 of the Convention.[49]

Nevertheless, this case illustrated that the Court was competent to consider and pronounce upon the legitimacy of a law that may inadvertently heighten the risk of statelessness. In the later, contentious case of *Yean and Bosico v. Dominican Republic* the same court did find fault with a state's interpretation and application of its citizenship laws where statelessness was the result.[50] The Court then ordered the authorities, among other things, to

> adopt within its domestic law [...] the legislative, administrative and any other measures needed to regulate the procedure and requirements for acquiring Dominican nationality based on late declaration of birth. This procedure should be simple, accessible and reasonable since, to the contrary, applicants could remain stateless. Also, an effective remedy should exist for cases in which the request is rejected.[51]

Moreover, under the rules regarding the compliance with decisions of the Inter-American Court in such contentious cases, the Dominican Republic is actually *required* to "guarantee implementation of the Court's ruling at the domestic level".[52] It is therefore far from inconceivable that international courts could have a very real impact on the prevention of statelessness in both general terms, through the consideration of domestic laws, and in individual cases by prescribing concrete remedies.[53]

---

[49] Inter-American Court on Human Rights, *Advisory Opinion on the Proposed Amendments to the Naturalisation Provision of the Constitution of Costa Rica,* OC-4/84, 19 January 1984, paragraphs 46-48.

[50] Recall that the court found "that for discriminatory reasons, and contrary to the pertinent domestic norms, the State failed to grant nationality to the children, which constituted an arbitrary deprivation of their nationality, and left them stateless for more than four years and four months, in violation of Articles 20 and 24 of the American Convention". Inter-American Court on Human Rights, *Case of Yean and Bosico v. Dominican Republic,* Series C, Case 130, 8 September 2005, paragraph 174.

[51] Inter-American Court on Human Rights, *Case of Yean and Bosico v. Dominican Republic,* Series C, Case 130, 8 September 2005, operative paragraph 7.

[52] Article 68, paragraph 1 of the Inter-American Convention on Human Rights. The court will continue to monitor whether the ruling it has given has been fully and correctly implemented. And in the case of this decision, the Dominican Republic has yet to satisfy the court that all of the prescribed measures have been carried out. See Inter-American Court on Human Rights, *Case of the Girls Yean and Bosico v. Dominican Republic – Monitoring Compliance with the Judgement,* Order of 28 November 2007.

[53] Human rights bodies on the African and European continents have also considered questions related to the prevention of statelessness. Recall, for instance, the *Decision as to the admissibility of Karassev v. Finland* before the European Court of Human Rights, cited in chapter V at note 60. Another case of interest is now pending before the European Court of Human Rights: the *Makuc and others v. Slovenia,* Application No. 26808/06. The African Commission on Human and Peoples' Rights ruled on a case in

So the human rights framework currently provides the best opportunity for supervising the implementation of relevant standards for the prevention of statelessness. The success or failure of such enforcement methods for actually shaping state's behaviour in this regard is then largely a factor of the strengths and weaknesses of these mechanisms generally.[54] However, there is also evidence that the various human rights bodies are rather cautious in finding against the state where domestic nationality policy is the subject of the dispute – perhaps exactly because human rights standards do not always offer unequivocal or precisely detailed norms for the allocation of responsibility in individual disputes relating to the realisation of the right to a nationality. This prudence is unmistakable in the Advisory Opinion of the Inter-American Court cited above on the naturalisation policy of Costa Rica where the court did not, or could not, find fault with a proposed amendment even after it conceded that it would contribute to the creation of (enduring) statelessness.[55] Various other cases have shown a similarly wide margin of appreciation being granted to states as far as nationality policy is concerned, even where statelessness threatens. For example in the *Case of Borzov v. Estonia,* the Human Rights Committee readily accepted that the refusal to grant the stateless applicant naturalisation for reasons of national security did not violate the terms of the ICCPR, largely on the basis of the finding that the applicant was at least offered a "genuine substantive review" of his case by the Estonian courts.[56]

There is one case in which the dilemma of enforcement *and* the aforementioned difficulties inherent in the lack of clear guidelines for establishing nationality or identifying the risk of statelessness come together: the noteworthy decision on admissibility in *Karassev v. Finland* before the European Court on Human Rights.[57] The dispute surrounded the applicability of Finland's domestic legal guarantees against statelessness at birth and therefore hinged on the finding that the child concerned "would otherwise be stateless", qualifying for citizenship *jus soli.* The Finnish authorities refused to apply this provision to the case at hand because they deemed the applicant to have received the nationality of the Russian Federation at birth. The European Court weighed the evidence before it on the plausibility of this assertion that the applicant had gained Russian citizenship - not with a view to determining whether the applicant had indeed obtained Russian nationality, but simply in order to ascertain whether the Finnish authorities' interpretation of the situation had been arbitrary. So, despite a declaration "signed by an attaché of the Embassy [stating] the applicant had never been a citizen of the Russian Federation" and only "ambiguous" evidence to the contrary, the Court

1997 that concerned access to citizenship, (*Case of John K. Modise v. Botswana,* Comm. No. 97/93) and there are currently two other relevant cases pending: *People v. Côte d'Ivoire* and *Yusuf Ali and others v. Kenya.* In addition, consider the plethora of comments and concluding observations of the UN treaty bodies relevant to the prevention of statelessness discussed throughout chapters IV to VII, as well as a number of individual decisions, including *Capena v. Canada* and *Stewart v. Canada,* decided by the Human Rights Committee.

[54] A question that falls beyond the scope of this study.

[55] See above at note 34.

[56] Human Rights Committee, *Case of Borzov v. Estonia,* CCPR/C/81/D/1136/2002, Geneva: 25 August 2004, paragraphs 7.1 - 7.4.

[57] European Court of Human Rights, *Decision as to the admissibility of Karassev v. Finland,* Application No. 31414/96, 12 January 1999.

found "that the decision of the Finnish authorities not to recognise the applicant as a citizen of Finland was not arbitrary in a way which could raise issues under Article 8 of the Convention".[58] The nationality status of the applicant thus remained unresolved. This case clearly demonstrates both the dangers of the wide margin of appreciation that is still often granted to states in nationality matters by international bodies and the ramifications of the absence of agreed procedures or rules of proof for the determination of nationality and identification of the risk of statelessness. With this in mind, the absence of a supervisory mechanism for the 1961 Convention on the Reduction of Statelessness is unquestionably regrettable, since this instrument does at least establish clear lines of responsibility where statelessness threatens and its provisions thereby lend themselves well for close supervision, leaving less discretion to states. Therefore if the international community takes up the challenge of improving and extending the normative framework for the prevention of statelessness, the issue of enforcement should be revisited and the idea of the establishment of a tribunal reconsidered. In the meantime, the relevant human rights bodies should continue to advise and adjudicate in matters relating the attribution of nationality and should be guided at all times by the ideal of the avoidance of statelessness.

5 Conclusion

In bringing the discussion of the prevention of statelessness to a close, it is important to pause briefly to consider the following warning:

> Nationality issues are intimately bound up with the very notion of identity and the nation. This century has taught us only too well that we should not treat such matters lightly. In every war and conflict that comes to mind, issues relating to nationality have played a critical role.[59]

The fight against statelessness is no trifling matter and there is no quick-fix solution. Yet there is an ever-growing realisation of the need tackle this challenge. And the international community is arguably better placed than ever before to do so because states have unmistakably allowed the interests of the individual to encroach, little by little, upon their freedom to attribute nationality however they deem fit.

In fact, the 1961 Convention on the Reduction of Statelessness is now just one of the many tools at the international community's disposal in its goal of preventing statelessness. In many respects, the arduous drafting process and the age of this instrument are reflected in its effectiveness with the result that, in some cases, the Convention fails to offer unconditional protection against statelessness and, in others, it prescribes no remedy whatsoever. Even where the Convention does offer solutions, we have seen that international human rights law has progressed to such an extent that in some areas it supersedes the Convention's

[58] European Court of Human Rights, *Decision as to the admissibility of Karassev v. Finland*, Application No. 31414/96, 12 January 1999.

[59] Guy de Vel, *Closing speech to the 1st European Conference on Nationality*, Director General for Legal Affairs of the Council of Europe, Strasbourg: 1999.

norms. Should institutions such as UNHCR and international non-governmental organisations be investing their energy in advocating for accession to this instrument and would this energy not be better spent elsewhere? It is certainly true that there are perhaps more pressing or more effective routes to pursue in an effort to stave off statelessness today – such as promoting universal birth registration and further developing the substantive and procedural protection offered by the prohibition of arbitrary deprivation of nationality. Yet despite it not being the ultimate solution to statelessness in all of its manifestations, the 1961 Statelessness Convention remains a useful tool in dealing with the – still widespread – problem of statelessness arising from technical causes and, as a specialised instrument dealing only with the prevention of statelessness, it focuses the attention of states on this (too often neglected) issue. Perhaps by revisiting the Convention and considering the options for the elaboration of a protocol to update and improve upon the text, a remedy will be found to the enduring low profile of this instrument.

Meanwhile, the sheer scale of the statelessness phenomenon and the severity of the situation of the stateless must spur the international community in utilising and developing alternative sources of standards for prevention. As the development of norms in relation to statelessness in the context of state succession has illustrated "the question is one of political will, not of undue legal or factual complexity".[60] Arguably even more critical than addressing the gaps in the *substantive* legal protection offered against statelessness, a major and urgent task is to tackle the concerns raised in the context of ensuring the full and effective implementation and enforcement of existing norms. Now, however, we must deal with the pressing conundrum that follows from the observation that cases of statelessness look set to continue to arise in years to come: the protection of the rights of the stateless. The following chapters will consider this question as we look more closely at the position of this vulnerable group under international law.

[60] Jeffrey Blackman, 'State Succession and Statelessness: The Emerging Right to an Effective Nationality under International Law', in *Michigan Journal of International law*, Vol. 19, 1998, page 1176.

PART 3

PROTECTING STATELESS PERSONS

CHAPTER IX

BACKGROUND TO PROTECTING STATELESS PERSONS

The time has come to consider the question of how much nationality *matters*. So far, we have discovered the many ways in which a person can end up without a nationality and we have developed a general notion that this is an undesirable state. But what exactly is the substance of nationality and what role does it play in an individual's enjoyment of fundamental rights? In other words: are stateless persons missing out because of their lack of a nationality and if so, to what degree? The answers to these questions reveal the extent to which additional measures are required to remedy the vulnerable situation of the stateless. This is the focus of the following chapters, where the international community's response to the enduring existence of statelessness is placed under the microscope and assessed as to its effectiveness. Mirroring the approach taken in Part II, the content of the tailor-made statelessness instruments is set off against the content of international human rights norms. Here however, attention is turned away from the 1961 Convention on the Reduction of Statelessness to look more closely at the 1954 Convention relating to the Status of Stateless Persons.[1] This introductory chapter begins by considering the meaning of citizenship, including that generally ascribed to it under contemporary international law, before introducing the 1954 Statelessness Convention – the instrument that has been specifically designed to protect the rights of those who have no nationality.

1 THE SUBSTANCE OF NATIONALITY: RIGHTS AND DUTIES

We have already seen that nationality is a legal bond that marks the membership of a state and is attributed to those who, for one reason or another, are considered to 'belong'. But what does the possession of a nationality actually mean for the individual? This is a question that we have not yet covered and it is appropriate to do so now. An oft-repeated portrayal of the substance of nationality is that which is attributed to US Supreme Court Chief Justice Earl Warren in the decision on the 1958 case of *Trop v. Dulles*: nationality is "the right to have rights".[2] Nationality

[1] The full text of the 1954 Convention relating to the Status of Stateless Persons can be found in Annex 2.

[2] US Supreme Court, *Trop v. Dulles, Secretary of State et. al.*, 356 US 86, 1958.

therefore provides not only a sense of membership - of belonging and of identity[3] - but it also paves the way for the enjoyment of various rights.[4] In the course of ruling on the case in question, the US Supreme Court went on to describe the impact of the revocation of citizenship and the condition of statelessness as:

> The total destruction of an individual's status in organised society [that] strips the citizen of his status in the national and international political community. His very existence is at the sufferance of the country in which he happens to find himself.[5]

While this is a very dramatic account of the importance of nationality, its sentiment has rung true and been echoed on many other occasions.[6] Historically, states have bestowed certain rights upon their people – often indeed limiting this protection to members only, excluding outsiders.[7] As far back as ancient Greece, communities reserved certain privileges for their citizens.[8] Thus, "to be deprived of citizenship of a state, when the state is the key distributor of social resources, is to be deprived of the basis of other rights".[9]

The question then arises: what rights accompany nationality? The answer is in principle to be found in the laws of each state. Just as we discovered that it has traditionally been domestic law that determines what constitutes a *genuine link* for the attribution of nationality, it is also domestic law that gives content to that status. It is the state, as a political community, that decides on the substance of nationality.[10] A citizen thus holds "all the rights [...] agreed upon in that particular state".[11] The basic contours are frequently outlined in a state's constitution and tend to include both civil freedoms and positive entitlements. For example, over a dozen

---

[3] UNHCR, "Statelessness and Citizenship" in *The State of the World's Refugees - A Humanitarian Agenda*, Oxford University Press, Oxford: 1997, page 225.

[4] For the full picture, nationality is in fact better described as resulting in "reciprocal rights and duties" on the part of the individual and the state concerned. International Court of Justice, *"Nottebohm Case" (Liechtenstein v. Guatamala)*, 1953; see also Donald Galloway, "Citizenship: A Jurisprudential Paradox" in Torre (ed) *European Citizenship - An Institutional Challenge*, Kluwer Law International, The Hague: 1998, page 80; Ruth Donner, "Chapter 1: Nationality Law in the Context of Public International Law" in *The Regulation of Nationality in International Law*, Transnational Publishers, New York: 1994, page 27; Yaffa Zilberschats, "Chapter 2 - Citizenship and International Law" in *The Human Right to Citizenship*, Transnational Publishers, Ardsley, NY: 2002, pages 34-36. This work is only concerned with the rights accorded or accessed on the basis of nationality and the corresponding duties of the state in that respect.

[5] US Supreme Court, *Trop v. Dulles, Secretary of State et. al.*, 356 US 86, 1958.

[6] Nationality is commonly described as a "necessary precursor to the exercise of other rights". See, for example, Carol Batchelor, 'Statelessness and the Problem of Resolving Nationality Status', in *International Journal of Refugee Law*, Vol. 10, 1998, page 159.

[7] Haro van Panhuys, "Section X.II: The Waning Significance of Nationality in Rules Concerning the Protection of Human Rights" in *The Role of Nationality in International Law*, A.W. Sijthoff's Uitgeversmaatschappij, Leiden: 1959, page 220.

[8] Mija Zagar, "Citizenship - Nationality: A Proper Balance Between the Interests of States and those of Individuals" in *Council of Europe's First European Conference on Nationality*, Strasbourg: 1999, page 94.

[9] Keith Faulks, *Citizenship*, Routledge, London: 2003, chapter 1, page 8.

[10] Keith Faulks, *Citizenship*, Routledge, London: 2003, chapter 3, page 81.

[11] Peter van Krieken, 'Disintegration and statelessness', in *Netherlands Quarterly of Human Rights,* Vol. 12, 1994, page 25.

provisions of the constitution of the People's Republic of China are devoted to the elaboration of the rights of its citizens including the right to freedom of religious belief and the right to "material assistance from the state and society when they are old, ill or disabled".[12] Further details as to the exact entitlements of nationals will subsequently be delineated in other municipal laws and policies. As a result, the content of nationality varies from one state to another and it also evolves over time.[13]

Nevertheless, there are two fundamental rights that ordinarily belong to the core substance of nationality. The first is the right to reside on the territory of the state. As a legally-affirmed member of the community, a national must be able to live within its borders. A citizen therefore has the automatic and absolute right to (re-)enter the state and to remain on its soil, offering the individual both stability and certainty.[14] The second is a right that accompanied the introduction of democracy. It is the right to join in with decision-making, to participate in the affairs of the state: "citizenship became the legal title for exercising political rights".[15] The opportunity to participate is provided through the right to vote, to be elected and to work in public service. Nationality thus came to mean empowerment.[16] As mentioned, beyond these two rights that are intrinsic to the function of nationality in this world of nation-states, many further rights and entitlements of citizens are laid out in states' municipal laws.

An additional, important component of the substance of nationality is diplomatic protection. Based on the notion that "whoever ill-treats a citizen indirectly injures the state",[17] states have the right to protect their citizens in the

[12] Articles 36 and 45 of the Constitution of the People's Republic of China, China Law no. 141, 1993. It should be noted that in response to developments in international human rights law – as will be discussed later - constitutional provisions are increasingly attributing fundamental rights to "everyone" and reserving just a select few to "citizens". China is one state that is lagging behind somewhat in these developments. See also David Weissbrodt, *Final Report on Prevention of Discrimination - The Rights of Non-Citizens,* E/CN.4/Sub.2/2003/23, 26 May 2003, paragraph 24.

[13] Haro van Panhuys, "Chapter VIII: The Traditional Function of Nationality in International Law (A Digest)" in *The Role of Nationality in International Law*, A.W. Sijthoff's Uitgeversmaatschappij, Leiden: 1959, page 181.

[14] This right of the national corresponds to a duty on the part of the state to (re-)admit its citizens. If a state fails or refuses to readmit its own citizens, this may result in the breach of another state's sovereignty as it is forced to continue to host foreign nationals. Paul Weis, *Nationality and Statelessness in International Law*, Kluwer Academic Publishers Group, Dordrecht: 1979, page 45.

[15] Mija Zagar, "Citizenship - Nationality: A Proper Balance Between the Interests of States and those of Individuals" in *Council of Europe's First European Conference on Nationality*, Strasbourg: 1999, page 98. The extent to which political rights could actually be exercised by the nationals of a state is something that has also varied over time and from country to country – consider the initial exclusion of women from suffrage. Nevertheless, the legal bond of nationality has been considered a necessary prerequisite for political participation.

[16] Advisory Board on Human Security (prepared by Constantin Sokoloff), *Denial of Citizenship: A Challenge to Human Security,* February 2005, page 6.

[17] Statement by Vattel, considered the father of the doctrine of state responsibility that is the foundation for the exercise of diplomatic protection. As cited in Carmen Tiburcio, "Chapter III. Development of the Treatment of Aliens from Diplomatic Protection to Human Rights" in *The human rights of aliens under international and comparative law*, Kluwer Law International, The Hague: 2001, page 35.

face of injuries committed by another state.[18] The state whose national has been wronged can exact some form of redress. Although the individual cannot demand such diplomatic protection, which is a right of the state and can thus be exercised at its discretion,[19] nationality thereby provides the gateway to another important measure for the protection of the individual.

2 INTERNATIONAL HUMAN RIGHTS LAW, THE SUBSTANCE OF NATIONALITY AND THE POSITION OF NON-NATIONALS

Whereas the extent to which a national enjoys any rights or entitlements was once purely a matter of municipal law, it has now also become the subject of international law. The major issue to surface in the wake of the devastation of World War II was one of protection - protection of individuals against the arbitrary whims of their own government. The protection afforded by national legislation and constitutions had proven to be inadequate since this law was susceptible to abuse by totalitarian regimes and could be employed as a weapon of persecution just as easily as being an instrument of protection. A new approach was deemed necessary, not only in the interest of the individuals involved, but also with the broader ideal of maintaining international peace and stability in mind. It was generally agreed that states which did not respect the fundamental rights of their own nationals would be much less likely to respect the rights of other peoples and territories, thus posing a greater threat to international security. [20] The international community put its faith in multilateral legal instruments and so the human rights regime was born: endowing individuals with certain basic rights directly on the basis of international law. Every state was obliged to recognise these rights with regards to their own nationals.[21] International law thereby began to replace (or at least set the broad parameters for) municipal law in delineating the substance of citizenship.

The rights in question were termed "human rights" – a label conveying the sentiment that they are owed to all people, everywhere, on the basis of their "humanity" rather than being conditional upon the possession of a particular legal status such as citizenship.[22] This was evident in the drafting of the Universal

[18] "The state exercises sovereignty over its territory and over its citizens *wherever they are located.* Thus if, State A harms the citizens of State B, State A infringes the sovereignty of State B and is consequently responsible to State B". Emphasis added, Yaffa Zilberschats, "Chapter 2 - Citizenship and International Law" in *The Human Right to Citizenship*, Transnational Publishers, Ardsley, NY: 2002, page 36; See also Guy Goodwin Gill, "The rights of refugees and stateless persons" in Saksena (ed) *Human rights perspectives & challenges (in 1900's and beyond)*, Lancers Books, New Delhi: 1994, page 392. Ruth Donner, "Chapter 1: Nationality Law in the Context of Public International Law" in *The Regulation of Nationality in International Law*, Transnational Publishers, New York: 1994, page 19.

[19] Paul Weis, *Nationality and Statelessness in International Law*, Kluwer Academic Publishers Group, Dordrecht: 1979, page 33.

[20] Ruth Donner, "Chapter 4: Human Rights Conventions and other Instruments" in *The Regulation of Nationality in International Law*, Transnational Publishers, New York: 1994 *page 186*

[21] Whereas previously, a minimum standard of treatment had existed only in relation to the treatment of foreign nationals by the host state, protected through the doctrines of state responsibility and diplomatic protection; Diana Elles, *International Provisions Protecting the Human Rights of Non-Citizens: Study*, New York: 1980.

[22] This is the basis of the claim that has been repeated time and time again, that human rights are *universal.* See for instance the 2005 World Summit Outcome document, where in paragraph 13 the

Declaration of Human Rights, the inspiration behind all other human rights instruments to date:

> When the subject first came up for discussion in the United Nations, the representative from Panama remarked that 'the rights of the individual do not spring from the fact that he is a citizen of a given state, but from the fact that he is a member of the human family'. That idea became the starting point for any consideration of Human Rights.[23]

So at a time when international law was beginning to delineate what rights citizens should enjoy, there was a simultaneous "denationalisation" of protection which deeply affected the very significance of nationality.[24] Rather than citizenship being the right to have rights, "the principles of human rights would maintain that being human is the right to have human rights".[25] A great illustration of this development is provided by the UN Human Rights Committee's General Comment on the position of non-nationals under the International Covenant on Civil and Political Rights. The Committee held that "the rights set forth in the Covenant apply to everyone, irrespective of reciprocity, and irrespective of his or her nationality or statelessness".[26] Indeed such observations have led many to point out that modern human rights norms now call into question the very relevance of nationality for the enjoyment of rights as *citizens* rights made way for *human* rights.[27] This vision is a utopia for the stateless who have no nationality to rely on.

---

world's states declared: "We reaffirm the universality, indivisibility, interdependence and interrelatedness of all human rights"; 2005 World Summit Outcome, United Nations document, A/60/L.1, 20th September 2005.

[23] UN, *Our rights as human beings: A discussion guide on the Universal Declaration of Human Rights,* New York: 1949, page 13. The preamble of the Universal Declaration of Human Rights reminds us that it deals with the "recognition of the inherent dignity and of the equal and inalienable rights of all members of the human family".

[24] Separate Opinion of Judge A.A. Cancado Trindade, Inter-American Court on Human Rights, *Case of Yean and Bosico v. Dominican Republic,* Series C, Case 130, 8 September 2005, paras. 7 and 11.

[25] David Weissbrodt; Clay Collins, 'The Human Rights of Stateless Persons', in *Human Rights Quarterly,* Vol. 28, 2006, page 248. See the example in Donner, *The regulation of nationality in international law,* on the right to petition: "it is granted to physical persons qua human beings, no bond of nationality or other form of allegiance is taken into account"; Ruth Donner, "Chapter 1: Nationality Law in the Context of Public International Law" in *The Regulation of Nationality in International Law,* Transnational Publishers, New York: 1994, page 14; see further David Weissbrodt, *Final Report on Prevention of Discrimination - The Rights of Non-Citizens,* E/CN.4/Sub.2/2003/23, 26 May 2003, page 5.

[26] Human Rights Committee, *CCPR General Comment No. 15: The Position of Aliens under the Covenant,* Geneva: 11 April 1986. See also Human Rights Committee, *General Comment 31: Nature of the General Legal Obligation imposed on States Parties to the Covenant,* CCPR/C/21/Rev.1/Add.13, Geneva: 26 May 2004, para. 10.

[27] See among others David Weissbrodt; Clay Collins, 'The Human Rights of Stateless Persons', in *Human Rights Quarterly,* Vol. 28, 2006; Keith Faulks, *Citizenship,* Routledge, London: 2003; Vincenzo Ferrari, "Citizenship: Problems, Concepts and Policies" in Torre (ed) *European Citizenship - An Institutional Challenge,* Kluwer Law International, The Hague: 1998; Richard Lillich, *The human rights of aliens in contemporary international law,* Manchester University Press, Manchester: 1984; Bard-Anders Andreassen, "Human Rights for Non-Citizens. Migrant Workers and the Trespassing of National Borders", *Joint sessions of workshops for the European Consortium for Political Research,*

If this were the case across the board – if human rights law did indeed guarantee and ensure the enjoyment of the full spectrum of rights for all people – the protection of the rights of the stateless would need no special provision. There would be no such thing as a gap in international protection in this regard, since each denial of rights would amount to an infringement of human rights obligations, whether committed against a national or a non-national. However, this conclusion is premature. Although the aim of the human rights regime was to circumvent the question of nationality to the extent that basic rights were granted to all individuals via international law, it did not intend to eliminate the need for a nationality entirely.[28] In particular, considerations of sovereignty and the need to respect the integrity of states ensured that nationality retained its place and importance. After all, it cannot be ignored that the world is organised into individual, sovereign states which each comprise a territory and a body of nationals for whom they are responsible.[29] So, while the Universal Declaration of Human Rights and the human rights instruments adopted in its wake grant each and every right that they contain to all persons everywhere, certain rights can only be exercised in relation to the country of citizenship.[30] For example, human rights law includes political rights such as the right to vote but these rights are guaranteed only with respect to the state of nationality.[31]

Therefore, while human rights instruments have at least "confined the rights afforded solely to citizens within a very short list",[32] in reality there are numerous ways in which the enjoyment of human rights by non-nationals may

Salzburg: 1984; Guy Goodwin-Gill, "The Rights of Refugees and Stateless Persons" in Saksena (ed) *Human Rights Perspectives & Challenges (in 1900's and beyond)*, Lancers Books, New Delhi: 1994.

[28] Ruth Donner, "Chapter 4: Human Rights Conventions and other Instruments" in *The Regulation of Nationality in International Law*, Transnational Publishers, New York: 1994, page 183-186.

[29] While the "draft [Universal] Declaration considers man as an isolated individual [...] this Declaration does not meet reality because man cannot be considered as an isolated entity. He is a member of certain communities and the concept of the individual man is contrary to social reality". Statement made by Yugoslavia at the plenary session of the General Assembly during the final debate on the Universal Declaration of Human Rights. In UN, *Our rights as human beings: A discussion guide on the Universal Declaration of Human Rights,* New York: 1949, page 28. For further treatment of the "struggle between the universal and the particular, between the principles of human rights and the sovereignty of a concrete people", see Seyla Benhabib, *Transformations of Citizenship - Dilemmas of the Nation State in the Era of Globalisation*, Koniklijke van Gorcum, Assen: 2001; See also Keith Faulks, *Citizenship*, Routledge, London: 2003.

[30] Indeed we also see a number of provisions and instruments geared especially to the rights of (certain groups of) non-nationals, including the UN Declaration on the Human Rights of Individuals Who are not Nationals of the Country in which They Live and the Convention on the Protection of the Rights of all Migrant Workers and Members of Their Families. These norms exemplify the notion that human rights are not just rights between states and their own nationals.

[31] See article 21 of the Universal Declaration of Human Rights and article 25 of the International Covenant on Civil and Political Rights. There are other examples of human rights norms that explicitly permit distinctions between nationals and non-nationals, such where the International Covenant on Economic, Social and Cultural Rights allows developing countries to "determine to what extent they would guarantee the economic rights recognised in the present Covenant to non-nationals" taking into account the country's economic situation. This provision is found in Article 2, paragraph 3 of the International Covenant on Economic, Social and Cultural Rights.

[32] Yaffa Zilberschats, "Chapter 2 - Citizenship and International Law" in *The Human Right to Citizenship*, Transnational Publishers, Ardsley, NY: 2002, page 34.

differ from that of nationals, both through divergence in the applicability of legal norms and through state practice. As long as every individual holds a nationality, the universality of these documents remains intact: everyone can enjoy these rights in relation to at least one country, so no one is excluded. This was a strong argument for including a right to a nationality among the human rights norms espoused in the Universal Declaration and other instruments.[33] Indeed human rights bodies still admit that:

> [Nationality] is one of the most important rights of man, after the right to life itself, because all other prerogative guarantees and benefits man derives from his membership in a political and social community – the states – stem from or are supported by this right.[34]

If the right to a nationality were fully realised, then no one would be without this legal bond and denied the enjoyment of the related rights. However, as we have seen, the full realisation of the right to a nationality for all is still a long way off. In practice then, the existence of statelessness interferes with the universal ambition of the human rights regime. In the absence of any special provision for their situation, such persons who lack the formal bond of nationality with any state are excluded outright from the enjoyment of certain human rights.[35]

Moreover, the *equal* enjoyment of rights by nationals and non-nationals is not an absolute norm as David Weissbrodt, UN Special Rapporteur on the rights of non-citizens, explains:

> The architecture of international human rights law is built on the premise that all persons, by virtue of their essential humanity, should enjoy all human rights *unless* exceptional distinctions, for example, between citizens and non-citizens, serve a legitimate State objective and are proportional to the achievement of that objective.[36]

Thus, although the general principles of "non-discrimination, together with equality before the law and equal protection of the law without any discrimination" are absolutely central to the human rights system as a whole,[37] distinctions between

---

[33] Paragraph 1 of Article 15 of the Universal Declaration of Human Rights reads: "Everyone has the right to a nationality".

[34] Inter-American Commission for Human Rights, *Third report on the situation of human rights in Chile,* OEA/Ser.L/V/II.40, doc. 10, 1977, as cited in Open Society Justice Initiative, *Written Comments on the Case of Dilcea Yean and Violeta Bosico v. Dominican Republic,* New York: April 2005, page 20.

[35] It should be noted that the position of migrants may also cause some concern from the point of view of human rights protection as they may not practicably be in a position to exercise all of their rights. However, their position can be resolved by their return to their state of nationality - admittedly an unfeasible option in the case of forced migrants and refugees - whereas that of the stateless requires the (re)instatement of citizenship.

[36] Emphasis added. David Weissbrodt, *Final Report on Prevention of Discrimination - The Rights of Non-Citizens,* E/CN.4/Sub.2/2003/23, 26 May 2003, para. 6.

[37] UN Human Rights Committee, *General Comment 18: Non-discrimination,* Geneva: 10 November 1989, paragraph 1.

nationals and non-nationals are not necessarily outlawed under these standards. Indeed, it has been said that one of "today's issues [is] the validity of the concept of alienage as a basis for discrimination in the protection of human rights".[38] And it is a pondering that cannot be immediately satisfied. On the one hand, for instance, the Convention on the Elimination of Racial Discrimination does not cover "distinctions, exclusions, restrictions or preferences made by a State Party to this Convention between citizens and non-citizens".[39] On the other hand, the Committee charged with overseeing the Convention declared that "human rights are, in principle, to be enjoyed by all persons [and] States parties are under an obligation to guarantee equality between citizens and non-citizens in the enjoyment of these rights to the extent recognised under international law".[40] The same Committee subsequently added that

> under the Convention, differential treatment based on citizenship or immigration status will constitute discrimination if the criteria for such differentiation, judged in the light of the objectives and purposes of the Convention, are not applied pursuant to a legitimate aim, and are not proportional to the achievement of this aim.[41]

Whether a distinction based on citizenship would pass muster or not therefore depends on the specific circumstances at hand – which instrument, which right, which facts - and is not by definition prohibited. As such, the position of the stateless may still be precarious. As we look more closely at different (categories of) rights over the course of the upcoming chapters, the extent to which the principles of equality and non-discrimination accept distinctions between citizens and non-citizens is a factor that must be taken into account.

In view of all of the foregoing it seems that in spite of the development of a comprehensive set of international human rights standards, nationality may not have lost its relevance in today's world. This means that – barring special remedies - the stateless may in fact find themselves in a protection gap as far as the enjoyment of rights is concerned. The challenge in the chapters to come is to find out exactly which rights are reliant on the bond of nationality for their (full) enjoyment

[38] Guy Goodwin-Gill, 'International Law and Human Rights: Trends Concerning International Migrants and Refugees', in *International Migration Review,* Vol. 23, 1989, page 546. A main reason for the current pertinence of this question is the fact that, according the International Organisations for Migration, "more people are on the move today than at any other point in human history". It is estimated that three percent of the world's population, or 192 million people are migrants. See for more information and up to date statistics on modern migration http://www.iom.int.

[39] Article 1, paragraph 2 of the Convention on the Elimination of All Forms of Racial Discrimination.

[40] UN Committee on the Elimination of Racial Discrimination, *General Recommendation 30: Discrimination against Non-citizens,* CERD/C/64/Misc.11/Rev.3, 2004, paragraph 3. Note that this recommendation has been described as building upon "all the previous protections for non-citizens and their interpretations not only by the Committee on the Elimination of Racial Discrimination, but also by the Human Rights Committee and other human rights institutions" and providing "a comprehensive elaboration of the human rights of non-citizens as a guide to all countries and particularly those that have ratified the Convention". Office of the High Commissioner of Human Rights, "The Rights of Non-citizens", prepared by David Weissbrodt, Geneva 2006.

[41] UN Committee on the Elimination of Racial Discrimination, *General Recommendation 30: Discrimination against Non-citizens,* CERD/C/64/Misc.11/Rev.3, 2004, paragraph 4.

according to current human rights law. In contrast, we must identify which rights are or may (to some extent) be restricted to citizens only. The work that has been done to date to document the difference in treatment between nationals and non-nationals under human rights law - by scholars such as Lillich, Tiburcio and Weissbrodt[42] - provides an invaluable source of information in this respect. The situation of the non-national is by and large representative of the stateless since, to put it plainly, stateless persons are non-nationals everywhere.

Nevertheless, the fact that the stateless are non-nationals *everywhere* adds a particular dimension to their plight that should not be overlooked. This makes them an "extremely vulnerable group of non-citizens".[43] It has been said of the refugee that he is

> an alien in any and every country to which he may go. He does not have the last resort which is always open to the 'normal alien' – return to his own country. The man who is everywhere an alien has to live in unusually difficult material and psychological conditions [...] Moreover, the refugee is not only an alien wherever he goes, he is also an 'unprotected alien' in the sense that he does not enjoy the protection of his country of origin.[44]

This dire predicament indeed befalls the refugee since the factual situation in the country of origin prevents him from returning home to exercise his rights as a national or calling in the assistance of his home country. However, where the stateless are concerned this fate is sealed in legal terms – only to be resolved through the attribution or restoration of the bond of nationality. Thus we must go further than scouring human rights law for any difference in treatment between nationals and non-nationals, we must also consider whether special provision is made for the situation of the stateless as non-nationals *everywhere.* In other words, we must reflect on whether the differentiation in treatment is indeed applicable to the particular situation of the stateless and whether this is in fact justifiable.[45]

3 The 1954 Convention relating to the Status of Stateless Persons

Out on the periphery of the human rights field as we know it, is a little-regarded instrument that was specially devised to protect the rights of the stateless: the 1954 Convention relating to the Status of Stateless Persons. Even as work was being completed on the Universal Declaration of Human Rights and the path was being laid for the future protection of all persons under international human rights law, the international community was second-guessing the effectiveness of this approach in

[42] Richard Lillich, *The human rights of aliens in contemporary international law*, Manchester University Press, Manchester: 1984 ; Carmen Tiburcio, *The human rights of aliens under international and comparative law*, Kluwer Law International, The Hague: 2001 ; David Weissbrodt, *Final Report on Prevention of Discrimination - The Rights of Non-Citizens,* E/CN.4/Sub.2/2003/23, 26 May 2003.

[43] David Weissbrodt, *Final Report on Prevention of Discrimination - The Rights of Non-Citizens,* E/CN.4/Sub.2/2003/23, 26 May 2003, Add.3, para. 7.

[44] Communication from the International Refugee Organisation to the Economic and Social Council, UN Doc. E/1392, 11 July 1949, App. I, as cited in James Hathaway, *The Rights of Refugees Under International Law*, Cambridge University Press, Cambridge: 2005, page 84.

[45] Or legitimate and proportional as suggested by Weissbrodt above. See note 36.

dealing with the massive humanitarian tragedy that had already unfolded. The implementation of international obligations and realisation of these international rights would still be reliant on the system of nation-states. As Hannah Arendt has vividly described:

> The rights of man had been defined as 'inalienable' because they were supposed to be independent of all governments, but it turned out that the moment human beings lacked their own government and had to fall back upon their minimum rights, no authority was left to protect them and no institution was willing to guarantee them.[46]

At that time there were vast numbers who were not in a position to rely on national protection[47] - millions of people who had become displaced by the Second World War or spontaneously found themselves residing in the territory of a different state because borders had been redrawn. Among these people, and others, some even found themselves stripped of the legal bond with their state thanks to denationalisation decrees or the legal consequences of state succession. Collectively known simply as the "unprotected", this destitute group presented the international community and the host countries with a serious challenge: who was to be responsible for their well-being, which rights could they rely on and to whom could they turn for protection? Such questions prompted the Economic and Social Council of the newly founded United Nations to commission a comprehensive study of the situation of the "stateless" on the grounds of which action could then be taken.[48]

As we briefly touched upon in chapter II, the *Study of Statelessness* marked the beginning of the process of according the stateless person - and the refugee - an independent definition and legal status. It was completed by the Secretary General in 1949 and, following its recommendation, an Ad Hoc Committee on Statelessness and Related Problems was established with the mandate of determining whether a new international instrument was needed to ensure the protection of both stateless persons and refugees.[49] This Committee decided that a convention was indeed desirable and set about the job of compiling a Draft Convention Relating to the Status of Refugees and a Protocol thereto Relating to the Status of Stateless Persons.[50] In 1951, a conference of plenipotentiaries unanimously adopted the

---

[46] Hannah Arendt, "The Decline of the Nation-State and the End of the Rights of Man" in *The origins of totalitarianism*, Harcourt Brace Jovanovich, New York: 1948, pages 291-292.

[47] Carol Batchelor, 'Stateless Persons: Some Gaps in International Protection', in *International Journal of Refugee Law,* Vol. 7, 1995 *page 239*

[48] UN, *A Study of Statelessness,* E/1112, New York: August 1949

[49] The Study of Statelessness was not in fact limited to considering statelessness as it is defined today. It included an assessment of the situation of other "unprotected persons", in particular refugees. Until then, the terms "stateless" and "refugee" were employed relatively indiscriminately to describe a person who could not rely on the protection of a state – both concepts had yet to be cordoned off. Nehemiah Robinson, *Convention relating to the status of stateless persons - Its history and interpretation,* UNHCR, Geneva: 1955 *Page 1*

[50] The preamble to the 1954 Convention relating to the Status of Stateless Persons would later explain that while reaffirming "the principle that human beings shall enjoy fundamental rights and freedoms without discrimination", further international agreement is needed "to assure stateless persons the widest possible exercise of these fundamental rights and freedoms".

Convention relating to the Status of Refugees.[51] The accompanying Draft Protocol on the Status of Stateless Persons was referred back to the General Assembly.[52] The refugee and the stateless person, who until then had "walked hand in hand"[53], thus embarked on diverging paths when the 1954 Convention relating to the Status of Stateless Persons was adopted by a second conference of plenipotentiaries some three years after the 1951 Refugee Convention.[54] However, the content of the Refugee Convention remained the point of departure in deciding which rights were to be granted to stateless persons. Consequently, the text of the 1954 Statelessness Convention closely resembles that of the 1951 Refugee Convention, with a number of exceptions where articles were either omitted, added or slightly modified. Indeed, in drafting the Statelessness Convention, "the prevailing view of the conference was that for a practical consideration (time) they should not engage in rewording the text of the Refugee Convention, except when this was justified by the difference between the two groups (refugees vs. stateless persons)".[55] In technique as well as in substance then, the two Conventions are highly similar and their parallel development has definitely left its mark. One helpful significance of this finding is that it allows us to also turn to reports and commentaries on the Refugee Convention to better understand the content of this 1954 Statelessness Convention.[56]

According to the "Information and Accession Package" which is used to promote ratification of the convention, the 1954 Convention is

[51] Hereafter referred to as the 1951 Refugee Convention.

[52] The decision to delay consideration of the Protocol – motivated by the time pressure to adopt an instrument to deal with refugees before the International Refugee Organisation was definitively dissolved - has had far-reaching consequences for the legal protection offered. The International Refugee Organisation (IRO) was established in 1947 and carried out the role of offering assistance to refugees until it was replaced by the Office of the United Nations High Commissioner for Refugees in 1951 alongside the adoption of the 1951 Refugee Convention; Carol Batchelor, 'Stateless Persons: Some Gaps in International Protection', in *International Journal of Refugee Law,* Vol. 7, 1995 *page 243*

[53] Guy Goodwin Gill, "The rights of refugees and stateless persons" in Saksena (ed) *Human rights perspectives & challenges (in 1900's and beyond)*, Lancers Books, New Delhi: 1994 *page 389*

[54] In the intervening period it became increasingly clear that the provisions relating to statelessness could no longer feasibly form a protocol to the Refugee Convention and so the document under consideration became a draft convention in its own right. It became obvious for example, that the rights which were to be bestowed on stateless persons were not entirely identical to the rights which were granted to refugees on the basis of the 1951 Refugee Convention and a protocol could not easily reflect the desired deviations. See further Nehemiah Robinson, *Convention relating to the status of stateless persons - Its history and interpretation*, UNHCR, Geneva: 1955 *Page 4-5*

[55] Nehemiah Robinson, *Convention relating to the status of stateless persons - Its history and interpretation*, UNHCR, Geneva: 1955, page 25.

[56] In particular, the 2005 work by James Hathaway offers an in depth analysis of the content and scope of the substantive rights of the 1951 Refugee Convention – as well as any counterpart guarantees under general human rights law – that will be utilised in upcoming chapters in the assessment of the 1954 Statelessness Convention.

> the primary international instrument adopted to date to regulate and improve the legal status of stateless persons and to ensure to stateless persons fundamental rights and freedoms without discrimination.[57]

To achieve this aim, the convention employs the same technique as the Refugee Convention: the individuals deserving of this protection are adorned the legal status of "stateless person". This status qualifies them for the guarantees that are laid out in the convention. The 1954 Statelessness Convention therefore opens with the official, internationally endorsed definition of statelessness:[58]

> The term "stateless person" means a person who is not considered as a national by any state under the operation of its law.[59]

After defining statelessness the 1954 Statelessness Convention goes straight on to delineate the rights - and duties - that accompany this newly created legal status.[60] The instrument does not spare any words on indicating how states are to undertake the process of identifying stateless persons for the purposes of applying the Convention's guarantees. No guidance is given as to the procedures by which the definition should be applied or where proof is to be sought of the satisfaction of the criteria outlined.[61] Just as we found for the 1961 Statelessness Convention, it is left entirely to states to organise the identification of cases which call for the implementation of these special protections. The prospects for a harmonised approach are therefore poor. And indeed, when surveyed, half of the respondent states reported having *neither* a specialised procedure for identifying cases of statelessness nor a mechanism for identifying stateless persons within the context of

---

[57] UNHCR, *Information and accession package: the 1954 Convention relating to the status of stateless persons and the 1961 Convention on the reduction of statelessness,* Geneva: January 1999, page 10.

[58] It is interesting to note that the original Draft Protocol to the Refugee Convention on the Status of Stateless Persons neglected to include a definition of statelessness which would have made the uniform application of its provisions impossible. Without a definition of a "stateless person" it would have been entirely for each state to decide whether an individual qualified for the protection offered under the Convention and what criteria would be used to make this determination. Nehemiah Robinson, *Convention relating to the status of stateless persons - Its history and interpretation*, UNHCR, Geneva: 1955, page 11.

[59] Article 1, 1954 Convention relating to the Status of Stateless Persons. For a full discussion of this definition of statelessness, see chapter II, section 4. Note further that the convention imitates the 1951 Refugee Convention again here by going on to exclude certain (groups of) persons from its scope of application including persons who are already receiving assistance from a United Nations agency other than the UNHCR, persons who are effectively treated as nationals by the country in which they reside and persons who have committed one of a variety of serious crimes. See on these grounds for exclusion Carol Batchelor The 1954 Convention relating to the Status of Stateless Persons: Implementation within the European Union Member States and Recommendations for Harmonisation 2004, pages 15-17.

[60] Indeed it starts by determining that "every stateless person has duties to the country in which he finds himself". Article 2 of the 1954 Convention relating to the Status of Stateless Persons. Rather than requiring a far-reaching allegiance to that state, the duties of the stateless person are restricted to conforming to its laws and refraining from disturbing public order.

[61] UNHCR and IPU, *Nationality and statelessness. A handbook for parliamentarians*, 2005, page 19.

asylum procedures.[62] This is likely to seriously impede the actual recognition as a stateless person and subsequently the enjoyment of any other rights emanating from the 1954 Statelessness Convention.

Some 30 provisions of the 1954 Statelessness Convention are then devoted to the improvement of the status of stateless persons by setting out a minimum standard of treatment for the stateless to enjoy, without discrimination.[63] There are two central observations to be made on how these substantive rights have been elaborated. The first is that not all of the rights are actually granted to all stateless persons. Eligibility for a particular entitlement is rendered further dependent on the relationship between the stateless person and the state in which he wishes to exercise that right. The Convention delineates five "levels of attachment" that the stateless person may enjoy in relation to the state.[64] The weakest level of attachment is simply being subject to the state's jurisdiction. From this position, a stateless person is guaranteed such rights as access to courts and education – assuming, of course, that his status as a stateless person has been established.[65] Thereafter, in order of strengthening attachment, the four other levels are: physical presence, lawful presence, lawful stay and durable residence. Thus a stateless person is, for example, entitled to identity papers and the freedom of religion in the state in which he is physically present, but only when such presence is also lawful is the freedom of movement within the state guaranteed.[66] Finally, as the connection between the individual and the state develops further and there is lawful stay or even durable

---

[62] UNHCR, *Final report concerning the Questionnaire on statelessness pursuant to the Agenda for Protection,* Geneva: March 2004, pages 26-27.

[63] Article 3 of the 1954 Statelessness Convention provides for the application of the non-discrimination principle to the guarantees offered under this instrument. For a discussion of this provision see Nehemiah Robinson, *Convention relating to the status of stateless persons - Its history and interpretation*, UNHCR, Geneva: 1955, pages 24-28. Meanwhile, article 5 determines that "nothing in this Convention shall be deemed to impair any rights and benefits granted by a Contracting State to stateless persons apart from this Convention" confirming that it sets out minimum standards beyond which states are free to extend additional protection and rights to (groups of) stateless persons. Brian Gorlick, *Human Rights and Refugees: Enhancing Protection through International Human Rights Law,* Geneva: October 2000, page 7; See also Nehemiah Robinson, *Convention relating to the status of stateless persons - Its history and interpretation*, UNHCR, Geneva: 1955, page 27.

[64] The system whereby rights are granted in accordance with the level of attachment to the state is identical to that adopted in the 1951 Convention relating to the Status of Refugees. This is outlined in detail in James Hathaway, *The Rights of Refugees Under International Law*, Cambridge University Press, Cambridge: 2005, pages 156-192. This "level of attachment" technique has also been referred to as the "criteria for entitlement". Guy Goodwin-Gill; Jane McAdam, *The refugee in international law*, Oxford University Press, Oxford: 2007, pages 524-528.

[65] Access to courts is guaranteed in article 16, paragraph 1 and the right to education in article 22 of the 1954 Statelessness Convention. Other rights that are granted to all stateless persons within a state's jurisdiction are: "non-discrimination" (article 3), "moveable and immoveable property" (article 13), "rationing" (article 20), "fiscal charges" (article 29) and "naturalisation" (article 32).

[66] The right to identity papers is found in article 27 and the freedom of religion in article 3 of the 1954 Statelessness Convention. Both articles delineate that contracting states must accord those rights to "stateless persons within their territories". The right to freedom of movement and choice of place of residence need only be guaranteed by a contracting state to "stateless persons lawfully in its territory". See article 26 of the 1954 Statelessness Convention.

residence, the stateless person will gain access to additional rights.[67] The entitlement of a stateless person to the rights offered by the 1954 Statelessness Convention is therefore largely dependent on his status and the connection that he enjoys with the state in question. The possession, for example, of an irregular immigration status severely curtails the enjoyment of rights under this instrument. This aspect of the regime must be taken into account later as we discuss the effectiveness of the Convention in protecting the various rights of the stateless.

The second essential observation with regard to the scope of the substantive rights in the 1954 Statelessness Convention is that the level of protection offered differs from one right to another. Under the Convention there are basically three levels of protection or "standards of treatment": treatment at least as favourable as that accorded to aliens generally, treatment on a par with nationals and absolute rights.[68] Thus stateless persons are entitled to the same level of enjoyment of such rights as self-employment and the right to housing as is attributed to aliens generally, although more favourable treatment is encouraged.[69] This is, in fact, the minimum standard of treatment ascribed to stateless persons under the 1954 Statelessness Convention: its article 7, paragraph 1 determines that

> except where this Convention contains more favourable provisions, a Contracting State shall accord to stateless persons the same treatment as is accorded to aliens generally.[70]

---

[67] These include, among others "wage-earning employment" (article 17) and "travel documents" (article 28) to which "stateless persons lawfully staying" in a state's territory are entitled and "artistic rights and industrial property" (article 14) which must be guaranteed to the stateless person "in the country in which he has his habitual residence". So-called "durable residence" refers to the additional criterion – alongside lawful stay – of a certain period of residence in a state. Thus article 7, paragraph 2 accords stateless persons exemption from legislative reciprocity after three years residence in the territory of a contracting state. Note that article 10 of the 1954 Statelessness Convention, on "continuity of residence" provides a special guarantee for the establishment of residence status or duration for those stateless persons who were forcibly displaced during World War II – sixty years on, this provision has become obsolete. See Nehemiah Robinson, *Convention relating to the status of stateless persons - Its history and interpretation*, UNHCR, Geneva: 1955, pages 46-47.

[68] This is the language used by Hathaway to describe the same system in the 1951 Refugee Convention. It should be noted that the Refugee Convention in fact has four standards of treatment – the fourth being the standard extended by the state to most-favoured nationals. This does not however feature in the 1954 Statelessness Convention where the two rights in question (association and wage-earning employment) demand treatment at least as favourable as non-nationals generally. For standards of treatment in the Refugee Convention, see James Hathaway, *The Rights of Refugees Under International Law*, Cambridge University Press, Cambridge: 2005, pages 228-238; Guy Goodwin-Gill; Jane McAdam, *The refugee in international law*, Oxford University Press, Oxford: 2007, pages 509-510.

[69] The right to property (article 13), the right to self-employment (article 18) and the right to housing (article 21) feature among the provisions that demand "treatment as favourable as possible and, in any event, not less favourable than that accorded to aliens generally in the same circumstances". Note that the encouragement to accord treatment as favourable as possible "imposes a duty on states to consider in good faith the exemption of [stateless persons] from even rules applied generally to non-citizens". James Hathaway, *The Rights of Refugees Under International Law*, Cambridge University Press, Cambridge: 2005, page 526.

[70] Note that under article 6 of the 1954 Statelessness Convention, where stateless persons are provided treatment on a par with non-nationals generally, "in the same circumstances", they are exempted from meeting requirements "which by their nature a stateless person is incapable of fulfilling". See

But with regard to other rights, such as rationing, education and freedom of religion, the Convention sets a higher standard by demanding that stateless persons be afforded "the same treatment as is accorded to nationals".[71] Among the absolute rights - those which are not contingent upon the treatment of any other group within the state but are guaranteed directly to stateless persons whether available to anyone else in the state or not[72] – are non-discrimination, access to courts, naturalisation and travel documents.[73] Similarly to the observation that not all rights in the 1954 Statelessness Convention are available to all stateless persons, this finding that the level of protection also varies from one right to another uncovers the complexity of the protection offered by this instrument and must be weighed into its evaluation in the chapters to come.

It is interesting to note that there is no discernable correlation between the level of attachment required for entitlement to one of the rights in the 1954 Statelessness Convention and the standard of treatment offered. This is clearly illustrated in the schematic overview provided in Annex 3 of the rights in the Convention by level of attachment needed and level of protection guaranteed.[74] Absolute rights are ascribed to stateless persons at each level of attachment, from merely being under a state's jurisdiction through to durable residence. Meanwhile, although lawful presence or lawful stay in a state does lead to the entitlement to more rights, it is not per definition the key to treatment on a par with nationals. Evidently both the level of attachment required and the level of protection offered have been independently deliberated, debated and determined in relation to each and every right that is included in the Convention and there is no all-explanatory logic to the system.

Beyond the impact of the level of attachment and the level of protection on the scope and content of the rights bestowed upon stateless persons, there are several additional comments to be made in this introduction to the protection offered by the 1954 Statelessness Convention. Firstly, it should be mentioned that the 1954 Statelessness Convention has succeeded in attracting more accessions than

---

Nehemiah Robinson, *Convention relating to the status of stateless persons - Its history and interpretation*, UNHCR, Geneva: 1955, pages 31-32; James Hathaway, *The Rights of Refugees Under International Law*, Cambridge University Press, Cambridge: 2005, pages 205-208. Moreover, under article 7, paragraphs 2 to 5, stateless persons are also exempted from the condition of reciprocity under certain circumstances, ensuring that their particular situation as non-nationals everywhere does not impede their enjoyment of the benefits of bi- and multilateral agreements between states. See Nehemiah Robinson, *The Universal Declaration of Human Rights. Its Origin, Significance, Application and Interpretation*, Institute of Jewish Affairs, New York: 1958, pages 32-39; James Hathaway, *The Rights of Refugees Under International Law*, Cambridge University Press, Cambridge: 2005, pages 200-205.

[71] In fact, article 4 on the freedom of religion goes further still by demanding that stateless persons be granted treatment "at least as favourable as that accorded to nationals".

[72] The rights which are made contingent on the entitlements available to other groups have also been referred to as "equated rights". Richard Lillich, *The human rights of aliens in contemporary international law*, Manchester University Press, Manchester: 1984, page 66.

[73] The formulation of many of these rights as absolute rights can be explained by the lack of an available counterpart or standard in the treatment of aliens or nationals since many of these are measures that are specifically geared to deal with the situation of the stateless. See James Hathaway, *The Rights of Refugees Under International Law*, Cambridge University Press, Cambridge: 2005, page 237.

[74] Annex 3 can be found on page 455.

its 1961 counterpart. To date, there are 62 state parties.[75] Nevertheless, this figure is far below the level of acceptance of the 1951 Refugee Convention – a striking fact given the shared history of these instruments.[76] Moreover, half of the state parties to the 1954 Statelessness Convention have exercised their right to submit either a declaration or reservations to its text upon ratification.[77] Even where reservations have not been lodged, the instrument itself allows for some restrictions to be placed on the enjoyment of certain Convention rights where this is necessitated by "national security or public order".[78] The limited acceptance of the 1954 Statelessness Convention and these further restrictions that may be placed on the rights that it houses should be kept in mind as we move on to consider how effective the 1954 Statelessness Convention is in protecting the fundamental rights of stateless persons.

Finally, we find that with regard to any dispute to arise on the interpretation or application of the 1954 Statelessness Convention, the question can be referred to the International Court of Justice for settlement.[79] However, as was discovered to be the case for the 1961 Convention on the Reduction of Statelessness, this option has never been utilised. The 1954 Statelessness Convention does include a general provision obliging state parties to

> communicate to the Secretary General of the United Nations the laws and regulations which they may adopt to ensure the application of this Convention.[80]

This article "stems from the right of every state party to a convention to be informed about its application by other parties" and was not necessarily conceived with a supervisory apparatus in mind.[81] Disappointingly then, this is the other only reference, albeit indirect, to the issue of enforcement.[82] There is no further mention of an enforcement or supervisory mechanism - a provision included in the 1951 Convention relating to the Status of Refugees on the duty of state parties to cooperate with the UN agency charged with overseeing the implementation of the

---

[75] The most recent spate of accessions was in 2006 when Belize, Montenegro, Romania and Rwanda became parties to the Convention.

[76] The 1951 Convention Relating to the Status of Refugees (and its 1967 Protocol) has attained 144 state parties, more than double the number of ratifications of the 1954 Statelessness Convention.

[77] Reservations are permitted to any of the articles of the 1954 Statelessness Convention with the exception of article 1 (definition), article 3 (non-discrimination), article 4 (religion), article 16,1 (access to courts) and articles 33-42 (final clauses).

[78] This is provided for in article 28 in relation to the provision of travel documents and in article 31 on expulsion.

[79] Article 34 of the 1954 Convention relating to the Status of Stateless Persons.

[80] Article 33 of the 1954 Convention relating to the Status of Stateless Persons (mimicking article 26 of the 1951 Refugee Convention).

[81] Nehemiah Robinson, *Convention relating to the status of stateless persons - Its history and interpretation*, UNHCR, Geneva: 1955

[82] According to Batchelor, "for procedural reasons, namely time, lack of authority, creation of an independent instrument and failure to raise the issue with governments or through reference back to the Refugee Convention, the matter of a supervisory body was never discussed". Carol Batchelor, 'Stateless Persons: Some Gaps in International Protection', in *International Journal of Refugee Law,* Vol. 7, 1995, page 247.

Convention was not transposed to the 1954 Statelessness Convention's text and there is no equivalent either to the provision in the 1961 Statelessness Convention that called for an agency to assist individuals with the task of claiming their rights.[83] Although UNHCR's mandate in relation to statelessness has now expanded to include the promotion of the rights of stateless persons,[84] enforcement remains an area of concern for the 1954 Statelessness Convention.

4 Purpose and Method of Part III

The following three chapters will build upon what has been said here as the international community's response to the protection needs of the stateless is discussed in detail. As a reminder, this quest is guided by the second of the research questions introduced in chapter 1:

> **How can the way in which international law deals with the *legal status and entitlements of stateless persons* be improved so as to ensure optimal protection of the individual's rights in the absence of nationality?**

To this end I will be assessing the value of the 1954 Convention relating to the status of stateless persons as well as general norms of international human rights law. While this is an ambitious aim, much work has inadvertently already been done by others in the detailed consideration of the rights of non-nationals under international human rights law and the in-depth analysis of the rights of refugees under both human rights norms and the 1951 Convention relating to the Status of Refugees. On these foundations it becomes possible to build a picture of the specific position of the stateless person as opposed to the non-national generally or the refugee. Moreover, it is prudent to be bear in mind that this investigation centres around the position of the stateless person and does not pretend to provide an exhaustive overall discussion of any of the individual topics covered.

In view of the elaborate and diverse catalogue of rights guaranteed under the 1954 Statelessness Convention it is absolutely vital to find a structured approach to dealing with its content.[85] One possibility would be to follow Hathaway and deal with the rights in categories according to the level of attachment required for their

[83] The refugee instrument determines that "the Contracting States undertake to cooperate with the Office of the United Nations High Commissioner for Refugees, or any other agency of the United Nations that may succeed it, in the exercise of its functions, and shall in particular facilitate its duty of supervising the application of the provisions of this Convention". Article 35, paragraph 1 of the 1951 Convention relating to the Status of Refugees. The second paragraph of this provision goes on to specify that the state parties must provide information and statistical data concerning "the condition of refugees; the implementation of this convention; and laws, regulations and decrees which are, or may hereafter be, in force relating to refugees". For a discussion of article 11 on the establishment of an agency to assist in the implementation of the 1961 Statelessness Convention, see chapter III, section 3.

[84] See for instance, UNHCR Executive Committee, *Conclusion on Identification, Prevention and Reduction of Statelessness and Protection of Stateless Persons, No. 106,* 57th Session, Geneva, 2006.

[85] As annex 3 shows, there is no discernible logic to the structure of the 1954 Statelessness Convention either in the grouping or ordering of rights.

enjoyment.[86] Another would be to group the rights according to the level of protection offered and deal with them that way.[87] However, I feel that neither will adequately facilitate the investigation into the overall protection offered to stateless persons and, in particular, the identification of gaps in that protection. I have therefore chosen a third route whereby the structure is inspired not by system of the 1954 Statelessness Convention itself, but by the system of international human rights law. So, while fully aware that the distinction between civil and political rights on the one hand and economic, social and cultural rights on the other is now considered largely artificial,[88] I feel that this traditional division does provide an appropriate framework for discussing the rights espoused in the 1954 Statelessness Convention. The rights contained in the Convention are therefore split according to the content of the International Covenant on Civil and Political Rights versus that of the International Covenant on Economic, Social and Cultural Rights: civil and political rights are dealt with in chapter X while economic, social and cultural rights are addressed in chapter XI. This approach makes it easier to identify the gaps in the protection offered by the 1954 Statelessness Convention – if any – and to assessing the overall enjoyment of each category of rights by stateless persons under contemporary international law. Once these rights have been separated and dealt with, there remains a residual category of provisions in the Convention that are dealt with in chapter XII under the heading "protecting the special needs of the stateless".[89] The findings from these three chapters are drawn together in chapter XIII where the strengths and weaknesses of the international community's approach to the protection of the stateless are laid out, the problems relating to implementation and enforcement of these norms reconsidered and suggestions made for future improvements.

[86] James Hathaway, *The Rights of Refugees Under International Law*, Cambridge University Press, Cambridge: 2005.

[87] This is the approach adopted in Richard Lillich, *The human rights of aliens in contemporary international law*, Manchester University Press, Manchester: 1984, pages 66-69.

[88] It is explained that: "These are not airtight categories. Many treaties declare rights that straddle the two basic covenants in these fields, or that fall clearly within the domains of both of them. Many rights are hard to categorise. Nonetheless, at their core, the conventional distinctions are clear, whatever the relationships and interdependency between the two categories". Henry Steiner; Philip Alston, *International Human Rights in Context. Law, Politics and Morals*, Oxford University Press, Oxford: 2000, page 136.

[89] Although this language is slightly ambiguous, since the entire convention is supposedly geared towards the special needs of the stateless, this expression was chosen for want of better language to indicate those additional measures that are prescribed alongside the attribution of 'traditional' rights to stateless persons. In the context of the refugee convention such matters have been described as "refugee-specific concerns" or "standards applicable to refugees as refugees". See James Hathaway, *The Rights of Refugees Under International Law*, Cambridge University Press, Cambridge: 2005, page 121; Guy Goodwin-Gill; Jane McAdam, *The refugee in international law*, Oxford University Press, Oxford: 2007, pages 510-524.

CHAPTER X

PROTECTING THE CIVIL AND POLITICAL RIGHTS OF THE STATELESS

This chapter deals with the international legal protection of the civil and political rights of stateless persons. Using the International Covenant on Civil and Political Rights (ICCPR) as a model, it was possible to identify which of the rights espoused in the 1954 Convention relating to the Status of Stateless Persons would generally be considered to fall within this category.[1] In the order in which they will shortly be discussed, these rights are: freedom of movement (articles 26 and 31), the right to legal personhood (article 12), access to courts (article 16), freedom of religion (article 4) and the right to property (article 13).[2] When contrasted with the provisions of the ICCPR – 27 substantive articles in all - this list is concise to say the least. In the process of this simple exercise we are thus immediately cautioned about the possible limitations of the 1954 Statelessness Convention in guaranteeing the civil and political rights of stateless persons. However, the protection of stateless persons' rights is not based on the 1954 Convention alone, it is the cumulative effect of this instrument and general human rights norms, to the extent that they are applicable to the situation of statelessness. Therefore, to uncover the full spectrum of stateless persons' civil and political rights, we must not only analyse the content of the 1954 Convention, but we must also compare and contrast these provisions with human rights law and consider the way in which the human rights field deals with those civil and political rights that the 1954 Statelessness Convention has overlooked. This will allow us to assess both the overall enjoyment of civil and political rights that is offered to stateless persons under international law and the role of the 1954 Statelessness Convention in guaranteeing these rights. In order to keep this investigation orderly and manageable, greatest attention will be

[1] The full text of the 1954 Convention relating to the Status of Stateless Persons is included as Annex 2.

[2] Article 29 that addresses fiscal charges and article 30 that deals with the transfer of assets are relevant for the scope of the right to property as guaranteed under the 1954 Statelessness Convention. This right is dealt with here, although it should be noted that the right to property also forms an important backbone to the enjoyment of economic, social and cultural rights. Note that the freedom of association could also be included among the civil and political rights attributed to stateless persons under the 1954 Statelessness Convention, however, this is a right that is very much situated on the boundary between the rights traditionally classed as civil and political and those classed as economic, social and cultural and can be found in both of the international covenants. In view of the formulation of this right in the 1954 Statelessness Convention– with its clear focus on the social aspect of membership of non-political associations such as trade unions– it will be dealt with in chapter XI when we turn to economic, social and cultural rights.

paid to those civil and political rights that are identified as particularly important in the specific context of statelessness.

1 NON-NATIONALS, NON-DISCRIMINATION AND THE ENJOYMENT OF CIVIL AND POLITICAL RIGHTS

As we commence consideration of the *civil and political rights* guaranteed to the stateless under international law it is helpful to make some general observations about the relevance of nationality for the enjoyment of this set of rights and the role of the principle of non-discrimination in this context. Firstly, recall that the enjoyment of the rights enumerated in the International Covenant on Civil and Political Rights

> is not limited to citizens of States Parties but must also be available to all individuals, *regardless of nationality or statelessness* [...] who may find themselves in the territory or subject to the jurisdiction of the State Party.[3]

Moreover, the Human Rights Committee has declared that

> the general rule is that each one of the rights of the Covenant must be guaranteed without discrimination *between* citizens and aliens.[4]

Read together these two statements imply that as far as *civil and political rights* go, non-citizens, including the stateless, not only benefit from the full catalogue of guarantees, but they are to enjoy the same level of protection as citizens. However, this conclusion is inaccurate – or at least incomplete – on both counts.

To begin with, a number of the rights contained in the ICCPR make their own distinctions, being explicitly concerned with only certain limited categories of person.[5] One such specialised or qualified provision addresses the right to participate in government found in article 25. As we have already noted, this right is offered to *citizens* rather than to *everyone* and thereby operates to the apparent exclusion of the stateless.[6] So within the realm of civil and political rights there is at least one area, if not more, in which (the possession of a) nationality continues to play a part.[7] This means that the personal scope of each right will have to be

---

[3] Human Rights Committee, *General Comment 31: Nature of the General Legal Obligation imposed on States Parties to the Covenant,* CCPR/C/21/Rev.1/Add.13, Geneva: 26 May 2004, paragraph 10; Human Rights Committee, *General Comment 15: The position of aliens under the covenant,* Geneva: Geneva: 11 April 1986, paragraph 1. See chapter IX, section.2.

[4] Emphasis added. Human Rights Committee, *General Comment 15: The position of aliens under the covenant,* Geneva: 11 April 1986, paragraph 2.

[5] See, for instance, article 6, paragraph 5 on the prohibition of the death penalty for *juvenile offenders* as well as for *pregnant women*.

[6] See chapter IX, section 2.

[7] The enumeration of the civil and political rights that *are* to be enjoyed by all non-nationals, including the stateless, has therefore been presented by the Human Rights Committee as follows: "Aliens thus have an inherent right to life, protected by law, and may not be arbitrarily deprived of life. They must not be subjected to torture or to cruel, inhuman or degrading treatment or punishment; nor may they be

investigated. The extent to which the explicit qualification of the right to participate in government - and perhaps others - places a restraint on its enjoyment by *stateless persons*, as a particular sub-group of non-citizens with its own specific traits, is something that will be studied closely as we move through the civil and political rights one by one over the course of this chapter. Meanwhile, since those rights that *are* elaborated to the enjoyment of everyone, regardless of nationality, may be qualified "by such limitations as may lawfully be imposed under the Covenant",[8] the extent to which restrictions are allowable will also need to be looked into.

A second issue is the precise impact of the principle of non-discrimination on the enjoyment of civil and political rights by non-nationals. The Human Rights Committee explains that

> the term 'discrimination' as used in the Covenant should be understood to imply any distinction, inclusion, restriction or preference which is based on any ground such as race, colour, sex, language, religion, political or other opinion, national or social origin, property, birth or other status, and which has the purpose of nullifying or impairing the recognition, enjoyment or exercise by all persons, on an equal footing, of all rights and freedoms.[9]

Article 2, paragraph 1 of the Covenant prohibits discrimination, as described above, in the protection of the civil and political rights set out in the instrument and the broad notion of "any other status" forms a potential basis for the prohibition of discrimination between citizens and non-citizens.[10] Thus in the case of *Gueye et al. v. France* where the Human Rights Committee was called upon to judge the

held in slavery or servitude. Aliens have the right to liberty and security of the person. If lawfully deprived of liberty, they shall be treated with humanity and with respect for the inherent dignity of their person. Aliens may not be imprisoned for failure to fulfil a contractual obligation. They have the right to liberty of movement and free choice of residence; they shall be free to leave the country. Aliens shall be equal before the courts and tribunals, and shall be entitled to a fair and public hearing by a competent, independent and impartial tribunal established by law in the determination of any criminal charge or of rights and obligations in a suit at law. Aliens shall not be subjected to retrospective penal legislation, and are entitled to recognition before the law. They may not be subjected to arbitrary or unlawful interference with their privacy, family, home or correspondence. They have the right to freedom of thought, conscience and religion, and the right to hold opinions and to express them. Aliens receive the benefit of the right of peaceful assembly and of freedom of association. They may marry when at marriageable age. Their children are entitled to those measures of protection required by their status as minors. In those cases where aliens constitute a minority within the meaning of article 27, they shall not be denied the right, in community with other members of their group, to enjoy their own culture, to profess and practice their own religion and to use their own language." Human Rights Committee, *General Comment 15: The position of aliens under the covenant,* Geneva: 11 April 1986, paragraph 7.

[8] Human Rights Committee, *General Comment 15: The position of aliens under the covenant,* Geneva: 11 April 1986, paragraph 7.

[9] Human Rights Committee, *General Comment 18: Non-discrimination,* Geneva: Geneva: 10 November 1989, paragraph 7.

[10] Meanwhile article 26 provides a similar, stand-alone guarantee for any field regulated and protected by public authorities. See also article 2 of the Convention on the Rights of the Child; article 14 of the European Convention on Human Rights and article 1 of Protocol No. 12 to the European Convention; Articles 1 and 24 of the American Convention on Human Rights; and Articles 2 and 19 of the African Charter on Human and Peoples' Rights.

compliance with the Covenant of a law that differentiated on the basis of nationality,

> it notes that nationality as such does not figure among the prohibited grounds for discrimination [but] in the Committee's opinion, this falls within the reference to "other status".[11]

The upshot of this finding is not that states may not differentiate between nationals and non-nationals in the protection of civil and political rights, but that such distinctions may be subject to scrutiny.[12]

Indeed, "the enjoyment of rights and freedoms on an equal footing [...] does not mean identical treatment in every instance".[13] Instead,

> the Committee observes that not every differentiation of treatment will constitute discrimination, if the criteria for such differentiation are *reasonable* and *objective* and if the aim is to achieve a purpose which is *legitimate* under the Covenant.[14]

---

[11] Human Rights Committee, *Case of Gueye et al. v. France,* Comm. No. 196/1985, Geneva: 1989, paragraph 9.4. See for instance also Human Rights Committee, *Case of Adam v. The Czech Republic,* Comm. No. 586/1994, Geneva: 1996; *Case of Blazek v. Czech Republic,* Comm. No. 857/1999, Geneva: 2001; *Case of Gratzinger v. Czech Republic,* Comm. No. 1463/2006, Geneva: 2007; and *Case of Zdenek v. Czech Republic,* Comm. No. 1533/2006, Geneva: 2007. Note that in these cases, the state was found to have violated article 26 of the ICCPR, the stand-alone guarantee of equal treatment before the law, because the differentiation on the grounds of citizenship was considered unreasonable in the specific context of the case at hand.

[12] The fact that article 25 of the ICCPR, by its own admission "guarantees certain political rights, *differentiating on grounds of citizenship*" is evidence that distinctions between nationals and non-nationals will not always be inappropriate or forbidden. Human Rights Committee, *General Comment 18: Non-discrimination,* Geneva: 10 November 1989, paragraph 8. See also Richard Lillich, *The human rights of aliens in contemporary international law*, Manchester University Press, Manchester: 1984, pages 45-46; Sarah Joseph; Jenny Schultz; Melissa Castan, *The International Covenant on Civil and Political Rights. Cases, Materials and Commentary*, Oxford University Press, Oxford: 2000, pages 529-530; James Hathaway, *The Rights of Refugees Under International Law*, Cambridge University Press, Cambridge: 2005, pages 123-147.

[13] Human Rights Committee, *General Comment 18: Non-discrimination,* Geneva: 10 November 1989, paragraph 8. Not all *distinctions* amount to *discrimination.* Recall also the discussion on the principle of non-discrimination in the context of the prohibition of arbitrary deprivation of nationality in chapter V.

[14] Human Rights Committee, *General Comment 18: Non-discrimination,* Geneva: 10 November 1989, paragraph 13. In other words, "*the principle of non-discrimination [...] places upon those who would make distinctions in the recognition or protection of rights the burden of showing that non-national status is a relevant basis for differentiation, that the distinction is implemented in pursuit of a reasonable aim or objective; that it is necessary, no alternative action being available; and that the discriminatory measures taken or contemplated are proportional to the end to be achieved*". Guy Goodwin-Gill, 'International Law and Human Rights: Trends Concerning International Migrants and Refugees', in *International Migration Review,* Vol. 23, 1989, page 532. Recall also the statement made by the Committee on the Elimination of Racial Discrimination in *General Recommendation 30: Discrimination against Non-citizens,* CERD/C/64/Misc.11/Rev.3, 2004, paragraph 4, as cited in chapter IX at note 40.

It is therefore difficult to make a general statement about how tolerant international law is of differentiation between nationals and non-nationals in the enjoyment of *civil and political rights*. The Human Rights Committee deals with the question on a right by right and case by case basis by putting the distinction employed by the state to the test as described above. Thus, in one of a series of cases brought against the Czech Republic involving differentiation between citizens and non-citizens in the recovery of confiscated property, the Committee first explained that "the criterion of citizenship is *objective*".[15] Thereafter, the Committee considered the question of whether "in the circumstances of these cases the application of the criterion to the authors would be *reasonable*".[16] Although here, the Committee found the differentiation on the grounds of citizenship to be *unreasonable,*[17] other cases, with other facts may present a different outcome. Indeed, according to Hathaway, the *reasonable and objective* test generally tends to be applied with regrettable lenience, to the detriment of the protection of non-citizens.[18]

Nevertheless, a case-specific application of the reasonable and objective test should allow consideration to be given to the particular circumstance of statelessness (as opposed to 'simple' non-citizenship) in determining the appropriateness of the distinction between nationals and non-nationals in the enjoyment of civil and political rights. In fact, consideration for the specific condition of statelessness in applying the principle of non-discrimination may call for positive measures in favour of stateless persons. The right not to be discriminated against in the enjoyment of the rights guaranteed under human rights treaties is also violated when states, without an objective and reasonable justification, fail to treat differently persons whose situations are significantly different:

> The Committee also wishes to point out that the principle of equality sometimes requires States parties to take affirmative action in order to diminish or eliminate conditions which cause or help to perpetuate discrimination prohibited by the Covenant. For example, in a State *where the general conditions of a certain part of the population prevent or impair their enjoyment of human rights, the State should take specific action to correct those conditions*. Such action may involve granting for a time to the part of the population concerned certain preferential treatment in specific matters as compared with the rest of the population.[19]

[15] Human Rights Committee, *Case of Blazek v. Czech Republic,* Comm. No. 857/1999 (2001), paragraph 5.7.

[16] Human Rights Committee, *Case of Blazek v. Czech Republic,* Comm. No. 857/1999 (2001), paragraph 5.7.

[17] The Committee found that, taking into account the role of the state in creating the situation whereby the claimants lacked Czech citizenship as required for restitution or compensation following the confiscation of property, the differentiation between citizens and non-citizens was *unreasonable*.

[18] For a full discussion of this question see James Hathaway, *The Rights of Refugees Under International Law*, Cambridge University Press, Cambridge: 2005, pages 129 –147.

[19] Human Rights Committee, *General Comment 18: Non-discrimination,* Geneva: 10 November 1989, paragraph 10.

The often vulnerable and deprived position of stateless persons may call for affirmative action to redress this disadvantage. This fact may influence not only the application of the norm of non-discrimination in cases involving stateless persons, but may even have an impact upon the very content or application of certain civil and political rights in the circumstances of statelessness.

The bottom line that can be distilled from this discussion is that to determine the enduring relevance of nationality for the enjoyment of *civil and political rights* and discover what treatment stateless persons can anticipate in this regard, a right-by-right exposition is unavoidable. Which rights are themselves prescribed to the exclusion of non-nationals? Which rights permit limitations that could be invoked to the exclusion of non-nationals? How has the principle of non-discrimination influenced the equal enjoyment of particular civil and political rights by non-nationals? And, most importantly, when presented with the concrete scenario of statelessness, how do or may the answers to each of these questions change? This final consideration (re)establishes the link to the issue of the role and value of the 1954 Convention relating to the Status of Stateless Persons, that is geared specifically to the protection of the stateless, within the broader human rights framework. Together, the questions presented will help to guide the discussion in the following sections.[20]

2 FREEDOM OF MOVEMENT

The first fundamental right to be addressed is the freedom of movement. When a person utilises his right to move freely from one place to another the freedom that he is exercising goes far beyond any simple change of address. It means the opportunity to leave a place where your political opinions are not accepted or to move to a place where you are able to enjoy an education. This is why the freedom of movement has also been described as the "right to 'vote with one's feet' [which] may be the ultimate means through which the individual may express his or her personal liberty".[21] Moreover, the freedom of movement is considered to "interact with several rights"[22] because it deals with the aspect of physical access – to a state's territory and thus jurisdiction or to particular opportunities, facilities and

[20] Note that in order to present a clear overview of the main points of relevance, the question of the relationship between nationality, the principle of non-discrimination and the enjoyment of civil and political rights was discussed in this section with reference to the International Covenant on Civil and Political Rights. However, other instruments and documents will also influence the answer to these questions, including the Convention on the Rights of the Child, the Convention on the Elimination of All Forms of Racial Discrimination, the Migrant Workers Convention, the UN Declaration on the Rights of Individuals Who are not Nationals of the Country in which They Live and regional human rights texts. These will be included, wherever relevant, in the right-by-right treatise in the rest of this chapter.

[21] Hurst Hannum, *The Right to Leave and Return in International Law and Practice*, Martinus Nijhoff Publishers, Dordrecht: 1987, page 4. See also *General Comment 27* of the Human Rights Committee where freedom of movement is described as "an indispensable condition for the free development of a person". Human Rights Committee, *General Comment 27: Freedom of Movement,* A/55/40 vol.1, Geneva: 2000 128, para. 1.

[22] Human Rights Committee, *General Comment 27: Freedom of Movement,* A/55/40 vol.1, Geneva: 2000 128, para. 1.

services. Curtailing a person's freedom of movement may subsequently hinder their access to other entitlements and, as we will see, part of the difficulty that stateless persons experience in accessing their rights indeed stems from problems related to the liberty of movement.

The freedom of movement actually encompasses two distinct elements: an internal and an international dimension. The first deals with the right to move freely within the territorial boundaries of a state while the second is concerned with the right to move across the international frontiers that separate one state from another. These two aspects of the freedom of movement are governed by different considerations and are regulated separately under international law. For this reason, they will now be dealt with in turn. Particular attention will be paid to the international dimension of the right to free movement, for the consideration of this issue plays a crucial role in shedding light on the overall protection system of the 1954 Statelessness Convention and uncovering a substantial underlying weakness. The upcoming paragraphs will thereby reveal just why the freedom of movement deserves this prominent position at the head of the discussion of the rights of the stateless.

2.1 Internal freedom of movement

As alluded to above, the freedom to move around within the borders of a state and to choose one's place of residence is of utmost importance as it will help to ensure access to all sorts of rights, facilities and services. For example, "impediments to freedom of movement [may] prevent persons entitled to vote from exercising their rights effectively".[23] And there are many other, comparable scenarios: the right of access to court, the right to work, to an education, to healthcare, to birth registration and many others may all be similarly affected. Yet it is not uncommon for restrictions to be placed on an individual's internal freedom of movement. One of the most straight-forward examples is the curtailment of the freedom of movement of prisoners – bound to remain within the confines of a detention facility for the duration of their sentence. Another is the employment of quarantine measures to contain the outbreak of an infectious disease. But states can also be found to limit the freedom of other (categories of) persons to choose their place of residence and move at liberty around the country for a wide variety of reasons.

Stateless persons are reportedly a common object of such restrictions and this has a severely negative impact on their enjoyment of other rights. In Thailand, restrictions placed on the freedom of movement of stateless and undocumented persons are impairing access to birth registration procedures as well as facilities such as healthcare and schooling.[24] In Bhutan, the stateless ethnic Nepalese are curtailed in their freedom of movement within the country and "adding insult to

---

[23] Human Rights Committee, *General Comment 25: The Right to Participate in Public Affairs, Voting Rights and the Right of Equal Access to Public Service,* A/51/40 vol.1, Geneva: 1996, para. 12.

[24] W. Courtland Robinson, *Thailand: Background paper on human rights, refugees and asylum seekers,* A Writenet Report commissioned by UNHCR, July 2004, pages 16-17. See also Laura van Waas, *Is Permanent Illegality Inevitable? The Challenges to Ensuring Birth Registration and the Right to a Nationality for the Children of Irregular Migrants - Thailand and the Dominican Republic,* Woking: 2006, page 38.

injury, people's inability to cross checkpoints makes it difficult for them to appeal their census status or otherwise claim their citizenship in Bhutan's capital".[25] While, in Myanmar

> the freedom of movement of the Rohingyas is severely restricted. They are virtually confined to their respective villages, unable to access medical and educational services, due, inter alia, to the fact that, should they wish to travel outside their respective villages, they would require official authorisation and must pay a fee which in many cases they cannot afford. This restriction, which is not applied to the Rakhine population in Rakhine State, seriously affects their standard of living, particularly with regard to food security. When Rohingyas nevertheless do attempt to travel without authorisation, if apprehended, they are reportedly arrested and imprisoned.[26]

Indeed, more broadly, the "treatment of the stateless has included internal relocation, often to harsh and inhospitable areas"[27] and similarly to refugees, stateless persons are also commonly subject to (immigration) detention or confinement to camps.[28] With some notion of the problems experienced by the stateless in practice, the following paragraphs will uncover what international law has to say about the internal freedom of movement of these persons.

2.1.1 The 1954 Convention relating to the Status of Stateless Persons

Stateless persons are guaranteed "freedom of movement" in article 26 of the 1954 Statelessness Convention. This provision in fact concentrates in its entirety on the internal aspect of freedom of movement and determines that

> each Contracting State shall accord to stateless persons lawfully in its territory the right to choose their place of residence and to move freely within its territory, subject to any regulations applicable to aliens generally in the same circumstances.[29]

---

[25] Human Rights Watch, *We don't want to be refugees again,* HRW Briefing Paper for the 14th Ministerial Joint Committee of Bhutan and Nepal, 19 May 2003, page 18.

[26] Recall that the Rohingyas are a stateless population group in Myanmar. Doudou Diène, *Report by the Special Rapporteur on contemporary forms of racism, racial discrimination, xenophobia and related intolerance, Addendum – Summary of cases transmitted to Governments and replies received,* A/HRC/4/19/Add.1, 5 June 2007, paragraph 126.

[27] UNHCR, *Stateless persons: a discussion note,* EC/1992/SCP/CRP.4, Geneva: 1 April 1992, para. 9.

[28] Consider, among others, the stateless Bihari living dispersed over 66 camps in Bangladesh and the stateless ethnic Nepalese from Bhutan living as refugees in camps in Nepal. See Refugees International, *Stateless Biharis in Bangladesh: A humanitarian nightmare,* RI Bulletin, 13 December 2004; UNHCR, *Unending Limbo: Warehousing Bhutanese Refugees in Nepal,* World Refugee Survey 2004, page 102. See also James Hathaway, *The Rights of Refugees Under International Law*, Cambridge University Press, Cambridge: 2005, pages 695 – 704; David Weissbrodt; Clay Collins, 'The Human Rights of Stateless Persons', in *Human Rights Quarterly,* Vol. 28, 2006, pages 267-268.

[29] Note that two states lodged reservations to this article upon ratification of the 1954 Statelessness Convention – both reserving the right to designate a place of residence for stateless persons. Zambia

The wording of this article betrays several weaknesses. Only stateless persons whose presence on the territory of the state in question is authorised are entitled to invoke this right. Stateless persons with an irregular immigration status are thus entirely excluded from the protection of the provision.[30] This may prove to be a serious limitation in practice since many of the world's stateless populations have an irregular or uncertain status in their host country – a problem that will be elucidated in section 2.2.

Meanwhile, even having met the precondition of lawful presence, stateless persons are not guaranteed an absolute right of free movement or choice of residence but are instead assimilated with other non-nationals. The Convention does not set any substantive limits to the measures that may be imposed. Wherever restrictions are placed on foreigners' freedom of internal movement, these may also apply to stateless persons, so long as the constraints do not deliberately target stateless persons.[31] This approach "was considered sufficient because free residence and movement are ordinarily granted all aliens".[32] Yet even then it was admitted that some states do enforce restrictions, a fact evidenced by the examples above.[33] As we now turn to look at the right to internal free movement under international human rights law we see that attention is also paid to the substance and purpose of restrictive measures, thereby potentially affording stateless persons broader protection.

2.1.2 International human rights law

The Universal Declaration of Human Rights includes a concise expression of the right to internal freedom of movement in article 13, paragraph 1: "Everyone has the right to freedom of movement and residence within the borders of each state". According to this formulation, nationality is irrelevant for the enjoyment of this right since it addresses the entitlement to "everyone" in respect of "each state". Neither, it would appear, is immigration status relevant.[34] As we turn to other sources of human rights norms, the terms narrow. The Civil and Political Rights Covenant determines that

---

reserved this right unconditionally while the Netherlands would only invoke this possibility where public interest is at stake.

[30] Basic guarantees against detention and certain restrictions on the freedom of movement for refugees who entered the state unlawfully were included in the 1951 Refugee Convention (article 31) where they form a compliment to its own article 26 that provides for internal freedom of movement and residence for lawfully present refugees in the same terms as adopted in the 1954 Statelessness Convention. However, article 31 was dropped from the 1954 Statelessness Convention, leaving the contracting parties to restrict the freedom of movement of unlawfully present stateless persons as they see fit.

[31] James Hathaway, *The Rights of Refugees Under International Law*, Cambridge University Press, Cambridge: 2005, page 712.

[32] Nehemiah Robinson, *Convention relating to the status of stateless persons - Its history and interpretation*, UNHCR, Geneva: 1955, page 78.

[33] Nehemiah Robinson, *Convention relating to the status of stateless persons - Its history and interpretation*, UNHCR, Geneva: 1955, page 78.

[34] Although since the provision only addresses movement *within* the borders or a state it is equally possible to conclude that this implies that a person must gain regular access to that state to claim this entitlement

> everybody lawfully within the territory of a State shall, within that territory, have the right to liberty of movement and freedom to choose his residence.[35]

This article explicitly embraces the precondition that a person must be lawfully within the territory of a state before he is entitled to liberty of movement and choice of residence within its borders. Eligibility to invoke this right is therefore dependent on immigration status rather than nationality. Nationals of the state in question will always meet this requirement since by virtue of their nationality their presence on state soil is automatically lawful.[36] Stateless persons (and all other non-nationals) must be lawfully present under domestic immigration regulations before they can rely on this provision. The ICCPR thus sets the same prerequisite for the enjoyment of the right to internal freedom of movement as the 1954 Statelessness Convention. However, once this precondition has been met, the level of protection offered by the International Covenant is higher than that provided for by the 1954 Statelessness Convention. The statelessness instrument prescribes treatment on a par with non-nationals generally while the ICCPR in principle entitles lawfully present non-nationals equal protection to nationals.[37]

The human rights norm does allow certain exceptions to the general rule of free movement within the borders of a state. The right housed in article 12 of the ICCPR is, in fact, qualified by a clause that closely succeeds it which allows for restrictions to free movement if they "are provided by law, are necessary to protect national security, public order (ordre public), public health or morals or the rights and freedoms of others, and are consistent with the other rights recognised in the present covenant".[38] Thus while the 1954 Statelessness Convention permits states to curtail the freedom of movement of non-nationals as they see fit, so long as they do not specifically target stateless persons, the human rights standard shows greater concern for the substance of any restrictions that encroach upon this basic liberty.

---

[35] Article 12 of the 1966 International Covenant on Civil and Political Rights. A comparable approach can be found in other human rights instruments and documents such as the Declaration on the Human Rights of Individuals Who are not Nationals of the Country in which They Live (article 5, paragraph 3); the Migrant Workers Convention (article 39); the American Convention on Human Rights (article 22); Protocol No. 4 to the European Convention on Human Rights (article 2); and the African Charter on Human and Peoples' Rights (article 12).

[36] This is inherent in the right of nationals to (re)enter and remain in the territory of the state of nationality that will be dealt with in greater detail in section 2.2. See also Human Rights Committee, *CCPR General Comment No. 27: Freedom of movement,* Geneva: 2 November 1999, para. 4.

[37] Human Rights Committee, *CCPR General Comment No. 15: The Position of Aliens under the Covenant,* Geneva: Geneva: 11 April 1986, para. 8. See also the case of *Tatishvili v. Russia* brought before the European Court of Human Rights. There, a *stateless* applicant successfully invoked article 2 of Protocol No. 4 to the European Convention on Human Rights to claim free movement and residence rights. The court determined the applicant to be lawfully resident – a fact that the Russian government strongly contested – and the fact of statelessness was then irrelevant to the enjoyment of free internal movement. European Court of Human Rights, *Case of Tatishvili v. Russia,* Application No. 1509/02, 22 February 2007.

[38] Article 12, paragraph 3 of the 1966 International Covenant on Civil and Political Rights. Similar clauses can also be found in the other human rights instruments referred in note 35.

So-called "permissible limitations"[39] must have the objective of protecting one of the values or interests set out - such as public order - and must *also* be necessary to achieve that goal *and* be provided by law *and* be in line with other fundamental rights.[40] Restrictions are therefore to be limited to "exceptional circumstances".[41] Although such broad notions as national security or public order can be invoked to cover a wide range of situations,[42] the requirement that the measures taken are also *necessary* serves to limit the possibilities of invoking this clause. This proportionality test necessitates that the measures be "appropriate to achieve their protective function [...] the least intrusive instrument amongst those which might achieve the desired result and [...] proportionate to the interest to be protected".[43] Any difference in treatment between nationals and lawfully present non-nationals - any measure that is specifically addressed to non-nationals or a particular group such as the stateless – is to be treated as a restriction to the general norm of liberty of movement and must satisfy all the aforementioned "demanding legal provisos".[44] This does not altogether rule out the possibility of imposing such restrictions but it does compel states to justify any relevant measures as specified. In this respect, human rights norms offer stateless persons stronger guarantees than the 1954 Statelessness Convention that the essence of the right to free movement and choice of residence within the territory of a state remain in tact.

2.2 International freedom of movement

Questions relating to the right of individuals to travel between territories and to settle on the soil of a foreign state - as well as the right of states to refuse or expel foreigners - have long been a favoured subject of debate by jurists and philosophers alike.[45] These matters are now dealt with under norms concerning the international dimension of the freedom of movement which has been further deconstructed into

[39] Sarah Joseph; Jenny Schultz; Melissa Castan, *The International Covenant on Civil and Political Rights. Cases, Materials and Commentary*, Oxford University Press, Oxford: 2000, page 256.

[40] In particular the principle of non-discrimination. Hurst Hannum, *The Right to Leave and Return in International Law and Practice*, Martinus Nijhoff Publishers, Dordrecht: 1987, page 44.

[41] Human Rights Committee, *CCPR General Comment No. 27: Freedom of movement,* Geneva: 2 November 1999, para. 11.

[42] See the examples in Sarah Joseph; Jenny Schultz; Melissa Castan, *The International Covenant on Civil and Political Rights. Cases, Materials and Commentary*, Oxford University Press, Oxford: 2000, pages 258-259.

[43] Human Rights Committee, *CCPR General Comment No. 27: Freedom of movement,* Geneva: 2 November 1999, para. 14. See also Hurst Hannum, *The Right to Leave and Return in International Law and Practice*, Martinus Nijhoff Publishers, Dordrecht: 1987, pages 26-27.

[44] James Hathaway, *The Rights of Refugees Under International Law*, Cambridge University Press, Cambridge: 2005, page 716. See further Human Rights Committee, *CCPR General Comment No. 15: The Position of Aliens under the Covenant,* Geneva: Geneva: 11 April 1986, para. 8; Human Rights Committee, *CCPR General Comment No. 27: Freedom of movement,* Geneva: 2 November 1999, para. 4; David Weissbrodt, *Final Report on Prevention of Discrimination - The Rights of Non-Citizens,* E/CN.4/Sub.2/2003/23, 26 May 2003, para. 39.

[45] See Hurst Hannum, *The Right to Leave and Return in International Law and Practice*, Martinus Nijhoff Publishers, Dordrecht: 1987, page 3; Carmen Tiburcio, "Chapter IX. Public Rights" in *The human rights of aliens under international and comparative law*, Kluwer Law International, The Hague: 2001, pages 210-211.

three specific individual entitlements: the right to enter (or return), the right to remain and the right to leave. For the stateless, these rights can be critical. We have already noted that many of the rights espoused in the 1954 Statelessness Convention are granted to a stateless person only once they have attained physical, lawful or even durable access to the territory of the contracting state.[46] Human rights norms also commonly require the individual to be within the territory of the state (or otherwise subject to its jurisdiction) to be invoked.[47] If a stateless person enjoys the right to enter or remain on the soil of a particular state, this can play a pivotal role in providing (continued) access to other rights.

However, as commented in chapter IX, the right to (re)enter and reside in a state has traditionally belonged to the substance and indeed the very function of nationality. This fact signals a grave potential difficulty for the stateless: no nationality so no automatic right to (re)enter or reside anywhere. With this observation in mind, the right to international free movement for the stateless is not only relevant to the ability to "vote with one's feet", as described in the introduction to this section, but indeed reveals a more basic dilemma: where do they have the right to live? As such, a review of the international legal framework relating to stateless persons' right to international free movement could not be more pertinent. It seeks to discover whether the international community has put in place the guarantees needed to protect the stateless from becoming the object of a game of human ping-pong – from facing life in physical as well as legal limbo, being passed from one state to another, with no officially acknowledged homeland to settle in.[48] Meanwhile, when a national travels abroad it is his citizenship that guarantees to the host state that, in whatever eventuality, there is always a state to which he can be returned and which is bound to accept him. In the absence of such an "escape clause" for the host state, the stateless may find themselves unwelcome and consequently their travel prospects limited. Moreover, in order to actually exercise free movement across an international frontier, "a passport has become a legal as well as a practical necessity"[49] and this all-important travel document is typically issued by the country of nationality.[50]

---

[46] See in particular the discussion of the different "levels of attachment" required for access to the 1954 Statelessness Convention rights in chapter IX, section 3.

[47] See for example article 2 of the 1966 International Covenant on Civil and Political Rights. A person may also be subject to the jurisdiction of a state through the bond of nationality, but the stateless do not enjoy this position with any state.

[48] See on the problems of detention and the ping-pong effect David Weissbrodt; Clay Collins, 'The Human Rights of Stateless Persons', in *Human Rights Quarterly,* Vol. 28, 2006, page 268; Stefanie Grant, "The Legal Protection of Stranded Migrants" in *International Migration Law,* R. Cholewinski, R. Perruchoud and E. MacDonald [Eds.], TMS Asser Press, The Hague 2007, pages 29-47.

[49] Hurst Hannum, *The Right to Leave and Return in International Law and Practice*, Martinus Nijhoff Publishers, Dordrecht: 1987, page 21. A passport provides the "prima facie guarantee that another state is prepared to accept an alien that the destination state may choose not to admit or to expel", thereby facilitating (temporary) entry into the state of destination. John Torpey, *The Invention of the Passport. Surveillance, Citizenship and the State*, Cambridge University Press, Cambridge: 2000, page 163.

[50] Carmen Tiburcio, "Chapter IX. Public Rights" in *The human rights of aliens under international and comparative law*, Kluwer Law International, The Hague: 2001, page 217. Note that the specific problem of access to (travel) documentation is dealt with in detail in return in greater detail in chapter XII where we consider the "special needs" of the stateless.

It is a painful irony then that statelessness and displacement often go hand-in-hand. For a start, migration has proven to be an instigating factor in the loss of nationality and the creation of statelessness.[51] Consider the situation of the Lhotsampas (ethnic Nepalese Hindus) of Bhutan whose statelessness was consolidated when they were forced to flee to neighbouring Nepal and were deemed, through this act, to have voluntarily forfeited their Bhutanese citizenship. They have subsequently been stuck in exile for over a decade, their stay tolerated but not officially recognised in Nepal and all calls for repatriation refused by the Bhutanese authorities.[52] How are such situations addressed in international standards on the right to enter, remain or leave a state? In other instances displacement has followed statelessness and is a consequence of the newly vulnerable status of the individuals concerned - the lack of a nationality may be just one manifestation of the severe treatment to which the population is exposed.[53] Here again, the fact of statelessness commonly presents an irreconcilable obstacle to eventual repatriation of refugees and other such displaced persons.[54] Yet neither does the circumstance of statelessness appear to provide any particular opportunities with respect to entry or residence in a host state.

Finally then, it is not uncommon for stateless groups or individuals to find themselves cast into an irregular situation or even expelled as a result of their loss of nationality. Consider the case of a man who was rendered stateless in the Netherlands through the withdrawal of his Dutch citizenship on the premise that he had failed to fulfil his commitment to renounce his Egyptian nationality, even though he had in fact managed to lose this other citizenship. The loss of his Dutch nationality brought with it the loss of an automatic right of residence and "in order to be readmitted as a foreign national, he had to return to Egypt to apply for a long-term visa, which was not possible because the applicant no longer had an Egyptian passport".[55] Meanwhile,

> incidents arousing international concern have included expulsion of large groups of stateless people from their countries of habitual residence [and] non-readmission by the countries of habitual residence of such groups.[56]

---

[51] Be reminded of the discussion of the link between migration and statelessness in chapter VII.

[52] Advisory Board on Human Security (prepared by Constantin Sokoloff), *Denial of Citizenship: A Challenge to Human Security,* February 2005, page 10; Hiram Ruiz and Michelle Berg, *Unending limbo: Warehousing Bhutanese Refugees in Nepal,* UNHCR World Refugee Survey 2004, pages 98-105; Michael Hutt, *Unbecoming Citizens. Culture, Nationhood, and the Flight of Refugees from Bhutan.*, Oxford University Press, New Delhi: 2005, pages 147-149 and 221. At the time of writing, efforts were underway to resolve this protracted situation through resettlement to various third countrys. See UNHCR, *Nepal: large-scale resettlement of refugees from Bhutan,* Briefing Notes, 25 March 2008.

[53] Frequently, "stateless and denaturalised populations are obliged to flee from their usual place of residence". UNHCR, "Statelessness and Citizenship" in *The State of the World's Refugees - A Humanitarian Agenda*, Oxford University Press, Oxford: 1997, page 244.

[54] UNHCR, "Statelessness and Citizenship" in *The State of the World's Refugees - A Humanitarian Agenda*, Oxford University Press, Oxford: 1997, page 246.

[55] Betty de Hart; Kees Groenendijk, "Multiple Nationality: The Practice of Germany and the Netherlands" in R. Cholewinski (ed) *International Migration Law*, TMC Asser Press, The Hague: 2007, page 99.

[56] UNHCR, *Stateless persons: a discussion note,* EC/1992/SCP/CRP.4, Geneva: 1 April 1992, para. 8.

For example, the mass expulsion of Bidoons from Kuwait contributed to the overall exodus of some 100,000 stateless persons from the country in the early 1990's while at around the same time Mauritania expelled some 60,000 black Africans, claiming that they were not Mauritanian nationals.[57] This begs the question whether the stateless are not protected from expulsion by international standards in the sphere of the right to international free movement, such as the right to *(re)enter* and to *remain*. Or in other words, in view of the foregoing, has the 1954 Statelessness Convention addressed the right to (re)enter a state for those who lack any citizenship and/or has this function of nationality in some way been superseded by developments in international human rights law – at least in relation to the stateless?

2.2.1 The 1954 Convention relating to the Status of Stateless Persons

While the 1954 Statelessness Convention requires physical, lawful or even durable presence on state territory for the enjoyment of many of the rights espoused, the instrument does not provide stateless persons with the right to enter a contracting party in order to claim the protection offered. Indeed, arguably the most noteworthy change made to the text of the 1951 Refugee Convention when it was transformed into the 1954 Statelessness Convention was the omission of an equivalent to article 33 on *non-refoulement*.[58] Central to the refugee protection regime, this article forms the basis for the entitlement of refugees to gain, or at least retain,[59] access to the territory of a state party. When read in conjunction with article 31 of the 1951 Refugee Convention on non-penalisation of unlawful entry – another provision omitted from the 1954 Statelessness Convention – the prohibition of refoulement provides "a limited right of (at least) temporary admission for asylum seekers to access fair and effective refugee status procedures".[60] Once refugee status has been recognised on the basis of the definition in article 1 of the Refugee Convention, the prohibition of refoulement ensures that the refugee has the right to remain in the

[57] UNHCR, "Statelessness and Citizenship" in *The State of the World's Refugees - A Humanitarian Agenda*, Oxford University Press, Oxford: 1997, pages 244-245. See also Human Rights Committee, *Concluding Observations: Kuwait*, A/55/40 vol.I, Geneva: 2000, paras. 477-479.

[58] A resolution was elaborated in the Final Act of the Conference which adopted the 1954 Convention relating to the Status of Stateless Persons recalling that the prohibition of *refoulement* (as housed in article 33 of the 1951 Refugee Convention) was considered to be a generally accepted principle and that to include an equivalent in the 1954 Statelessness Convention was unnecessary.

[59] Evident already in the debate surrounding the formulation of the 1951 Refugee Convention, there remains some contention to this day as to whether the principle of *non-refoulement* encompasses a duty for states to admit refugees to their territory rather than strictly a duty not to return refugees. Nevertheless, Goodwin-Gill concludes that: "By and large, States in their practice and in their recorded views, have recognised that *non-refoulement* applies to the moment at which asylum seekers present themselves for entry, either within a state or at its border. Certain factual elements may be necessary before the principle is triggered, but the concept now encompasses both non-return and non-rejection". Guy Goodwin-Gill, *The Refugee in International Law*, Oxford University Press, Oxford: 2007, page 208.

[60] Guy Guy Goodwin-Gill, *The Refugee in International Law*, Oxford University Press, Oxford: 2007, page 384. It is important to note that such admission for the purposes of determining refugee status must be considered to amount to lawful presence for the purposes of the application of the convention rights. See also James Hathaway, *The Rights of Refugees Under International Law*, Cambridge University Press, Cambridge: 2005, pages 177-179 and page 301.

host state so long as the risk of persecution endures.[61] In contrast, the 1954 Statelessness Convention "doesn't oblige States to grant a legal stay to an individual while his/her request for recognition as a stateless person is being assessed",[62] nor once this status has been determined. Obviously, if a stateless person is also a refugee, his right to enter or remain in the host state will be determined on the basis of the 1951 Refugee Convention.[63] But without provision for lawful entry or regularisation of a stateless person's immigration status under the 1954 Statelessness Convention, state parties are free to treat the non-refugee stateless as any other non-national and subject them to the regular provisions of domestic immigration law. There is nothing in the convention to prevent a state from refusing entry to a stateless person.[64] And if he nevertheless enters the state – unauthorised – he may be deported or subjected to whatever penalties domestic immigration law imposes.[65] In order for a stateless person to become eligible for the rights proclaimed in the 1954 Statelessness Convention on the condition of (lawful) presence or a closer level of attachment, he must satisfy the conditions set in municipal immigration law.

These facts uncover what is arguably the core weakness of the 1954 Statelessness Convention: that with no state compelled to allow a stateless person to enter or settle on its territory, these individuals are stuck in a true legal limbo. They may be passed from one state to another, kept in indefinite detention pending the possibility of deportation or be forever informally "tolerated" without achieving a lawful status (the essential precondition for access to many of the rights housed in the Convention itself). In a Handbook for dealing with statelessness, UNHCR has determined that

> once an individual is on a State's territory, a determination of his/her nationality status may be the only way to identify a solution to his/her plight. If the individual is determined to be stateless, and if there is no possibility of return to the country of former habitual residence or if there

[61] James Hathaway, *The Rights of Refugees Under International Law*, Cambridge University Press, Cambridge: 2005, page 302.

[62] UNHCR and IPU, *Nationality and statelessness. A handbook for parliamentarians*, 2005, pages 20–21.

[63] If a person qualifies both as a refugee under the definition in the 1951 Refugee Convention and as a stateless person under the definition in the 1954 Statelessness Convention, the Refugee Convention is applicable: "this follows from the purpose of the Stateless Persons Convention to cover such person to whom the Refugee Convention is not applicable". Nehemiah Robinson, *Convention relating to the status of stateless persons - Its history and interpretation*, UNHCR, Geneva: 1955, page 8.

[64] The only persons that may be able to claim some right of (re)entry into a state on the basis of the 1954 Statelessness Convention are "stateless persons regularly serving as crew members on board a ship flying the flag of a Contracting State". But even in these very limited cases, the state is only required to "give sympathetic consideration" to admitting the stateless individual – obliging the state to consider such requests but by no means providing an absolute or secure guarantee. See article 11 of the 1954 Convention relating to the Status of Stateless Persons.

[65] As previously noted, the 1954 Statelessness Convention does not include an equivalent to article 31 of the 1951 Refugee Convention which elaborates a norm on the non-imposition of penalties on refugees on account of their unlawful entry or presence.

> is no such country, then admittance to the State and some type of legal stay may be the only solution.[66]

While this may indeed be the only conceivable solution for the individual, the 1954 Statelessness Convention fails to set out any such guarantee.[67]

Once a state has recognised the lawful presence of a stateless person, however, the right to remain becomes relatively secure. Article 31 of the Convention devotes its first paragraph to the general rule that "Contracting States shall not expel a stateless person lawfully in their territory save on grounds of national security or public order".[68] States retain full discretion to expel stateless persons who have no authorisation to be on their territory,[69] but

> once a stateless person has been admitted or legalised, he is entitled to stay in the country indefinitely and can forfeit this right only by becoming a national security risk or by disturbing public order.[70]

There must be "exceptional circumstances" for the exceptions to non-expulsion to be invoked.[71] Where expulsion is envisaged on national security grounds, such exceptional circumstances may be at stake when the presence or actions of the individual in question "give rise to an objectively reasonable, real possibility of directly or indirectly inflicted substantial harm to the host state's most basic interests, including the risk of an armed attack on its territory or its citizens or the destruction of its democratic institutions".[72] For public order to be a ground for

---

[66] UNHCR and IPU, *Nationality and statelessness. A handbook for parliamentarians*, 2005, page 21.

[67] UNHCR therefore calls upon states to at least ensure that detention with a view to expulsion is not unduly prolonged and that where expulsion is found to be impracticable, "states should consider giving [stateless] delinquents the same treatment as national delinquents" rather than concentrating on giving effect to the order. UNHCR Executive Committee, *Conclusion No. 7: Expulsion,* 28th session, Geneva 1977, paras. (d)-(e).

[68] Since the entire article was adopted – eventually and after much debate – in the same wording as it is included in the 1951 Refugee Convention, we can once again turn to the discussions of this instrument for further explanation of the content of this provision. Nehemiah Robinson, *Convention relating to the status of stateless persons - Its history and interpretation*, UNHCR, Geneva: 1955, pages 95 and 98. Note that objections by many states to the format of this article were not entirely dispelled by the decision to stick to the text as adopted in the 1951 Refugee Convention. This article of the 1954 Statelessness Convention on expulsion went on to attract a substantial number of reservations as states ratified the instrument. See the overview of *Declarations and Reservations to the 1954 Convention relating to the Status of Stateless Persons* provided by the UNHCR.

[69] Nevertheless, thanks also to the resolution included in the Final Act to the Convention, the principle of *non-refoulement* may have some bearing on the freedom of states to expel stateless persons even when unlawfully present. See note 58.

[70] Nehemiah Robinson, *Convention relating to the status of stateless persons - Its history and interpretation*, UNHCR, Geneva: 1955, pages 96-97.

[71] UNHCR Executive Committee, *Conclusion No. 7: Expulsion,* 28th session, Geneva: 1977, para. (a).

[72] James Hathaway, *The Rights of Refugees Under International Law*, Cambridge University Press, Cambridge: 2005, page 679.

expulsion, a stateless person would have to have committed a serious crime or caused severe offence to the social norms of the host state.[73]

Alongside this substantive aspect of article 31 of the 1954 Statelessness Convention is a procedural dimension that further strengthens the protection against expulsion of lawfully present stateless persons. Not only are states compelled to enact an expulsion order only "in pursuance of a decision reached in accordance with due process of law", but they must also provide the opportunity to seek a review of this decision.[74] The final paragraph of article 31 deals with the position of the stateless person once the state has made the final decision to expel. The individual must be given some opportunity to seek *legal admission* to another country. This is to prevent the situation where the stateless person is forced to enter another territory illegally or clandestinely – being without a nationality, there is no state that is obliged to admit him. In the meantime, the stateless person may be detained or subject to other restrictions.[75] Considering that in reality the implementation of an expulsion order is often unfeasible,[76] there is a danger that detention becomes indefinite.[77]

Although article 31 of the 1954 Statelessness Convention does therefore attempt to provide basic substantive and procedural guarantees against the expulsion of stateless persons, its value in practice is questionable since it does not resolve the problem of lawful access to a state in the first place. In this respect, the conclusion drawn by Special Rapporteur Maurice Kamto when studying the provision in the context of work on the "Expulsion of Aliens" for the International Law Commission is insightful:

> It seems that the rules for the expulsion of stateless persons too easily reproduce the wording of the rules for the expulsion of refugees.[78]

---

[73] Nehemiah Robinson, *Convention relating to the status of stateless persons - Its history and interpretation*, UNHCR, Geneva: 1955, page 99; James Hathaway, *The Rights of Refugees Under International Law*, Cambridge University Press, Cambridge: 2005, pages 685-686.

[74] Article 31, paragraph 2 of the 1954 Convention relating to the Status of Stateless Persons. Note that adherence to due process of law is *always* required in the decision-making procedure, while the opportunity to seek a review of the decision may be restricted for "compelling reasons of national security". See also James Hathaway, *The Rights of Refugees Under International Law*, Cambridge University Press, Cambridge: 2005, page 675. The specification that states must allow the stateless person to appeal against the expulsion order is of great importance. In section 4 of this chapter we will see that while the 1954 Statelessness Convention offers a basic right of access to courts, there is no guarantee that a state's judiciary will have subject-matter jurisdiction over all matters that may affect stateless persons. Thanks to article 31, states are required to provide at least some form of review by a competent body of decisions on expulsion – although admittedly this need not necessarily be a court of law.

[75] "The Contracting States reserve the right to apply during that period such internal measures as they may deem necessary". Article 31, paragraph 3 of the 1954 Convention relating to the Status of Stateless Persons.

[76] Nehemiah Robinson, *Convention relating to the status of stateless persons - Its history and interpretation*, UNHCR, Geneva: 1955, page 100; Guy Goodwin-Gill, *The Refugee in International Law*, Oxford University Press, Oxford: 2007, page 264.

[77] A problem that will be looked at in more detail in section 7.1 below.

[78] International Law Commission, *Third report on the expulsion of aliens,* prepared by Special Rapporteur Maurice Kamto, A/CN.4/581, 19 April 2007, page 31.

Recall that the latter are contained within an instrument that does broach the problem of admission alongside the question of non-expulsion.

Finally, there is one other provision in the 1954 Statelessness Convention that should be mentioned since it has some bearing on a stateless person's right to *re-enter* the territory of a state from abroad. That is article 28 on travel documents. Once a stateless person is already *lawfully staying* within a state party, he is entitled to "travel documents for the purposes of travel outside their territory". According to paragraph 13 of the Schedule that applies to such documents, the papers issued shall in principle enable him to "re-enter the territory of the issuing State at any time during the period of its validity".[79] To a greatly limited extent, this provision allows stateless persons to benefit from the same right to return as is granted to nationals of the host state, which – together with the travel documents themselves – will enable the stateless to exercise the right to leave and will facilitate international travel.[80]

2.2.2 International human rights law

A study of contemporary international standards relating to the admittance, non-admittance and expulsion of non-nationals by Special Rapporteur Maurice Kamto for the International Law Commission concluded that customary international law recognises the right of every state to "set the conditions for the entry and residence of aliens in its territory" as well as "the right to expel them".[81] This means that, in principle, an individual may be refused admittance to – or expelled from – a state of which he is not a national.[82] For the stateless: *every* state. The international freedom of movement of the stateless may therefore be severely curtailed.[83] However, this

[79] It should be noted that "compelling reasons of national security or public order" may be invoked by a state party in order to refuse travel documents to a lawfully staying stateless person. Article 28 of the 1954 Convention relating to the Status of Stateless Persons. Furthermore, it is possible for states to elaborate a statement on the travel document issued that waives the duty to re-admit the stateless person. Paragraph 13, section 1 of the Schedule to Article 28 of the 1954 Convention relating to the Status of Stateless Persons.

[80] The provision of documentation to stateless persons under the 1954 Convention relating to the Status of Stateless Persons is discussed further in chapter XII, section 2.1.

[81] International Law Commission, *Preliminary report on the expulsion of aliens,* prepared by Special Rapporteur Maurice Kamto, A/CN.4/554, 2 June 2005, pages 6-7. In other words, international law does not "spell out specific criteria for the granting of residence permits". Human Rights Committee, *Case of Tsjarov v. Estonia,* CCPR/C/91/D/1223/2003, Geneva: 14 November 2007, paragraph 7.5.

[82] This is a corollary of the fact that, as introduced in chapter IX, section 1, one of the inherent functions of nationality is the right of access to the respective state's territory - nationals are free to enter and remain in *their* state.

[83] Note that all human rights documents are in agreement in granting the right to leave to *everyone* in respect of *any state.* Nationality has become irrelevant to this question. See Article 13, paragraph 2 of the Universal Declaration of Human Rights; Article 12, paragraph 2 of the International Covenant on Civil and Political Rights; Article 5, paragraph (d)(ii) of the Convention on the Elimination of All Forms of Racial Discrimination; Article 8, paragraph 2 of the Convention on the Protection of All Migrant Workers and Members of Their Families; Article 2, paragraph 2 of the Fourth Protocol to the European Convention on Human Rights; Article 22, paragraph 2 of the American Convention on Human Rights; and Article 12, paragraph 2 of the African Charter on Human and Peoples' Rights. Moreover, included in the right to leave is the entitlement to the requisite travel documents. See Human

statement requires some nuance, for states' discretion in these matters is not absolute and the overall international standard is more appropriately summarised as follows:

> The admission of aliens is in the discretion of each state – except where a State is bound by treaty to accord such admission.[84]

Human rights law has begun to encroach upon the freedom of states to admit, refuse or expel non-nationals at will. Yet the right to move freely across state borders is still rather complicated as far as international human rights law is concerned because its content continues to be greatly influenced by a tension between consideration for the position of the individual and respect for the sovereignty and territorial supremacy of states – a tension that is particularly fraught in the context of immigration policy.[85] Nevertheless, stateless persons may now be able to benefit from a variety of human rights norms in seeking to enter or remain in a particular country.

Rights Committee, *CCPR General Comment No. 27: Freedom of movement,* Geneva: 2 November 1999, para. 9. States may impose restrictions on the right to leave where this is necessary for reasons such as national security, but the measures must meet the same strict conditions as were outlined above with respect to limitations imposed on the internal freedom of movement (section 2.1.2). However, the greatest practical limitation in effectuating the right to leave, in particular for stateless persons, is presented by the fact that there is not necessarily a corresponding right to enter another country – and with the world comprehensively divided into a patchwork of states, this question of access to territory is crucial. See further on the right to leave Hurst Hannum, *The Right to Leave and Return in International Law and Practice*, Martinus Nijhoff Publishers, Dordrecht: 1987.

[84] Paul Weis, *Nationality and Statelessness in International Law*, Kluwer Academic Publishers Group, Dordrecht: 1979, page 45. Note that the state may also be bound by obligations arising from customary international law. The UN Declaration on the Human Rights of Individuals Who are not Nationals of the Country in which They Live provides a similar account of the overall obligation of states in article 2, paragraph 1 where it determines that none of its provisions shall "be interpreted as restricting the right of any State to promulgate laws and regulations concerning the entry of aliens and the terms and conditions of their stay [...] However, such laws and regulations shall not be incompatible with the international legal obligations of that state".

[85] It is of interest to note that since the early 1960s there have been numerous unsuccessful attempts to further elaborate the content of the right to international freedom of movement. See the three studies prepared for the UN Sub-Commission on Prevention of Discrimination and Protection of Minorities (in 1963, 1988 and 1997); the *Draft Principles on Freedom and Non-Discrimination in respect of the Right of Everyone to Leave Any Country, including His Own, and to Return to His Country,* prepared by Special Rapporteur José Ingles in 1963; a document of the same name approved by the UN Sub-Commission on Prevention of Discrimination and Protection of Minorities in 1963; the *Declaration on the Right to Leave and the Right to Return,* adopted by Uppsala Colloquium of legal and human rights experts in Uppsala, Sweden in 1972; and the *Strasbourg Declaration on the Right to Leave and Return,* adopted at a meeting of international lawyers convened by the International Institute of Human Rights in Strasbourg in 1986. The text of the draft declarations can be found in Hurst Hannum, *The Right to Leave and Return in International Law and Practice*, Martinus Nijhoff Publishers, Dordrecht: 1987, pages 142-158. The most recent efforts focus on the "expulsion of aliens" and are being undertaken by the International Law Commission under the guidance of Special Rapporteur Maurice Kamto. At the time of writing he had submitted his third report on the subject which included a number of draft articles. International Law Commission, *Preliminary report on the expulsion of aliens,* prepared by Special Rapporteur Maurice Kamto, A/CN.4/554, 2 June 2005; *Second report on the expulsion of aliens*, A/CN.4/573, 20 July 2006; *Third report on the expulsion of aliens*, A/CN.4/581, 19 April 2007.

The Human Rights Committee has identified three initial norms that restrict the aforementioned freedom of states to refuse entry to or expel non-nationals, including stateless persons, in its General Comment on the position of aliens under the ICCPR:

> It is in principle a matter for the State to decide who it will admit to its territory. However, in certain circumstances an alien may enjoy the protection of the Covenant even in relation to entry or residence, for example, when considerations of non-discrimination, prohibition of inhuman treatment and respect for family life arise.[86]

States are therefore prevented from maintaining immigration policies that unjustifiably differentiate between different groups – for example on the grounds of religion or gender – by the international norm of non-discrimination or equality of treatment.[87] The prohibition of *refoulement,* a fundamental principle of international law that is espoused in numerous documents,[88] protects all non-nationals (including stateless persons) from being "deported to a country in which they may be subjected to persecution or abuse".[89] Finally, norms addressing the respect for and protection of family life – and *private* life - may provide a right to remain for non-nationals, including stateless persons, in certain circumstances.[90] Indeed, in a case before the

---

[86] Human Rights Committee, *CCPR General Comment No. 15: The Position of Aliens under the Covenant,* Geneva: Geneva: 11 April 1986, para. 5. See also UN Committee on the Elimination of Racial Discrimination, *General Recommendation 30: Discrimination against Non-citizens,* CERD/C/64/Misc.11/Rev.3, New York: 2004, paras. 9, 25, 27 and 28. See for instance the case of *Aumeeruddy-Cziffra v. Mauritius* where the Human Rights Committee ruled that domestic immigration law that placed greater restrictions on the right of access to state territory for the non-national husbands of Mauritian women than for the non-national wives of Mauritian men violated the principle of equal treatment of the sexes and therefore constituted a violation of articles 2 (1), 3 and 26 of the ICCPR. Human Rights Committee, *Case of Shirin Aumeeruddy-Cziffra and 19 other Mautitian women v. Mauritius,* Communication No. 35/1978, Geneva: 9 April 1981. See also European Court of Human Rights, *Family K and W v. The Netherlands,* Application No. 11278/84, 1 July 1985. Both cases are discussed in UN Division for the Advancement of Women, *Women, nationality and citizenship,* June 2003, pages 12-13.

[87] UN Committee on the Elimination of Racial Discrimination, *General Recommendation 30: Discrimination against Non-citizens,* CERD/C/64/Misc.11/Rev.3, New York: 2004, paras. 9 and 25. Carmen Tiburcio, "Chapter IX. Public Rights" in *The human rights of aliens under international and comparative law,* Kluwer Law International, The Hague: 2001, page 216; See also the discussion of the *East African Asians cases* before the European Court of Human Rights in Richard Lillich, *The human rights of aliens in contemporary international law,* Manchester University Press, Manchester: 1984, pages 95-96.

[88] The principle of *non-refoulement* can be found in article 33 of the 1951 Convention relating to the status of Refugees and Article 22, paragraph 8 of the American Convention on Human Rights. It is also implicit in article 3 of the Convention Against Torture; article 7 of the International Covenant on Civil and Political Rights; article 3 of the European Convention of Human Rights; and article 12, paragraph 3 of the African Charter on Human and Peoples' Rights.

[89] David Weissbrodt, *Final Report on Prevention of Discrimination - The Rights of Non-Citizens,* E/CN.4/Sub.2/2003/23, 26 May 2003, para. 54.

[90] The relevant provisions are articles 17, 23 and 24 of the International Covenant on Civil and Political Rights; Article 9 of the Convention on the Rights of the Child; Article 8 of the European Convention on Human Rights; Article 17 of the American Convention on Human Rights; and Article 18 of the African

UN Human Rights Committee, the two stateless parents of an Australian child successfully challenged the deportation order enacted by the Australian authorities, on the basis of rights related to the protection of the family and of the child.[91] And in a series of remarkable cases brought against Latvia, the European Court of Human Rights found that the deportation of – or the prolonged refusal to grant a permanent residence status to – the stateless applicants violated their right to private life.[92]

In addition to these three avenues that may offer stateless persons the right to enter or remain in a particular state in very specific circumstances, standards that relate to the expulsion of non-nationals generally may be relevant. According to these norms, collective expulsion is prohibited[93] and (lawfully present) foreigners

---

Charter on Human and Peoples' Rights. The UN Declaration on the Human Rights of Individuals Who are not Nationals of the Country in which They Live also provides (in article 5, paragraph 4) for certain rights relating to entry and residence in a state on the basis of protection of the family unit. Some ILO standards are also relevant to the right to reunification of families, including Migrant Workers Recommendation No. 151 of 1975. According to the Human Rights Committee, "the right to found a family implies, in principle, the right to procreate and live together [and] the possibility to live together implies the adoption of appropriate measures, both at the internal level and *as the case may be, in cooperation with other States, to ensure the unity or reunification of families*". Human Rights Committee, *General Comment No. 19: Protection of the family, the right to marriage and equality of the spouses*, Geneva: 27 July 1990, paragraph 5.

[91] Human Rights Committee, *Winata and Lan Li v. Australia,* CCPR/C/72/D/930/2000, Geneva: 2001, as cited in David Weissbrodt, *Final Report on Prevention of Discrimination - The Rights of Non-Citizens,* E/CN.4/Sub.2/2003/23, 26 May 2003, para. 56. The European Court of Human Rights has developed extensive case law with respect to article 8 of the European Convention and its impact on the right to enter or remain in a state. See also David Weissbrodt, *Final Report on Prevention of Discrimination - The Rights of Non-Citizens,* E/CN.4/Sub.2/2003/23, 26 May 2003, paras. 49-51 and Add.2, paras. 9-11; Carmen Tiburcio, "Chapter V. Private Rights" in *The human rights of aliens under international and comparative law*, Kluwer Law International, The Hague: 2001, pages 118-128.

[92] The construction of the argument by the court in three cases is very similar. The court considered first that "during their time in Latvia the applicants have developed the personal, social and economic ties that make up the private life of every human being" and that the deportation order or refusal to grant permanent residence constituted an interference with that private life. Thereafter, the court declares that in those circumstances "only reasons of a particularly serious nature" could justify the state's action. In all of the cases, the court found that the Latvian authorities exceeded their margin of appreciation in this sphere and did not strike a fair balance between the legitimate aim of the protection of national security / preventing disorder and the interest of the protection of the applicant's right to private life (article 8 of the European Convention on Human Rights). European Court of Human Rights, *Case of Slivenko v. Latvia,* Application No. 48321/99, 9 October 2003; *Case of Sisojeva and others v. Latvia,* Application No. 60654/00, 16 June 2005; *Case of Kaftailova v. Latvia,* Application No. 59643/00, 22 June 2006.

[93] This is explicitly elaborated in article 22, paragraph 1 of the Migrant Workers Convention; article 4 of the Fourth Protocol to the European Convention on Human Rights; article 22, paragraph 9 of the American Convention on Human Rights; and article 12, paragraph 5 of the African Charter on Human and Peoples' Rights. It is implicit in the procedural protection offered against expulsion of aliens in article 13 of the International Covenant on Civil and Political Rights. See Human Rights Committee, *CCPR General Comment No. 15: The Position of Aliens under the Covenant,* Geneva: Geneva: 11 April 1986, para. 10; Human Rights Committee, *Concluding Observations: Dominican Republic,* A/48/40 vol. I, Geneva: 1993, para. 460 and A/56/40 vol. I, Geneva: 2001, para. 78(16); See also UN Committee on the Elimination of Racial Discrimination, *General Recommendation 30: Discrimination against Non-citizens,* CERD/C/64/Misc.11/Rev.3, New York: 2004, para. 26. It is also of interest to note that the European Court of Human Rights following its case law in which it clarified that *collective*

may only be expelled in accordance with a decision that is accompanied by due process guarantees.[94] The procedural protection prescribed is of particular interest here for two reasons. Firstly, unlike in the 1954 Statelessness Convention, human rights law does not necessarily reserve procedural guarantees to *lawfully present* non-nationals. This is of critical importance since it is precisely in the context of the refusal to grant lawful admission, the decision to revoke an individual's lawful immigration status or the issuance of an order to expel him, that the value of procedural protection lies. It is true that the formulation chosen for most of the relevant treaty articles refers to "aliens *lawfully* in the territory of a state party". However, the Migrant Workers Convention does not make this distinction and the pertinent article is located in Part III of the Convention where the rights of *all* migrant workers – regular and irregular – are housed.[95] The African Commission on Human and Peoples' Rights has also deemed that even in the context of the (proposed) expulsion of unlawfully present immigrants, provision should be made for those who are subject to deportation to "plead their case before the competent national courts", basing its conclusion on "the spirit and letter of the [African] Charter and international law".[96] Moreover, both the Human Rights Committee and the European Court of Human Rights have remarked on the fundamental importance of the opportunity to challenge both expulsion orders and the refusal to

---

expulsion refers to "any measure compelling aliens, as a group, to leave a country, except where such a measure is taken on the basis of a reasonable and objective examination of the particular case of each individual alien in the group", it found a violation of the prohibition of collective expulsion of aliens (article 4 of the 4th Protocol to the European Convention) in a case concerning the expulsion of just four people. David Weissbrodt, *Final Report on Prevention of Discrimination - The Rights of Non-Citizens,* E/CN.4/Sub.2/2003/23, 26 May 2003, Add. 2, para. 13. In addition, in a case dealing with the mass expulsion of people from Angola in 1996, the African Commission on Human and Peoples' Rights determined that the deportation may amount to a violation of numerous additional rights set out in the African Charter on Human and Peoples' Rights such as the right to property, right to work, right to education and right to family life. See Magdalena Sepulveda; Theo van Banning; Gudrun Gudmundsdotter; Christine Chamoun, *Universal and Regional Human Rights Protection: Cases and Commentaries*, University for Peace, Ciudad Colon: 2004, pages 377-378. See also the findings of the Inter-American Commission on Human Rights with regard to the expulsion of Haitians and Haitian-Dominicans from the Dominican Republic. Inter-American Commission on Human Rights, *Chapter V – Situation of Haitians in the Dominican Republic,* in "Annual Report 1991", OAE/Ser.L/V/II.81, Doc. 6, Rev. 1, 14 February 1992; and Inter-American Commission on Human Rights, *Chapter IX – Situation of Haitian migrant workers and their families in the Dominican Republic,* in "Report on the situation of human rights in the Dominican Republic", OAE/Ser.L/V/II.014, Doc. 49, Rev. 1, 7 October 1999.

[94] Article 13 of the International Covenant on Civil and Political Rights; article 1 of Protocol No. 7 to the European Convention on Human Rights; article 22, paragraph 6 of the American Convention on Human Rights; and Article 12, paragraph 4 of the African Charter on Human and Peoples' Rights. Similar guarantees can be found in article 22, paragraphs 2-9 of the Migrant Workers Convention. See also article 7 of the UN Declaration on the Human Rights of Individuals Who are not Nationals of the Country in which They Live.

[95] Be reminded once again, however, that stateless persons are in principle excluded from the scope of application of the Migrant Workers Convention.

[96] See Magdalena Sepulveda; Theo van Banning; Gudrun Gudmundsdotter; Christine Chamoun, *Universal and Regional Human Rights Protection: Cases and Commentaries*, University for Peace, Ciudad Colon: 2004, pages 377-378.

issue a residence permit on the basis of other human rights norms.[97] These development suggest that the scope for relying on procedural protections under general human rights law is broader than that offered by the tailor-made statelessness instrument.

Secondly, unlike the 1954 Statelessness Convention, the relevant human rights norms are strictly procedural and do not determine that expulsion must also be substantively justified,[98] such as on the basis national security or public order considerations. The only exception is article 8 of the European Convention on Human Rights which specifies that an interference with the right to family or private life – for example through expulsion – must be justified on one of a number of grounds.[99] Not withstanding this observation, in this respect, the Statelessness Convention seems to trump the protection offered under the general human rights framework. However, the overall procedural protection espoused under human rights law is also clearly designed to prevent arbitrary or abusive decision-making. Thus, bound up in the availability of a review of an expulsion order is the opportunity to consider the substance of the decision and determine whether it was lawful and justified. So, even in the absence of pre-set criteria for making this determination, the procedural guarantees actually allow the decision to expel to be tested against the three standards outlined above - non-discrimination, *non-refoulement* and protection of family or private life - as well as any other human rights-based considerations.

Meanwhile, the Human Rights Committee has also suggested that a foreigner who is to be expelled "must be allowed to leave for any country that

---

[97] In a case brought against Estonia for the refusal to issue a residence permit to the stateless applicant for national security considerations, the Human Rights Committee ruled that there had been no violation of the right to equal protection before the law (article 26), in part because the individual "had a right to have the denial of his application for permanent residence reviewed by the State party's courts". Human Rights Committee, *Case of Tsarjov v. Estonia,* CCPR/C/91/D/1223/2003, 14 November 2007, at paragraph 7.5. The European Court of Human Rights found – again in a case involving a stateless individual - that even where the provision devoted to procedural guarantees in the context of expulsion of non-nationals (article 1 of Protocol 7 to the European Convention on Human Rights) cannot be invoked, "where there is an arguable claim that such an expulsion may infringe the foreigner's right to respect for family life, article 13 in conjunction with article 8 of the Convention requires that States must make available to the individual concerned the effective possibility of challenging the deportation or refusal-of-residence order and of having the relevant issues examined with sufficient procedural safeguards and thoroughness by an appropriate domestic forum offering adequate guarantees of independence and impartiality". European Court of Human Rights, *Case of Al-Nashif v. Bulgaria,* Application No. 50963/99, 20 June 2002, at paragraph 133.

[98] Richard Lillich, *The human rights of aliens in contemporary international law*, Manchester University Press, Manchester: 1984, page 47.

[99] The grounds listed are: "national security, public safety or the economic well-being of the country, for the prevention of disorder or crime, for the protection of health or morals, or for the protection of the rights and freedoms of others". Article 8, paragraph 2 of the European Convention on Human Rights. Moveover, such substantive requirements resurface in the draft articles on Expulsion of Aliens prepared for the International Law Commission and "danger to the community of the state" (evidenced by a conviction for a "particularly serious crime or offence" has been added to the list of grounds justifying expulsion. "Terrorism" has also been pencilled in as a grounds for further debate. See Draft article 6 on "Non-expulsion of stateless persons" in International Law Commission, *Third report on the expulsion of aliens,* prepared by Special Rapporteur Maurice Kamto, A/CN.4/581, 19 April 2007.

agrees to take him"[100] – offering the stateless person, in a similar fashion to the 1954 Statelessness Convention, the opportunity to choose his state of destination within the boundaries of the possibilities that are available to him. Furthermore, in the case of *Harabi v. The Netherlands,* the European Commission on Human Rights determined that

> the repeated expulsion of an individual, whose identity was impossible to establish, to a country where his admission is not guaranteed, may raise an issue under Article 3 of the Convention [...] Such an issue may arise, a fortiori, if an alien is, over a long period of time, deported repeatedly from one country to another without any country taking measures to regularise his situation.[101]

Therefore, within the European framework at least, human rights law provides an ultimate remedy against the worst cases of stateless persons stranded in a game of human ping-pong.

If none of the standards discussed offers any solace to stateless persons seeking to enter or remain in a state then human rights law offers one more prospect. This lies in the discovery that the basic right to enter and remain in a country has two different formulations in human rights law.[102] The first and narrower expression is that included in the European and American human rights conventions as well as one universal instrument – the Migrant Workers Convention.[103] Following the traditional view of the matter, the relevant provisions determine that everyone has the right to enter and remain in *the state of which he is a national.*[104] Lacking any nationality, the stateless will not enjoy this right in respect of any state. However, an alternative formulation offers more hope. It can be found in the Universal Declaration of Human Rights, the International Covenant on Civil and Political Rights, the Convention on the Elimination of Racial

---

[100] Human Rights Committee, *CCPR General Comment No. 15: The Position of Aliens under the Covenant,* Geneva: Geneva: 11 April 1986, para. 9; Human Rights Committee, *CCPR General Comment No. 27: Freedom of movement,* Geneva: 2 November 1999, para. 8.

[101] Article 3 of the European Convention on Human Rights provides that "no one shall be subjected to torture or to inhuman or degrading treatment or punishment". European Commission on Human Rights, *Case of Harabi v. The Netherlands,* Application No. 10798/84, 5 March 1986, page 112.

[102] Note that the right to remain (freedom from expulsion) is mentioned explicitly in the European and American regional human rights instruments while it is considered implicit in the right to enter or return as formulated in the other human rights texts. Therefore, if an individual is entitled to the right to enter a certain country, he or she also enjoys the right to remain and reside there. See Human Rights Committee, *CCPR General Comment No. 27: Freedom of movement,* Geneva: 2 November 1999, para. 19; See also Human Rights Committee, *Stewart v. Canada,* CCPR/C/58/D/538/1993, para. 12.2.

[103] Article 3 of the Fourth Protocol to the European Convention on Human Rights; Article 22, paragraph 5 of the American Convention on Human Rights and Article 8, paragraph 2 of the Convention on the Rights of All Migrant Workers and Members of Their Families.

[104] Note that although the provision on freedom of movement in the Migrant Workers Convention refers not to the *state of nationality* but to the *country of origin,* this is defined elsewhere in the same instrument as meaning the country of which the person concerned is a national. See article 8, paragraph 2 in conjunction with article 6, paragraph (a) of the Convention on the Rights of All Migrant Workers and Members of Their Families.

Discrimination and the African Human Rights Charter.[105] The norm provides in essence that everyone has the right to enter or return to (and remain in) *his own country.*[106] This wording appears broader in scope and may arguably entitle non-nationals to be (re)admitted to (or protected from expulsion from) a given state under certain circumstances.

The extent to which non-nationals are indeed considered co-beneficiaries of this latter provision remained a subject of serious contention for quite some time. Proponents in both camps – those who considered *his own country* to refer solely to the country of citizenship and the opposing group that interpreted the text more expansively, to also include the country with which an individual has a particularly close connection – argued their case on the basis of the same *travaux préparatoires* of the ICCPR.[107] It was the treaty body responsible for monitoring the implementation of the ICCPR that eventually brought clarity to the situation. By the early 1990s, the Human Rights Committee had acknowledged that the notion "his own country" is broader than the concept of the country of nationality although its jurisprudence also betrayed some lasting disagreement on the precise scope of the norm.[108] Then in 1999, the Committee issued a General Comment on the freedom of movement that elucidated and built on its jurisprudence on the subject. Importantly, this General Comment includes several statements on the scope of the right to enter "one's own country" that are directly relevant to the situation of many stateless populations:

---

[105] Article 13, paragraph 2 of the Universal Declaration of Human Rights; Article 12, paragraph 4 of the International Covenant on Civil and Political Rights; Article 5, paragraph (d)(ii) of the Convention on the Elimination of All Forms of Racial Discrimination and Article 12, paragraph 2 of the African Charter on Human and Peoples' Rights.

[106] The formulation in the International Covenant on Civil and Political Rights deviates somewhat from that of the other instruments in providing – in place of an absolute right to enter or return – that "no one shall be arbitrarily deprived of the right to enter his own country". The Human Rights Committee has explained that there are nevertheless "few, if any, circumstances in which deprivation of the right to enter one's own country could be reasonable". Human Rights Committee, *CCPR General Comment No. 27: Freedom of movement,* Geneva: 2 November 1999, para. 21. Note moreover, that unlike the right to move freely within the borders of a state – and the right to leave any country – this right to enter is not subject to any restrictions on grounds such as national security or public health. See section 2.1.2 above at note 38.

[107] Hurst Hannum, *The Right to Leave and Return in International Law and Practice*, Martinus Nijhoff Publishers, Dordrecht: 1987, pages 56-60. Note that "while in the drafting of article 12, paragraph 4 of the [Civil and Political Rights] Covenant the term 'country of nationality' was rejected, so was the suggestion to refer to the country of one's permanent home". The meaning of *one's own country* therefore lies somewhere between these two counter poles. See Human Rights Committee, *Stewart v. Canada,* CCPR/C/58/D/538/1993, para. 12.5.

[108] See Human Rights Committee, *Stewart v. Canada,* CCPR/C/58/D/538/1993 including the dissenting opinions by E. Evatt, C. Quirogay, F. Urbina, C. Chanet and J. Vallejo; Human Rights Committee, *Canepa v. Canada,* CCPR/C/59/D/558/1993 including the concurring opinion by M. Scheinin and the dissenting opinions by E. Evatt, C. Quirogay and C. Chanet. See also Sarah Joseph; Jenny Schultz; Melissa Castan, *The International Covenant on Civil and Political Rights. Cases, Materials and Commentary*, Oxford University Press, Oxford: 2000, pages 261-267; David Weissbrodt, *Final Report on Prevention of Discrimination - The Rights of Non-Citizens,* E/CN.4/Sub.2/2003/23, 26 May 2003, para 40.

> The scope of 'his own country' is broader than the concept 'country of his nationality'. It is not limited to nationality in a formal sense, that is, nationality acquired at birth or by conferral; it embraces, at the very least, an individual who, because of his or her special ties to or claims in relation to a given country, cannot be considered to be a mere alien. This would be the case, for example, of nationals of a country who have been stripped of their nationality in violation of international law, and of individuals whose country of nationality has been incorporated in or transferred to another national entity, whose nationality is being denied them. The language of article 12, paragraph 4, moreover, permits a broader interpretation that might embrace other categories of long-term residents, including but not limited to stateless persons arbitrarily deprived of the right to acquire the nationality of the country of such residence.[109]

This statement may be seen as an expression of the principle of non-discrimination which calls both for the same treatment in equal cases and for different treatment in clearly different cases.[110] Thus, it would be *unreasonable* to treat all non-nationals equally where some, "because of his or her special ties or claims in relation to a given country, cannot be considered to be a mere alien" and the personal scope of the right to enter *his own country* must reflect this.[111]

The three examples given by the Human Rights Committee – and these should be considered illustrative, rather than exhaustive[112] – of circumstances in which a right to (re)enter and remain in a country could be claimed by a non-national are all situations that are very familiar by now since they have already come up in the discussion of the statelessness phenomenon. Thus a stateless person whose nationality was lost through an act of denationalisation that ran counter to a state's international obligations - such as the prohibition of arbitrary deprivation of nationality - will be entitled to (re)enter or remain in that state regardless of the loss

---

109 Human Rights Committee, *CCPR General Comment No. 27: Freedom of movement,* Geneva: 2 November 1999, para. 20.

110 Recall the discussion of positive measures or *affirmative action* based on the principle of non-discrimination in section 1 at note 19 .

111 Moreover, while the European Court of Human Rights is not able to interpret the guarantee housed in Article 3 of the Fourth Protocol to the European Convention on Human Rights expansively, because it clearly refers to *nationality*, the Court has found other ways of offering the same, broad protection to persons who have developed a connection with a country of which they are not a national. In the aforementioned cases brought against Latvia, the Court used article 8 on the right to private life to offer protect the stateless persons in question from expulsion or non-issancce of a residence permit. European Court of Human Rights, *Case of Slivenko v. Latvia,* Application No. 48321/99, 9 October 2003; *Case of Sisojeva and others v. Latvia,* Application No. 60654/00, 16 June 2005; *Case of Kaftailova v. Latvia,* Application No. 59643/00, 22 June 2006. See further note 92 above.

112 In its *Concluding Observations* to the periodic report of Japan, the Human Rights Committee has referred to another category of person who may benefit from the guarantees under article 12, paragraph 4 of the ICCPR. The Committee determined that depriving "foreigners who are second- or third-generation permanent residents in Japan and whose activities are based in Japan" of their right to re-enter the country is incompatible with article 12, paragraph 4 of the Covenant. Human Rights Committee, *Concluding Observations: Japan,* A/54/40 vol. I (1999) 36, para. 160. See also Human Rights Committee, *Concluding Observations: New Zealand,* A/57/40 vol. I (2002) 63, para. 81(12).

of citizenship.[113] Where state succession has created statelessness, these individuals will also enjoy the right to (re)enter and reside in the successor state despite their lack of nationality.[114] Finally, where statelessness is prolonged due to enduring denial of citizenship by the country of residence, this state is nevertheless to be considered the individual's "own country" for the purposes of enjoying the right to (re)admission and residence. This category also encompasses the successive generations of stateless children who owe their situation to the continued refusal of nationality by the state.[115]

In each of the situations outlined, there is a link with a state that clearly *should* have been formalised through the attribution or continuation of citizenship and the absence of this bond of nationality is deemed not to excuse the state of its responsibilities towards the individual. So, a stateless person does not enjoy the right to enter or remain in any and every state by virtue of his statelessness, but only with respect to the state that has unjustifiably withheld or withdrawn citizenship. In view of the complexity of the international norms dealing with the attribution of nationality – as we saw in Part 2 – the task of identifying the state responsible and indeed enforcing this right of (re)admission or residence where the right to a nationality has broken down may not always be easy. Nevertheless, this progression towards a broader interpretation of the right to enter a country to the benefit of certain groups of stateless persons is of enormous importance because it offers an opportunity for (renewed) access to the territory of a state and by consequence provides the individuals in question with the chance to access and claim other rights – including those granted under the 1954 Statelessness Convention where the state

[113] It is important to note that should the denationalisation of an individual be enacted in order for the state to shirk its obligation to allow the person to (re)enter or remain on its soil, this act may amount to a violation of the right to enter as protected under, for example, article 12, paragraph 4 of the International Covenant on Civil and Political Rights: "A State party must not, by stripping a person of nationality or by expelling an individual to a third country, arbitrarily prevent this person from returning to his or her own country". Human Rights Committee, *CCPR General Comment No. 27: Freedom of movement,* Geneva: 2 November 1999, para. 21. See also Human Rights Committee, *Concluding Observations: Syrian Arab Republic,* A/56/40 vol. I (2001) 70, para. 81(21). Moreover, it has been argued that if denationalisation was combined with deprivation of the right to remain or return, this would necessarily result in an infringement of another state's territorial supremacy by forcing non-nationals upon them and refusing to re-admit them. Thus for the "maintenance of peaceful relations among States [...] loss of nationality by denationalisation should [...] not entail the loss of the right of sojourn; it should not relieve the State from the obligation to receive the former national back on its territory". Paul Weis, *Nationality and Statelessness in International Law*, Kluwer Academic Publishers Group, Dordrecht: 1979, page 54. See also Hurst Hannum, *The Right to Leave and Return in International Law and Practice*, Martinus Nijhoff Publishers, Dordrecht: 1987, pages 60-63.

[114] This is reaffirmed in Human Rights Committee, *Concluding Observations: Croatia,* A/56/40 vol. I (2001) 65, para. 80 (15). See also article 20 of the European Convention on Nationality.

[115] See the comments of the Committee on the situation of the Bedoons in Kuwait: "The treatment of the Bedoons (included in the category of stateless persons) in Kuwait, who number several thousand, is of grave concern. In view of the fact that many of these people are born in or have been living in Kuwaiti territory for decades [...] the sweeping statement of the delegation characterising Bedoons generally as 'illegal residents' is of grave concern. That many Bedoons long resident in Kuwait who left the country during the Iraqi occupation in 1990/91 are not permitted to return to Kuwait is of concern". Human Rights Committee, *Concluding Observations: Kuwait,* A/55/40, vol. I (2000) 65, para. 477.

has ratified that instrument.[116] Moreover, with the unbridled right to remain an implicit component of this right to enter, if a stateless person is found to enjoy the right to enter a particular state, he must also be deemed to enjoy protection from expulsion from that state.[117] Many of the situations in which the withdrawal or refusal of nationality has been accompanied by (the threat of) deportation are thus likely to be in breach of this norm.[118] This development, together with the other human rights standards that impact upon an individual's international free movement – as discussed above – is a firm, positive step towards the assurance of a right for stateless persons to live somewhere. Nevertheless, more will need to be done to truly take advantage of the possibilities offered to the stateless under human rights law and to further clarify the application of these norms in the specific situation of statelessness.

3 LEGAL PERSONHOOD

The next issue to be considered is the right to legal personhood or the right to be recognised as a person before the law. The notion is that while "'personality' implies factual existence, 'legal personality' implies legal existence".[119] Legal personality is therefore required for an individual to be recognised as the bearer of rights – including human rights – and duties. As such, legal personhood is a basic requirement for the capacity to engage in various legal transactions, including contracting marriage, purchasing, selling or inheriting property or staking a claim in

---

[116] To this end, it is certainly advantageous that the underlying norm is contained in one of the major *universal* human rights instruments - enjoying wide acceptance and not being limited in geographical application to a particular region only. Of interest to note is the fact that this provision attracted only one reservation (by the United Kingdom) from among all of the 160 state parties to the International Covenant on Civil and Political Rights. Moreover, the 1951 Convention relating to the Status of Refugees also implicitly acknowledges that stateless persons enjoy the right to return to their country of habitual residence, even in the absence of the bond of nationality. In assessing whether a stateless person falls within the definition of a "refugee", it is the country of former habitual residence that is looked to (in place of the country of nationality). Guy Goodwin-Gill, *The Refugee in International Law*, Oxford University Press, Oxford: 2007, pages 67-70.

[117] Some authors have even gone so far as to assert that customary international law precludes the expulsion of any non-national who "by virtue of long residence, have prima facie acquired the effective nationality of the host state if no state allows them entry". Yaffa Zilberschats, "Chapter 2 - Citizenship and International Law" in *The Human Right to Citizenship*, Transnational Publishers, Ardsley, NY: 2002, page 43.

[118] Consider the case mentioned in the introduction to this issue where the Mauritanian nationality of 60,000 black Africans was spontaneously disputed and they were subsequently expelled from the country. The situation in Ethiopia/Eritrea is another example of an infringement of this norm: denationalisation and expulsion of population groups both preceded and accompanied the conflict and even in the wake of independence, the non-recognition of nationality claims and deportations continued. See Maureen Lynch, *Lives on hold: The human cost of statelessness,* Washington: 2005, page 28; Human Rights Watch, *The Horn of Africa: Mass Expulsions and the Nationality Issue,* 30 January 2003.

[119] Anna Meijknecht, *Towards International Personality: The Position of Minorities and Indigenous Peoples in International Law,* Intersentia, Antwerp: 2001, page 26.

court.[120] As a result, the recognition of a person's legal existence is critical to these and many other facets of his life.

It has been said that today, "no country expressly denies to aliens legal personality".[121] Nevertheless, since the capacity to acquire and exercise rights rests upon the recognition of legal personhood, many of the problems that stateless populations report could point to an underlying issue of denial of legal personality. One reported fact that is illustrative here is that crimes committed against stateless individuals are not always investigated. Indeed,

> if someone robs or rapes them, they may find they cannot lodge a complaint, because legally they do not exist and because the police require proof that they do before they can open an investigation.[122]

However, it is unclear how widespread this complaint is and what factors have contributed to the non-investigation of crimes. Yet, it is certainly arguable that this problem, as well as the difficulties experienced by stateless persons with regards to respect for family life (including the official recognition and documentation of marriage and the registration of a child's birth), property ownership, indefinite detention and many other areas, could be considered evidence of a lesser or lack of regard for their basic legal personhood. This is enough to warrant a brief investigation of the extent to which international law prescribes the recognition of the legal personality of stateless persons.

3.1 The 1954 Convention relating to the Status of Stateless Persons

The 1954 Statelessness Convention addresses the right to legal personhood indirectly in its article 12 that deals with "personal status". According to the instrument's commentary, the term personal status as used here refers to an individual's:

> Legal capacity (age of majority, the rights of persons under age, capacity to marry, capacity of married women, the instances when a person may lose his legal capacity), their family rights (marriage, divorce, recognition and adoption of children, the powers of parents over their children or of husband over his wife and their mutual rights to support), the matrimonial regime (the mutual rights of spouses to property, for instance), and succession and inheritance (whom succeeds whom, what are the consequences of a will, who is considered to have survived in case of unknown date of death, etc).[123]

---

[120] Just what rights a person holds and is entitled to exercise – his actual legal *capacity* - is regulated elsewhere in international and domestic law.

[121] Carmen Tiburcio, "Chapter V. Private Rights" in *The human rights of aliens under international and comparative law*, Kluwer Law International, The Hague: 2001, page 114.

[122] Philippe Leclerc and Rupert Colville, "In the shadows. Millions seek to escape the grim world of the stateless", in *Refugees* Magazine, No. 147, Issue 3, 2007, page 6. See also Maureen Lynch and Perveen Ali, *Buried Alive. Stateless Kurds in Syria,* Report for Refugees International, January 2006, page 3.

[123] Nehemiah Robinson, *Convention relating to the status of stateless persons - Its history and interpretation*, UNHCR, Geneva: 1955, pages 48-49.

However, the provision addresses the question of jurisdiction rather than of rights or substance.[124] It determines which state's domestic law governs a particular stateless person's personal status[125] and provides for the recognition of "rights previously acquired by a stateless person and dependent on personal status, more particularly rights attaching to marriage".[126] The article thereby skips the question of whether stateless persons have legal personhood and moves straight onto the issue of jurisdiction in matters of personal status. This suggests that the 1954 Statelessness Convention considers the legal personality of stateless persons as a given and not in question. Furthermore, this implicit affirmation of the right to legal personhood for stateless persons is reinforced by the overall approach taken in the instrument whereby rights are prescribed on the basis of the legal status of "stateless person" – a status that could not be enjoyed unless the beneficiaries legal existence were also acknowledged.

3.2 International human rights law

When human rights law is consulted, we find that the right to legal personality has been dealt with explicitly.[127] For instance, article 6 of the Universal Declaration of Human Rights proclaims that "everyone has the right to recognition everywhere as a person before the law" – a provision that is echoed in, among other instruments, the International Covenant on Civil and Political Rights.[128] The insertion of the word "everywhere" indicates that the right to legal personhood does not stop at the border - it is not territorially bound. Non-nationals also have the right to be recognised as a person before the law.[129] Moreover, the very concept of human

[124] The need to deal with the question of jurisdiction stems from the fact that in countries where the personal status of a foreigner is governed by the law of the country of nationality, "a person without a nationality (particularly if he never possessed one) does not possess, in theory, any status whatsoever, unless the law contains special provisions for stateless persons". Nehemiah Robinson, *Convention relating to the status of stateless persons - Its history and interpretation*, UNHCR, Geneva: 1955, page 49

[125] According to paragraph 1 of article 12: "1. The personal status of a stateless person shall be governed by the law of the country of his domicile or, if he has no domicile, by the law of the country of his residence".

[126] Paragraph 2 of article 12.

[127] International law also knows a whole body of standards – *private* international law – that address jurisdictional questions related to personal status and other issues.

[128] The right to legal personhood can be found in article 16 of the International Covenant on Civil and Political Rights. It can moreover be traced in article 24 of the Migrant Workers Convention, article 12 of the Convention on the Rights of Persons with Disabilities, article 3 of the American Convention on Human Rights and article 5 of the African Charter on Human and Peoples' Rights. The Committee on the Rights of the Child has also read the right to be recognised as a person before the law into article 7 of the Convention on the Rights of the Child; see, among others, Committee on the Rights of the Child, *Concluding Observations: Jamaica,* CRC/C/38, Geneva: 1995, paragraph 148; *Nicaragua,* CRC/C/43, Geneva: 1995, paragraph 43; *Nepal,* CRC/C/54, Geneva: 1996, paragraph 180.

[129] Interestingly, according to Tiburcio it is the historical position of non-nationals that spurred the elaboration of the right to legal personhood in modern human rights instruments: "In Antiquity, aliens were not recognised as such, for they were denied the enjoyment and acquisition of all rights. Therefore many international conventions still emphasise this right". Carmen Tiburcio, "Chapter V. Private

rights presupposes legal personhood by bestowing people with substantive rights. Indeed the right to legal personhood is considered to be of such primary significance, for nationals and non-nationals alike, that it is among the non-derogable standards that cannot be limited at all, under any circumstances.[130] In conclusion then, on the basis of human rights law, any laws and practices that prevent stateless persons or any other group from "being treated or from functioning as full legal persons" should be eradicated.[131] The 1954 Statelessness Convention and international human rights framework are thus in full agreement on this matter.

4 ACCESS TO COURTS

The right of access to courts is one element of a broader set of rights and principles that include the right to an effective remedy, the right to a fair trial and the principle of due process of law.[132] These notions play a central role in the legitimacy of government and the individual enjoyment of rights. Indeed, the right of access to courts and related procedural rights "are of fundamental importance for they guarantee compliance with all other rights".[133] They provide an avenue for individuals to complain about - and seek redress for - arbitrary acts of government, but also means for settling a dispute that arises between private individuals or for ensuring the fair and impartial prosecution of criminal offences. Furthermore, access to court has long been considered pivotal in the protection of individual rights,[134] including for non-nationals through the regime of diplomatic protection. There,

> the idea that individuals have a right to resort to local courts whenever their rights are violated is the basis of the local remedies rule in the context of diplomatic protection, according to which aliens have first to vindicate their rights in local courts before invoking their national State protective apparatus.[135]

Rights" in *The human rights of aliens under international and comparative law*, Kluwer Law International, The Hague: 2001, page 112.

[130] See article 4, paragraph 2 of the International Covenant on Civil and Political Rights.

[131] See Human Rights Committee, *General Comment 28: Equality of Rights between Men and Women*, CCPR/C/21/Rev.1/Add.10, Geneva: 29 March 2000, paragraph 19.

[132] Magdalena Sepulveda; Theo van Banning; Gudrun Gudmundsdotter; Christine Chamoun, *Universal and Regional Human Rights Protection: Cases and Commentaries*, University for Peace, Ciudad Colon: 2004, pages 477-560.

[133] Carmen Tiburcio, "Chapter X. Procedural Rights" in *The human rights of aliens under international and comparative law*, Kluwer Law International, The Hague: 2001, page 245.

[134] In other words, "human rights cannot be secured effectively without protection by effective, independent and impartial tribunals". Magdalena Sepulveda; Theo van Banning; Gudrun Gudmundsdotter; Christine Chamoun, *Universal and Regional Human Rights Protection: Cases and Commentaries*, University for Peace, Ciudad Colon: 2004, page 560.

[135] Carmen Tiburcio, "Chapter X. Procedural Rights" in *The human rights of aliens under international and comparative law*, Kluwer Law International, The Hague: 2001, page 246.

Similarly, the exhaustion of local remedies is a precondition for access to international human rights complaints bodies such as the UN Human Rights Committee,[136] the European Court on Human Rights[137] and the Inter-American Commission on Human Rights.[138]

In the specific context of statelessness, this key right gains even greater value. Firstly, as a vulnerable group the stateless are known to commonly experience substantial human rights violations, heightening the need for access to courts as a means of redressing such treatment.[139] For example, stateless persons may be subjected to lengthy or indefinite detention due to their status and the opportunity to contest such detention is an important tool in combating this conduct.[140] Secondly, access to court provides the opportunity to contest the very decision(s) on attribution of nationality that have caused the (continued) statelessness of the individual. Where we have identified concrete obligations of states in the context of the right to a nationality, such as the prohibition of discriminatory deprivation of nationality, access to a court will enable the persons affected to actually enforce these guarantees. For instance, in a case in the Netherlands where a man was rendered stateless by the withdrawal of his Dutch nationality – after he had renounced his prior Egyptian citizenship – it was a domestic court that ensured that his nationality was reinstated.[141] Finally, the right of access to courts also offers the stateless the opportunity to invoke their specific entitlements as "stateless persons". To gain access to the rights attributed to stateless persons under the 1954 Statelessness Convention and elsewhere in international law, some form of status determination is needed.[142] Where a state rejects an application by a stateless person for recognition as such, the prospect of demanding a review of the correctness and lawfulness of this decision becomes crucial.[143] And, of course, it is also important that stateless persons are able to rely a state's courts in the same way as any other individual, for the purpose of resolving civil and criminal cases.

---

[136] Article 5, paragraph 2 of the Optional Protocol to the International Covenant on Civil and Political Rights, 1976.

[137] Article 35, paragraph 1 of the European Convention on Human Rights.

[138] Article 46, paragraph 1 of the American Convention on Human Rights.

[139] Just as "in practice, refugees have often looked to their host country's courts to secure respect for their rights", this avenue provides similar opportunities to stateless persons. James Hathaway, *The Rights of Refugees Under International Law*, Cambridge University Press, Cambridge: 2005, page 628.

[140] Maureen Lynch, *Lives on hold: The human cost of statelessness,* Washington: 2005, page 7 ; Carol Batchelor The 1954 Convention relating to the Status of Stateless Persons: Implementation within the European Union Member States and Recommendations for Harmonisation 2004; UNHCR, *Stateless persons: a discussion note,* EC/1992/SCP/CRP.4, Geneva: 1 April 1992, para 9 and annex. The specific problem of detention – and the opportunity to appeal the lawfulness of detention – is discussed in section 7 below.

[141] Betty de Hart; Kees Groenendijk, "Multiple Nationality: The Practice of Germany and the Netherlands" in R. Cholewinski (ed) *International Migration Law*, TMC Asser Press, The Hague: 2007 This case was introduced in chapter IV at note 155.

[142] See UNHCR and IPU, *Nationality and statelessness. A handbook for parliamentarians*, 2005, pages 19-21.

[143] Compare what has been said of the role of the right of access to courts for an individual seeking recognition as a refugee in James Hathaway, *The Rights of Refugees Under International Law*, Cambridge University Press, Cambridge: 2005, page 630.

In practice, access to states' judicial systems has reportedly been a problem for stateless persons as well as for non-citizens in general. For example, in the Advisory Board on Human Security's study on the denial of citizenship it was reported that the difficulties experienced by non-citizens and the human rights violations they face are "further compounded by inadequate access to justice".[144] UN Special Rapporteur on the rights of non-citizens, David Weissbrodt, has added that:

> Discrimination [against non-citizens] is aggravated when combined with insufficient possibilities to bring complaints and obtain reparation.[145]

Disappointingly, neither of these reports elaborates any further on this problem.[146] Yet references to the difficulty that stateless persons face in accessing judicial systems and legal remedies can also be found in documents compiled by UNHCR and NGOs.[147] Further investigation into state practice in this respect would be useful in mapping the implications of statelessness because these references are overwhelmingly brief and superficial. Here, however, the task is to give closer consideration to the international legal standards on the right of access to courts – and related rights - for stateless persons, starting with where it is espoused in the 1954 Convention relating to the Status of Stateless Persons.

4.1 The 1954 Convention relating to the Status of Stateless Persons

The right of access to courts was included in the 1954 Convention relating to the Status of Stateless Persons in precisely the same terms as in the 1951 Refugee Convention whereby "stateless person" was simply substituted for "refugee".[148] Thus, the first paragraph of article 16 decrees that

---

[144] Advisory Board on Human Security (prepared by Constantin Sokoloff), *Denial of Citizenship: A Challenge to Human Security*, February 2005, page 20.

[145] David Weissbrodt, *Final Report on Prevention of Discrimination - The Rights of Non-Citizens*, E/CN.4/Sub.2/2003/23, 26 May 2003, Add.3, para. 3.

[146] In this context it should be noted that the content of the UN Special Rapporteur's report on "Examples of practices in regard to non-citizens" – the inclusion of some issues and the exclusion of others – was guided by methodological considerations rather than any allocation of priority to certain problems over others. The fact that the issue of access to courts was not discussed in detail in this document should not be interpreted as an appraisal of the (lack of) seriousness or importance of this matter. See David Weissbrodt, *Final Report on Prevention of Discrimination - The Rights of Non-Citizens*, E/CN.4/Sub.2/2003/23, 26 May 2003, Add.3, para. 1.

[147] See for example UNHCR, "Statelessness and Citizenship" in *The State of the World's Refugees - A Humanitarian Agenda*, Oxford University Press, Oxford: 1997, page 225; UNHCR Executive Committee, *Conclusion on Identification, Prevention and Reduction of Statelessness and Protection of Stateless Persons, No. 106*, 57th Session, Geneva, 2006, para. (v); Maureen Lynch, *Lives on hold: The human cost of statelessness*, Washington: 2005, page 3; Maureen Lynch and Perveen Ali, *Buried Alive. Stateless Kurds in Syria*, Report for Refugees International, January 2006, page 2; Youth Advocate Program International, *Stateless Children - Youth Who are Without Citizenship*, Washington: 2002, page 7.

[148] This provision was, in turn, derived from the refugee instruments that preceded the 1951 Refugee Convention – the 1933 Convention relating to the International Status of Refugees and the 1938

> a stateless person shall have free access to the courts of law on the territory of all Contracting States.[149]

This basic right to access the courts of law of any state party is granted to the stateless person directly and absolutely.[150] It is not in any way dependent on the treatment accorded by the state to other groups of persons (nationals or non-nationals). The level of attachment required to exercise this right is that of simple jurisdiction only. The only requirement is that the court be competent – have subject-matter jurisdiction – to try the case in question.[151] Presence, lawful or otherwise, on the soil of the state party is not required. This is important because the right of access to courts may, for example, be invoked by a stateless person who faces detention, expulsion or other difficulties on the grounds of his unlawful status. It may also be possible for the aspirant stateless person to invoke the right of access to court in the context of the determination of his status, if such an opportunity is provided for under domestic law.

However, states are not compelled, under the 1954 Statelessness Convention to ensure that their courts are competent to adjudicate in nationality matters. It can be recalled that the other statelessness instrument, the 1961 Convention on the Reduction of Statelessness, does provide for the opportunity for a review of at least some decisions relating to nationality – but concerns were raised about the limited scope of those guarantees and it is regrettable to see that the 1954 Statelessness Convention does not redress these.[152] More troublesome is the failure of the 1954 Statelessness Convention to elaborate a concrete right to a judicial remedy in the context of a "stateless person status" determination exercise, particularly in view of the difficulties inherent in the identification of statelessness.[153] The only situation in which the 1954 Statelessness Convention actually calls for provision to be made for some kind of legal review of a decision – although not necessarily through access to court – is where an expulsion order for a lawfully present stateless person has been enacted.[154] This fact significantly limits the value of this provision.

Convention concerning the Status of Refugees coming from Germany. James Hathaway, *The Rights of Refugees Under International Law*, Cambridge University Press, Cambridge: 2005, page 644.

149 Article 16, paragraph 1 of the 1954 Convention relating to the Status of Stateless Persons.

150 The Convention explicitly determines that no reservations may be made to this paragraph of article 16, containing the core right of access to courts. See article 38 of the 1954 Convention relating to the Status of Stateless Persons. Furthermore, the provision is very straight-forward and requires little interpretation. Only the word "free" may be somewhat ambiguous, but the *travaux préparatoires* quickly clarify that it is *ready* access to court that is envisaged rather than access free of fees or charges. A stateless person may therefore be subject to the same fees as are levied against nationals. See also article 29 on the imposition of duties, charges and taxes. 1954 Convention relating to the Status of Stateless Persons. Paul Weis, *The Refugee Convention, 1951*, Cambridge University Press, Cambridge: 1995, pages 131-134.

151 James Hathaway, *The Rights of Refugees Under International Law*, Cambridge University Press, Cambridge: 2005, pages 645-647.

152 See chapter V, section 2.1.

153 As discussed in chapter II, section 2 and chapter IX, section 3.

154 The right to due process within the particular circumstance of expulsion from state territory is established separately in article 31 of the 1954 Convention relating to the Status of Stateless Persons.

Having established that all stateless persons have the right to petition a court, article 16 then makes an effort to facilitate the enjoyment of this right by tackling certain practical obstacles:[155]

> A stateless persons shall enjoy in the Contracting State in which he has his habitual residence the same treatment as a national in matters pertaining to access to the courts, including legal assistance and exemption from *cautio judicatum solvi.*[156]

In comparison with the first paragraph, as cited above, both the level of attachment needed for enjoyment of this entitlement and the level of protection offered differ dramatically: the level of attachment required is habitual residence and the standard of protection offered is that on a par with the country's nationals.[157] By compelling states to treat stateless persons as though they were nationals, the provision can attain its objective of removing the practical difficulties that specifically affect non-nationals when trying to gain access to courts. Two such issues are raised explicitly. Firstly, to the extent that legal assistance is available to nationals, this must also be made available to stateless persons. Here again, there is the limitation that the Convention does not oblige states to establish a system of legal aid generally or for stateless persons specifically, but stateless persons must enjoy access to any existing system on the same terms as nationals. The second matter dealt with is the *cautio judicatum solvi*: a security deposit that has historically been required of a non-national who brings a case before the court to cover the expenses of the

---

The question of expulsion has already been dealt with in considering the right to freedom of movement in section 2.2 of this chapter.

155 Nehemiah Robinson, *Convention relating to the status of stateless persons - Its history and interpretation*, UNHCR, Geneva: 1955, page 60; James Hathaway, *The Rights of Refugees Under International Law*, Cambridge University Press, Cambridge: 2005, page 656.

156 Article 16, paragraph 2 of the 1954 Convention relating to the Status of Stateless Persons.

157 There is some contention as to the interpretation of the expression "habitual residence" in the context of the 1954 Convention relating to the Status of Stateless Persons – a similar ambiguity to that traced with regard to the use of this term in the 1961 Convention on the Reduction of Statelessness. There we found some evidence to support the possibility that habitual residence does not necessarily imply lawful residence. If that were the case here, then *habitual residence* would be an additional, hybrid level of attachment: a presence in the state that is comparable in durability to *lawful stay,* yet does not presuppose *lawfulness*. See chapter VII, at note 123. Nevertheless, Hathaway categorises this right together with those that specify *lawful stay*, thereby suggesting that stateless persons who are in a contracting state irregularly, for whatever duration, would be excluded. James Hathaway, *The Rights of Refugees Under International Law*, Cambridge University Press, Cambridge: 2005. Irregular stateless persons would have to fall back on article 7 of the 1954 Convention which offers them the same level of treatment as is granted to aliens generally. Sadly, the *traveaux preparatiores* of the Convention do not settle the matter one way or another, nor does the commentary to the text. Paul Weis, *The Refugee Convention, 1951*, Cambridge University Press, Cambridge: 1995, pages 117-123; Nehemiah Robinson, *Convention relating to the status of stateless persons - Its history and interpretation*, UNHCR, Geneva: 1955, page 55. States may certainly be able to take advantage of this enduring ambiguity and interpret the terms narrowly, to the exclusion of those stateless persons who are durably, but unlawfully, within their territory. Even if the expression is not subjected to this strict interpretation, it may be difficult for unlawfully present stateless persons to establish their habitual residence in practice.

opposing party in the event the non-national loses the case.[158] To the extent that this is required of non-nationals by virtue of their possession of a foreign nationality, stateless persons must be exempted.[159]

Thanks to the broad formulation of this provision, its benefits may extend beyond the two particular entitlements mentioned, which are clearly included as examples.[160] Thus where nationals enjoy additional protection in relation to their access to courts, habitually resident stateless persons are entitled to the same treatment. Moreover, where a national enjoys certain advantages in accessing the courts in another state, the habitually resident stateless person must enjoy those same advantages.[161] However, the guarantee of access to courts as contained within the 1954 Statelessness Convention fails to go beyond the question of access to existing remedies and address the need for, nature or quality of the judicial procedures that must be in place. It does dissolve any disadvantage experienced by the stateless on the basis of their lack of any nationality but stops disappointingly short of offering concrete prospects of a remedy against a violation of their rights. As we turn to alternative sources of protection of this civil right within the human rights field, we will see that these aspects come much more to the fore.

4.2 International human rights law

Turning to international human rights law and its treatment of the right of access to courts, we find that this issue is dealt with in two separate yet complimentary sets of provisions: those dealing with the right to an *effective remedy* and those providing for the right to a *fair trial*. This is illustrated well by the Universal Declaration of Human Rights, where article 8 determines that

---

[158] "The origins of the security deposit – *cautio judicatum solvi* – lie in Roman Law [...] At its origin, this deposit was due by any author, Roman or otherwise, as a guarantee to the defendant, who at the end of the suit could receive money as payment for costs and expenses incurred, in the case of the author losing the plea. Thus, this caution was necessary whenever the author was not solvent – mainly when the author was an alien and his property was located abroad. In the 16th century this institution changed its nature in most countries and was understood as linked to the status of being an alien". Carmen Tiburcio, "Chapter X. Procedural Rights" in *The human rights of aliens under international and comparative law*, Kluwer Law International, The Hague: 2001, page 260.

[159] It has been noted that this explicit reference to the security deposit "has a psychological effect only, because nationals of the country where the court is located are not required to pay the *cautio*; therefore once a stateless person is assimilated to a national he could not be required to pay *cautio judicatum solvi*". Nehemiah Robinson, *Convention relating to the status of stateless persons - Its history and interpretation*, UNHCR, Geneva: 1955, page 60. However, some countries have chosen to adopt a system whereby all insolvents and suspected insolvents are required to post a *cautio* – be they nationals or non-nationals. Carmen Tiburcio, "Chapter X. Procedural Rights" in *The human rights of aliens under international and comparative law*, Kluwer Law International, The Hague: 2001, page 264.

[160] At the time, these were "the two practical impediments of greatest concern to the drafters". James Hathaway, *The Rights of Refugees Under International Law*, Cambridge University Press, Cambridge: 2005, page 910.

[161] This is prescribed by the third paragraph of article 16: "A stateless person shall be accorded in the matters referred to in paragraph 2 in countries other than that in which he has his habitual residence the treatment granted to a national of the country of his habitual residence". 1954 Convention relating to the Status of Stateless Persons.

> everyone has the right to an effective remedy by the competent national tribunals for acts violating the fundamental rights granted him by the constitution or by law.

The purpose of the article is to provide individuals with a means of complaining and seeking redress for any violation of the rights attributed to them under domestic law.[162] Thereafter, article 10 sets out that

> everyone is entitled in full equality to a fair and public hearing by an independent and impartial tribunal, in the determination of his rights and obligations and of any criminal charge against him.[163]

The Universal Declaration is, therefore, concerned with both access to and quality of judicial remedies. The wording of these provisions – granting the rights involved to everyone – allows nationals, non-nationals and stateless persons alike to benefit from the protection offered.[164]

Other major human rights documents follow suit with the Universal Declaration. The right to an effective remedy is housed, for instance, among the "fundamental principles" codified in Part II of the International Covenant on Civil and Political Rights. It calls for a system to be set in place for the alleged violations of the convention rights to be considered and redressed.[165] Although these provisions do not unequivocally provide for access to a *court* for the consideration

---

[162] Thereby indirectly also the rights espoused under international (human rights) law to the extent that these have direct effect in the state in question or have been transposed into municipal law. It should be noted that the formulation of this provision has raised some concerns for it provides only for access to courts to assert a right that has been granted under domestic law, while "it should be the role of the courts to verify whether the individual has or has not the right under dispute, that is to say, the right of access to courts should be granted anyway". Carmen Tiburcio, "Chapter X. Procedural Rights" in *The human rights of aliens under international and comparative law*, Kluwer Law International, The Hague: 2001, page 247.

[163] Article 11 then adds certain guarantees related specifically to criminal proceedings. It determines that a criminal trial be public and that the defendant be assured "all the guarantees necessary for his defence". Article 11, paragraph 1 of the Universal Declaration of Human Rights.

[164] The irrelevance of nationality for the enjoyment of this right is reaffirmed in another non-binding yet important human rights document: the Declaration on the Human Rights of Individuals Who are not Nationals of the Country in which They Live. Article 5 of this Declaration promulgates the right of non-nationals "to be equal before the courts, tribunals and all other organs and authorities administering justice" as well as the additional entitlement to the aid of an interpreter in criminal – and possibly other – proceedings.

[165] The article calls upon state parties to undertake: "To ensure that any person whose rights or freedoms as herein recognised are violated shall have an effective remedy [and] to ensure that any person claiming such a remedy shall have his right thereto determined by competent judicial, administrative or legislative authorities". Article 2, paragraph 3 (a) and (b) of the ICCPR. Equivalent articles detailing the requirement of an effective remedy can be found in instruments such as the Convention on the Elimination of All Forms of Racial Discrimination (article 6); the Migrant Workers Convention (article 83); the European Convention on Human Rights (article 13), the American Convention on Human Rights (article 25); and the African Charter on Human and Peoples' Rights (article 7).

of a complaint,[166] this right to an effective remedy is of great importance to nationals and non-nationals since "the enjoyment of the rights recognised, without discrimination, will often be appropriately promoted [...] through the provision of judicial or other effective remedies".[167] There is no indication that the right to an effective remedy could be restricted to nationals. These provisions thereby provide an avenue for stateless persons to seek redress for difficulties that they encounter in their enjoyment of the rights elaborated – including indeed their right to a nationality[168] and arguably also the specific entitlements due to them as stateless persons.[169]

The right to a *fair trial* can be found in the International Covenant on Civil and Political Rights. Its article 14 concerns itself with the procedural guarantees that are to ensure "the proper administration of justice".[170] Although this article does not explicitly provide for the right of access to courts, this right is intrinsic to the concepts of a fair hearing and equality before the courts:

> It is inconceivable that international human rights instruments should prescribe in detail the procedural guarantees afforded to parties in a pending proceeding without guaranteeing that which alone makes it possible for them to benefit from such guarantees. The fair, public and expeditious characteristics of a judicial proceeding are of no value at all if there is no judicial proceeding. Accordingly, the right to a fair trial embodies the 'right to a court'; of which the right to institute proceedings, i.e. the right of access, constitutes one aspect.[171]

[166] The phrasing of these articles implies that the existence of a procedure for administrative review may also satisfy the requirement of affording persons an effective remedy against the violation of their rights – there need not necessarily be recourse to a court. See also Carmen Tiburcio, "Chapter X. Procedural Rights" in *The human rights of aliens under international and comparative law*, Kluwer Law International, The Hague: 2001, page 256.

[167] Committee on Economic, Social and Cultural Rights, *General Comment 3: The Nature of States Parties Obligations,* E/1991/23, New York and Geneva: 1990, para. 5. The Committee on Economic, Social and Cultural Rights argued that the importance of an effective remedy is not limited to the context of the enjoyment of civil and political rights (generally considered more readily justiciable) but that states should equally aspire to ensuring an effective remedy in relation to certain economic, social and cultural rights "which would seem to be capable of immediate application by judicial and other organs in many national systems". So, although the International Covenant on Economic, Social and Cultural Rights does not promulgate the right to an effective remedy, the Committee has read this into the overall human rights system.

[168] The relevance of these guarantees in the context of nationality disputes has already been dealt with in chapter V, section 2.2.

[169] Recall the statement made by the ESC Committee and cited in the previous note whereby even in the context of the International Covenant on Economic, Social and Cultural Rights, which does not have its own provision on the right to an effective remedy, such a remedy must be made available by states.

[170] Human Rights Committee, *General Comment 32 on Article 14: Right to equality before courts and tribunals and to a fair trial,* CCPR/C/GC/32, Geneva: 23 August 2007, para. 2 (Replacing *General Comment 13 on Article 14: Equality before the courts and the Right to a Fair and Public Hearing by an Independent Court Established by Law,* A/39/40, 13 April 1984).

[171] Nihal Jayawickrama, "The Judicial Application of Human Rights Law", Cambridge University Press, Cambridge: 2002, pages 481-481; as cited in James Hathaway, *The Rights of Refugees Under International Law*, Cambridge University Press, Cambridge: 2005, page 650.

Thus article 14 of the ICCPR "encompasses the right of access to courts in the determination of criminal charges and rights and obligations in a suit at law".[172] Similar guarantees can be found in many other human rights instruments.[173] Nowhere is there any suggestion that the enjoyment of the right to a (fair) hearing may be restricted to nationals only.[174] In fact, the Human Rights Committee has now declared that

> The right of access to courts and tribunals and equality before them is not limited to citizens of State parties, but must also be available to all individuals, regardless of nationality or statelessness, or whatever their status, whether asylum seekers, refugees, migrant workers, unaccompanied children or other

[172] Article 14, paragraph 1 of the ICCPR. Human Rights Committee, *General Comment 32 on Article 14: Right to equality before courts and tribunals and to a fair trial,* CCPR/C/GC/32, Geneva: 23 August 2007, para. 9. See also James Hathaway, *The Rights of Refugees Under International Law*, Cambridge University Press, Cambridge: 2005, page 648; Magdalena Sepulveda; Theo van Banning; Gudrun Gudmundsdotter; Christine Chamoun, *Universal and Regional Human Rights Protection: Cases and Commentaries*, University for Peace, Ciudad Colon: 2004, page 527; Sarah Joseph; Jenny Schultz; Melissa Castan, *The International Covenant on Civil and Political Rights. Cases, Materials and Commentary*, Oxford University Press, Oxford: 2000, page 283. Recall that the guarantees encompassed in the right to a fair hearing are not necessarily directly applicable to the context of disputes on nationality attribution as these may not be deemed to fall within the ambit of criminal or civil suits. See chapter V, section 2.

[173] Article 6, paragraph 1 of the European Convention on Human Rights; Article 8 of American Convention on Human Rights (that explicitly promulgates the fundamental right of every person to a hearing); and article 7 of the African Charter on Human and Peoples' Rights. In fact, in all, "the Universal Declaration of Human Rights and the Civil and Political Covenant have inspired fair trial provisions in no less than 20 global and regional human rights treaties and other instruments". David Weissbrodt, *The Right to a Fair Trial*, Martinus Nijhoff Publishers, The Hague: 2001, page 153.

[174] The Human Rights Committee included the right to a fair trial among the list of rights to which aliens are entitled under the covenant in its *General Comment 15: The position of aliens under the covenant,* Geneva: 11 April 1986, para. 7. The UN Special Rapporteur on the Rights of Non-Citizens, David Weissbrodt, concurs in his 2005 report on the rights of non-citizens that "they shall be equal before the courts and tribunals and shall be entitled to a fair and public hearing". David Weissbrodt, *The Rights of Non-Citizens,* Office of the United Nations High Commissioner for Human Rights, HR/PUB/05/1, Geneva 2005, para. 41. See also Diana Elles, *International Provisions Protecting the Human Rights of Non-Citizens: Study,* New York: , page 35; Magdalena Sepulveda; Theo van Banning; Gudrun Gudmundsdotter; Christine Chamoun, *Universal and Regional Human Rights Protection: Cases and Commentaries*, University for Peace, Ciudad Colon: 2004, page 546. Beyond the unambiguous conferral of this right on "all persons" there are numerous additional signals that such differentiation of treatment between nationals and non-nationals would be considered at odds with the right to equality before the courts and a fair hearing. Indeed a comparative study of domestic practice also uncovered that "as regards access to courts, the great majority of countries grant [...] this right to everyone, without distinctions" so to both nationals and non-nationals (including stateless persons) alike. See also the examples of state legislation provided. Carmen Tiburcio, "Chapter X. Procedural Rights" in *The human rights of aliens under international and comparative law*, Kluwer Law International, The Hague: 2001, pages 252-253. Moreover, the importance attributed to the right of access to courts and the right to a fair trial has led to several aspects of this right being recognised as non-derogable. See David Weissbrodt, *The Right to a Fair Trial*, Martinus Nijhoff Publishers, The Hague: 2001, page 154.

> persons, who may find themselves in the territory or subject to the jurisdiction of the State party.[175]

So all stateless persons, whatever their status in their host state, should be able to rely on the courts in the context of civil and criminal suits, on a basis of equality. This clear-cut statement shows that human rights law thereby negates the, somewhat more ambiguous, protection offered under the 1954 Statelessness Convention, as described above.

International human rights law therefore guarantees stateless persons the fundamental right of access to courts (in the context of civil and criminal cases) and the right to an effective remedy in the event of a violation of their human rights. But are there also human rights norms that have the effect of removing some of the practical obstacles that may impair the access to court for non-nationals? On this question, human rights law is less forthcoming. Arguably, the overall guarantee of equality before the courts will limit the freedom of states to treat nationals and non-nationals differently with regard to the conditions for petitioning a court and related matters. It can therefore be asked whether requiring (only) non-nationals to post a security deposit in order to bring a case before the court - the *cautio judicarum* solvi - can be maintained in the contemporary human rights climate. Demanding a security deposit of non-nationals, because they are non-nationals, would amount to discriminatory treatment.[176] Where a *cautio* is demanded of insolvents or suspected insolvents, this condition must be applied to nationals and non-nationals equally. This means that stateless persons may not be wholly exempt from posting a security deposit, but may be subjected to this requirement on the same terms as a national. Human rights law has an identical impact on the rules for the provision of legal aid. The right of access to court "must be substantive, not just formal"[177] and may therefore require positive obligations from the state. Any assistance that is provided must be available to nationals and non-nationals on equal terms.[178] Stateless persons can, therefore, rely on the overall human rights field for the same guarantees as are explicitly set down in article 16 of the 1954 Statelessness Convention.

---

[175] Human Rights Committee, *General Comment 32 on Article 14: Right to equality before courts and tribunals and to a fair trial,* CCPR/C/GC/32, Geneva: 23 August 2007, para. 9.

[176] Carmen Tiburcio, "Chapter X. Procedural Rights" in *The human rights of aliens under international and comparative law*, Kluwer Law International, The Hague: 2001, pages 264-265. See also the 1954 Hague Convention on Civil Procedure and the 1980 Hague Convention on International Access to Justice which determine that a *cautio* cannot be demanded of a non-national purely on the basis of their foreign nationality. These Conventions were developed within the forum of the Hague Conference on Private International Law but have not been widely ratified (they currently count 44 and 22 state parties respectively).

[177] Magdalena Sepulveda; Theo van Banning; Gudrun Gudmundsdotter; Christine Chamoun, *Universal and Regional Human Rights Protection: Cases and Commentaries*, University for Peace, Ciudad Colon: 2004, page 546.

[178] In the context of criminal proceedings, for instance, the relevant human rights norms even determine that the state must provide legal assistance free of charge if the defendant does not have sufficient means to pay for it. Article 14, paragraph 3(d) of the ICCPR; Article 18, paragraph 3(d) of the CMW; Article 6, paragraph 3(c) of the ECHR; Article 8, paragraph 2(e) of the American Convention on Human Rights. The 1954 Hague Convention on Civil Procedure and the 1980 Hague Convention on International Access to Justice explicitly determine that free legal aid be granted to non-nationals under the same conditions as to nationals in both civil and criminal proceedings.

Moreover, the international human rights regime introduces a wide range of additional guarantees regarding the nature and quality of judicial remedies. Human rights law is concerned not only with the availability of a trial but also with ensuring that the composition of the tribunal and course of the procedure are such that the hearing can be deemed *fair*. Thanks to human rights instruments, stateless persons can put their case to a court and are guaranteed that this court is "competent, independent and impartial [and] established by law".[179] The hearing must be public and – particularly in the event of the determination of a criminal charge – a number of procedural safeguards must also be in place.[180] If a stateless person raises a complaint against a violation of his rights and the competent (judicial or administrative) authorities find in his favour, the state must also "undertake [...] to ensure that the competent authorities shall enforce such remedies when granted".[181] Human rights law has thereby added further substance to the fundamental right of access to courts, going beyond the terms of the 1954 Statelessness Convention.

5 Freedom of Religion

It has been suggested that "the struggle for the freedom of religion precedes every other, in the history of human rights"[182] and it undoubtedly retains its importance to this day. The liberty to determine and practice your own beliefs - closely bound up with the more general freedoms of thought and of expression - is central to core human needs.[183] This is a fact that we will see reflected in the terms in which the freedom of religion is protected under international law. Although stateless persons are not generally reported to experience difficulties in practicing their freedom of religion as a direct consequence of their statelessness, restrictions on the religious freedom of non-nationals are not uncommon. A report by then United Nations Special Rapporteur on Religious Intolerance in 1989 "identified Bulgaria,

[179] Article 14, paragraph 1 of the ICCPR.

[180] See for example article 14, paragraphs 2-7 of the ICCPR. For a discussion of the "qualitative requirements" of article 14, see also James Hathaway, *The Rights of Refugees Under International Law*, Cambridge University Press, Cambridge: 2005, pages 653-655. See further David Weissbrodt, *The Right to a Fair Trial*, Martinus Nijhoff Publishers, The Hague: 2001; Sarah Joseph; Jenny Schultz; Melissa Castan, *The International Covenant on Civil and Political Rights. Cases, Materials and Commentary*, Oxford University Press, Oxford: 2000, pages 277-339.

[181] Article 2, paragraph 3(c) of the ICCPR. The right to an effective remedy also embodies the possibility of offering effective interim measures wherever necessary. See the discussion of the case of *Mamatkulov and Abdurasulovic v. Turkey* before the European Court of Human Rights, 2003, in Magdalena Sepulveda; Theo van Banning; Gudrun Gudmundsdotter; Christine Chamoun, *Universal and Regional Human Rights Protection: Cases and Commentaries*, University for Peace, Ciudad Colon: 2004, pages 537-545.

[182] Carmen Tiburcio, "Chapter IX. Public Rights" in *The human rights of aliens under international and comparative law*, Kluwer Law International, The Hague: 2001, page 205.

[183] A person's religion or belief has been described as "one of the fundamental elements of his conception of life". Fourth preamble to the UN Declaration on Elimination of All Forms of Intolerance and of Discrimination Based on Religion or Belief, adopted by the General Assembly on 25 November 1981. See on the content and value of this Declaration Henry Steiner; Philip Alston, *International Human Rights in Context. Law, Politics and Morals,* Oxford University Press, Oxford: 2000, pages 469-473.

Byelorussia, Cape Verde, Finland, Pakistan, Rwanda, Sudan, Syria, Ukraine and the United States as countries in which the religious freedom of non-citizens is less fully guaranteed than is that of citizens."[184] And the freedom of religion is certainly under no less pressure today than it was then – in fact, if anything, the tolerance for the religious beliefs and habits of foreigners has deteriorated since 11 September 2001 and the attack on the World Trade Centre. It cannot be ruled out that stateless persons are among the groups affected. In fact, where statelessness afflicts a particular minority group, targeting on the basis of religion may be an element of the problem – think of the denationalisation of the Rohingya *Muslim* minority in Myanmar.[185] In such cases, discrimination on religious grounds or attempts to suppress the religious beliefs or practices of the persons involved may surround the formal denial of citizenship.[186]

5.1 The 1954 Convention relating to the Status of Stateless Persons

The article housing the freedom of religion was given a position of honour right at the start of the 1954 Convention relating to the Status of Stateless Persons, in the chapter elaborating "general provisions". Article 4 provides that

> the Contracting States shall accord to stateless persons within their territories treatment at least as favourable as that accorded to their nationals with respect to freedom to practice their religion and freedom as regards the religious education of their children.[187]

The weight attributed to the freedom of religion is illustrated not only by this article's positioning in the instrument, but also by the determination that no reservations to the provision are permitted.[188] Importantly, it espouses both the freedom of stateless persons to practice their religion and the freedom to teach their beliefs to their children. This also implies the freedom to choose one's religion. And, these rights are attributed to the stateless as soon as they are physically present in the state – there is no precondition of *lawful* presence or residence. Furthermore, the wording used is unique to this provision in that it generates a special standard of treatment that is not found elsewhere: treatment *at least as favourable* as that

184 James Hathaway, *The Rights of Refugees Under International Law*, Cambridge University Press, Cambridge: 2005, page 569. Reference is made to the report by Elizabeth Benito, *Elimination of All Forms of Intolerance and Discrimination Based on Religion or Belief*, UN Doc. E.89.XIV.3, 1989, paras. 35-46. Tiburcio also points out a number of countries that formally grant religious freedom to citizens only. See Carmen Tiburcio, "Chapter IX. Public Rights" in *The human rights of aliens under international and comparative law*, Kluwer Law International, The Hague: 2001, page 209.

185 Maureen Lynch, *Lives on hold: The human cost of statelessness*, Washington: 2005, pages 31-32.

186 See also Asma Jahangir, *Annual Report of the Special Rapporteur on freedom of religion or belief*, E/CN.4/2005/61, 20 December 2004, para. 36 and the case of the Maldives in Abdelfattah Amor, *Annual Report of the Special Rapporteur on Religious Intolerance*, E/CN.4/2000/65, 15 February 2000, para. 64; Asma Jahangir, *Annual Report of the Special Rapporteur on freedom of religion or belief*, A/HRC/4/21, 26 December 2006, para. 16.

187 Note that the wording is identical to its counterpart in the 1951 Convention relating to the Status of Refugees.

188 Article 38 of the 1954 Convention relating to the Status of Stateless Persons.

accorded to nationals.[189] The assertion of this standard stems from concern – expressed in particular by the Holy See at the time – that national treatment "would not do in countries where religious liberty was circumscribed".[190]

However, as Hathaway explains in relation to the 1951 Refugee Convention, the ultimate aim was not to grant a privileged position to refugees over a state's own nationals but rather to ensure that there is "substantive equality of religious freedom for refugees [... achieved by obliging states...] to take account of the specificity of the religious needs of refugees".[191] But, this does not necessarily mean that individuals can claim "material facilities and economic assistance" for the purposes of practicing of their religion on the basis of this norm.[192] Meanwhile, with regard to the freedom of religious education, a similar duty to respect – rather than necessarily fulfil – this right is envisaged by the 1954 Statelessness Convention: stateless parents

> are free (if they have the resources) to enrol their children in schools which provide the preferred form of religious instruction; and if they are not able to fund education of that kind, they enjoy the liberty to withdraw their children from any non-preferred form of religious instruction provided within the public school system.[193]

Finally, it should be noted that the freedom of religion, as elaborated in the 1954 Statelessness Convention, is not boundless. In accordance with article 2 of the same Convention, states may take measures "for the maintenance of public order" that may in effect impose restrictions on the freedom of stateless persons to *practice* or *teach* their religion.[194]

---

[189] In chapter IX we saw that the 1954 Statelessness Convention prescribes three basic standards of treatment for the enjoyment of rights by stateless persons: treatment at least as favourable as aliens generally, national treatment and absolute rights. This is the only provision that deviates slightly from this overall approach.

[190] Nehemiah Robinson, *Convention relating to the status of stateless persons - Its history and interpretation*, UNHCR, Geneva: 1955, page 29.

[191] These comments are equally valid with respect to the 1954 Statelessness Convention into which, as noted, the provision on religious freedom was transposed unchanged. James Hathaway, *The Rights of Refugees Under International Law*, Cambridge University Press, Cambridge: 2005, pages 572-573.

[192] Nehemiah Robinson, *Convention relating to the status of stateless persons - Its history and interpretation*, UNHCR, Geneva: 1955, page 29.

[193] James Hathaway, *The Rights of Refugees Under International Law*, Cambridge University Press, Cambridge: 2005, page 583. The right of stateless children to an education – and thus to access the public school system - is also dealt with in the 1954 Convention relating to the Status of Stateless Persons and will be dealt with in chapter XI, section 6.

[194] James Hathaway, *The Rights of Refugees Under International Law*, Cambridge University Press, Cambridge: 2005, page 578. Note that in this context, "*Public order* is the translation of the French *ordre public* which has acquired a particular meaning in French and is also being used in international documents [...] It covers everything essential to the life of the country, including its security". Nehemiah Robinson, *Convention relating to the status of stateless persons - Its history and interpretation*, UNHCR, Geneva: 1955, page 24.

5.2 International human rights law

Guided by the Universal Declaration of Human Rights, which includes the freedom of religion in its article 18, all major human rights instruments promulgate the freedom of "thought, conscience and religion".[195] This right is clearly and unambiguously granted to *everyone* – the possession of a (particular) nationality is irrelevant for its enjoyment.[196] In fact, the recognition of the freedom to practice the religion of one's own choosing has been described as "one of the first signs of non-discrimination between nationals and aliens [...] as it implies the idea of tolerance towards others".[197] Under international human rights law, a stateless person therefore enjoys the freedom to

> have or to adopt a religion or belief of [his] choice, and freedom, either individually or in community with others and in public or private, to manifest his religion or belief in worship, observance, practice or teaching.[198]

The right is elaborated in direct terms, so nationals and non-nationals alike are to be guaranteed freedom of religion in accordance with this international standard – an obvious advantage over the provision in the 1954 Statelessness Convention that still effectively renders the enjoyment of freedom of religion contingent on the treatment by the state of nationals generally. Human rights law also protects the freedom to choose and change one's religion which was not explicitly included in the 1954 Statelessness Convention.[199] In addition, human rights instruments protect

---

[195] Article 18 of the International Covenant on Civil and Political Rights; Article 14 of the Convention on the Rights of the Child; Article 5, paragraph (d)(vii) of the Convention on the Elimination of Racial Discrimination; Article 12 of the Migrant Workers Convention; Article 9 of the European Convention on Human Rights; Article 12 of the American Convention on Human Rights; Article 8 of the African Charter of Human and Peoples' Rights. Also relevant are the UN Declaration on Elimination of All Forms of Intolerance and of Discrimination Based on Religion or Belief; Article 27 of the ICCPR and Article 30 of the Convention on the Rights of the Child on the freedom of religion for members of minority groups; Article 13, paragraph 3 of the International Covenant on Economic, Social and Cultural Rights on the freedom to ensure the religious education of one's children; and all non-discrimination provisions, whereby religion is a prohibited ground for differential treatment.

[196] David Weissbrodt, *Final Report on Prevention of Discrimination - The Rights of Non-Citizens,* E/CN.4/Sub.2/2003/23, 26 May 2003, para. 47. Note in this regard also article 5, paragraphs 1 (e) and (f) of the UN Declaration on the Human Rights of Individuals Who are not Nationals of the Country in which They Live.

[197] Carmen Tiburcio, "Chapter IX. Public Rights" in *The human rights of aliens under international and comparative law*, Kluwer Law International, The Hague: 2001, page 206.

[198] Article 18, paragraph 1 of the International Covenant on Civil and Political Rights. Note that in accordance with article 4, paragraph 2 of the Covenant, this right is to be protected - and cannot to be derogated from - even in the event of an emergency. See for further details of the content of the norm on the freedom of religion also article 6 of the UN Declaration on Elimination of All Forms of Intolerance and of Discrimination Based on Religion or Belief.

[199] Paragraph 2 of article 18 of the ICCPR even expressly prohibits the use of coercion to effect adherence to – or recantation of - a particular religion or belief. See also Human Rights Committee, *General Comment 22: The Right to Freedom of Thought, Conscience and Religion,* A/48/40 vol. I, Geneva: 1993, para. 5.

everyone's right to freedom of opinion and expression,[200] an important guarantee closely related to the freedom of religion that cannot be found in the 1954 Statelessness Convention.

However, there is a highly significant aspect to the freedom of religion as protected under international human rights law that has yet to be mentioned. As far as the right to *manifest* one's religion is concerned – the "active component of one's religious freedom"[201] – this is not guaranteed entirely without qualification. Under the International Covenant on Civil and Political Rights, restrictions may be placed on the freedom to manifest one's beliefs on the grounds of "public safety, order, health or morals or the fundamental rights and freedoms of others".[202] When comparing the opportunity to restrict the freedom of religion under human rights law to the terms of the 1951 Refugee Convention – and by extension the 1954 Statelessness Convention – Hathaway expressed concern at what he described as the sanctioning of "other forms of limitation" that were in some cases even "specifically rejected by the drafters of the Refugee Convention".[203] He suggests that the refugee (or statelessness) convention offers broader protection than general human rights law and that a refugee (or stateless person) could "avoid the impact of [...] limitations on religious freedom by invoking the Refugee Convention".[204] But, as we have already noted, the refugee and statelessness conventions do not offer blanket protection of freedom of religion - they prescribe, at a minimum, national treatment. Therefore, where states have curtailed the freedom of religion generally on one of these grounds, there is nothing to stand in the way of also applying such

[200] Article 19 of the Universal Declaration of Human Rights; Article 19 of the International Covenant on Civil and Political Rights; Article 13 of the Convention on the Rights of the Child; Article 5, paragraph (d)(viii) of the Convention on the Elimination of Racial Discrimination; Article 13 of the Migrant Workers Convention; Article 10 of the European Convention on Human Rights; Article 13 of the American Convention on Human Rights; Article 9 of the African Charter on Human and Peoples' Rights.

[201] As opposed to the "*passive* component, which consists of mere adherence to certain beliefs". Sarah Joseph; Jenny Schultz; Melissa Castan, *The International Covenant on Civil and Political Rights. Cases, Materials and Commentary*, Oxford University Press, Oxford: 2000, page 375.

[202] Article 18, paragraph 3 of the International Covenant on Civil and Political Rights. Such limitations are only permitted so long as they are prescribed by law and necessary to protect the value for which they are invoked. The list of limitations is to be interpreted strictly and is limitative. Moreover, with regard to the term "morals" it is important to note that this concept "derives from many social, philosophical and religious traditions; consequently, limitations on the freedom to manifest a religion or belief for the purpose of protecting morals must be based on principles not deriving exclusively from a single tradition". This ground cannot therefore be invoked in favour of the majority religion against the beliefs of minority groups. See Human Rights Committee, *General Comment 22: The Right to Freedom of Thought, Conscience and Religion,* A/48/40 vol. I (1993), para. 8. See further Sarah Joseph; Jenny Schultz; Melissa Castan, *The International Covenant on Civil and Political Rights. Cases, Materials and Commentary*, Oxford University Press, Oxford: 2000, pages 376-379. Note that the Convention on the Rights of the Child, the Migrant Workers Convention and the American Convention on Human Rights maintain the same grounds while the European Convention on Human Rights has omitted public safety from the list and the African Charter refers only to "law and order".

[203] As we saw, the 1951 Refugee Convention and the 1954 Statelessness Convention only admit restrictions on the grounds of "public order". James Hathaway, *The Rights of Refugees Under International Law*, Cambridge University Press, Cambridge: 2005, pages 579-580.

[204] James Hathaway, *The Rights of Refugees Under International Law*, Cambridge University Press, Cambridge: 2005, page 581.

restrictions to stateless persons. Moreover, it can be questioned whether to invoke the 1954 Statelessness Convention in favour of a more sweeping norm on freedom of religion would really be to the benefit of the overall human rights standard. Freedom of religion would certainly be advanced, but the other values which the ICCPR and similar instruments strive to protect through the allowance of restrictions on grounds such as the "rights and freedom of others" would then be endangered.[205] From this perspective I would argue that the concern expressed by Hathaway at the scope of permissible limitations to the freedom of religion under general human rights law is, in fact, unwarranted and that the Statelessness Convention has no added benefit alongside the forceful, well-balanced and detailed norm contained in human rights instruments.

6 RIGHT TO PROPERTY

While reports describing the plight of stateless populations across the globe are relatively silent on issues relating to their freedom of religion, they are much more vocal on the difficulties that stateless persons face in renting, buying, inheriting or retaining property.[206] For example, in Syria, it was reported that

> with no nationality, Kurds cannot obtain property deeds or register cars or businesses [...] Some register their property under the names of friends or relatives who are nationals to circumvent these issues. Yet this arrangement forces them to rely upon the good faith of such persons, and the problem still remains that they cannot pass on ownership of property to their children.[207]

Gaining legal title to land or other immovable assets – and protecting these from confiscation – appears to be a particular problem for stateless persons.[208] Numerous countries impose restrictions on the ownership or real estate by non-nationals or simply forbid them outright from owning land.[209] These policies stem from

---

205 Consider the importance for the protection of other fundamental rights – such as the right to be free from torture and the right to life - of being able to prohibit such practices as female genital mutilation, even where this is exercised on the basis of a certain religious belief. Henry Steiner; Philip Alston, *International Human Rights in Context. Law, Politics and Morals*, Oxford University Press, Oxford: 2000, page 473.

206 See for example UNHCR, "Statelessness and Citizenship" in *The State of the World's Refugees - A Humanitarian Agenda*, Oxford University Press, Oxford: 1997, page 241; Maureen Lynch, *Lives on hold: The human cost of statelessness,* Washington: 2005, page 23.

207 Maureen Lynch and Perveen Ali, *Buried Alive. Stateless Kurds in Syria,* Report for Refugees International, January 2006, pages 6-7.

208 This has been reported with regard to the Banyarwanda in the Democratic Republic of Congo, the Hill Tribes in Thailand, the Rohingya in Myanmar, the Black Africans in Mauritania, the ethnic Chinese in Brunei and the Meskhetian Turks in Russia. See Maureen Lynch, *Lives on hold: The human cost of statelessness,* Washington: 2005; Advisory Board on Human Security (prepared by Constantin Sokoloff), *Denial of Citizenship: A Challenge to Human Security,* February 2005, page 20.

209 James Hathaway, *The Rights of Refugees Under International Law*, Cambridge University Press, Cambridge: 2005, page 516; Carmen Tiburcio, "Chapter V. Private Rights" in *The human rights of aliens under international and comparative law*, Kluwer Law International, The Hague: 2001, pages 137-144. See also Human Rights Committee, *Case of Adam v. The Czech Republic,* Comm. No.

considerations of sovereignty and national security.[210] But ownership of other types of property may also be restricted.[211] Are these practices in line with contemporary international law?

6.1 The 1954 Convention relating to the Status of Stateless Persons

The 1954 Statelessness Convention deals with the issue of property ownership in article 13, which states:

> The Contracting States shall accord to a stateless person treatment as favourable as possible and, in any event, not less favourable than that accorded to aliens generally in the same circumstances, as regards the acquisition of movable and immovable property and other rights pertaining thereto, and to leases and other contracts relating to movable and immovable property.

Knowing by now what to look for, we can immediately ascertain that the level of attachment required for the enjoyment of this right is the lowest that is set by the Statelessness Convention (being subject to the jurisdiction of the state is enough), but that the standard of protection offered is also the weakest (not less favourable than aliens generally), although a higher standard is encouraged.[212] No absolute right to acquire property can be garnered from this article. Two further observations can be made to clarify the scope of protection offered under this provision. Firstly, "it must be assumed that the word 'property' is used in the broad sense of the word, including not only tangible property but also the so-called 'property rights', for instance, securities, moneys, bank accounts".[213] This is important in view of the difficulties experienced by stateless persons in practice, as mentioned above. And secondly, where reference is made to the *rights pertaining to* moveable and immoveable property, this means that "sale, exchange, mortgaging, pawning,

---

586/1994 (1996). This fact contributes to overcrowding in areas where the presence of stateless persons is tolerated - such as dedicated camps - and also has an impact on the individuals' freedom of movement and right to (adequate) housing. See for example the account of the living conditions of the Bihari in Bangladesh in Maureen Lynch; Thatcher Cook, *Citizens of nowhere. The stateless Biharis of Bangladesh,* Washington: 2006.

210 Carmen Tiburcio, "Chapter V. Private Rights" in *The human rights of aliens under international and comparative law*, Kluwer Law International, The Hague: 2001, page 138.

211 One of the issues faces by the erased in Slovenia was reportedly the "denial of rights to property ownership, founding a company, opening bank accounts, mobile telephone subscriptions, register a car in their own name". Brad Blitz, 'Statelessness and the Social (De)Construction of Citizenship: Political Restructuring and Ethnic Discrimination in Slovenia', in *Journal of Human Rights,* Vol. 5, 2006, page 464. Consider also the case of *Ivcher Bronstein v. Peru* brought before the Inter-American Court of Human Rights (Series C, No. 74, 6 February 2001) whereby Mr. Ivcher denationalised in order to subsequently deprive him of the ownership and therefore control of a television station. The underlying motivation was to suppress certain programming. See Magdalena Sepulveda; Theo van Banning; Gudrun Gudmundsdotter; Christine Chamoun, *Universal and Regional Human Rights Protection: Cases and Commentaries*, University for Peace, Ciudad Colon: 2004, pages 393-394.

212 Note that no reservations have been made by contracting states to this provision.

213 Nehemiah Robinson, *Convention relating to the status of stateless persons - Its history and interpretation*, UNHCR, Geneva: 1955, page 53.

administration [and] income"[214] are also covered. Stateless persons are therefore accorded not only the right to acquire property on terms at least as favourable as those accorded to aliens generally; they also enjoy the full use of that property by way of these related "contractual interests".[215] Following up on this last remark, it should be noted that article 30 of the 1954 Statelessness Convention is also relevant to the right to property because it elaborates the specific right to transfer assets out of the country in the context of resettlement.[216]

6.2 International human rights law

In considering how international human rights law deals with the issue, it should be noted from the outset that the right to property is "one of the more controversial and complex human rights".[217] Indeed, enduring disagreement on the need to protect private property as a value – a discussion that was long fuelled by the "capitalist-socialist philosophical divide"[218] – has inevitably had an enormous impact on the way that this right is proclaimed under human rights law. Although elaborated in several major regional instruments,[219] the right to property as such has not been codified at the universal level beyond a very general formulation in the Universal Declaration of Human Rights and a similar statement in the UN Declaration on the Rights of Non-Nationals:

> 1. Everyone has the right to own property alone as well as in association with others.
> 2. No one shall be arbitrarily deprived of his property.[220]

---

[214] Nehemiah Robinson, *Convention relating to the status of stateless persons - Its history and interpretation*, UNHCR, Geneva: 1955, page 53.

[215] James Hathaway, *The Rights of Refugees Under International Law*, Cambridge University Press, Cambridge: 2005, page 524.

[216] Article 30 of the 1954 Convention relating to the Status of Stateless Persons determines the following: "1. A Contracting State shall, in conformity with its laws and regulations, permit stateless persons to transfer assets which they have brought into its territory, to another country where they have been admitted for the purposes of resettlement. 2. A Contracting State shall give sympathetic consideration to the application of stateless persons for permission to transfer assets wherever they may be and which are necessary for their resettlement in another country to which they have been admitted".

[217] Magdalena Sepulveda; Theo van Banning; Gudrun Gudmundsdotter; Christine Chamoun, *Universal and Regional Human Rights Protection: Cases and Commentaries*, University for Peace, Ciudad Colon: 2004, page 373. See also Theo van Banning, *The Human Right to Property*, Intersentia, Antwerp: 2002, pages 2-6.

[218] James Hathaway, *The Rights of Refugees Under International Law*, Cambridge University Press, Cambridge: 2005, page 518. See also Catarina Krause, "The right to property" in Rosas (ed) *Economic, Social and Cultural Rights*, Martinus Nijhoff Publishers, Dordrecht: 1995, page 144.

[219] Article 1 of the Protocol No. 1 to the European Convention on Human Rights; Article 21 of the American Convention on Human Rights; and Article 14 of the African Charter on Human and Peoples' Rights. For a detailed discussion of the development of the right to property in regional context, see Theo van Banning, *The Human Right to Property*, Intersentia, Antwerp: 2002.

[220] Article 17 of the Universal Declaration of Human Rights. Similar content can be traced in article 5, paragraph 2(d) and article 9 of the UN Declaration on the Human Rights of Individuals Who are not Nationals of the Country in which They Live. The Migrant Workers Convention also includes a prohibition of arbitrary deprivation of property in its article 15. Note that although the ICCPR does not enunciate the right to property, issues relating to the enjoyment of property and property rights have

To the extent that human rights law deals with the right to property, it is to be enjoyed by both nationals and non-nationals alike. However, neither this provision in the Universal Declaration, nor the right to property as formulated under the aforementioned regional instruments, specify a right to *acquire* property. Stateless persons are therefore unable to rely on human rights law for an absolute right to acquire property that would clarify (or replace) their entitlement under the 1954 Statelessness Convention which is contingent on the state's treatment of non-nationals generally.

Instead, international human rights law – in particular through the relevant regional documents – provides for "the use and enjoyment of property, once it is acquired".[221] Protection of the "use and enjoyment" of property includes protection against restrictions on the capacity to invoke what were described in the 1954 Statelessness Convention as *rights pertaining to* the right to property such as sale and mortgaging.[222] Any interference with the peaceful enjoyment of property, or indeed deprivation or confiscation of property, will amount to a violation of this norm unless it can be justified under the permissible exceptions.[223] As such, the interference or confiscation must serve the *public need* or the *general interest*, be provided for by law and be proportional – "a balance needs to be struck between the interests of the community and the fundamental rights of the individual".[224] Overall

---

indirectly been dealt with by the Human Rights Committee on the basis of several provisions in the ICCPR, including article 14 (fair trial), article 26 (equal treatment) and article 27 (rights of minorities). Magdalena Sepulveda; Theo van Banning; Gudrun Gudmundsdotter; Christine Chamoun, *Universal and Regional Human Rights Protection: Cases and Commentaries*, University for Peace, Ciudad Colon: 2004, page 421. Nevertheless, "property rights are not a specifically protected interest under the Civil and Political Covenant". James Hathaway, *The Rights of Refugees Under International Law*, Cambridge University Press, Cambridge: 2005, page 520.

[221] Carmen Tiburcio, "Chapter V. Private Rights" in *The human rights of aliens under international and comparative law*, Kluwer Law International, The Hague: 2001, page 137. Protection of the right to property as "*merely* a civil liberty without any *social elements*". Catarina Krause, "The right to property" in Rosas (ed) *Economic, Social and Cultural Rights*, Martinus Nijhoff Publishers, Dordrecht: 1995, page 149.

[222] See Magdalena Sepulveda; Theo van Banning; Gudrun Gudmundsdotter; Christine Chamoun, *Universal and Regional Human Rights Protection: Cases and Commentaries*, University for Peace, Ciudad Colon: 2004, pages 378-383. Note that with regard to the right to transfer assets abroad, found in article 30 of the 1954 Statelessness Convention in the context of resettlement of stateless persons, this also has a more explicit counterpart under human rights law. Article 5, paragraph 1(g) of the UN Declaration on non-nationals provides for "the right to transfer abroad earnings, savings or other personal monetary assets, subject to domestic currency regulations" and article 32 of the Migrant Workers Convention also offers some guarantees along these lines.

[223] These rights relating to the enjoyment of property and the protection from deprivation of property have been invoked in situations where the ownership of the property in question has not been formalised. See the discussion of the case before the European Court of Human Rights of *The Holy Monestaries v. Greece* (Appl. Nr. 13092/87 and 13984/88, 9 December 1994) in Magdalena Sepulveda; Theo van Banning; Gudrun Gudmundsdotter; Christine Chamoun, *Universal and Regional Human Rights Protection: Cases and Commentaries*, University for Peace, Ciudad Colon: 2004, pages 389-393.

[224] Magdalena Sepulveda; Theo van Banning; Gudrun Gudmundsdotter; Christine Chamoun, *Universal and Regional Human Rights Protection: Cases and Commentaries*, University for Peace, Ciudad Colon: 2004, page 384. These criteria are also bound up in the notion of arbitrariness found in the

though, states are generally afforded a wide margin of appreciation in determining the legitimacy of an interference with acquired property rights to serve a public need.[225]

Nevertheless, to the extent that international law or indeed national law recognises a right to property, this is to be guaranteed without discrimination. Although universal instruments were found to be relatively unforthcoming in professing a general right to property, they have been clear and explicit in prohibiting discrimination in the enjoyment of property rights.[226] Moreover, on the basis of the overall right to equal treatment before the law[227] and the mention (albeit summarily) of rights relating to property in such instruments as the UN Declaration on the Rights of Non-Nationals and the Migrant Workers Convention, it has been concluded that

> general international law provides that aliens should not be discriminated against in their enjoyment of property rights once they have been acquired. If alien property is nationalised whereas the property of nationals remains unaffected then that act is discriminatory and prohibited under international law.[228]

So while stateless persons cannot rely on human rights law for a right to acquire property, in respecting the peaceful and continued enjoyment of property and any rights attributed by the state in this context, any differential treatment between nationals and non-nationals must pass muster as being "based on reasonable and justified criteria".[229] The same is true of distinctions between different categories of non-nationals, such as those that would operate to the particular detriment of

---

provisions dealing with the right to property in the Universal Declaration and the UN Declaration on the Rights of Non-nationals. For the proportionality test to be met, compensation may be required. See in this respect also article 15 of the Migrant Workers Convention and article 21, paragraph 2 of the American Convention on Human Rights where compensation is explicitly required in the event of confiscation or deprivation of property. The extent to which this is recognised to be an absolute precondition for the legitimacy of deprivation of property is still subject to debate. See Catarina Krause, "The right to property" in Rosas (ed) *Economic, Social and Cultural Rights*, Martinus Nijhoff Publishers, Dordrecht: 1995, page 151.

225 Catarina Krause, "The right to property" in Rosas (ed) *Economic, Social and Cultural Rights*, Martinus Nijhoff Publishers, Dordrecht: 1995, page 153.

226 See in particular article 5, paragraphs d (v) and (vi) of the Convention on the Elimination of Racial Discrimination and numerous provisions of the Convention on the Elimination of Discrimination Against Women.

227 As espoused, for example, in article 26 of the International Covenant on Civil and Political Rights. See also section 1 of this chapter.

228 Warwick McKean, *Equality and discrimination under international law*, Clarendon Press, Oxford: 1983, page 195. See also Catarina Krause, "The right to property" in Rosas (ed) *Economic, Social and Cultural Rights*, Martinus Nijhoff Publishers, Dordrecht: 1995, page 148; Theo van Banning, *The Human Right to Property*, Intersentia, Antwerp: 2002, page 49; James Hathaway, *The Rights of Refugees Under International Law*, Cambridge University Press, Cambridge: 2005, pages 521-522.

229 Recall the jurisprudence of the Human Rights Committee as discussed in section 1, in particular Human Rights Committee, *Case of Gueye et al. v. France,* Comm. No. 196/1985 (1989), para. 9.4; Human Rights Committee, *Case of Adam v. The Czech Republic,* Comm. No. 586/1994 (1996), para. 12.4.

stateless persons. The fact that a right to property stemming from human rights law cannot necessarily be relied on has no impact on this conclusion.[230] In other words, where domestic law *does* offer non-nationals the right to *acquire* (certain types of) property, the same general norm of equal treatment under the law may be invoked to ensure that stateless persons benefit from this opportunity on equal terms with other non-nationals. Therefore, where the 1954 Statelessness Convention deals with the right to property by prescribing treatment for stateless persons equal to that of non-nationals generally, rather than an absolute right to acquire or enjoy property, its value over and above contemporary human rights standards is negligible.

7 Civil and Political Rights Absent from the 1954 Statelessness Convention

As mentioned in the introduction to this chapter, even a superficial comparison of the content of the 1954 Statelessness Convention with such documents as the International Covenant on Civil and Political Rights is sufficient to reveal that a number of internationally recognised civil and political rights were not included in the statelessness instrument. Among these are some of the most fundamental of civil rights and freedoms such as the right to life, the freedom from torture, arbitrary arrest and detention, and the prohibition of slavery.[231] It is reported that the drafters deemed it unnecessary to reiterate these rights in an instrument geared to a particular category of persons (first refugees in the 1951 Convention and later stateless persons in this 1954 text) since the universal character of these norms was already accepted.[232] Yet numerous human rights documents that have since been adopted *have* elected to reaffirm these rights in respect of particular groups, including children, persons with disabilities, non-nationals and migrant workers, which effectively nullifies this argument.[233] Even less clear is why the right to privacy and to family life also remained absent from the 1954 Statelessness Convention.[234] In view of its aim of establishing a minimum standard of treatment for stateless persons, it would have been favourable for the overall impact of - and

---

[230] Human Rights Committee, *General Comment 18: Non-discrimination,* Geneva: 10 November 1989, para. 12. See also Human Rights Committee, *Case of Gueye et al. v. France,* Comm. No. 196/1985 (1989), para. 9.4. After noting that "the Covenant does not protect the right to a pension as such", the Committee went on to subject the policy in question to the test of reasonableness and objectiveness, finding a violation of article 26 of the ICCPR.

[231] Found, for example, in articles 6, 7 and 8 of the ICCPR respectively.

[232] James Hathaway, *The Rights of Refugees Under International Law*, Cambridge University Press, Cambridge: 2005, page 94; Yaffa Zilberschats, "Chapter 2 - Citizenship and International Law" in *The Human Right to Citizenship*, Transnational Publishers, Ardsley, NY: 2002, page 41.

[233] See the Convention on the Rights of the Child, the Convention on the Rights of Persons with Disabilities, UN Declaration on the Human Rights of Individuals Who are Not Nationals of the Country in which They Live and the Migrant Workers Convention as well as instruments as the Convention on the Rights of the Child and the Convention on the Elimination of Racial Discrimination.

[234] Note that a recommendation promoting respect for family life and family unity that was elaborated in the Final Act of the 1951 Refugee Convention (Recommendation "B") was not transposed to the Final Act accompanying the 1954 Statelessness Convention. This is regrettable in view of the reports that statelessness may lead to situations of indefinite family separation. See UNHCR, *Statelessness in Canadian Context – A Discussion Paper,* Ottawa, July 2003, page 3.

the message sent by - the instrument had the 1954 Statelessness Convention reiterated these most basic rights and freedoms.

For all of these issues, the only avenue open to stateless persons under the 1954 Statelessness Convention is to rely on the broad and general provision in article 7 requiring equal treatment as accorded to non-nationals generally.[235] Contemporary human rights law has helped to give content to the obligations of states in respect of non-nationals by firmly establishing that everyone – nationals and non-nationals – is entitled to the protection of all of the fundamental rights mentioned above.[236] Thus, if restrictions are to be placed on the exercise of these rights by stateless persons, they must be legitimated under the applicable system of permissible limitations provided for by the human rights regime itself. And, in fact, several of the rights in question are non-derogable with the result that they are not subject to restriction on any ground, even in exceptional circumstances such as a state of national emergency.[237] Generally speaking then, the decision not to add provisions on these matters to the catalogue of rights elaborated in the 1954 Statelessness Convention is of little consequence for the actual protection offered by international law as a whole.

7.1 Freedom from arbitrary detention

Some further comments are, nevertheless, due with regard to one of the rights listed above: freedom from arbitrary detention. There are two reasons for singling out this issue. Firstly, because one of the major problems facing stateless persons is (the threat of) prolonged or indefinite detention, as mentioned in section 2 above in the context of internal and international freedom of movement. Indeed, it has been reported that "unnecessary imprisonment is one of the most pervasive and most difficult problems faced by stateless persons".[238] The second noteworthy point about this subject is that - unlike the 1954 Statelessness Convention - the 1951 Refugee Convention does to some extent deal with the question of arrest and

---

[235] Article 7, paragraph 1 of the 1954 Convention relating to the Status of Stateless Persons.

[236] The Human Rights Committee reaffirmed that these rights are in no way dependent on the possession of the nationality of the state and should be respected with respect to nationals and non-nationals alike. Human Rights Committee, *CCPR General Comment No. 15: The Position of Aliens under the Covenant,* Geneva: Geneva: 11 April 1986, para. 7. Note further that some of these fundamental rights establish their authority not only on the basis of texts like the Universal Declaration of Human Rights and such instruments as the ICCPR, they also have roots in norms of customary international law, even to some extent *jus cogens.* Consider the prohibition of slavery and of genocide and the freedom from torture. Carmen Tiburcio, "Chapter IV. Fundamental Rights" in *The human rights of aliens under international and comparative law*, Kluwer Law International, The Hague: 2001, page 76; Ian Brownlie, *Principles of Public International Law*, Oxford University Press, Oxford: 2003, page 537.

[237] Carmen Tiburcio, "Chapter IV. Fundamental Rights" in *The human rights of aliens under international and comparative law*, Kluwer Law International, The Hague: 2001, pages 75-77.

[238] David Weissbrodt; Clay Collins, 'The Human Rights of Stateless Persons', in *Human Rights Quarterly,* Vol. 28, 2006, page 267. Garbiela Rodriguez Pizarro, *Specific Groups and Individuals - Migrant Workers,* Geneva: 30 December 2002, paragraph 37; Refugees International, "Refugee Voices: Detained Stateless People in Kuwait", 24 September 2007; Stephanie Grant, "The Legal Protection of Stranded Migrants" in R. Cholewinski (ed) *International Migration Law*, TMC Asser Press, The Hague: 2007, pages 29-47.

detention by limiting the freedom of contracting states to impose penalties on refugees for unlawful entry in the country and allowing only provisional detention to be imposed for unlawfully present refugees until such time as their refugee status is determined.[239] In this manner, the refugee instrument offers guidance as to what must be considered *arbitrary* in relation to the *arbitrary detention* of *refugees*. Since a similar determination of the specific application of standards dealing with arbitrary detention has not been made for situations involving stateless persons through the 1954 Statelessness Convention, the stateless must rely on the general human rights system.

Human rights norms do not provide a blanket prohibition of arrest or detention. To the contrary, depriving an individual of his or her liberty is considered to be a legitimate action by the state in a variety of circumstances, so long as certain procedural guarantees are met.[240] One of the instances in which detention of a person is considered permissible is "to prevent his effecting an unauthorised entry into the country or of a person against whom action is being taken with a view to deportation or extradition".[241] In practice, the detention of stateless persons will often stem precisely from their uncertain or unlawful immigration status:

> Without proof of identity or nationality, stateless persons often cannot re-enter their state of habitual residence. Furthermore, the detaining state cannot resolve the question of where to deport the stateless detainee, and it is unwilling to let them illegally reside within its territory. In such cases, stateless persons have been held in prolonged or 'indefinite detention' only because the question of where to send them remains unresolved.[242]

---

[239] See James Hathaway, *The Rights of Refugees Under International Law*, Cambridge University Press, Cambridge: 2005, page 370 onwards.

[240] See the provisions on freedom from arbitrary detention or the right to liberty and security of the person: Article 9 of the Universal Declaration of Human Rights; Article 9 of the International Covenant on Civil and Political Rights; Article 37 of the Convention on the Rights of the Child; Article 16 of the Migrant Workers Convention; Article 7 of the American Convention on Human Rights; Article 5 of the European Convention on Human Rights; and Article 6 of the African Charter on Human and Peoples' Rights.

[241] See article 5, paragraph 1 of the European Convention on Human Rights which provides an exhaustive list of the circumstances in which a person may be deprived of his liberty. This particular situation can be found in sub-paragraph f. In practice, "migrants are particularly vulnerable to deprivation of liberty. On the one hand there is a tendency to criminalise violations of immigration regulations and to punish them severely, in an attempt to discourage irregular migration. On the other hand, a great number of countries resort to administrative detention of irregular migrants pending their deportation". Garbiela Rodriguez Pizarro, *Specific Groups and Individuals - Migrant Workers,* Geneva: 30 December 2002, para. 65. See also Shyla Vohra, "Detention of Irregular Migrants and Asylum Seekers" in R. Cholewinski (ed) *International Migration Law*, TMC Asser Press, The Hague: 2007, page 49.

[242] Moreover, "the problem of prolonged or unwarranted imprisonment is often exacerbated when states, having failed to resolve the question of where to send a particular stateless person, nonetheless attempt to rid themselves of the stateless person by deporting him or her to another state that is also unwilling to receive the person. In such cases, a stateless person may spend years in detention, being passed from state to state like an unwanted pariah". David Weissbrodt; Clay Collins, 'The Human Rights of Stateless Persons', in *Human Rights Quarterly,* Vol. 28, 2006, pages 267-268.

With this in mind, the failure to transpose the provision on the non-imposition of penalties for unlawful entry from the 1951 Refugee Convention to the 1954 Statelessness Convention becomes all the more regrettable and the discussion of a stateless person's right to enter or return to "his own country" all the more pertinent.[243] The prohibition of arbitrary detention, as established within the broader human rights framework, does nonetheless include some elements of protection that can be vital for the stateless. One such guarantee is "the right to control by a court of the legality of detention [which] applies to all persons deprived of their liberty by arrest or detention".[244] And since a review of the arbitrariness of detention also includes such considerations as *appropriateness* and *justice*, human rights law hereby provides an opportunity to take the specific circumstance of statelessness into account.[245] Moreover, this question as to the legality and non-arbitrariness of detention is something that should be subject to *continuous* review. Detention that was lawful and reasonable to begin with may become arbitrary if it becomes too prolonged, as the Human Rights Committee explained in a succession of cases brought by detained non-citizens against Australia: in order not to be characterised as arbitrary, "detention should not continue beyond the period for which a State party can provide appropriate justification".[246] Therefore, while human rights law does not rule out the detention of stateless persons in the context of immigration regulations, it does present an avenue for stateless persons to challenge the permissibility of *unduly prolonged* or *indefinite* detention.[247] Similarly, human rights norms offer protection against continued detention when there is no (longer any) real prospect of expelling the individual.[248] Finally, human rights law does also

---

243 The intrinsic link between this latter question and the protection of stateless persons from arbitrary detention should therefore not be overlooked. See section 2.2 above.

244 Human Rights Committee, *General Comment No. 8: Right to liberty and security of persons,* Geneva: 30 June 1982, paragraph 1.

245 "'Arbitrariness' is not to be equated with 'against the law', but must be interpreted more broadly to include elements of inappropriateness, injustice, lack of predictability and due process of law". Human Rights Committee, *Case of Van Alphen v. The Netherlands,* Comm. No. 305/1988, Geneva: 23 July 1990, paragraph 5.8. Moreover, the Working Group on Arbitrary Detention has urged that "alternative and non-custodial measures, such as reporting requirements, should always be considered before resorting to detention".UN Working Group on Arbitrary Detention, *Report of the visit of the Working Group to the United Kingdom on the issue of immigrants and asylum seekers,* E/CN.4/1999/63/Add.3, 18 December 1998, paragraph 33.

246 Human Rights Committee, *Case of A. v. Australia,* Comm. No. 560/1993, Geneva: 3 April 1997, paragraph 9.4; *Case of C. v. Australia,* Comm. No. 900/1999, Geneva: 28 October 2002, paragraph 8.2; *Case of Baban et. al. v. Australia,* Comm. No. 1014/2001, Geneva: 6 August 2003, paragraph 7.2; *Case of Bakhtiyari v. Australia,* Comm. No. 1069/2002, Geneva: 29 October 2003, paragraph 9.2; *Case of D and E. v. Australia,* Comm. No. 1050/2002, Geneva: 11 July 2006, paragraph 7.2; *Case of Shams et. al. v. Australia,* Comm No. 1255, 1256, 1259, 1260, 1266, 1268, 1270, 1288/2004, Geneva: 20 July 2007, paragraph 7.2. See also Garbiela Rodriguez Pizarro, *Specific Groups and Individuals - Migrant Workers,* Geneva: 30 December 2002, paragraphs 35-38; Shyla Vohra, "Detention of Irregular Migrants and Asylum Seekers" in R. Cholewinski (ed) *International Migration Law,* TMC Asser Press, The Hague: 2007, pages 58-60.

247 In the cases listed above, the Human Rights Committee found a violation of article 9, paragraph 1 of the ICCPR where the claimants (all non-citizens) were subjected to anywhere upwards of two years of detention.

248 Human Rights Committee, *Case of Jalloh v. The Netherlands,* Comm. No. 794/1998, Geneva: 23 March 2002, para. 8.2. See also Human Rights Committee, *Concluding observations: United Kingdom,*

offers a broad range of standards relating to the *conditions* of detention which may be relied upon by any detained person – stateless or otherwise.[249]

7.2 Freedom of opinion, expression and (political) assembly

The absence of political rights as well as rights that can be perceived as politically-tinted from the text of the 1954 Statelessness Convention requires more reflection. Whereas the aforementioned "oversights" involved norms that may have been considered so evidently universal that their reaffirmation would be an unnecessary exercise, this is not the case for the other rights that the Convention has neglected. To begin with, all attempts to codify the freedom of opinion and expression as well as the freedom of (political) assembly were deliberately rejected. While these are perhaps not strictly-speaking political rights – being those rights which enable a person to have "a *direct* influence in the structure of the State"[250] – they may be exercised to the benefit of political activity in the broadest possible sense and certainly play an important role in the overall empowerment of an individual.[251] The exclusion of these rights from the final text of the Convention was, therefore, motivated by a desire to allow states to restrict the political activity of stateless persons on their territory.[252] Through this choice, the instrument also fails to offer

CCPR A/57/40 vol. I, Geneva: 2002, para. 16; European Court of Human Rights, *Case of Chahal v. the United Kingdom,* 23 EHRR 413, 15 November 1996; European Commission on Human Rights, *Case of Caprino v. the United Kingdom,* Application No. 6871/75, 3 March 1978.

[249] Article 10 of the International Covenant on Civil and Political Rights; Article 5 of the American Convention on Human Rights; Article 3 of the European Convention on Human Rights; Article 5 of the African Charter on Human and Peoples' Rights. See also Human Rights Committee, *General Comment No. 21: Replaces general comment 9 concerning humane treatment of persons deprived of liberty,* Geneva: 10 April 1992 and the UN Body of Principles for the Protection of All Persons under Any Form of Detention or Imprisonment, Adopted by General Assembly Resolution 43/173, 9 December 1988. For a further discussion of the problem of detention of persons who do not hold a regular immigration status, see Shyla Vohra, "Detention of Irregular Migrants and Asylum Seekers" in R. Cholewinski (ed) *International Migration Law*, TMC Asser Press, The Hague: 2007.

[250] Carmen Tiburcio, "Chapter VIII. Political Rights" in *The human rights of aliens under international and comparative law*, Kluwer Law International, The Hague: 2001, page 177.

[251] The Human Rights Committee explains that "freedom of expression, assembly and association are essential conditions for the effective exercise of the right to vote". Human Rights Committee, *General Comment No. 25: The right to participate in public affairs, voting rights and the right of equal access to public service,* Geneva: 12 July 1996, paragraph 12. The entire set of political and quasi-political rights have also been collectively referred to as "democratic rights" – even including the freedom of movement. Susan Marks, Andrew Clapham, *International Human Rights Lexicon,* Oxford University Press, Oxford: 2005, page 64.

[252] This is another example of a decision that was taken in the drafting process of the 1951 Refugee Convention that went on to have an indelible effect on the content of the 1954 Statelessness Convention, without there necessarily being any consideration for the difference in characteristics and needs of the two groups. Note that article 2 of both conventions - where the general obligations orfrefugees and stateless persons are set out – was also introduced with a particular view to affording states the opportunity to curtail the political activities of these individuals. Nehemiah Robinson, *Convention relating to the status of stateless persons - Its history and interpretation*, UNHCR, Geneva: 1955, pages 23-24. See also James Hathaway, *The Rights of Refugees Under International Law*, Cambridge University Press, Cambridge: 2005, pages 94 and 887. It is conceivable that a similar motivation also underlies the failure to lay down the right to privacy in the Convention.

the stateless the right to assemble or to freely hold and express opinions in relation to other, non-political matters.

However, the omission of these politically-tinged rights from the 1954 Statelessness Convention is now obviated by general human rights law which proclaims each of these rights to the benefit of all, nationals and non-nationals alike. If a state is concerned about the political activities of stateless persons on its territory – or indeed of any individual or sub-set of the population – then restrictions may be imposed within the constraints of the limitation clauses established in the relevant human rights provisions. For example, where article 19 of the International Covenant on Civil and Political Rights provides for the freedom of opinion and of expression (paragraphs 1 and 2) it also recognises that there may be reason to restrict these rights in order to protect other esteemed values such as the rights of others or national security (paragraph 3). States may therefore continue to restrict the political activities of non-nationals under certain circumstances, so long as the policy falls within the ambit of the permissible limitations.[253] However, a blanket denial of these quasi-political rights to stateless persons could not be legitimated under such clauses.[254] Cases such as the reported arrest and detention of stateless Kurds in Syria for openly campaigning for the reinstatement of their nationality are also clearly a violation of these international standards.[255] Moreover, the Human Rights Committee has explicitly expressed concern about "legislation prohibiting non-citizens from being members of political parties".[256] Human rights law hereby makes an important contribution to the overall protection of the rights of the stateless by guaranteeing their right to express their opinion on their own situation and granting them some basic tools of empowerment that will allow them to stand up for their own needs and rights.

7.3 Right to participate in government

As we go on to consider the protection offered to stateless persons in the enjoyment of "true" political rights – the right to vote, to be elected and to work in public service[257] – we can immediately observe that the 1954 Statelessness Convention does not touch upon these rights in any way. Since we have already established that states were keen to clamp down on the political activities of stateless persons by omitting even the most basic politically tinged rights discussed above, it comes as

[253] The European Convention on Human Rights provides even more leeway to states in this matter by explicitly admitting that despite the guarantees of freedom of expression, freedom of assembly and prohibition of discrimination, states remain free to impose restrictions on the political activity of non-nationals. Article 16 of the European Convention on Human Rights.

[254] See, for example, Human Rights Committee, *Concluding observations: Estonia,* A/51/40, Geneva: 1996 paragraph 120.

[255] Maureen Lynch and Perveen Ali, *Buried Alive. Stateless Kurds in Syria,* Report for Refugees International, January 2006, pages 8-9; Human Rights Committee, *Concluding observations: Syrian Arab Republic,* CCPR/CO/84/SYR, 9 August 2005, paragraph 13.

[256] Human Rights Committee, *Concluding observations: Estonia,* A/58/40, Geneva: 2003, paragraph 79 (17).

[257] Public service functions include such jobs as cabinet minister, diplomat and judge. Diana Elles, *International Provisions Protecting the Human Rights of Non-Citizens: Study,* New York: 1980, page 38.

little surprise that the right to directly participate in government is not granted to the stateless, even at the highest level of attachment. This means, once again, falling back on the general clause in article 7 of the Convention requiring stateless persons to be treated not less favourably than non-nationals generally. In looking to see how contemporary human rights law demands that states treat non-nationals generally, we find political rights to be expressed in (variations of) the following terms:

> Every citizen shall have the right and the opportunity [...] to take part in the conduct of public affairs, directly or through freely chosen representatives; to vote and to be elected [...]; to have access, on general terms of equality, to public service in his country.[258]

The norm applies to everyone but offers these political rights only in relation to a person's country of citizenship. States are fully entitled to exclude non-nationals from these rights.[259] As such, human rights law as it stands today does not provide the stateless with any claim - direct or indirect - to the right to participate in government.

Let us consider the implications of this finding. With the stateless unable to exercise political rights in any country - thanks to their status as non-nationals *everywhere* - neither the 1954 Statelessness Convention nor general human rights law have taken a stand against their lack of empowerment. Unlike other non-nationals, the stateless do not have the option of returning to their country of citizenship to reclaim their political rights or exercising them long-distance through special arrangements.[260] Formally voiceless and disenfranchised, the stateless are without access to the necessary procedures that would enable them to defend themselves against any (perceived) injustices they suffer and influence policy that affects them.

Leaving aside any moral arguments, there are to my mind a number of very tangible objections to this state of affairs. Firstly, in countries with large stateless populations, this absolute lack of empowerment may ultimately be a greater threat to national security - a common ground for restricting the political activity of non-nationals - than there would be in granting political rights. With normal routes for

[258] Article 25 of the International Covenant on Civil and Political Rights. See also article 21 of the Universal Declaration of Human Rights; Article 2; Article 23 of the American Convention on Human Rights; and Article 13 of the African Charter on Human and Peoples' Rights. The Human Rights Committee explains that this is one of the human rights which is exceptionally reserved for citizens. Human Rights Committee, *CCPR General Comment No. 15: The Position of Aliens under the Covenant,* Geneva: Geneva: 11 April 1986, para. 2; Human Rights Committee, *CCPR General Comment No. 25: The right to participate in public affairs, voting rights and the right of equal access to public service,* Geneva: 12 July 1996, para. 3.

[259] In other words, the "disqualification of aliens from exercising political rights has never been held to be discriminatory but a legitimate and reasonable restriction". Warwick McKean, *Equality and discrimination under international law*, Clarendon Press, Oxford: 1983, page 199; See also Diana Elles, *International Provisions Protecting the Human Rights of Non-Citizens: Study,* New York: , page 42; Yaffa Zilberschats, "Chapter 2 - Citizenship and International Law" in *The Human Right to Citizenship*, Transnational Publishers, Ardsley, NY: 2002, page 59.

[260] See for example also article 41 of the Migrant Workers Convention that provides for the facilitation of the exercise of political rights by migrant workers in their country of origin (state of citizenship).

effectuating change closed to them, in every state, the stateless may resort to much more destructive means of attracting attention to their need and opinions and conflict may result.[261] Secondly, if the participation of foreign nationals in government is restricted because it is perceived as a threat to national security or other values on the grounds of their allegiance to *another* state, [262] this particular reasoning should not stand in the way of granting political rights to stateless persons. The stateless differ from other non-nationals in that they do not owe formal allegiance to a foreign country so the idea that they may engage in subversive or malignant action against the state as pawns of a foreign authority is unfounded. Recall, in this context, the discussion of the principle of non-discrimination in section 1 of the present chapter, where it was made clear that *different* cases should also be treated *differently*. Then, there is the danger that a state will use the tool of denial of citizenship in order to deliberately effectuate the disenfranchisement of individuals or groups: anyone whose political activity is considered unfavourable or a threat to the policy of the ruling power. It has already been noted that political motivations underlie many cases of denial of citizenship and that this is becoming a common feature in states that have newly introduced a multi-party democratic system.[263] If a state has withdrawn or withheld citizenship in contravention of international legal standards, it should be possible to also qualify the subsequent exclusion of the stateless person from the political process as a violation of human rights. The importance of this is that it may allow the person concerned to access additional mechanisms for redressing his situation.[264] The approach adopted by the UN Human Rights Committee to the personal scope of the right to enter, as discussed earlier in this chapter, would seem a more appropriate model for the attribution of political rights than an outright exclusion of all non-nationals.[265] And

---

[261] For instance, it has been widely reported that the denial of citizenship of much of the Banyarwanda population in the Democratic Republic of Congo (DRC) – was a major contributor to the many conflicts that have plagued the Great Lakes Region. Advisory Board on Human Security (prepared by Constantin Sokoloff), *Denial of Citizenship: A Challenge to Human Security,* February 2005, page 20 and 26-27. See on the link between statelessness and civil unrest also Dorothy Jean Walker, "Statelessness: Violation or Conduit for Violation of Human Rights?" in *Human Rights Quarterly,* Vol. 3, No. 1, 1981, pages 107-108.

[262] It is asserted that non-nationals are excluded from certain professions because these require loyalty to the state, "which only citizens owe" and the same argument partly underscores the attribution of political rights to nationals only. Yaffa Zilberschats, "Chapter 2 - Citizenship and International Law" in *The Human Right to Citizenship*, Transnational Publishers, Ardsley, NY: 2002, pages 34 and 38. See on the link between "loyalty" and political rights also Diana Elles, *International Provisions Protecting the Human Rights of Non-Citizens: Study,* New York: , pages 37-38 Alexander Aleinikoff; Douglas Klusmeyer, *Citizenship Policies for an Age of Migration*, Carnegie Empowerment for International Peace, Washington D.C.: 2002, page 47.

[263] See chapter V, including the case of the denationalisation of Kenneth Kaunda, former president of Zambia.

[264] For example, while the International Covenant on Civil and Political Rights does not elaborate standards relating to the attribution of nationality (beyond the general right of every child to acquire a nationality), it does provide for the political rights of citizens. Submitting a complaint against the violation of the right to participate in government – even though technically citizenship is required for a claim - would be a means for a stateless person to nevertheless access the individual complaints procedure before the Human Rights Committee.

[265] See section 2.2.2.

finally, I submit that a more tempered approach to restricting the political rights and activities of non-nationals that allows account to be taken of the specific situation of the stateless would be in better keeping with the overall system of human rights protection. As was explained in chapter IX, the universality of the human rights regime in spite of the inclusion of some "citizens rights", is only kept intact thanks to the elaboration of the right to a nationality. Where states are failing – individually or collectively – to ensure that everyone enjoys the bond of citizenship somewhere, this assertion of universality begins to crumble unless special provision is made for those persons who find themselves excluded by the system: the stateless.

It is clear, however, that to start to dislocate political rights from citizenship is such a radical step, that even the aforementioned considerations may be insufficiently persuasive. Political participation is an issue that is intrinsically linked not only with notions such as allegiance and national security, but also with the fundamental concept of sovereignty. Only those who are "members" of the sovereign body are entitled to a say in the decision-making.[266] The world is currently arranged in a particular way, with sovereignty resting at state level and nationality being the mark of membership. Yet the world is also changing and with it are the notions of sovereignty and membership.[267] There is a trend towards the recognition of new levels of membership that can also result in the enjoyment of (certain) political rights. For example, an increasing number of countries grant non-national residents the right to vote or be elected in local elections.[268] Within the European Union, the special voting rights of "EU citizens" have been formalised: all EU citizens are entitled to vote in and stand for local elections of any member

---

266 The right to self-determination strengthens this consideration by providing for "the right of all peoples to pursue freely their economic, social and cultural development *without outside interference* [linked to] the right of every *citizen* to take part in the conduct of public affairs". Emphasis added, Committee on the Elimination of Racial Discrimination, *CERD General Recommendation XXI: Right to Self-Determination,* A/51/18, New York: 1996, para. 9. Although again, the question must be raised whether the stateless can really be perceived as an *outside influence* since they hold no (other) allegiance.

267 Sovereignty is becoming more a "elastic" as opposed to "absolute" concept in this age of globalisation and this is in turn effecting notions of citizenship. Yaffa Zilberschats, "Chapter 2 - Citizenship and International Law" in *The Human Right to Citizenship*, Transnational Publishers, Ardsley, NY: 2002, page 170. This has prompted much discussion on the meaning that is or should be attributed to citizenship today. See for example Guy Goodwin-Gill, 'International Law and Human Rights: Trends Concerning International Migrants and Refugees', in *International Migration Review*, Vol. 23, 1989, pages 531-532; Yasemin Soysal, *Limits of citizenship - Migrants and postnational membership in Europe*, The University of Chicago Press, Chicago: 1994; Vincenzo Ferrari, "Citizenship: Problems, Concepts and Policies" in Torre (ed) *European Citizenship - An Institutional Challenge*, Kluwer Law International, The Hague: 1998; Stephen Castles; Alastair Davidson, *Citizenship and Migration. Globalisation and the Politics of Belonging*, Macmillan Press, London: 2000; Douglas Klusmeyer; Alexander Aleinikoff, *From Migrants to Citizens: Membership in a Changing World*, Carnegie Endowment for International Peace, Washington, DC: 2000; Seyla Benhabib, *Transformations of Citizenship - Dilemmas of the Nation State in the Era of Globalisation*, Koniklijke van Gorcum, Assen: 2001; Alexander Aleinikoff; Douglas Klusmeyer, *Citizenship Policies for an Age of Migration*, Carnegie Empowerment for International Peace, Washington D.C.: 2002; Keith Faulks, *Citizenship*, Routledge, London: 2003.

268 This is largely in reaction to increasing levels of international migration and therefore growing numbers of non-nationals.

state in which they have acquired residence.[269] But also elsewhere, countries have granted political rights at the local-level to non-nationals who meet certain conditions.[270] This new type of membership – somewhere between citizenship and non-citizenship – is described as denizenship or quasi-citizenship.[271] The UN treaty bodies, in particular the Committee on the Elimination of Racial Discrimination, have been very encouraging of these and other developments towards the increased participation of non-nationals in political processes.[272]

However, the disentanglement of nationality and political rights for the purposes of local level politics is by no means a universal trend, nor is it necessarily suggestive of a broader move away from nationality as a precondition for exercising other political rights. One important point that has been made is that local politics are considered to be a very different sort of matter to national politics:

> At local level, the political process pertains only to matters which may affect normal living, such as urbanisation, matters related to education and health services, for instance, while participation at national level would mean giving access to the alien to influence the foreign policy of the country, national security, public debt, the making of national legislation and other issues, considered beyond aliens' interests.[273]

---

[269] All EU citizens are also entitled to vote in and stand for European Parliament elections – an embodiment of "membership" at a regional level that brings with it corresponding political rights. Note that EU citizenship, although a regional concept, is actually dependent upon "membership" at national level. An EU citizen is any person who is a national of one of the EU member states. Articles 17 and 19 of the Treaty Establishing the European Community. See Stephen Castles; Alastair Davidson, *Citizenship and Migration. Globalisation and the Politics of Belonging*, Macmillan Press, London: 2000, pages 97-100; Yaffa Zilberschats, "Chapter 6 - Recent Political Changes and Citizenship" in *The Human Right to Citizenship*, Transnational Publishers, Ardsley, NY: 2002, pages 171-176. Moreover, there have been moves to expand the political rights attributed on the basis of EU citizenship and residence, as opposed to nationality. For a discussion of the suggestions tabled, see Helen Staples, *The Legal Status of Third Country Nationals Resident in the European Union*, Kluwer Law International, The Hague: 1999, pages 335-355; Kay Hailbronner, "Free Movement of EU Nationals and Union Citizenship" in R. Cholewinski (ed) *International Migration Law*, TMC Asser Press, The Hague: 2007, page 325.

[270] These include Israel, Paraguay and Argentina. Many European countries also extend local-level political rights to non-nationals who are not EU citizens. See Carmen Tiburcio, "Chapter VIII. Political Rights" in *The human rights of aliens under international and comparative law*, Kluwer Law International, The Hague: 2001, pages 181-182; Alexander Aleinikoff; Douglas Klusmeyer, *Citizenship Policies for an Age of Migration*, Carnegie Empowerment for International Peace, Washington D.C.: 2002, pages 51-54.

[271] Stephen Castles; Alastair Davidson, *Citizenship and Migration. Globalisation and the Politics of Belonging*, Macmillan Press, London: 2000, page 94.

[272] Committee on the Elimination of Racial Discrimination, *Concluding Observations: Sweden,* A/52/18, New York: 1997, para. 499; *Estonia,* A/55/18, New York: 2000, para. 77; *Lithuania,* A/57/18 New York: 2002, para. 167; *Liechtenstein,* CERD A/57/18, New York: 2002, para. 149. Human Rights Committee, *Concluding Observations: Portugal,* A/52/40 vol. 1 Geneva: 1997, paras. 322 and 326; *Switzerland,* A/57/40 vol. 1, Geneva: 2002, para. 76. See also article 42, paragraph 3 of the Convention on the Rights of Migrant Workers.

[273] Carmen Tiburcio, "Chapter VIII. Political Rights" in *The human rights of aliens under international and comparative law*, Kluwer Law International, The Hague: 2001, page 182.

Nevertheless, the possibility of bypassing the requirement of citizenship for the exercise of political rights for specific persons or in particular circumstances has effectively been tabled by the emergence of denizenship.

Furthermore, when calling upon states to provide information on the implementation of any such policies in their periodic reports, the Committee on the Elimination of Racial Discrimination appears open to the possibility that further steps may be taken towards uncoupling citizenship from political rights:

> State parties should report whether any groups, *such as* permanent residents, enjoy [political] rights on a limited basis, *for example*, by having the right to vote in local elections or to hold particular public service positions.[274]

Meanwhile, in the context of the protection of the rights of minorities, the need to consider ways in which ensure the effective participation of persons belonging to minorities in "decisions on the national and, where appropriate, regional level concerning the minority to which they belong or the regions in which they live"[275] has added a new dimension to the question of offering political participation in the absence of nationality. As Asbjorn Eide explains in a paper on minority rights and non-citizens:

> Non-citizens do not under international human rights law have an unconditional right to elect and be elected to public office. Nevertheless, where sizeable and stable minorities exist with many of their members being non-citizens, States should seek ways to involve their representatives, at least on a consultative basis, in decisions affecting them as a group.[276]

In future, this problem of the participation of minorities may further contribute to interest in the concept of denizenship and the process of uncoupling nationality from political rights.

It seems then that it is no longer entirely inconceivable that (at least some) political rights could be separated from the formal concept of nationality[277] - if not generally, then at least to the benefit of the stateless in view of their particular situation and the arguments raised above. If a new or additional instrument were to be envisaged for the protection of the rights of the stateless then states may now be more receptive to the idea of filling the gap left by the 1954 Statelessness Convention. This move could be founded upon a greater understanding of the plight

---

[274] Emphasis added, Human Rights Committee, *CCPR General Comment No. 25: The right to participate in public affairs, voting rights and the right of equal access to public service,* Geneva: 12 July 1996, para. 3.

[275] Article 2.3 of the UN Declaration on the Rights of Persons Belonging to National, Ethnic, Religious or Linguistic Minorities,18 December 1992.

[276] Asbjorn Eide, "Citizenship and the minority rights of non-citizens", Working Paper prepared for the UN Sub-Commission on Prevention of Discrimination and Protection of Minorities, E/CN.4/Sub.2/AC.5/1999/WP.3, 15 April 1999, paragraph 53.

[277] "A franchise for noncitizens is not a utopian goal; is has become a democratic norm in several countries". Alexander Aleinikoff; Douglas Klusmeyer, *Citizenship Policies for an Age of Migration,* Carnegie Empowerment for International Peace, Washington D.C.: 2002, page 45.

of the stateless (as distinct from the situation of refugees), the objections presented above to the enduring exclusion of stateless persons from political rights and the opportunities created by the concept of denizenship. Again, the carefully-tailored approach that human rights law is now taking to the right to enter – an expansive interpretation that favours particular groups of stateless persons – could provide the model for such a new approach to political rights.

7.4 Minority rights

At the close of this section on civil and political rights that were omitted from the 1954 Statelessness Convention I would like to make a few comments about one further provision that appears in the International Covenant on Civil and Political Rights but was not given a place in the statelessness instrument: the article on minority rights. Article 27 of the ICCPR proclaims that

> in those States in which ethnic, religious or linguistic minorities exist, persons belonging to such minorities shall not be denied the rights, in community with the other members of their group, to enjoy their own culture, to profess and practice their own religion, or to use their own language.[278]

The UN Independent Expert on Minorities reports that "evidence demonstrates that discriminatory denial or deprivation of citizenship disproportionately affects persons belonging to minorities".[279] So, a great many of the world's larger stateless communities are ethnic, religious or linguistic minorities who have long resided in the state in which they are found. The Hill Tribes in Thailand and the Russians in Latvia and Estonia are just two examples.

According to the wording of article 27 of the ICCPR, the statelessness of these minority groups should not be a bar to their enjoyment of minority rights – no precondition of nationality may be set. This interpretation has been confirmed by the Human Rights Committee.[280] However, many countries continue to enforce

---

[278] Note that "this article establishes and recognizes a right which is conferred on individuals belonging to minority groups and which is distinct from, and additional to, all the other rights which, as individuals in common with everyone else, they are already entitled to enjoy under the Covenant". Human Rights Committee, *General Comment No. 23: The Rights of Minorities,* Geneva: 8 April 1994, para. 1.

[279] Gay McDougall, *Promotion and Protection of all Human Rights, Civil, Political, Economic, Social and Cultural Rights, Including the Right to Development – Report of the Independent Expert on Minority Issues,* A/HRC/7/23, 28 February 2008, para. 15.

[280] In the context of the broader discussion of the rights of non-nationals, the Committee declared that "in those cases where aliens constitute a minority within the meaning of article 27, they shall not be denied the right, in community with other members of their group, to enjoy their own culture, to profess and practice their own religion and to use their own language". Human Rights Committee, *General Comment 15: The position of aliens under the covenant,* Geneva: 11 April 1986, paragraph 7. Later, the Committee explained that specifically with regard to minority rights, "the individuals designed to be protected need not be citizens of the State party. In this regard, the obligations deriving from article 2.1 are also relevant, since a State party is required under that article to ensure that the rights protected under the Covenant are available to all individuals within its territory and subject to its jurisdiction, except rights which are expressly made to apply to citizens, for example, political rights under article

policies whereby only citizens can be recognised as belonging to a minority and granted rights accordingly, thereby fuelling the ongoing debate on the definition of a "minority" or "national minority".[281] With the close relationship between the two issues – "most stateless persons today are members of minority groups"[282]- it would have been beneficial to the protection of minority rights for the statelessness instrument to have explicitly referred to the capacity of stateless persons to claim such entitlements. The decision, for whatever reason,[283] not to include the issue of minority rights in the 1954 Statelessness Convention is therefore a further disappointment.

8 Conclusion

The exercise of going through each of the civil and political rights contained within the 1954 Convention relating to the Status of Stateless Persons clearly reveals just how much of an impression the drafting process has left on the instrument. On the one hand, as a result of the decision to stick closely to the text of the 1951 Refugee Convention, the two documents appear indistinguishable at first, apart from the obvious difference in the delineation of personal scope. Certainly many of the civil and political rights have simply been transposed directly from the Refugee Convention into the Statelessness Convention without any alterations. Moreover, the Statelessness Convention only deals with those issues that were already

25. A State party may not, therefore, restrict the rights under article 27 to its citizens alone". Human Rights Committee, *General Comment No. 23: The Rights of Minorities,* Geneva: 8 April 1994, para. 5.1. See also Yvonne Donders, *Towards a Right to Cultural Identity?*, Intersentia, Oxford: 2002, page 170; David Weissbrodt, *Final Report on Prevention of Discrimination - The Rights of Non-Citizens,* E/CN.4/Sub.2/2003/23, 26 May 2003, para. 42.

[281] The creation of special instruments on the rights of national minorities within the context of the Council of Europe and the Organisation for Security and Cooperation in Europe has not resolved this debate on definition. Among the countries that continue to consider the term "national minority" to refer only to citizens is Estonia, where the stateless Russians cannot claim the benefit of such instruments as the Council of Europe Framework Convention on National Minorities to which Estonia is a party. See for further discussion of this issue Ineta Ziemele, *State Continuity and Nationality: The Baltic States and Russia. Past, Present and Future as Defined by International Law*, Martinus Nijhoff Publishers, Leiden: 2005, pages 375-380; For details on how "citizenship" factors into the definition of or approach to minorities adopted by various international mechanisms see Rianne Letschert, *The Impact of Minority Rights Mechanisms. The OSCE High Commissioner on National Minorities, the UN Working Group on Minorities and the CoE Advisory Committee on Minorities*, T.M.C. Asser Press, The Hague: 2005, pages 64, 101 and 174.

[282] Gay McDougall, *Promotion and Protection of all Human Rights, Civil, Political, Economic, Social and Cultural Rights, Including the Right to Development – Report of the Independent Expert on Minority Issues,* A/HRC/7/23, 28 February 2008, summary.

[283] Be reminded once more that it was the content of the 1951 Refugee Convention that largely pre-determined what the 1954 Statelessness Convention would and would not deal with. Perhaps in the formulation of the refugee instrument it was felt that the refugee would could not be considered a minority in this sense because he is by definition a newcomer to the state of refuge. This may be a valid argument for the refugee - although there are now also situations conceivable where refugees form a "new" minority similarly to other migrants in their host state, in particular where protracted refugee situations are concerned, and may be entitled to minority rights on that basis. However, the plight of the stateless is not always directly comparable to that of the refugee and as mentioned, statelessness has afflicted pre-existing minority groups in many states.

carefully debated and approved as part of the refugee instrument. This approach appears to have had a somewhat damaging effect on the protection offered to stateless persons because in practice the assumption that the situation of stateless populations is largely comparable to that of refugees has proven unfounded. For example, where a provision on the right to freedom of opinion and expression was rejected in the drafting process of the 1951 Refugee Convention because of the desire to allow states to control the political activities of foreigners, this reasoning is not appropriate for excluding the article from an instrument geared towards stateless persons. So too the failure to include a reference to minority rights – perhaps a logical choice for a tool that addresses refugee situations, but a dubious one for a document upon which large stateless minority groups may wish to rely. Had the drafters started from scratch or fully re-opened the debate on each civil and political right (both those present in the draft and those rejected), it is feasible that the outcome may have been quite different and indeed more relevant.

On the other hand, the areas in which the text of the 1954 Statelessness Convention do deviate from that of its precursor raise even greater concern. Each of the changes amounts to a weakening of the protection offered – most notably through the omission of one particular guarantee that is absolutely central to the overall system of the Convention. I refer here to the right to enter and remain. The prohibition of *non-refoulement* espoused in the 1951 Refugee Convention indirectly provides the refugee with an avenue for claiming (continued) access to the territory of the state of asylum. The Convention itself establishes the possibility of gaining and maintaining physical and even lawful presence for the purposes of accessing the remainder of the rights espoused. However the 1954 Statelessness Convention provides no such opportunity. State parties to the Statelessness Convention are free to refuse, detain or expel any stateless person seeking access to their soil without the proper authorisation. This is in spite of the fact that physical, lawful and even durable presence is still set as a precondition for accessing the vast majority of the substantive guarantees contained in the instrument. Thus, the failure to deal with the issue of entry and residence rights is arguably the single greatest flaw of the 1954 Statelessness Convention. The stateless are thereby compelled to rely on the goodwill of a state party for (continued) access to its territory in order to claim their convention rights.

With this in mind it became all the more pressing to search the international human rights framework for alternative and supplementary protection. It was noted that access to territory is also important for the enjoyment of rights under human rights law - not because human rights norms tend to set the precondition of lawful residence, but because as long as the state remains free to expel the stateless person at will, it can choose to purge the stateless person from its jurisdiction at any moment, making it impossible to physically access any rights. And since no other state is necessarily compelled to admit a stateless person, this can result in indefinite detention or the "ping-pong" effect of enduring limbo where the individual is passed from one state to another indefinitely or, alternatively, trapped in indefinite detention. Although human rights law, in principle, only recognises the right of a person to enter or remain in "his own country" and this generally refers to the country of nationality, recent developments suggest the beginnings of an answer to the plight of the stateless in this respect. In particular, the UN Human Rights Committee has determined that in various cases a state must act as a person's "own country" even in the absence of a bond of nationality.[284] It will not necessarily be easy to identify which state should be obliged to admit, regularise or refrain from expelling a particular stateless person because this effectively involves identifying the state that arguably should be attributing its nationality to that person (closest genuine connection) and this, in turn, means falling back on the complex norms relating to the prevention of statelessness discussed in Part 2. However, there is scope to build upon the initiative taken by the Human Rights Committee to interpret the term "his own country" in a broad manner and guidelines could be developed to further elucidate these ideas and apply them to the specific situation of the stateless.[285] This would rectify the oversight committed by the 1954 Statelessness Convention and in fact render the instrument instantly more effective.

In this chapter it was also suggested that the failure of the 1954 Statelessness Convention to address the lack of empowerment of stateless persons – the omission of any political rights – could be dealt with along similar lines.[286] This would admittedly be a radical move and unlikely to garner widespread support at this time. However, the system of modern human rights law and the changing practices of states with regard to political rights at the local level both suggest that the granting of political rights in the absence of citizenship where the circumstances so demand is not entirely and definitively out of the question. Once all of the dimensions of the protection of the stateless have been discussed, we will be able to consider the manner in which these and other ideas to improve upon the protection offered could be further developed and implemented.[287]

For now I would like to draw a conclusion on the existing content of the 1954 Convention relating to the Status of Stateless Persons and its role in protecting the substantive rights of the stateless. On the basis of the assessment made over the course of this chapter, the unavoidable verdict seems to be that the contribution of the 1954 Statelessness Convention to the enjoyment of *civil and political rights* by the stateless is virtually nil. The instrument proclaims a somewhat random and notably incomplete selection of civil and political rights. The decision to omit various fundamental issues (that *are* dealt with in human rights law) is neither logical nor necessarily appropriate. Each one of the rights that *is* elaborated can be found in similar or stronger wording in contemporary human rights instruments. Those provisions with the greatest value and significance in its precursor, the 1951 Refugee Convention, find no counterpart in the text of the 1954 Statelessness

[284] The three situations covered explicitly were: where denationalisation has been implemented in violation of a state's international obligations, where nationality is denied following state succession and where there is an enduring denial of citizenship to long-term residents. In each case, the state that *should* have attributed or maintained citizenship is deemed to owe the stateless person the right to enter and remain on its territory.

[285] For example, where more than one state is identified as being "responsible" for a particular stateless persons, bilateral negotiations or the implementation of a right of option would be possible avenues to determining in which country the stateless person may enjoy residence.

[286] Hence once the state has been identified in which the stateless person should be entitled to enjoy (continued) residence, this state could also be required or at least encouraged to afford the stateless person certain political rights – for example, only the right to work in public service or also the right to vote and be elected. Additional conditions could be set such as a minimum period of residence before these political rights can be exercised.

[287] This will be done in chapter XIII.

Convention - these key articles were simply deleted. And the instrument fails to deal with some of the most fundamental issues of concern that face stateless persons as a specific vulnerable group, such as the right to (continued) residence (including the right to return), protection from arbitrary detention and the right to political participation. In the following chapters the value of this 1954 Statelessness Convention for the protection of first the economic, social and cultural rights and then the special needs of the stateless will be assessed before coming to an overall conclusion on the role of this instrument in the protection of stateless persons today.

CHAPTER XI

PROTECTING THE ECONOMIC, SOCIAL AND CULTURAL RIGHTS OF THE STATELESS

The second major category of substantive provisions in the 1954 Convention relating to the Status of Stateless Persons comprises economic, social and cultural rights (ESC rights). Here, the International Covenant on Economic, Social and Cultural Rights (ICESCR) forms the reference point for grouping the articles. The economic, social and cultural rights thus found within the 1954 Statelessness Convention – in the order in which they will be dealt with below – are: the right to work and labour-related rights (articles 17, 18, 19 and 24, paragraph 1(a)), freedom of association (article 15), right to social security and assistance (articles 23 and 24), right to an adequate standard of living (articles 20 and 21), right to education (article 22) and intellectual property rights (article 14).[1] It is an impressive array of provisions - in fact double the number that is devoted to civil and political rights in this statelessness instrument. This is a promising discovery, but the stateless are nevertheless reported to experience widespread difficulties in exercising a range of economic, social and cultural rights[2] and it is not until the content of these articles has been analysed that any conclusions can be drawn on their value. In the upcoming paragraphs, the rights will be dealt with in turn in order to assess the role of the 1954 Statelessness Convention within the system of contemporary human rights law for the protection of the ESC rights of the stateless. At the same time, we will be on the lookout for areas in which the overall system is perhaps letting down

---

[1] Be reminded once more that the distinction between civil and political rights, on the one hand, and economic, social and cultural rights, on the other, is largely artificial. Particularly evident in reference to such rights as the right to property (dealt with in chapter 10 among the civil and political rights, yet a fundamental guarantee for the enjoyment of economic, social and cultural rights) and the freedom of association (which is a fundamental freedom that may be exercised to the benefit of political activities and is closely tied up with the freedom of assembly yet is dealt with in this chapter among the economic, social and cultural rights in view of its role in backing up labour-related rights).

[2] The problem is illustrated well by a quote from a stateless Bidoon living in the United Arab Emirates: "We can't get jobs, we can't move, we are like boats without ports. Access to education and healthcare are also problems. I couldn't finish high school or go to college. I can only see a doctor in a private hospital, not in the government ones." cited in UNHCR and IPU, *Nationality and statelessness. A handbook for parliamentarians*, 2005, page 17. See also UNHCR, "Statelessness and Citizenship" in *The State of the World's Refugees - A Humanitarian Agenda*, Oxford University Press, Oxford: 1997, page 241; Maureen Lynch, *Lives on hold: The human cost of statelessness,* Washington: 2005, page 3; Advisory Board on Human Security (prepared by Constantin Sokoloff), *Denial of Citizenship: A Challenge to Human Security,* February 2005, pages 20-21.

the stateless and consider ways in which the protection of the rights of this vulnerable group could be enhanced.

1 Non-nationals, non-discrimination and the enjoyment of economic, social and cultural rights

Before we discuss the content of these rights in detail, we must pause again to consider the influence of the principle of non-discrimination on the position of non-nationals, this time within the overall system of *economic, social and cultural rights*. Most fundamentally, as with civil and political rights, the ICESCR and other relevant standard-setting instruments are firmly founded on the notion of universality and elaborate protections to the benefit of "everyone". In principle then, non-citizens including stateless persons, are also entitled to enjoy economic, social and cultural rights.[3] Yet, in an identical approach to that taken in the International Covenant on Civil and Political Rights, the ICESCR does not explicitly prohibit distinctions based on nationality in its enunciation of the principle of non-discrimination.[4] This means that such distinctions would have to be assessed under the heading of "other status". The difficulty is that:

> Non-nationals cannot necessarily count on receiving the treatment enjoyed by citizens, as neither treaty monitoring body of the two Covenants [ICCPR and ICESCR] has unequivocally held that non-nationals are to enjoy all *social and economic rights* without distinction with nationals.[5]

Nevertheless, the Committee on Economic, Social and Cultural Rights[6] not entirely refrained from considering the legitimacy of differential treatment between citizens and non-citizens. In fact, it has taken an active stance in assessing the compliance

[3] David Weissbrodt, *Preliminary Report on the Rights of Non-Citizens,* E/CN.4/Sub.2/2001/20, Geneva: 6 June 2001, para. 56.

[4] Article 2, paragraph 2 of the ICESCR states: "The States Parties to the present Covenant undertake to guarantee that the rights enunciated in the present Covenant will be exercised without discrimination of any kind as to race, colour, sex, language, religion, political or other opinion, national or social origin, property, birth or other status". The list of prohibited grounds is identical to that found in article 2, paragraph 1 and article 26 of the ICCPR

[5] Emphasis added. John Dent, *Research Paper on the Social and Economic Rights of Non-Nationals in Europe,* Brussels: 1998, page 12. See also Matthew Craven, *The International Covenant on Economic, Social and Cultural Rights. A Perspective on its Development*, Clarendon Press, Oxford: 1998, page 173; Tang Lay Lee, "Statelessness, Human Rights and Gender. Irregular migrant workers from Burma in Thailand", Martinus Nijhoff Publishers, Leiden 2005, page 93. The recently elaborated General Comment on the right to social security is the only instance in which the ESC Committee plainly declares that "Article 2(2) proscribes discrimination on ground of nationality". See ESC Committee, *General Comment No. 19 - The Right to Social Security,* Advanced unedited version, 4 February 2008, para. 36. This stands in marked contrast to the position of the UN Human Rights Committee in its general comment on the position of aliens under the ICCPR on the permissibility of distinctions between citizens and non-citizens in the enjoyment of civil and political rights where a much harder stance is taken against such distinctions. See chapter X, section 1.

[6] Hereafter referred to as the ESC Committee.

with the Covenant of such situations.[7] To sum up the position of the Committee: "even though equality of treatment is not necessarily prescribed, discrimination on the basis of nationality is by no means legitimate".[8] When it comes to it, this question of legitimacy can only be answered by reference to the content of the particular ESC right in relation to which the differential treatment is established. And this is where the nature of ESC rights comes into play.

The resource-intensive character of many (aspects of) ESC rights impedes the prospect of their direct implementation and their prescription with immediate binding force. In contrast to the system of civil and political rights then, the ICESCR allows for flexibility by enunciating most rights in such a way as to demand *progressive* rather than immediate achievement:

> Each State Party to the present Covenant undertakes to take steps [...] to the maximum of its available resources, with a view to *achieving progressively* the full realization of the rights recognized in the present Covenant by all appropriate means.[9]

No overall timeframe is set as to when full realisation is to be achieved (nor is it made clear what full realisation exactly entails) and states are generally granted a wide margin of discretion in determining what resources are available for improving the enjoyment of these rights. Because states are thereby afforded greater discretion in the implementation of these norms, it is difficult to claim a very concrete entitlement under many ESC rights and harder for supervising bodies such as courts to determine where there has been a violation. And, for the stateless, this basically flexible nature of many ESC rights complicates the question of whether states are bound to afford non-nationals – and the stateless – the same level of protection as their own citizens.

Nevertheless, the flexibility inherent in the demand to work towards *progressive* achievement is not limitless. The ESC Committee has determined that "a minimum core obligation to ensure the satisfaction of, at the very least, minimum essential levels of each of the rights is incumbent upon every State Party".[10] Failure to fulfil such a minimum core obligation amounts to a *prima facie* violation of the Covenant that can only exceptionally be justified.[11] Breaking down each ESC right

---

[7] As we will see over the course of this chapter, the Committee on Economic, Social and Cultural Rights - as well as the Committee on the Elimination of Racial Discrimination and the Committee on the Rights of the Child - have considered questions relating to the enjoyment of ESC by non-nationals on numerous occasions both in the formulation of general comments and in response to state party reports.

[8] Matthew Craven, *The International Covenant on Economic, Social and Cultural Rights. A Perspective on its Development*, Clarendon Press, Oxford: 1998, page 174.

[9] Article 2, paragraph 1 of the ICESCR. Compare this to article 2, paragraph 1 of the ICCPR which determines that "each State party to the present Covenant undertakes to *respect and to ensure* to all individuals within its territory and subject to its jurisdiction the rights recognised in the present Covenant".

[10] ESC Committee, *General Comment No. 3: The nature of state parties obligations*, E/1991/23, 14 December 1990, para. 10.

[11] Ibid. More recently, in the context of the right to health, the ESC Committee has even held that "a State party cannot, under any circumstances whatsoever, justify its non-compliance with the core

into those components that are considered to be "core obligations" and those that are considered subject to progressive realisation is thus an invaluable interpretative mechanism for assessing compliance with the Covenant. This characteristic trait of ESC rights has an impact on the way in which the principle of non-discrimination is applied, in particular in relation to non-citizens, because

> the Committee on Economic, Social and Cultural Rights has forcefully asserted that *no group* should be denied the 'minimum core content' of the ICESCR rights.[12]

Thus non-nationals, including stateless persons, enjoy the minimum standards at the heart of each ESC right and the failure to ensure their enjoyment of this core content will be considered a *prima facie* breach of the Covenant. Beyond these minimum core obligations, states may offer their own citizens a greater level of protection of ESC rights. Nevertheless, any differentiation in treatment between nationals and non-nationals in an area that does not belong to the minimum core content must still pass a basic "reasonableness" test.[13]

Deconstructing each ESC right into elements that are considered to be core obligations and those that may be achieved progressively is therefore the first step towards understanding the influence of the non-discrimination principle on the enjoyment of these rights by stateless persons. Where an assessment must be made of the reasonableness of distinctions between nationals and non-nationals outside the sphere of the core minimum content, there are a number of further interpretative tools that can be helpful. In the first place, where the ESC Committee has elaborated on the interpretation of a norm and the protection to be enjoyed by (certain categories of) non-nationals, either through general comments and recommendations or through its response to the situation on the ground in state parties, this is a direct source of information on the influence of the non-discrimination principle in that particular context.

Secondly, account must be taken of a remarkable statement found early on in the ICESCR, namely paragraph 3 of its second article:

> Developing countries, with due regard to human rights and their national economy, may determine to what extent they would guarantee the economic rights recognized in the present Covenant to non-nationals.

Developing states are hereby expressly permitted to restrict the *economic* rights of non-citizens – and thereby also stateless persons – on their territory. At first, it

---

obligations [...] which are non-derogable". ESC Committee, *General Comment No. 14: The right to the highest attainable standard of health,* E/C.12/2000/4, 11 August 2000, para. 47.

[12] Emphasis added. John Dent, *Research Paper on the Social and Economic Rights of Non-Nationals in Europe,* Brussels: 1998, page 12. See also Matthew Craven, *The International Covenant on Economic, Social and Cultural Rights. A Perspective on its Development,* Clarendon Press, Oxford: 1998, page 174.

[13] Note that the distinction drawn on the basis of citizenship must also not be implemented in such a way as to amount to *de facto* or indirect discrimination on one of the prohibited grounds set out in article 2, paragraph 2 of the ICESCR. John Dent, *Research Paper on the Social and Economic Rights of Non-Nationals in Europe,* Brussels: 1998, page 12.

seems difficult to place this provision in the overall system of ESC rights. It has been described as elaborating the exception to a general rule of equality in the enjoyment of ESC rights.[14] However, we have already seen that the application of the principle of non-discrimination to non-nationals in the context of ESC rights has not resulted in an outright prescription of equality with citizens. How then, does this extraordinary clause contribute to the overall picture? The historical background to this paragraph does not shed much light on this question,[15] although it is of interest to note that it was only narrowly adopted, which suggests that the subject was already highly controversial at the time.[16] This may explain the use of what has been described as "unconscionably vague"[17] terminology – the references to developing countries[18] and economic rights[19] - that is not defined anywhere within

[14] David Weissbrodt, *Final Report on Prevention of Discrimination - The Rights of Non-Citizens,* E/CN.4/Sub.2/2003/23, 26 May 2003, para. 19. The express allowance for restrictions to the economic rights of non-nationals contained in article 2, paragraph 3 of the ICESCR has been hailed in some instances as evidence of a general rule of equality between citizens and non-citizens in the enjoyment of ESC rights in all other situations. Matthew Craven, *The International Covenant on Economic, Social and Cultural Rights. A Perspective on its Development*, Clarendon Press, Oxford: 1998, pages 172-173; Carmen Tiburcio, "Chapter VI. Social and Cultural Rights" in *The human rights of aliens under international and comparative law*, Kluwer Law International, The Hague: 2001, page 147.

[15] The only explanation offered is that "the sole aim of the proposals in question was to rectify the situation which frequently existed in the developing countries particularly those which recently won their independence. In such countries, the influence of non-nationals on the national economy – a heritage of the colonial era – was often such that nationals were not in a position to fully enjoy the economic rights set forth in the draft covenant". From the report of the Third Committee of the General Assembly on the drafting of the ICESCR as cited in E. Dankwa, 'Working Paper on Article 2(3) of the International Covenant on Economic, Social and Cultural Rights', in *Human Rights Quarterly,* Vol. 9, 1987, page 235. See also Carmen Tiburcio, "Chapter VII. Economic Rights" in *The human rights of aliens under international and comparative law*, Kluwer Law International, The Hague: 2001, page 171.

[16] The amendment which introduced paragraph 3 to article 2 of the ICESCR was adopted by 41 votes to 38, with 12 abstentions. E. Dankwa, 'Working Paper on Article 2(3) of the International Covenant on Economic, Social and Cultural Rights', in *Human Rights Quarterly,* Vol. 9, 1987, page 236.

[17] Warwick McKean, *Equality and discrimination under international law*, Clarendon Press, Oxford: 1983, page 201.

[18] Although the concept of *developing* countries does enjoy widespread usage, there is no single, authoritative source which elaborates a list of (criteria to identify) states that belong to this category. This leaves article 2, paragraph 3 open to misuse. See E. Dankwa, 'Working Paper on Article 2(3) of the International Covenant on Economic, Social and Cultural Rights', in *Human Rights Quarterly,* Vol. 9, 1987, pages 236-238.

[19] There is no agreement as to the categorisation of particular norms as *economic* rights, as distinct from *social* and *cultural* rights. The ICESCR does not group its provisions along these lines. At one end of the spectrum, scholars such as Elles include the rights to work, to form trade unions, to social security, to adequate standard of living and to health among so-called *economic* rights. At the other end, Tiburcio considers only the right to invest or take part in profitable activities to be categorised as an *economic* right for the purposes of this provision – qualifying most other rights as *social.* Even the description of *economic* rights provided by Dankwa as "rights that enable a person to earn a living or that relate to that process" does not fully settle the discussion as to which matters are to be included. Again, states may take advantage of this lack of clarity and deliberately construe the category of *economic* rights broadly. Diana Elles, *International Provisions Protecting the Human Rights of Non-Citizens: Study,* New York: 1980, pages 30-34; Carmen Tiburcio, "Chapter VII. Economic Rights" in *The human rights of aliens under international and comparative law*, Kluwer Law International, The Hague: 2001; Carmen

the Covenant's text and remains ambiguous to this day.[20] The Committee on Economic, Social and Cultural Rights has yet to elaborate a general comment on either the scope of these terms for the purposes of the application of this provision or the intent and effect of the paragraph as a whole.[21] Would reliance on this provision allow developing countries to deprive non-nationals of even the core minimum content of economic rights? Considering the emphasis placed on the importance of always ensuring that minimum essential levels of each ESC right are guaranteed as outlined above, this would be an extremely undesirable and indeed highly improbable understanding of the norm. Instead I would suggest that the explicit acceptance of restrictions upon the economic rights of non-nationals by developing countries should be used as an interpretative tool in assessing the appropriateness or "reasonableness" of a distinction between citizens and non-citizens in the enjoyment of everything beyond the core content of this category of rights. Thus, if the ESC Committee is called upon to assess the compliance with the Covenant of a restriction on the enjoyment by non-nationals of what it determines (for the purposes of the case) to be an economic right by a state that it determines (for the purposes of the case) to be a developing country, the state shall be afforded a wider margin of discretion and the reasonableness test will be more lax.

A final consideration that may assist in delineating the scope of the "reasonableness" test for differential treatment between citizens and non-citizens is the question whether - and in what form - the ESC right involved also appears in the Convention on the Rights of the Child, the Migrant Workers Convention or other relevant instruments. The Convention on the Rights of the Child, for instance, elaborates both civil and political rights and economic, social and cultural rights in much the same way, to the benefit of *all* children. The principle of non-discrimination again enjoys a prominent position and is enunciated in article 2 of the Convention. Although the terms of the prohibition of discrimination in the enjoyment of child rights are the same as those of the non-discrimination provision in the ICESCR, the Committee on the Rights of the Child has gone to great lengths to affirm that:

Tiburcio, "Chapter VI. Social and Cultural Rights" in *The human rights of aliens under international and comparative law*, Kluwer Law International, The Hague: 2001; E. Dankwa, 'Working Paper on Article 2(3) of the International Covenant on Economic, Social and Cultural Rights', in *Human Rights Quarterly,* Vol. 9, 1987, pages 239-240; Matthew Craven, *The International Covenant on Economic, Social and Cultural Rights. A Perspective on its Development*, Clarendon Press, Oxford: 1998, page 172; James Hathaway, *The Rights of Refugees Under International Law*, Cambridge University Press, Cambridge: 2005, pages 488 and 601.

[20] It is, however, suggested that the provision as a whole should be "narrowly construed", an assertion that would favour a strict interpretation of these undefined concepts. David Weissbrodt, *Final Report on Prevention of Discrimination - The Rights of Non-Citizens,* E/CN.4/Sub.2/2003/23, 26 May 2003, para. 19.

[21] Nor has the recent work of the special-rapporteur on the rights of non-citizens clarified this question. James Hathaway, *The Rights of Refugees Under International Law*, Cambridge University Press, Cambridge: 2005, page 151. There are several possible explanations for the lack of elaboration on this issue by the Committee. The issue could be too controversial to be settled at this time or it could be a deliberate stance of the Committee in order to retain flexibility in assessing state policies under this provision in light of the overall system of protection of ESC rights.

> The enjoyment of rights stipulated in the Convention is not limited to children who are citizens of a State party and must therefore, if not explicitly stated otherwise in the Convention, also be available to all children [...] irrespective of their nationality, immigration status or statelessness.[22]

So where a certain ESC right is also espoused in the Convention on the Rights of the Child, the "reasonableness" test as to distinctions between national and non-national children must be applied more strictly, leaving less room for state discretion. As an instrument addressed to (a particular subsection of) non-nationals, the Migrant Workers Convention can also be instrumental in determining the extent to which certain ESC rights are extended to non-nationals and under what terms. So too can the UN Declaration on the Rights of Individuals Who are not Nationals of the Country in which They Live and additional standards set for example within the forum of the International Labour Organisation. In sum, the question of the tolerance of the human rights regime for restrictions on the enjoyment of ESC rights by non-nationals is a complex one that depends on many different factors. These considerations will be taken into account as we look more closely at the enjoyment by stateless persons of the full range of economic, social and cultural rights over the course of the rest of this chapter.

2 Right to Work and Labour-Related Rights

Employment is arguably one of the most fundamental issues dealt with in the field of economic, social and cultural rights. Together with the right to education and the right to social security or assistance, the right to work ensures that an individual has the tools that are needed to provide for his or her basic needs and the subsistence of his or her family.[23] In addition, labour is now viewed as an important value, playing a central role in a person's "self-realisation and the development of human personality".[24] In accordance with this perspective, the right to work as we understand it today is not only about access to employment and the right to earn a living, it is also concerned with freedom from forced labour, freedom of choice in employment and freedom to work independently (self-employed). Work-related

---

[22] Committee on the Rights of the Child, *General Comment No. 6: Treatment of unaccompanied and separated children outside their country of origin,* 1 September 2005, para. 12. See also Thomas Hammarberg, "Children" in Rosas (ed) *Economic, Social and Cultural Rights*, Martinus Nijhoff Publishers, Dordrecht: 1995, page 293; Geraldine van Bueren, *The International Law on the Rights of the Child*, Martinus Nijhoff, Dordrecht: 1995, page 362; John Dent, *Research Paper on the Social and Economic Rights of Non-Nationals in Europe,* Brussels: 1998, page 32. This interpretation has been put into practice by the Committee on the Rights of the Child in, for example, Committee on the Rights of the Child, *Concluding Observations: Kyrgyzstan,* CRC/C/97, Geneva: 2000, para. 288 and 289.

[23] It has even been argued that in view of this role, these social rights can be seen as "a prerequisite to the enjoyment of civil and political rights". Carmen Tiburcio, "Chapter VI. Social and Cultural Rights" in *The human rights of aliens under international and comparative law*, Kluwer Law International, The Hague: 2001, page 147.

[24] Krysztof Drzewicki, "The Right to Work and Rights in Work" in Rosas (ed) *Economic, Social and Cultural Rights*, Martinus Nijhoff Publishers, Dordrecht: 1995, page 194.

rights then add to this picture the right to a safe and healthy work environment and other rights relating to the assurance of just and favourable labour conditions.[25]

Stateless persons are reported to experience difficulties in many of the areas that have just been outlined. As non-citizens, they fall within the category of individuals that commonly encounter

> poor working conditions, including difficult, dangerous, and dirty jobs; verbal abuse; violence; racism; discriminatory attitudes; cramped living conditions; intimidating workplace environments; and low salaries (which are often withheld).[26]

Furthermore, there are widespread accounts of stateless groups being subjected to restrictions in accessing (lawful) employment.[27] In some instances, the stateless are prevented from taking a job in a particular field or engaging in certain professions.[28] In others, the measures are more extreme. During the late 1980s in Kuwait for example, the authorities set in motion a policy whereby the country's stateless Bidoons were dismissed from government jobs and private employers were subsequently obliged to follow suit.[29] Such deliberate curtailment of access to the formal labour market and the influence that the overall situation of statelessness has on employment prospects compels many individuals to seek their livelihood through participation in the informal circuit.[30] This pattern serves only to add to their (economic) marginalisation and their vulnerability to the troublesome practices mentioned.[31]

---

[25] See for a full overview of the components of the right to work Magdalena Sepulveda; Theo van Banning; Gudrun Gudmundsdottir; Christine Chamoun; Willem van Genugten, *Human Rights Reference Handbook*, University for Peace, Ciudad Colon: 2004, pages 259-260.

[26] David Weissbrodt, *Final Report on Prevention of Discrimination - The Rights of Non-Citizens,* E/CN.4/Sub.2/2003/23, 26 May 2003, Add.3, para. 11.

[27] UNHCR, "Statelessness and Citizenship" in *The State of the World's Refugees - A Humanitarian Agenda*, Oxford University Press, Oxford: 1997, page 225; David Weissbrodt, *Final Report on Prevention of Discrimination - The Rights of Non-Citizens,* E/CN.4/Sub.2/2003/23, 26 May 2003, Add.3, para. 11; Open Society Justice Initiative, *Racial Discrimination and the Rights of Non-Citizens. Submission to the UN Committee on the Elimination of Racial Discrimination on the occasion of its 64th Session,* New York: 2004; Maureen Lynch, *Lives on hold: The human cost of statelessness,* Washington: 2005, page 3.

[28] Maureen Lynch, "Syria: Follow Through on Commitment to Grant Citizenship to Stateless Kurds" *Refugees International Bulletin,* Washington: 2005

[29] Open Society Justice Initiative, *Racial Discrimination and the Rights of Non-Citizens. Submission to the UN Committee on the Elimination of Racial Discrimination on the occasion of its 64th Session,* New York: 2004.

[30] Advisory Board on Human Security (prepared by Constantin Sokoloff), *Denial of Citizenship: A Challenge to Human Security,* February 2005, page 20;

[31] For example, the stateless refugees from Bhutan who live in camps in Nepal are forced to work illegally due to the restrictions in place and "they are vulnerable to extortion and discrimination, and generally have weakened bargaining power". Hiram Ruiz; Michelle Berg, "Unending Limbo: Warehousing Bhutanese Refugees in Nepal" in UNHCR (ed) *World Refugee Survey 2004*, UNHCR, Geneva: 2004, page 102. There are also cases of stateless persons being subjected to forced labour, for example, the Rohingya in Myanmar. Open Society Justice Initiative, *Racial Discrimination and the Rights of Non-Citizens. Submission to the UN Committee on the Elimination of Racial Discrimination on the occasion of its 64th Session,* New York: 2004.

2.1 The 1954 Convention relating to the Status of Stateless Persons

The 1954 Convention relating to the Status of Stateless Persons contains three full provisions relating to the right to work, housed in their own chapter on "gainful employment". The first, article 17, addresses access to wage-earning employment and declares that

> the Contracting States shall accord to stateless persons lawfully staying in their territory treatment as favourable as possible and, in any event, not less favourable than that accorded to aliens generally in the same circumstances, as regards the right to engage in wage-earning employment.[32]

Adopting the same technique as in the previous chapter and identifying the level of attachment and standard of treatment set out here, we can immediately establish that only the stateless who are *lawfully staying* in a state will benefit from this norm and that they are assimilated to *aliens generally* for the enjoyment of this aspect of the right to work, although more favourable treatment is encouraged. The provision thus combines a relatively stringent level of attachment with a level of protection that in effect goes no further than the general rule of article 7 of the Convention whereby stateless persons are to be treated in an equal manner to non-nationals generally. However, there follows a second paragraph in which contracting states pledge to give "sympathetic consideration to assimilating the rights of all stateless persons with regard to wage-earning employment to those of nationals".[33] States are thereby obliged to give due consideration to any request by a stateless person (whether lawfully staying or otherwise) to be treated on a par with the country's nationals for the purposes of the right to engage in wage-earning employment and deny such a request only with proper motivation.[34] In spite of the explicit encouragement to provide treatment as favourable as possible or even national treatment to stateless persons in their enjoyment of this element of the right to work, this remains a discretionary standard. If the article is distilled such that only the binding norm remains then the foregoing observation still stands: the provision lacks teeth and adds nothing to the general rule set out in article 7 of the Statelessness Convention. It is somewhat of a mystery then why *lawful stay* is required before the stateless can benefit under this article.[35]

---

[32] Article 17, paragraph 1 of the 1954 Convention relating to the Status of Stateless Persons.

[33] The provision adds that this is encouraged in particular for "those stateless persons who have entered their territory pursuant to programmes of labour recruitment or under immigration schemes". Article 17, paragraph 2 of the 1954 Convention relating to the Status of Stateless Persons. Note that there are no requirements set with regard to the level of attachment that must be met.

[34] Nehemiah Robinson, *Convention relating to the status of stateless persons - Its history and interpretation*, UNHCR, Geneva: 1955, page 48.

[35] It is of interest to note that in spite of the "weak" approach to the right to work, several countries still felt the need to submit reservations to this article. See UNHCR, *Declarations and Reservations to the 1954 Convention relating to the Status of Stateless Persons,* accessible via http://www.unhcr.org/protect/PROTECTION/416114164.pdf.

This disappointing finding becomes all the more noteworthy when the wording of the article is compared with its counterpart in the 1951 Refugee Convention. To begin with, we find that *refugees* are guaranteed an higher overall standard of treatment with regards to their right to engage in wage-earning employment: "the most favourable treatment accorded to nationals of a foreign country".[36] Then, an entire additional paragraph ensures that refugees are exempted from any restrictions imposed on the access of non-nationals to the national labour market if they meet one of a number of criteria such as the completion of three years' residence.[37] Governments somehow managed to wave aside all of the usual concerns relating to the competition between non-nationals and citizens for domestic employment opportunities that "could very easily have resulted in either the failure to guarantee refugees the right to work, or no more than a minimalist commitment at the lowest common denominator".[38] What the drafters of the 1951 Refugee Convention achieved instead was a bold step and a huge innovation over previous refugee instruments in establishing a far-reaching right of refugees to participate in the domestic workforce.[39] Yet when this article came up for discussion in the drafting of the 1954 Statelessness Convention, it was dismantled and weakened until only a *minimalist commitment at the lowest common denominator* remained: treatment on a par with non-nationals generally – the baseline standard of treatment offered by the instrument.[40] This has had a significant impact on the value of the 1954 Statelessness Convention in guaranteeing stateless persons' right to work as well as

---

[36] Article 17, paragraph 1 of the 1951 Convention relating to the status of Refugees. This standard of treatment amounts to "the best treatment which is given to nationals of any other country by treaty or usage" and is not to be found anywhere in the 1954 Statelessness Convention. Nehemiah Robinson, *Convention relating to the status of stateless persons - Its history and interpretation*, UNHCR, Geneva: 1955, page 56. Be reminded that the proviso "in the same circumstances" that is included in the article on the right to engage in wage-earning employment in both the 1951 Refugee Convention and the 1954 Statelessness Convention ensures that refugees and stateless persons respectively may nevertheless be held to "obtain work permits, or otherwise satisfy the routine administrative requirements for the employment of non-citizens". James Hathaway, *The Rights of Refugees Under International Law*, Cambridge University Press, Cambridge: 2005, page 753.

[37] Other qualifying factors for exemption are that it had already been granted to the refugee before entry into force of the Convention or that the refugee is married to a national of the country in question or has a child who is a national of that country. Such exemption applies only to measures that have the purpose of protecting the domestic labour market from foreign competition. Article 17, paragraph 2 of the 1951 Convention relating to the Status of Refugees. Note that the duty to give sympathetic consideration to according national treatment in respect of the right to engage in wage-earning employment is found in the *third* paragraph of article 17 of the 1951 Refugee Convention in the same terms as it is included in the 1954 Statelessness Convention where it is paragraph 2.

[38] James Hathaway, *The Rights of Refugees Under International Law*, Cambridge University Press, Cambridge: 2005, page 744.

[39] James Hathaway, *The Rights of Refugees Under International Law*, Cambridge University Press, Cambridge: 2005, pages 742-747.

[40] A report of the discussions surrounding the drafting of article 17 of the 1954 Statelessness Convention can be found in Nehemiah Robinson, *Convention relating to the status of stateless persons - Its history and interpretation*, UNHCR, Geneva: 1955, pages 61-62. Consider also the comments made by delegations in favour of the most-favoured-national treatment included in the 1951 Refugee Convention as recounted in James Hathaway, *The Rights of Refugees Under International Law*, Cambridge University Press, Cambridge: 2005, page 750.

the overall standard set by international law, as we will see when we turn to the human rights regime in the following section.

Meanwhile, the other two articles that are housed in the chapter on "gainful employment" in the 1954 Statelessness Convention address self-employment[41] and the right to work within the sphere of the liberal professions.[42] Rather than going into a detailed discussion on the content of these norms, it is sufficient to point out that all three articles on the right to work provide the same low level of protection, calling for treatment as favourable as possible while determining that the minimum standard is that accorded to non-nationals generally. For the purposes of the 1954 Statelessness Convention then, "in practice, it will make little difference [...] whether a person is labelled 'professional' or 'self-employed' or a 'wage-earner', because the treatment is the same".[43]

Having dealt with the articles that relate to the right to work and access to various types of employment, we can now move on to consider the standards set for the conditions of work – the labour-related rights. Article 24 of the 1954 Statelessness Convention obliges states to afford *lawfully staying* stateless persons *the same treatment as nationals* in the following matters:

> remuneration, hours of work, overtime arrangements, holidays with pay, restrictions on home work, minimum age of employment, apprenticeship and training, women's work and the work of young persons, and the enjoyment of the benefits of collective bargaining.[44]

---

[41] Article 18 of the 1954 Convention relating to the Status of Stateless Persons. This provides the stateless with the right to engage independently in agriculture, industry, handicrafts and commerce in order to earn their keep.

[42] Article 19 of the 1954 Convention relating to the Status of Stateless Persons. This article deals with employment as, for example, a doctor, dentist, lawyer, teacher or architect. Note that the category "liberal profession" remains undefined, so "the local authorities will decide in each case whether a person falls under the rubric 'liberal profession' or any other heading". Nehemiah Robinson, *Convention relating to the status of stateless persons - Its history and interpretation*, UNHCR, Geneva: 1955, page 65. See also James Hathaway, *The Rights of Refugees Under International Law*, Cambridge University Press, Cambridge: 2005, pages 798-799.

[43] The only substantive differences are the level of attachment required (which is lower in the case of self-employment - only lawful presence is required) and the inclusion of an additional condition for the practicing of a liberal profession (the possession of a recognised, requisite diploma). Nehemiah Robinson, *Convention relating to the status of stateless persons - Its history and interpretation*, UNHCR, Geneva: 1955, page 65. Hathaway's assessment of the role of the same article within the 1951 Refugee Convention differs due to the divergence between the norms on wage-earning employment between the two instruments. He concludes that "in pith and substance, [article 19 is] most appropriately understood not so much as a source of refugee entitlement, but as a clawback provision directed to a subset of refugees who would otherwise have been able to invoke the more generous provisions of either Art. 17 on wage-earning employment or Art. 18 on self-employment". James Hathaway, *The Rights of Refugees Under International Law*, Cambridge University Press, Cambridge: 2005, page 794.

[44] To the extent that "such matters are governed by laws or regulations or are subject to the control of administrative authorities". Article 24, paragraph 1(a) of the 1954 Convention relating to the Status of Stateless Persons.

States agreed to grant a high standard of protection - national treatment - with respect to these labour-related rights. This was, however, thanks as much to economic protectionism as to any moral arguments or concern for individual rights:

> The placing of foreigners and national workers on the same footing not only met the demands of equity but was in the interests of national wage-earners who might have been afraid that foreign labour, being cheaper that their own, would have been preferred.[45]

As we go on to consider the scope and content of work-related rights as set down in human rights instruments, we will uncover to what extent this line of thought has permeated the overall international legal regime. On the basis of the 1954 Statelessness Convention at least, once a stateless person has achieved lawful stay in a state *and* has gained access to the labour market, he must enjoy the same basic working conditions as citizens. The irregularly situated stateless person will, however, miss out on these work-related guarantees.

2.2 International human rights law

Labour and labour-related rights are issues that the international community has long taken an interest in. The development of labour standards took place both through and in parallel to the development of human rights. By the time that the Universal Declaration of Human Rights elaborated the right to work and to just and favourable work conditions,[46] the International Labour Organisation (ILO) had already achieved the codification of a wide range of work-related issues in almost 100 specialised conventions.[47] As of the time of writing, 187 Conventions have been settled within the forum of the ILO and these now form an indispensable compliment to the human rights framework. Centre stage of the human rights system "proper" for the purposes of this section – and indeed the rest of this chapter – is the International Covenant on Economic, Social and Cultural Rights. The right to work can be found in article 6 of this instrument while labour-related rights are elaborated in article 7.[48] Importantly, the point of departure for both the ICESCR

[45] James Hathaway, *The Rights of Refugees Under International Law*, Cambridge University Press, Cambridge: 2005, page 765. See also Nehemiah Robinson, *Convention relating to the status of stateless persons - Its history and interpretation*, UNHCR, Geneva: 1955, page 72.

[46] See articles 23 and 24 of the Universal Declaration of Human Rights, 1948.

[47] The International Labour Organisation (ILO) was founded in 1919 with the specific aim of promoting "decent and productive work in conditions of freedom, equity, security and human dignity". ILO, *About the ILO,* information retrieved from http://www.ilo.org/global/About_the_ILO/lang--en/index.htm. The instruments settled cover everything from minimum age for employment to hours of work and from forced labour to paid holidays. According to the Preamble to the Constitution of the International Labour Organisation, one specific area of concern is the protection of non-national workers. Note that the ILO instruments dealing with the rights of migrant workers do not allow for the exclusion of stateless persons from the scope of application in the way that the Migrant Workers Convention does, so they may be a source of direct rights for the stateless.

[48] Provisions dealing with (some aspect of) the right to work and labour standards can also be found in article 5, paragraph e(i) of the Convention on the Elimination of Racial Discrimination; Article 11 of the Convention on the Elimination of Discrimination Against Women; Articles 25, 52, 54 and 55 of the Convention on the Rights of Migrant Workers; Articles 1-8 of the European Social Charter; Article 26

and the aforementioned ILO labour standards is the attribution of these rights to "everyone", irrespective of citizenship, and thereby also to the stateless.[49] However, the question of the enjoyment of a right to work and of labour-related rights by non-nationals cannot be answered that easily. We must also consider to what extent the non-discrimination norm, as described above, influences our understanding of the application of these international human rights provisions to the situation of the stateless.

It is time to look more closely at the content of the right to work. According to article 6 of the ICESCR:

> The States Parties to the present Covenant recognize the right to work, which includes the right of everyone to the opportunity to gain his living by work which he freely chooses or accepts, and will take appropriate steps to safeguard this right.[50]

Since the right to work is formulated in such a way as to require progressive realisation – as encapsulated by the pledge to "recognise" the right to work - [51] it is important to be on the lookout for any core minimum obligations that this right may entail as we discuss its content. Central to the discussion here is the question of access to employment.[52] The ESC Committee has determined that the right of *non-*

---

of the American Convention on Human Rights read in conjunction with article 34, paragraph g of the Charter of the Organisation of American States (refers to labour conditions only) and Articles 6 and 7 of the Additional Protocol to the American Convention on Human Rights in the Area of Economic, Social and Cultural Rights; and article 15 of the African Charter on Human and Peoples' Rights. The prohibition of forced labour is dealt with separately in these and other human rights instruments. Note that stateless persons cannot rely on the protection offered by the European Social Charter because its personal scope is limited to nationals of contracting states.

[49] John Dent, *Research Paper on the Social and Economic Rights of Non-Nationals in Europe*, Brussels: 1998, page 4; David Weissbrodt, *Final Report on Prevention of Discrimination - The Rights of Non-Citizens*, E/CN.4/Sub.2/2003/23, 26 May 2003, para. 15; Matthew Craven, *The International Covenant on Economic, Social and Cultural Rights. A Perspective on its Development*, Clarendon Press, Oxford: 1998, page 153; Carmen Tiburcio, "Chapter VI. Social and Cultural Rights" in *The human rights of aliens under international and comparative law*, Kluwer Law International, The Hague: 2001, page 146; James Hathaway, *The Rights of Refugees Under International Law*, Cambridge University Press, Cambridge: 2005, page 485.

[50] Article 6, paragraph 1 of the ICESCR. In paragraph 2 of this provision, some of the steps that state parties should take towards realising the right to work are outlined, such as the provision of technical and vocational guidance. Note that the right to work "encompasses all forms of work, whether independent work or dependent wage-paid work" so this provision deals in one go with all of the categories of employment that the 1954 Statelessness Convention addressed. Committee on Economic, Social and Cultural Rights, *General Comment No. 18: The Right to Work,* E/C.12/GC/18, 6 February 2006, para. 6. The Migrant Workers Convention also deals with both employed and self-employed workers. ILO standards on the rights of migrants are, however, only applicable to those who are employed "otherwise than on his own account".

[51] The right to work "should not be understood as an absolute and unconditional right to obtain employment". Committee on Economic, Social and Cultural Rights, *General Comment No. 18: The Right to Work,* E/C.12/GC/18, 6 February 2006, para. 6.

[52] The right to work as provided for under the ICESCR encompasses several elements. Craven lists three main aspects to the right to work – access to employment, freedom of choice in employment and protection against dismissal - although there are other (sub)elements. Matthew Craven, *The*

discriminatory access to employment belongs to the core and immediately effective obligations of the right to work.[53] If non-nationals have the right to enjoy this minimum core content, it would seem that they also enjoy the right to access employment. However, the minimum core content refers to equality of access, not access itself - it merely requires that where non-nationals *are* granted access to employment, this should be on the basis of non-discrimination.[54] And although the "core obligation" elaborated by the ESC Committee also requires states to "ensure the right of access to employment, especially for disadvantaged and marginalised groups, permitting them to live in dignity", which could arguably include the stateless,[55] it has been suggested that the Committee is in fact

> likely to allow States considerable latitude to differentiate in favour of their citizens [...] in the right to access work, unless such differentiations are 'unreasonable'.[56]

The Committee on the Elimination of Racial Discrimination also recognises that states "may refuse to offer jobs to non-citizens without a work permit".[57] Nevertheless, the ESC Committee has recently determined that "the labour market must be open to everyone under the jurisdiction of State parties".[58] Thus, while states are free to regulate the access of non-nationals to their territory (and thereby jurisdiction) through immigration policy,[59] this statement suggests that once access has been granted, access to the labour market should follow. However, there are many groups of non-citizens, in particular temporary visitors such as tourists or persons in transit, who are admitted to state soil but for whom access to employment may be inappropriate. A more considered reading of the ESC Committee's general comment on the right to work leads to the understanding that

---

International Covenant on Economic, Social and Cultural Rights. A Perspective on its Development, Clarendon Press, Oxford: 1998, page 205. See also Committee on Economic, Social and Cultural Rights, *General Comment No. 18: The Right to Work,* E/C.12/GC/18, 6 February 2006, para. 6.

[53] Committee on Economic, Social and Cultural Rights, *General Comment No. 18: The Right to Work,* E/C.12/GC/18, 6 February 2006, paras. 19 and 31. This norm is reinforced by article 5, paragraph e(i) of the Convention on the Elimination of Racial Discrimination.

[54] Note that nationality as a ground of discrimination is also absent from the list proscribed by the ILO Convention No. 111 concerning Discrimination in Employment and Occupation (1958).

[55] Emphasis added. Committee on Economic, Social and Cultural Rights, *General Comment No. 18: The Right to Work,* E/C.12/GC/18, 6 February 2006, para. 31 (a).

[56] John Dent, *Research Paper on the Social and Economic Rights of Non-Nationals in Europe,* Brussels: 1998, page 45. Other scholars have even held that it is still "readily accepted that foreign workers may be required to obtain special authorisations (or permits) in order to work". Matthew Craven, *The International Covenant on Economic, Social and Cultural Rights. A Perspective on its Development*, Clarendon Press, Oxford: 1998, page 213. See also Diana Elles, *International Provisions Protecting the Human Rights of Non-Citizens: Study,* New York: 1980, page 30.

[57] Committee on the Elimination of Racial Discrimination, *General Recommendation 30: Discrimination against Non-Citizens*, New York: 1 October 2004, para. 35. The Migrant Workers Convention also admits that states may set conditions for both the granting of entry into the state and of authorisation to work. See for example articles 37, 49 and 55.

[58] Committee on Economic, Social and Cultural Rights, *General Comment No. 18: The Right to Work,* E/C.12/GC/18, 6 February 2006, para. 12.

[59] Within certain constraints. See chapter X, section 1.2.

it is "migrant workers and members of their families" – a sub-category of non-citizens - for whom access to the labour market should be ensured.[60]

Under the current state of international human rights law, it would therefore seem that stateless persons will only benefit from the right to access employment if they have gained lawful access to the state's jurisdiction[61] and will have the best chance of claiming protection under the human rights regime if they also fall into the category of migrant workers or members of their families.[62] This will not always provide solace to the situation of the stateless. So although the ESC Committee has occasionally taken an interest in the access of non-citizens to the labour market,[63] and the Committee on the Elimination of Racial Discrimination is calling for the removal of obstacles "that prevent the enjoyment of economic, social and cultural rights by non-citizens, notably in the [area] of [...] employment",[64] the underlying norm remains too narrow and too uncertain to be heralded as a decisive aid for the stateless. Moreover, thanks to article 2, paragraph 3 of the ICESCR, any state that plays the card of the "developing country" could potentially further curtail any of its obligations towards non-nationals in respect of the right to work that is widely acknowledged to be an economic right.[65] Exclusion from employment opportunities only serves to seriously compound the overall marginalisation and disempowerment of the stateless. Had the 1954 Statelessness Convention followed the line taken in the 1951 Refugee instrument, it would have been a valuable asset to the protection of the right to work for stateless persons.[66] As it stands, this opportunity was lost.

---

[60] Committee on Economic, Social and Cultural Rights, *General Comment No. 18: The Right to Work*, E/C.12/GC/18, 6 February 2006, paras. 18 and 23.

[61] This is further indicated by the fact that for non-nationals, *lawful* presence on state territory is required for the protection of other elements of the right to work such as the (limited) freedom of choice of work under the Migrant Workers Convention, including recognition of diploma's to that effect (articles 52 and 53) and protection against dismissal, in the Migrant Workers Convention (article 54) or ILO Convention No. 143 concerning Migrant Workers (1975).

[62] Note that while the Migrant Workers Convention explicitly excludes stateless persons from the personal scope of application, the term "migrant worker" is of more widespread usage and stateless persons may thus benefit as migrant workers from the protections of such instruments as the ICESCR and ILO standard-setting convention. Under ILO Convention No. 143 concerning Migrant Workers (1975), the term migrant worker is defined as "a person who migrates or who has migrated from one country to another with a view to being employed otherwise than on his own account" (article 11). Note that the concept of a migrant worker generally excludes the self-employed.

[63] ESC Committee, *Concluding observations: Finland*, E/1997/22, New York and Geneva: 1996, para. 307; *Denmark*, E/2000/22, New York and Geneva: 1999, para. 115; *Italy*, E/2005/22, New York and Geneva: 2004, para. 435.

[64] Committee on the Elimination of Racial Discrimination, *General Recommendation 30: Discrimination against Non-Citizens*, New York: 1 October 2004, para 29. The Committee has also addressed this matter in reaction to numerous state reports. See for example CERD, *Concluding observations: Norway*, A/49/18, New York: 1994, para. 264; *Latvia*, A/58/18, New York: 2003, para. 451.

[65] See James Hathaway, *The Rights of Refugees Under International Law*, Cambridge University Press, Cambridge: 2005, pages 740-742. It is regrettable that the ESC Committee did not address the impact of article 2, paragraph 3 of the ICESCR on the right to work in its General Comment on this topic.

[66] Hathaway is (quite rightly) full of praise for the impact of article 17 of the 1951 Convention relating to the Status of Refugees in setting a standard on the right to work that explicitly benefits refugees and goes beyond the terms of the ambiguous standard set for non-nationals generally under human rights

The situation as far as labour-related rights are concerned is less troublesome since the applicability of relevant human rights norms to the situation of non-nationals is more clearly defined. Article 7 of the International Covenant on Economic, Social and Cultural Rights outlines the main components that make up the "just and favourable conditions of work" that everyone is to enjoy. These include issues such as fair remuneration, safe and healthy working conditions and adequate rest.[67] This provision is, in fact, worded in such a way as to demand immediate, rather than progressive, realisation and there is no indication that non-nationals cannot benefit from the guarantees on equal footing to nationals.[68] In its general comment on non-citizens, the Committee on the Elimination of Racial Discrimination explicitly stated that "all individuals are entitled to the enjoyment of labour and employment rights [...] once an employment relationship has been initiated until it is terminated".[69] Rather than being attached to citizenship, labour rights are thus attributed on the basis of the existence of an *employment relationship*: to be enjoyed by all workers as workers.[70] A plethora of ILO instruments addressing labour-related rights vouch for this fact.[71] The Migrant Workers Convention provides that migrant workers are entitled to treatment on a par with the host state's nationals for the purposes of the enjoyment of labour-related rights[72] and, unlike the 1954 Statelessness Convention, bestows these rights regardless of the (ir)regularity of the individual's situation.[73] The Inter-American Court of Human Rights has also held that labour rights are to be respected regardless of immigration status.[74] So, "the right of non-nationals to equal treatment

law. See James Hathaway, *The Rights of Refugees Under International Law*, Cambridge University Press, Cambridge: 2005, page 741 onwards.

67 The list differs somewhat from that found in the 1954 Statelessness Convention – which mimics the ILO standards - but can be considered largely comparable. For an in depth comparison of the content of these norms see James Hathaway, *The Rights of Refugees Under International Law*, Cambridge University Press, Cambridge: 2005, pages 765-769.

68 The ESC Committee has yet to issue a General Comment on article 7 of the ICESCR. Although admitting that this norm is interdependent with article 6 on the right to work, the Committee expressed the preference to deal with it separately. Committee on Economic, Social and Cultural Rights, *General Comment No. 18: The Right to Work,* E/C.12/GC/18, 6 February 2006, para. 8. However, the Committee has considered and expressed concern at the working conditions faced by non-nationals or the curtailment of labour rights of non-citizens in its assessment of country reports, for example in ESC Committee, *Concluding Observations: Libyan Arab Jamariya,* E/C.12/1/Add.15, New York and Geneva: 1997, para. 16; *Portugal,* E/C.12/1/Add.53, New York and Geneva: 2000, para. 11.

69 Committee on the Elimination of Racial Discrimination, *General Recommendation 30: Discrimination against Non-Citizens*, New York: 1 October 2004, paras. 33 and 35.

70 See also Inter-American Court of Human Rights, *Advisory Opinion on Juridical Condition and the Rights of Undocumented Migrants,* OC-18/03, 17 September 2003, paragraph 148.

71 See also David Weissbrodt, *Final Report on Prevention of Discrimination - The Rights of Non-Citizens,* E/CN.4/Sub.2/2003/23, 26 May 2003, para. 15.

72 Article 25 of the Migrant Workers Convention.

73 The provision is located in Part III of the CMW where the rights of *all* migrant workers, both regular and irregular, are housed.

74 The Court found "that the migratory status of a person cannot constitute a justification to deprive him of the enjoyment and exercise of human rights, including those of a labour-related nature. When assuming an employment relationship, the migrant acquires rights that must be recognised and ensured because he is an employee, irrespective of his regular or irregular status in the State where he is employed. These rights are a result of the employment relationship". Inter-American Court of Human

in conditions of work [...] is well entrenched"[75] and can generally be expected to benefit stateless persons regardless of their immigration status.[76] So, labour-related rights are attributable to everyone equally, regardless of citizenship and the 1954 Statelessness Convention therefore simply reflects – in weaker terms – the existing international norm with respect to the enjoyment of labour standards.[77]

3 Freedom of Association

The next ESC right to be discussed is considered to be closely linked to the right to work and is sometimes even described as a labour-related right: the freedom of association.[78] It is dealt with in a separate section here because it is a multidimensional right that has a political and cultural aspect alongside its strong social and economic role and, as such, warrants independent consideration.[79] A major element is the right to associate in the form of trade unions in order to

---

Rights, *Advisory Opinion on Juridical Condition and the Rights of Undocumented Migrants*, OC-18/03, 17 September 2003, decisions of the court, paragraph 8.

[75] John Dent, *Research Paper on the Social and Economic Rights of Non-Nationals in Europe*, Brussels: 1998, page 45.

[76] Under human rights law, "states are required to [...] provide minimum legal protection to migrant workers whose situations are irregular; basic human rights are not conditional upon the circumstances of residence". These include norms relating to basic labour conditions. Guy Goodwin-Gill, 'International Law and Human Rights: Trends Concerning International Migrants and Refugees', in *International Migration Review*, Vol. 23, 1989, page 535. A minor incongruity can be found in the ILO standards on migrant workers (article 6 of the ILO Convention No. 97 concerning Migration for Employment) – which also provide for national treatment in respect of labour conditions – and the UN Declaration on the Human Rights of Individuals Who are not Nationals of the Country in which They Live (article 8). These texts are more cautious and attribute the respective labour-related rights to lawfully present non-citizens only. However, the beneficiaries of the general labour standards set out in other ILO Conventions and Recommendations are such categories as "all employed persons" or "all workers" in a particular industry – confirming the overriding approach that these rights are attributed to workers as workers.

[77] It has been argued that the added value of a provision relating specifically to the stateless (or rather to refugees for it was in reference to the 1951 Refugee Convention) lies in the universal application of this norm. If developing states were to try to evade their obligations with respect to the labour-related rights of non-nationals on the basis of article 2, paragraph 3 of the ICESCR, all lawfully-residing stateless persons would be exempted from this restricted protection. However, in view of the inclusion of these work-related rights in numerous other international instruments from which non-nationals may also benefit - and indeed the possible adverse effect on local labour that would be created if non-citizens have the "competitive edge" because labour standards need not be respected – it seems an unlikely scenario that this provision could be relied upon to justify differential treatment between nationals and non-nationals for the purposes of *protecting the national economy*. See James Hathaway, *The Rights of Refugees Under International Law*, Cambridge University Press, Cambridge: 2005, page 769.

[78] Committee on Economic, Social and Cultural Rights, *General Comment No. 18: The Right to Work*, E/C.12/GC/18, 6 February 2006, para. 8.

[79] Be reminded that the freedom of association could have been considered in the previous chapter, as it is closely related to the freedom of expression and of assembly. It is a norm that can be found in both the ICCPR and the ICESCR and the extent to which it is considered a civil and political right or an ESC right depends very much on the circumstances in which it operates. The decision was taken to deal with this right here because of the formulation of the norm in the 1954 Statelessness Convention with its focus on the social and economic dimension..

promote and protect social and economic rights and interests.[80] In this context, it includes the right to strike.[81] Yet the freedom of association also "allows individuals to join together to pursue and further collective interests in groups, such as sports clubs, political parties [and] NGOs".[82] Importantly for non-nationals and minority groups, associations may also be formed in order to facilitate the preservation of a language, culture or religious belief.[83] Therefore, as a vehicle for defending or advancing a wide variety of concerns, the freedom of association is of vital interest to all individuals and groups, but in particular to vulnerable populations like the stateless. Yet it is not unheard of for the stateless to experience difficulties in respect of this right, as they do in so many other areas. One example is offered by the Kuwaiti government's treatment of the country's stateless Bidoon: all "private clubs and associations" were reportedly ordered to dismiss any Bidoon members.[84] Let us consider the scope of the international norms that have a bearing on such practices.

3.1 The 1954 Convention relating to the Status of Stateless Persons

The freedom of association is guaranteed to stateless persons by the 1954 Statelessness Convention's article 15:

> As regards non-political and non-profit-making associations and trade unions the Contracting States shall accord to stateless persons lawfully staying in their territory treatment as favourable as possible and, in any event, not less favourable than that accorded to aliens generally in the same circumstances.[85]

The drafting history of this provision once again reveals a pattern of weakening of language and narrowing of protection offered. When the draft article was first put forward for debate in the context of the formulation of the 1951 Refugee Convention, the freedom of association was expressed in absolute terms – rather than being made contingent upon the protection offered to any other group – and

[80] "The right to form and join trade unions [...] is a particular aspect of the right to freedom of association joined with the right to work. This right includes, for instance, the right of unions to administer their own affairs, join federations and international organisations and draw up their own rules. It encompasses the rights of persons to be elected to and act within unions without intimidation and the right not to join without fear of retribution". Magdalena Sepulveda; Theo van Banning; Gudrun Gudmundsdottir; Christine Chamoun; Willem van Genugten, *Human Rights Reference Handbook*, University for Peace, Ciudad Colon: 2004, page 303.

[81] Carmen Tiburcio, "Chapter IX. Public Rights" in *The human rights of aliens under international and comparative law*, Kluwer Law International, The Hague: 2001, page 237

[82] Magdalena Sepulveda; Theo van Banning; Gudrun Gudmundsdottir; Christine Chamoun; Willem van Genugten, *Human Rights Reference Handbook*, University for Peace, Ciudad Colon: 2004, page 302.

[83] James Hathaway, *The Rights of Refugees Under International Law*, Cambridge University Press, Cambridge: 2005, page 875.

[84] Open Society Justice Initiative, *Racial Discrimination and the Rights of Non-Citizens. Submission to the UN Committee on the Elimination of Racial Discrimination on the occasion of its 64th Session*, New York: 2004.

[85] Note that no reservations have been lodged in reference to this article by contracting states.

was granted to all refugees regardless of status.[86] While the text that was eventually adopted for the refugee instrument already lowered the standard of treatment to that of most favoured non-citizen and raised the level of attachment required to *lawful stay*, the wording eventually reverted to in the 1954 Statelessness Convention establishes for *lawfully staying* stateless persons only the same level of treatment as non-nationals generally - although again more preferential treatment is encouraged. In the main, the steady stripping down of the norm until only minimal guarantees remain can be explained by reference to the political tinge that the freedom of association has and the desire of state governments to restrict the political activities of (refugees and later) stateless persons.[87]

The motives that caused states to elevate the level of attachment and lower the standard of protection in respect of the freedom of association have also had an impact on the scope of the norm. Rather than expressing an overall right to associate, the provision only protects association in *non-political and non-profit-making associations and trade unions*. Once more, the main objective pursued through this approach is the exclusion of political association from the sphere of activities protected. While the freedom of association for economic, social and cultural pursuits is maintained, the deliberate exclusion of political activities (as well as the omission of the freedom of assembly from the 1954 Statelessness Convention) is disappointing.[88] Hathaway said of this right in the Refugee Convention that

> overall, the best that can be said for Art. 15 is that it is an important affirmation of the right of refugees – at least once they are lawfully staying and to the same extent as most-favoured foreigners – to undertake quite a broad range of associational activities, including not only the right to join trade unions, but also to participate in the activities of a diverse array of associations, including those with cultural, sporting, social or philanthropic aims.[89]

Yet even this only marginally positive conclusion must be tempered further in relation to the Statelessness Convention which did not manage to hold onto the most-favoured-foreigner treatment. In order to discover the standard of treatment prescribed for non-nationals generally – and thereby also the stateless - under international law, we must turn once again to the relevant human rights (and ILO) standards.

[86] James Hathaway, *The Rights of Refugees Under International Law*, Cambridge University Press, Cambridge: 2005, page 881.
[87] For an account of the modifications made to this norm during the drafting process of the 1951 Refugee Convention and the reasoning behind the changes, see James Hathaway, *The Rights of Refugees Under International Law*, Cambridge University Press, Cambridge: 2005, pages 881-888; For the 1954 Statelessness Convention see Nehemiah Robinson, *Convention relating to the status of stateless persons - Its history and interpretation*, UNHCR, Geneva: 1955, pages 57-58.
[88] See further on this matter chapter X, section 7.
[89] James Hathaway, *The Rights of Refugees Under International Law*, Cambridge University Press, Cambridge: 2005, page 891.

3.2 International human rights law

Under human rights law, the freedom of association enjoys a privileged position as it is included in both the civil and political rights and ESC rights instruments. Thus, article 22 of the ICCPR and article 8 of the ICESCR are both relevant to the protection of this right under human rights law and, as such, will be discussed together here. Plus, there are many additional instruments that espouse one or more aspects of the freedom of association.[90] In principle, non-citizens are to benefit from the guarantees offered by each of these norms and are considered to enjoy the freedom of association.[91] However, as we look more closely at the actual scope of the protection offered to non-nationals, the picture becomes greatly complicated and is riddled with inconsistencies.

We will start with the provision found in the International Covenant on Civil and Political Rights. Article 22 provides for a broad freedom of association – including participation in trade unions - that can be relied upon to protect the participation in any form of (political, social, cultural or economic) association.[92] On the basis of this article, which attributes the right to everyone, it has been asserted that even "membership in political parties, for example, should be open to non-citizens".[93] So the freedom of association as guaranteed under the ICCPR deals with a much wider range of associational activities than the 1954 Statelessness Convention (that explicitly excludes political and profit-making associations). Moreover, individuals may not only join such associations, they may also form

[90] In the Universal Declaration on Human Rights, the freedom of association and of assembly are espoused in one and the same provision, article 20. The Convention on the Elimination of Racial establishes non-discriminatory enjoyment of both the freedom of assembly and of association in article 5, paragraph d (ix), where they are categorised as civil rights, then the right to form and join trade unions in article 5, paragraph e(ii) which is grouped with the ESC rights. Other sources of these rights are article 15 of the Convention on the Rights of the Child; Articles 26 and 40 of the Migrant Workers Convention; Article 11 of the European Convention on Human Rights; Article 16 of the American Convention on Human Rights (which mentions association for "ideological, religious, political, economic, labour, social, cultural, sports, or other purposes") and article 8 of the Additional Protocol to the American Convention on Human Rights in the Area of Economic, Social and Cultural Rights; and Article 10 of the African Charter on Human and Peoples' Rights. We will also be looking at ILO standards, in particular the ILO Convention No. 87 concerning Freedom of association and Protection of the Right to Organise (1948).

[91] Human Rights Committee, *CCPR General Comment No. 15: The Position of Aliens under the Covenant,* Geneva: 11 April 1986, para. 7; David Weissbrodt, *Final Report on Prevention of Discrimination - The Rights of Non-Citizens,* E/CN.4/Sub.2/2003/23, 26 May 2003, para. 48; Carmen Tiburcio, "Chapter IX. Public Rights" in *The human rights of aliens under international and comparative law*, Kluwer Law International, The Hague: 2001, page 239; James Hathaway, *The Rights of Refugees Under International Law*, Cambridge University Press, Cambridge: 2005, page 895.

[92] The freedom of association is found in article 22 of the ICCPR where the purpose to be served is simply the protection of "interests" which is further unspecified. Thus, "religious societies, political parties, commercial undertakings and trade unions are as protected by art. 22 as cultural or human rights organisations, soccer clubs or associations of stamp collectors". From Nowak's commentary on the ICCPR as cited in James Hathaway, *The Rights of Refugees Under International Law*, Cambridge University Press, Cambridge: 2005, page 895.

[93] David Weissbrodt, *Final Report on Prevention of Discrimination - The Rights of Non-Citizens,* E/CN.4/Sub.2/2003/23, 26 May 2003, para. 48.

them. Since non-nationals benefit equally from this provision,[94] any restrictions on their enjoyment of the freedom of association must be justified through the system of permissible limitations outlined in its second paragraph.[95] In this regard, we can note that the ICCPR is comparably lenient in allowing for curtailment of this right: "public safety" and "public health or morals" are grounds that can be invoked under the ICCPR but are not admitted elsewhere in the context of limitations to the freedom of association.[96]

Next, in the ICESCR, the freedom of association is declared in much narrower terms. Its article 8 refers only to the right to participate in trade unions, with the more limited aim of the "promotion and protection of [...] economic and social interests".[97] Again though, it is both the right to join and to form such associations that is protected. As ever we must be mindful of the nature of ESC rights in assessing the scope of protection offered to non-nationals under this norm. Unlike the provision where the right to work is "recognised" and which is therefore a matter for progressive realisation, this article is worded as an obligation that is subject to immediate implementation.[98] As such, the entire provision could be qualified as the "minimum core obligation" in the field of trade union rights and non-nationals are to benefit fully from its terms.[99] Restrictions on the exercise of these rights may only be imposed on citizens and non-citizens through the system of permissible limitations.[100] Meanwhile, in view of the very particular perspective of this article, with its focus on associational rights in the employment and thus economic sphere, it is conceivable that developing states may try to curtail the

[94] Human Rights Committee, CCPR General Comment No. 15: The Position of Aliens under the Covenant, Geneva: 11 April 1986, para. 7; Committee on the Elimination of Racial Discrimination, General Recommendation 30: Discrimination against Non-Citizens, New York: 1 October 2004, para. 35.

[95] "No restrictions may be placed on the exercise of this right other than those which are prescribed by law and which are necessary in a democratic society in the interests of national security or public safety, public order (*ordre public*), the protection of public health or morals or the protection of the rights and freedom of others". Article 22, paragraph 2 of the International Covenant on Civil and Political Rights.

[96] See in this respect article 8, paragraph 1(a) of the ICESCR; Article 26, paragraph 2 and article 40, paragraph 2 of the Migrant Workers Convention and Article 8, paragraph 1(b) of the UN Declaration on the Rights of Non-nationals.

[97] Meanwhile, participation in *cultural* associations may be protected under article 15, paragraph 1 of the ICESCR where the right to participate in cultural life is recognised. This right will be discussed in more detail in section 7 below.

[98] Matthew Craven, *The International Covenant on Economic, Social and Cultural Rights. A Perspective on its Development*, Clarendon Press, Oxford: 1998, pages 249 and 251.

[99] The ESC Committee has, on several occasions, determined that blanket restrictions on the participation of non-nationals in trade unions violate article 8 of the ICESCR. See ESC Committee, *Concluding Observations: Costa Rica,* E/1991/23, New York and Geneva: 1990, para. 194; *Panama,* E/1992/23, New York and Geneva: 1991, para. 138; *Senegal,* E/1994/23, New York and Geneva: 1993, para. 266 and E/2002/22, New York and Geneva: 2001, para. 348. See also Matthew Craven, *The International Covenant on Economic, Social and Cultural Rights. A Perspective on its Development*, Clarendon Press, Oxford: 1998, pages 265-266. Nevertheless, a general comment on this article is still outstanding and would be valuable in clarifying the exact nature and scope of the right, including the position of non-nationals in this regard.

[100] Be reminded that this is identical to the system found in the ICCPR provision, with the exclusion of the grounds of public safety and public health or morals.

enjoyment of these rights by non-citizens by relying on article 2, paragraph 3 of the ICESCR.[101] However, since the freedom of association is also espoused in the ICCPR (which does not provide for special measures for the treatment of non-nationals by developing states) any aspects of article 8 of the ICESCR that overlap with the provision in the ICCPR should be considered exempted from the sphere of influence of article 2, paragraph 3 of the ICESCR.[102]

While the ICCPR and the ICESCR permit the curtailment of the freedom of association under certain circumstances, at the same time they expressly remind states that the ILO standards that have been elaborated in this area must also be respected. Both provisions determine that

> nothing in this article shall authorise State Parties to the International Labour Organisation Convention of 1948 concerning Freedom of Association and Protection of the Right to Organise to take legislative measures which would prejudice, or apply the law in such a manner as would prejudice, the guarantees provided for in that Convention.[103]

The ILO Convention referred to here (No. 87) has now been ratified by 149 states – almost as many as are a party to the two international Covenants.[104] Since the ILO instrument grants associational rights to all "workers and employers, without distinction whatsoever",[105] non-nationals are irrefutably deemed to benefit from its provisions. They are thus assured the right to both join and form associations which are geared to "furthering and defending the interests of workers or of employers",[106] the most prevalent of which are trade unions. The ICCPR and ICESCR agree that this ILO document establishes a basic minimum standard that must be respected, regardless of nationality.

So far, the position of non-nationals under the various provisions on the freedom of association discussed is relatively straight forward and has yet to show any major inconsistencies. Yet the complex picture for which I have forewarned at the beginning of this section has yet to be coloured in. The difficulties arise in connection with those human rights and ILO documents that specifically address the rights of (certain categories of) non-nationals. First there is the Migrant Workers Convention. On a positive note, this instrument protects a broad freedom of association – not only for economic pursuits but also for "cultural and other interests" that may be interpreted to include political associations.[107] However, irregular migrant workers are only attributed the right to *join* such associations, a regular migratory status being required for the enjoyment of the right to *form*

---

[101] See James Hathaway, *The Rights of Refugees Under International Law*, Cambridge University Press, Cambridge: 2005, page 897.

[102] For example, the right to join and form trade unions is protected in both the ICCPR and the ICESCR whereas the right to strike is only explicitly guaranteed in the ICESCR.

[103] Article 22, paragraph 3 of the ICCPR and article 8, paragraph 3 of the ICESCR.

[104] Be reminded that the ICCPR currently has 162 state parties and the ICESCR has 159.

[105] Article 2 of ILO Convention No. 87 concerning Freedom of Association and Protection of the Right to Organise (1948).

[106] Article 10 of ILO Convention No. 87 concerning Freedom of Association and Protection of the Right to Organise (1948).

[107] See article 26, paragraph 1 and article 40, paragraph 1 of the Migrant Workers Convention.

associations.[108] This approach suggests that states may restrict the rights of non-nationals to form associations without having to rely on the regime of permissible limitations, so long as those non-nationals are not lawfully present – a step backwards from the terms of the ICCPR and ICESCR and towards the less generous terms of the 1954 Statelessness Convention. The UN Declaration on the rights of Non-nationals goes even further along this path and adds to the confusion by offering non-citizens only the right to join associations and trade unions (albeit likely in the pursuit of all interests) and only once lawful residence has been acquired.[109] The ILO standards elaborated specifically for migrant workers are similarly restrictive, granting national treatment only in respect of membership of trade unions and only to lawfully present migrant workers.[110]

It is fortunate that the more favourable and expansive norms are to be found in those instruments that enjoy a much wider acceptance, as evidenced by the higher level of ratification, and are thereby more likely to reflect the current standing of international law on this matter. Nevertheless, the reluctance to directly transpose these standards into documents that deal specifically with the rights of non-citizens – a trend that was already set with the drafting of the relevant provision in the 1951 Refugee Convention and the 1954 Statelessness Convention – is cause for concern. We have seen that several of the human rights treaty bodies have expressed the opinion that non-citizens are protected under the norms on freedom of association. So, there is certainly potential for guaranteeing to stateless persons all aspects of the freedom of association on the basis of the ICCPR and the ICESCR.[111] However, there remains a need for clarification of the scope of the provisions found in these instruments and their application to the situation of non-nationals in order to prevent the divergence in standards uncovered from enabling states to reduce their obligations to the lowest common denominator to the detriment of non-nationals, including the stateless.

4 Right to social security

Social security programmes are designed to function as a safety net for those whose circumstances temporarily or permanently prevent them from providing for themselves. Social security thus means income security in times of economic or social distress. It is all about ensuring the "minimum conditions for survival"[112] or,

[108] Article 26 elaborates the right to *join* trade unions and other associations. It is housed in the section of the Convention devoted to the rights of *all* migrant workers regardless of status. Meanwhile article 40 contributes the right to *form* associations and trade unions, but this is found in the section on the rights of *regular* migrant workers.

[109] Article 8, paragraph 1(b) of the UN Declaration on the rights of Non-nationals.

[110] Article 6, paragraph 1 a (ii), of ILO Convention No. 97 concerning Migration for Employment (1948).

[111] Hathaway is optimistic about the role of these norms, in particular the ICCPR provisions, in redressing some of the damage done by the incorporation of such limited terms into the refugee (and stateless) convention(s). James Hathaway, *The Rights of Refugees Under International Law*, Cambridge University Press, Cambridge: 2005, pages 891-892.

[112] Magdalena Sepulveda; Theo van Banning; Gudrun Gudmundsdottir; Christine Chamoun; Willem van Genugten, *Human Rights Reference Handbook*, University for Peace, Ciudad Colon: 2004, page 262.

more precisely, enabling everyone to enjoy an adequate standard of living.[113] *Social security* should be seen as an umbrella term that covers two different phenomena. The first - also referred to as social security in the narrow sense or social insurance - comprises compensation or benefits that are financed through a social insurance system closely linked to employment. In other words, it addresses "contribution-based initiatives designed to compensate workers unable to continue working".[114] The second kind of social security programme - often termed social or public assistance, relief or welfare - is a separate form of "needs-based assistance from public funds, raised through tax revenues".[115] In reality, the two types of scheme will often be required to work in conjunction in order to meet the needs of all persons who are not in a position to earn their own living.

Before we look at how the right to social security is framed under the 1954 Statelessness Convention and international human rights law, a few brief comments can be made on the problems experienced by non-nationals generally and stateless persons specifically in accessing social security benefits. To begin with, it is important to note that social security is a typical area in which the treatment of non-nationals has been shaped by the conclusion of reciprocal agreements whereby a citizen of country A is granted social security benefits in country B on a par with that state's nationals, so long as country A offers the same treatment to nationals of country B.[116] As we will see, this approach can also be identified in a number of multilateral instruments, including some ILO documents. Without any nationality, the stateless have no country of their own that can offer to reciprocate the favoured treatment and are therefore not in a position to benefit from any such agreements. We will be looking to see whether the instruments in question take this predicament of the stateless into account. Leaving aside the question of reciprocity, access to social security is another area in which the stateless are generally reported to experience difficulties. The lack of a nationality is said to present an obstacle to making use of "public services"[117] and is barring access to social security for groups like the Meskhetians in Russia[118] and the Hill Tribes in Thailand.[119] With this in mind, it is time again to consider the content of the relevant international norms.

---

[113] The right to an adequate standard of living is another well-established ESC right and will be dealt with in section 5 of this chapter.

[114] James Hathaway, *The Rights of Refugees Under International Law*, Cambridge University Press, Cambridge: 2005, page 775. See also John Dent, *Research Paper on the Social and Economic Rights of Non-Nationals in Europe,* Brussels: 1998, page 63.

[115] Martin Scheinin, "The Right to Social Security" in Rosas (ed) *Economic, Social and Cultural Rights*, Martinus Nijhoff Publishers, Dordrecht: 1995, page 159.

[116] Diana Elles, *International Provisions Protecting the Human Rights of Non-Citizens: Study,* New York: 1980, page, page 32; James Hathaway, *The Rights of Refugees Under International Law*, Cambridge University Press, Cambridge: 2005, page 773.

[117] UNHCR, "Statelessness and Citizenship" in *The State of the World's Refugees - A Humanitarian Agenda*, Oxford University Press, Oxford: 1997, page 225.

[118] Open Society Justice Initiative, *Racial Discrimination and the Rights of Non-Citizens. Submission to the UN Committee on the Elimination of Racial Discrimination on the occasion of its 64th Session,* New York: 2004.

[119] Maureen Lynch, *Lives on hold: The human cost of statelessness,* Washington: 2005, page 8.

4.1 The 1954 Convention relating to the Status of Stateless Persons

In addressing the right of the stateless to social security, the 1954 Convention relating to the Status of Stateless Persons splits this overall entitlement into its two component parts. Thus article 23 deals with the right to "public relief and assistance" and article 24 looks at access to "social security".[120] The two provisions (both transposed word-for-word from the text of the 1951 Refugee Convention) offer the same basic standard of treatment and agree on the level of attachment required for eligibility to this protection: *lawfully staying* stateless persons are to enjoy *national treatment*. While the level of attachment required may pose problems for a lot of stateless individuals, the prescription of national treatment is a higher standard than offered in respect of many of the Convention's rights. Furthermore, by making the protection offered contingent on national treatment, rather than the treatment of (particular categories of) non-nationals, the 1954 Statelessness Convention neatly bypasses any difficulties that might otherwise have been raised by the requirement of reciprocity for the enjoyment of rights.[121] However, since the actual protection offered is still contingent upon the treatment of the state's own nationals and there is no absolute obligation to provide for a system of either social security or public relief, the stateless may still be unassisted by these provisions.[122] Furthermore, both articles were the subject of ardent debate during the drafting of the convention – their inclusion having to eventually be agreed by vote – and have since attracted a significant number of reservations, thereby limiting their impact.[123] And, as we look more closely at the details set out under each provision, there is another troubling discovery in store.

Turning first to the article on social security, we find that the guarantees elaborated are applicable to

> legal provisions in respect of employment injury, occupational diseases, maternity, sickness, disability, old age, death, unemployment, family responsibilities and any other contingency which according to national laws or regulations, is covered by a social security scheme.[124]

The content of the concept of social security is thereby identified on the basis of the type of measure and appears indifferent to whether the benefits are funded through a contribution-based scheme or from the public coffers. Following this definition of terms are two sub-paragraphs in which permissible limitations to the general standard of *national treatment* are elaborated.[125] The most noteworthy of these is

[120] Recall that paragraph 1(a) of article 24 deals with labour-related rights, while the rest of the provision addresses social security matters.

[121] Recall that, as mentioned in chapter IX, at note 70, the 1954 Statelessness Convention also specifically exempts the stateless from the requirement of reciprocity in certain cases.

[122] See also James Hathaway, *The Rights of Refugees Under International Law*, Cambridge University Press, Cambridge: 2005, page 809.

[123] A total of 8 states have submitted some form of reservation to article 23, while 11 states have made reservations to (one or more of) the paragraphs dealing with the right to social security in article 24.

[124] Article 24, paragraph 1(b) of the 1954 Convention relating to the Status of Stateless Persons.

[125] The rest of article 24 (paragraphs 2 to 4) is devoted to detailed arrangements for certain situations in which social security benefits may be accumulated and paid out. See on the content of these provisions

the determination that states may restrict the enjoyment by stateless persons of "such portions of the social security benefits which are payable wholly out of public funds".[126] Although this limitation is reportedly designed to allow governments to refuse stateless persons *supplementary* benefits,[127] the clause is formulated in much broader terms. And it is here, where the provision on social security touches upon the right of the stateless to access benefits paid for by public moneys, that a certain tension with article 23 on public relief can be traced.

While article 23 establishes national treatment for lawfully staying stateless persons in respect of "public relief and assistance", it actually fails to elaborate on the meaning of this expression.[128] The scope of protection offered is thus effectively left to domestic law and can cover the full spectrum of assistance provided for through public funds. Various parties have attempted to offer examples of measures that (could) fall under the term "public relief", referring, amongst other things, to benefits bestowed for sickness, invalidity and old age.[129] In substance then, it appears possible that "public relief" may overlap, in part, with "social security", rendering it very hard to establish how a particular measure should be qualified. With this in mind, it has nonetheless been suggested that "no difficulties will, as a rule, arise in practice concerning the delimitation between public relief and assistance, on the one hand, and social security, on the other, because the Convention provides for the same treatment, in both instances".[130] However, the same commentary goes on to confess that the treatment does differ where the restrictions admitted by article 24 come into play.[131] The broader implications of this observation are not considered, yet an important question thus arises as to the reach of the permissible exception to national treatment found in article 24.[132] Can

Nehemiah Robinson, *Convention relating to the status of stateless persons - Its history and interpretation*, UNHCR, Geneva: 1955, pages 72-73 and James Hathaway, *The Rights of Refugees Under International Law*, Cambridge University Press, Cambridge: 2005, pages 777 and 781-785.

[126] Nehemiah Robinson, *Convention relating to the status of stateless persons - Its history and interpretation*, UNHCR, Geneva: 1955, page 72.

[127] James Hathaway, *The Rights of Refugees Under International Law*, Cambridge University Press, Cambridge: 2005, page 781.

[128] This was a deliberate decision by the drafters of the 1951 Refugee Convention who felt that it would not be possible to enumerate a complete list of situations covered by or beneficiaries of public relief. James Hathaway, *The Rights of Refugees Under International Law*, Cambridge University Press, Cambridge: 2005, page 810.

[129] James Hathaway, *The Rights of Refugees Under International Law*, Cambridge University Press, Cambridge: 2005, page 810.

[130] Nehemiah Robinson, *Convention relating to the status of stateless persons - Its history and interpretation*, UNHCR, Geneva: 1955, page 70.

[131] Nehemiah Robinson, *Convention relating to the status of stateless persons - Its history and interpretation*, UNHCR, Geneva: 1955, page 70. In his extensive commentary of the 1951 Refugee Convention, Hathaway comes to the same conclusion in respect of this instrument's identical provisions. See James Hathaway, *The Rights of Refugees Under International Law*, Cambridge University Press, Cambridge: 2005, page 811.

[132] Note that the entire text of article 24, paragraph 1(b), including permissible limitations, was derived from a pre-existing ILO instrument. See article 6, paragraph 1(b) of ILO Convention No. 97 Concerning Migration for Employment (1949). This may help to explain the lack of attention for any incongruity between articles 23 and 24 of the 1954 Statelessness Convention at the time of its adoption, since the ILO document deals only with social security and "need-based basic subsistence benefits [...] to a large extent fall outside the ILO concept of social security". Martin Scheinin, "The Right to Social

public relief granted through a state-funded system be withheld from the stateless so long as the state in question labels the benefit "social security"?

If we must defer to domestic legislation in order to determine whether a particular measure is categorised as social security or as public relief there is a definite risk of misuse of the indistinctness of the two concepts under the 1954 Statelessness Convention and of the permissible limitation admitted by article 24. The existence of an obligation to grant national treatment without exception in the field of public relief may arguably negate the rule included in the provision on social security whereby the stateless can be excluded from enjoying publicly funded benefits. At the very least, it calls for highly reserved usage of this permissible exception. Nevertheless, alongside the issues raised by the substantial number of reservations to both articles 23 and 24 and the high level of attachment required before either provision can be relied upon, this ambiguity of obligation may severely weaken the impact of the 1954 Statelessness Convention on the protection of the overall right to social security for stateless persons. Time now to see how this approach compares with that taken under human rights law generally.

4.2 International human rights law

After the detailed elaboration of the right to social security in not one, but two provisions of the 1954 Statelessness Convention, it comes as something of a surprise to find that the International Covenant on Economic, Social and Cultural Rights contents itself with the following statement:

> The State Parties to the present Covenant recognise the right of everyone to social security, including social insurance.[133]

While this delineation is certainly concise and appears rather vague, the Committee has clarified that it covers such "branches" as "medical care, cash sickness benefits, maternity benefits, old-age benefits, invalidity benefits, survivors' benefits, employment injury benefits, unemployment benefits [and] family benefits".[134] Again, it is a right that is in principle guaranteed to "everyone".[135] Moreover, the

Security" in Rosas (ed) *Economic, Social and Cultural Rights*, Martinus Nijhoff Publishers, Dordrecht: 1995, page 163.

[133] Article 9 of the ICESCR. The right to social security is also dealt with in articles 22 and 25 of the Universal Declaration of Human Rights; Article 5, paragraph e (iv) of the Convention on the Elimination of Racial Discrimination; Article 26 of the Convention on the Rights of the Child; Articles 27, 43, 45 and 54 of the Migrant Workers Convention; Article 9 of the Additional Protocol to the American Convention on Human Rights in the Area of Economic, Social and Cultural Rights; Articles 12, 13 and 14 of the European Social Charter and various ILO instruments including Convention No. 102 concerning Social Security (Minimum Standards) (1952) and Convention No. 118 concerning Equality of Treatment (Social Security) (1962).

[134] ESC Committee, *Revised general guidelines regarding the form and contents of reports to be submitted by state parties under articles 16 and 17 of the International Covenant on Economic, Social and Cultural Rights*, E/C.12/1991/1, 17 June 1991. This list is virtually identical to that set out in the 1954 Statelessness Convention and the relevant ILO standards.

[135] The UN treaty bodies have been active in encouraging access to social security benefits for non-nationals and expressing concern where the enjoyment of these rights by non-citizens is restricted. Examples from recent years are: Committee on the Elimination of Racial Discrimination, *Concluding*

right housed in this article is given further body by a number of closely related norms that all have a bearing on the obligation to provide a basic safety-net for dignified human survival. Among these are the right to life, the right to an adequate standard of living, the right to health, the right to protection of the family, including special provision for the protection of mother and child and even the prohibition of torture.[136] Yet the right to social security remains an independent concept, concerned with access to benefits with a view to the (continued) enjoyment of the other rights mentioned and thereby often plays a central role in their realisation.[137]

The wording of the right to social security in the ICESCR immediately clarifies two important points in respect of this norm. Firstly, that since states "recognise" the right to social security, it is progressive realisation that is envisaged rather than an obligation with immediate binding force. This means that beyond any minimum core obligations, states will be allowed some leeway in determining to what extent non-nationals may benefit from this provision. The second significant observation that can be made is that the right to social security *includes* social insurance systems, but its scope is not limited to such schemes. In other words, the measures taken to realise this right can include both contribution-based schemes (such as social insurance), and non-contributory schemes (such as universal schemes or targeted social assistance schemes).[138] Therefore, the right to social security under international human rights law matches the 1954 Statelessness Convention by touching upon both social security in its narrower sense as social insurance and what the Statelessness Convention termed "public relief". What we must consider here is the scope of protection offered to non-nationals – or indeed specifically to stateless persons – with regard to both types of scheme.

Observations: Saudi Arabia, A/58/18, New York: 2003, para. 206; *Slovenia,* A/58/18, New York: 2003, para. 241; *France,* A/60/18, New York: 2005, para. 118. Human Rights Committee, *Concluding Observations: Thailand,* A/60/40 vol. I, Geneva: 2005, para. 95(23). ESC Committee, *Concluding Observations: Israel,* E/2004/22, New York and Geneva: 2003, para. 251; *Kuwait,* E/2005/22, New York and Geneva: 2004, para. 193; *Spain,* E/2005/22, New York and Geneva: 2004, para. 230. Committee on the Rights of the Child, *Concluding Observations: Uzbekistan,* CRC/C/111, Geneva: 2001, para. 549; *Republic of Korea,* CRC/C/124, Geneva: 2003, paras. 136-137.

[136] Martin Scheinin, "The Right to Social Security" in Rosas (ed) *Economic, Social and Cultural Rights,* Martinus Nijhoff Publishers, Dordrecht: 1995, pages 160-161; John Dent, *Research Paper on the Social and Economic Rights of Non-Nationals in Europe,* Brussels: 1998, page 64; James Hathaway, *The Rights of Refugees Under International Law,* Cambridge University Press, Cambridge: 2005, page 807; Magdalena Sepulveda; Theo van Banning; Gudrun Gudmundsdottir; Christine Chamoun; Willem van Genugten, *Human Rights Reference Handbook,* University for Peace, Ciudad Colon: 2004, page 264; ESC Committee, *General Comment No. 19 - The Right to Social Security,* Advanced unedited version, 4 February 2008, para. 1. The close relationship between the right to social security and these other fundamental rights has allowed social security matters to be addressed on occasion through the numerous related international norms.

[137] "Benefits, whether in cash or in kind, must be *adequate* in amount and duration in order that everyone can realise his or her rights to family protection and assistance, an adequate standard of living and adequate access to health care [...] but other measures are necessary to compliment the right to social security". ESC Committee, *General Comment No. 19 - The Right to Social Security,* Advanced unedited version, 4 February 2008, paras. 22 and 28.

[138] ESC Committee, *General Comment No. 19 - The Right to Social Security,* Advanced unedited version, 4 February 2008, para. 4. The Committee goes on to suggest that "in almost all state parties, non-contributory schemes will be required since it is unlikely that every person could be adequately covered through an insurance-based system".

Where social security is offered through a system of social insurance, there is a growing indication that non-nationals must enjoy equal protection under such schemes as nationals. Although this is an area in which states have traditionally granted national treatment to foreigners on the basis of *reciprocal* bilateral or multilateral arrangements,[139] there are indications that stateless persons should be exempted from the demands of reciprocity. For example, the relevant ILO Convention expressly waives the condition of reciprocity with respect to the stateless (and refugees) so that they enjoy an absolute right to national treatment in social security matters under the instrument.[140] Meanwhile, human rights law generally operates on the idea that entitlement to social insurance benefits is actually accrued through participation in the contributory mechanism, similarly to the way in which labour-related rights are entitlements attributed to workers. As long as a non-national makes the requisite contribution to the particular social insurance fund, he or she must be free to access the benefits that flow from it. This entitlement should not be contingent on the possession of a (specific) nationality.[141] This was brought to the fore in a case before the UN Human Rights Committee in which the petitioners complained against France's differential treatment of pension entitlements for former soldiers, between persons who held French citizenship and those who possessed Senegalese nationality. The Committee found a violation of article 26 of the ICCPR, the principle of equal treatment, by determining that

> [since] it was not the question of nationality which determined the granting of pensions to the authors but the services rendered by them in the past [...] a subsequent change in nationality cannot by itself be considered as a sufficient justification for different treatment, since the basis for the grant of the pension was the same service which both they and the soldiers who remained French had provided.[142]

[139] Consider the reference to "applicable bilateral and multilateral treaties" in the article dealing with the enjoyment of social security in the Migrant Workers Convention – migrant workers must meet the requirements of any such treaties if they are to enjoy equal treatment to nationals; See also Article 12, paragraph 4(a) of the European Social Charter and ILO Convention No. 118 concerning Equality of Treatment (Social Security) (1962) both of which provides for equality of treatment on the basis of reciprocity between state parties.

[140] Article 10 of ILO Convention No. 118 concerning Equality of Treatment (Social Security) (1962). Note that this instrument has been ratified by only 37 states and each state is, in fact, entitled to establish upon ratification which types of social security are to be covered by its terms, so the scope of obligations is different for each state party.

[141] ESC Committee, *General Comment No. 19 - The Right to Social Security,* Advanced unedited version, 4 February 2008, para. 36. Note that this General Comment on social security is somewhat ambiguous on the question of access to social insurance schemes, skipping this question and moving straight on to the enjoyment of benefits under such schemes, *where* non-nationals have participated. However, it seems unlikely that states would want to prevent non-nationals from contributing to social insurance schemes, since this would create an uneven playing field in the domestic labour market (see the motivation behind the attribution of equal labour-related rights) and would leave the non-nationals uninsured for such situations as employment injury and thereby reliant on public assistance paid for from tax revenue.

[142] UN Human Rights Committee, *Case of Gueye v. France (196/1985),* A/44/40, 3 April 1989, para. 9.5.

Moreover, the enjoyment of social insurance benefits is protected not only by the right to social security but also by the right to property.[143] This offers additional scope for tackling social insurance benefits made contingent upon nationality. Even the European Court on Human Rights has thus been able to rule on the permissibility of nationality-based distinctions in the field of social security – in spite of the absence of any right to social security under the Convention or its protocols – and has found such measures to be in violation of article 14 of the Convention (non-discrimination) and article 1 of the first protocol (right to property).[144] On the basis of these observations it can be concluded that human rights law widely acknowledges the right of stateless persons to the same treatment as nationals under any contribution-based social security scheme in which they are participating, thereby echoing the guarantee set out in the 1954 Statelessness Convention.

The enjoyment by non-nationals of non-contributory social security is a less straightforward matter. Both the UN Declaration on the Rights of Non-nationals and the Migrant Workers Convention offer non-citizens certain guarantees with regards to "social services"[145] or "social and health services [and] unemployment benefits".[146] These provisions arguably include non-contribution based social assistance. Yet the articles are only applicable to non-nationals who are lawfully present or residing and even then states are free to set additional preconditions for the enjoyment of these benefits.[147] Yet the UN Committee on Economic, Social and Cultural Rights has noted the need for social assistance for all population groups, including non-citizens, that is "adequate to ensure a minimum standard of living".[148] This would suggest that human rights law does prescribe access to at least basic social assistance from non-contributory schemes as a means of ensuring that this standard is met. Regrettably little more has been formally undertaken to

---

[143] Martin Scheinin, "The Right to Social Security" in Rosas (ed) *Economic, Social and Cultural Rights*, Martinus Nijhoff Publishers, Dordrecht: 1995, pages 160-161.

[144] European Court of Human Rights, *Case of Gaygusuz v. Austria,* No. 17371/90, 16 September 1996. As Tiburcio explains, the court "examined the refusal of Austrian authorities to provide a Turkish unemployed with an advance on his pension in the form of 'emergency assistance'. In this case the individual complied with all legal requirements to benefit from this measure and the Court verified that the refusal was due only to the fact that he did not have Austrian nationality, which was required under the Emergency Insurance Act". Carmen Tiburcio, "Chapter VI. Social and Cultural Rights" in *The human rights of aliens under international and comparative law*, Kluwer Law International, The Hague: 2001, page 165.

[145] Article 8, paragraph 1(c) of the UN Declaration on the Rights of Non-nationals.

[146] Article 43, paragraph 1(e); article 45, paragraph 1(c); and article 54, paragraph 1(b) of the Migrant Workers Convention.

[147] Moreover, in the case of the UN Declaration, the enjoyment of such benefits is only prescribed so long as "undue strain is not placed on the resources of the State". This is a remarkable provision given the general categorisation of social security as a *social* right whereby it is not subject to specific restrictions against non-nationals (by developing states) by reference to the national economy under article 2, paragraph 3 of the ICESCR.

[148] Committee on Economic, Social and Cultural Rights, *Concluding Observations: Ukraine,* E/1996/22 (1995) 50, para. 266.

clarify the scope of the norm and its application to non-nationals,[149] so this is an area of international (human rights) law that remains shrouded in "imprecision and lack of objectivity".[150]

The General Comment on social security by the ESC Committee does provide some much-needed clarification. The Comment confirms that "access to a social security scheme that provides a minimum essential level of benefits to all individuals and families that will enable them to acquire at least essential health care, basic shelter and housing, water and sanitation, foodstuffs, and the most basic forms of education" belongs to the minimum core obligations of the right to social security.[151] As such, this basic protection should also be available to stateless persons. Moreover, for the first time in any General Comment by the ESC Committee, the situation of the stateless is explicitly dealt with:

> Refugees, *stateless persons* and asylum-seekers, and other disadvantaged and marginalized individuals and groups, should enjoy equal treatment in access to non-contributory social security schemes, including reasonable access to health care and family support, consistent with international standards.[152]

While this pronouncement does unequivocally affirm that stateless persons may be entitled to public assistance, its terms are regrettably ambiguous. In particular, it is unclear what is meant by "equal treatment" in this context. A literal reading would suggest that states are obliged to grant the same treatment to refugees, asylum seekers and stateless persons, without distinction between or within these groups. However, this would be a very hollow guarantee as it would in no way proscribe restrictions on access to social security for *all* of these vulnerable groups. This interpretation would seem to contradict the overall gist garnered from an earlier section of the General Comment whereby non-nationals are seen as one of the vulnerable groups who "traditionally faced difficulties in exercising [the right to social security]" and for which special attention is needed.[153] It is therefore arguable that the proper interpretation of "equal treatment" here is *national* treatment.[154]

---

[149] Note, for example, that the CERD does not mention (access to) social security in its General Recommendation on the rights of non-citizens. Committee on the Elimination of Racial Discrimination, *General Recommendation 30: Discrimination against Non-Citizens*, New York: 1 October 2004.

[150] Carmen Tiburcio, "Chapter VI. Social and Cultural Rights" in *The human rights of aliens under international and comparative law*, Kluwer Law International, The Hague: 2001, page 165. See also James Hathaway, *The Rights of Refugees Under International Law*, Cambridge University Press, Cambridge: 2005, page 136.

[151] ESC Committee, *General Comment No. 19 - The Right to Social Security,* Advanced unedited version, 4 February 2008, para. 59 (a).

[152] ESC Committee, *General Comment No. 19 - The Right to Social Security,* Advanced unedited version, 4 February 2008, para. 38. Note that paragraph 37 of the same General Comment provides for access of non-nationals generally to "non-contributory schemes for income support, affordable access to health care and family support" and that "any restrictions, including a qualification period, must be proportionate and reasonable".

[153] ESC Committee, *General Comment No. 19 - The Right to Social Security,* Advanced unedited version, 4 February 2008, para. 31.

[154] This interpretation is also in line with the provisions of the 1951 Refugee Convention and the 1954 Statelessness Convention.

In conclusion it would seem that human rights law does offer a certain minimum standard of non-contributory social security to all, including non-nationals, and that there is an increasing onus on states to carefully justify differences in treatment between citizens and non-citizens in the enjoyment of any social assistance that goes beyond this basic level of protection. Nevertheless, until such questions are fully elucidated, the 1954 Statelessness Convention will retain some value in prescribing *national treatment* with respect to this public assistance, with the proviso that all effort is made to ensure that the impact of this statelessness instrument is not irreparably impaired by difficulties of interpretation as discussed above.

5 Right to an adequate standard of living

The right to an adequate standard of living is concerned with providing for every individual's basic needs so as to ensure that "every individual shall be able, without shame and without unreasonable obstacles, to be a full participant in ordinary, everyday interaction with other people".[155] In this respect, it is very closely related to the right to social security and equally central to dignified human survival.[156] Since much has thus already been said about the right to the fulfilment of basic needs, here the focus will be on the scope of those subsistence needs and additional state obligations - alongside norms relating to social security - geared towards their realisation. Where social security dealt largely with the provision of "benefits" generally, the right to an adequate standard of living looks specifically at the availability of several primary necessities of life: food (including water), clothing and housing.[157] The right to an adequate standard of living is also said to encapsulate the right to adequate health(care) and education, but these will be dealt with at a later stage since they are detailed in separate articles of the ICESCR.[158]

Food (including water) and shelter (i.e. clothing and housing) are such elemental human needs that the elaboration of an international norm to ensure their fulfilment seems almost bizarre. But the same feeling may be conjured by many other human rights and reality has betrayed the fact that none is so universally respected and enjoyed as to render its elaboration as a legal norm nonsensical. And indeed it has been found that

> the right to an adequate standard of living has been violated 'more comprehensively and systematically than probably any other right' [and] that the realisation of the right is overlaid by issues of economic

[155] Asbjorn Eide, "The Right to an Adequate Standard of Living Including the Right to Food" in Rosas (ed) *Economic, Social and Cultural Rights*, Martinus Nijhoff Publishers, Dordrecht: 1995, page 89.
[156] Matthew Craven, *The International Covenant on Economic, Social and Cultural Rights. A Perspective on its Development*, Clarendon Press, Oxford: 1998, pages 287.
[157] Asbjorn Eide, "The Right to an Adequate Standard of Living Including the Right to Food" in Rosas (ed) *Economic, Social and Cultural Rights*, Martinus Nijhoff Publishers, Dordrecht: 1995, pages 89 - 91; Magdalena Sepulveda; Theo van Banning; Gudrun Gudmundsdottir; Christine Chamoun; Willem van Genugten, *Human Rights Reference Handbook*, University for Peace, Ciudad Colon: 2004, page 267.
[158] In fact, the right to health also distinguishes itself by its absence from the 1954 Convention relating to the Status of Stateless Persons. It will be addressed in section 8 of this chapter.

> development, agrarian reform, principles of nutrition, international trade and aid (to name but a few).[159]

The stateless once again show their colours as a vulnerable group and report difficulties in their enjoyment of the right to an adequate standard of living.[160] Inadequate access to housing is a particular problem - as we already saw when looking at the right to property, the stateless are often unable to buy immovable property or land and there have been cases of confiscation of this property.[161] But inadequate food can also be a serious issue and the stateless may find themselves the victims of multiple neglect:

> While the Bangladesh government has hosted stateless Bihari for more than three decades, the already desperate living conditions worsened over the last year [2004]. The delivery of government-subsidised food aid was ended, and there was a substantial loss of homes to tornado, fire and eviction.[162]

This segment of a report from a mission by Refugees International to document the plight of the stateless in Bangladesh is illustrative of how hard it can be for stateless groups across the world to assert their right to dignified human survival.[163]

5.1 The 1954 Convention relating to the Status of Stateless Persons

In the previous section we discovered that the 1954 Convention relating to the Status of Stateless Persons includes a broadly formulated provision attributing *national treatment* to stateless persons in respect of public relief and assistance. This article offers some scope for ensuring that the stateless enjoy an adequate standard of living, but it provides for national treatment and not an absolute right to (benefits that allow for) adequate housing, food and clothing. Moreover, it can only

---

[159] Matthew Craven, *The International Covenant on Economic, Social and Cultural Rights. A Perspective on its Development*, Clarendon Press, Oxford: 1998, pages 288.

[160] It has been pointed out that "asylum seekers, refugees and displaced persons do not have the same opportunity as others to achieve an adequate standard of living on the basis of their own efforts. They therefore require, to a larger extent than the ordinary public, direct provisions, until conditions are established in which they can obtain their own entitlements". Asbjorn Eide, "The Right to an Adequate Standard of Living Including the Right to Food" in Rosas (ed) *Economic, Social and Cultural Rights*, Martinus Nijhoff Publishers, Dordrecht: 1995, page 105. The same assessment can be made of the circumstances in which the stateless live – they too have been shown to experience difficulties in earning their own living.

[161] See chapter X, section 6.

[162] Maureen Lynch, *Lives on hold: The human cost of statelessness,* Washington: 2005, page 13.

[163] Other examples include situations in Syria, where the stateless Kurds cannot access food subsidies; in Côte d'Ivoire, where thousands of non-citizens were evicted from their homes; and in Russia, where the revocation of land from the stateless Meskhetian Turks "brought them to the brink of famine" because they no were no longer able to grow their own food. Maureen Lynch, *Lives on hold: The human cost of statelessness,* Washington: 2005, pages 40-43 and 46; David Weissbrodt, *Final Report on Prevention of Discrimination - The Rights of Non-Citizens,* E/CN.4/Sub.2/2003/23, 26 May 2003, Add.3, para. 24; Advisory Board on Human Security (prepared by Constantin Sokoloff), *Denial of Citizenship: A Challenge to Human Security,* February 2005, page 21.

be relied upon by stateless persons who are lawfully staying on state territory. Here then, we will consider the alternatives offered under the 1954 Statelessness Convention to ensuring that the stateless enjoy an adequate standard of living. There are just two short articles in the 1954 Statelessness Convention that in some way touch upon (aspects of) this issue: article 20 that deals with "rationing" and article 21 on "housing".

In the provision on "rationing", the 1954 Statelessness Convention offers stateless persons *national treatment* in accessing any system "which applies to the population at large and regulates the general distribution of products in short supply".[164] Food is a commodity that has historically been subjected to rationing during periods of scarcity, but rationing may impact upon access to any consumer good,[165] including for example clothing. In this sense it has a bearing on the ability to enjoy an adequate standard of living. The stateless are granted equal treatment as nationals at the lowest level of attachment – as soon as they are subject to the state's jurisdiction, even if this is by way of unlawful presence in the territory. However, all that is offered is equal treatment under an existing rationing system. There is no guarantee of access to adequate food or other goods, nor any obligation to provide these commodities to the stateless free of charge.[166] Regrettably, this provision

> is therefore not a basis for [stateless persons] to assert a right of access to public welfare or comparable systems which allocate basic necessities (or funds to acquire them) on the basis of economic need, rather than because of the scarcity of the products themselves.[167]

It is in relation to this article then, that the 1954 Statelessness Convention is most evidently – and lamentably - a product of its time: post World War II, when rationing was in place in many countries. As we will see, international human rights law has moved ahead greatly in elaborating the right to an adequate standard of living and a plethora of state obligations flowing from it to ensure that basic subsistence needs are met. So although article 20 of the Statelessness Convention initially appears to address access to food and other basic goods, the actual contribution of this outdated provision is now questionable.

As far as its substantive scope is concerned, article 21 of the Statelessness Convention on "housing" appears to be much more promising. It is applicable to any housing matter that is "regulated by laws or regulations or is subject to the

[164] Article 20 of the 1954 Convention relating to the Status of Stateless Persons. Note that this article is identical to its counterpart in the 1951 Refugee Convention, was accepted without debate and has not been the subject of any reservations by state parties.

[165] Nehemiah Robinson, *Convention relating to the status of stateless persons - Its history and interpretation*, UNHCR, Geneva: 1955, page 66; James Hathaway, *The Rights of Refugees Under International Law*, Cambridge University Press, Cambridge: 2005, page 468.

[166] Nehemiah Robinson, *Convention relating to the status of stateless persons - Its history and interpretation*, UNHCR, Geneva: 1955, page 66; James Hathaway, *The Rights of Refugees Under International Law*, Cambridge University Press, Cambridge: 2005, page 467.

[167] James Hathaway, *The Rights of Refugees Under International Law*, Cambridge University Press, Cambridge: 2005, page 470. This statement originally pertained to refugees and the 1951 Refugee Convention but it is applicable to the identically worded text of the article in the 1954 Statelessness Convention.

control of public authorities".[168] Unlike rationing, which has largely gone out of fashion, housing regulation in one form or another is pervasive to this day, so the article is still very relevant. And the broad wording of the provision allows it to be invoked in the context of any housing question regulated by any public authority at any level of government, from "rent control and assignment of apartments" to "any social welfare measures taken by States with a view to providing housing accommodation".[169] However, to draw an entitlement from this article, the stateless person must first meet the high level of attachment required – lawful stay – and will, even then, benefit only from a guarantee to treatment on a par with non-nationals generally. There is no absolute right to housing or any qualitative guarantee as to the nature of housing that must be available or the matters that should be regulated. In effect then, this provision adds little to what is already offered to stateless persons elsewhere in the Convention.

To begin with, we have seen that under article 13, on the right to property, the stateless benefit from all housing-related property rights on equal terms to non-nationals generally (and at a much lower level of attachment), which would arguably include such matters as rent control.[170] Furthermore,

> initiatives which provide housing benefits to sub-populations on the basis of need should be deemed in pith and substance to be forms of relief or assistance subject to the requirements of Art. 23.[171]

This means that in the context of housing assistance, the stateless should enjoy *national* treatment under article 23 on public relief – and at the same level of attachment as is set in the provision specifically geared to housing. So the inclusion of article 21 on housing in the terms in which it is expressed in fact introduces a certain risk as far as the enjoyment by the stateless of an adequate standard of living is concerned. The danger is that states will refer to this article in any housing-related matter and offer the stateless treatment on a par with non-nationals generally rather than acknowledging that under article 23 on public assistance they are obliged to satisfy a higher level of protection. All in all then, the 1954 Statelessness Convention is found to lack any satisfactory expression of the right to an adequate standard of living, or any of its substantive elements, beyond what has already been discussed in section 4 in the context of the right to social security.[172]

---

[168] Article 21 of the 1954 Convention relating to the Status of Refugees. Identically to article 20 on rationing, this provision on housing was adopted in the same terms as it is included in the 1951 Refugee Convention, it was passed without discussion and has attracted no reservations from state parties.

[169] Nehemiah Robinson, *Convention relating to the status of stateless persons - Its history and interpretation*, UNHCR, Geneva: 1955, page 67; James Hathaway, *The Rights of Refugees Under International Law*, Cambridge University Press, Cambridge: 2005, pages 823-824.

[170] See chapter X, section 6.1.

[171] James Hathaway, *The Rights of Refugees Under International Law*, Cambridge University Press, Cambridge: 2005, page 824.

[172] Here again, the absence of an equivalent to article 33 of the 1951 Refugee Convention in the statelessness instrument is clearly felt: "In some cases, depriving refugees of the necessities of life may give rise to a breach of the duty of *non-refoulement*. Repatriation under coercion, including situations in which refugees are left no real option but to leave, is in breach of Art. 33 of the Refugee Convention". James Hathaway, *The Rights of Refugees Under International Law*, Cambridge University Press,

5.2 International human rights law

In contrast to the 1954 Statelessness Convention, the International Covenant on Economic, Social and Cultural Rights and indeed its Committee, have had much more to say on the right to an adequate standard of living – as a right independent from the right to social security. Thus article 11 of the Covenant opens with the following declaration:

> The States Parties to the present Covenant recognise the right of everyone to an adequate standard of living for himself and his family, including adequate food, clothing and housing, and to the continuous improvement of living conditions.[173]

Here explicit mention is made of the rights to adequate food, clothing and housing that are inherent in the concept of the right to an adequate standard of living, although the overall obligation is, again, one of progressive realisation. The ESC Committee has gone on to elaborate on the content of both the right to food and to housing, as well as the right to water which is also considered to stem from this provision.[174] These documents are instrumental in determining the scope of state obligations generally and with regards to non-nationals and the stateless specifically.

As far as the right to adequate food is concerned, we find that the second paragraph of this article in the ICESCR already provides some clues as to the core minimum content of the norm: state parties also recognise "the fundamental right of everyone to be free from hunger".[175] In view of this, "States have a core obligation

---

Cambridge: 2005, page 464. No such ultimate fall-back clause can be found in the 1954 Statelessness Convention.

[173] Article 11, paragraph 1 of the International Covenant on Economic, Social and Cultural Rights. Note that as a *social* right, the right to an adequate standard of living is not subject to the terms of article 2, paragraph 3 of the ICESCR. Other sources of (elements of) the right to an adequate standard of living are article 25 of the Universal Declaration of Human Rights; Article 5, paragraph e(iii) of the Convention on the Elimination of All Racial Discrimination; Articles 24 and 27 of the Convention on the Rights of the Child; Articles 43 and 70 of the Migrant Workers Convention; Article 12 of the Additional Protocol to the American Convention on Human Rights in the Area of Economic, Social and Cultural Rights (right to food); Articles 30 and 31 of the European Social Charter; and Article 20, paragraph 2 of the African Charter on the Rights and Welfare of the Child. Note that neither the overall right to an adequate standard of living, nor any of its constituent parts, is elaborated in the UN Declaration on the Rights of Non-nationals.

[174] ESC Committee, *General Comment 4: The right to adequate housing*, 13 December 1991; ESC Committee, *General Comment 7: The right to adequate housing – forced evictions*, 20 May 1997; ESC Committee, *General Comment 12: The right to adequate food*, 12 May 1999; and ESC Committee, *General Comment 15: The right to water*, 20 January 2003. The right to adequate clothing, as an aspect of the right to an adequate standard of living, has had "little attention either from the Committee or independent commentators [and] the impression given is that clothing is not a matter in which the State may exercise a great deal of control, nor one that the Committee feels is of great importance". Matthew Craven, *The International Covenant on Economic, Social and Cultural Rights. A Perspective on its Development*, Clarendon Press, Oxford: 1998, page 349.

[175] Article 11, paragraph 2 of the International Covenant on Economic, Social and Cultural Rights.

to take the necessary action to mitigate and alleviate hunger [...] even in times of natural or other disasters".[176] There is a concrete and immediate obligation for states to prevent starvation, strengthened by the connection with the right to life espoused elsewhere in human rights instruments.[177] But the core minimum content of the right to food stretches further, encompassing obligations linked to the requirement that the food be *adequate*. This adds another dimension by prescribing

> the availability of food in a quantity and quality sufficient to satisfy the dietary needs of individuals, free from adverse substances, and acceptable within a given culture.[178]

Such food must be available and accessible to everyone, including non-nationals and stateless persons.[179] Moreover, "inextricably related" to the right to food is the right to water and this is also protected under article 11 of the ICESCR.[180] The ESC Committee has detailed the core obligations that are encapsulated within this norm as well, which include the obligation

> to ensure access to the minimum essential amount of water, that is sufficient and safe for personal and domestic uses to prevent disease; to ensure the right of access to water and water facilities and services on a non-discriminatory basis, especially for disadvantaged and marginalized groups [and] to adopt relatively low-cost targeted water programmes to protect vulnerable and marginalized groups.[181]

These core minimum standards are to be enjoyed by "*everyone* without discrimination, within the jurisdiction of the State party"[182] and the Committee acknowledges that special measures may be needed to ensure the full enjoyment of

---

[176] ESC Committee, *General Comment 12: The right to adequate food*, 12 May 1999, para. 6. In paragraph 14 of the General Comment the Committee confirms the applicability of this minimum core content to everyone, regardless of nationality: "Every State is obliged to ensure for everyone under its jurisdiction access to the minimum essential food which is sufficient, nutritionally adequate and safe, to ensure their freedom from hunger".

[177] Matthew Craven, *The International Covenant on Economic, Social and Cultural Rights. A Perspective on its Development*, Clarendon Press, Oxford: 1998, page 307.

[178] ESC Committee, *General Comment 12: The right to adequate food*, 12 May 1999, para. 8. The meaning of each of the components of this phrase is then elaborated upon in some detail by the Committee. See also Asbjorn Eide, "The Right to an Adequate Standard of Living Including the Right to Food" in Rosas (ed) *Economic, Social and Cultural Rights*, Martinus Nijhoff Publishers, Dordrecht: 1995, page 90; Magdalena Sepulveda; Theo van Banning; Gudrun Gudmundsdottir; Christine Chamoun; Willem van Genugten, *Human Rights Reference Handbook*, University for Peace, Ciudad Colon: 2004, pages 270-271.

[179] Note that the accessibility of food refers to both "economic accessibility" and "physical accessibility" and that vulnerable groups may require assistance in either or both areas through special programmes. ESC Committee, *General Comment 12: The right to adequate food*, 12 May 1999, para. 13.

[180] ESC Committee, *General Comment 15: The right to water*, 20 January 2003, para. 3.

[181] The Committee lists six further core obligations relating to the right to water. ESC Committee, *General Comment 15: The right to water*, 20 January 2003, para. 37.

[182] ESC Committee, *General Comment 15: The right to water*, 20 January 2003, para. 12(c).

these standards by various vulnerable groups, including minority groups, refugees, asylum seekers and migrant workers.[183] By extension then, the stateless are also to benefit fully from this norm. The right to an adequate standard of living as espoused under the ICESCR and elsewhere therefore offers the stateless a detailed and sturdy basis for the protection of two basic subsistence needs: adequate food and water.[184]

The right to adequate housing also contains certain elements that are deemed to be *core obligations*, but these are less clearly enunciated than the minimum core standards relating to the right to adequate food and water.[185] The two General Comments elaborated by the ESC Committee to "identify the principle issues" fail to fully elucidate the question of core obligations.[186] The Committee does explain that it is more than pure "shelter" that is envisioned by the right to adequate housing, it is "the right to live somewhere in security, peace and dignity".[187] Thereafter, numerous instructions are provided as to how to determine the *adequacy* of accommodation for the purposes of the (eventual) full realisation of this norm.[188] This has been described as the core content of the right to adequate housing,[189] however it is not presented as such in the General Comment. Instead, this core content is more likely to be formed by what the Committee describes as "steps which must be taken immediately" by states which include "a commitment to facilitating 'self-help' by affected groups" and "the abstention by the Government from certain practices [... in particular...] forced eviction".[190] At least with respect

[183] ESC Committee, *General Comment 15: The right to water*, 20 January 2003, para. 16.

[184] Note that the specific issue of the enjoyment by non-nationals of the right to adequate food and/or water has yet to raise significant attention in the consideration of state reports by the UN treaty bodies, although concern has been expressed at the level of enjoyment of these rights by groups such as the Roma (which may include stateless persons), internally displaced persons and refugees. See for example Committee on the Elimination of Racial Discrimination, *Concluding Observations: Albania,* A/ 58/18, New York: 2003, para. 315; Human Rights Committee, *Concluding Observations: Slovakia,* A/59/18, Geneva: 2004, para. 388; Committee on the Rights of the Child, *Concluding Observations: Greece,* CRC/C/114, Geneva: 2002, para. 156; ESC Committee, *Concluding Observations: Serbia and Montenegro,* E/2006/22, New York and Geneva: 2005, para. 290 and *Azerbaijan,* E/2005/22, New York and Geneva: 2004, para. 517.

[185] James Hathaway, *The Rights of Refugees Under International Law*, Cambridge University Press, Cambridge: 2005, page 504.

[186] ESC Committee, *General Comment 4: The right to adequate housing*, 13 December 1991; ESC Committee, *General Comment 7: The right to adequate housing – forced evictions*, 20 May 1997. See also John Dent, *Research Paper on the Social and Economic Rights of Non-Nationals in Europe,* Brussels: 1998, page 108.

[187] ESC Committee, *General Comment 4: The right to adequate housing*, 13 December 1991, para. 6.

[188] This includes considerations such as the availability of services, materials, facilities and infrastructure as well as the affordability of the housing. See ESC Committee, *General Comment 4: The right to adequate housing*, 13 December 1991, para. 8.

[189] Magdalena Sepulveda; Theo van Banning; Gudrun Gudmundsdottir; Christine Chamoun; Willem van Genugten, *Human Rights Reference Handbook*, University for Peace, Ciudad Colon: 2004, page 272.

[190] ESC Committee, *General Comment 4: The right to adequate housing*, 13 December 1991, paras. 10 and 18. For a full discussion of the scope of the prohibition of forced eviction, see ESC Committee, *General Comment 7: The right to adequate housing – forced evictions*, 20 May 1997.

to these dimensions of the right to adequate housing, there is no question that the stateless are to benefit from the relevant human rights norms.[191] In addition,

> a State in which any significant number of individuals is deprived of [...] basic shelter and housing is, *prima facie*, failing to discharge its obligations under the Covenant.[192]

This must be deemed the case whether the individuals concerned possess the nationality of the state or not. Beyond these core commitments, it remains somewhat ambiguous what scope of protection is offered to non-nationals, including stateless persons. Nevertheless, the UN treaty bodies have taken a broader interest in the housing situation of non-nationals, beyond this narrowly construed core content, discussing instead their overall enjoyment of the right to adequate housing.[193]

Moreover, the Committee on the Elimination of Racial Discrimination has called upon states to "guarantee *equal enjoyment* of the right to adequate housing for citizens and non-citizens".[194] It appears then that there is a strong onus on states to offer non-nationals and stateless persons the same treatment with respect to all aspects of the right to adequate housing, including those geared towards progressive realisation, as is offered to citizens. In fact, with respect to the right to an adequate standard of living generally, the human rights regime shows a substantial commitment to non-citizens, which offers far greater scope for the protection of the stateless than under the narrow and outdated terms of the 1954 Statelessness Convention.

---

191 Consider the concern expressed at the (circumstances of the) eviction of non-citizens in Slovenia. See Committee on the Elimination of Racial Discrimination, *Concluding Observations: Slovenia,* A/58/18, New York: 2003, para. 241;

192 ESC Committee, *General Comment 3: The nature of State parties obligations (Art. 1, par. 1)*, 1990, para. 10; See also Scott Leckie, "The Right to Housing" in Rosas (ed) *Economic, Social and Cultural Rights*, Martinus Nijhoff Publishers, Dordrecht: 1995, page 112.

193 See for example Committee on the Elimination of Racial Discrimination, *Concluding Observations: France,* A/60/18, New York: 2005, para. 106; *Luxembourg,* A60/18, New York: 2005, para. 198. ESC Committee, *Concluding Observations: Azerbaijan,* E/2005/22, New York and Geneva: 2004, paras 517 and 519; Committee on the Rights of the Child, *Concluding Observations: Estonia,* CRC/C124 (2003) 9, para. 45. See also Matthew Craven, *The International Covenant on Economic, Social and Cultural Rights. A Perspective on its Development*, Clarendon Press, Oxford: 1998, page 338; David Weissbrodt, *Final Report on Prevention of Discrimination - The Rights of Non-Citizens,* E/CN.4/Sub.2/2003/23, 26 May 2003, para. 67.

194 Emphasis added. Committee on the Elimination of Racial Discrimination, *General Recommendation 30: Discrimination against Non-Citizens*, New York: 1 October 2004, para. 32. See also the decision of the Committee in CERD, *Case of F.A. v. Norway,* CERD/C/58/D/18/2000, 21 March 2001. Note in addition that the Migrant Workers Convention provides for *national* treatment in relation to "access to housing, including social housing schemes, and protection against exploitation in respect of rents". Later, the same instrument compels states to offer migrant workers the same assistance as nationals in promoting "living conditions [...] in keeping with the standards of fitness, safety, health and principles of human dignity". However it must be recalled that these provisions benefit migrant workers with a *regular* status only. See article 43, paragraph 1(d) and article 70 of the Migrant Workers Convention.

6 RIGHT TO EDUCATION

By now we are familiar with the interconnectedness of human rights and the role that one right may play in ensuring the enjoyment of another. So it comes as no surprise that the right to education is another norm that is considered absolutely pivotal in the overall system of human rights – it is said to "epitomise the indivisibility and interdependence of all human rights".[195] This is because education offers human beings the basic knowledge and understanding needed for the full enjoyment of rights such as the freedom of opinion or the right to work, while at the same time promoting "increased awareness of human rights and mutual tolerance".[196] As we will see in more detail in a moment, because of the many roles that education plays, this is a complex and multidimensional right. It deals with a variety of issues from access to basic schooling to the freedom of choice in cultural or religious education.

In conjunction, there are a multitude of ways in which the stateless can – and do - experience difficulties in the field of education.[197] The number of cases in which access to education is reportedly obstructed, restricted or simply denied to stateless populations is genuinely worrying and the geographical spread of the problem spans the globe.[198] Since education has also been described as a "vehicle for empowerment",[199]

> if governments wish to prevent certain groups from equally participating in the political, social, economic or cultural life in their countries, one of the most efficient methods is to deny them equal access to education.[200]

The problems that the stateless encounter in enjoying an education thus contribute to their progressive and enduring disempowerment and marginalisation, in turn

---

195 ESC Committee, *General Comment 11: Plans of action for primary education,* 10 May 1999, para. 2.

196 Manfred Nowak, "The Right to Education" in Rosas (ed) *Economic, Social and Cultural Rights*, Martinus Nijhoff Publishers, Dordrecht: 1995, pages 188-189. On the importance of education as a human right, see also Advisory Board on Human Security (prepared by Constantin Sokoloff), *Denial of Citizenship: A Challenge to Human Security,* February 2005, page 22.

197 Access to education is a generally-reported issue for the stateless. See for example UNHCR, "Statelessness and Citizenship" in *The State of the World's Refugees - A Humanitarian Agenda*, Oxford University Press, Oxford: 1997, page 241; Maureen Lynch, *Lives on hold: The human cost of statelessness,* Washington: 2005, pages 3 and 21; UNHCR and IPU, *Nationality and statelessness. A handbook for parliamentarians*, 2005, page 6; Youth Advocate Program International, *Stateless Children - Youth Who are Without Citizenship,* Washington: 2003, pages 6-7.

198 Access to (some forms of) education is reported to be a problem for stateless populations in Bangladesh, Syria, Myanmar, the Dominican Republic, Ukraine, the United Arab Emirates, Russia, Turkmenistan and many other places, including in particular for Roma populations across Europe. See Maureen Lynch, *Lives on hold: The human cost of statelessness,* Washington: 2005, pages 27 – 46.

199 It is explained that "education can give marginalized adults and children a means to escape from poverty and participate meaningfully in society". Magdalena Sepulveda; Theo van Banning; Gudrun Gudmundsdottir; Christine Chamoun; Willem van Genugten, *Human Rights Reference Handbook*, University for Peace, Ciudad Colon: 2004, page 291.

200 Manfred Nowak, "The Right to Education" in Rosas (ed) *Economic, Social and Cultural Rights*, Martinus Nijhoff Publishers, Dordrecht: 1995, page 202.

presenting a growing obstacle to the resolution of their plight.[201] Enough cause then, to delve into the international legal protection of the right of the stateless to education.

6.1 The 1954 Convention relating to the Status of Stateless Persons

Sandwiched between the right to housing and the right to public relief in the 1954 Statelessness Convention is an article that deals exclusively with the right to education. The provision is composed of two distinct parts, the first addressing "elementary education" while the second is applicable to all other levels or forms of education.[202] Thus, paragraph 1 of article 22 states:

> The Contracting States shall accord to stateless persons the same treatment as is accorded to nationals with respect to elementary education.[203]

This is one of the strongest provisions in the 1954 Statelessness Convention, offering stateless persons *national treatment* without first requiring a stringent level of attachment to be met. As far as elementary education is concerned, the stateless must be treated on a par with nationals, whatever their status in the country concerned. The second paragraph of article 2 is also applicable to all stateless persons as soon as they are subject to a state's jurisdiction. However, it provides for treatment at least as favourable as non-nationals generally, in the same circumstances. So wherever non-elementary education is concerned, in particular "access to studies, the recognition of foreign school certificates, diplomas and degrees, the remission of fees and charges and the award of scholarships",[204] the stateless can only claim treatment on a par with similarly situated non-citizens and this may be greatly influenced by their immigration status in the country concerned.

Although this article on the right to education is largely straightforward, a few comments should be made as to the exact scope of protection offered. Firstly, in view of the title that was given to the provision as a whole – "public education" – its terms are only considered to be applicable to education that is provided by public authorities or funded or subsidised by public funds.[205] Private schooling is entirely beyond the scope of the obligations contained in both paragraphs and so the stateless cannot discern any entitlement to access private education from the 1954 Statelessness Convention. This limitation may have an impact on the enjoyment by the stateless of the freedom of choice in education (including the freedom to found

[201] Advisory Board on Human Security (prepared by Constantin Sokoloff), *Denial of Citizenship: A Challenge to Human Security*, February 2005, page 22.

[202] Note that the wording of the entire article is identical to that found in the 1951 Refugee Convention and that this provision was adopted by a convincing vote after only minimal discussion. Nehemiah Robinson, *Convention relating to the status of stateless persons - Its history and interpretation*, UNHCR, Geneva: 1955, page 68.

[203] Just one reservation has been lodged with respect of article 22: by Zambia, to the effect that this first paragraph will be treated as a recommendation only.

[204] Article 22, paragraph 2 of the 1954 Convention relating to the Status of Stateless Persons.

[205] Nehemiah Robinson, *Convention relating to the status of stateless persons - Its history and interpretation*, UNHCR, Geneva: 1955, pages 68 – 69.

educational institutes), another major component of the right to education as we will see when we turn to human rights law.[206] A second clarification of scope centres on the expression "elementary education". No definition is given in the instrument itself, leaving it open to debate whether the term addresses only "primary education" or covers all "fundamental education". The former is a term used to differentiate a certain level of schooling from secondary or higher education, while the latter is a more open notion that takes in "basic education in all its forms (including, for example, adult education}".[207] In the event, by neglecting to clarify this point, the 1954 Statelessness Convention leaves it to states to establish what "elementary education" is under domestic law and accordingly to determine the level of protection that must be attributed to the stateless.[208] The statelessness instrument therefore grants states substantial discretion to determine first to what extent non-primary education is to be considered *elementary* for the purposes of the Convention and thereafter to restrict access to non-elementary education, so long as non-nationals are generally subjected to such a policy. Finally, it is important to note that in prescribing a contingent standard of treatment with regard to both elementary and other forms of education, the 1954 Statelessness Convention remains silent on vital questions as to the actual availability of schooling generally and the type and quality of education that must be offered. As we come to consider human rights law, we find that these are details that do come to the fore in the relevant instruments.

6.2 International human rights law

In order to "eliminate practices of depriving any person or group access to education",[209] some fifty years ago the international community adopted an independent legal instrument dedicated to outlawing discrimination in education: the UNESCO Convention against Discrimination in Education. This instrument - settled even before the ICESCR was elaborated - demands that resident non-citizens be provided equal access to education as a state's own nationals.[210] This first step towards ensuring that all individuals enjoy the right to an education, regardless of nationality, provided the basis for an ever-growing catalogue of affirmations to this effect in international legal instruments and the work of the UN treaty bodies.[211]

---

[206] Note that article 4 of the 1954 Convention relating to the Status of Stateless Persons was found to offer freedom of choice in *religious* education as a component of the overall prescription of the freedom of religion. See chapter X, section 5.1.

[207] James Hathaway, *The Rights of Refugees Under International Law*, Cambridge University Press, Cambridge: 2005, pages 596-597.

[208] Nehemiah Robinson, *Convention relating to the status of stateless persons - Its history and interpretation*, UNHCR, Geneva: 1955, page 68.

[209] Manfred Nowak, "The Right to Education" in Rosas (ed) *Economic, Social and Cultural Rights*, Martinus Nijhoff Publishers, Dordrecht: 1995, page 202.

[210] Article 3, paragraph e of the UNESCO Convention against Discrimination in Education, 14 December 1960. At the time of writing, the Convention counted 94 state parties, all of which have accepted the instrument's obligations in full (reservations are not permitted according to article 9 of the Convention).

[211] One or more aspects of the right to education can be found in Article 26 of the Universal Declaration of Human Rights; Articles 13 and 14 of the International Covenant on Civil and Political Rights; article

Thus where the ICESCR attributes the right to education to "all persons" in its voluminous article 13, the full spectrum of rights elaborated – from the right to enjoy an education as such, to the need for such education to be directed towards certain aims such as the "full development of the human personality" and the importance of free choice in education - is to be enjoyed by everyone, citizens and non-citizens alike.[212]

The ESC Committee has confirmed this interpretation on numerous occasions, both through its General Comments and its response to state party reports. For example, a core obligation is the prohibition of discrimination in all aspects of education and this applies to "all persons of school age residing in the territory of a State party, including non-nationals, and irrespective of their legal status".[213] The position that lack of citizenship should not in any way effect a persons' enjoyment of the right to education has led the Committee to express concern at instances of impeded or unequal access to education for non-citizens across the globe, from Sri Lanka to Switzerland and from Italy to Canada.[214] Not only must there be equal enjoyment of (free and compulsory) primary education – another core obligation of the right to education[215] – but access to secondary and higher education must also be assured.[216] Thus,

---

5, paragraph e(v) of the Convention on the Elimination of Racial Discrimination; Articles 28 and 29 of the Convention on the Rights of the Child; Articles 30, 43 and 45 of the Migrant Workers Convention; Article 2 of the first Protocol to the European Convention on Human Rights and Article 17 of the European Social Charter; Articles 13 and 16 of the Additional Protocol to the American Convention on Human Rights in the Area of Economic, Social and Cultural Rights; Article 17 of the African Charter on Human and Peoples' Rights and many other instruments.

[212] Diana Elles, *International Provisions Protecting the Human Rights of Non-Citizens: Study*, New York: 1980, page 34; David Weissbrodt, *Final Report on Prevention of Discrimination - The Rights of Non-Citizens*, E/CN.4/Sub.2/2003/23, 26 May 2003, para. 66. For a breakdown of the elements of the right to education, use can be made of the "right to education matrix" devised by Coomans, see Magdalena Sepulveda; Theo van Banning; Gudrun Gudmundsdottir; Christine Chamoun; Willem van Genugten, *Human Rights Reference Handbook*, University for Peace, Ciudad Colon: 2004, pages 293-294.

[213] ESC Committee, *General Comment 13: The right to education,* 8 December 1999, para. 34.

[214] See, among others, ESC Committee, *Concluding Observations: Sri Lanka,* E/1999/22, New York and Geneva: 1998, para. 72; *Switzerland,* E/1999/22, New York and Geneva: 1998, para. 371; *Italy,* E/2005/22, New York and Geneva: 2004, para. 435; *Canada,* E/1999/22 , New York and Geneva: 1998, paras. 414 and 424.

[215] See article 13, paragraph 2(a) of the ICESCR and ESC Committee, *General Comment 13: The right to education,* 8 December 1999, para. 57. Moreover, under article 14 of the ICESCR, where compulsory and free primary education has yet to be fully achieved, for example due to inadequate funds, state parties are "unequivocally" required to adopt a plan of action to ensure the swift realisation of this core obligation. See also ESC Committee, *General Comment 11: Plans of action for primary education,* 10 May 1999, para. 2. The ESC Committee has since for example expressed concern that Azerbaijan "does not provide free compulsory education to non-Azerbaijani children". See also ESC Committee, *Concluding Observations: Azerbaijan,* E/2005/22, New York and Geneva: 2004, para. 498; *China,* E/2006/22, New York and Geneva: 2005, para. 195.

[216] Consider the call for the Canadian government to "develop and expand adequate programmes to address the financial obstacles to post-secondary education for low-income students, without any discrimination on the basis of citizenship status". ESC Committee, *Concluding Observations: Canada,* E/1999/22, New York and Geneva: 1998, para. 424. And for the Swiss government to promote "equal

> while poorer states may rely on the Economic Covenant's general duty of progressive implementation to justify an overall insufficiency of secondary education opportunities or the failure to progressively make such education free of charge, there must be no discrimination against non-citizens in granting access to [...] education.[217]

Again, the Committee holds that the immigration status of non-citizens is irrelevant for the enjoyment of this right.[218] The protection offered of the right to education under the ICESCR thereby surpasses that which is guaranteed under the 1954 Statelessness Convention.

Under the Convention on the Rights of the Child, where the right to education is housed in articles 28 and 29, the same stance has been taken on the right of non-nationals to education. As we have seen earlier, the Committee on the Rights of the Child has made it clear that the Convention elaborates entitlements to be enjoyed by *all* children, regardless of citizenship or statelessness.[219] In responding to state party reports, the Committee on the Rights of the Child has been even more active than the ESC Committee in asserting the need for non-citizens to be granted equal protection of the right to education. Over the last decade, the Committee has expressed praise for states for the adoption of measures to promote the fuller enjoyment of education by non-nationals and concern over impeded access to (satisfactory) education on over a dozen occasions.[220] In one instance, the Committee even explicitly referred to the irrelevance of statelessness for the enjoyment of an education, where it recommended that Iran

---

access to higher education for [...] immigrants". ESC Committee, *Concluding Observations: Switzerland,* E/1999/22, New York and Geneva: 1998, para. 371.

[217] James Hathaway, *The Rights of Refugees Under International Law*, Cambridge University Press, Cambridge: 2005, pages 611-612. Elsewhere, Hathaway admits that there may be scope for arguing that (some aspects of) the right to an education falls into the category of "economic rights", allowing developing states to rely on article 2(3) of the ICESCR to restrict the enjoyment of this right by non-nationals. Indeed the ESC Committee has declared that the right to education "has been variously classified as an economic right, a social right and a cultural right". However, in view of the approach taken by the ESC Committee in its assessment of state practice, an appeal to this exception clause is nevertheless unlikely to hold water in relation to the right to education. See James Hathaway, *The Rights of Refugees Under International Law*, Cambridge University Press, Cambridge: 2005, page 601; ESC Committee, *General Comment 11: Plans of action for primary education,* 10 May 1999, para. 2.

[218] China is called upon to "amend its legislation to provide for the right to education of all school-age children in its jurisdiction, including children of migrants without the leave to remain". ESC Committee, *Concluding Observations: China,* E/2006/22, New York and Geneva: 2005, paras. 218 and 230.

[219] Committee on the Rights of the Child, *General Comment No. 6: Treatment of unaccompanied and separated children outside their country of origin,* 1 September 2005, para. 12. See also section 1 of this chapter.

[220] See for example Committee on the Rights of the Child, *Concluding Observations: Panama,* CRC/C/62, Geneva: 1997, para. 115; *Belize,* CRC/C/84, Geneva: 1999, para. 75; *Djibouti,* CRC/C/97, Geneva: 2000, para. 556; *Spain,* CRC/C/118, Geneva: 2002, para. 509; *Iceland,* CRC/C/124, Geneva: 2003, para. 496; *Krgyzstan* CRC/C/143, Geneva: 2004, para. 294.

> ensure that all children, including refugee children, have equal opportunities on all levels of the education system without discrimination based on gender, religion, ethnic origin, nationality or statelessness.[221]

On the basis of recommendations made to numerous other state parties, it is clear that this Committee also considers restrictions imposed on the grounds of immigration status to be contrary to state obligations.[222] Moreover, the obligation to ensure that non-nationals fully enjoy the right to education may require the states concerned to take particular account of their situation in providing educational opportunities, for example by ensuring that the "system of education [is] adequate to their cultural values and identity"[223] or that non-nationals are "not disadvantaged by the educational programme and teaching methods [including through] language problems".[224] Under international human rights law, it is therefore not enough that states provide for equal access to educational facilities, they must also take steps to ensure that non-nationals enjoy "equal access to the *same standard of services* [as nationals] in the field of education".[225] Furthermore, all of the foregoing is confirmed by the work of the Committee on the Elimination of Racial Discrimination.[226]

While we have already ascertained that ESC rights are generally expounded to the benefit of everyone, it is clear that with respect to the right to education, every effort has been taken to ensure that this right really is universally and equally enjoyed. Here, the irrelevance of citizenship status has been clearly and frequently pronounced. And, not only should the lack of a(ny) nationality have no impact on the enjoyment of education, but the right to education as such is also defined in detail. Under human rights law, stateless persons should be able to enjoy not just

[221] Committee on the Rights of the Child, *Concluding Observations: Iran,* CRC/C/146, Geneva: 2005, para. 496.

[222] Committee on the Rights of the Child, *Concluding Observations: Russian Federation,* CRC/C/90, Geneva: 1999, para. 113; *Argentina,* CRC/C/121, Geneva: 2001, para. 81; *Ukraine,* CRC/C/121, Geneva: 2002, para. 355; *The Netherlands (Netherlands and Aruba),* CRC/C/137, Geneva: 2004, para. 367; *Krgyzstan* CRC/C/143, Geneva: 2004, para. 294

[223] Committee on the Rights of the Child, *Concluding Observations: Panama,* CRC/C/62, Geneva: 1997, para. 115.

[224] Committee on the Rights of the Child, *Concluding Observations: Luxembourg,* CRC/C/146, Geneva: 2005, para. 206.

[225] Emphasis added. Committee on the Rights of the Child, *Concluding Observations: Luxembourg,* CRC/C/146, Geneva: 2005, para. 207.

[226] Committee on the Elimination of Racial Discrimination, *General Recommendation 30: Discrimination against Non-Citizens,* New York: 1 October 2004, para. 30. See also CERD, *Concluding Observations: Sweden,* A/52/18, New York: 1997, para. 500; *Finland,* A/54/18, New York: 1999, para. 71; *Canada,* A/57/18, New York: 2002, para. 337; *Republic of Korea,* A/58/18, New York: 2003, para. 489; *Argentina,* A/59/18, New York: 2004, para. 235. As to the equal entitlement to the right to education regardless of residence status, note also that article 30 of the Migrant Workers Convention guarantees access to education to the children of regular and irregular migrant workers alike. It is unfortunate that the UNESCO Convention Against Discrimination in Education only guarantees *resident* foreigners equality of treatment with nationals in respect of access to education and that the UN Declaration on Non-nationals offers an even more limited provision concerning the right to education (article 8, paragraph 1(c)). However, these instruments predate the developments mentioned above that firmly illustrate which path has since been carved out by modern human rights law.

"access to public educational institutions and programmes" at all levels,[227] but the education offered must meet certain standards – be directed towards certain goals[228] – and the stateless are to enjoy freedom of choice in education, including the freedom to establish educational institutions.[229] Human rights law therefore duplicates and moves unmistakably beyond the guarantees made to stateless persons under the 1954 Statelessness Convention.

7 THE RIGHT TO INTELLECTUAL PROPERTY

The term "intellectual property" refers to all of the "legal rights which result from intellectual activity in the industrial, scientific, literary and artistic fields".[230] One of the main purposes of intellectual property rights is to protect the moral and material interests of inventors and authors.[231] From a human rights perspective, the right to intellectual property forms one element of a cluster of rights broadly referred to as the right to participate in or enjoy cultural life or simply "cultural rights". The proclamation of these rights is grounded on the understanding that culture forms an indispensable attribute of human identity:

> The basic source of identity for human beings is often found in cultural traditions into which he or she is born and brought up. The preservation of that identity can be of crucial importance to well-being and self-respect.[232]

For the stateless, a cultural identity distinct from that of the majority of the state population is often a contributing factor to their plight – in many cases "citizenship inequalities and citizenship denial are historically and *culturally* produced"[233] – and

---

[227] At primary and secondary level education should be made "generally available and accessible to all". Article 13, paragraph 2 (a) and (b) of the ICESCR and article 28, paragraph 1(a) and (b) of the Convention on the Rights of the Child. Meanwhile, higher education "shall be made equally accessible to all, on the basis of capacity", allowing states to deny access to those who do not possess the required expertise. Article 13, paragraph 2(c) of the ICESCR and article 28, paragraph 1(c) of the Convention on the Rights of the Child. States must also "take measures to encourage regular attendance at schools and the reduction of drop-out rates". Article 28, paragraph 1 (e) of the Convention on the Rights of the Child.

[228] See article 13, paragraph 1 of the ICESCR and article 29, paragraph 1 of the Convention on the Rights of the Child.

[229] See article 13, paragraphs 3 and 4 of the ICESCR and article 29, paragraph 2 of the Convention on the Rights of the Child.

[230] World Intellectual Property Organisation, *WIPO Intellectual Property Handbook: Policy, Laws and Use,* WIPO Publication No. 489(E), Geneva 2004, page 3.

[231] Another broad goal of intellectual property law has been to "promote, as a deliberate act of Government policy, creativity and the dissemination and application of its results and to encourage fair trading which would contribute to economic and social development". World Intellectual Property Organisation, *WIPO Intellectual Property Handbook: Policy, Laws and Use,* WIPO Publication No. 489(E), Geneva 2004, page 3.

[232] Asbjorn Eide, "Cultural Rights as Individual Human Rights" in Rosas (ed) *Economic, Social and Cultural Rights*, Martinus Nijhoff Publishers, Dordrecht: 1995, page 231.

[233] Emphasis added. Advisory Board on Human Security (prepared by Constantin Sokoloff), *Denial of Citizenship: A Challenge to Human Security,* February 2005, page. 35.

difficulties enjoying that distinct cultural life are not uncommon.[234] However, cultural rights have a long and complicated history that has been marred by controversy and today this area remains the subject of much disagreement and the norms involved are poorly defined.[235] Instead the importance of cultural considerations has strongly infiltrated the overall human rights regime through the protection of other rights, such as the right to education, the freedom of expression and minority rights, which have already been dealt with.[236] With this in mind, a very brief investigation will suffice. Meanwhile, intellectual property rights have tended to be the subject of international agreements outside the human rights field[237] – rescuing them in a sense from the overall cultural rights impasse – and this will also be touched upon in the following assessment of the state of play of international law.

7.1 The 1954 Convention relating to the Status of Stateless Persons

In this section we come to consider the last ESC right housed in the 1954 Statelessness Convention, indeed the last substantive provision that can be classed as an expression of either a civil and political right or an economic, social and cultural right. Article 14 is entitled "artistic rights and industrial property"[238] and provides for the right to intellectual property in the following terms:

> In respect of the protection of industrial property, such as inventions, designs or models, trade marks, trade names, and of rights in literary, artistic and scientific works, a stateless person shall be accorded in the country in which he has his habitual residence the same protection as is accorded to nationals of that country.[239]

The purpose of this article is to provide protection of "the totality of creations of the human mind".[240] As the type of protection remains unspecified, we can assume that *all* aspects of protection are covered, whether they relate to economic or moral

[234] As a minority group in many countries, the stateless experience severe difficulties in expressing and retaining their culture. For example, the Syrian government is reported to enforce a prohibition of Kurdish cultural celebrations. Maureen Lynch, *Lives on hold: The human cost of statelessness,* Washington: 2005, page 46.

[235] Magdalena Sepulveda; Theo van Banning; Gudrun Gudmundsdottir; Christine Chamoun; Willem van Genugten, *Human Rights Reference Handbook*, University for Peace, Ciudad Colon: 2004, page 296.

[236] See chapter X, section 7 and section 6 of the present chapter.

[237] From the late 19th century onwards, intellectual property rights have been the subject of multilateral conventions. The system is now coordinated through the World Intellectual Property Organisation (WIPO) – one of the UN's specialised agencies.

[238] Industrial property and artistic rights (also known as copyright) are the two main fields of intellectual property. World Intellectual Property Organisation, *WIPO Intellectual Property Handbook: Policy, Laws and Use,* WIPO Publication No. 489(E), Geneva 2004, page 3.

[239] Note that this article was adopted in identical wording to the equivalent provision in the 1951 Refugee Convention. No reservations have been lodged in respect of this provision by state parties to the 1954 Statelessness Convention.

[240] Nehemiah Robinson, *Convention relating to the status of stateless persons - Its history and interpretation*, UNHCR, Geneva: 1955, page 55.

interests in the intellectual property. Moreover, for the purposes of such protection of intellectual property, it is unimportant what mechanism the state has introduced, be it copyrighting, patenting or another system.[241] What is, however, relevant is that in order to benefit from this provision, a stateless person must have acquired *habitual residence* in the state in question. As we have previously noted, there is every potential for this phrase to be interpreted as a highly demanding level of attachment, requiring not only "residence of a sufficiently long duration to consider him as locally connected with the country",[242] but also lawfulness of stay.[243]

Once a stateless person has established his status as a habitual resident, he will, nevertheless, be able to enjoy *national treatment*. In addition, thanks to the second sentence of this provision, the stateless person is to be treated by other state parties as if he or she is a national of the country of habitual residence for the purposes of intellectual property rights.[244] This means that the stateless can benefit from reciprocal agreements that may be in place even though they lack a formal bond of nationality. However, without obtaining the status of a habitual resident – for example through lack of lawful stay – a stateless person is unable to benefit from either of these guarantees and will enjoy only that treatment which is generally accorded to similarly situated non-nationals.[245] Furthermore, article 15 limits its attention to intellectual property rights and does not deal with cultural rights more generally. Nor is there any other provision in the 1954 Statelessness Convention that explicitly addresses this subject. And as to those rights which may indirectly touch upon the right to enjoy or participate in cultural life, the 1954 Statelessness Convention also comes up considerably short. It fails to offer any protection of minority rights, the freedom of expression or, for example, a guarantee of the qualitative aspect of education.[246] The only solace is that provided by the articles on the freedom of religion and the freedom of association.[247]

7.2 International human rights law

The right to intellectual property can be found in article 15 of the International Covenant on Economic, Social and Cultural Rights, where paragraph 1(c) declares:

---

[241] James Hathaway, *The Rights of Refugees Under International Law*, Cambridge University Press, Cambridge: 2005, page 834.

[242] Nehemiah Robinson, *Convention relating to the status of stateless persons - Its history and interpretation*, UNHCR, Geneva: 1955, page 55.

[243] See the previous discussion of this difficulty the discussion of the right of access of to courts in chapter X, at note 157.

[244] The second sentence of article 14 of the 1954 Convention relating to the Status of Stateless Persons reads: "In the territory of any other Contracting State, he shall be accorded the same protection as is accorded in that territory to nationals of the country in which he has his habitual residence".

[245] This is the "residual standard" prescribed by article 7, paragraph 1 of the 1954 Statelessness Convention. See also James Hathaway, *The Rights of Refugees Under International Law*, Cambridge University Press, Cambridge: 2005, page 839. Note again that under article 7, paragraphs 2-5, the stateless may benefit from an exemption from reciprocity. See chapter IX.

[246] See chapter X, section 7 and section 6.1 of the present chapter.

[247] See chapter X, section 5.1 and section 3.1 of the present chapter.

> The States Parties to the present Covenant recognise the right of everyone [...] to benefit from the protection of the moral and material interests resulting from any scientific, literary or artistic production of which he is the author.[248]

As we found in the context of the 1954 Statelessness Convention, the protection envisaged relates to all "creations of the human mind".[249] Just as the provision indicates, the "protection" covers moral and material interests, which means both the right to be recognised as the author of a work and to object to its misuse as well as the right to benefit economically from the work produced with a view to the enjoyment of an adequate standard of living.[250] With regards to the question to what extent non-nationals may invoke this right, the simple answer lies in the understanding that intellectual property rights are attributed to authors of such works, as "authors", so citizenship should not be relevant.[251] Moreover, according to the ESC Committee, the core content of this right includes the obligation to protect the moral interests of authors, respect and protect the material interests of authors in order to allow them to enjoy an adequate standard of living and "ensure equal access [...] to administrative, judicial or other appropriate remedies enabling authors to seek and obtain redress in case their moral and material interests have been infringed".[252] These basic standards apply to everyone - nationals, non-nationals and stateless persons.

However, beyond this enunciation of the core minimum obligations, the Committee on Economic, Social and Cultural Rights has evaded the question of the scope of protection offered by article 15, paragraph 1(c) of the ICESCR to non-

[248] This provision was clearly inspired by the identically worded article 27, paragraph 2 of the Universal Declaration of Human Rights. The only other source of this right in a major human rights instrument is article 14, paragraph 1(c) of the Additional Protocol to the American Convention on Human Rights in the Area of Economic, Social and Cultural Rights.

[249] ESC Committee, *General Comment No. 17: The right of everyone to benefit from the protection of the moral and material interests resulting from any scientific, literary or artistic production of which he or she is the author*, E/C.12/GC/17, 12 January 2006, para. 9.

[250] ESC Committee, *General Comment No. 17: The right of everyone to benefit from the protection of the moral and material interests resulting from any scientific, literary or artistic production of which he or she is the author*, E/C.12/GC/17, 12 January 2006, paras. 13 and 15. The right to property (dealt with in chapter X, section 6) is also relevant for the enjoyment of the material rights connected to intellectual property. See also Asbjorn Eide, "Cultural Rights as Individual Human Rights" in Rosas (ed) *Economic, Social and Cultural Rights*, Martinus Nijhoff Publishers, Dordrecht: 1995, page 232.

[251] Throughout the general comment on this article, the ESC Committee refers to the rights enjoyed by "authors" and no-where is citizenship mentioned. ESC Committee, *General Comment No. 17: The right of everyone to benefit from the protection of the moral and material interests resulting from any scientific, literary or artistic production of which he or she is the author*, E/C.12/GC/17, 12 January 2006. More generally, all "cultural rights" are considered to be espoused to the benefit of nationals and non-nationals alike. Diana Elles, *International Provisions Protecting the Human Rights of Non-Citizens: Study,* New York: 1980, page 34; David Weissbrodt, *Final Report on Prevention of Discrimination - The Rights of Non-Citizens,* E/CN.4/Sub.2/2003/23, 26 May 2003, para. 47; Committee on the Elimination of Racial Discrimination, *General Recommendation 30: Discrimination against Non-Citizens*, New York: 1 October 2004, para. 37.

[252] ESC Committee, *General Comment No. 17: The right of everyone to benefit from the protection of the moral and material interests resulting from any scientific, literary or artistic production of which he or she is the author*, E/C.12/GC/17, 12 January 2006, para. 39.

nationals. This is neither dealt with in the General Comment on this provision, nor touched upon in any concluding observations on state party reports – whether for lack of interest or lack of any problems to comment on, it is difficult to say.[253] What the Committee has clearly asserted, is that it is "important not to equate intellectual property rights with the human right recognised in article 15, paragraph 1(c)".[254] Although there is undoubtedly a significant substantive overlap, the exact content and purpose of this human rights provision differs from the content and purpose of intellectual property rights and agreements elaborated independently of the human rights regime. The relationship between the two systems is a complex question that continues to occupy various scholars and institutions.[255] In the meantime, the ESC Committee seems to have adopted the position that the regulation of intellectual property rights is a matter to be dealt with under the specialised regime that is watched over by the World Intellectual Property Organisation (WIPO).[256] Nowhere does the ESC committee contest the legitimacy of the approach taken under the numerous intellectual property conventions, which generally establish a system of reciprocity for the recognition and enjoyment of intellectual property rights.[257] Under this system, the lack of a nationality through which to invoke the benefits of a reciprocal agreement places the stateless in a severely disadvantaged position. Yet upon closer inspection, the two main intellectual property conventions at least, also

---

[253] In fact, the subject of intellectual property rights is generally very rarely raised in response to state party reports – these focus much more on issues relating to the preservation and enjoyment of cultural identities. Note moreover that in their treatment of "cultural rights", the issue of intellectual property rights tends also to receive only a passing mention by human rights scholars. See for example Magdalena Sepulveda; Theo van Banning; Gudrun Gudmundsdottir; Christine Chamoun; Willem van Genugten, *Human Rights Reference Handbook*, University for Peace, Ciudad Colon: 2004, pages 296-298 and Asbjorn Eide, "Cultural Rights as Individual Human Rights" in Rosas (ed) *Economic, Social and Cultural Rights*, Martinus Nijhoff Publishers, Dordrecht: 1995, pages 233 and 236.

[254] ESC Committee, *General Comment No. 17: The right of everyone to benefit from the protection of the moral and material interests resulting from any scientific, literary or artistic production of which he or she is the author*, E/C.12/GC/17, 12 January 2006, para. 3.

[255] Lauwence Helfer, *Human Rights and Intellectual Property: Conflict or Coexistence?* in Minnesota Journal of Law, Science & Technology, Vol. 5, 2003, pages 47-61. For example, the World Intellectual Property Organization (WIPO) collaborated with the Office of the United Nations High Commissioner for Human Rights to organise a panel discussion on "Intellectual Property and Human Rights" in 1998. A full report of this event and the background papers discussed can be found at http://www.wipo.int/tk/en/hr/paneldiscussion/. See in particular Silke von Lewinski, *Intellectual Property, Nationality and Non-Discrimination*, paper presented at the "Panel Discussion on Intellectual Property and Human Rights", Geneva, 9 November 1998. See also the UN Sub-Commission on Human Rights, *Resolution on Intellectual Property and Human Rights,* 25th Meeting, Geneva, 17 August 2000.

[256] 24 treaties relating to intellectual property are currently administered by the WIPO.

[257] Since intellectual property rights are traditionally dealt with at the domestic level, they tend to be limited territorially: "they exist and can be exercised only within the jurisdiction of the country or countries under whose laws they are granted". In order to secure a more uniform practice between states and the regulation of intellectual property rights across borders, international conventions have been settled. The contracting states agree to accord *national treatment* to one another's citizens on the basis of reciprocity through participation in the requisite multilateral agreement. See World Intellectual Property Organisation, *WIPO Intellectual Property Handbook: Policy, Laws and Use,* WIPO Publication No. 489(E), Geneva 2004, page 7; Silke von Lewinski, *Intellectual Property, Nationality and Non-Discrimination*, paper presented at the "Panel Discussion on Intellectual Property and Human Rights", Geneva, 9 November 1998, section 3.

provide for *national treatment* for certain categories of people who are not the citizens of a participating state. This may enable the stateless to invoke the protection offered – providing that they meet the conditions set which, similarly to the 1954 Statelessness Convention, relate to the residence status of the individuals concerned. Indeed a protocol to the Universal Copyright Convention now explicitly provides for national treatment for habitually resident stateless persons.[258] Thus between the minimum core obligations elaborated in this area under the ICESCR and the possibilities that the international intellectual property regime offer for protecting stateless persons, the added value of the stateless-specific protection of intellectual property rights as outlined in the 1954 Statelessness Convention is limited.[259]

In the meantime, where the 1954 Statelessness Convention failed to address any other "cultural rights", international human rights law shows a much greater interest in this subject. The rest of article 15 of the ICESCR is devoted to these rights, which include

> the right to participate in cultural life; the right to enjoy culture; the right to choose to belong to a group; linguistic rights; and protection of cultural and scientific heritage.[260]

---

[258] Protocol concerning the application of that Convention to works of Stateless Persons and Refugees (adopted in Paris on the 24th of July 1971) to the Universal Copyright Convention, adopted in Geneva on the 6th of September 1952 (and revised in 1971). Meanwhile, the Paris Convention for the Protection of Industrial Property, adopted on the 20th of March 1883 (and since revised on several occasions), provides in article 3 that citizens of non-state parties, a category that should include the stateless, shall enjoy national treatment if they "are domiciled or [...] have real and effective industrial and commercial establishments in the territory of one of the [state parties]". And the Berne Convention for the Protection of Literary and Artistic Works, adopted on the 9th of September 1886 (and since revised on several occasions), establishes in its article 3 that the stateless (or any national of a non-state party) shall benefit from the terms of the convention if they either have their habitual residence in a state party or where their work is first published in a state party.

[259] Upon a comparison of the 1951 Refugee Convention with the terms of various instruments of the international intellectual property regime, Hathaway concludes that "in sum, the primary purpose of Art. 14 as conceived by the drafters – to allow refugees to enforce their literary and artistic rights outside their country of citizenship despite the prevalence of reciprocity agreements – is today largely superseded by the amended Berne Convention. But Art. 14 remains of value in ensuring that the industrial property rights of refugees who are habitually resident, even if not domiciled, in a state party can be enforced outside the asylum country. It also ensures that refugees benefit from new forms of intellectual property protection [...] even when [...] non-citizens are not otherwise enfranchised". His assessment is equally applicable to the 1954 Statelessness Convention. James Hathaway, *The Rights of Refugees Under International Law*, Cambridge University Press, Cambridge: 2005, page 840.

[260] Yvonne Donders, *Towards a Right to Cultural Identity?*, Intersentia, Oxford: 2002, page 15; Magdalena Sepulveda; Theo van Banning; Gudrun Gudmundsdottir; Christine Chamoun; Willem van Genugten, *Human Rights Reference Handbook*, University for Peace, Ciudad Colon: 2004, page 297. For an in depth analysis of the content of these norms see generally Yvonne Donders, *Towards a Right to Cultural Identity?* Intersentia, Oxford: 2002; and Asbjorn Eide, "Cultural Rights as Individual Human Rights" in Rosas (ed) *Economic, Social and Cultural Rights*, Martinus Nijhoff Publishers, Dordrecht: 1995, pages 233-240. See also the rights set out in article 27 of the Universal Declaration of Human Rights; Article 5, paragraph e(vi) of the Convention on the Elimination of Racial Discrimination; Article 31 of the Convention on the Rights of the Child; Article 45 of the Migrant Workers Convention; Article 14 of the Additional Protocol to the American Convention on Human

These rights are elaborated to the benefit of everyone, including non-citizens, and the UN Committee on the Elimination of Racial Discrimination has explicitly asked states to "take the necessary measures to prevent practices that deny non-citizens their cultural identity".[261] Moreover, the UN Declaration on the Rights of Non-nationals provides to all non-citizens, regardless of immigration status, the right "to retain their own language, culture and tradition".[262] Sadly, the continuing controversy surrounding cultural rights has impeded the ESC Committee from adopting a general comment with respect to these dimensions of article 15 of the ICESCR.[263] However, as mentioned in the introduction to this section, the recognition of the importance of preserving culture and promoting participation in cultural life has infiltrated many other areas of human rights law and is having an enormous influence on the interpretation of such matters as the right to health and the right to education.[264] So, while there is still great scope for the clarification of "cultural rights" and the obligations imposed on states with respect to (nationals and) non-nationals, the stateless should already be benefiting from this overall recognition of the intrinsic human need to enjoy culture where the 1954 Statelessness Convention remains silent.

8 Economic, social and cultural rights absent from the 1954 Statelessness Convention

In the foregoing sections we identified several areas in which the 1954 Statelessness Convention was found to come up short in the protection of (aspects of) the economic, social and cultural rights of the stateless. It is now time to consider an area which the convention has overlooked almost entirely: the right to health. While it is true that provision for hospital care or some forms of (ill)health-related benefits may indirectly be addressed by the article of the Convention that deals broadly with "public relief" or indeed social security, these norms in no way guarantee that states will address this issue under either type of programme.[265] Where the 1954 Statelessness Convention did go on to at least touch upon, for example, the right to

Rights in the Area of Economic, Social and Cultural Rights; and Article 17 of the African Charter on Human and Peoples' Rights.

261 Committee on the Elimination of Racial Discrimination, General Recommendation 30: Discrimination against Non-Citizens, New York: 1 October 2004, para. 37. See also David Weissbrodt, Final Report on Prevention of Discrimination - The Rights of Non-Citizens, E/CN.4/Sub.2/2003/23, 26 May 2003, para. 47.

262 Article 5, paragraph 1(f) of the UN Declaration on the Rights of Non-nationals.

263 Magdalena Sepulveda; Theo van Banning; Gudrun Gudmundsdottir; Christine Chamoun; Willem van Genugten, *Human Rights Reference Handbook*, University for Peace, Ciudad Colon: 2004, page 296.

264 Asbjorn Eide, "Cultural Rights as Individual Human Rights" in Rosas (ed) *Economic, Social and Cultural Rights*, Martinus Nijhoff Publishers, Dordrecht: 1995, page 232. A Day of General Discussion was held on article 15 of the ICESCR in 1992 but this has regrettably not yet been succeeded by a General Comment. See also Yvonne Donders, *Towards a Right to Cultural Identity?*, Intersentia, Oxford: 2002, pages 154-156.

265 See section 4.1 above and James Hathaway, *The Rights of Refugees Under International Law*, Cambridge University Press, Cambridge: 2005, page 810.

adequate food and housing,[266] there is no mention whatsoever of the need to protect the health of the stateless. Yet health(care) is another area in which the stateless report grave difficulties.[267] This fact is made all the more troubling by the understanding that the circumstances in which many stateless populations live can contribute to susceptibility to poor general health – due to inadequate housing, food and sanitation – as well as mental health problems:

> Denial of citizenship has also severe consequences on mental health. Those confined to camps are particularly vulnerable to depression, which in turn leads to violence, suicide and increased emotional and psychological strain on the community. The mental health of many Lhotshampas men living in the refugee camps of South East Nepal has degraded over the past ten years and alcoholism, domestic violence and suicide are not uncommon.[268]

The last question to be answered in this chapter on ESC rights is therefore to what extent human rights law steps in to compensate for the omission of the right to health from the 1954 Statelessness Convention.

The right to health is enshrined in article 12 of the ICESCR, which opens with the declaration that "the State Parties to the present Covenant recognise the right of everyone to the enjoyment of the highest attainable standard of physical and mental health".[269] The wording of this paragraph indicates that the right to health is another typical ESC right which requires largely progressive realisation. It also shows that the human rights regime is not just concerned with access to health*care* but with a

[266] See section 5.1 of this chapter.

[267] Restricted access to or a blanket exclusion from health care services has been reported in relation to many stateless populations, including the Meskhetian Turks in Russia, the Rohingya in Myanmar, the Estate Tamils in Sri Lanka, Kurds in Syria, Haitians in the Dominican Republic and the Biharis in Bangladesh. See Open Society Justice Initiative, *Racial Discrimination and the Rights of Non-Citizens. Submission to the UN Committee on the Elimination of Racial Discrimination on the occasion of its 64th Session,* New York: 2004; Maureen Lynch, *Lives on hold: The human cost of statelessness,* Washington: 2005; Advisory Board on Human Security (prepared by Constantin Sokoloff), *Denial of Citizenship: A Challenge to Human Security,* February 2005, page 20. Specific problems have also been cited in relation to access to child healthcare, including vaccination programmes. See Youth Advocate Program International, *Stateless Children - Youth Who are Without Citizenship,* Washington: 2003, page 6.

[268] Be reminded that the Lhotshampas are a group made stateless by Bhutan, many of whom are still living as refugees in neighbouring Nepal. Advisory Board on Human Security (prepared by Constantin Sokoloff), *Denial of Citizenship: A Challenge to Human Security,* February 2005, page 22.

[269] Article 12, paragraph 1 of the International Covenant on Economic, Social and Cultural Rights. Expressions of the right to health can also be found in Article 25, paragraph 1 of the Universal Declaration of Human Rights; Article 5, paragraph e(iv) of the Convention on the Elimination of Racial Discrimination; Article 24 of the Convention on the Rights of the Child; Articles 28, 43 and 45 of the Migrant Workers Convention; Article 26 of the American Convention on Human Rights read in conjunction with article XI of the American Declaration on the Rights and Duties of Man and Article 10 of the Additional Protocol to the American Convention on Human Rights in the Area of Economic, Social and Cultural Rights; Article 11 of the European Social Charter; and Article 16 of the African Charter on Human and Peoples' Rights. For a concise analysis of these provisions, see Magdalena Sepulveda; Theo van Banning; Gudrun Gudmundsdottir; Christine Chamoun; Willem van Genugten, *Human Rights Reference Handbook,* University for Peace, Ciudad Colon: 2004, pages 284-286.

person's overall physical *and* psychological or social well-being.[270] Importantly though, the right to health "is not to be understood as the right to be *healthy*".[271] It is about promoting the enjoyment of the *highest attainable standard* of health, a standard that "obviously varies in time and place".[272] What has been established, however, is the scope of the minimum core obligations in respect of the right to health, which states must assure to everyone and for which non-compliance is considered unjustifiable in any circumstances.[273] These core obligations include the duty to ensure non-discriminatory access to healthcare as well as to ensure access to basic food, shelter, housing, sanitation and potable water and to provide certain essential drugs.[274] Besides elaborating these minimum guarantees that non-citizens and stateless persons should also benefit from, the ESC Committee has explicitly determined that states must refrain from

> denying or limiting equal access for all persons, including [...] asylum seekers and illegal immigrants, to preventive, curative and palliative health services.[275]

Lack of citizenship (and even legal status in the state) should therefore not be a ground for restricting access to existing healthcare opportunities.[276] Moreover, with

---

[270] Among the steps that the ICESCR goes on to outline for the realisation of this right is, for example, "the improvement of all aspects of environmental and industrial hygiene" (article 12, paragraph 2(b) of the ICESCR). The Convention on the Rights of the Child also mentions measures to "combat disease and malnutrition, including within the framework of primary health care, through, *inter alia*, the application of readily available technology and through the provision of adequate nutritious foods and clean drinking water, taking into consideration the dangers and risks of environmental pollution" (article 24, paragraph 2(c)). See also Katarina Tomasevski, "Health Rights" in Rosas (ed) *Economic, Social and Cultural Rights*, Martinus Nijhoff Publishers, Dordrecht: 1995, pages 125-126 and 128.

[271] ESC Committee, *General Comment No. 14: The right to the highest attainable standard of health*, E/C.12/2000/4, 11 August 2000, para. 8.

[272] Katarina Tomasevski, "Health Rights" in Rosas (ed) *Economic, Social and Cultural Rights*, Martinus Nijhoff Publishers, Dordrecht: 1995, page 125. See also John Dent, *Research Paper on the Social and Economic Rights of Non-Nationals in Europe,* Brussels: 1998, page 80; James Hathaway, *The Rights of Refugees Under International Law*, Cambridge University Press, Cambridge: 2005, page 511.

[273] See ESC Committee, *General Comment No. 14: The right to the highest attainable standard of health,* E/C.12/2000/4, 11 August 2000, para. 47.

[274] ESC Committee, *General Comment No. 14: The right to the highest attainable standard of health,* E/C.12/2000/4, 11 August 2000, para. 43. This core content has been derived from the work of the World Health Organisation. Beyond these minimum standards, the ESC Committee has also set out a number of obligations that should be implemented as a matter of priority (found in paragraph 44 of the same General Comment). See also Magdalena Sepulveda; Theo van Banning; Gudrun Gudmundsdottir; Christine Chamoun; Willem van Genugten, *Human Rights Reference Handbook*, University for Peace, Ciudad Colon: 2004, page 283.

[275] ESC Committee, *General Comment No. 14: The right to the highest attainable standard of health,* E/C.12/2000/4, 11 August 2000, para. 34. The Committee on the Elimination of Racial Discrimination made a similar statement in Committee on the Elimination of Racial Discrimination, *General Recommendation 30: Discrimination against Non-Citizens*, New York: 1 October 2004, para. 36. See also ESC Committee, *General Comment No. 19 - The Right to Social Security,* Advanced unedited version, 4 February 2008, para. 38.

[276] This is a matter that the two UN treaty bodies have taken up on a number of occasions in their comments on state practice. See for example ESC Committee, *Concluding Observations: Nepal,* E/2002/22, New York and Geneva: 2001, para. 545. Committee on the Elimination of Racial

regards to child health and emergency medical care, the possession of a (certain) nationality is also irrelevant.[277] The stateless should therefore garner substantial protection of the right to health from contemporary human rights law – thus resolving this particular oversight of the 1954 Statelessness Convention.

9 Conclusion

In the previous chapter, as the consideration of civil and political rights was drawn to a close, we were forced to conclude that the contribution of the 1954 Convention relating to the Status of Stateless Persons in offering the stateless a basis for enjoying such rights was negligible. It was on a note of optimism then, that this chapter opened with the discovery that the 1954 Statelessness Convention devoted twice as much attention (double the number of provisions) to economic, social and cultural rights. And we did indeed find that the statelessness instrument covers most ESC rights, at least to some extent, whereas it overlooked quite a number of civil and political rights.[278] However, as the analysis of the content of the relevant articles got underway and their position in the overall scheme of the international legal protection of the ESC rights of the stateless became clearer, this optimism made way for disillusionment. The, by now familiar, weaknesses in the approach taken to the elaboration of rights once again came to the fore: many of the rights are conditioned by a high level of attachment – all but two of the ESC rights require at least lawful presence[279] - and all of them prescribe a certain level of contingent treatment rather than absolute rights. Moreover, we again identified a significant

Discrimination, *Concluding Observations: Saudi Arabia,* A/58/18, New York: 2003, para. 206; *Argentina,* A/59/18, New York: 2004, para. 235; *Bahrain,* A/60/18, New York: 2005, para. 84. See also David Weissbrodt, *Final Report on Prevention of Discrimination - The Rights of Non-Citizens,* E/CN.4/Sub.2/2003/23, 26 May 2003, paras. 66 and 68; James Hathaway, *The Rights of Refugees Under International Law*, Cambridge University Press, Cambridge: 2005, pages 512-514.

[277] Recall the previous comments on the application of the Convention on the Rights of the Child to *all* children, regardless of citizenship. It has further been commented that "the priority accorded to children's rights is evidenced in the high degree of consensus concerning the protection of their health and their access to health care" and that Article 24 of the Convention on the Rights of the Child provides a clear obligation for state parties to "extend to *all* children access to facilities for the treatment of illness and rehabilitation of health". Katarina Tomasevski, "Health Rights" in Rosas (ed) *Economic, Social and Cultural Rights*, Martinus Nijhoff Publishers, Dordrecht: 1995, pages 134-135. See also John Dent, *Research Paper on the Social and Economic Rights of Non-Nationals in Europe,* Brussels: 1998, page 87 and Committee on the Rights of the Child, *Concluding Observations: Panama,* CRC/C/62, Geneva: 1997, para. 116; *Kyrgyzstan,* CRC/C/97, Geneva: 2000, para. 311; *Djibouti,* CRC/C/97, Geneva: 2000, para. 551; *France,* CRC/C/140, Geneva: 2004, para. 621. With regards to access to emergency medical care, article 28 of the Migrant Workers Convention determines that all migrant workers and members of their families, whether in a regular or irregular situation have the right to receive "any medical care that is urgently required for the preservation of their life or the avoidance of irreparable harm to their health on the basis of equality of treatment with nationals of the State concerned".

[278] Compare chapter X, section 7 and section 8 of this chapter.

[279] Only the provision that deals with rationing (which, as discussed, is somewhat obsolete in this day and age) and that addressing the right to education were elaborated to the benefit of *all* stateless persons, regardless of status. In contrast, the civil and political rights protected under the 1954 Statelessness Convention were generally less demanding in respect of the level of attachment required for their enjoyment. See also annex 3.

watering down of protection as the norms from the 1951 Refugee Convention were transposed into this statelessness instrument. The terms of some of the more forceful and valuable provisions of the 1951 Refugee Convention – such as article 17 on the right to work - were redrafted with detrimental effect. The combined result of offering only a diluted, contingent standard of treatment at a high level of attachment casts severe doubt upon the overall value of the 1954 Statelessness Convention for the protection of ESC rights.[280]

The nature of ESC rights and the manner in which they are guaranteed under human rights law makes this conclusion all the more rueful. There are many areas in which the exact treatment owed to non-nationals in their enjoyment of ESC rights through the human rights regime remains uncertain: the core minimum standards have not been universally elucidated and the scope of the principle of non-discrimination in respect of distinctions between citizens and non-citizens is not entirely clear in each case. Thus

> while non-nationals are clearly beneficiaries of ICESCR rights, the exact treatment owed to them by States Parties is not well defined.[281]

In addition, article 2, paragraph 3 of the ICESCR grants "developing countries" the opportunity to restrict the enjoyment of "economic rights" by non-nationals, a provision clouded by ambiguous terms that may be (mis)used to deny a variety of rights to stateless persons.[282] This is particularly worrying in the context of the protection of statelessness, since many of the large populations of stateless persons live in countries that could play this "developing country" card.[283] In an area where a stateless-specific instrument could therefore have made an invaluable contribution to enunciating and clarifying the protection to be enjoyed by the stateless, the 1954 Statelessness Convention stops woefully short of fulfilling this purpose. By prescribing a contingent standard, *particularly* where this is limited to treatment on a par with non-nationals generally, the 1954 Statelessness Convention does nothing more than simply force us to turn back to other sources of international law to determine what actual protection this standard of treatment entails. The conclusion to be drawn as to the role of this statelessness instrument in guaranteeing the basic rights of the stateless is therefore the same as that in chapter X: its added value in light of contemporary human rights law is negligible.

Meanwhile, the search for norms relating to the enjoyment of ESC rights by non-nationals and stateless persons in the overall human rights field revealed a complex picture that is difficult to decipher in places. In some areas, the UN treaty

---

[280] One possible exception is the elaboration of a right to public assistance on a par with nationals since this is an area in which the human rights norms are less clear. However, the impact of the standards set by the 1954 Statelessness Convention may be severely restricted due to the ambiguous relationship between the article dealing with public assistance and that dealing with social security financed from public funds. See section 4.1 above.

[281] John Dent, *Research Paper on the Social and Economic Rights of Non-Nationals in Europe*, Brussels: 1998, page 45.

[282] See also James Hathaway, *The Rights of Refugees Under International Law*, Cambridge University Press, Cambridge: 2005, pages 122-123.

[283] See the overview of "The World's Stateless People" in *Refugees Magazine*, No. 147, Issue 3, 2007, pages 8-9.

bodies have taken a clear stance on the importance of ensuring that non-citizens enjoy the applicable rights and are actively monitoring and reacting to the treatment of non-nationals across the world. The right to an adequate standard of living and the right to education provide examples of this approach. In contrast, the question of what scope of protection must be offered to non-nationals remains considerably neglected in respect of various other ESC rights, like the right to work or cultural rights. Nor has much attention been devoted to the specific plight and needs of the *stateless,* as a distinct group, in any area. Here and there are signs of acknowledgement of the fact that the particular nature of statelessness is such that it warrants a differentiated approach from that set out for non-citizens generally. Consider, for instance, the recently adopted General Comment of the ESC Committee on social security that explicitly includes the stateless among the marginalized groups in need of special attention.[284] Moreover, the motivation for according the stateless protection that is more commensurate with their situation also remains active in the minds of human rights scholars – as it was at the time that the 1954 Statelessness Convention was adopted with a view to achieving this very goal.[285] However, we have yet to see this reasoning fully permeate the system of economic, social and cultural rights as protected under human rights law.

[284] See section 4.2 above.

[285] Human rights scholar Asbjorn Eide is one voice that has clearly enunciated the need to distinguish carefully between different groups of non-nationals and has expressed the need, also with regard to economic and social rights, to accord treatment that takes into account the specifics of their situation. See Asbjorn Asbjorn Eide, "Economic, Social and Cultural Rights as Human Rights" in Rosas (ed) *Economic, Social and Cultural Rights*, Martinus Nijhoff Publishers, Dordrecht: 1995, pages 34-35.

CHAPTER XII

PROTECTING THE SPECIAL NEEDS OF THE STATELESS

After separating the protection offered to the stateless into the two main classes of human rights and dealing with both in some depth, the question arises what more there is to discuss. This brings us to a residual category of guarantees elaborated in the 1954 Convention relating to the Status of Stateless Persons that is best referred to as protecting the "special needs" of the stateless. Thus, alongside the promulgation of various minimum (human rights) standards for the stateless to enjoy – and thereby following once more in the footsteps of the 1951 Refugee Convention - the statelessness instrument offers the stateless certain "facilities"[1] that are necessitated by their very statelessness.[2] These can be found in Chapter V of the Statelessness Convention entitled *Administrative Measures*.[3]

Arguably the greatest special need of the stateless is the decisive resolution of their plight through the bestowal of citizenship. In line with this reasoning, the most important of the special measures included in the 1954 Statelessness Convention is article 32 that deals with naturalisation and thereby with access to a nationality. In the upcoming section we will look closely at the obligations of states to undertake to resolve statelessness under the 1954 Statelessness Convention and compare these with the duties that emanate from general international (human rights) law. Thereafter, the Convention's approach to a second special need of the stateless will be discussed: documentation. And, finally, we must consider whether there are further concerns that affect the stateless *as* stateless persons that the 1954 Statelessness Convention has neglected to attend to and whether other areas of international law compensate for any such oversight.

---

[1] Guy Goodwin-Gill, *The Refugee in International Law*, Oxford University Press, Oxford: 2007, page 512.

[2] These special measures have also been described, in the context of the 1951 Refugee Convention, as "standards applicable to refugees as refugees" or "refugee-specific concerns". See Guy Goodwin-Gill, *The Refugee in International Law*, Oxford University Press, Oxford: 2007, pages 510 – 524 and James Hathaway, *The Rights of Refugees Under International Law*, Cambridge University Press, Cambridge: 2005, page 121.

[3] The internal freedom of movement, expulsion, fiscal charges and transfer of assets are also dealt with in the chapter of the 1954 Statelessness Convention on "Administrative Measures" but have already been addressed in chapter X, sections 2 and 6 in the context of the freedom of movement and the right to property.

1 NATURALISATION

It goes without saying that the prospect of naturalisation would be hugely beneficial to all stateless persons since the conferral of nationality is tantamount to lifting them out of this severely vulnerable group.[4] Naturalisation is thus an indispensable tool in working towards the resolution of the ultimate "special need" of the stateless - addressing their actual lack of a nationality. Meanwhile, the elaboration of a (facilitated) right or opportunity to gain citizenship through naturalisation, is effectively also an expression of the right to a nationality. As such, it could have been presented for consideration in chapter X where we looked at the civil and political rights attributed to stateless persons through the 1954 Statelessness Convention and other instruments. However, the issue was set aside for consideration in the present chapter to allow the measures prescribed to be evaluated in their proper context. We are not concerned here with the right to a nationality in general terms or the bearing it has on the prevention of statelessness – matters dealt with in detail in part 2[5] – but with naturalisation as a means to meet the need of existing stateless populations. It is from this perspective that an assessment will be made of the scope of protection offered under the 1954 Statelessness Convention and other areas of international law.

It is important to realise that naturalisation policies vary substantially from one state to the next in accordance with the (perceived) national identity and state interests.[6] The enduring lack of sufficient willpower or mettle to redress situations of (large-scale) statelessness finds its roots in the overwhelming sensitivity of this question as to which outsiders are worthy of admission to full membership of the political community. Political motivations can thus contribute to the adoption of a restrictive naturalisation policy and the prescription of rigorous conditions for eligibility to citizenship.[7] In extreme cases, we have discovered that the conditions elaborated for naturalisation may be deliberately exclusionary so as to manipulate or impede access to citizenship for particular groups.[8] However, even where the requirements set are not particularly stringent, they may, at times, be difficult to

---

[4] "The condition of being stateless will *ipso facto* terminate when one acquires a nationality". Carol Batchelor The 1954 Convention relating to the Status of Stateless Persons: Implementation within the European Union Member States and Recommendations for Harmonisation 2004, page 17. For an introduction to the concept attribution of nationality through naturalisation, see chapter III.

[5] Whereby the separate 1961 Convention on the Reduction of Statelessness which is focussed on the prevention of statelessness and the realisation of the right to a nationality was discussed.

[6] Manley Hudson, *Report on Nationality, including Statelessness,* A/CN.4/50, 21 February 1952, page 57; Paul Weis, *Nationality and Statelessness in International Law*, Kluwer Academic Publishers Group, Dordrecht: 1979, page 100; Ruth Donner, "Chapter 2: The Principle of the "Link" in Nationality Law" in *The Regulation of Nationality in International Law*, Transnational Publishers, New York: 1994, pages 33-34; Douglas Klusmeyer; Alexander Aleinikoff, *From Migrants to Citizens: Membership in a Changing World*, Carnegie Endowment for International Peace, Washington, DC: 2000, page 14.

[7] A strong notion of national identity can have a similar impact, contributing to the enduring exclusion of minority groups. Thus, while "integration would ideally require citizenship [...] citizenship is sometimes made conditional on requirements that in effect demand assimilation". Asbjorn Eide, "Citizenship and the minority rights of non-citizens", Working Paper prepared for the UN Sub-Commission on Prevention of Discrimination and Protection of Minorities, E/CN.4/Sub.2/AC.5/1999/WP.3, 15 April 1999, paragraph 5.

[8] See chapter V, section 1 on arbitrary deprivation of nationality.

meet. Consider the common condition of a prolonged period of (lawful and habitual) residence: difficult for numerous categories of non-citizens to achieve and for the stateless especially so because of the difficulties inherent in gaining or retaining access to a state's territory in the absence of the bond of nationality.[9] Furthermore, states may also make certain stipulations in their naturalisation policy that "create particular difficulties in the naturalisation of stateless persons", such as the need to prove the absence of any other bond of citizenship or to produce an assortment of documents.[10]

These interrelated problems of technical impediments and the issue of political will contribute to a poor overall prospect for the acquisition of nationality by stateless persons. Consequently, in many instances – in particular where large caseloads are involved – statelessness has proven to be a long, drawn-out affair. Consider the stateless Russian minority in Latvia and Estonia for whom the acquisition of citizenship by naturalisation (or otherwise) proved untenable until the laws were relaxed many years down the line[11] or the Kurds in Syria who are still waiting for a (real) opportunity to acquire nationality.[12] And there are a plethora of other examples of the protracted nature of the phenomenon of statelessness.[13] Naturalisation then, although an obvious solution to this dramatic form of non-citizenship, is by no means an easy one. Yet the attribution of citizenship under the domestic laws and regulations of a state is the only viable solution to statelessness. Only the state itself is empowered to actually confer nationality and this task cannot be assumed by another state or an international organisation.[14] And there is no alternative to domestic citizenship – the idea of developing a form of international

[9] For a discussion of problems relating to residence status for stateless persons, see chapter X, section 2.2. Manley Hudson, *Report on Nationality, including Statelessness,* A/CN.4/50, 21 February 1952, page 57. In his 1950s report, Hudson also listed the following issues that can commonly impair naturalisation: complicated and expensive procedures and stringent requirements as to the possession of property. These days, proof of integration through language and history or civics exams often also proves to be a challenging requirement for newcomers or members of a minority group to meet.

[10] Manley Hudson, *Report on Nationality, including Statelessness,* A/CN.4/50, 21 February 1952, page 57; Rosa da Costa, *Rights of Refugees in the Context of Integration: Legal Standards and Recommendations,* Geneva: June 2006, page 188.

[11] The group of ethnic Russians and former citizens of the Soviet Union became stateless in the aftermath of the dissolution of the Soviet Union and the independence of Latvia and Estonia. They were not granted an automatic right of citizenship and prospects for naturalisation were initially severely restricted: many categories of person were excluded outright and others were required to meet very stringent language and other requirements. These laws were later relaxed, partly as a result of the EU and NATO accession process. See Nida Gelazis, "An Evaluation of International Instruments that Address the Condition of Statelessness: A Case Study of Estonia and Latvia" in R. Cholewinski (ed) *International Migration Law,* T.M.C. Asser Press, The Hague: 2007, pages 297 – 308.

[12] The Kurds in Syria can trace their statelessness back to a 1962 government census. Maureen Lynch, "Syria: Follow Through on Commitment to Grant Citizenship to Stateless Kurds" *Refugees International Bulletin,* Washington: Date 2005; Curtis Doebbler, 'A Human Rights Approach to Statelessness in the Middle East', in *Leiden Journal of International Law,* Vol. 15, 2002, page 545.

[13] This is in spite of the finding in the 2003 Questionnaire on statelessness that 59.5% of respondent states do provide for facilitated naturalisation for stateless persons who are lawfully and permanently resident. UNHCR, *Final report concerning the Questionnaire on statelessness pursuant to the Agenda for Protection,* Geneva: March 2004, page 30.

[14] Carol Batchelor, 'Statelessness and the Problem of Resolving Nationality Status', in *International Journal of Refugee Law,* Vol. 10, 1998, page 174.

citizenship, although raised many times, never gained any real ground.[15] It will therefore be of great interest to see to what extent a right to a solution has been delineated under international law and whether – and in what circumstances – the stateless may now enjoy a *right* to (be considered for) naturalisation under the relevant norms.

While naturalisation is an important route towards the resolution of statelessness, it is not the only mechanism through which existing cases can be redressed. The acquisition of nationality may also be achieved automatically by operation of the law or through a simple procedure of registration, declaration or option.[16] A state may, for instance, adopt new legislation with a view to reducing the incidence of statelessness on its territory. This was seen in Sri Lanka where parliament passed the "Grant of Citizenship to Persons of Indian Origin Act" in 2003 to confer nationality upon the country's stateless Estate Tamils. Individuals were able to acquire citizenship under this law through one of two routes: automatically, by the entry into force of the law itself if they are stateless and meet the basic conditions set or through a straight-forward declaration exercise if they hold a defunct Indian passport.[17] In other cases, it may be the re-visiting of the

[15] Roberto Córdova discusses the notion of an international nationality in his 1954 report. Roberto Córdova, *Nationality, Including Statelessness. Third Report on the Elimination or Reduction of Statelessness by Roberto Córdova, Special Rapporteur,* A/CN.4/81, New York: 11 March 1954, page 29. Since then, other scholars have investigated the theory of this concept. See for example Haro van Panhuys, "Chapter XI: Final Reflections" in *The Role of Nationality in International Law*, A.W. Sijthoff's Uitgeversmaatschappij, Leiden: 1959; Vincenzo Ferrari, "Citizenship: Problems, Concepts and Policies" in Torre (ed) *European Citizenship - An Institutional Challenge*, Kluwer Law International, The Hague: 1998; Seyla Benhabib, *Transformations of Citizenship - Dilemmas of the Nation State in the Era of Globalisation*, Koniklijke van Gorcum, Assen: 2001; Rainer Bauböck, *Transnational Citizenship. Membership and Rights in International Migration*, Edward Elgar, Cheltenham: 2002. The only development that remotely reflects such ideas is the introduction of "European Union citizenship". However, although trans-national in scope, this form of citizenship is essentially based on regular domestic nationality – Union citizenship is enjoyed once one of the members of the EU attributes domestic citizenship. To this day there is therefore no replacement for nationality as conferred by nation-states.

[16] Automatic conferral of citizenship on an existing population is a technique that is generally adopted in the context of state succession because such cases involve the delineation of the initial body of citizens that constitute the (new) state. In other instances, automatic conferral of citizenship by operation of the law, other than at birth, has been described as *imposition* of nationality and may run counter to international law where it is realised without the consent of the individual involved. See Ruth Donner, "Chapter 3: The Imposition and Withdrawal of Nationality" in *The Regulation of Nationality in International Law*, Transnational Publishers, New York: 1994. Nevertheless, where the automatic or compulsory conferral of nationality involves persons who were initially stateless, this is more widely considered to be acceptable under international law. See Paul Weis, *Nationality and Statelessness in International Law*, Kluwer Academic Publishers Group, Dordrecht: 1979, pages 101-115; and Article 8, paragraph 2 of the Draft Articles on nationality in relation to state succession, International Law Commission, 'Draft Articles on Nationality of Natural Persons in Relation to the Succession of States - With Commentaries', in *Yearbook of the International Law Commission,* Vol. II, 1999, page 31. It is therefore a viable means of resolving cases of statelessness.

[17] "Any person of Indian origin who, on the date of the coming into operation of this act, (a) has been a permanent resident of Sri Lanka since October 30, 1964; or (b) is a descendent, resident in Sri Lanka, of a person who has been a permanent resident of Sri Lanka since October 30, 1964, shall be granted the status of citizen of Sri Lanka, with effect from such date [...] provided however, the grant of status of a

regulations that underlie problems of statelessness in the country, such as a gender-sensitive *jus sanguinis* law, that provides an opportunity for dealing with existing cases of statelessness. Thus, in Morocco, where the nationality code was modified in 2007 so as to allow women to transmit citizenship to their children, provision was made for the retrospective application of this amendment. It has been reported that "many children born to foreign fathers have already requested Moroccan nationality and have been able to acquire it".[18] The automatic conferral of nationality or acquisition of citizenship through registration, declaration or option are therefore also recognised tools in tackling statelessness. Indeed these mechanisms may be a more foolproof alternative to naturalisation since they require that prospective citizens meet only basic conditions for eligibility and do not leave the room for discretion that naturalisation procedures acknowledge. Nevertheless, in this section we will concentrate on *naturalisation* as a right of solution prescribed, for example, by the 1954 Statelessness Convention. The use of alternative mechanisms for the (re)instatement of nationality was already covered by default in part 2, since it is the rules that were discussed there in the context of the prevention of statelessness that can, by extension, be applied for the purposes of the reduction of existing cases.[19]

1.1 1954 Convention relating to the Status of Stateless Persons

Before discussing how the 1954 Convention relating to the Status of Stateless Persons deals with the question of conferral of citizenship it is of interest to once more delve into the historical development of the international statelessness instruments. We have already discussed how the 1954 and 1961 Statelessness Conventions were developed and adopted,[20] but the subject of a third potential

---

citizen of Sri Lanka to a permanent resident, who on the date of coming into operation of this Act, holds an Indian passport or other similar document, shall be effective only on his forwarding to the Commissioner a declaration [...] stating his intention to voluntarily acquire citizenship of Sri Lanka". Article 2 of the Grant of Citizenship to Persons of Indian Origin Act, 2003.

[18] Mark Manly, "Sorry, wrong gender" in *Refugees Magazine,* Number 147, Issue 3, 2007, page 25.

[19] In some cases, the *reduction* of statelessness through the use of the norms relating to the *prevention* of statelessness is explicitly elaborated. See, for instance, chapter IV where the possibility was discussed of "preventing" statelessness at birth by offering nationality *jus soli,* while actually confer this citizenship only at a later date upon application by the individual concerned. And chapter VI where the use of option was discussed in the context of the attribution of nationality following state succession. In reality, all of the rules that are espoused for the prevention of statelessness can equally be invoked for the resolution of existing cases, where the origin of statelessness is a violation of one of these norms. Thus, for example, where a person loses his citizenship as a result of a criminal conviction and is thereby rendered stateless, he could challenge this decision before a court and achieve an order for the reinstatement of his nationality. Involving, as it does, an individual who is already stateless, this type of situation does, in a sense, deal with the resolution of existing cases. Even where the resolution of statelessness involves the adoption of a new law to rectify a long-standing injustice (such as in the example of Sri Lanka given above where statelessness followed state succession), such a law may be seen achieve the delayed implementation of standards for the prevention of statelessness. Clearly then, there is a fine line between prevention and reduction. In this chapter, where the focus is on naturalisation, we are especially interested in "new" opportunities for stateless persons to acquire a nationality – as distinct from the reliance on international standards for the prevention of statelessness.

[20] See chapters III (section 3) and IX (section 3).

document deliberated over by the international community has yet to be raised. Roberto Córdova, Special Rapporteur to the International Law Commission on nationality, including statelessness, also prepared draft texts on the reduction or elimination of *present* statelessness.[21] The proposals essentially involved attributing citizenship (or a special status of "protected national") to various categories of stateless person, in order to fully restore their rights. Naturalisation was also encouraged under these draft documents. However, "in view of the great difficulties of a non-legal nature which beset the problem of present statelessness", by the time these proposals were put before the General Assembly it was accepted that an international instrument of any kind may be beyond reach and governments should simply view the articles as "suggestions".[22] Thereafter, the General Assembly did not take any action on the issue of existing cases of statelessness – a decision that was motivated in part by reference to the recent successful adoption of the 1954 Convention relating to the Status of Stateless Persons.[23] And no action has since been taken on the matter.

Meanwhile, the protection offered to stateless persons through the 1954 Convention relating to the Status of Stateless Persons was actually always envisaged as an interim measure to ensure that certain minimum standards are enjoyed until such time as a nationality can be procured.[24] So, perhaps the most important provision of the 1954 Statelessness Convention, and the very last of its substantive guarantees, is article 32 which offers that crucial "right of solution" by considering access to citizenship.[25] It addresses the naturalisation of stateless persons, as follows:

---

[21] Four draft instruments were prepared in all, allowing for a choice to be made on the basic substance (between a far-reaching instrument aimed at *eliminating* present statelessness and a less extreme variant devised to reduce present statelessness) and on the form (between an independent convention and a protocol to the convention that would go on to be adopted as the 1961 Convention on the Reduction of Statelessness). It was the draft *convention* on the *reduction* of present statelessness that went on to be considered by the International Law Commission. For the text of all four proposals, see Roberto Córdova, *Nationality, Including Statelessness. Third Report on the Elimination or Reduction of Statelessness by Roberto Córdova, Special Rapporteur,* A/CN.4/81, New York: 11 March 1954.

[22] UN, 'Statelessness', in *Yearbook of the United Nations,* Vol. 1954, page 417.

[23] UN, 'Statelessness', in *Yearbook of the United Nations,* Vol. 1954, pages 418-419.

[24] The protection offered under the 1954 Convention relating to the Status of Stateless Persons was never intended to be a substitute for granting nationality. UNHCR and IPU, *Nationality and statelessness. A handbook for parliamentarians*, 2005, page 26.

[25] James Hathaway, *The Rights of Refugees Under International Law*, Cambridge University Press, Cambridge: 2005. According to Hathaway, the 1951 Refugee Convention proposes four rights of solution – repatriation, voluntary reestablishment, resettlement and naturalisation. Although there is some indication that resettlement may also be constructive in the context of statelessness - for example through the retention of provisions dealing with the transfer of assets and the movement of a stateless person from one (contracting) state to another – "there is only one durable solution to the problem of statelessness, and that is the acquisition of nationality". This may of course be preceded and facilitated by resettlement. Carol Batchelor, "The International Legal Framework Concerning Statelessness and Access for Stateless Persons", *European Union Seminar on the Content and Scope of International Protection: Panel 1 - Legal basis of international protection,* Madrid: 2002, page 6. See also UNHCR Executive Committee, *Conclusion No. 95: General Conclusion on International Protection,* Geneva: 10 October 2003, para. (v); UNHCR and IPU, *Nationality and statelessness. A handbook for parliamentarians*, 2005, page 26; and UNHCR, *Resettlement Handbook,* Geneva, November 2004, chapter 5.1 on Stateless Persons.

> The Contracting States shall as far as possible facilitate the assimilation and naturalisation of stateless persons. They shall in particular make every effort to expedite naturalisation proceedings and to reduce as far as possible the charges and costs of such proceedings.[26]

This is the only provision to deal with the resolution of statelessness. Nowhere does the 1954 Statelessness Convention elaborate a right to acquire a nationality by other means, such as registration, declaration or option.[27] Furthermore, from the phraseology chosen for this article it is immediately clear that it is not a *right* to (be considered for) naturalisation that is envisaged for the stateless but, at most, an *opportunity* to enjoy *facilitated* naturalisation. Stateless persons cannot demand access to a naturalisation procedure or even insist upon the lowering of the requisite conditions in their favour. Under the 1954 Statelessness Convention, states are strongly urged to facilitate naturalisation, but it remains within their discretion to do so.[28] Offering a solution to statelessness through access to citizenship never becomes obligatory, even in severely protracted cases.[29] Nor does the specific reference to the expedition of proceedings and the reduction of related costs mean that either of these measures are mandatory – states must simply (be seen to) "make every effort" to assist stateless persons in these procedural matters.

Nevertheless, the encouragement of naturalisation through this article is considered to be of value and the provision

> has real legal force in at least extreme cases [where stateless persons] are effectively barred without sound reasons from accessing the usual process to acquire citizenship.[30]

---

[26] Only one state party – Mexico – has lodged a reservation to this article of the 1954 Statelessness Convention. Note further that where the provision refers to "assimilation", this word "is not used in the usual meaning of loss of the specific identity of the persons involved but in the sense of integration into the economic, social and cultural life of the community". Nehemiah Robinson, *Convention relating to the status of stateless persons - Its history and interpretation*, UNHCR, Geneva: 1955, page 102. See also James Hathaway, *The Rights of Refugees Under International Law*, Cambridge University Press, Cambridge: 2005, pages 983-984.

[27] Stateless individuals will have to fall back on the 1961 Convention relating to the Status of Stateless Persons as discussed in part 2 for any opportunity to acquire citizenship through simple application.

[28] Nehemiah Robinson, *Convention relating to the status of stateless persons - Its history and interpretation*, UNHCR, Geneva: 1955, page 101; Carol Batchelor, "The International Legal Framework Concerning Statelessness and Access for Stateless Persons", *European Union Seminar on the Content and Scope of International Protection: Panel 1 - Legal basis of international protection,* Madrid: 2002, page 6.

[29] A recent conclusion elaborated by the Executive Committee of the UNHCR on, among other things, the reduction of statelessness confirms this reading of the 1954 Statelessness Convention. The Committee "encourages States to actively disseminate information regarding access to citizenship, including naturalisation procedures" - implying that such procedures should be available to stateless persons but in no way suggesting that they enjoy a *right* to access nationality. UNHCR Executive Committee, *Conclusion No. 106: Conclusion on Identification, Prevention and Reduction of Statelessness and Protection of Stateless Persons,* Geneva: 6 October 2006, para. (r).

[30] James Hathaway, *The Rights of Refugees Under International Law*, Cambridge University Press, Cambridge: 2005, page 989.

What is more, the provision applies broadly to all stateless persons – it is framed, in that sense, in absolute terms. It does not address itself only to the state, if any, in which the stateless person is lawfully and habitually residing, it addresses all contracting states without further specification. This means that stateless persons may be able to benefit from facilitated naturalisation on grounds other than *lawful* and habitual residence, for example on the basis of a connection with the state through birth or marriage, or even simple *de facto* habitual residence. On the other hand, through this technique, the provision omits any indication as to the form or content that should be given to naturalisation procedures generally or for the stateless specifically. And even where it encourages the "facilitation" of naturalisation, it does not offer any suggestion as to which pre-conditions for eligibility for naturalisation are considered legitimate and which may not justifiably be required of the stateless.[31] It will be interesting to see whether international (human rights) law provides more concrete guidance in this respect or indeed a stronger legal norm for resolving statelessness.

1.2 International (human rights) law

Looking to other sources of contemporary international law for norms relating to the conferral of nationality to the stateless, we automatically arrive at provisions that elaborate or are related to the right to a nationality.[32] We therefore find that the question of a right to (be considered for) *naturalisation* has already been raised in part 2 where we discussed the international legal response to the various causes of statelessness. It was there that we discovered that international law limits state discretion in setting naturalisation policy[33] and that the prohibition of arbitrary deprivation of nationality can have a particular bearing on this matter. So while this issue has already been given some consideration,[34] here we will be looking more closely at naturalisation as a "right of solution" and, thereby, at access to naturalisation procedures specifically for stateless persons *as* stateless persons.

Then we see that there is evidence of a progressive development towards a *right* to (be considered for) naturalisation for stateless persons – and certain other categories of non-nationals - under human rights law. This observation stems from a number of sources. Firstly, the explicit comment by the UN Human Rights

---

[31] This is in spite of the work prepared prior to elaboration of the Convention by Special Rapporteur Hudson in identifying substantive areas in which the stateless may experience difficulties. See Manley Hudson, *Report on Nationality, including Statelessness,* A/CN.4/50, 21 February 1952, page 57. It may be possible to interpret the explicit encouragement given to the expedition of proceedings expansively as an appeal to states to not only ensure that the process of applying for citizenship is not unduly time-consuming but also that where a number of years residence is required for eligibility to apply for nationalisation, this period be shortened for the stateless. See James Hathaway, *The Rights of Refugees Under International Law*, Cambridge University Press, Cambridge: 2005, page 986.

[32] For an overview of the relevant articles, see chapter III, section 2.

[33] Be reminded of the ruling given within the Inter-American human rights system: Inter-American Court on Human Rights, *Advisory Opinion on the Proposed Amendments to the Naturalisation Provision of the Constitution of Costa Rica,* OC-4/84, 19 January 1984, para. 36. Cited above in chapter V, section 1.2.

[34] See in particular chapter V, section 1.2 and chapter VII, section 2.2.

Committee in the case of *Stewart v. Canada* that it is possible for a stateless person to be arbitrarily deprived of his "right to acquire the nationality of the country of residence".[35] Secondly, the recommendation by the UN Committee on the Elimination of Racial Discrimination that states should "pay due attention to possible barriers to naturalisation that may exist for long-term or permanent residents"[36], suggesting that non-nationals develop a *right* to naturalise after a certain period of residence. And thirdly, the clear acknowledgement in the European Convention on Nationality that residence will, over time, lead to a *right* to apply for nationality through naturalisation procedures.[37]

After a certain period of time then, a stateless person may be able to claim a right to apply for naturalisation in the state in which he has established lawful and habitual residence, on the basis of developing international norms.[38] Moreover, various texts and bodies have begun to elaborate on a number of substantive questions relating to naturalisation, including on the appropriateness – in general or in the specific context of statelessness – of various conditions for eligibility. One example of a very concrete standard is provided by the European Convention on Nationality which determines that states may not demand more than ten years of lawful residence as a pre-condition to naturalisation.[39] Another is the determination by the Committee on the Elimination of Racial Discrimination that states should refrain from

> practices that deny non-citizens their cultural and ethnic identity, such as requirements that non-citizens change their name in order to be naturalised.[40]

Consider also the overall impact of the principle of non-discrimination and standards of due process on state discretion in naturalisation procedures, as discussed in chapter V. And a further possible limitation to the freedom of states to set the conditions for naturalisation has been argued on the basis of article 15 of the ICCPR. It is suggested that where the conviction for a criminal offence forms a bar for the opportunity to apply for naturalisation, this amounts to "*ex post facto*

---

[35] UN Human Rights Committee, *Individual complaint of Stewart v. Canada,* case number 538/1993, A/52/40, vol. II, 1 November 1996, para. 12.4.

[36] CERD General Recommendation 30: Discrimination against Non-Citizens 2004, para. 13.

[37] Article 6, paragraph 3 of the European Convention on Nationality. For a discussion of the place and importance of the European Convention on Nationality in contemporary international law, please refer to Chapter III, Section 2. See also Carol Batchelor, 'Statelessness and the Problem of Resolving Nationality Status', in *International Journal of Refugee Law,* Vol. 10, 1998, pages 162-163 and Carol Batchelor, "Developments in International law: The Avoidance of Statelessness Through Positive Application of the Right to a Nationality" in *Council of Europe's First Conference on Nationality,* Strasbourg: 2001, page 56. In contrast, however, it should be noted that neither the UN Declaration on the Rights of Non-nationals or the Convention on Migrant Workers mentions (a right to) naturalisation.

[38] For a discussion of the problems associated with access to naturalisation for individuals holding an irregular immigration status, see chapter VII, section 2.

[39] Article 6, paragraph 3 of the European Convention on Nationality.

[40] Office of the High Commissioner for Human Rights, "The Rights of Non-citizens", prepared by David Weissbrodt, Geneva 2006. See also Committee on the Elimination of Racial Discrimination, *Concluding observations: Japan,* A/56/18, New York: 2001, paragraph 176.

punishment to the individual who committed the crime" which is outlawed under the aforementioned article.[41]

For the benefit of stateless persons *as* stateless persons, several additional standards may be helpful in their quest for naturalisation. To begin with, we have seen that a state may not discriminate against any *particular* group or nationality in determining the conditions for access to naturalisation.[42] Where a state directly or indirectly blocks access to naturalisation procedures for stateless persons specifically – as opposed to other groups of non-nationals – this would amount to an unreasonable and thus prohibited distinction. Let us also recall that, more generally, states may not uphold "unreasonable impediments" to the achievement of citizenship through naturalisation.[43] This submission can be an important interpretative tool in assessing the compliance with human rights standards of any obstacles that stateless persons encounter within the context of naturalisation. It becomes possible to evaluate naturalisation procedures on two levels: firstly to consider whether the conditions set may generally be considered appropriate and secondly, whether the requirements, while initially deemed legitimate, in fact amount to *unreasonable* impediments when applied with respect to the stateless. For instance, while states may reasonably demand that non-nationals produce various documents to support their application for naturalisation, to insist that a stateless person presents the full range of documentation – without for example allowing alternative forms of evidence to be utilised where certain documents cannot be delivered – may nevertheless be unreasonable.[44] Thus by taking into account the circumstance of statelessness the expression "unreasonable impediments" gains a very specific content and a form of facilitated naturalisation can be promoted for persons belonging to this vulnerable group.

Again, the European Convention on Nationality goes one step further and delineates a concrete obligation for states to facilitate the naturalisation of stateless persons.[45] Unlike the commentary to the 1954 Statelessness Convention, the accompanying explanatory report to the European Convention on Nationality

---

[41] Human Rights Watch, *Roma in the Czech Republic Foreigners in Their Own Land,* 1 June 1996.

[42] Article 1, paragraph 3 of the Convention on the Elimination of all Forms of Racial Discrimination; CERD General Recommendation 30: Discrimination against Non-Citizens 2004, para. 13. See chapter V, section 1.2.

[43] UN Human Rights Committee, *Individual complaint of Capena v. Canada,* case number 558/1993, A/52/40, vol. II, 3 April 1997, para. 11.3. Again, see also chapter V, section 1.2.

[44] Recall the identification by Hudson of problematic areas for the stateless in the context of naturalisation in Manley Hudson, *Report on Nationality, including Statelessness,* A/CN.4/50, 21 February 1952, page 57. Consider here the development of standards in the context of the attribution of nationality following the succession of states, where the Council of Europe Convention on the avoidance of statelessness in relation to State succession determined that the documentary requirements usually set may not be "reasonable" in the context of the avoidance of statelessness. These standards (discussed in chapter VI, section 3) could also be a useful interpretative device for applying this notion of "unreasonable impediments" in the overall context of the naturalisation of the stateless. See also Rosa da Costa, *Rights of Refugees in the Context of Integration: Legal Standards and Recommendations,* Geneva: June 2006, pages 186-191.

[45] Article 6, paragraph 4 (g) of the European Convention on Nationality. Note that the Council of Europe Convention on the avoidance of statelessness in relation to State succession (article 9) also prescribes the facilitated naturalisation of persons who, in spite of the various guarantees, were rendered stateless in the context of state succession.

discusses the substantive implications of this duty to facilitate the acquisition of nationality by the stateless. In particular, it means ensuring that there are "favourable conditions" in place, which may include

> a reduction of the length of required residence, less stringent language requirements, an easier procedure and lower procedural fees.[46]

Here the cost and complexity of naturalisation procedures is addressed – as it was in the 1954 Statelessness Convention – but so too is the lowering of other conditions. In 1999, the Council of Europe's Committee of Ministers elaborated on the idea of facilitated naturalisation for the stateless in a recommendation on the "Avoidance and Reduction of Statelessness".[47] Again, the cost and complexity of procedures, the pre-condition of a certain period of residence and a certain level of knowledge of the language are addressed. In addition, the recommendation calls upon states to

> ensure that offences, when they are relevant for the decision concerning the acquisition of nationality, do not unreasonably prevent stateless persons seeking the nationality of a state.[48]

The message that the Council of Europe is thereby sending is that, unlike in the context of "regular" naturalisation procedures, where the naturalisation of *stateless persons* is concerned, the objective of tackling statelessness should be weighed into the equation at all times. Thus, any barriers to the naturalisation of stateless persons must be especially carefully considered and justified.

The overall picture painted by international (human rights) law as it stands today is that states may be required to simplify or relax some of their naturalisation requirements to facilitate – or at least not impede – access to citizenship for the stateless. International law is thereby much more concerned with how the substance of naturalisation policy affects the stateless and provides more guidance as to what may be considered to be reasonable requirements and what are seen as inappropriate, even unlawful, stipulations. However, there is one common theme that can be traced throughout the references to naturalisation in the human rights field: for the stateless, or any non-national, to benefit from a right to (facilitated) naturalisation, they must first establish lawful and habitual residence on the territory of the state in question. At most, states may be obliged to admit stateless persons to their naturalisation procedures after a condensed period of residence, but nowhere is it suggested that the stateless should have access to naturalisation *without* first gaining (lawful and habitual) residence. This is perhaps a logical approach, since

---

[46] This is a list of examples of "favourable conditions" and should not be considered exhaustive. Council of Europe, *European Convention on Nationality: Explanatory report,* Strasbourg: 1997, page 35.

[47] Council of Europe, Recommendation R (1999) 18 of the Committee of Ministers to Member States on the Avoidance and Reduction of Statelessness, Strasbourg, 17 September 1999.

[48] Paragraph (d) of section IIB. Council of Europe, Recommendation R (1999) 18 of the Committee of Ministers to Member States on the Avoidance and Reduction of Statelessness, Strasbourg, 17 September 1999. Consider in this respect also the arguments raised above with respect to the appropriateness of allowing the conviction for a criminal offence to stand in the way of an opportunity for naturalisation.

naturalisation is most commonly offered on the basis of *jus domicilli*, whereby the acquisition of citizenship reflects the genuine link that is developed between the individual and his state of residence.[49] Nevertheless, this approach poses a serious problem. As we have seen in chapter X, it can be very difficult for stateless persons to achieve lawful residence – a matter which is neither provided for under the 1954 Statelessness Convention nor decisively settled in human rights instruments.[50] And indeed, if a *right* to (facilitated) naturalisation is earned after a certain period of lawful and habitual residence, states may become even less willing to formally admit stateless persons to their territory. Dealing with the interaction between statelessness, immigration law and naturalisation policy is therefore central to the ultimate resolution of (protracted) cases of statelessness.[51] In the meantime, it is important to recall that long-term residence is not the only credible indicator of a genuine link between an individual and a state that could form the basis of a claim to citizenship.[52] From this point of view, the more general formulation used in the 1954 Statelessness Convention may provide more scope for assisting the stateless to access naturalisation for it does not limit its attention to resident stateless persons. However, since this provision is drafted in such facultative terms, states must still volunteer to offer access to (facilitated) naturalisation to unlawfully present stateless persons - albeit on the grounds of another real connection - and this is highly unlikely.

2 Documentation

The second special need of the stateless that is addressed in the 1954 Convention relating to the Status of Stateless Persons can be summarised as the need for "documentation". As UNHCR explains:

> The need for some form of personal documentation is a constant of daily life in most modern societies [...] Establishing one's identity may be essential for a wide range of activities, including the registration of births and deaths, contracting marriages, obtaining employment, housing, hospital care or rations, qualifying for social benefits, entering educational institutions, or requesting the issuance of official documents and permits.[53]

---

[49] See chapter III, section 1.

[50] See chapter X, section 2.2.

[51] Attuning immigration and citizenship policy is also important from the point of view of ensuring that where the stateless are granted lawful residence in a state, the actual *status* attributed is compatible with naturalisation requirements. See Rosa da Costa, *Rights of Refugees in the Context of Integration: Legal Standards and Recommendations,* Geneva: June 2006, page 187.

[52] Consider the proposed instruments on the reduction or elimination of present statelessness that also used *jus soli* and *jus sanguinis* connections to promote the attribution of nationality in existing cases of statelessness. See Roberto Córdova, *Nationality, Including Statelessness. Third Report on the Elimination or Reduction of Statelessness by Roberto Córdova, Special Rapporteur,* A/CN.4/81, New York: 11 March 1954

[53] UNHCR, "Identity documents for Refugees", UN Doc. EC/SCP/33, Geneva, 20 July 1984, paragraph 1.

To this list, we can add "travel" as another aspect of life for which the proper papers are essential.[54] For the stateless, who earn special entitlements on the basis of their status as a stateless person, documentation gains a heightened importance as a tool for accessing these benefits.[55]

Similarly to the subject of naturalisation, we have already touched upon this issue of documentation - albeit indirectly - in the consideration of related issues. Thus, in chapter X, section 2.2, where we discussed international freedom of movement we raised the importance of the passport for travel across international frontiers, noting that since passports are normally issued by a state to its citizens the stateless are typically unable to obtain this important document.[56] Access to travel documents is therefore one aspect of the "special needs" of the stateless as far as documentation is concerned. Another is access to a more general type of document: identity papers. Again, commonly issued by the authorities of the state of nationality, identity documents can play a crucial role in accessing a host of rights and facilities by attesting to various key aspects of an individual's personal particulars. Proof of statelessness is especially indispensable and proof of lawful immigration status (if held) equally so. Other important documents are those that give evidence of civil status and other facts such as date and place of birth or educational and professional qualifications.[57]

Where do the stateless currently stand in relation to this "special need"? In response to a 2003 survey by the UNHCR, almost four out of five respondent states declared that they provided identity and travel documents to stateless persons lawfully and permanently resident on their territory.[58] Nevertheless, for many stateless populations around the world, in particular those with an uncertain immigration status, the acquisition of any documents – for travel or proof of identity or status – is reportedly very difficult and costly, if not impossible.[59] And earlier in this work we have already seen what a problem access to birth and marriage certificates can pose for the stateless.[60] In the upcoming sections we will

---

[54] Recall in particular the quote that "a passport has become a legal as well as a practical necessity" for travel between states. Hurst Hannum, *The Right to Leave and Return in International Law and Practice*, Martinus Nijhoff Publishers, Dordrecht: 1987, page 21.

[55] A similar conclusion was drawn with reference to the situation of refugees: "The refugee, in order to benefit from treatment in accordance with internationally accepted standards, needs to be able to establish vis-à-vis government officials not only his identity but also his refugee character". UNHCR, "Identity documents for Refugees", UN Doc. EC/SCP/33, Geneva, 20 July 1984, paragraph 2.

[56] Hurst Hannum, *The Right to Leave and Return in International Law and Practice*, Martinus Nijhoff Publishers, Dordrecht: 1987, page 21; John Torpey, *The Invention of the Passport. Surveillance, Citizenship and the State*, Cambridge University Press, Cambridge: 2000, page 161; Carmen Tiburcio, "Chapter IX. Public Rights" in *The human rights of aliens under international and comparative law*, Kluwer Law International, The Hague: 2001, page 217.

[57] Such papers may even play a role in the fight against (the perpetuation or continuation of) statelessness and have, therefore, already been dealt with to some extent in Part 2.

[58] UNHCR, *Final report concerning the Questionnaire on statelessness pursuant to the Agenda for Protection,* Geneva: March 2004, page 29. Be reminded that only 74 states completed this questionnaire.

[59] See the description of the situation of, among others, the Bidoon in the United Arab Emirates, the Batwa in Burundi and the stateless ethnic Chinese in Indonesia. Maureen Lynch, *Lives on hold: The human cost of statelessness,* Washington: 2005.

[60] See chapter VII, section 1.

therefore consider how effectively the 1954 Statelessness Convention and other sources of international law address the documentation needs of the stateless.

2.1 1954 Convention relating to the Status of Stateless Persons

In considering access to documentation for the stateless, we come to the final three provisions of the 1954 Convention relating to the Status of Stateless Persons to be discussed. We also will pause for one last time to consider the historical origins of this instrument because it was in fact precisely the issue of documentation that first induced the international community to settle international agreements to deal with refugees and later the stateless. The system of "Nansen certificates" or "Nansen passports", developed in the 1920s, was a means of offering refugees travel papers and proof of identity and status as a refugee.[61] These international documents issued in lieu of a national passport

> represented the first step toward resolving at the supranational level the internal contradictions of a system of movement controls rooted in national membership.[62]

An accompanying task bestowed upon the League of Nations was to offer "surrogate consular protection" to refugees and provide them with other forms of documentation as needed, like proof of civil status or educational qualifications.[63] These arrangements became the inspiration for the provisions of the 1951 Refugee Convention that address the documentation needs of refugees – and these, in turn, were transposed to become articles 25, 27 and 28 of the 1954 Statelessness Convention. The result is that when "read together, these three articles form a single system of protection of the [stateless person's] entitlement to identity and documentation".[64] Working in reverse order, so starting with article 28, the content and scope of these provisions will now be presented.

In order to ensure that stateless persons would be empowered to travel outside their host state, the 1954 Statelessness Convention offers the stateless the opportunity – and in some cases the right – to obtain a Convention Travel Document or "CTD" equivalent to that provided to refugees under the 1951 Refugee Convention.[65] States must provide these papers to a stateless person who is

---

[61] Nehemiah Robinson, *Convention relating to the status of stateless persons - Its history and interpretation*, UNHCR, Geneva: 1955, page 80; Guy Goodwin-Gill, *The Refugee in International Law*, Oxford University Press, Oxford: 2007, pages 513 - 516.

[62] John Torpey, *The Invention of the Passport. Surveillance, Citizenship and the State*, Cambridge University Press, Cambridge: 2000, page 129.

[63] James Hathaway, *The Rights of Refugees Under International Law*, Cambridge University Press, Cambridge: 2005, page 85.

[64] Guy Goodwin-Gill, *The Refugee in International Law*, Oxford University Press, Oxford: 2007, page 512.

[65] Article 28 of the 1954 Convention relating to the Status of Stateless Persons reproduces paragraph 1 of article 28 of the Refugee Convention word-for-word. Paragraph 2 was not transposed to the statelessness instrument for the simple reason that it deals with the recognition of documents issued under previous *refugee* agreements so has no relevance for the situation of the stateless. Note that article 28 of the 1954 Statelessness Convention has attracted just one blanket reservation (Finland) and

lawfully staying in their territory and wishes to make an international journey – be it for business, pleasure or resettlement purposes.[66] In such a case, the issuance of a travel document may only be refused if there are "compelling reasons of national security or public order".[67] Meanwhile, states are free to supply travel documents to stateless persons who are *not* lawfully staying at their own discretion,[68] so it is possible that the benefits of holding a CTD could be extended to any stateless person. One of these benefits is detailed in paragraph 1 of the "Schedule to Article 28" that elaborates the further terms relating to the issuance and recognition of travel documents:

> The travel document referred to in article 28 of this Convention shall indicate that the holder is a stateless person under the terms of the Convention.[69]

So the Convention Travel Document is not only about facilitating travel,[70] it provides evidence of the individual's status as a stateless person and should help to ensure access to the privileges that accompany this status when the stateless person is abroad.[71] It should nevertheless be noted that the documentation of the status of

---

one declaration restricting the scope of application of the provision (Czech Republic, acknowledges a right to travel documents for *permanently* resident stateless persons only).

[66] James Hathaway, *The Rights of Refugees Under International Law*, Cambridge University Press, Cambridge: 2005, page 846.

[67] Article 28 of the 1954 Convention relating to the Status of Stateless Persons. The word "compelling" indicates that the national security or public order issue must be very serious for the stateless person to be denied a travel document and that this restriction to the right to such a document should be interpreted restrictively. Nehemiah Robinson, *Convention relating to the status of stateless persons - Its history and interpretation*, UNHCR, Geneva: 1955, page 82; Guy Goodwin-Gill, *The Refugee in International Law*, Oxford University Press, Oxford: 2007, page 516.

[68] In the final segment of text in article 28 of the 1954 Statelessness Convention, states are explicitly encouraged to provide travel documents where the stateless person in question is unable to acquire such papers from their country of lawful residence.

[69] Paragraph 1, section 1 of the Schedule to Article 28 of the Convention relating to the Status of Stateless Persons.

[70] To that end, Contracting States are obliged to recognise the validity of travel documents issued under the 1954 Statelessness Convention (paragraph 7 of the Schedule to Article 28). See Nehemiah Robinson, *Convention relating to the status of stateless persons - Its history and interpretation*, UNHCR, Geneva: 1955, page 88. Note that paragraph 14 of the Schedule to Article 28 clarifies that the possession of a Convention Travel Document does not in any way affect the authority of states to delineate and impose their own immigration policy, it merely functions in lieu of a passport while the stateless person is still required to meet whatever conditions may be set for admission to the territory of another state. However, as mentioned briefly in chapter X, section 2.2.1, another important quality of the CTD is that, in principle, it vouches for an entitlement to re-enter the territory of the state that issued it: a stateless person may re-enter the issuing state for as long as the CTD is valid, unless the document contains a specific statement to the contrary. Paragraph 13, section 1 of the Schedule to Article 28 of the 1954 Convention relating to the Status of Stateless Persons.

[71] This is a step forward from the terms of the equivalent Schedule attached to the 1951 Refugee Convention that does not specify that the Convention Travel Document issued to refugees should also indicate the possession of refugee status. In reality, although "not designed to be proof of refugee status or any other status" the Convention Travel Document issued to refugees has been widely recognised as evidence of refugee status. See James Hathaway, *The Rights of Refugees Under International Law*,

the stateless person through the provision of travel documents in no way affects "the status of the holder, particularly as regards nationality".[72]

In the event that a stateless person does not acquire a Convention Travel Document – or any other form of travel papers – article 27 of the 1954 Statelessness Convention introduces the guarantee of at least some basic form of identity document:

> the Contracting States shall issue identity papers to any stateless person in their territory who does not possess a valid travel document.

Whereas states are only obliged to issue travel documents to *lawfully staying* stateless persons (and even then there are two approved grounds for non-issuance), this back-up article prescribes an absolute right to an identity document for stateless persons to be issued by the state in which the person is physically present.[73] The two provisions are intended to act in conjunction to ensure that every stateless person benefits from one form of documentation or another.[74] The identity papers envisaged in article 27 fulfil a dual purpose: on the one hand, establishing certain facts relating to the identity of the person while, on the other hand, vouching for his or her status as a stateless person.[75] Again, this second dimension is of paramount importance for it ensures that the stateless are able to effectively lay claim to the entitlements bestowed upon them by virtue of their status. Similarly to the Convention Travel Document, an identity document does not have any affect on the status of the stateless person. Thus, while unlawfully present stateless persons may

---

Cambridge University Press, Cambridge: 2005, pages 851-853; UNHCR and IPU, *Nationality and statelessness. A handbook for parliamentarians*, 2005, page 24.

[72] Paragraph 15 of the Schedule to Article 28 of the 1954 Convention relating to the Status of Stateless Persons. This can be taken to mean that the provision of a travel document does not amount to the conferral of nationality. It is of interest to note that on the model travel document, as set out under the 1954 Statelessness Convention, the following line would be included: "This document is issued solely with a view to providing the holder with a travel document which can serve in lieu of a national passport. It is without prejudice to and in no way affects the holder's nationality". This statement has been transposed word-for-word from the model travel document for refugees (as elaborated under the 1951 Refugee Convention). While it is not difficult to infer that what is meant here is, again, that the issuance of such a document does not result in the attribution of citizenship. However, the wording is peculiar when read in the context of *statelessness*: the document will in no way affect "the holder's nationality" even though the stateless, by definition, do not hold a nationality. In practice, this minor detail is of no consequence, but it is further evidence of the haste in which the provisions of the 1951 Refugee Convention were recycled into the 1954 Statelessness Convention with little added thought to the difference in circumstances between these two groups.

[73] Note that this article has attracted five reservations by state parties: Germany and Latvia elaborating a blanket reservation to the provision while Romania, Slovakia and the Czech Republic have limited the personal scope to those stateless persons who are permanent residents only.

[74] Guy Goodwin-Gill, *The Refugee in International Law*, Oxford University Press, Oxford: 2007, page 515. See on the deliberate separation of the entitlement to travel documents and to identity papers, James Hathaway, *The Rights of Refugees Under International Law*, Cambridge University Press, Cambridge: 2005, page 619.

[75] James Hathaway, *The Rights of Refugees Under International Law*, Cambridge University Press, Cambridge: 2005, pages 620-623.

acquire identity papers on the basis of article 27 of the 1954 Statelessness Convention, these documents do not provide a right to stay in the country.[76]

The 1954 Convention relating to the Status of Stateless Persons is clearly keen to ensure that those individuals who qualify for protection under its terms are provided with documentation attesting to their status as stateless persons. With this in mind, it is once more rather astounding to reflect that the instrument provides absolutely no guidance as to how "stateless person status" is to be established or when it is considered to be proven.[77] When addressing the documentation of stateless persons the Convention skirts once more around this issue, although clearly it is only once a stateless person has been identified as such that his status can be documented. And, realistically, it is only after he has acquired proof of his status that he will be able to invoke the corresponding rights and benefits. This is an issue that undeniably requires further consideration and we will come back to it again in the next chapter.[78]

Lastly we come to article 25 entitled "administrative assistance". Based on the concept of "surrogate consular protection" that existed under the League of Nations refugee regime,[79] this article allows stateless persons to enjoy services and obtain a range of other sorts of documents that usually require the involvement of the state of nationality. As examples of what is deemed to fall within the scope of this article, Robinson lists:

> Services which nationals of a country ordinarily receive from their juridical, administrative or consular authorities [including issuance] of documents relating to their family position (birth, marriage, adoption, death, or divorce certificates) or their special position (school or professional certificates), certifications (copies or translations of documents, regularity of documents or their conformity with the law of the country) [and] identity.[80]

Such services and related documentation shall be provided by (or through) the state in which the stateless person is residing.[81] The article is worded in such a way as to

[76] Nehemiah Robinson, *Convention relating to the status of stateless persons - Its history and interpretation*, UNHCR, Geneva: 1955, page 79. The eligibility of unlawfully present stateless persons to identity documents is nevertheless crucial since several of the rights elaborated in the 1954 Statelessness Convention are accrued on the basis of statelessness status or simple presence alone. See also James Hathaway, *The Rights of Refugees Under International Law*, Cambridge University Press, Cambridge: 2005, page 626; UNHCR and IPU, *Nationality and statelessness. A handbook for parliamentarians*, 2005, page 24.

[77] Recall chapter IX, section 3.

[78] Chapter XIII, section 4.

[79] Above at note 61. See also James Hathaway, *The Rights of Refugees Under International Law*, Cambridge University Press, Cambridge: 2005, page 94.

[80] Nehemiah Robinson, *Convention relating to the status of stateless persons - Its history and interpretation*, UNHCR, Geneva: 1955, page 74.

[81] Note that this is a move away from the system in place under the League of Nations whereby it was the League of Nations High Commissioner for Refugees that fulfilled this role. See James Hathaway, *The Rights of Refugees Under International Law*, Cambridge University Press, Cambridge: 2005, pages 627-628. Nine states have elaborated reservations to – all or part of – article 25 of the 1954 Statelessness Convention although it is important to observe that these are mainly common law

suggest that stateless persons may invoke its terms at a low level of attachment – habitual residence or even lawful presence is not required, the reference to the state of *residence* of the stateless merely serves to settle the question of jurisdiction for the implementation of this norm.[82] The documents issued "shall stand in stead of the official documents" which they serve to replace and are presumed to establish the correct facts unless evidence to the contrary surfaces.[83] On the basis of this provision it should be possible for any pressing documentary needs of the stateless to be satisfied. Overall then, the 1954 Statelessness Convention responds well to this particular "special need" of the stateless, providing opportunities for accessing travel and identity papers as well as a host of other documents. Time now, to look to other areas of international law to see how they compare and whether any additional guarantees can be found.

2.2 International (human rights) law

Within the human rights field, recognition has also been given to the importance of documentation. In particular, human rights bodies have acknowledged the vital role that documentation plays in claiming rights-related entitlements. The following quote from a report by the Committee on Economic, Social and Cultural Rights is a case in point:

> The Committee is concerned that the non-issue of personal documentation to refugees and asylum-seekers by the State authorities seriously hinders their enjoyment of economic, social and cultural rights, including the rights to work, health and education.[84]

The Committee confirms that access to various rights and services is not just affected by the fact of being a refugee or asylum seeking – or a stateless person - but also by the lack of documentation that commonly afflicts them. However, nowhere does any human rights instrument proclaim an all-encompassing right to documentation. Instead, this question has been addressed to one extent or another on the basis of a number of individual norms. We have seen evidence of this in the consideration of the freedom of international movement and the attention paid within that context to the issue of travel papers.[85] In addition, we have discovered the value attributed to the documentation of certain events or facts such as through

---

countries that, as such, maintain a system of affidavits for establishing these facts and do not require the documents involved. See also Guy Goodwin-Gill, *The Refugee in International Law*, Oxford University Press, Oxford: 2007, page 514.

[82] James Hathaway, *The Rights of Refugees Under International Law*, Cambridge University Press, Cambridge: 2005, pages 637-639.

[83] Article 25, paragraph 3 of the Convention relating to the Status of Stateless Persons. See also Nehemiah Robinson, *Convention relating to the status of stateless persons - Its history and interpretation*, UNHCR, Geneva: 1955, page 77.

[84] ESC Committee, *Concluding Observations: Venezuela*, E/2002/22, New York and Geneva: 2001, para. 84. See also Committee on the Rights of the Child, *Concluding Observations*: *Thailand,* CRC/C/80, Geneva: 1998 35, para. 71; *Kyrgyzstan,* CRC/C/97, Geneva: 2000, paras. 320-321; *Mauritania,* CRC/C/111, Geneva: 2001, paras. 74-75; *Lebanon,* CRC/C/114, Geneva: 2002, para. 82.

[85] See chapter X, section 2.2.

the registration and certification of births and marriages.[86] This means that we have already uncovered and discussed several of the relevant standards. In this section, we will be recalling what has been said about these norms and taking a fresh overall look at how the human rights regime addresses the documentation needs faced by the stateless.

Let us begin once more with access to travel documents. This issue was brought to the fore by the Human Rights Committee in its General Comment on the freedom of movement where a right to travel documents was coupled to the right to leave any country, including one's own.[87] We can recall from chapter X, section 2.2.2 that the Committee acknowledged the importance of travel documents for movement between states and in consequence declared that "the right to leave a country must include the right to obtain the necessary travel documents".[88] Although in the same paragraph, the Committee explicitly refers to passports and acknowledges that "the issuing of passports is *normally incumbent* on the State of nationality of the individual",[89] it does not rule out the possibility that a state may be required to offer travel documents to non-nationals in order to guarantee their right to leave.[90] Indeed, since the right to leave – as opposed to the right to enter – is very clearly granted to everyone in respect of any state,[91] the stateless should also be able to invoke the relevant provisions in order to obtain travel documents.[92] Restrictions may only be placed on the right to leave and thereby also on the issuance of travel documents if they are "necessary to protect national security,

---

[86] Important also with a view to preventing statelessness. See chapter VII, section 1.2.

[87] The right to leave is espoused in article 13, paragraph 2 of the Universal Declaration of Human Rights; article 12, paragraph 2 of the International Covenant on Civil and Political Rights; article 2, paragraph 2 of the Fourth Protocol to the European Convention on Human Rights; Article 22, aparagraph 2 of the American Convention on Human Rights; article 12, paragraph 2 of the African Charter on Human and Peoples' Rights. See also article 5, paragraph (d)(ii) of the Convention on the Elimination of All Forms of Racial Discrimination and article 8, paragraph 2 of the Convention on the Protection of All Migrant Workers and Members of Their Families.

[88] Human Rights Committee, *CCPR General Comment No. 27: Freedom of movement,* Geneva: 2 November 1999, para. 9. See also the "Uruguayan passport cases" before the Human Rights Committee, as cited in Sarah Joseph; Jenny Schultz; Melissa Castan, *The International Covenant on Civil and Political Rights. Cases, Materials and Commentary*, Oxford University Press, Oxford: 2000, pages 250-251. Human Rights Committee, *Concluding Observations: Belarus,* A/47/40, Geneva: 1992, para. 560; *Mongolia,* A/47/40, Geneva: 1992, para. 601; *Azerbaijan,* A/49/40 vol. I, Geneva: 1994, para. 300; *Zimbabwe,* A/53/40 vol. I, Geneva: 1998, para. 228. Indeed, "the refusal to issue travel documents is permissible only in those special circumstances in which the individual's right to travel may be restricted". Hurst Hannum, *The Right to Leave and Return in International Law and Practice*, Martinus Nijhoff Publishers, Dordrecht: 1987, page 21.

[89] Emphasis added, Human Rights Committee, *CCPR General Comment No. 27: Freedom of movement,* Geneva: 2 November 1999, para. 9.

[90] See in this respect also Committee on the Elimination of Racial Discrimination, *Concluding Observations: Latvia,* A/54/18, New York: 1999, para. 398.

[91] Hurst Hannum, *The Right to Leave and Return in International Law and Practice*, Martinus Nijhoff Publishers, Dordrecht: 1987, page 60.

[92] Whether they are subsequently able to actually travel to another state will nevertheless depend upon whether they meet the conditions set by that state's domestic immigration law. See chapter X, section 2.2.2.

public order, public health or morals and the rights and freedoms of others".[93] None of these grounds can be invoked in order to justify a blanket refusal to issue travel documents to stateless persons. The jurisprudence of the Human Rights Committee confirms that a refusal, without proper justification, of a travel document violates the terms of the International Covenant on Civil and Political Rights.[94] At the same time, the Committee noted that where the situation involved a citizen who is resident abroad – whose status there is that of a non-national – both the country of citizenship *and* the country of residence have a duty to protect his right to leave and coinciding right to travel documents.[95] It is therefore conceivable to argue that the country of residence of a stateless person, or the country identified as "his own country" for the purposes of the right to (re)enter the state,[96] could be held accountable for the provision of travel documents. However, an unambiguous norm prescribing such a duty towards the stateless has yet to crystallise and with the current focus of human rights bodies on the role of the state of nationality in these matters, the reality is that it may still be difficult for the stateless to rely on human rights instruments for access to a travel document.

The contribution that the human rights regime can make to ensuring the acquisition of identity documents by the stateless is even less clear. It may be possible, for example, to distil a right to identity papers for children at least from the guarantee in the Convention on the Rights of the Child relating to the preservation of identity.[97] More generally, proof of identity may also be seen as a component of the recognition of legal personhood.[98] And it is true that, as the citation above illustrated, organs such as the Committee on the Rights of the Child and the ESC Committee have expressed criticism on the non-issuance of identity

---

[93] Article 12, paragraph 3 of the International Covenant on Civil and Political Rights. The Human Rights Committee has actively monitored the implementation of these restrictions, commenting on policies relating to the issuance of passports in many states. See for example, Human Rights Committee, *Concluding Observations: Azerbaijan,* A/49/40 vol. I, Geneva: 1994, para. 300; *Morocco,* A/55/40 vol. I, Geneva: 2000, para. 114; *Syrian Arab Republic,* A/56/40 vol. I, Geneva: 2001, para. 81 (21). See also Colin Harvey; Robert Barnidge, 'Human Rights, Free Movement, and the Right to Leave in International Law', in *International Journal of Refugee Law,* Vol. 19, 2007, page 6.

[94] See, for example, Human Rights Committee, *Case of El Ghar v. Libyan Arab Jamahiriya,* 1107/2002, A/60/40 vol. II, Geneva: 2 November 2004, para. 8.

[95] Human Rights Committee, *Case of Martins v. Uruguay,* R.13/57, A/37/49, Geneva: 23 March 1982, para. 7; *Case of Lichtensztejn v. Uruguay,* R.19/77, A/38/40, Geneva: 3 March 1983, paras. 6.1 and 8.3. See for a full discussion of these and other "Uruguayan passport cases", Sarah Joseph; Jenny Schultz; Melissa Castan, *The International Covenant on Civil and Political Rights. Cases, Materials and Commentary,* Oxford University Press, Oxford: 2000, pages 250-251; Colin Harvey; Robert Barnidge, 'Human Rights, Free Movement, and the Right to Leave in International Law', in *International Journal of Refugee Law,* Vol. 19, 2007, pages 7-9. See also the consideration of state party reports by the Human Rights Committee, for instance in *Concluding Observations: Syrian Arab Republic,* CCPR, A/56/40, Geneva: 2001, paragraph 81 (21).

[96] Chapter X, section 2.2.2.

[97] Under article 8 of the Convention on the Rights of the Child, "States Parties undertake to respect the right of the child to preserve his or her identity, including nationality, name and family relations as recognized by law without unlawful interference". See also Committee on the Rights of the Child, *Concluding Observations: Rwanda,* CRC/C/140, Geneva: 2004 36, paras. 189-192.

[98] See, for instance, Committee on the Rights of the Child, *General Comment 3: HIV/AIDS and the Rights of the Child,* CRC/GC/2003/3, Geneva: 17 March 2003, para. 32.

documents to certain categories of individuals, including refugees.[99] However, the general association of identity documents with access to rights and services has not yielded the promulgation of a concrete right to such papers in any human rights instrument. In fact, when reflecting on the lack of documentation of refugees, the UN treaty bodies appear to rely on the provisions of the 1951 Refugee Convention as the legal foundation for access to identity papers.[100] There is certainly no other legal basis for the acquisition of (identity) papers attesting to statelessness status than the 1954 Statelessness Convention itself – the very instrument that brings this status into being. It is not without reason then that the tailor-made refugee and statelessness instruments were so deliberate in their attention to documentation needs. For identity papers – and to a large extent also travel documents – the importance of regulating these matters through a specially-designed legal regime seems not to have lost its significance even with the developments traced in human rights law.[101]

An area in which contemporary human rights law does provide comprehensive protection, including for the stateless, is with respect to the issuance of documentation relating to births and marriages. In chapter VII we uncovered a global consensus on the right to birth registration – including the issuance of a birth certificate – as a right of *every* child, regardless of (immigration) status or nationality.[102] Equally, although less attention has been paid to the right to marriage registration and documentation, where this is espoused there is no indication that the stateless could not benefit from the relevant norms.[103] Yet, the documentation of births and marriages were just two examples of the types of assistance that the stateless could rely on under article 25 of the 1954 Statelessness Convention. The certification of educational or professional qualifications and the translation of official documents are matters for which a basis for protection under human rights law is far less apparent. No doubt where the lack of (recognition of) requisite documents impedes stateless persons' access to work, (further) education or other rights, this subject may be taken up in the overall assessment of the conformity of

---

[99] See for example Committee on the Rights of the Child, *Concluding Observations: Kyrgyzstan,* CRC/C/97, Geneva: 2000, paras. 320-321 and ESC Committee, *Concluding Observations: Venezuela,* E/2002/22, New York and Geneva: 2001, para. 84.

[100] See for example Committee on the Rights of the Child, *Concluding Observations: Lebanon,* CRC/C/114, Geneva: 2002, para. 82.

[101] Nevertheless, the human rights framework does appear to provide new avenues for enforcing the right to documentation as espoused under the 1954 Statelessness Convention – the human rights treaty bodies may simply remind states of their commitments under this instrument in the same way as they have taken to referring to the 1951 Convention relating to the Status of Refugees. We will be looking more closely at the opportunities for enforcement of the various norms for the protection of statelessness in chapter XIII, section 4.

[102] Recall for example Committee on the Rights of the Child, *Concluding observations: Bosnia and Herzegovina,* CRC/C/15/Add.259, Geneva: 2005, para. 33; Committee on the Rights of the Child, *General Comment No.6: Treatment of unaccompanied and separated children outside their country of origin,* Geneva: 1 September 2005, para. 12; and article 29 of the Migrant Workers Convention.

[103] Recall in this respect UN Committee on the Elimination of Discrimination Against Women, *General Recommendation 21: Equality in marriage and family relations,* A/49/38 (1994) at para. 39; Committee on the Elimination of Discrimination Against Women, *Concluding Observations: Namibia,* A/52/38/Rev.1 Part II, New York: 1997, paras. 110 and 125; *India,* A/55/38 part I, New York: 2000, para. 62.

the situation with human rights norms. But to date, this question has yet to be raised and it is fair to conclude that the 1954 Statelessness Convention retains its value on this point.

3 Special needs for which the 1954 Statelessness Convention has not provided

So far in this chapter we have seen that in drafting the 1954 Statelessness Convention governments not only considered the access of the stateless to various (human) rights, but also took notice of certain special needs which arise from the very circumstances of this vulnerable group. However, there is one issue that can be considered to fall within this category of "special needs" for which the statelessness instrument neglected to provide: diplomatic protection. As we introduced the concept and function of nationality in chapter IX, we already broached the subject of diplomatic protection as one of the areas of law for which citizenship has particular importance. Indeed, we discovered that an exceptional element of the bond of nationality is the right that it creates on the part of the state to seek redress for any injury committed against one of its citizenry.[104] If local remedies have not provided adequate means for redressing the injury, diplomatic protection provides a route to nevertheless guaranteeing that the situation is correctly resolved.[105] Diplomatic protection is thus an important mechanism in ensuring that nationals receive fair and proper treatment abroad.

Although, with the advent of human rights law - espousing rights to the benefit of everyone and introducing various enforcement mechanisms - there is a reduced need for diplomatic protection, it is of enduring relevance to the protection of the interests of non-nationals.[106] And there are certainly conceivable scenarios, even real-life cases, in which diplomatic protection could play an important role in helping stateless persons to assert their rights. For instance, following the partition and independence of Eritrea from Ethiopia and the accompanying hostilities, property confiscations and expulsions, a Claims Commission was established to

> decide through binding arbitration all claims for loss, damage or injury by one Government against the other, and by nationals [...] of one party against the

[104] Yaffa Zilberschats, "Chapter 2 - Citizenship and International Law" in *The Human Right to Citizenship*, Transnational Publishers, Ardsley, NY: 2002, page 36; Guy Goodwin Gill, "The rights of refugees and stateless persons" in Saksena (ed) *Human rights perspectives & challenges (in 1900's and beyond)*, Lancers Books, New Delhi: 1994, page 392; Ruth Donner, "Chapter 1: Nationality Law in the Context of Public International Law" in *The Regulation of Nationality in International Law*, Transnational Publishers, New York: 1994, page 19. Recall, as noted in chapter IX, that diplomatic protection is generally considered to be aright of the state, rather than a right of the individual.

[105] For a discussion of the exhaustion of local remedies as a precondition to the exercise of diplomatic protection, see Ian Brownlie, *Principles of Public International Law*, Oxford University Press, Oxford: 2003, pages 472-481.

[106] Carmen Tiburcio, "Conclusion" in *The human rights of aliens under international and comparative law*, Kluwer Law International, The Hague: 2001, page 267; International Law Commission, *Report to the General Assembly on the work of the fiftieth session,* Yearbook 1998, Volume II, Part 2, pages 46-47.

> Government of the other party or entities owned or controlled by the other party.[107]

Since the same circumstances of hostilities, expulsions and state succession also contributed to nationality disputes and cases of statelessness, ensuring that such persons were also able to benefit from diplomatic protection was fundamental to making sure that all individuals who were wronged by the conflict were able to benefit from the facilities offered by this Claim Commission.[108]

The difficulty is that the long-standing doctrine of diplomatic protection is such that states may *only* exercise it with respect to their nationals.[109] This approach would exclude stateless persons outright, yet international tribunals have, in the past, often elected to follow this route of caution and dismiss any claim where the bond of nationality is either not present or insufficiently proven. In a particularly remarkable ruling in 1931, the *Dickson Car Wheel Company v. United Mexican States* case, an international arbitration panel even declared that

> a state [...] does not commit an international delinquency in inflicting an injury upon an individual lacking nationality, and consequently, no State is empowered to intervene or complain on his behalf either before or after the injury.[110]

In other instances, most notably the widely-cited *Nottebohm* ruling, courts have taken this matter further still, by asking not only if nationality is present but also testing the substance of that nationality: Friedrich Nottebohm's factual ties with Liechtenstein were determined to be insufficient for his Liechtenstein nationality to

---

[107] Article 5, paragraph 1 of the Agreement Between the Government of the Federal Democratic Republic of Ethiopia and the Government of the State of Eritrea, signed in Algiers, 22 December 2000.

[108] See also Human Rights Watch, *The Horn of Africa War: Mass Expulsions and the Nationality Issue,* 30 January 2003.

[109] "A normal and important function of nationality is to establish the legal interest of a state when nationals [...] receive injury or loss at the hands of another state. The subject-matter of the claim is the individual and his property: the claim is that of the state. Thus if the plaintiff state cannot establish the nationality of the claim, the claim is inadmissible because of the absence of any legal interest of the claimant". Ian Brownlie, *Principles of Public International Law*, Oxford University Press, Oxford: 2003, pages 459-460. See also Permanent Court of International Justice, *Panevezys-Saldutiskis Railway case,* P.C.I.J. Series A/B, No. 76, 28 February 1939; Haro van Panhuys, "Chapter VIII: The Traditional Function of Nationality in International Law (A Digest)" in *The Role of Nationality in International Law*, A.W. Sijthoff's Uitgeversmaatschappij, Leiden: 1959, pages 182-183; Paul Weis, *Nationality and Statelessness in International Law*, Kluwer Academic Publishers Group, Dordrecht: 1979, pages 32-35; Carmen Tiburcio, "Chapter III. Development of the Treatment of Aliens from Diplomatic Protection to Human Rights" in *The human rights of aliens under international and comparative law*, Kluwer Law International, The Hague: 2001, pages 37-39.

[110] *Dickson Car Wheel Co. (USA) v. United Mexican States*, UNRIAA, vol. IV, (Sales No. 1951.V.1), July 1931, page 678. See also Johannes Chan, 'The Right to a Nationality as a Human Right - The Current Trend Towards Recognition', in *Human Rights Law Journal,* Vol. 12, 1991, page 9; Curtis Doebbler, 'A Human Rights Approach to Statelessness in the Middle East', in *Leiden Journal of International Law,* Vol. 15, 2002, page 530; International Law Commission, *Report of the 54th Session,* UN General Assembly Official Records, 57th Session, Supplement No. 10, A/57/10, New York 2002, page 188.

be recognised for the purposes of international law and the exercise of diplomatic protection.[111] The International Court of Justice hereby ruled in favour of statelessness – at least for the purposes of international relations – and against protection. This finding "underlines how deeply rooted, for the admissibility of diplomatic protection, is the requirement that the person involved must be a full-fledged member of the population of the complainant state".[112]

However there are understood to be some exceptions to the general rule requiring the presence of a bond of nationality, resting on a "genuine link", for the exercise of diplomatic protection. In particular, "a right to protection of non-nationals may arise from treaty or an *ad hoc* arrangement establishing an agency".[113] Or in other words:

> Protection may be accorded and is in fact granted to non-nationals, but the exercise of such protection need be recognised by other states only if it is consistent with international custom or treaties. Protection of nationals is distinct from any such protection accorded to non-nationals in that it is unconditional, and unlimited as to time.[114]

From the outset, the 1954 Convention relating to the Status of Stateless Persons had the potential to provide just such a special arrangement. During the drafting of the document a Belgian proposal would have resulted in an explicit reference to the diplomatic protection of stateless persons, in the following terms: "Each Contracting State shall be entitled to ensure the protection of both the property and the person of stateless persons domiciled or resident in its territory". If adopted this amendment would have established the legal basis for the exercise of diplomatic protection by states on behalf of stateless persons – thus in the absence of the bond of nationality. The proposal received a mixed review and was eventually narrowly rejected by vote.[115] In the end, the 1954 Statelessness Convention mentions

---

[111] International Court of Justice, *"Nottebohm Case" (Liechtenstein v. Guatamala)*, 1953. See also Ruth Donner, "Chapter 2: The Principle of the "Link" in Nationality Law" in *The Regulation of Nationality in International Law*, Transnational Publishers, New York: 1994, pages 59-64; Ian Brownlie, *Principles of Public International Law*, Oxford University Press, Oxford: 2003, pages 396-406.

[112] Haro van Panhuys, "Chapter VIII: The Traditional Function of Nationality in International Law (A Digest)" in *The Role of Nationality in International Law*, A.W. Sijthoff's Uitgeversmaatschappij, Leiden: 1959, page 187.

[113] Richard Lillich, *The human rights of aliens in contemporary international law*, Manchester University Press, Manchester: 1984, page 64; Ian Brownlie, *Principles of Public International Law*, Oxford University Press, Oxford: 2003, page 391. See, for instance, article 20 of the Treaty Establishing the European Community which declares that "Every citizen of the Union shall, in the territory of a third country in which the Member State of which he is a national is not represented, be entitled to protection by the diplomatic or consular authorities of any Member State, on the same conditions as the nationals of that State".

[114] Paul Weis, *Nationality and Statelessness in International Law*, Kluwer Academic Publishers Group, Dordrecht: 1979, page 43. Weis also provides a number of historic examples of specific arrangements whereby non-nationals could be granted diplomatic protection by a state "in lieu of protection by the State of nationality". See ibid, pages 39-40.

[115] The votes came in as 5 against, 4 in favour and 4 abstentions. See for the presentation of this question Nehemiah Robinson, *Convention relating to the status of stateless persons - Its history and interpretation*, UNHCR, Geneva: 1955, page 92.

diplomatic protection only in the context of the issuance of travel documents where it declares that the delivery of such a document "does not in any way entitle the holder to the protection of the diplomatic or consular authorities of the country of issue, and does not *ipso facto* confer on these authorities a right of protection".[116] The Convention thereby defers the question back to the states involved, neither providing a legal basis for, nor necessarily outlawing, the exercise of diplomatic protection.[117] The time was clearly not yet ripe for more decisive action on this point. Nor do contemporary human rights instruments offer any answers to this dilemma.[118]

Nevertheless, today there are signs that the doctrine of diplomatic protection is developing to be more conducive to the needs of the stateless. This is especially evident in the work that has been taken up by the International Law Commission over the last decade. Commencing in 1997, the ILC has undertaken a (renewed) attempt to codify the customary norms that relate to diplomatic protection.[119] Throughout its work, the ILC clearly acknowledges the importance of nationality as the principle link through which jurisdiction to exercise diplomatic protection is created. However, it also confirms the existence of exceptions to this rule of thumb and gives substantial thought to the position of the stateless (and refugees). In particular, the ILC recalls the 1931 ruling cited above where it was "held that a stateless person could not be the beneficiary of diplomatic protection" before going on to declare that "this dictum no longer reflects the accurate position of international law for both stateless persons and refugees".[120] From the outset, the

---

[116] Paragraph 16 of the Schedule to article 28 of the 1954 Convention relating to the Status of Stateless Persons.

[117] "While the issue of a travel document by the authorities of a state does not *per se* authorise the consular or diplomatic representatives of that state to provide protection to the stateless person abroad during his travel, there is no prohibition to do so, if these authorities do desire and the states in which the stateless person travels do not object thereto". Nehemiah Robinson, *Convention relating to the status of stateless persons - Its history and interpretation*, UNHCR, Geneva: 1955, page 91. See also Guy Goodwin-Gill, *The Refugee in International Law*, Oxford University Press, Oxford: 2007, pages 519-520.

[118] The Migrant Workers Convention is the only instrument that mentions diplomatic protection but it does not settle the question of access to diplomatic protection for (particular categories of) non-nationals. See article 23 of the Migrant Workers Convention. Recall further that the human rights regime has developed its own monitoring and enforcement mechanisms – that are not dependent on state intervention – and is, therefore, not reliant on the system of diplomatic protection.

[119] The International Law Commission placed the subject of diplomatic protection on its agenda in 1996, a decision that was validated by the UN General Assembly later the same year in Resolution 51/160 of 16 December 1996 – and work got underway the following year. For a discussion of previous, unsuccessful attempts by the ILC to codify the rules relating to diplomatic protection – as well as the elaboration of draft norms relating to state responsibility generally - see Carmen Tiburcio, "Chapter III. Development of the Treatment of Aliens from Diplomatic Protection to Human Rights" in *The human rights of aliens under international and comparative law*, Kluwer Law International, The Hague: 2001, pages 53-57.

[120] Commentary to article 8 of the Draft Articles on Diplomatic Protection, International Law Commission, *Report of the work of its 58th Session,* UN General Assembly Official Records, 61st Session, Supplement No. 10, A/61/10, New York 2006, page 48. Interestingly, this vision of the current state of international law is founded in particular on the development of instruments to protect the rights and interests of the stateless (and refugees), such as the 1961 Convention on the Reduction of Statelessness and the 1954 Convention relating to the Status of Stateless Persons.

ILC has therefore included a provision dealing with access to diplomatic protection for the stateless in the draft articles that it prepared on the subject.[121] The article, as adopted by the ILC and submitted to the UN General Assembly for consideration reads:

> A state may exercise diplomatic protection in respect of a stateless person who, at the date of injury and at the date of the official presentation of the claim, is lawfully and habitually resident in that state.[122]

The ILC correctly recognises that "lawful and habitual residence" is a stringent condition and that some individuals will subsequently still go without protection but considers this to be a legitimate requirement in view of the exceptional position of this "new" rule with regard to the overall doctrine of diplomatic protection. This is a regrettable, but indeed perhaps currently necessary, constraint on the protection offered.

Once lawful and habitual residence is attained, the article will effectively place such stateless persons on a par with nationals. Firstly, the same temporal requirement must be met: the connection of nationality, or in this case lawful and habitual residence, must be present at both the time that the injury is committed and the time that the claim is made. And secondly, it remains within the discretion of states to decide whether or not to actually accord diplomatic protection (encapsulated by the use of the word "may").[123] To date, the response of governments to this "progressive development of the law"[124] have been unanimously positive and encouraging.[125] So if the articles are formally adopted in their present state, for example as recommended by the ILC in the form of a Convention on Diplomatic Protection,[126] this particular provision is unlikely to meet much resistance. But until such a time, the question of access to diplomatic protection for the stateless will remain uncertain. Just as the 1954 Statelessness Convention declared: there is nothing to stop states presenting a claim in reaction to an injury suffered by a stateless person, but there is also nothing to stop the respondent state from attempting to have the claim dismissed on the grounds of the

[121] The first draft of this provision can be found in International Law Commission, *Report on the work of its 52nd Session,* UN General Assembly Official Records, 56th Session, Supplement No. 10, A/55/10, New York 2000, page 83.

[122] Article 8, paragraph 1 of the Draft Articles on Diplomatic Protection, International Law Commission, *Report of the work of its 58th Session,* UN General Assembly Official Records, 61st Session, Supplement No. 10, A/61/10, New York 2006 page 47. Note that for the purposes of defining statelessness in order to implement this provision, reference is made in the commentary to the draft article to the definition espoused in the 1954 Statelessness Convention which is said to be "considered as having acquired a customary nature".

[123] See Commentary to article 8 of the Draft Articles on Diplomatic Protection, International Law Commission, *Report of the work of its 58th Session,* UN General Assembly Official Records, 61st Session, Supplement No. 10, A/61/10, New York 2006, pages 48-51.

[124] In addressing access to diplomatic protection for the stateless – and refugees - the International Law Commission is taking a step beyond the existing customary norms relating to diplomatic protection.

[125] International Law Commission, *Diplomatic Protection – Comments and observations received from governments,* UN Doc. A/CN.4/561, 26 January 2006, pages 24-26.

[126] International Law Commission, *Report of the work of its 58th Session,* UN General Assembly Official Records, 61st Session, Supplement No. 10, A/61/10, New York 2006, page 15.

absence of the legal connection of nationality. Considering the support expressed for the draft article on diplomatic protection of stateless persons (as discussed above), we can assume that it will become increasingly uncommon for states to object to the exercise of diplomatic protection by a state on behalf of their resident stateless population.[127] Yet as it stands, there is no rule of international customary or treaty law that establishes such a move as an irrefutable right of the state concerned.

4 Conclusion

As an instrument purposefully crafted to address the difficulties that arise for individuals who find themselves without a nationality, expectations were high going into this chapter that the 1954 Convention relating to the Status of Stateless Persons would offer appropriate solutions to the "special needs" of the stateless. In the end, the convention receives a mixed report in this respect. On the one hand, this chapter identified an area in which the 1954 Statelessness Convention very clearly retains its value, even in the light of contemporary international (human rights) law: it decisively addresses the problem of obtaining various forms of documentation and this, in turn, can have a positive knock-on effect on the enjoyment of many other rights and facilities. On the other hand, the 1954 Statelessness Convention missed two important opportunities: dealing hesitantly with the question of naturalisation – and thereby the very resolution of statelessness - and failing to tackle the issue of diplomatic protection. Let us reflect briefly upon (the implications of) these observations.

It has long been acknowledged that "the problem of *existing* statelessness has so many grave political, social and even racial aspects that it should be treated with utmost care".[128] Thus, addressing the *statelessness* of stateless persons or attributing a right to (be considered for) naturalisation is a complex matter. We found evidence of this in the discovery that not only did the international community decline an initiative to set down specific rules relating to the resolution of *existing* cases of statelessness, but the standard on the naturalisation of stateless persons delineated by the 1954 Statelessness Convention is largely vague and

[127] Evidence to support this view can already, for instance, be found in the *Purulia arms case* dating from the late 1990s whereby Latvia provided diplomatic protection to five stateless residents for the purposes of a dispute with the authorities of India, in Ineta Ziemele, *State Continuity and Nationality: The Baltic States and Russia. Past, Present and Future as Defined by International Law*, Martinus Nijhoff Publishers, Leiden: 2005, page 165. Another example is provided by the rules surrounding the Eritrea-Ethiopia Claims Commission, introduced above, whereby "in appropriate cases, each party may file claims on behalf of persons of Eritrean or Ethiopian origin who may not be its nationals [and] such claims shall be considered by the Commission on the same basis as claims submitted on behalf of that party's nationals". Article 5, paragraph 9 of the Agreement Between the Government of the Federal Democratic Republic of Ethiopia and the Government of the State of Eritrea, signed in Algiers, 22 December 2000. This approach was clearly prompted by the nationality disputes surrounding and following the independence of Eritrea. See also Human Rights Watch, *The Horn of Africa War: Mass Expulsions and the Nationality Issue*, 30 January 2003.

[128] Emphasis added. Roberto Córdova, *Nationality, Including Statelessness. Third Report on the Elimination or Reduction of Statelessness by Roberto Córdova, Special Rapporteur*, A/CN.4/81, New York: 11 March 1954, page 27.

discretionary. Meanwhile, although it is possible to find evidence of the development within the human rights field of a right to (facilitated) naturalisation for the stateless, this issue is, as yet, far from settled. Human rights standards do already prevent states from deliberately targeting the stateless with a restrictive naturalisation policy or from upholding manifestly unreasonable impediments. However, there are no universally accepted, palpable, positive rules establishing the conditions under which the stateless can claim a right to naturalisation and which additional requirements may or may not be set by the state in this context. Moreover, since the current trend is towards recognition of a right to commence naturalisation proceedings that is contingent upon attaining (a certain period of) lawful and habitual residence, for this to provide a real answer to existing cases of statelessness, something must be done to address the enduring issue of access to a lawful immigration status.[129]

So, where to from here? In order to provide an effective response to the "special need" of the stateless that is their very lack of nationality, more will have to be done to develop a truly credible solution. In view of the finding that efforts to prevent statelessness are not yet fool-proof and what is now known about the protracted nature of statelessness, it is clear that such a solution is overdue. Now is therefore the time to reflect upon the advances that human rights law has made over the last 50 years in dealing with access to naturalisation and to revive discussion on the resolution of existing statelessness by building upon these foundations. The most promising source of concrete standards for naturalisation is the European Convention on Nationality and this could be used as a basis for further developing stateless-specific norms. Renewed thought must also be given to the questions raised by the problem of access to residence as a basic prerequisite for access to naturalisation and consideration should be given to the elaboration of norms that allow other "genuine links" to be translated into the bond of citizenship.[130] In addition, new avenues could be investigated, as we now see in the context of avoiding statelessness in the event of state succession,[131] such as the possibility of introducing international consultation or even arbitration[132] as a tool to identifying an appropriate connection to open up a route to naturalisation. Keep in mind that at all times, these possibilities should be seen in parallel to the opportunities offered by the standards relating to the prevention of statelessness for tackling existing cases of statelessness through the (retrospective) conferral or reinstatement of nationality.

---

[129] This was raised in chapter X.

[130] It may be helpful to go back to the draft instruments on the reduction or elimination of *present* statelessness prepared by Roberto Córdova in the 1950s and reconsider the feasibility of suggestions made there in the light of more recent developments. See Roberto Córdova, *Nationality, Including Statelessness. Third Report on the Elimination or Reduction of Statelessness by Roberto Córdova, Special Rapporteur,* A/CN.4/81, New York: 11 March 1954.

[131] See the provisions on international consultation and exchange of information in the ILC Draft Articles on Nationality of Natural Persons in relation to the Succession of States and the Council of Europe Convention on the avoidance of statelessness in relation to State succession as discussed in chapter VI, section 3.

[132] Manley Hudson, *Report on Nationality, including Statelessness,* A/CN.4/50, 21 February 1952, page 58.

The other concern that the tailor-made statelessness instrument neglects to tackle with sufficient vigour is diplomatic protection. It is deeply regrettable that a provision that would have provided the legal basis needed for states to exercise diplomatic protection on behalf of a stateless person was excluded from the final text of the 1954 Statelessness Convention. As it stands, the Convention simply does not pronounce either way on the matter. Presently, international law does not allow states to rely on an unequivocal right to exercise diplomatic protection in respect of an injury committed against a stateless person and the claim may simply be quashed on the grounds of the absence of the connection of nationality. This is a pity since diplomatic protection can be a helpful addition to the arsenal of available remedies for the protection of individual rights. The draft article presented by the International Law Commission would rectify this situation in favour of the protection of the stateless - at least for those who can establish lawful and habitual residence – by establishing a legal basis for the claim. Therefore, if other considerations (further) delay the adoption of an instrument dealing with diplomatic protection in its entirety,[133] it would be advisable for the international community to push ahead with the codification of at least the basic contours of these norms and specifically approve the provision dealing with stateless persons. Alternatively - or indeed additionally - the issue of diplomatic protection of the stateless could be taken up elsewhere, for example within an instrument updating and supplementing the protection offered to the stateless under the 1954 Statelessness Convention.[134]

As mentioned at the beginning of this section, the 1954 Statelessness Convention fares much better on the matter of documentation. The instrument offers a basic guarantee of identity papers for *all* stateless persons – documents to attest not only to the personal particulars of the holder, but also to his or her stateless status. In addition, stateless persons may be able to obtain travel documents under the provisions of the 1954 Statelessness Convention – lawfully staying stateless persons can even invoke a right to such documents – and these papers again serve both to facilitate travel *and* to vouch for the statelessness of the individual. Moreover, thanks to the same Convention the stateless can also rely on their state of residence for the issuance of any other forms of documentation or certification that they require. In sum, the 1954 Convention relating to the Status of Stateless Persons offers a comprehensive set of guarantees that, together, ensure that the stateless are issued with the basic documents needed to access any rights and facilities - related to their status or otherwise. And even though human rights law recognises the importance of documentation and may even provide a route to claiming various types of papers, to date these developments in no way negate the relevant provisions of the statelessness-specific instrument. This is because the 1954 Statelessness Convention establishes a concrete entitlement to the different documents. Plus it identifies which state is mandated to issue them as well as calling into being the status of "stateless person" and ensuring the documentation of individuals accordingly. Nevertheless, there is no escaping the fact that what the statelessness instrument fails to do – and this will present a major practical obstacle

[133] See note 118.

[134] Suggestions as to the scope, content and form of such an instrument will be presented and illustrated in chapter XIII upon reflection on the full set of observations drawn from the analysis in chapters X, XI and XII.

to the enjoyment of a right to documentation and to subsequently unlocking the further protection granted – is to provide guidance on how to identify cases of statelessness and actually establish a person's status as a stateless person. In this respect, the 1954 Statelessness Convention is a serious let-down and this is an area that will need much greater consideration in future if the instrument is to be truly effective in its aims. With this serious issue in mind, it is time to progress to the overall evaluation of the value of the 1954 Convention relating to the Status of Stateless Persons and consider – in light also of what contribution human rights law has been found to make – to what extent supplementary instruments or guidelines are necessary if the stateless are to enjoy adequate protection of their rights and needs. This is the task of the following chapter.

CHAPTER XIII

INTERNATIONAL LAW AND THE PROTECTION OF STATELESS PERSONS

One of the most frequently cited descriptions of nationality and how much it *matters* is the assertion that citizenship amounts to "the right to have rights".[1] When statelessness is considered in this light we face the worrying possibility that, without any nationality, the stateless are deemed to have no right to have rights and can be (mis)treated accordingly, without consequence. Just how dire the picture of statelessness then becomes was painted very powerfully by Arendt:

> The prolongation of their lives is due to charity and not to right, for no law exists which could force the nations to feed them; their freedom of movement, if they have it at all, gives them no right to residence which even the jailed criminal enjoys as a matter of course; and their freedom of opinion is a fool's freedom, for nothing they think matters anyhow.[2]

Fortunately over the course of the last three chapters it became clear that this gloomy scenario is not (any longer) a true reflection of the status of this vulnerable group. The 1954 Convention relating to the Status of Stateless Persons establishes a minimum standard of treatment for the stateless - elaborating and conferring a catalogue of basic rights – while the development of human rights norms has heralded the progressive advance of "humanity" over "nationality" as the foundation of the right to have rights.

So, the position of the stateless today is simultaneously less ominous and more complex. While they are certainly not entirely right-less, their lack of any nationality does continue to raise difficulties – not just in practice, but even according to the letter of international law as it now stands. The purpose of the investigation conducted in the foregoing chapters was to shed some light on the intricacies of this issue in order to answer the following research question:

---

1 See chapter IX, section 1.

2 Hannah Arendt, "The Decline of the Nation-State and the End of the Rights of Man" in *The origins of totalitarianism*, Harcourt Brace Jovanovich, New York: 1948, page 296. Be reminded also of the decision by the international arbitration panel in *Dickson Car Wheel Company v. United Mexican States* which pronounced states free to inflict injuries upon stateless persons without this amounting to an international delinquency.

How can the way in which international law deals with the *legal status and entitlements of stateless persons* be improved so as to ensure optimal protection of the individual's rights in the absence of nationality?

On the one hand then, we weighed up the contribution made by the 1954 Statelessness Convention to assuring the stateless the enjoyment of the full range of human rights. On the other hand, we considered the progress made within the broader human rights field towards guaranteeing that the stateless are not disadvantaged by their lack of a nationality. The following pages offer a reflection upon the observations made in the preceding chapters; establish the independent value of the tailor-made statelessness instrument and the role of human rights law in protecting the stateless; ponder any gaps identified in the protection offered that call for a (further) response from the international community; and pause once more to consider the potential for the implementation and enforcement of the relevant standards before drawing to an overall conclusion.

1 Value of the 1954 Convention Relating to the Status of Stateless Persons in the protection of stateless persons

The process of systematically deliberating upon each right and guarantee housed in the 1954 Convention relating to the Status of Stateless Persons allowed us to pick up on particular points of interest and proceed gradually towards an overall assessment of the effectiveness of the instrument's approach to appeasing the situation of the stateless. One of the foremost observations to be made about this instrument is that in order to better understand its content a basic concept of its origins and drafting history is absolutely indispensable. The development of the text in parallel to the 1951 Convention relating to the Status of Refugees has left an indelible impression on the approach taken to the problem of statelessness. We found that debate on the appropriateness of particular paragraphs or details within the specific context of statelessness - as a problem very much distinct from refugee-hood - was regrettably minimal. The provisions of the statelessness instrument largely echo those of the Refugee Convention even though this has not always proven to be the most suitable route to alleviating the specific difficulties faced by the stateless. Nevertheless, we also discovered a number of significant modifications to the guarantees offered: some subtle, such as a change in standard of protection and some dramatic such, as the deletion of the provision on non-punishment for unlawful entry. In each and every case, however, the upshot of the amendment was a *deterioration* of the protection offered. We are thus forced to conclude that this drafting process had an irreversibly detrimental impact upon the effectiveness of the 1954 Statelessness Convention – a fact that was evidenced time and again as we reflected upon the scope and content of each individual provision.

As we ran through the provisions of the 1954 Statelessness Convention one by one, it became increasingly apparent that the instrument's characteristic approach to the elaboration of rights is in fact its greatest weakness.[3] Firstly, the Convention attributes the majority of rights not to all stateless persons within the

[3] Again, the approach mimics the 1951 Refugee Convention and is therefore characteristic of both instruments.

jurisdiction of a state party, but to a smaller subset of this group: for example only to those who are lawfully present or even only to those who are lawfully resident. The level of attachment required as a precondition for the enjoyment of protection under the instrument is of clear concern for a substantial number of the rights espoused. Achieving entitlement to the various economic, social and cultural rights housed in the 1954 Statelessness Convention is particularly endangered by this formula since the majority require at least lawful presence if not an even more substantial connection with a state.[4] And since the Convention itself does not address the question of access to a state's jurisdiction or to a particular status, contracting states are under no obligation to promote stateless persons to a higher level of attachment and thereby ensure that they are (gradually) entitled to the full set of rights promulgated.[5]

The second major trait – and flaw - of the 1954 Statelessness Convention's approach to the protection of the stateless is the elaboration of a contingent rather than an absolute standard of protection. A handful of provisions do contain absolute rights or guarantees, such as the right of access to courts and the articles that deal with the "special needs" of the stateless.[6] However, the majority of articles declare that the stateless must enjoy either treatment on a par with nationals or, much less helpfully, "treatment at least as favourable as aliens generally". This technique was found to be a major drawback in relation to both the civil and political and the economic, social and cultural rights that the 1954 Statelessness Convention sets out. Indeed, rather than providing an immediate and enforceable standard of its own, this approach effectively defers the question of the content to be given to the respective rights back to the states concerned or to other international norms such as the human rights standards that were subsequently investigated. In particular, the elaboration of a series of rights for which the stateless may rely only upon treatment *on a par with non-nationals generally* is an irrefutable shortcoming because it ignores the crux of the issue: the stateless are non-citizens everywhere and can thus never rely on rights beyond those offered to foreigners generally unless special provision is made to that effect. Instead, those provisions that offer the stateless *national treatment* are much better suited to the realisation of the purpose of the instrument – to overcoming problems associated with the specific circumstances of statelessness, characterised by the absence of any nationality. With this in mind, it is perhaps unfair to be overly critical of those rights that are promulgated at this standard. Still, it can be questioned whether this approach is appropriate in the contemporary human rights environment because it does not compel states to guarantee any of these rights, just to treat stateless persons and citizens equally (well or badly). Other areas of international law - in particular relevant human rights norms - will still need to be invoked, in conjunction with the relevant

---

[4] See, among others, articles 15, 17, 23 and 24 of the 1954 Convention relating to the Status of Stateless Persons.

[5] As noted in chapter X, section 2.2, this approach to the elaboration of rights was transposed from the 1951 Refugee Convention which, through the inclusion of the principle of *non-refoulement* does at least provide some basis for moving up through the various levels of attachment and achieving a progressively closer connection with the host state which in turn serves to open the door to the enjoyment of the full spectrum of rights.

[6] See, among others, article 16, paragraph 1 and article 27 of the 1954 Convention relating to the Status of Stateless Persons.

provisions of the 1954 Statelessness Convention, to give this standard of treatment any true meaning.

It is the combination of these two trademark techniques that serves an especially severe blow to the effectiveness of the 1954 Statelessness Convention. For example, the freedom of association and the right to housing are guaranteed only to those stateless individuals who have reached an advanced – often unattainable – level of attachment (lawful stay) and even then, the actual substance of the right attributed is made contingent upon the standard enjoyed by non-nationals generally. So, while the 1954 Statelessness Convention *appears* to tackle a wide range of concerns, each provision must be read very carefully. Through this approach to standard-setting, the instrument stops sadly short of reaching its full potential. Moreover, even if we set to one side the problems related to the *conditional* attribution of *contingent* rights, many of the provisions are still substantively inadequate. In some cases the terminology is vague or ambiguous,[7] in others it is simply not thorough or forceful enough to ensure that the needs or interests of the stateless are optimally protected.[8] A prime example of this failure to elaborate appropriately clear and decisive norms is article 32 on naturalisation: this crucial "right of solution" is formulated in awkwardly imprecise, open and facultative language with the result that it is doubtful whether the stateless can claim any benefit from it at all.

As well as expressing serious discontent about the existing content of the 1954 Convention relating to the Status of Stateless Persons on a number of counts, we were forced to admit that the instrument's deficiencies are further compounded by the oversights that it commits. By structuring this study such that we considered one category of guarantees at a time, identifying the topics that have been overlooked entirely by the 1954 Statelessness Convention was relatively straightforward. In each chapter we came across at least one issue that the instrument failed to address whereas, with a view to offering the stateless a comprehensive protection regime, it arguably should have. From among these concerns, four particular subjects stand out. The first is international freedom of movement or, more precisely, the right to enter, remain in and return to the territory of a state. Being without any nationality, the stateless cannot rely on the automatic right of entry and residence that this status brings with respect to the country of citizenship.[9] Meanwhile as mentioned above the ability to attain or retain a certain status (or level of attachment) within a state is crucial for accessing a great number of the 1954 Statelessness Convention's benefits and, equally importantly, for rescuing the stateless from becoming part of

[7] For example, the ambiguous relationship between the provision relating to "administrative assistance"(article 25) and that dealing with "social security" (article 24) may cause difficulties in implementation, to the detriment of the protection offered.

[8] Consider the limited scope of, among others, the right of access to courts (chapter X, section 4.1) and the freedom of association (chapter XI, section 3.1).

[9] Remember that the importance of the right to enter lies not in the fact that stateless persons necessarily desire to travel or migrate, but to ensure that they are entitled to live *somewhere* and indeed ideally in that place with which they have a real connection. So, the right to enter ensures that expulsion cannot follow denationalisation; that if the stateless are forced to flee or migration has been part of the problem leading up to statelessness they are ensured a right to return; and that they are not just 'tolerated' forever but are able to enjoy a regular immigration status which may allow them to enjoy additional rights and benefits. Recall chapter X, section 2.2.

an international "ping-pong" match whereby they are forever shunted back and forth while their status remains in limbo. Yet the document does not tackle the problem of gaining (lawful) entry into or residence in a state. This oversight has a severe knock-on effect for the enjoyment of so many of the other rights elaborated in the 1954 Statelessness Convention – because these are linked to lawful presence or residence - that it jeopardises the effectiveness of the entire instrument. The second and related omission is a set of guarantees to protect stateless persons from arbitrary or indefinite detention – including in the context of the difficulties relating to their immigration status. Meanwhile, just as the right to enter or remain in a state is a traditional function of nationality - and is, as such, *precisely* the type of issue that we would expect an instrument addressing the position of the stateless to touch upon - the last two topics that are very notably absent from the 1954 Statelessness Convention are also matters that are inherent in concept of citizenship: political rights (or indeed even quasi-political rights) and diplomatic protection.[10]

At the time that the instrument was being drafted states were clearly not prepared to prescribe measures that would circumvent nationality entirely and attribute such rights and privileges to the stateless as would normally be founded upon the bond of citizenship. So, although tailor-made to redress the protection gap presented by the specific circumstance of statelessness, the 1954 Convention relating to the Status of Stateless Persons had to limit its ambition to the protection of a basic, minimum standard of treatment. The idea was not that the measures prescribed by the instrument would replace the need for a nationality, but that the stateless would not suffer too much hardship or indignity while awaiting the definitive resolution of their plight through the attribution or restoration of nationality. The 1954 Statelessness Convention even manages to enunciate a "right of solution" to encourage this process. However, as mentioned in chapter XII (section 1.1), access to naturalisation as a right of solution is put forward in such vague and discretionary terms that even here the instrument fails to really grasp the issue with sufficient vigour. I contend that the 1954 Statelessness Convention cannot be forgiven on both counts: it must either present an effective route towards resolving cases of statelessness – in which case it can be excused for pursuing a minimum standard of treatment as an interim status – or it must deal resolutely with all those difficulties that the stateless face by virtue of their statelessness by prescribing something far better than *treatment on a par with non-nationals generally* (preferably national treatment or even absolute rights) across the board. In contrast, it has become apparent over the course of the foregoing chapters that international (human rights) law has moved on in great strides since the adoption of the 1954 Statelessness Convention and today it is possible to trace the necessary starting-points from which to develop a more appropriate response to statelessness through either or both of these routes.

After such stern critique, we must ask: has the 1954 Convention relating to the Status of Stateless Persons no positive attributes? On balance I would have to conclude that the instrument has two main plus points. First and foremost of these is the fact that the document defines statelessness and establishes the international

[10] See on political and quasi-political rights chapter X, section 7 and on diplomatic protection chapter XII, section 3.

status of "stateless person" to which certain rights can be attached.[11] The Convention thereby focuses states' attention on the vulnerability of those who lack any nationality and the importance of responding to their particular protection needs. Just as "refugees" and "migrant workers" have also become categories of special concern to the international community, by formally introducing "statelessness" to international legal terminology the instrument provides a vital reference point for discussing the issue at hand, implementing measures addressed towards the persons concerned and monitoring their treatment. The second and closely related pro of the 1954 Statelessness Convention is that it not only introduces the status of stateless person but also provides for the documentation of stateless persons *as* stateless persons. A strong and thorough set of guarantees elaborated in the closing provisions of the convention

- ensures that the stateless have access to at least basic identity papers which establish both the personal particulars and the statelessness of the individual;

- mandates contracting states to also provide any other basic documentation which may be required to access rights or services; and

- offers the possibility of a travel document to function in lieu of a passport.[12]

In this way, the 1954 Statelessness Convention provides the basic building blocks of a system that has the potential to offer the stateless the protection that they need. And the instrument does go on to detail a selection of civil and political *and* economic, social and cultural rights for the stateless to enjoy. Had the content of these provisions been clearer, more forceful and taken the specific plight of the stateless into greater consideration, the conclusion as to the overall effectiveness of the Convention would have been very different.

If the 1954 Convention relating to the Status of Stateless Persons existed in isolation it could be considered a valuable instrument, warts and all, precisely because it does lay down the elementary foundations of a protection regime purposely geared towards this vulnerable group – bearing in mind, nonetheless, the limitations inherent in offering a contingent standard of treatment. However, the 1954 Statelessness Convention is just one small cog in the vast machine that is international law today. When situated within its proper context, much of the added value of the document fades away. Since its adoption in 1954, the Convention has been largely outmanoeuvred by developments in the human rights field. Ratification of the 1954 Statelessness Convention therefore amounts to little more than a reaffirmation that the stateless enjoy the various rights that are elaborated elsewhere and to which states have therefore already committed. In effect, this means that there is also nothing in the content of the 1954 Statelessness Convention that states could consider contentious or objectionable and prevent them from becoming a party to the instrument – a finding that may be useful in campaigning for

[11] See chapter IX, section 3.
[12] See chapter XII, section 2.1.

ratification of the text since any concerns that may be raised by states with respect to particular norms can be readily pacified through reference to the corresponding human rights standards that the state has already acknowledged.[13]

However, in view of all of the criticism expressed at the content on the 1954 Statelessness Convention, would it in fact be a useful exercise to attempt to boost the number of state parties of this largely outdated instrument with the help of the observations that have just been made? Perhaps somewhat surprisingly, in my view, the answer to this question is: yes, advocating for wider acceptance of this instrument is still worthwhile. This is because it puts the stateless on the map as a group who hold a particular status and are entitled to treatment that caters for their specific needs, be it on the basis of the 1954 Statelessness Convention itself or broader human rights norms, as well as guaranteeing the acquisition of documentation that can be the key to claiming these exclusive (and any other) benefits. Meanwhile, it is important to be forever conscious of the limitations of the 1954 Statelessness Convention. Rather than seeing it as the definitive answer to the conundrum of the protection of stateless persons, we should be aware of what the document can and cannot contribute to addressing their plight. And where the instrument is let down by vague terminology or references to contingent standards of treatment, rather than casting the text aside we should not be afraid to utilise developing human rights standards to bring more clarity or body to the guarantees.

This does not detract from the fact that serious contemplation will have to be given to a number of outstanding issues identified over the course of this investigation that seriously jeopardise the effectiveness of any efforts to attribute rights to the stateless on the basis of the 1954 Statelessness Convention. In particular the problem of ensuring a right to reside somewhere,[14] but also the difficult question of identifying cases of statelessness on the basis of the definition as a precursor to setting in motion all of the guarantees that accompany that status[15] and the overall challenge of enforcement.[16] We will return to these residual issues in the upcoming sections as we take a conclusive look at the contribution made by human rights law to the protection of stateless persons, the remaining normative gaps and the potential for implementation and enforcement of all of the standards traced.

2 The role of international (human rights) law in the protection of stateless persons

For numerous decades now, the progressive development of human rights standards has been eroding the foundations of the notion that *nationality* is the right to have rights and replacing it with a concept of humanity or human dignity as the basis for the enjoyment of rights:

[13] For example through their acceptance of the International Covenants or the Convention on the Rights of the Child – all of which count many more state parties than the 1954 Statelessness Convention.

[14] Recall chapter X, section 2.2.1.

[15] See in particular chapter II, section 1 and chapter IX, section 3.

[16] Recall the comments made in chapter IX, section 3.

> With the passage of time, it became evident that the nationality regime was not always sufficient to provide protection under any and every circumstance (as evidenced, for example, by the situation of stateless persons). Throughout the twentieth century and to date, international human rights law has sought to remedy this deficiency or vacuum, by denationalising protection (and thus including every individual, even stateless persons).[17]

Thanks to this development, human rights law now forms a second important source of norms for the protection of the rights and interests of the stateless - alongside the stateless-specific instrument discussed above. But, although citizenship is not (any longer) that relevant for the enjoyment of basic rights, the foregoing chapters have made clear that it would be premature to assert that nationality is entirely *irrelevant* in the contemporary human rights environment. In fact, modern human rights law – just like the 1954 Statelessness Convention – receives a mixed report when its response to the particular plight of the stateless is put under the microscope.

On the one hand, human rights norms have achieved a breadth of scope and an intensity of detail that far outreaches the 1954 Statelessness Convention: many topics that were absent from the statelessness instrument are dealt with in universal and regional human rights documents alike and thanks to the efforts of human rights institutions like the UN treaty bodies, each entitlement has been worked out in considerable depth. Since the vast majority of the rights espoused are attributed to "everyone", the stateless should also be able to benefit from the protection offered in the human rights field. Indeed, on numerous occasions, human rights bodies have considered and remarked upon the enjoyment by non-nationals – including stateless persons – of rights such as the right to (enjoy) property, the right to education and a plethora of others. On the other hand, human rights law continues to admit the possibility that non-nationals be treated differently to nationals. Distinctions between citizens and non-citizens are not necessarily outlawed under the principles of equality and non-discrimination. This contributes a tinge of uncertainty to the position of the stateless and the exact extent of the protection offered to them. Moreover, some human rights norms are actually better described as *citizen's* rights since they can ordinarily be relied upon only with respect to the state of nationality, to the apparent exclusion of the stateless.

So there remain a number of key areas in which international (human rights) law has yet to satisfactorily address the vulnerable situation of the stateless – although there are also markedly positive developments, the potential of which should not be underestimated. To begin with, where we saw that international law acknowledges that the right to enter and remain in a state is still reserved, in principle, to nationals, there are numerous norms on which stateless individuals may nevertheless be able to rely in a bid to gain (re)admission to a state, regularisation of status or protection from expulsion. These included the principle of *non-refoulement,* the right to family and private life, the prohibition of collective or arbitrary expulsion and, with arguably the greatest potential to help stateless

[17] Separate opinion of Judge A.A. Cancado Trindade, Inter-American Court on Human Rights, *Case of Yean and Bosico v. Dominican Republic,* Series C, Case 130, 8 September 2005.

persons in a wide variety of situations, the expanding interpretation of the right to enter *his own country*.[18] Nevertheless, the human rights regime has yet to offer concrete standards that will enable all stateless persons to secure a right of entry and residence in an appropriate state and put an end to related problems of indefinite detention or serial expulsion.[19]

Similarly, human rights law guarantees to everyone, including stateless persons, the basic building blocks for political empowerment that were omitted from the 1954 Statelessness Convention: the freedom of opinion, expression and assembly. Any measures that states impose that encroach upon these freedoms - whether geared towards the stateless, all non-nationals or everyone - must fall within the scope of the permissible limitations that the human rights instruments themselves delineate. Moreover, we found evidence of an increasing generosity towards the attribution of true political rights (the right to vote, stand for election or work in public service) to certain categories of non-nationals. EU citizenship is one example where the link between national citizenship and political rights has become less direct, but we found other cases of "denizenship" where the uncoupling of nationality and political participation is even more apparent. And the human rights community has reacted very positively to such developments. Yet, in spite of this interesting progression and the various arguments that could easily be brought in favour of special treatment for the stateless – as a distinct group - where political rights are concerned, this has nonetheless so far failed to generate any corresponding international norms. According to human rights law as it stands today, political rights are still guaranteed to everyone, but only in respect of their country of citizenship, and any more charitable or liberal policy on the part of states is welcomed rather than obliged.[20]

The assessment of the human rights framework uncovered much the same picture in respect of many other issues. For instance, while stateless persons are to benefit, along with everyone else, from economic, social and cultural rights, the nature of these guarantees (commonly directed towards progressive rather than immediate realisation) and the explicit authorisation to *developing countries* to restrict the *economic rights* of non-nationals in the interest of their domestic economy complicate the picture. States may thereby be accorded a much wider margin of appreciation in determining the appropriateness of distinctions between nationals and non-nationals in respect of these rights, putting the stateless in a delicate position.[21] Meanwhile with regard to a right of solution, although international law does not dictate the conditions for naturalisation, it does appear that a window of opportunity has opened within the human rights framework for the assertion of a right for stateless persons to (be considered for) naturalisation under given circumstances. It is certainly clear that *unreasonable impediments* to naturalisation are to be avoided as well as that the fact of statelessness must be taken into account and may oblige states to facilitate procedures or lower

[18] See chapter X, section 2.2.2.

[19] Although we also found that the human rights framework provides both some substantive and some procedural guarantees against arbitrary or indefinite detention. See chapter X, section 7.

[20] These issues were discussed in depth in chapter X, section 7.

[21] See chapter XI, section 1.

requirements.[22] There are even signs of change in relation to diplomatic protection where the so-called "nationality of the claims" has traditionally been an inescapable pre-condition for a state to assert its right to diplomatic protection. In fact, if the international community pushes ahead with the rules elaborated on this issue by the International Law Commission, the legal basis for states to exercise diplomatic protection over stateless persons - on the grounds of the connection of habitual residence rather than nationality – will be assured. This will transform the shape of the doctrine of diplomatic protection to the benefit of the stateless as a specific, vulnerable category of non-nationals.[23]

Overall then, what is perhaps most interesting about the role of contemporary international (human rights) law in the protection of stateless persons is the incredible potential afforded by advancements achieved over the course of the past few decades. Already, the general human rights framework offers equal, if not stronger, guarantees to those elaborated in the 1954 Statelessness Convention on virtually all issues. And the foundations have now been laid for protection that would go much further and come much closer to the ideal of filling the gaps in the enjoyment of rights that stateless persons would otherwise face due to their lack of a nationality. The difficulty is that the interpretation of human rights standards in such a way as to be progressively more sympathetic to the position of the stateless has not necessarily been guided by concern for the particular quandary of this group. To solidify these developments in favour of the protection of stateless persons it will therefore be necessary to (re)focus attention on their specific plight and (re)evaluate how these individuals can be assisted through a pro-active application of existing trends. Some suggestions as to how this could be achieved are submitted in the next section.

3 Normative gaps in the protection of stateless persons under international law and suggested remedies

It is strict but fair to conclude that, to date, international law has failed to fully remedy any of the *core* difficulties that are presented by the situation of statelessness. Yes, there is a specially devised instrument that offers a minimum standard of treatment to be enjoyed by the stateless. And yes, human rights law has progressively denationalised protection with the result that the "rights gap" into which the stateless tumble is narrowing. Yet the "big issues" remain outstanding. Those rights and entitlements that traditionally belong to the very heart and function of citizenship still generally hover just beyond the reach of the stateless: the right to enter and remain in a state, the right to participate in government and the opportunity to enjoy diplomatic protection. Moreover, there are many – less sensitive - areas in which the exact treatment owed to stateless persons remains uncertain and a clarification of the scope and content of the various norms, as they apply to the stateless, would be hugely beneficial. And it would be similarly invaluable to reaffirm and elucidate a decisive right of solution for stateless persons. I therefore feel that in order to offer the stateless an appropriate answer to their plight, a new international instrument is needed in which all of these questions are

[22] As discussed in chapter XII, section 1.2.
[23] See chapter XII, section 3.

brought together and codified. Although this would be a major project, the necessary foundations can already be found in existing (human rights) texts, decisions and comments, as well as in the 1954 Statelessness Convention itself. Plus, within the human rights field there is a growing body of instruments directed towards the protection of particular vulnerable groups, for example migrant workers, persons with disabilities and indigenous persons.[24] It would therefore be in keeping with this pattern to elaborate a full catalogue of international norms relating specifically to the treatment of stateless persons – based on standards that have already been developing independently within the human rights context since the inception of the 1954 Statelessness Convention - in a new human rights instrument.

An internationally-recognised definition of statelessness was already brought into being by the 1954 Statelessness Convention and has been repeated in various other instruments, so this definition could simply be copied across to any new document addressing statelessness, thereby delineating the scope of application of the norms. After opening with the question of definition, the new instrument should also pause to address the problem of actually identifying cases of statelessness and reaffirm the guarantees that are set out in the 1954 Statelessness Convention with respect to basic identity documentation, vouching for both status and other personal details.[25] Immediately thereafter, another definitional problem must be tackled. The text will need to assert some means of establishing which state, for the purposes of the instrument, is to be regarded as the stateless person's "own country" even in the absence of the formal bond of nationality. This is undoubtedly the most challenging and contentious matter to be dealt with because this determination can subsequently be used to identify the state in which the stateless person is owed a number of important rights – the most crucial of which is the right to enter (and thereby reside in) the state's territory.

The pronouncements of the Human Rights Committee are arguably the most fruitful source of guidance in this delicate matter. In the context of interpreting the scope of a person's *own country* for the purposes of the right to enter, the Committee made a start with the task of delineating which state, in the absence of nationality, can nevertheless be considered connected to an individual in such a way as to warrant recognition. The crux of the matter seems to be in establishing which state is "responsible" for an individual's statelessness. This requires the application of the norms relating to the prevention of statelessness, which are themselves in need of some further crystallisation and clarification.[26] As it stands, it will not necessarily always be possible to identify one particular state that is responsible.

[24] Recall the Convention on the Protection of the Rights of All Migrant Workers and Members of Their Families (entered into force in July 2003), the Convention on the Rights of Persons with Disabilities (not yet in force) and the Declaration on the Rights of Indigenous Peoples (adopted in September 2007).

[25] See article 27 of the 1954 Convention relating to the Status of Stateless Persons. Note that where I have proposed to transpose various useful provisions of the 1954 Statelessness Convention to the new instrument devised to improve and update the protection offered to the stateless, it would also be possible to simply refer to the relevant articles of the "original" Convention. The reason that I have suggested that the new instrument start from scratch and include all aspects of the protection of the stateless is that this route would not be reliant on states' concurrent ratification of the 1954 Statelessness Convention for its own effectiveness.

[26] See part 2.

There are obviously some clear-cut cases, as the examples given by the Committee itself has illustrated. Thus, in the event of the denationalisation of an individual in contravention of international norms on arbitrary deprivation of nationality it is the state which withdrew citizenship that should be regarded as the person's *own country*.[27] Where the situation is less straightforward and there is perhaps more than one state that could be deemed to be the stateless person's *own country*, the most appropriate solution would be to assure the individual concerned the right to opt for one or the other of the states to function as his *own country*.

Having dealt with this final question of definition, the instrument can begin to elaborate the rights that are to be enjoyed by stateless persons generally and in relation to the state that has been identified as their *own country*. To begin with then, the instrument should reaffirm the full application of existing international law and human rights standards to the situation of the stateless. This could be achieved through a restatement of the entire catalogue of relevant rights, a technique employed in other instruments such as the Convention on the Rights of the Child, the Migrant Workers Convention and the Convention on the Rights of Persons with Disabilities. By taking each right in turn, the instrument can clarify the scope of everything from the right of access to courts to the right to work for the specific context of statelessness, building upon developments in the field of non-citizens rights generally and taking into account the very special circumstance of the lack of *any* nationality that afflicts the beneficiaries of protection.[28] In some cases, the technique of offering stateless persons treatment on a par with nationals may still be useful – an approach that is also employed in the Migrant Workers Convention - especially in elucidating the privileged position of stateless persons with regard to their *own country*. Thus, all states should assure the stateless person the right to education or to legal personhood, but the right to enter a state need only be guaranteed with respect to the stateless person's *own country*, whereupon he should be treated equally to that state's nationals. Another area in which the guarantees may focus on the protection to be offered by the stateless person's *own country* include the right to participate in government. The stateless person could be assured full political rights, on a par with nationals, with respect to his *own country* or, if this is a too radical step, at least offered the right to participate in local government while the state is also *encouraged* to extend national-level political rights.[29] In

[27] Recall that the other examples offered by the Committee involved situations where nationality was refused in the context of state succession or where stateless long-term residents were arbitrarily deprived of the right to acquire nationality.

[28] The text can continue the ambitions of the 1954 Statelessness Convention by addressing both civil and political as well as economic, social and cultural rights. Such instruments as the Migrant Workers Convention and the Convention on the Rights of Persons with Disabilities again provide a model for this approach by showing how a subtle adjustment of the wording can achieve the desired result. Thus, some provisions (in particular the traditional civil and political rights) are formulated such that the right is attributed directly to the stateless person while others (in particular those that would be classed as typical ESC rights) are worded along the following lines: "state parties recognise the right..." or "state parties shall take effective and appropriate measures to enable...".

[29] In fact, another helpful system generally, again also evident in the Migrant Workers Convention, would be to adopt a dual approach, elaborating mandatory and then facultative elements for some of the rights and issues addressed. This would allow a balance to be struck between the need to move forward in the quest to better elucidate the (already widely acknowledged) rights of the stateless and the

addition, the instrument should lay down clear guidelines on the access of stateless persons to naturalisation[30] and could also establish the required legal basis for the exercise by a state of diplomatic protection on behalf of a stateless person.[31]

If these suggestions were to be implemented and stateless persons were to enjoy the right to (re)enter and remain in a state, the right to participate in the government of that state and even diplomatic protection, all in the absence of the legal bond of nationality, then the question arises whether citizenship retains any meaning once it can be bypassed so comprehensively. As we begin to uncouple nationality from those rights and privileges that are traditionally attributed to this bond of membership – that are inherent to the very function of nationality – then are we in fact attacking the very concept of citizenship which plays such a central role in the world as it is currently organised? I would argue that no, we are not negating the need for and purpose of citizenship, we are simply devising a pragmatic, tailor-made solution for the situation of those who find themselves without *any* nationality. The enduring existence of statelessness already runs counter to the general right of everyone to a nationality and the principle that statelessness should be avoided, so the exclusion of such individuals from the enjoyment of other rights should, as far as possible, be avoided. The stateless, as a closed group, would be the beneficiaries of such a policy and the rights would only be recognised in relation to the particular state that is identified as answerable for their plight – the state that should have allowed the individual to obtain or retain citizenship in the first place. In this manner, the state in question is prevented from shirking its responsibilities towards individuals or groups within its population by way of its nationality policy. The logic of the human rights regime as a whole, whereby the inclusion of "citizens rights" is only justified because the right to be a citizen is also guaranteed, would support such a response to the plight of the stateless as a means to maintain its asserted universality (human rights as the rights of all persons, everywhere). The approach suggested would also have the added benefit of discouraging states from misusing their citizenship policy in order to exclude people from political rights and the right to (re)enter or reside on state soil. The denial of these rights, even in the absence of the formal bond of nationality, would still amount to a violation of the applicable norm and the state could still be held accountable, rendering the denial of citizenship immaterial.

For these proposals to come to fruition, a significant commitment on the part of the international community to the protection of stateless persons is called for. It may take some time to muster up support for such a drastic step as the elaboration of a new instrument – and indeed there is likely to be some resistance to the very idea of devoting a second text to the protection of stateless persons, particularly in view of existing criticism regarding repetition in and proliferation of international

ultimate challenge of achieving progress in respect of the more controversial or sensitive issues that face the stateless. See, for instance, article 42 of the Migrant Workers Convention. A similar result can also be achieved through the specification of where reservations may and may not be elaborated.

[30] This should include an elucidation, on the one hand, of what may be considered *unreasonable impediments*, and what, on the other hand, is deemed to satisfy the call for *facilitated naturalisation.*

[31] This could follow the standards currently being developed by the International Law Commission and allow diplomatic protection to be exercised on the basis of *habitual residence* (rather than citizenship) in the case of the stateless. Alternatively, the instrument could accord the state that is identified as the stateless person's *own country* the right to exercise diplomatic protection.

conventions. If the latter concerns win out over the need to further elucidate the standards relating to the protection of stateless persons, or until such a time as a new or revised instrument can be adopted, a number of less radical measures should be considered. The human rights community has already taken a clear interest in the problems faced by non-citizens generally – and in some cases by the stateless specifically. But, as we have seen, the treatment that is owed to the stateless must presently be gleaned from a whole variety of instruments and corresponding reports and jurisprudence. Moreover, human rights bodies have not always been consistently thorough in considering the treatment specifically enjoyed by or owed to stateless persons, as opposed to other (categories of) non-nationals. There is therefore a need to focus and indeed mainstream attention to the plight of the stateless within the existing human rights system. The UN treaty bodies could, for instance, lead the way by elaborating upon the relevant stateless-specific standards in a joint general comment and should certainly commit to paying greater attention to the problems faced by the stateless when considering state party reports. Another possibility would be to establish, under the auspices of the UN Human Rights Council, a *Special Rapporteur* on the rights of the stateless to give impetus to this objective of mainstreaming attention to their plight and realising a harmonised approach to their rights.[32] Such measures would help to consolidate recent developments and facilitate the identification and application of standards relevant to the specific situation of statelessness.

4 Prospects for the implementation and enforcement of norms for the protection of stateless persons

Despite uncovering various areas in which there is undoubtedly room for improvement, the international standards relating to the protection of the stateless that were discussed over the course of the preceding chapters do offer many opportunities to tackle the plight of this group. Nevertheless, on the basis of reports describing the enduringly poor treatment of stateless persons we are forced to concede that the implementation and enforcement of these norms presents greater difficulties than the content of the standards themselves. So the time has come to consider the potential that the overall international legal framework offers for the application and supervision of the relevant standards – a similar quest to that which was undertaken in part 2 in the context of the *prevention* of statelessness. Here we find, once again, that the challenges inherent in the *identification* of statelessness to a large extent underlie both problems of implementation and enforcement.

The identification of statelessness, the very determination or recognition of stateless person status, is not addressed in the 1954 Convention relating to the Status of Stateless Persons. And as a result of states being left to their own devices

[32] See also Guy Goodwin-Gill, "The Rights of Refugees and Stateless Persons" in Saksena (ed) *Human Rights Perspectives & Challenges (in 1900's and beyond)*, Lancers Books, New Delhi: 1994, pages 400-401; Maureen Lynch, *Lives on hold: The human cost of statelessness*, Washington: 2005, page 26; Office of the High Commissioner of Human Rights, "The Rights of Non-citizens", prepared by David Weissbrodt, Geneva 2006; and David Weissbrodt, "The Protection of Non-Citizens in International Human Rights Law" in R. Cholewinski (ed) *International Migration Law*, TMC Asser Press, The Hague: 2007, page 233.

in addressing the problem of identification, we saw that there is no unified approach to this task (and indeed, in many instances, the authorities have failed to ensure that there is a mechanism in place for tackling it at all).[33] In fact, there is even a divergence in the definition of a stateless person at the domestic level – including between state parties to the 1954 Statelessness Convention.[34] This, in spite of the warning that

> if, however, States do not approach article 1 with a common interpretation or application, it will be impossible to harmonise implementation of the Convention overall or, indeed, for decisions taken by one State party to be recognised as between State parties. This could mean that a single case will arrive at varying results depending on the State in which the stateless person makes an application. As one key objective of the 1954 Convention is to promote the acquisition of a legal identity for a stateless person in one State, which will be widely recognised by other states, a lack of harmonised interpretation and implementation of article 1 risks limiting the benefits of this instrument for both States and individuals concerned.[35]

Clearly then, the proper identification of cases of statelessness is key to the implementation of the standards relating to the protection of stateless persons. The absence of any concrete guidelines to states results not only in the lack of a harmonised approach but also, inevitably, in some persons being unable to access the protection that they deserve. Yet such guidelines have never developed, not even in the form of an agreed advisory handbook or toolkit.[36] This stands in marked contrast to the detailed elaboration of standards relating to Refugee Status Determination (RSD) which help states and UNHCR to establish whether a person is a refugee under the 1951 Convention relating to the Status of Refugees – a similar type of legal status to that of stateless person.[37] Even within the European

---

[33] See chapter IX, section 3.

[34] See for example the discussion of the definition of statelessness under domestic law in the member states of the Council of Europe in Roland Schärer, *Promoting acquisition of citizenship as a means to reduce statelessness – feasibility study,* prepared for the Bureau of the European Committee on Legal Co-operation of the Council of Europe, CDCJ-BU (2006) 18, Strasbourg: 2006, pages 13-14; see also UNHCR and IPU, *Nationality and statelessness. A handbook for parliamentarians*, 2005, pages 19-20.

[35] Carol Batchelor The 1954 Convention relating to the Status of Stateless Persons: Implementation within the European Union Member States and Recommendations for Harmonisation 2004, para. 28.

[36] At most, UNHCR's Executive Committee has called upon the agency to "actively disseminate information and, where appropriate, train government counterparts on appropriate mechanisms for identifying, recording, and granting a status to stateless persons". UNHCR Executive Committee, *Conclusion on Identification, Prevention and Reduction of Statelessness and Protection of Stateless Persons, No. 106,* 57th Session, Geneva, 2006, para. (t). And in the Handbook for Parliamentarians on the issue of statelessness there are some basic suggestions as to who should be empowered to make the determination of stateless person status and what types of procedural guarantees should be in place. UNHCR and IPU, *Nationality and statelessness. A handbook for parliamentarians*, 2005, pages 19-21.

[37] See in particular UNHCR, *Handbook on Procedures and Criteria for Determining Refugee Status under the 1951 Convention and the 1967 Protocol relating to the Status of Refugees,* HCR/IP/Eng/Rev.1, 1979 (re-edited 1992); UNHCR, *Guidelines on International Protection,* No. 1-7, adopted between 2002 and 2006; a whole host of UNHCR Executive Committee *Conclusions on*

Union for instance, where many states have acceded to the 1954 Statelessness Convention and extensive agreements have been elaborated for a harmonised approach to RSD in order to implement the 1951 Refugee Convention,[38] the recognition of stateless person status remains a highly uncoordinated area of policy.[39]

Nor has the broader human rights framework been able to offer much to stem the wide divergence of practices in relation to the identification of stateless persons. It is not possible to readily extract any general instructions as to procedures, competences or the burden of proof from the comments or jurisprudence concerning the protection of the stateless. This is not to say that human rights bodies have never been faced with the task of assessing a person's claim to a certain nationality or indeed to stateless person status for the purposes of deciding a case. For instance, in a case brought before the European Court of Human Rights, the citizenship of the applicant was again a crucial factor in the appraisal of the situation and its compliance with human rights law. In *Tatishvili v. Russia,* the state's defence against an alleged violation of the right to free movement within the country rested on the assertion that the applicant was unlawfully present in Russia because she held Georgian nationality and did not hold the requisite entry visa. After considering the facts and the relevant laws submitted to the court, it ruled that

> in so far as the Russian authorities claimed that the applicant needed an entry visa as a Georgian citizen, the Court observes that the applicant maintained as her citizenship that of the former USSR. She denied that she had ever acquired Georgian citizenship. Neither in the domestic proceedings nor before the Court did the Russian authorities produce *any evidence in support of their claim that the applicant had been a Georgian citizen.* The registration of the applicant's residence in Tbilisi dating back to early 1990s had no automatic bearing on *determination of her citizenship under either Russian or Georgian laws* [...] The Government's allegation that the applicant was of Georgian citizenship has *no evidentiary basis.*[40]

The court clearly considers itself competent to weight up the evidence of nationality brought before it, just as it is competent to consider other facts. However, since the court does not entirely elucidate the steps taken to reach its decision it is difficult to distil principles or rules on the appropriate procedures or standards of proof for the establishment of nationality from this case. The court plainly recognises that the relevant citizenship laws are indispensable in determining a person's nationality and has examined the content of these laws accordingly. What the court fails to describe

---

International Protection; and UNHCR, *Self-study module 2: Refugee Status Determination. Identifying who is a refugee,* September 2005.

[38] See Council Directive 8043/04 of 27 April 2004 on minimum standards for the qualification and status of third country nationals and stateless persons as refugees or as persons who otherwise need international protection and content of the protection granted.

[39] Carol Batchelor The 1954 Convention relating to the Status of Stateless Persons: Implementation within the European Union Member States and Recommendations for Harmonisation 2004, paras. 49-82.

[40] Emphasis added, European Court of Human Rights, *Case of Tatishvili v. Russia,* Application No 1509/02, Strasbourg, 22 February 2007, paragraph 40.

is what "supporting evidence" the Russian authorities could have provided in order to come to a different conclusion about the position of the individual in question under the relevant citizenship laws.

Meanwhile, in the previously discussed case of *Yean and Bosico v. Dominican Republic,* the Inter-American Court of Human Rights began by ascertaining that the state denied the claimants nationality and

> placed them outside the State's juridical system and kept them stateless, which placed them in a situation of extreme vulnerability, as regards the exercise and enjoyment of right.[41]

In this case, the court based the identification of statelessness on the rejection of their application for late birth registration, going on to explain that when the Dominican Republic did eventually grant the children birth certificates, this resulted in the conferral of citizenship.[42] The court hereby confirms that birth registration and the details recorded through this process is one means of certifying a person's nationality – a fact that we came across earlier when considering the importance of birth registration in staving off statelessness.[43] However, it is important to realise that in the Dominican Republic there is a particularly close connection between birth registration and nationality, thanks to the state's *ius soli* laws,[44] and neither the initial refusal of a birth certificate or the resulting temporary statelessness were in fact disputed by the state in this case. The fact that the court based its assessment of the children's nationality solely on their lack of birth registration cannot therefore be seen to suggest that birth registration is anything more than *one* type of proof of nationality that can be brought forward. Again, the message is that international human rights bodies are able to rule on the nationality status of an individual where this is relevant to the facts of the case – and are sometimes called to do so – but the limited jurisprudence that exists fails to reveal more than a very basic insight into how this determination must be made.

Nevertheless, this brings us neatly to the broader issue of the enforcement of the rights of the stateless. At the outset, it is important to realise that enforcement has always been something of a dilemma where international human rights norms are concerned. When the first major human rights instruments were being prepared

---

[41] Inter-American Court on Human Rights, *Case of Yean and Bosico v. Dominican Republic,* Series C, Case 130, 8 September 2005, operative paragraph 166. Thereafter, the court went on to rule that the circumstance of statelessness contributed to the violation of a number of further rights, including article 3 (right to legal personhood), article 18 (right to a name) and article 19 (rights of the child) and article of the American Convention on Human Rights. See paragraphs 167-187 of the judgement.

[42] Inter-American Court on Human Rights, *Case of Yean and Bosico v. Dominican Republic,* Series C, Case 130, 8 September 2005, operative paragraph 147. The court also based this finding on the Constitution of the Dominican Republic where the rules for the attribution of citizenship at birth are laid down. See paragraph 109 of the decision.

[43] See the references to the connection between birth registration and nationality in chapter VII, section 1.

[44] Laura van Waas, *Is Permanent Illegality Inevitable? The Challenges to Ensuring Birth Registration and the Right to a Nationality for the Children of Irregular Migrants - Thailand and the Dominican Republic,* Woking: 2006.

after the Second World War, "measures of implementation" (supervisory mechanisms) were a contentious issue:

> While the Universal Declaration of Human Rights was adopted as early as December 10, 1948, it took until 16 December 1966 for the International Covenant on Economic, Social and Cultural Rights and the International Covenant on Civil and Political Rights to be adopted by the General Assembly of the United Nations. The controversial views on the nature of measures of implementation which would be incorporated into the Covenants was one of the major reasons for this delay.[45]

To this day, the supervisory machinery within the international human rights framework continues to evolve and debate on new developments remains impassioned.[46] And, as we saw, the 1954 Statelessness Convention failed to create an accompanying supervisory mechanism to assist or compel state parties to comply with their obligations or to arbitrate in individual cases.[47]

Yet we also saw that the right to an effective remedy, as promulgated under numerous human rights instruments, provides a useful, broad guarantee that stateless persons will be able to present a claim where they feel that their rights have been violated. States are thereby committed to helping with the enforcement of rights within their jurisdiction by ensuring the availability of complaints procedures or judicial review within their own domestic legal system.[48] Moreover, there are now many enforcement procedures and mechanisms in place under both universal and regional human rights instruments. Whatever the method or focus of these mechanisms - whether they are directed towards monitoring and ensuring state-wide compliance with human rights commitments or handling individual cases – the fact that stateless persons benefit generally under human rights law means that they are also afforded an opportunity, through these procedures, to ensure that they receive the protection that they are due. Generally speaking then, stateless persons can simply rely on the same supervisory apparatus as non-stateless persons for the protection of their rights. The only current exception to this rule is the availability of diplomatic protection as an additional option for the realisation of treatment in accordance with their rights – as we have seen, there is as yet no firm legal basis for the exercise by a state of diplomatic protection on behalf of a stateless person, although this possibility is not outlawed entirely.[49]

So the enforcement dilemma for the protection of stateless persons is arguably less severe than the challenge of monitoring the *prevention* of statelessness. The rights that stateless persons seek to invoke in the context of *protection* are familiar human rights norms that the supervisory machinery is highly familiar and

---

[45] Paul Weis, "Diplomatic protection of nationals and international protection of human rights" in *International Journal of Refugee Law*, 1991, p. 654.

[46] Consider the ongoing debate on the possibility of establishing an indifidual complaints mechanism for the International Covenant on Economic, Social and Cultural Rights. See the work of the Open-Ended Working Group to consider options regarding the elaboration of an Optional Protocol to the International Covenant on Economic, Social and Cultural Rights.

[47] See chapter IX, section 3.

[48] See chapter X, section 4.

[49] See chapter XII, section 3.

comfortable with. The fact of statelessness is not necessarily even relevant - for example when finding a violation of the freedom of religion or the right to education. And indeed, over the course of the foregoing chapters we have become aware of the role that is already being played by a variety of human rights bodies and institutions in delineating and supervising the rights of the stateless. We have seen that the protection of stateless persons has been taken into account in country reporting procedures and that stateless persons have been able to access individual complaints mechanisms.[50] If the protection owed to stateless persons *as* stateless persons under existing human rights instruments such as the ICCPR and ICESCR is further elucidated and the question of how to *identify* situations of statelessness is clarified, then the current human rights framework provides adequate opportunity for the enforcement of these rights. If, on the other hand, a new universal instrument that concentrates on the rights of the stateless were to be elaborated, careful thought would have to be given to the question of enforcement. In that case, and in keeping with the development of treaty bodies within the United Nations system,[51] a new committee could be created and tasked with monitoring compliance with – as well as offering an authoritative interpretation of – the text.

5 Conclusion

The stateless are, in some respects, uniquely vulnerable. The human rights system itself seems to abhor their very existence since it severely challenges the ambition of the universal enjoyment of human rights: stateless persons are, by definition, unable to enjoy those rights that are accorded only in relation to the state of citizenship. And although nationality is no longer a pre-condition for the attribution of most human rights, in practice it is often still a requirement for the *exercise* of such rights, for example due to problems in relation to documentation and the lack of any official "home country" in which residence rights are guaranteed:

> A person without a passport or nationality [...] faces the horrifying prospect of spending literally his entire life being shunted from one frontier to another in the desperate hope that some State for some reason may be induced to accept him.[52]

The legal or even physical limbo that threatens stateless persons is perhaps the greatest challenge to their protection. It is therefore of utmost importance that their right to live somewhere is assured – hence the pointed focus on the right to enter "one's own country" as the key to the instigation of a comprehensive protection

[50] In particular, over the past decade, the European Court of Human Rights has seen numerous procedures brought before it by stateless persons against different states. For example *Slavov v. Sweden,* Application No. 44828/98, 29 June 1999; *Okonkwo v. Austria,* Application No. 35117/97, 22 May 2001; *Al-Nashif v. Bulgaria,* Application No. 50963/99, 20 June 2002. In each of these cases, the court opens the description of the facts by noting that the applicant is a stateless person. This finding clearly has no direct influence on the admissibility of the claim since it is the jurisdiction of the state – not nationality – that is relevant.

[51] Each of the major UN human rights instruments has its own committee or treaty body.

[52] Richard Lillich, *The human rights of aliens in contemporary international law,* Manchester University Press, Manchester: 1984, page 64.

regime. Once this issue is resolved, the human rights system and even the 1954 Statelessness Convention itself offers much greater scope for effectively protecting the rights of the stateless and access to naturalisation as a right of solution also becomes a more workable possibility.

Meanwhile, the challenge of protecting stateless persons rests on the enduring notion, apparent even within the modern human rights framework, that states may legitimately treat nationals and non-nationals differently. Indeed, it has been noted that the scope and content of the protection offered to non-nationals has been strongly influenced by the perception that non-citizenship is by and large a voluntary choice:

> The less-developed nature of the prohibition against discrimination on the grounds of citizenship reflects public opinion in many countries. A broad consensus disfavours differential treatment based on immutable characteristics such as race and ethnicity. By contrast, not withstanding the reality of forced migration, refugees fleeing persecution and persons made stateless against their will, status as a non-citizen is considered the product of voluntary choice – something which states may properly take into account in rationing the distribution of rights and benefits.[53]

So, while absolute non-discrimination between citizens and non-citizens is admittedly neither realistic nor appropriate - nationality is an existing and relevant legal status in today's world - the specific circumstance of statelessness does require a moderated approach. In striving to ensure that everyone enjoys the full spectrum of rights, the stateless may be owed some form of *positive* discrimination that takes into account the particular conundrum presented by their lack of nationality: differential treatment towards non-nationals that may generally be considered legitimate requires renewed reflection and assessment where the stateless are affected by it. Of course, with this in mind, the *identification* of situations of statelessness remains an absolutely critical task and one that deserves far greater consideration than it has achieved to date.

Meanwhile, since there is a noticeable progression towards the recognition of links other than nationality as a basis for the exercise of even those rights that have traditionally belonged to the very function of nationality (right to enter, diplomatic protection, even political rights), where is it more appropriate to take advantage of these developments if not to the benefit of stateless persons who would otherwise be left out? Nevertheless, it is important to remember that the ultimate form of protection that stateless persons can enjoy is the *resolution* of their plight. To this end, alongside a pro-active application of the norms relating to the prevention of statelessness,[54] naturalisation can be a indispensible tool. States and the international community alike should recall that, whatever the protection extended to stateless persons, the "lack or denial of citizenship creates conditions for human

[53] Open Society Justice Initiative, *Racial Discrimination and the Rights of Non-Citizens. Submission to the UN Committee on the Elimination of Racial Discrimination on the occasion of its 64th Session*, New York: 2004.

[54] Discussed in part 2.

insecurity".[55] So within the challenge of the protecting stateless persons lies the task of the further concretisation of a right of solution.

[55] Advisory Board on Human Security (prepared by Constantin Sokoloff), *Denial of Citizenship: A Challenge to Human Security,* February 2005, page 6.

PART 4

WHAT FUTURE FOR THE STATELESSNESS CONVENTIONS?

CHAPTER XIV

FINAL OBSERVATIONS

Roughly half a century ago, in an important study on nationality and statelessness prepared for the International Law Commission, statelessness was described as a "deep-rooted evil".[1] These are troubling words indeed. Equally so, is an account of similar vintage by the US Supreme Court of the "destruction" caused by the withdrawal of nationality and resultant statelessness:

> There may be involved no physical mistreatment, no primitive torture. There is instead the total destruction of the individual's status in organised society. It is a form of punishment more primitive than torture for it destroys for the individual the political existence that was centuries in the development. The punishment strips the citizen of his status in the international political community. His very existence is at the sufferance of the country in which he happens to find himself. While any one country may accord his some rights, and presumably as long as he remained in this country he would enjoy the limited rights of an alien, no country need do so because he is stateless. Furthermore, his enjoyment of even the limited rights of an alien might be subject to termination at any time by reason of deportation. In short, the expatriate has lost the right to have rights.[2]

Invoking, as it does, such imposing language, it is little wonder that the international community has taken an active – if, at times, uneven – interest in tackling statelessness.[3] The last 400-odd pages have been devoted to assessing this international response and thereby refreshing the picture of statelessness. In particular, through a detailed study of the relevant international legal framework we have considered the following question:

---

[1] Roberto Córdova, *Nationality, Including Statelessness. Third Report on the Elimination or Reduction of Statelessness by Roberto Córdova, Special Rapporteur,* A/CN.4/81, New York: 11 March 1954, page 28.

[2] US Supreme Court, *Trop v. Dulles, Secretary of State et. al.*, 1958. Recall also chapter III, section 1.

[3] For a concise overview of the international response to statelessness since World War II, see chapter II, section 3.

How can the way in which international law deals with the issue of statelessness be improved so as to ensure optimal protection of the individual and his rights?

We focused first on the actual avoidance or *prevention* of statelessness – as the most favourable outcome – and later on the *protection* of the rights of those persons who nevertheless find themselves stateless. This approach led to two sets of conclusions, to be found in chapters VIII and XIII respectively. The task for this closing chapter is to recap some of these findings (section 1) as well as to offer some broader reflections on the direction in which international law relating to the issue of statelessness has developed and on the challenges that remain to be fully answered (sections 2 to 4).

1 Nationality and Statelessness in the 21st Century

In the fifty years that have elapsed since the US Supreme Court ruling cited above, and indeed since the adoption of the two Statelessness Conventions, the international legal framework relating to nationality and statelessness has undergone a rather major evolution. According to the letter of international law, as it stands today, statelessness is no longer tantamount to the "total destruction of an individual's status in organised society" or the loss of the "right to have rights".[4] Nor are states as free as they once were to leave an individual without any citizenship or withdraw his only nationality.[5] Many of the necessary normative tools are now in place to prevent statelessness and, failing that, to protect the fundamental rights of the stateless. These are provided not only - indeed no longer even chiefly - by the tailor-made Statelessness Conventions, but also by a plethora of human rights and human rights-inspired instruments. Based on the findings in foregoing chapters, what follows below is a brief reflection upon the main strengths and weaknesses of the international response to questions of nationality and statelessness in the 21st century.

International law today reflects a mounting intolerance for statelessness. There are two main principles that are gaining ever more ground: the avoidance of statelessness at birth and the avoidance of denationalisation resulting in statelessness. Ultimately, these two standards are all that is needed to secure the prevention of statelessness since they focus on ensuring that every individual

[4] Recall the discussion of the impact of human rights law on the role of citizenship versus humanity in underpinning the "right to have rights". See chapter IX, section II.

[5] As illustrated by the fundamental change in perspective on the influence of international law in limiting states' freedom to attribute nationality as they deem fit, from the 1923 *Tunis and Morocco Nationality Decrees Case* of the Permanent Court of International Justice to the *Case of Yean and Bosico v. Dominican Republic,* settled by the Inter-American Court of Human Rights in 2005. The adoption of the 1930 Hague Convention on Certain Questions relating to the Conflict of Nationality Laws marked the beginning of an ongoing process of concretisation of the principle of the avoidance of statelessness. Later, the inclusion of the right to a nationality among the articles of the Universal Declaration on Human Rights provided fresh momentum for the battle to limit or indeed eradicate cases of statelessness. The provision, article 15, provided the inspiration for the elaboration of the right to a nationality in many other human rights instruments as well as for the formulation of the 1961 Convention on the Reduction of Statelessness. See chapter III, section 2.

acquires a nationality at the start of his lifetime and that this nationality is not lost unless another nationality is acquired. And both principles are reflected in the 1961 Convention on the Reduction of Statelessness and numerous human rights instruments. In the former, the principles have been transformed into a series of intricate provisions that detail which state is responsible for conferring nationality or for refraining from withdrawing citizenship and under which circumstances.[6] In the latter, we traced mainly more broadly stated norms, such as the right of every child to acquire a nationality and the prohibition of arbitrary deprivation of nationality.[7] But the 1961 Statelessness Convention clearly limits its ambitions to *reducing* the incidence of statelessness - thereby failing to provide for the unequivocal bestowal or retention of nationality where statelessness threatens - and fails to deal with a number of issues either persuasively or indeed at all.[8] Meanwhile the wider human rights framework offers sweeping standards that, in places, lack the detail that is required to ensure their full, correct and harmonised application – and the truly interesting and innovative developments that were traced are still in their infancy.[9] So, neither approach turned out to be infallible. Nor is the combined impact of the two sets of standards a guarantee that all causes of statelessness will be nipped in the bud.

As we moved on to look at the international legal framework for the protection of stateless persons, we found a similar story. The development of human rights law has resulted in an increasing move away from citizenship as the right to have rights, as described by the US Supreme Court, and towards the "denationalisation" of protection. Yet the recognition of the *right to a nationality* as a human right also reaffirmed the enduring relevance of nationality: the human rights system can only maintain its aspiration of universality with the guarantee that every human will also hold a nationality. Although then, there is perhaps less need for a stateless-specific instrument today than there was prior to the advent of the major human rights instruments, it has not become redundant. The 1954 Statelessness Convention attempts to answer to this need, but falls short on quite a number of counts - in particular thanks to the trademark technique of offering different rights at different "levels of attachment" and often only to a weak, contingent standard.[10] Meanwhile, within the human rights framework itself, standards have begun to develop that address the situation of non-nationals or even stateless persons specifically. But the exact treatment owed to these groups under contemporary human rights law is still hazy in many areas, for example with respect to economic, social and cultural rights and in particular in developing countries.[11]

---

[6] See, in particular, the discussion of the 1961 Statelessness Convention's response to the technical causes of statelessness in chapter IV.

[7] Only in such instruments as the European Convention on Nationality, the Council of Europe Convention on the avoidance of statelessness in relation to State succession and the ILC Draft Articles on Nationality of Natural Persons in relation to the Succession of States – those documents that are geared specifically to nationality questions – was the same level of detail traced as that found in the 1961 Convention on the Reduction of Statelessness.

[8] See chapter VIII, section 1.

[9] See chapter VIII, section 2.

[10] See chapter XIII, section 1.

[11] See chapter XIII, section 2.

Unmistakably then, a number of challenges remain – not least of which is to ensure the full implementation and enforcement of all of the existing norms.[12] But numerous gaps were also found in the normative frameworks for the prevention of statelessness and protection of stateless persons.[13] Consequently, various suggestions were raised for the further clarification and elaboration of standards with a view to *improving the way in which international law deals with the issue of statelessness so as to ensure optimal protection of the individual and his rights.*[14] In the context of both prevention and protection, we were able to trace certain current and relevant developments that helped to show the way forward. For instance, where the prevention of statelessness is concerned, the recently formulated texts addressing nationality and statelessness in the context of state succession were found to provide inspiration for standards that could be applied much more broadly and to great effect. Thus, it was suggested that the procedural guarantees elaborated and the notion of a right of option as a way of preventing ongoing disputes on nationality attribution - and promoting the acquisition of the most appropriate nationality - be implemented across the board as general tools in the prevention of statelessness.[15] Then, for the protection of stateless persons, instruments such as the Migrant Workers Convention offer an example of how the current international framework for the protection of stateless persons could be revisited and a new document elaborated to build upon the standards set by the 1954 Statelessness Convention.[16]

One of the most pervasive issues to be dealt with is the nexus between inclusion and exclusion on the basis of nationality, and inclusion and exclusion on the basis of immigration status. An enduring, fundamental function of nationality is providing the holder with a "home", a state to which they can always return and in which they have an irrefutable right to reside. On the one hand, this implies that stateless persons have no undisputed right to live anywhere – and indeed we saw that gaining and retaining lawful access to the territory of a(ny) state presents serious difficulties to the stateless.[17] This, in turn results in problems relating to detention, family separation and access to rights and services - including many of those elaborated in the 1954 Statelessness Convention - as the connection of habitual or permanent residence is increasingly recognised as an alternative basis to citizenship for the enjoyment of rights.[18] On the other hand, we discovered a connection between statelessness and displacement,[19] as well as the fact that the possession of an unlawful or ambiguous immigration status can contribute to the

[12] See chapter VIII, section 4 and chapter XIII, section 4 and sections 3 and 4 of this chapter below.

[13] See chapter VIII, sections 2 and 3 and chapter XIII, sections 2 and 3.

[14] The overall research question for this study, as cited at the beginning of this chapter. See for the full discussion of ways to improve the normative framework for the prevention of statelessness chapter VIII, section 3 and, for the protection of stateless persons, chapter XIII, section 3.

[15] See chapter VIII, section 3.

[16] See chapter XIII, section 3.

[17] See chapter X, the introduction to section 2.2.

[18] Consider the example of diplomatic protection where the "nationality of the claim" has for a very long time been critical and where the possibility is now being considered of recognising habitual residence as a sufficient connection with a state, in lieu of nationality, for the stateless. See chapter XII, section 3.

[19] See chapter II, section 2.

creation and perpetuation of statelessness.[20] This underlines the urgency of securing the stateless a right to live somewhere. Of all of the potential, supplementary standard-setting activities that I have discussed, this is the area that is at once one of the most imperative and the most complex. As explained in chapter XIII, there is ample scope to build upon the UN Human Rights Committee's efforts to identify an individuals *own country,* regardless of the question of citizenship, for the purposes of the enjoyment of the right to enter and reside.[21] The stateless are evidently the group *par excellence* to benefit from the further development of this notion as without this construction, they will continue to lack an *own country* and the very basic security that this offers. Remember though, that a further crystallisation and clarification of the norms relating to the prevention of statelessness is absolutely indispensable to this quest of ascertaining which state is to be considered a stateless person's *own country* – because this quest is tantamount to establishing which country is "responsible" for an individual's statelessness, in violation of international standards.[22]

Subsequently, once a stateless person's *own country* is established, there is great scope for ensuring that they enjoy the full spectrum of human rights. Indeed, this process can be likened to the creation of an *international* concept of nationality for the purpose of applying *international* legal protections. Support for this approach can be found in the jurisprudence relating to international claims. In determining whether a state is entitled to exercise diplomatic protection in a particular case – thus, in establishing whether the bond of nationality is present – international tribunals have been known to disregard the municipal finding of nationality. Where the tribunal determines that nationality has been acquired by fraud or in a manner that is "inconsistent with the provisions of international treaties governing questions of nationality [or] contrary to the general principles of the Law of Nations on nationality",[23] it has discounted this nationality for the purposes of applying international law relating to diplomatic protection. And

> in doing so, [the tribunals] deviated from the general rule of international law that questions of nationality are determined by the State concerned under its own law.[24]

In such cases, by disregarding the municipal finding of nationality, the tribunals have created a kind of "functional statelessness" for the purpose of international law.[25] In contrast, in order to offer optimal protection to the stateless, it may be possible to use the broadening concept of *own country* to create a kind of

---

[20] See in particular chapter VII, section 2.

[21] See chapter XIII, section 3.

[22] See chapter X, section 2.2.2.

[23] Paul Weis, *Nationality and Statelessness in International Law*, Kluwer Academic Publishers Group, Dordrecht: 1979, page 212.

[24] Paul Weis, *Nationality and Statelessness in International Law*, Kluwer Academic Publishers Group, Dordrecht: 1979, page 220.

[25] Recall also the "Nottebohm Case" where the International Court of Justice ruled that the naturalisation of the applicant was to be disregarded for the purposes of applying international law and thereby the exercise of diplomatic protection. International Court of Justice, *"Nottebohm Case" (Liechtenstein v. Guatamala)*, 1953. See chapter XII, section 3.

"functional nationality" for the purposes of international law. Thus, where a state has denationalised an individual, rendering him stateless, in a manner that is *inconsistent with the provisions of international treaties governing questions of nationality [or] contrary to the general principles of the Law of Nations on nationality,* the denationalisation could be disregarded and the state held fully accountable for the treatment of the individual as though he were a national. The identification of a stateless person's *own country* could thereby procure him access to the full range of rights that are to be enjoyed by citizens, including those linked to political participation, on the basis of non-discrimination with all other nationals of the state. If this approach were to be adopted, it would help to promote not only the protection of stateless persons, but also the prevention of statelessness. Any state policy that would deliberately render a person or group stateless – in disregard of the relevant international norms - with a view to restricting their exercise of rights (i.e. subsequently denying them the right to remain and expelling them or preventing them from participating in an election) would become a futile exercise. The state would still be fully accountable for the subsequent treatment of the individual or group on the basis of the "functional nationality" attributed for the purposes of international law. So, the 21st century international legal framework relating to nationality and statelessness offers enormous potential for tackling even the more demanding issues relating to prevention and protection, if existing developments such as those described in this section were to be pursued further. But an effective response to statelessness may demand more than prevention and protection measures, as will be discussed next.

2 Prevention, protection and more

The opening paragraphs of this book described how the phrase "nationality matters", the book's title, offers a superb depiction of the dual nature of the response to statelessness: prevention and protection. Thereafter, the discussion has indeed been focused either on *nationality* matters - on what contemporary international law has to say about the freedom of states to set their own rules on the attribution of nationality (part 2); or on the extent to which nationality *matters* - on the enduring importance of nationality within the current international legal setting (part 3). Having arrived at the stage of offering some final reflections on the findings from this investigation, it is time to also reconsider this basic premise of a two-dimensional response to statelessness. In fact, it is time to admit that an effective response to statelessness may equally be deemed to demand not two, but four complimentary strategies. Firstly, within both the context of the prevention of statelessness and the protection of stateless persons, we uncovered an underlying need for the *identification* of cases of statelessness or situations where statelessness threatens. And secondly, we found that where prevention strategies have failed, the protection of stateless persons *as* stateless persons should be seen only as an intermediate response, with the *resolution* of statelessness through the (re)acquisition of nationality the ultimate goal.

The notion of a four-dimensional response can actually be traced in UNHCR's current policy towards its statelessness mandate.[26] In the most comprehensive Conclusion on statelessness to date, adopted by UNHCR's Executive Committee in 2006, the four elements are clearly enunciated: the *identification*, *prevention* and *reduction* (i.e. resolution of cases) of statelessness and the *protection* of stateless persons.[27] This Conclusion sets out the contours of UNHCR's strategy towards statelessness for the years to come, describing what it considers to be the agency's main tasks under each of these four components of the overall response.[28] The question is, how do we reconcile this new, four-dimensional concept of the problem of statelessness with the apparently two-dimensional approach taken to the issue under international law and indeed reflected in this manuscript?

It is true that there are just two universal, tailor-made statelessness instruments, the 1961 and 1954 Statelessness Conventions, and that these Conventions address prevention and protection respectively. It is also true that this manuscript echoed the dualistic approach by dividing the overall research question in two and offering first an analysis of the international legal framework for the prevention of statelessness and then of the framework for the protection of stateless persons. Yet we saw that even when following the structure of the Statelessness Conventions, the other two aspects naturally become part of the discussion. The question of identification was actually raised very early on when we considered the initial dilemma of defining statelessness for the purposes of establishing the scope of application of the specialised legal regime that addresses the issue.[29] Thereafter, the challenge of identifying cases that call for the application of international norms relating to statelessness came up for discussion again when drawing conclusions on the effectiveness of the legal regime for both prevention[30] and protection.[31] Meanwhile, in accordance with the way in which this book is structured - to put the Statelessness Conventions centre stage throughout the investigation - the resolution or reduction of statelessness was flagged as an issue in the chapter on the "special needs" of the stateless.[32] The reduction of statelessness, i.e. the opportunity to

---

[26] As we have seen, the history of UNHCR's involvement in the issue of statelessness dates back to 1974, when the UN General Assembly bestowed UNHCR with various tasks in relation to the supervision of the 1961 Convention on the Reduction of Statelessness. In the decades since, UNHCR's mandate on statelessness gradually expanded, on the basis of subsequent General Assembly resolutions, to include *all* states and an increasing array of activities and responsibilities. See chapter III, section 3 and chapter IX, section 3.

[27] UNHCR Executive Committee, *Conclusion on Identification, Prevention and Reduction of Statelessness and Protection of Stateless Persons, No. 106,* 57th Session, Geneva, 2006.

[28] The agency is expected together with states and other international partners, to pursue "targeted activities to support the identification, prevention and reduction of statelessness and to further the protection of stateless persons". The idea is that all four dimensions will be included in future planning, strategy-setting and reporting materials and reflected in the agency's operational response to statelessness around the world. See UNHCR Executive Committee, *Conclusion on Identification, Prevention and Reduction of Statelessness and Protection of Stateless Persons, No. 106,* 57th Session, Geneva, 2006, paragraph (a).

[29] See chapter II, section 4.

[30] See chapter VIII, section 4.

[31] See chapter XIII, section 4.

[32] In assessing the international legal framework for the protection of stateless persons, we discussed three categories of protection: civil and political rights; economic, social and cultural rights; and

(re)acquire a nationality, was thus largely discussed as an element of the overall protection response since it was the 1954 Statelessness Convention that put forward a right of solution.[33] So, what this study has shown is that, in practice, whether you categorise the international response to statelessness as two or four-dimensional is neither here nor there.[34] The only question of any consequence remains whether international law provides an appropriate answer to the "additional" challenges of identification and resolution of statelessness.

As far back as chapter II, concerns were raised that the international legal framework may provide insufficient guidance for the identification of statelessness. We saw, for instance, that the lack of (uniform) procedures for the identification of cases of statelessness was hampering the collection of data on the scale of the phenomenon.[35] And we noted that the debate on the aptness of the international definition of "stateless person" could in fact be answered through a comprehensive framework for the identification of statelessness – without touching the definition itself.[36] Therefore, in the process of discerning the global magnitude of statelessness and discussing the contention that surrounds the definition of statelessness, we found evidence to suggest that the appropriate tools for the arduous task of identifying statelessness may be lacking. Later, we tested this speculation when we looked for principles, procedures or guidelines relating to the identification of (the threat of) statelessness within the international legal framework for the prevention of statelessness and the protection of stateless persons.

Disappointingly, we found the prediction to be largely accurate. Neither of the Statelessness Conventions offers any suggestion as to how to identify stateless persons or cases in which the individual would "otherwise be stateless" – precisely those situations that call for the application of the norms espoused. Meanwhile, the broader field of international human rights law provided only a few very basic clues as to how states are to go about the process of identification of statelessness and what types of evidence of nationality – or of statelessness – can be taken into account. Thus, in the context of prevention we discovered that the European Convention on Nationality obliges state parties to cooperate and exchange information,[37] two techniques that can assist in the challenge of identification.[38] We also noted with interest the innovative provision in the Council of Europe Convention on the avoidance of statelessness in relation to State succession that calls upon states to *lower* the standard of proof in order to facilitate the prevention

"special needs". This last set of norms relates to certain rights or facilities that the stateless require by virtue of their very statelessness. See chapter XII.

33 See chapter XII, section 1.

34 In other words, whether you view *identification* as a given - as inherent in both prevention and protection - and *reduction* as an element of protection or whether you deem each of these aspects to be a strategy or response in its own right.

35 See chapter II, section 2.

36 See chapter II, section 4.

37 Articles 23 and 24 of the European Convention on Nationality.

38 See chapter VIII, section 4. Note that the duty to cooperate internationally would be beneficial not only for the identification of statelessness and of situations where statelessness threatens, but also in realising the subsequent prevention of statelessness or resolution of existing cases of statelessness.

of statelessness in the context of state succession[39] – although the same instrument does not describe how the standard of proof should generally be established.[40] In the context of protection, we discovered that even though international courts have undertaken the task of identifying an individual's nationality or statelessness for the purposes of deciding a case on a protection issue, such jurisprudence is limited and offers only a minor insight into the question of proof of nationality or statelessness. The courts looked at the pertinent domestic law and considered the "evidence" relating to the position of the applicants under this law – one element of which may be birth registration – but did not discuss what kinds of evidence may generally be admitted or where the burden of proof lies.[41] The only conclusion that can be drawn on the basis of these observations is that the international legal framework does not adequately address the challenge of identification that is critical to the prevention (and reduction) of statelessness and the protection of stateless persons. Until more effort is put into this aspect of the response to statelessness, the actual implementation and enforcement of all of the existing standards in this field is likely to continue to suffer. In the following section, I will offer some thoughts on how to progress on this matter.

In the meantime, we can note that the findings with regards to the resolution or reduction of statelessness were more encouraging. Although the international community rejected a proposal for a convention devoted to the reduction or elimination of "present" statelessness,[42] both the international legal framework on the prevention of statelessness and that which addresses the protection of stateless persons offer some standards that are relevant to the resolution of existing cases. On the one hand, the norms that have been espoused for the purposes of the prevention of statelessness - in the 1961 Convention on the Reduction of Statelessness and elsewhere - can be used, by extension, to resolve situations of statelessness. In fact, the distinction between prevention and reduction is not finite. For instance, where a state withdraws an individual's citizenship, for whatever reason, only to discover afterwards that this was the person's only nationality, the subsequent reinstatement of nationality in order to avoid statelessness - perhaps following a successful appeal of the decision - could rightly be described as either prevention or reduction.[43] Similarly, if a state adopts legislation to correct the gender imbalance in its *jus sanguinis* laws in order to prevent statelessness from arising where the father's nationality is absent or unknown, by providing for retroactive application, the new law that is geared towards prevention can also achieve the resolution of cases of

[39] Article 8 of the Council of Europe Convention on the avoidance of statelessness in relation to State succession.
[40] See chapter VIII, section 4.
[41] See chapter XIII, section 4.
[42] See chapter XII, section 1.1.
[43] Consider the example of the man who was rendered stateless in the Netherlands through the withdrawal of his Dutch citizenship on the premise that he had failed to fulfil his commitment to renounce his Egyptian nationality, even though he had in fact managed to lose this other citizenship. The domestic court subsequently found the withdrawal of Dutch citizenship to be contrary to the law, thereby ensuring the reinstatement of the mans nationality. This example is discussed in chapter IV, section 4 (on loss of nationality as a cause of statelessness) and chapter V, section 2 (on illegal deprivation of nationality). The case is also cited in chapter X, section 4 when the access to courts for stateless persons is considered.

statelessness that have arisen in the past.[44] On the other hand, where a pro-active application of the standards relating to the prevention of statelessness is not possible or offers no solace in a particular case, international law also offers some scope for the acquisition by a stateless person of a nationality through a newly formed bond with a state. Within the *protection* framework of the 1954 Convention relating to the Status of Stateless Persons, alongside the provisions prescribing a certain standard of treatment to be enjoyed by stateless persons during their statelessness, we found an article addressing a "right of solution". The 1954 Statelessness Convention thereby adds facilitated naturalisation to the toolbox for the reduction of statelessness.[45] And the broader field of international (human rights) law confirms that this option should be available to stateless persons - at least to the extent that states may not uphold *unreasonable impediments* to naturalisation as well as that a person's statelessness must be taken into account and may call for facilitation of procedures or relaxation of criteria for naturalisation.[46]

Thus, in spite of the lack of a specialised instrument on the reduction of statelessness, the international legal framework does provide some highly relevant norms that may assist with the resolution of cases. However, neither of the routes described above - using the international legal standards relating to prevention or protection – offers a sure-fire solution, as is arguably evidenced by the enduring existence of statelessness on a large scale. To begin with, in part 2 we found that the norms relating to the prevention of statelessness still exhibit a number of gaps and ambiguities with the result that the task of pinpointing the "responsible" state and "reversing" the situation may not always be straight forward.[47] And this problem clearly grows more acute the longer statelessness endures since the details surrounding the origins of statelessness may become (further) obscured and the population in question may, through displacement or migration, develop an increasingly close connection with another – perhaps previously uninvolved – state. Then the adoption of a law or policy of (re)instatement of nationality for the reduction of statelessness that is based on international standards relating to prevention is neither a simple avenue to pursue, nor necessarily one that is in the best interests of the persons concerned. Nor would it be appropriate to rely entirely on naturalisation as the means of resolving cases of statelessness. A major impediment for many stateless persons in seeking naturalisation in order to resolve their situation is the need to first secure *lawful* residence in a state.[48] As we have repeatedly discussed, this is no easy feat.[49] Even when lawful residence has been attained, notwithstanding what has been said above about the prohibition of unreasonable impediments to naturalisation and the clear call for states to facilitate the naturalisation of stateless persons, states are still largely free to set the

[44] The legislative changes in 2007 in Morocco were given as an example of this type of combined strategy of prevention and reduction. See chapter XII, section 1.

[45] Article 32 of the 1954 Convention relating to the Status of Stateless Persons. Note, however, that this provision is formulated in vague and facultative language whereby its added value can be questioned. See chapter XII, section 1.1 and chapter XIII, section 1.

[46] See chapter XII, section 1.2 and chapter XIII, section 2.

[47] See on the remaining gaps in the normative framework for the prevention of statelessness chapter VIII, in particular section 3.

[48] See chapter XII, sections 1 and 4.

[49] See chapter X, section 2.2, chapter XIII and section 1 of the present chapter.

conditions for naturalisation and so it is not always a real possibility for the stateless population. Moreover, naturalisation – even if facilitated – is by definition a less powerful tool than a policy of automatic conferral of nationality for the qualifying population:

> Typically naturalisation procedures contain an element of discretion and tend to be lengthy, whereas the right of option into the nationality can take place immediately through registration and is, in principle, not possible to reject on discretionary grounds.[50]

The clarification of standards concerning the prevention of statelessness[51] as well as of those that relate to access to naturalisation for stateless persons[52] would undoubtedly help to further guide reasonable and appropriate strategies to address existing cases of statelessness around the world.[53] In addition, it would be hugely beneficial to explore other avenues for the reduction of statelessness. In particular the increased use of a right of option should be promoted as a means of tackling any ongoing dispute between states on the ultimate "responsibility" for a certain situation of statelessness and as an alternative to facilitated naturalisation.[54] Nevertheless, in practice, before any existing or future standards for the prevention or reduction of statelessness and the protection of stateless persons can be applied, renewed efforts must be made to identify those situations in which the norms are applicable, which brings us back to the "fourth dimension", identification.

3 Meeting the Challenge of Identification

One of the major challenges that was raised early on in this study, and has been a recurring concern throughout, is the *identification* of statelessness. Identifying situations where statelessness threatens is obviously a fundamental preliminary step towards applying any norms that seek to prevent statelessness. And identifying

---

[50] Carol Batchelor, "Transforming international legal principles into national law: the right to a nationality and the avoidance of statelessness" in *Refugee Survey Quarterly,* 2006, pages 15-16.

[51] See suggestions raised in chapter VIII, section 3.

[52] See chapter XIII, section 3.

[53] Note that the further enhancement of the international legal framework to guide the resolution of cases of statelessness is not, of itself, a quick-fix answer to existing stateless situations. Much also depends on the political and practical realities, including the willpower of the government to adopt any necessary legislative changes, the availability of the required resources for the implementation of a perhaps large-scale reduction strategy and the attitude of the population towards the "solution" that is presented to them. For some notion of the complexities involved in a (large-scale) project to resolve statelessness, see the description of the campaign to reduce statelessness in Sri Lanka in Sulakshani Perera, "Sri Lankan Success Story", in *Refugees Magazine,* Number 147, Issue 3, 2007, pages 20-23 and "Statelessness in Sri Lanka", specially devoted UNHCR webpage, accessible via http://www.unhcr.org.

[54] A right of option is currently prescribed within the context of state succession but is a valuable tool for the prevention and reduction of statelessness across the full spectrum of cases and should therefore be pursued further. A right of option assures not only that a nationality is genuinely acquired (lacks the discretionary characteristic of naturalisation), but also helps to ensure that the individual ends up with the nationality of the state with which he is most closely connected. See chapter VI, section 3 and chapter VIII, section 3.

cases of statelessness is evidently a critical precursor to promoting the enjoyment of standards relating specifically to the protection of stateless persons as well as the reduction of statelessness – and indeed to identifying other individuals who are at risk of statelessness through their connection to a stateless person. As such, the task of identification forms an inherent part of any response to statelessness. Yet, as explained,[55] identification is also the activity for which the least guidance is provided by the international legal framework relating to statelessness. As a result, we found cases in which individuals have failed to rely on back-up clauses that were in place to prevent statelessness[56] and discovered a wide divergence – or even lack – of procedures for the determination of "Stateless Person Status" for the purposes of accessing the relevant rights and benefits.[57] Therefore, arguably the greatest threat to the whole system that has developed for the prevention (and reduction) of statelessness and the protection of stateless persons is the inability to identify the situations in which these specialised norms are to be applied. Fortunately, if we expand our search for clues, there are some avenues that could be pursued in an effort to build upon the meagre set of suggestions for undertaking the task of identification of statelessness that has been extracted from the international legal framework relating to statelessness.[58] Indeed, there are two main areas in which to seek further, valuable guidance or information in order to meet the challenge of identification: the principles and guidelines for Refugee Status Determination and jurisprudence relating to international claims (diplomatic protection).

Refugee Status Determination (RSD) is the process whereby an individual gains recognition as a refugee under the terms of the 1951 Refugee Convention, thereby unlocking access to the rights bestowed on the basis of this instrument. It is the subject of various detailed handbooks and guidelines.[59] In the absence of similar guidelines on - or a harmonised approach to – "Stateless Person Status Determination", we can fall back on some of the instructions relating to RSD to gain an understanding of how to tackle the identification of statelessness. A first lesson that can be extracted relates to the burden of proof – the question as to whose responsibility it is, in principle, to establish evidence of refugee or stateless person status. Recalling that "it is a general legal principle that the burden of proof lies on the person submitting a claim", UNHCR's Handbook on RSD determines that "the

[55] In section 2 of the present chapter.

[56] Recall the "Baby Andrew" case presented in chapter III, section 3 and the case of *Karassev v. Finland,* discussed in chapter VIII, section 4.

[57] See chapter XIII, section 4.

[58] See section 2 above.

[59] These include UNHCR, *Handbook on Procedures and Criteria for Determining Refugee Status under the 1951 Convention and the 1967 Protocol relating to the Status of Refugees,* HCR/IP/Eng/Rev.1, Reedited January 1992; UNHCR, *Refugee Status Determination – Identifying who is a refugee,* Self-study module No. 2, September 2005; A series of UNHCR *Guidelines on International Protection* that deal with specific aspects of the refugee definition, including on Gender-Related Persecution (HRC/GIP/02/01, 7 May 2002), Membership of a particular social group (HRC/GIP/02/02, 7 May 2002), Internal Flight or Relocation Alternative (HRC/GIP/03/04, 23 July 2003) and Religion-Based Refugee Claims (HRC/GIP/04/06, 28 April 2004).

relevant facts of the individual case will have to be furnished in the first place by the applicant himself".[60] But then, the Handbook goes on to admit that

> often, however, an applicant may not be able to support his statements by documentary or other proof [...] thus, while the burden of proof in principle rests on the applicant, the duty to ascertain and evaluate all the relevant facts is shared between the applicant and the examiner. Indeed, in some cases, it may be for the examiner to use all the means at his disposal to produce the necessary evidence in support of the application.[61]

The task of establishing statelessness is arguably similarly arduous: to prove statelessness "the individual must demonstrate something that is *not* there".[62] The applicant for stateless person status may therefore be unable to furnish, of his own accord, satisfactory evidence that he is not considered a national by any state under the operation of its law. Therefore, the approach to the burden of proof that is outlined above could also be adopted in Stateless Person Status Determination as well as in cases where statelessness threatens (i.e. to establish the fact that the person would "otherwise be stateless"). The applicant would be required to cooperate fully by presenting all relevant facts and documents, while the authority that is charged with assessing the application would also be obliged to take an active role in ascertaining the status of the applicant.[63] The importance of international cooperation and consultation in the identification of statelessness is thereby reaffirmed - a course that should be initiated, if necessary, by the authority charged with Stateless Person Status Determination.

Another important point is that, in the context of Refugee Status Determination, states are also compelled to consider the nationality of the person in question. One element of the definition of a refugee is *displacement* and in order to determine whether the individual is outside his country of nationality, that nationality must first be identified. Moreover, stateless persons may also fall within the definition of a refugee, whereby the displacement and well-founded fear of persecution must be established with respect to his country of former habitual residence – necessitating both a finding of statelessness and the identification of said country. So, since the adoption of the 1951 Refugee Convention, government (immigration) authorities and UNHCR have indirectly been called upon to establish the nationality of many millions of people.[64] Yet relatively little guidance has been

---

[60] UNHCR, *Handbook on Procedures and Criteria for Determining Refugee Status under the 1951 Convention and the 1967 Protocol relating to the Status of Refugees,* HCR/IP/Eng/Rev.1, Reedited January 1992, paragraphs 195 and 196.

[61] UNHCR, *Handbook on Procedures and Criteria for Determining Refugee Status under the 1951 Convention and the 1967 Protocol relating to the Status of Refugees,* HCR/IP/Eng/Rev.1, Reedited January 1992, paragraph 196.

[62] Carol Batchelor The 1954 Convention relating to the Status of Stateless Persons: Implementation within the European Union Member States and Recommendations for Harmonisation 2004, page 13.

[63] See also Carol Batchelor The 1954 Convention relating to the Status of Stateless Persons: Implementation within the European Union Member States and Recommendations for Harmonisation 2004, page 15.

[64] In fact, it is within the context of Refugee Status Determination that many cases of statelessness are flagged for the first time – in particular in the absence of any separate procedures devoted to the

provided on how to undertake this aspect of the RSD[65] - the real crux of the issue in RSD being the identification of a well-founded fear of persecution on one of the grounds enumerated in the 1951 Refugee Convention.[66] Various materials produced by UNHCR on RSD nevertheless offer a few helpful tips. The first is that the determination that a person is outside his country of nationality or, if stateless, is outside his country of habitual residence – and thereby, by default, the identification of that nationality or statelessness – is

> to be established on the basis of documents, statements or any other information submitted by the applicant or obtained from other sources.[67]

The UNHCR Handbook on RSD then explains that

> nationality may be proved by the possession of a national passport. Possession of such a passport creates a *prima facie* presumption that the holder is a national of the country of issue, unless the passport itself states otherwise.[68]

For Refugee Status Determination then, the individual's passport is the clear port of call in establishing nationality. This is unsurprising in view of what has been said about the contemporary role of the passport in vouching for a persons nationality and thereby his right to re-admission to the issuing state.[69] In the context of identifying (a threat of) statelessness, the *prima facie* presumption of nationality created by a passport can help to establish the position of the individual and those connected to him or her under the relevant domestic laws. For instance, it will help to determine whether any descendents run the risk of statelessness in view of the applicable laws and the further circumstances of their birth. Regrettably, the Handbook does not delineate what evidence of nationality should be considered in the absence of a passport. Nor is it suggested that the simple inability to produce a passport creates a *prima facie* presumption of statelessness. Such a policy may in fact be highly undesirable as it could open the door to abuse, with individuals

---

identification of statelessness. UNHCR and IPU, *Nationality and statelessness. A handbook for parliamentarians*, 2005, page 19.

[65] This may explain the fact that, notwithstanding what was said in the previous note, when surveyed, almost 50% of respondent states reported that within their Refugee Status Determination procedures they had no way of identifying stateless applicants. UNHCR, *Final report concerning the Questionnaire on statelessness pursuant to the Agenda for Protection,* Geneva: March 2004, page 27.

[66] Note that, for the same reason, the literature also pays little attention paid to the assessment of the fact of being "outside the country of nationality". See for instance James Hathaway, *The Rights of Refugees Under International Law*, Cambridge University Press, Cambridge: 2005; and Guy Goodwin-Gill; Jane McAdam, *The refugee in international law*, Oxford University Press, Oxford: 2007.

[67] UNHCR, *Refugee Status Determination – Identifying who is a refugee,* Self-study module No. 2, September 2005, page 29.

[68] UNHCR, *Handbook on Procedures and Criteria for Determining Refugee Status under the 1951 Convention and the 1967 Protocol relating to the Status of Refugees,* HCR/IP/Eng/Rev.1, Reedited January 1992, paragraph 93.

[69] See chapter X, section 2.2 and chapter XII, section 2. Moreover, Weis confirms that the administrative practice of states is such that "a foreign national passport is, as a rule, accepted as *prima facie* evidence of the holder's nationality". Paul Weis, *Nationality and Statelessness in International Law*, Kluwer Academic Publishers Group, Dordrecht: 1979, page 228.

deliberately destroying or refusing to present their passport in order to access protection as a stateless person.

Meanwhile, if a person in possession of a passport nevertheless asserts a claim to statelessness, he must "substantiate his claim, for example, by showing that the passport is a so-called 'passport of convenience' (an apparently regular national passport that is sometimes issued by a national authority to non-nationals)".[70] Just what evidence can be brought forward is not discussed.[71] However, some pertinent comments can be found in a separate paragraph on the position of a person who appears to hold more than one nationality:

> In examining the case of an applicant with dual or multiple nationality, it is necessary [...] to distinguish between the possession of a nationality in the legal sense and the availability of protection by the country concerned. There will be cases where the applicant has the nationality of a country in regard to which he alleges no fear, but such nationality may be deemed ineffective as it does not entail the protection normally granted to nationals. In such circumstances, the possession of the second nationality would not be inconsistent with refugee status. As a rule, there should have been a request for, and a refusal of, protection before it can be established that a given nationality is ineffective. If there is no explicit refusal of protection, absence of a reply within reasonable time may be considered a refusal.[72]

Admittedly, this notion of discounting an individual's *second* nationality if it is deemed to be "ineffective" can be considered to be very specific to the refugee context.[73] Nevertheless, the steps described for the establishment of an "ineffective

[70] UNHCR, *Handbook on Procedures and Criteria for Determining Refugee Status under the 1951 Convention and the 1967 Protocol relating to the Status of Refugees,* HCR/IP/Eng/Rev.1, Reedited January 1992, paragraph 93.

[71] The Handbook does foresee a role for the issuing authority in clarifying the situation, but, depending on the response, this is not necessarily decisive: "In certain cases, it might be possible to obtain information from the authority that issued the passport. If such information cannot be obtained, or cannot be obtained within reasonable time, the examiner will have to decide on the credibility of the applicant's assertion in weighing all other elements of his story". UNHCR, *Handbook on Procedures and Criteria for Determining Refugee Status under the 1951 Convention and the 1967 Protocol relating to the Status of Refugees,* HCR/IP/Eng/Rev.1, Reedited January 1992, paragraph 93. According to Weis, the proof of nationality provided by a passport "can be rebutted by other evidence that the holder does not possess the nationality indicated by his passport, in particular if there is good reason to believe that he obtained the passport by fraud or misrepresentation". Paul Weis, *Nationality and Statelessness in International Law*, Kluwer Academic Publishers Group, Dordrecht: 1979, page 228.

[72] UNHCR, *Handbook on Procedures and Criteria for Determining Refugee Status under the 1951 Convention and the 1967 Protocol relating to the Status of Refugees,* HCR/IP/Eng/Rev.1, Reedited January 1992, paragraph 107. The self-study module on RSD explains that the second nationality is only relevant "if it carries with it the full range of rights normally enjoyed by citizens of the country [...] this is not always the case, and decision-makers must distinguish between the possession of nationality merely in a legal sense and the actual availability of protection in the country, or countries, concerned". UNHCR, *Refugee Status Determination – Identifying who is a refugee,* Self-study module No. 2, September 2005, page 29.

[73] It has to do with the fact that "national protection takes precedence over international protection", so when there is a real alternative source of national protection - a second, effective nationality - the

nationality" in the context of RSD may be used, by extension, as a tool in the identification of statelessness. Thus, if there has been "a request for, and a refusal of, protection" or the "absence of a reply within reasonable time", this may be factored in as evidence towards substantiating an individual's claim that - perhaps even despite the possession of a passport - he is not considered by that state to be a national.[74] Batchelor has followed this line of reasoning in her reflections on the standard of proof in identifying statelessness and suggests that

> from a practical perspective, it might be assumed that if a State refuses to indicate that a person *is* a national, this itself is a form of evidence which could have a bearing on the claim because States normally extend diplomatic services and protection to their nationals.[75]

Such facts would obviously have to be weighed up alongside any other relevant and available evidence.

Another area of law that requires the determination of an individual's nationality is the settlement of international claims, whereby the "nationality of the claim" - the basis for the exercise of diplomatic protection by a state - must generally be established before the case can be considered on its merits.[76] Jurisprudence relating to such international claims is therefore a further useful source of information about how nationality can be established. Weis has conducted a detailed study of such cases and his findings are of great interest.[77] According to his research, there is no significant uniformity in the way in which international tribunals deal with this problem.[78] He did, however, discover that such tribunals admitted (at least) four types of evidence:

> (1) proof of facts from which the possession of nationality follows according to municipal law; [...]
>
> (2) direct proof, usually by documentary evidence, that the competent authority had determined the person to be a national or had certified his nationality with conclusive effect; [...]

---

individual cannot rely on international protection. UNHCR, *Handbook on Procedures and Criteria for Determining Refugee Status under the 1951 Convention and the 1967 Protocol relating to the Status of Refugees,* HCR/IP/Eng/Rev.1, Reedited January 1992, paragraph 106. Moreover, keep in mind that the finding that national protection is lacking is only one basic element of the refugee definition, the individual must also exhibit a well-founded fear of persecution on one of the grounds listed in the 1951 Refugee Convention in order to be considered a refugee.

[74] Recall, once again, the comments made in chapter II, section 4 on the role that the establishment of an ineffective nationality can play in identifying cases of statelessness under the official definition.

[75] Carol Batchelor The 1954 Convention relating to the Status of Stateless Persons: Implementation within the European Union Member States and Recommendations for Harmonisation 2004, page 15.

[76] See on the doctrine of diplomatic protection and the role of nationality chapter XII, section 3.

[77] Paul Weis, *Nationality and Statelessness in International Law*, Kluwer Academic Publishers Group, Dordrecht: 1979, Chapter 13 on "Proof of Nationality, pages 204-236. See also chapter II, section 4.

[78] Paul Weis, *Nationality and Statelessness in International Law*, Kluwer Academic Publishers Group, Dordrecht: 1979, page 215.

(3) evidence, as a rule documentary, that an authority of the State concerned was satisfied that the person possessed the nationality of that State; [and]

(4) proof of facts from which it could be inferred that the person was considered as a national by a competent of authority of the State.[79]

Weis hereby leads the way to many concrete sources of evidence relating to a person's nationality and thereby potentially also to where to look for proof of (the threat of) statelessness.[80]

First on the list above is proof of facts that are relevant to the establishment of nationality under the applicable domestic law. A clear example is birth registration, which provides evidence of place and date of birth and of parentage, all of which can be key to the (failure of) acquisition of nationality under domestic law.[81] Based on what we have learned about the way in which nationality is attributed, other types of documentary evidence that attest to potentially key facts include marriage registration (proof of the bond between husband and wife and of the legitimacy of children born to the union)[82], adoption certificates[83] and civil, residence or household registration (proof of place and duration of residence).[84] According to Weis, witness testimony or affidavits have also been accepted as proof of relevant facts, either "in the absence of other evidence or as corroborative evidence".[85] The second kind of evidence, direct proof of nationality status, is comprised of an attestation by the competent authority that the individual in question is – or is not – a national.[86] Obvious examples are naturalisation or citizenship certificates or documents attesting to the withdrawal or renunciation of nationality, issued by the

---

[79] Paul Weis, *Nationality and Statelessness in International Law*, Kluwer Academic Publishers Group, Dordrecht: 1979, page 221.

[80] Again, recall that in order to establish that an applicant would "otherwise be stateless" if nationality is withheld or withdrawn by the state, the identification of the individual's present nationality status and/or that of those persons with whom he is connected is critical. See chapter VIII, section 4.

[81] The importance of birth registration in certifying a child's claim to nationality and indeed in lowering the very risk of statelessness is something that was raised many times over the course of this study. See in particular chapter VII, section 1 and chapter XIII, section 4.

[82] On the role of marriage and the registration of marriage in issues of statelessness, see chapter IV, sections 1 and 3 as well as chapter VII, section 1.

[83] See chapter IV, section 3.

[84] Tracing residence in a state back beyond a certain date can be of particular importance when a state introduces new legislation, establishing its initial body of citizens, for example following state succession. See chapter VI, section 1.

[85] Paul Weis, *Nationality and Statelessness in International Law*, Kluwer Academic Publishers Group, Dordrecht: 1979, page 216.

[86] Domestic law delineates not only the rules for the attribution of nationality but also sets out which organ of the state is competent to apply these rules and to confirm the nationality status of individuals. Weis offers a number of examples, looking at the United Kingdom, the United States and France. See Paul Weis, *Nationality and Statelessness in International Law*, Kluwer Academic Publishers Group, Dordrecht: 1979, pages 215-216. A highly contemporary example can be found in the Interim Constitution of Nepal 2063 (2007), where article 11 determines that a "Citizenship Distribution Team" shall have the authority to "provide citizenship to the persons eligible to acquire citizenship as provided for in the laws in force". A document issued by this team, attesting to the Nepali nationality of the holder, amounts to such direct proof of nationality.

authority in question. Evidence of the third type may consist of documents or statements emanating from any other state body that attest to a person's nationality status. Weis offers the example of a consular certificate: a document that is issued by a state's consular officers abroad, certifying that the person has been "entered in the register of nationals resident within the area for which the consulate is competent".[87] Inclusion in a state's electoral roll or entry as a national in a population census or civil register may also be considered to be evidence of this sort. Thus, the refusal to enter an individual in a consular register or on an electoral roll, or to record him as a national in a census or civil register, may contribute important evidence for the identification of statelessness.[88] Meanwhile, a passport could be deemed to contribute evidence of the second or third type listed, depending on the competence of the issuing authority under municipal law – although its special status as establishing *prima facie* evidence of nationality should not be overlooked. Finally, the fourth type of evidence discussed by Weis is the proof of certain facts from which nationality status may be inferred, "such as voting in elections, holding public office, etc".[89] As suggested in chapter II, it is conceivable that statelessness could be proven – or at least corroborated in part – by a clear denial of these and any other privileges that are granted to nationals under the state's domestic law.[90] On the basis of this overview, it becomes apparent that there are many possible sources of evidence on a person's nationality, statelessness or risk of statelessness.

Now is the time to draw together the findings on identifying (the threat of) statelessness that were discussed over the course of this section and the rest of the study. Thus, the following ideas should be incorporated into any future guidelines on how to meet the challenge of identification:

- The burden of proof lies, in principle, with the applicant seeking recognition of Stateless Person Status. The authority charged with status

[87] Paul Weis, *Nationality and Statelessness in International Law*, Kluwer Academic Publishers Group, Dordrecht: 1979, page 230.

[88] Note that the value of existing data collections such as birth, marriage and other civil registers, electoral rolls and population censuses is not only to be found in offering secondary evidence of nationality status in the context of identifying individual cases of (a threat of) statelessness. It is also possible to tap into such data sets and extract information that can be used to create a clearer picture of the stateless or at risk population across a whole area, country or region. UNHCR and other actors have come to recognise the enormous potential that is locked away in these data collections - especially if the inclusion rate and reliability of information relating to nationality and statelessness can be improved. For instance, UNHCR's Executive Committee has called on the agency to "continue to work with interested Governments to engage in or to renew efforts to identify stateless populations and populations with undetermined nationality residing in their territory, in cooperation with other United Nations agencies, in particular UNICEF and UNFPA as well as DPA, OHCHR and UNDP within the framework of national programmes, which may include, as appropriate, processes linked to birth registration and updating of population data". UNHCR Executive Committee, *Conclusion on Identification, Prevention and Reduction of Statelessness and Protection of Stateless Persons, No. 106*, 57th Session, Geneva, 2006, paragraph (b).

[89] Paul Weis, *Nationality and Statelessness in International Law*, Kluwer Academic Publishers Group, Dordrecht: 1979, page 216.

[90] See chapter II, section 4.

determination must also, if necessary, take an actively engage in the collection of evidence.[91]

- The content of domestic nationality law is central to the identification of (persons at risk of) statelessness.[92] Upon request, states should provide information on the content, interpretation and application of their nationality law to other states and international bodies.[93]

- A passport or document issued by the state authority competent to determine nationality matters that attests to the nationality of the holder is to be considered *prima facie* evidence of nationality.

- Upon receipt of a request from an individual, another state organ, an international body or a third state, the state authority competent to determine nationality matters shall confirm whether the individual in question holds the nationality of the state. In the event of a refusal or prolonged lack of response to such a request, this fact shall be admitted as *prima facie* evidence that the individual in question is *not* a national of the state concerned.

- Official data collections such as birth, marriage or other civil registers, electoral rolls, consular registers and population censuses – and the details recorded – can be admitted as secondary evidence of the position an individual under domestic nationality law.

- Documentation or witness testimony attesting to any relevant fact can be admitted as secondary evidence of the position of an individual under domestic nationality law. This includes documentation or witness testimony relating to the (in)ability to exercise those rights and privileges that are accorded to nationals under municipal law.

- States should consider relaxing the usual standard of proof in nationality matters when the prevention or resolution of statelessness and the protection of stateless persons is at stake.[94]

What concrete step forward should now be envisaged? The most ideal measure at this stage would therefore be the formulation of a handbook on the question of identification, taking the aforementioned issues into account. The handbook should consist of a number of principles relating to establishing proof of nationality and identifying statelessness and these principles should be accompanied by detailed

[91] Following the approach taken to the burden of proof in Refugee Status Determination.
[92] This is also apparent from the definition of statelessness: a stateless person is a person who is not considered a national by any state *under the operation of its law* See chapter II, section 4.
[93] See articles 23 and 24 of the European Convention on Nationality on co-operation between state parties and exchange of information. Chapter VIII, section 4.
[94] Following the example of the Council of Europe Convention on the avoidance of statelessness in relation to State succession. See chapter VIII, section 4.

guidelines that describe how they should be implemented in practice. With statelessness now firmly anchored into the mandate of the United Nations High Commissioner for Refugees, it is this agency that is best placed to compose, disseminate and promote the use of such a handbook. By doing so, the prospects for the implementation and enforcement of the existing international legal framework in response to statelessness would receive an immediate and much-needed boost. Since identification is a necessary precursor to implementing standards relating either to prevention, reduction or protection, the elaboration of an identification handbook will help states to pinpoint situations that call for the application of their stateless-related obligations – be that under the 1961 Convention on the Reduction of Statelessness, the 1954 Convention relating to the Status of Stateless Persons or otherwise. The same handbook will also assist existing supervisory bodies, such as the human rights courts and UN treaty bodies, in their task of overseeing the implementation by states of their commitments in this field.

Meanwhile, as explained in chapter XIII, there is a need for a new international instrument to update and further consolidate the regime for the *protection* of stateless persons and to clarify the question of access to nationality as a right of solution (i.e. *reduction* of statelessness).[95] There it was suggested that one of the main tasks of this instrument would be to elucidate how cases of (potential) statelessness are to be identified. Admittedly, such a step is not likely to be attainable short-term as the adoption of a new international agreement demands a serious investment of both time and government willpower. However, ultimately, this would be a highly appropriate way of formally codifying the basic contours of procedures and principles for the establishment of nationality and the identification of (the threat of) statelessness. This would help to ensure a harmonised approach to the application of the new instrument. Moreover, if the creation of a new human rights convention for the protection of stateless persons were to be accompanied by the creation of a specially-designated supervisory committee, as suggested in chapter XIII,[96] then the elaboration of standards relating to identification would also lend a hand towards the effective monitor of the implementation of the instrument's norms by this body.

4 What future for the Statelessness Conventions?

The reality of today's world, a reality that cannot simply be brushed aside or ignored, is that we have organised ourselves into communities of states, with nationality the badge of membership:

> Citizenship is derived from the division of the world into States. Division into States reflects a reality in which diverse human societies are positioned alongside each other. In this reality, it is not possible for everyone in the world to be a stranger to the other or for everyone in the world to be a member of a

[95] See chapter XIII, section 3.
[96] See chapter XIII, sections 3 and 4.

> single society. In the reality of the existence of States, a division exists between citizens who are members of a State and foreigners who are not.[97]

And in this same reality, the existence of statelessness appears almost inevitable. With inclusion comes the possibility of exclusion, and with the possibility of exclusion from one state comes the possibility of exclusion from each and every state. This is not a fact to which we must resign ourselves, but it is a truth of which we must be aware. At the same time, we must acknowledge another important truth:

> Nationality did not always exist. It is an invention of lawyers, philosophers and politicians. An invention which only emerged four centuries ago [...] We are free to redefine nationality. It is our own invention.[98]

So, nationality is not a static concept. Our approach to nationality - the way in which nationality can be gained and lost and the substance of this bond of membership - can be remoulded to reflect emerging interests and values. A fundamental, contemporary interest is the avoidance of statelessness (i.e. the enjoyment of the right to a nationality) or, failing that, the minimisation of the consequences of statelessness for the individual (i.e. the enjoyment of the full spectrum of human rights by everyone, everywhere). And these are the values that we see reflected in the 1961 Convention on the Reduction of Statelessness and the 1954 Convention relating to the Status of Stateless Persons as well as elsewhere in international law today.

The problem that we were forced to acknowledge back in the introductory chapters to this book is that the system for the prevention of statelessness and the protection of stateless persons is breaking down somewhere between the general enunciation of these lofty ideals and the actual situation on the ground. There are still vast numbers of stateless persons around the world and the treatment that they experience continues to range from minor annoyances to severe rights violations - enough reason to question the international response to statelessness. On the basis of the findings of this study, it is fair to conclude that these difficulties arise both from gaps and ambiguities in the normative framework and from the substantial challenge of implementation and enforcement of the existing standards. And from within the overall international legal setting for the response to statelessness, the Statelessness Conventions stood out. Not as the mainstay or strength of the system, but as instruments that, despite their ambitions, lack the forcefulness and foresight to really address the issues - or even, in places, to make any clear contribution to tackling statelessness over and above the content of the broader human rights framework.

---

[97] Yaffa Zilberschats, "Chapter 3 - The Horizontal Aspect of Citizenship" in *The Human Right to Citizenship*, Transnational Publishers, Ardsley, NY: 2002, page 71. It has also been said that "So far as organised human communities go, the heterogeneous nation-state under the rule of law and equipped with democratic institutions is the greatest constitutional achievement in history. It is not the last word, but it is the best one for the time being". Ralf Dahrendorf, *The changing quality of citizenship,* in "The condition of citizenship", B. van Steenbergen (Ed.), Sage Publications, London: 1994, page 17.

[98] Pieter Boeles, "What is the use of nationality?" Valedictory lecture, Leiden University, 29 June 2007.

I have already discussed, in some detail, what can be done to improve the overall international legal framework for addressing statelessness.[99] The question with which I would like to draw this manuscript to a close is this: *what future is there for the Statelessness Conventions?* After all, these are the tailor-made instruments with which the international community proposed to deal with statelessness. And, with the growing realisation that statelessness is a phenomenon of some consequence that will not resolve itself, it is to the Statelessness Conventions that many bodies and organisations are again turning in their renewed aspirations to tackle the issue.

As stated in chapter VIII, "it is not easy to offer one, all-encompassing answer to this question".[100] It is, of course, easy to point to the situation on the ground as evidence that the Statelessness Conventions have been failing to do their job adequately for the past half-century. There are also a number of clear gaps in the protection offered by the instruments against and in statelessness.[101] Moreover, as suggested above, it would be fair to say that the overall impression of the Statelessness Conventions is of two catalogues of provisions that lack strength[102] – are at times even sloppy[103] – and have clearly suffered from being a product of the (now outdated) conceptions of nationality, statelessness and sovereignty that presided at the time of their adoption.[104]

Nevertheless, we determined that both of the Statelessness Conventions retain some value, even in the contemporary international legal setting. We saw that the 1961 Statelessness Convention is the only universal instrument to deal in purposeful detail with the prevention of statelessness. With regard to the so-called "technical causes" of statelessness, the instrument was even found to have clear added value. As we move into the future, the measures prescribed for the avoidance of statelessness arising from technical causes will continue to be of importance, in particular for the prevention of statelessness at birth and thereby also the further perpetuation of statelessness within existing populations.[105] Meanwhile, the 1954 Statelessness Convention firmly places the stateless on the map as a specific vulnerable group, with very particular needs to which the international community

[99] See chapter VIII, section 3, chapter XIII, section 3 and the discussion in the present chapter.
[100] See chapter VIII, section 1.
[101] See in particular chapter VII, chapter X, section 7, chapter XI, section 8 and chapter XII, section 3.
[102] Consider the example of the articles in the 1961 Statelessness Convention that address the prevention of statelessness from loss of nationality later in life, but fail to provide unequivocally for the retention of nationality where statelessness threatens. Recall also, for instance, the "right of solution" formulated in the 1954 Statelessness Convention, yet in very ambiguous and facultative language. See chapter VIII, section 1 and chapter XIII, section 1.
[103] Recall the comments made about the way in which some of the provisions of the 1951 Refugee Convention were transposed to the 1954 Statelessness Convention with little thought for the practical differences between the situation of refugees and stateless persons. Another example of the sloppiness of the 1954 Statelessness Convention is its failure to address the issue of gaining or retaining lawful access to a state's territory, while at the same time elaborating rights on the basis of lawful presence or residence. See chapter XIII, section 1.
[104] The fact, for instance, that the 1961 Statelessness Convention was a product of its time and that this has done some damage to the enduring value of the instrument was evident in the lack of attention paid to a number of sources of statelessness that were only acknowledged after the instrument was adopted. See chapter VII and chapter VIII, section 1.
[105] See chapter VIII, section 1.

must respond. It offers the opportunity for recognition and documentation of Stateless Person Status as the basis for protection. And it reminds states that the resolution of the plight of the stateless through the acquisition of nationality must remain the "right of solution" to which efforts should ultimately be devoted.[106]

Looking ahead then, I would say that the two Statelessness Conventions do have a future. Indeed, by advocating for increased accession to these instruments, one of their shared flaws would be resolved: the pitifully low number of state parties that have been attracted to date. With an increased acceptance of the Statelessness Conventions comes increased scope for their implementation around the world – an objective that would be further stimulated by the elaboration of guidelines addressing the challenge of identification.[107] The uncertainty that surrounds the task of identifying stateless persons and situations where an individual would "otherwise be stateless" is currently hampering the effective implementation of both Statelessness Conventions. Furthermore, with renewed efforts to implement the terms of the Statelessness Conventions, across a broader spectrum of countries and with the assistance of a handbook on identification, there will be greater scope to consider or review the remaining normative gaps and the residual question of enforcement (again, an issue for both instruments).[108] Neither Convention should be seen, in isolation, to be the definitive answer to statelessness - to prevention and protection respectively - and the other avenues for improving the international response to statelessness that were outlined over the course of this study should also be pursued. In the meantime though, boosting the number of state parties to the Statelessness Conventions is a worthwhile cause and one that is decidedly easier today than half a century ago, since in the current international legal setting the content of the instruments can no longer be considered to be radical or objectionable.

Let me finish by saying that the incentives for dealing with statelessness, whether by following the suggestions outlined in this study or otherwise, are as persuasive as ever. It is a matter of justice, of human dignity and of peace and stability. As one scholar eloquently explains,

> global justice does not necessarily imply a duty on States to open their borders to whomsoever wishes to enter and become a citizen of the State. But global justice does imply that it is the duty of every State to see that citizenship, full membership in society, should be granted to each and every person, if not by that State then at least by another [...] Membership of a society is a basic human need. Societies are organised under a system of States. Regimes cannot act arbitrarily or fail to act at all in the allocation of such membership. Indeed, a

[106] See chapter XIII, section 1.
[107] See the suggestions made in section 3 of the present chapter.
[108] In other words, once the implementation of existing international standards has been facilitated by giving states the tools to meet the challenge of identification, it will be easier to (re)assess the following questions: how well the statelessness conventions address the prevention, reduction and protection issues in practice and to what extent additional enforcement mechanisms – besides domestic courts and UNHCR – are really needed in this context.

> person's dignity is violated if he leads his life knowing that he will never become a full member of the state in which he resides.[109]

Over the course of this book, it has become evident that statelessness is a quintessential human rights issue, putting the *human* in "human rights" to the ultimate test. In some ways, the very legitimacy of the human rights framework rests upon its capacity to either ensure that everyone does enjoy the right to a nationality (prevent statelessness) or to ensure that those who do not are not unreasonably disadvantaged by their plight (protect stateless persons). Moreover, there is an important flip-side to the "justice" argument: unless we find a way to deal fairly and appropriately with the issue of statelessness, there is the potential for abuse - not just by states that are seeking to shirk their responsibility over an undesirable individual or segment of the population, but also by individuals seeking to take advantage of the possibilities offered by the status of stateless person. It is not unheard of, for instance, for individuals to renounce their only nationality after migrating to a new country in order to obstruct their deportation and thereby create an opportunity to remain.[110] Nor is it inconceivable that individuals will "choose" statelessness in order to avoid military conscription, take advantage of a regime that provides for facilitated naturalisation of stateless persons or even avoid prosecution.[111] With effective guarantees in place for the prevention of statelessness and a carefully considered response to the protection of stateless persons, the scope for abuse on the part of states and individuals is minimised. And finally, we must not forget the stark warning that came early on in this investigation – that statelessness and nationality issues can escalate into a matter of national or even international security if left to fester. With all of these considerations in mind, there is no disputing the need to reinvigorate prevention and protection – or indeed prevention, protection, identification *and* reduction – efforts. I hope that this study has shed some light on how to tackle this ongoing challenge.

---

[109] Yaffa Zilberschats, "Chapter 2 - Citizenship and International Law" in *The Human Right to Citizenship*, Transnational Publishers, Ardsley, NY: 2002, pages 67 and 179.

[110] For example, in the case of *Slavov v. Sweden,* the European Court of Human Rights found the complaint to be inadmissible because "the applicant lost his Bulgarian citizenship after his latest conviction and after his expulsion had been ordered. It appears that his application to have his citizenship repealed was made in an attempt to obstruct his expulsion. In these circumstances, it was not unreasonable for the Swedish authorities to secure that the applicant would be received in Bulgaria". European Court of Human Rights, *Slavov v. Sweden,* Application No. 44828/98, Decision on admissibility, 29 June 1999. See also the case of *Mogos and Krifka v. Germany* before the European Court of Human Rights, Application No. 78084/01, Decision on admissibility, 27 March 2003.

[111] See, for instance, the discussion of the impact of statelessness on the potential for prosecution under the statute of the International Criminal Court in Zsuzsanna Deen-Racsmany, "The Nationality of the Offender and the Jurisdiction of the International Criminal Court", in *The American Journal of International Law,* Vol. 95, No. 3, 2001, pages 616-618.

ANNEX 1

THE 1961 CONVENTION ON THE REDUCTION OF STATELESSNESS

Considering it desirable to reduce statelessness by international agreement,

Have agreed as follows:

Article 1

1. A Contracting State shall grant its nationality to a person born in its territory who would otherwise be stateless. Such nationality shall be granted:
(a) At birth, by operation of law, or
(b) Upon an application being lodged with the appropriate authority, by or on behalf of the person concerned, in the manner prescribed by the national law. Subject to the provisions of paragraph 2 of this article, no such application may be rejected. A Contracting State which provides for the grant of its nationality in accordance with subparagraph (b) of this paragraph may also provide for the grant of its nationality by operation of law at such age and subject to such conditions as may be prescribed by the national law.
2. A Contracting State may make the grant of its nationality in accordance with subparagraph (b) -of paragraph I of this article subject to one or more of the following conditions:
(a) That the application is lodged during a period, fixed by the Contracting State, beginning not later than at the age of eighteen years and ending not earlier than at the age of twenty-one years, so, however, that the person concerned shall be allowed at least one year during which he may himself make the application without having to obtain legal authorization to do so;
(b) That the person concerned has habitually resided in the territory of the Contracting State for such period as may be fixed by that State, not exceeding five years immediately preceding the lodging of the application nor ten years in all;
(c) That the person concerned has neither been convicted of an offence against national security nor has been sentenced to imprisonment for a term of five years or more on a criminal charge;
(d) That the person concerned has always been stateless.
3. Notwithstanding the provisions of paragraphs I (b) and 2 of this article, a child born in wedlock in the territory of a Contracting State, whose mother has the nationality of that State, shall acquire at birth that nationality if it otherwise would be stateless.

4. A Contracting State shall grant its nationality to a person who would otherwise be stateless and who is unable to acquire the nationality of the Contracting State in whose territory he was born because he has passed the age for lodging his application or has not fulfilled the required residence conditions, if the nationality of one of his parents at the time of the person's birth was that of the Contracting State first above-mentioned. If his parents did not possess the same nationality at the time of his birth, the question whether the nationality of the person concerned should follow that of the father or that of the mother shall be determined by the national law of such Contracting State. If application for such nationality is required, the application shall be made to the appropriate authority by or on behalf of the applicant in the manner prescribed by the national law. Subject to the provisions of paragraph 5 of this article, such application shall not be refused.
5. The Contracting State may make the grant of its nationality in accordance with the provisions of paragraph 4 of this article subject to one or more of the following conditions:
(a) That the application is lodged before the applicant reaches an age, being not less than twenty-three years, fixed by the Contracting State;
(b) That the person concerned has habitually resided in the territory of the Contracting State for such period immediately preceding the lodging of the application, not exceeding three years, as may be fixed by that State;
(c) That the person concerned has always been stateless.

Article 2
A foundling found in the territory of a Contracting State shall, in the absence of proof to the contrary, be considered to have been born within that territory of parents possessing the nationality of that State.

Article 3
For the purpose of determining the obligations of Contracting States under this Convention, birth on a ship or in an aircraft shall be deemed to have taken place in the territory of the State whose flag the ship flies or in the territory of the State in which the aircraft is registered, as the case may be.

Article 4
1. A Contracting State shall grant its nationality to a person, not born in the territory of a Contracting State, who would otherwise be stateless, if the nationality of one of his parents at the time of the person's birth was that of that State. If his parents did not possess the same nationality at the time of his birth, the question whether the nationality of the person concerned should follow that of the father or that of the mother shall be determined by the national law of such Contracting State. Nationality granted in accordance with the provisions of this paragraph shall be granted:
(a) At birth, by operation of law, or
(b) Upon an application being lodged with the appropriate authority, by or on behalf of the person concerned, in the manner prescribed by the national law. Subject to the provisions of paragraph 2 of this article, no such application may be rejected.

2. A Contracting State may make the grant of its nationality in accordance with the provisions of paragraph I of this article subject to one or more of the following conditions:
(a) That the application is lodged before the applicant reaches an age, being not less than twenty-three years, fixed by the Contracting State;
(b) That the person concerned has habitually resided in the territory of the Contracting State for such period immediately preceding the lodging of the application, not exceeding three years, as may be fixed by that State;
(c) That the person concerned has not been convicted of an offence against national security;
(d) That the person concerned has always been stateless.

Article 5
1. If the law of a Contracting State entails loss of nationality as a consequence of any change in the personal status of a person such as marriage, termination of marriage, legitimation, recognition or adoption, such loss shall be conditional upon possession or acquisition of another nationality.
2. If, under the law of a Contracting State, a child born out of wedlock loses the nationality of that State in consequence of a recognition of affiliation, he shall be given an opportunity to recover that nationality by written application to the appropriate authority, and the conditions governing such application shall not be more rigorous than those laid down in paragraph 2 of article I of this Convention.

Article 6
If the law of a Contracting State provides for loss of its nationality by a person' s spouse or children as a consequence of that person losing or being deprived of that nationality, such loss shall be conditional upon their possession or acquisition of another nationality.

Article 7
1. (a) If the law of a Contracting State entails loss or renunciation of nationality, such renunciation shall not result in loss of nationality unless the person concerned possesses or acquires another nationality;
(b) The provisions of subparagraph (a) of this paragraph shall not apply where their application would be inconsistent with the principles stated in articles 13 and 14 of the Universal Declaration of Human Rights approved on 10 December 1948 by the General Assembly of the United Nations.
2. A national of a Contracting State who seeks naturalization in a foreign country shall not lose his nationality unless he acquires or has been accorded assurance of acquiring the nationality of that foreign country.
3. Subject to the provisions of paragraphs 4 and 5 of this article, a national of a Contracting State shall not lose his nationality, so as to become stateless, on the ground of departure, residence abroad, failure to register or on any similar ground.
4. A naturalized person may lose his nationality on account of residence abroad for a period, not less than seven consecutive years, specified by the law of the Contracting State concerned if he fails to declare to the appropriate authority his intention to retain his nationality.

5. In the case of a national of a Contracting State, born outside its territory, the law of that State may make the retention of its nationality after the expiry of one year from his attaining his majority conditional upon residence at that time in the territory of the State or registration with the appropriate authority.
6. Except in the circumstances mentioned in this article, a person shall not lose the nationality of a Contracting State, if such loss would render him stateless, notwithstanding that such loss is not expressly prohibited by any other provision of this Convention.

Article 8
1. A Contracting State shall not deprive a person of his nationality if such deprivation would render him stateless.
2. Notwithstanding the provisions of paragraph 1 of this article, a person may be deprived of the nationality of a Contracting State:
(a) In the circumstances in which, under paragraphs 4 and 5 of article 7, it is permissible that a person should lose his nationality;
(b) Where the nationality has been obtained by misrepresentation or fraud.
3. Notwithstanding the provisions of paragraph I of this article, a Contracting State may retain the right to deprive a person of his nationality, if at the time of signature, ratification or accession it specifies its retention of such right on one or more of the following grounds, being grounds existing in its national law at that time:
(a) That, inconsistently with his duty of loyalty to the Contracting State, the person:
(i) Has, in disregard of an express prohibition by the Contracting State rendered or continued to render services to, or received or continued to receive emoluments from, another State, or
(ii) Has conducted himself in a manner seriously prejudicial to the vital interests of the State;
(b) That the person has taken an oath, or made a formal declaration, of allegiance to another State, or given definite evidence of his determination to repudiate his allegiance to the Contracting State.
4. A Contracting State shall not exercise a power of deprivation permitted by paragraphs 2 or 3 of this article except in accordance with law, which shall provide for the person concerned the right to a fair hearing by a court or other independent body.

Article 9
A Contracting State may not deprive any person or group of persons of their nationality on racial, ethnic, religious or political grounds.

Article 10
1. Every treaty between Contracting States providing for the transfer of territory shall include provisions designed to secure that no person shall become stateless as a result of the transfer. A Contracting State shall use its best endeavours to secure that any such treaty made by it with a State which is not a Party to this Convention includes such provisions.
2. In the absence of such provisions a Contracting State to which territory is transferred or which otherwise acquires territory shall confer its nationality on such

persons as would otherwise become stateless as a result of the transfer or acquisition.

Article 11
The Contracting States shall promote the establishment within the framework of the United Nations, as soon as may be after the deposit of the sixth instrument of ratification or accession, of a body to which a person claiming the benefit of this Convention may apply for the examination of his claim and for assistance in presenting it to the appropriate authority.

Article 12
1. In relation to a Contracting State which does not, in accordance with the provisions of paragraph I of article I or of article 4 of this Convention, grant its nationality at birth by operation of law, the provisions of paragraph I of article I or of article 4, as the case may be, shall apply to persons born before as well as to persons born after the entry into force of this Convention.
2. The provisions of paragraph 4 of article I of this Convention shall apply to persons born before as well as to persons born after its entry into force.
3. The provisions of article 2 of this Convention shall apply only to foundlings found in the territory of a Contracting State after the entry into force of the Convention for that State.

Article 13
This Convention shall not be construed as affecting any provisions more conducive to the reduction of statelessness which may be contained in the law of any Contracting State now or hereafter in force, or may be contained in any other convention, treaty or agreement now or hereafter in force between two or more Contracting States..

Article 14
Any dispute between Contracting States concerning the interpretation or application of this Convention which cannot be settled by other means shall be submitted to the International Court of Justice at the request of any one of the parties to the dispute.

Article 15
1. This Convention shall apply to all non-self-governing, trust, colonial and other non-metropolitan territories for the international relations of which any Contracting State is responsible; the Contracting State concerned shall, subject to the provisions of paragraph 2 of this article, at the time of signature, ratification or accession, declare the non-metropolitan territory or territories to which the Convention shall apply ipso facto as a result of such signature, ratification or accession.
2. In any case in which, for the purpose of nationality, a non-metropolitan territory is not treated as one with the metropolitan territory, or in any case in which the previous con sent of a non-metropolitan territory is required by the constitutional laws or practices of the Contracting State or of the non-metropolitan territory for the application of the Convention to that territory, that Contracting State shall endeavour to secure the needed consent of the non-metropolitan territory within the period of twelve months from the date of signature of the Convention by that

Contracting State, and when such consent has been obtained the Contracting State shall notify the Secretary General of the United Nations. This Convention shall apply to the territory or territories named in such notification from the date of its receipt by the Secretary-General.
3. After the expiry of the twelve-month period mentioned in paragraph 2 of this article, the Contracting States concerned shall inform the Secretary-General of the results of the consultations with those non-metropolitan territories for whose international relations they are responsible and whose consent to the application of this Convention may have been withheld.

Article 16
1. This Convention shall be open for signature at the Headquarters of the United Nations from 30 August 1961 to 31 May 1962.
2. This Convention shall be open for signature on behalf of:
(a) Any State Member of the United Nations;
(b) Any other State invited to attend the United Nations Conference on the Elimination or Reduction of Future Statelessness;
(c) Any State to which an invitation to sign or to accede may be addressed by the General Assembly of the United Nations.
3. This Convention shall be ratified and the instruments of ratification shall be deposited with the Secretary-General of the United Nations.
4. This Convention shall be open for accession by the States referred to in paragraph 2 of this article. Accession shall be effected by the deposit of an instrument of accession with the Secretary-General of the United Nations.

Article 17
1. At the time of signature, ratification or accession any State may make a reservation in respect of articles 11, 14 or 15.
2. No other reservations to this Convention shall be admissible.

Article 18
1. This Convention shall enter into force two years after the date of the deposit of the sixth instrument of ratification or accession.
2. For each State ratifying or acceding to this Convention after the deposit of the sixth instrument of ratification or accession, it shall enter into force on the ninetieth day after the deposit by such State of its instrument of ratification or accession or on the date on which this Convention enters into force in accordance with the provisions of paragraph I of this article, whichever is the later.

Article 19
1. Any Contracting State may denounce this Convention at any time by a written notification addressed to the Secretary-General of the United Nations. Such denunciation shall take effect for the Contracting State concerned one year after the date of its receipt by the Secretary-General.
2. In cases where, in accordance with the provisions of article 15, this Convention has become applicable to a non-metropolitan territory of a Contracting State, that State may at any time thereafter, with the consent of the territory concerned, give notice to the Secretary-General of the United-Nations denouncing this Convention

separately in respect to that territory. The denunciation shall take effect one year after the date of the receipt of such notice by the Secretary-General, who shall notify all other Contracting States of such notice and the date of receipt thereof.

Article 20

1. The Secretary-General of the United Nations shall notify all Members of the United Nations and the non-member States referred to in article 16 of the following particulars:
(a) Signatures, ratifications and accessions under article 16;
(b) Reservations under article 17;
(c) The date upon which this Convention enters into force in pursuance of article 18;
(d) Denunciations under article 19.
2. The Secretary-General of the United Nations shall, after the deposit of the sixth instrument of ratification or accession at the latest, bring to the attention of the General Assembly the question of the establishment, in accordance with article 11, of such a body as therein mentioned.

Article 21

This Convention shall be registered by the Secretary-General of the United Nations on the date of its entry into force.
IN WITNESS WHEREOF the undersigned Plenipotentiaries have signed this Convention.
DONE at New York, this thirtieth day of August, one thousand nine hundred and sixty-one, in a single copy, of which the Chinese, English, French, Russian and Spanish texts are equally authentic and which shall be deposited in the archives of the United Nations, and certified copies of which shall be delivered by the Secretary-General of the United Nations to all members of the United Nations and to the non-member States referred to in article 16 of this Convention

ANNEX 2

THE 1954 CONVENTION RELATING TO THE STATUS OF STATELESS PERSONS

PREAMBLE

The High Contracting Parties,

Considering that the Charter of the United Nations and the Universal Declaration of Human Rights approved on 10 December 1948 by the General Assembly of the United Nations have affirmed the principle that human beings shall enjoy fundamental rights and freedoms without discrimination,

Considering that the United Nations has, on various occasions, manifested its profound concern for stateless persons and endeavoured to assure stateless persons the widest possible exercise of these fundamental rights and freedoms,

Considering that only those stateless persons who are also refugees are covered by the Convention relating to the Status of Refugees of 28 July 1951, and that there are many stateless persons who are not covered by that Convention,

Considering that it is desirable to regulate and improve the status of stateless persons by an international agreement, Have agreed as follows:

CHAPTER I

GENERAL PROVISIONS

Article 1.-Definition of the term "stateless person"
1. For the purpose of this Convention, the term "stateless person" means a person who is not considered as a national by any State under the operation of its law.
2. This Convention shall not apply:
(i) To persons who are at present receiving from organs or agencies of the United Nations other than the United Nations High Commissioner for Refugees protection or assistance so long as they are receiving such protection or assistance;
(ii) To persons who are recognized by the competent authorities of the country in which they have taken residence as having the rights and obligations which are attached to the possession of the nationality of that country;

(iii) To persons with respect to whom there are serious reasons for considering that:
(a) They have committed a crime against peace, a war crime, or a crime against humanity, as defined in the international instruments drawn up to make provisions in respect of such crimes;
(b) They have committed a serious non-political crime outside the country of their residence prior to their admission to that country;
(c) They have been guilty of acts contrary to the purposes and principles of the United Nations.

Article 2.-General obligations

Every stateless person has duties to the country in which he finds himself, which require in particular that he conform to its laws and regulations as well as to measures taken for the maintenance of public order.

Article 3.-Non-discrimination

The Contracting States shall apply the provisions of this Convention to stateless persons without discrimination as to race, religion or country of origin.

Article 4. -Religion

The Contracting States shall accord to stateless persons within their territories treatment at least as favourable as that accorded to their nationals with respect to freedom to practise their religion and freedom as regards the religious education of their children.

Article 5. - Rights granted apart from this Convention

Nothing in this Convention shall be deemed to impair any rights and benefits granted by a Contracting State to stateless persons apart from this Convention.

Article 6. - The term "in the same circumstances"

For the purpose of this Convention, the term " in the same circumstances" implies that any requirements (including requirements as to length and conditions of sojourn or residence) which the particular individual would have to fulfil for the enjoyment of the right in question, if he were not a stateless person, must be fulfilled by him, with the exception of requirements which by their nature a stateless person is incapable of fulfilling.

Article 7. - Exemption from reciprocity

1. Except where this Convention contains more favourable provisions, a Contracting State shall accord to stateless persons the same treatment as is accorded to aliens generally.
2. After a period of three years' residence, all stateless persons shall enjoy exemption from legislative reciprocity in the territory of the Contracting States.
3. Each Contracting State shall continue to accord to stateless persons the rights and benefits to which they were already entitled, in the absence of reciprocity, at the date of entry into force of this Convention for that State.
4. The Contracting States shall consider favourably the possibility of according to stateless persons, in the absence of reciprocity, rights and benefits beyond those to which they are entitled according to paragraphs 2 and 3, and to extending

exemption from reciprocity to stateless persons who do not fulfil the conditions provided for in paragraphs 2 and 3.
5. The provisions of paragraphs 2 and 3 apply both to the rights and benefits referred to in articles 13, 18, 19, 21 and 22 of this Convention and to rights and benefits for which this Convention does not provide.

Article 8. - Exemption from exceptional measures
With regard to exceptional measures which may be taken against the person, property or interests of nationals or former nationals of a foreign State, the Contracting States shall not apply such measures to a stateless person solely on account of his having previously possessed the nationality of the foreign State in question. Contracting States which, under their legislation, are prevented from applying the general principle expressed in this article shall, in appropriate cases, grant exemptions in favour of such stateless persons.

Article 9. - Provisional measures
Nothing in this Convention shall prevent a Contracting State, in time of war or other grave and exceptional circumstances, from taking provisionally measures which it considers to be essential to the national security in the case of a particular person, pending a determination by the Contracting State that that person is in fact a stateless person and that the continuance of such measures is necessary in his case in the interests of national security.

Article 10. - Continuity of residence
1. Where a stateless person has been forcibly displaced during the Second World War and removed to the territory of a Contracting State, and is resident there, the period of such enforced sojourn shall be considered to have been lawful residence within that territory.
2. Where a stateless person has been forcibly displaced during the Second World War from the territory of a Contracting State and has, prior to the date of entry into force of this Convention, returned there for the purpose of taking up residence, the period of residence before and after such enforced displacement shall be regarded as one uninterrupted period for any purposes for which uninterrupted residence is required.

Article 11. - Stateless seamen
In the case of stateless persons regularly serving as crew members on board a ship flying the flag of a Contracting State, that State shall give sympathetic consideration to their establishment on its territory and the issue of travel documents to them or their temporary admission to its territory particularly with a view to facilitating their establishment in another country.

CHAPTER II

JURIDICAL STATUS

Article 12. - Personal status
1. The personal status of a stateless person shall be governed by the law of the country of his domicile or, if he has no domicile, by the law of the country of his residence.
2. Rights previously acquired by a stateless person and dependent on personal status, more particularly rights attaching to marriage, shall be respected by a Contracting State, subject to compliance, if this be necessary, with the formalities required by the law of that State, provided that the right in question is one which would have been recognized by the law of that State had he not become stateless.

Article 13. - Movable and immovable property
The Contracting States shall accord to a stateless person treatment as favourable as possible and, in any event, not less favourable than that accorded to aliens generally in the same circumstances, as regards the acquisition of movable and immovable property and other rights pertaining thereto, and to leases and other contracts relating to movable and immovable property.

Article 14. - Artistic rights and industrial property
In respect of the protection of industrial property, such as inventions, designs or models, trade marks, trade names, and of rights in literary, artistic and scientific works, a stateless person shall be accorded in the country in which he has his habitual residence the same protection as is accorded to nationals of that country. In the territory of any other Contracting State, he shall be accorded the same protection as is accorded in that territory to nationals of the country in which he has his habitual residence.

Article 15. - Right of association
As regards non-political and non -profit- making associations and trade unions the Contracting States shall accord to stateless persons lawfully staying in their territory treatment as favourable as possible, and in any event, not less favourable than that accorded to aliens generally in the same circumstances.

Article 16. - Access to courts
1. A stateless person shall have free access to the courts of law on the territory of all Contracting States.
2. A stateless person shall enjoy in the Contracting State in which he has his habitual residence the same treatment as a national in matters pertaining to access to the courts, including legal assistance and exemption from cautio judicatum solvi.
3. A stateless person shall be accorded in the matters referred to in paragraph 2 in countries other than that in which he has his habitual residence the treatment granted to a national of the country of his habitual residence.

CHAPTER III

GAINFUL EMPLOYMENT

Article 17. - Wage-earning employment

1. The Contracting States shall accord to stateless persons lawfully staying in their territory treatment as favourable as possible and, in any event, not less favourable that that accorded to aliens generally in the same circumstances, as regards the right to engage in wage-earning employment.
2. The Contracting States shall give sympathetic consideration to assimilating the rights of all stateless persons with regard to wage-earning employment to those of nationals, and in particular of those stateless persons who have entered their territory pursuant to programmes of labour recruitment or under immigration schemes.

Article 18. - Self-employment

The Contracting States shall accord to a stateless person lawfully in their territory treatment as favourable as possible and, in any event, not less favourable than that accorded to aliens generally in the same circumstances, as regards the right to engage on his own account in agriculture, industry, handicrafts and commerce and to establish commercial and industrial companies.

Article 19. - Liberal professions

Each Contracting State shall accord to stateless persons lawfully staying in their territory who hold diplomas recognized by the competent authorities of that State, and who are desirous of practising a liberal profession, treatment as favourable as possible and, in any event, not less favourable than that accorded to aliens generally in the same circumstances.

CHAPTER IV

WELFARE

Article 20. - Rationing

Where a rationing system exists, which applies to the population at large and regulates the general distribution of products in short supply, stateless persons shall be accorded the same treatment as nationals.

Article 21. - Housing

As regards housing, the Contracting States, in so far as the matter is regulated by laws or regulations or is subject to the control of public authorities, shall accord to stateless persons lawfully staying in their territory treatment as favourable as possible and, in any event, not less favourable than that accorded to aliens generally in the same circumstances.

Article 22. - Public education
1. The Contracting States shall accord to stateless persons the same treatment as is accorded to nationals with respect to elementary education.
2. The Contracting States shall accord to stateless persons treatment as favourable as possible and, in any event, not less favourable than that accorded to aliens generally in the same circumstances, with respect to education other than elementary education and, in particular, as regards access to studies, the recognition of foreign school certificates, diplomas and degrees, the remission of fees and charges and the award of scholarships.

Article 23. -Public relief
The Contracting States shall accord to stateless persons lawfully staying in their territory the same treatment with respect to public relief and assistance as is accorded to their nationals.

Article 24. - Labour legislation and social security
1. The Contracting States shall accord to stateless persons lawfully staying in their territory the same treatment as is accorded to nationals in respect of the following matters:
(a) In so far as such matters are governed by laws or regulations or are subject to the control of administrative authorities; remuneration, including family allowances where these form part of remuneration, hours of work, overtime arrangements, holidays with pay, restrictions on home work, minimum age of employment, apprenticeship and training, women's work and the work of young persons, and the enjoyment of the benefits of collective bargaining;
(b) Social security (legal provisions in respect of employment injury, occupational diseases, maternity, sickness, disability, old age, death, unemployment, family responsibilities and any other contingency which, according to national laws or regulations, is covered by a social security scheme), subject to the following limitations:
(i) There may be appropriate arrangements for the maintenance of acquired rights and rights in course of acquisition;
(ii) National laws or regulations of the country of residence may prescribe special arrangements concerning benefits or portions of benefits which are payable wholly out of public funds, and concerning allowances paid to persons who do not fulfil the contribution conditions prescribed for the award of a normal pension.
2. The right to compensation for the death of a stateless person resulting from employment injury or from occupational disease shall not be affected by the fact that the residence of the beneficiary is outside the territory of the Contracting State.
3. The Contracting States shall extend to stateless persons the benefits of agreements concluded between them, or which may be concluded between them in the future, concerning the maintenance of acquired rights and rights in the process of acquisition in regard to social security, subject only to the conditions which apply to nationals of the States signatory to the agreements in question.
4. The Contracting States will give sympathetic consideration to extending to stateless persons so far as possible the benefits of similar agreements which may at any time be in force between such Contracting States and non-contracting States.

CHAPTER V

ADMINISTRATIVE MEASURES

Article 25. - Administrative assistance

1. When the exercise of a right by a stateless person would normally require the assistance of authorities of a foreign country to whom he cannot have recourse, the Contracting State in whose territory he is residing shall arrange that such assistance be afforded to him by their own authorities.
2. The authority or authorities mentioned in paragraph I shall deliver or cause to be delivered under their supervision to stateless persons such documents or certifications as would normally be delivered to aliens by or through their national authorities.
3. Documents or certifications so delivered shall stand in the stead of the official instruments delivered to aliens by or through their national authorities and shall be given credence in the absence of proof to the contrary.
4. Subject to such exceptional treatment as may be granted to indigent persons, fees may be charged for the services mentioned herein, but such fees shall be moderate and commensurate with those charged to nationals for similar services.
5. The provisions of this article shall be without prejudice to articles 27 and 28.

Article 26. - Freedom of movement

Each Contracting State shall accord to stateless persons lawfully in its territory the right to choose their place of residence and to move freely within its territory, subject to any regulations applicable to aliens generally in the same circumstances.

Article 27. - Identity papers

The Contracting States shall issue identity papers to any stateless person in their territory who does not possess a valid travel document.

Article 28. - Travel documents

The Contracting States shall issue to stateless persons lawfully staying in their territory travel documents for the purpose of travel outside their territory, unless compelling reasons of national security or public order otherwise require, and the provisions of the schedule to this Convention shall apply with respect to such documents. The Contracting States may issue such a travel document to any other stateless person in their territory; they shall in particular give sympathetic consideration to the issue of such a travel document to stateless persons in their territory who are unable to obtain a travel document from the country of their lawful residence.

Article 29. - Fiscal charges

1. The Contracting States shall not impose upon stateless persons duties, charges or taxes, of any description whatsoever, other or higher than tho se which are or may be levied on their nationals in similar situations .
2. Nothing in the above paragraph shall prevent the application to stateless persons of the laws and regulations concerning charges in respect of the issue to aliens of administrative documents including identity papers.

Article 30. - Transfer of assets

1. A Contracting State shall, in conformity with its laws and regulations, permit stateless persons to transfer assets which they have brought into its territory, to another country where they have been admitted for the purposes of resettlement. 2. A Contracting State shall give sympathetic consideration to the application of stateless persons for permission to transfer assets wherever they may be and which are necessary for their resettlement in another country to which they have been admitted. Article 31. - Expulsion

1. The Contracting States shall not expel a stateless person lawfully in their territory save on grounds of national security or public order.

2. The expulsion of such a stateless person shall be only in pursuance of a decision reached in accordance with due process of law. Except where compelling reasons of national security otherwise require, the stateless person shall be allowed to submit evidence to clear himself, and to appeal to and be represented for the purpose before competent authority or a person or persons specially designated by the competent authority.

3. The Contracting States shall allow such a stateless person a reasonable period within which to seek legal admission into another country. The Contracting States reserve the right to apply during that period such internal measures as they may deem necessary.

Article 32. - Naturalization

The Contracting States shall as far as possible facilitate the assimilation and naturalization of stateless persons. They shall in particular make every effort to expedite naturalization proceedings and to reduce as far as possible the charges and costs of such proceedings.

CHAPTER VI

FINAL CLAUSES

Article 33. - Information on national legislation

The Contracting States shall communicate to the Secretary-General of the United Nations the laws and regulations which they may adopt to ensure the application of this Convention.

Article 34. - Settlement of disputes

Any dispute between Parties to this Convention relating to its interpretation or application, which cannot be settled by other means, shall be referred to the International Court of Justice at the request of any one of the parties to the dispute.

Article 35. - Signature, ratification and accession

1. This Convention shall be open for signature at the Headquarters of the United Nations until 31 December 1955.

2. It shall be open for signature on behalf of:

(a) Any State Member of the United Nations;

(b) Any other State invited to attend the United Nations Conference on the Status of Stateless Persons; and
(c) Any State to which an invitation to sign or to accede may be addressed by the General Assembly of the United Nations.
3. It shall be ratified and the instruments of ratification shall be deposited with the Secretary-General of the United Nations.
4. It shall be open for accession by the States referred to in paragraph 2 of this article. Accession shall be effected by the deposit of an instrument of accession with the Secretary-General of the United Nations.

Article 36. - Territorial application clause
1. Any State may, at the time of signature, ratification or accession, declare that this Convention shall extend to all or any of the territories for the international relations of which it is responsible. Such a declaration shall take effect when the Convention enters into force for the State concerned.
2. At any time thereafter any such extension shall be made by notification addressed to the Secretary-General of the United Nations and shall take effect as from the ninetieth day after the day of receipt by the Secretary-General of the United Nations of this notification, or as from the date of entry into force of the Convention for the State concerned, whichever is the later.
3. With respect to those territories to which this Convention is not extended at the time of signature, ratification or accession, each State concerned shall consider the possibility of taking the necessary steps in order to extend the application of this Convention to such territories, subject, where necessary for constitutional reasons, to the consent of the Governments of such territories.

Article 37. - Federal clause
In the case of a Federal or non-unitary State, the following provisions shall apply
(a) With respect to those articles of this Convention that come within the legislative jurisdiction of the federal legislative authority, the obligations of the Federal Government shall to this extent be the same as those of Parties which are not Federal States;
(b) With respect to those articles of this Convention that come within the legislative jurisdiction of constituent States, provinces or cantons which are not, under the constitutional system of the Federation, bound to take legislative action, the Federal Government shall bring such articles with a favourable recommendation to the notice of the appropriate authorities of States, provinces or cantons at the earliest possible moment;
(c) A Federal State Party to this Convention shall, at the request of any other Contracting State transmitted through the Secretary-General of the United Nations, supply a statement of the law and practice of the Federation and its constituent units in regard to any particular provision of the Convention showing the extent to which effect has been given to that provision by legislative or other action.

Article 38. - Reservations
1. At the time of signature, ratification or accession, any State may make reservations to articles of the Convention other than to articles 1, 3, 4, 16 (1) and 33 to 42 inclusive.

2. Any State making a reservation in accordance with paragraph I of this article may at any time withdraw the reservation by a communication to that effect addressed to the Secretary-General of the United Nations.

Article 39. - Entry into force
1. This Convention shall come into force on the ninetieth day following the day of deposit of the sixth instrument of ratification or accession.
2. For each State ratifying or acceding to the Convention after the deposit of the sixth instrument of ratification or accession, the Convention shall enter into force on the ninetieth day following the date of deposit by such State of its instrument of ratification or accession.

Article 40. - Denunciation
1. Any Contracting State may denounce this Convention at any time by a notification addressed to the Secretary-General of the United Nations.
2. Such denunciation shall take effect for the Contracting State concerned one year from the date upon which it is received by the Secretary-General of the United Nations.
3. Any State which has made a declaration or notification under article 36 may, at any time thereafter, by a notification to the Secretary- General of the United Nations, declare that the Convention shall cease to extend to such territory one year after the date of receipt of the notification by the Secretary-General.

Article 41. - Revision
1. Any Contracting State may request revision of this Convention at any time by a notification addressed to the Secretary-General of the United Nations.
2. The General Assembly of the United Nations shall recommend the steps, if any, to be taken in respect of such request.

Article 42. - Notifications by the Secretary-General of the United Nations
The Secretary-General of the United Nations shall inform all Members of the United Nations and non-member States referred to in article 35:
(a) Of signatures, ratifications and accessions in accordance with article 35;
(b) Of declarations and notifications in accordance with article 36;
(c) Of reservations and withdrawals in accordance with article 38;
(d) Of the date on which this Convention will come into force in accordance with article 39;
(e) Of denunciations and notifications in accordance with article 40;
(f) Of request for revision in accordance with article 41.
IN FAITH WHEREOF the undersigned, duly authorized, have signed this Convention on behalf of their respective Governments.
DONE at New York, this twenty-eighth day of September, one thousand nine hundred and fifty-four, in a single copy, of which the English, French and Spanish texts are equally authentic and which shall remain deposited in the archives of the United Nations, and certified true copies of which shall be delivered to all Members of the United Nations and to the non-member States referred to in article 35.

Annex 3

Schematic overview of the rights in the 1954 Statelessness Convention

	Subject to a state's jurisdiction	Physical presence	Lawful presence	Lawful stay	Durable residence
Treatment at least as favourable as aliens generally	- moveable and immoveable property (art.13)		- self-employment (art.18) - liberal professions (art.19) - freedom of movement (art.26)	- right of association (art.15) - wage-earning employment (art.17) * - housing (art.21)	
National treatment	- rationing (art.20) - education (art.22) - fiscal charges (art.29)	- religion (art.4)		- artistic rights and industrial property (art.14) - access to courts (art.16(2,3)) - public relief (art.23) - labour legislation and social security (art.24)	
Absolute rights	- non-discrimination (art.3) - legal personhood (article 12)** -access to courts (art.16(1)) - naturalisation (art.32) ***	- identity papers (art.27) - transfer of assets (art.30)****	- expulsion (art.31)	- administrative assistance (art.25) - travel documents (art.28)	- exemption from legislative reciprocity (art.7(2))

* With the proviso that under article 17, paragraph 2 the contracting states are required to "give sympathetic consideration to assimilating the rights of all stateless persons with regard to wage-earning employment to those of nationals".

** This article addresses the question of legal jurisdiction in regulating the "personal status" of stateless persons and deals only implicitly with the right to legal personhood.

*** Although this provision does not demand (lawful) residence or even physical presence, nothing in this article restricts the rights of states to set the condition of (a certain period of) lawful and habitual residence for eligibility to naturalisation, although it does encourage a lowering of such conditions for stateless persons.

**** This right has been categorised under those enjoyed through physical presence in a contracting state since it deals with assets that a stateless person has "brought into its territory". Under paragraph 2 contracting states are also called upon to "give sympathetic consideration to the application of stateless persons for permission to transfer assets wherever they may be" which would require only jurisdiction of the state over the assets and not the presence of the stateless person on state territory.

SUMMARY

It is a familiar and irrefutable fact that the world we live in today is marked with divisions. Border posts, frontier patrols and even elaborate fencing establish the dividing lines between the territory of one state and the next. Meanwhile, partitions have also been created between people. Individuals do not (just) exist as isolated beings, they are connected to one state or another through the legal bond of membership, *nationality*. But these divisions are not watertight. Just as there is the occasional slither of no-man's land between two countries, so too, are there individuals who remain unclaimed by any state. These are the world's *stateless persons* – also variously described as outcasts, legal-ghosts and non-persons in recognition of their precarious position as outsiders in this modern, well-ordered world. It is their anomalous situation which formed the subject matter of this book.

In the opening chapters it quickly became apparent that the issue of statelessness is neither theoretical nor trifling – it is a very real and pressing problem, afflicting as many as 15 million people worldwide. It stems from a wide variety of causes, leaving no region untouched. More often than not, statelessness proves to be a highly persistent problem with individuals spending years, decades or even their whole lives in this legal limbo. Statelessness can also be self-perpetuating, passed on helplessly from one generation to the next. And even a brief perusal of reports on stateless populations is enough to reveal that, while the impact that the lack of a nationality has on these individuals' lives varies, the overall picture is sincerely troubling. Statelessness impairs a person's ability to effectuate a wide range of rights and lays him or her bare to abuse in both the public and private sphere. The individual insecurity and marginalisation experienced by stateless persons can also have a dramatic knock-on effect on the individual's family and the wider community. Furthermore, nationality disputes and statelessness can be a major contributing factor to forced displacement, domestic or international instability and even conflict.

At the turn of the millennium, a deepening understanding of the severity and potential implications of statelessness – as well as the emergence of several large, new caseloads of stateless persons – spurred the international community to renew its attempts to tackle the issue. Half a century previously, statelessness also captured the international community's attention. When the Second World War ended, it left a mammoth humanitarian crisis in its wake. One of the many challenges involved the vast numbers of people who had, in one way or another, become uprooted and were in need of protection. A series of studies and debates eventually led to the adoption of three independent legal instruments to respond to this problem of the "unprotected": the 1951 Convention relating to the Status of Refugees, the 1954 Convention relating to the Status of Stateless Persons and the 1961 Convention on the Reduction of Statelessness. While the 1951 Refugee Convention quickly gained wide acceptance and, to this day, forms the cornerstone of international refugee protection, the Statelessness Conventions suffered a long period of neglect. Indeed, generally-speaking, interest in statelessness went into swift decline, only to be re-ignited in the 1990s as alluded to above.

By then, however, several decades had elapsed since the Statelessness Conventions were adopted – or indeed, since any comprehensive study was made of the phenomenon. As the international community turned its attention back to statelessness, it gained new insights into this complex problem, raising the question of whether the Statelessness Conventions that had fallen into disregard still – or had in fact ever – offered an appropriate response. Moreover, with the realisation that the overall international legal setting had changed significantly, thanks especially to the advent and development of human rights law, came the question as to the enduring value of the antiquated statelessness-specific instruments.

More fundamentally, the concern is whether the international community has the necessary tools at its disposal to respond effectively to the issue of statelessness. The current, growing preoccupation with the plight of the stateless offered an opportune moment to reflect upon this question, to pin-point the gaps in the international legal framework and to submit suggestions as to how these may be remedied. In short:

> **How can the way in which international law deals with the issue of statelessness be improved so as to ensure optimal protection of the individual and his rights?**

To facilitate and structure this research, the approach taken in the Statelessness Conventions, whereby *prevention* and *protection* are dealt with separately, was mimicked. Thus, part 2 was devoted to an analysis of the international norms relating to the prevention of statelessness (with a particular focus on the 1961 Convention on the Reduction of Statelessness) and part 3 looked at the standards relating to the protection of stateless persons (with a particular focus on the 1954 Convention relating to the Status of Stateless Persons). Thereafter, part 4 reflected on the overarching lessons learned, considered what future lays ahead for the Statelessness Conventions and discussed some of the remaining challenges.

In order to assess the international legal framework for the prevention of statelessness, each of the causes of statelessness was considered in turn: technical causes (i.e. administrative practices and conflicts of laws), arbitrary deprivation of nationality, statelessness in the context of state succession and the "new" causes of statelessness (those that were recognised *after* the 1961 Statelessness Convention was drafted). In the end, it was concluded that international law today reflects a mounting intolerance for statelessness, with two main principles gaining ever more ground: the avoidance of statelessness at birth and the avoidance of denationalisation resulting in statelessness. Ultimately, these two standards are all that is needed to secure the prevention of statelessness since they focus on ensuring that every individual acquires a nationality at the start of his or her lifetime and that this nationality is not lost unless another nationality is acquired. Both principles are reflected in the 1961 Convention on the Reduction of Statelessness and numerous human rights instruments. In the former, the principles have been transformed into a series of intricate provisions that detail which state is responsible for conferring nationality, or for refraining from withdrawing citizenship, and under which circumstances. In the latter, mainly more broadly stated norms were traced, such as the right of every child to acquire a nationality and the prohibition of arbitrary deprivation of nationality. But the 1961 Statelessness Convention clearly limits its ambitions to *reducing* the incidence of statelessness – thereby failing to provide for the unequivocal bestowal or retention of nationality where statelessness threatens – and fails to deal with a number of issues either persuasively or indeed at all. Meanwhile the wider human rights framework offers sweeping standards that, in places, lack the detail that is required to ensure their full, correct and harmonised application – and the truly interesting and innovative developments that were traced are still in their infancy. So, neither approach turned out to be infallible. Nor is the combined impact of the two sets of standards a guarantee that all causes of statelessness will be nipped in the bud.

This finding reaffirmed the importance of norms for the protection of stateless persons, which were next to go under the microscope – first civil and political rights, then economic, social and cultural rights and, lastly, the "special needs" of the stateless. The result was a similarly mixed story to that uncovered for the prevention of statelessness. The development of human rights law *has* resulted in an increasing move away from citizenship as the right to have rights, as famously described by the US Supreme Court, and towards the "denationalisation" of protection. Yet the recognition of the *right to a nationality* as a human right also reaffirms the enduring relevance of nationality: the human rights system can only maintain its aspiration of universality with the guarantee that every human will also hold a nationality. So although there is perhaps less need for a stateless-specific instrument today than there was prior to the advent of the major human rights instruments, it has not become redundant. The 1954 Statelessness Convention attempts to answer to this need, but falls short on quite a number of counts. The instruments is particularly let down by its own trademark technique of offering different rights at different "levels of attachment" (for example, only to stateless persons who are lawfully present or lawfully staying) and often only to a weak, contingent standard (for instance, only to the same extent as enjoyed by non-nationals generally). Meanwhile, within the human rights framework itself, standards have begun to develop that address the situation of non-nationals or even stateless persons specifically. But the exact treatment owed to these groups under contemporary human rights law is still hazy in many areas, for example with respect to economic, social and cultural rights and in particular in developing countries.

Unmistakably then, a number of challenges remain – not least of which is to ensure the full implementation and enforcement of all of the existing norms. However, numerous gaps were also found in the normative frameworks for the prevention of statelessness and protection of stateless persons. Consequently, various suggestions were raised for the further clarification and elaboration of standards with a view to *improving the way in which international law deals with the issue of statelessness so as to ensure optimal protection of the individual and his rights*. In the context of both prevention and protection, it was possible to trace certain current and relevant developments that helped to show the way forward.

One of the most pervasive issues to be dealt with is the nexus between inclusion and exclusion on the basis of nationality, and inclusion and exclusion on the basis of immigration status. An enduring, fundamental function of nationality is providing the holder with a "home", a state to which they can always return and in which they have an irrefutable right to reside. On the one hand, this implies that stateless persons have no undisputed right to live anywhere – and indeed gaining and retaining lawful access to the territory of a(ny) state was found to present serious difficulties to the stateless in practice. This, in turn, results in problems relating to detention, family separation and lack of access to rights and services, including many of those elaborated in the 1954 Statelessness Convention. On the other hand, statelessness has been found to lead to displacement. Plus, the possession of an unlawful or ambiguous immigration status can contribute to the creation and perpetuation of statelessness. These facts underline the urgency of securing the stateless a right to live somewhere. Thus, of all of the potential, supplementary standard-setting activities discussed, this is the area that is at once one of the most imperative and the most complex. It was suggested that the most appropriate avenue to pursue in this regard is to build upon the UN Human Rights Committee's efforts to identify an individuals *own country,* regardless of the question of citizenship, for the purposes of the enjoyment of the right to enter and reside. The stateless are evidently the group *par excellence* to benefit from the further development of this notion as, without this construction, they will continue to lack an *own country* and the very basic security that this offers. It was also noted that a further crystallisation and clarification of the norms relating to the prevention of statelessness is absolutely indispensable to the quest of ascertaining which state is to be considered a stateless person's *own country* – because this quest is tantamount to establishing which country is "responsible" for an individual's statelessness, in violation of international standards.

A second, even more fundamental, challenge that has yet to be met with an adequate response is the identification of stateless persons and individuals at risk of statelessness. This is a necessary precursor to the application of standards relating to the prevention of statelessness, the protection of stateless persons and, ultimately, the resolution of existing cases of statelessness. Yet this matter is wholly overlooked by the two Statelessness Conventions and has received regrettably little attention from the international community to date. Even the most recent, highly progressive examples of international instruments dealing with questions of nationality and statelessness barely touch upon the problem of identification. And where human rights bodies have been called upon to ascertain the nationality or statelessness of an applicant in a case, they have done so in an ad hoc – and, at times, somewhat inaccessible – fashion, without attempting to elaborate rules or procedures for future or general use. In order to nevertheless begin to piece together such guidelines, in the closing chapter of this study, the search for any relevant international practice was widened and lessons were extracted from the areas of Refugee Status Determination and international claims jurisprudence. In order to provide people with a real opportunity to benefit from international norms relating to statelessness, this initial input for guidelines for identification will have to be further elucidated and laid down in an appropriate document – an identification handbook, to begin with, but later, potentially, a supplementary international instrument that also addresses other existing gaps in the international legal framework.

Looking ahead, it was submitted that the two Statelessness Conventions do have a future. Indeed, by advocating for increased accession to these instruments, one of their shared flaws would be resolved: the pitifully low number of state parties that have been attracted to date. With an increased acceptance of the Statelessness Conventions comes increased scope for their implementation around the world – an objective that would be further stimulated by the elaboration of guidelines addressing the challenge of identification. Furthermore, with renewed efforts to implement the terms of the Statelessness Conventions, across a broader spectrum of countries and with the assistance of an identification handbook, there will be greater scope to review the remaining normative gaps and to consider what additional measures are needed to facilitate the enforcement of these standards. Neither Convention should be seen, in isolation, to be the definitive answer to statelessness – to prevention and protection respectively – and the other avenues for improving the international response to statelessness that were outlined over the course of this study should also be pursued. In the meantime though, boosting the number of state parties to the Statelessness Conventions is a worthwhile cause and one that is decidedly easier today than half a century ago, since in the current international legal setting the content of the instruments can no longer be considered to be either radical or objectionable. It is also an unmistakeably worthwhile pursuit, from the individual, the state and the international community's standpoint, especially in view of the realisation that statelessness and nationality issues can escalate into a matter of national or even international security if left to fester.

Samenvatting

Het is een bekend en onbetwistbaar feit dat de wereld waarin wij leven bepaald wordt door scheidslijnen. Grensposten, grenspatrouilles en zelfs uitgebreide afscheidingen bakenen het territorium van staten af ten opzichte van hun buurstaten. Ook tussen mensen zijn scheidsmuren opgeworpen. Mensen bestaan niet (alleen) als afzonderlijk individu: ze zijn aan een bepaalde staat verbonden door het wettig lidmaatschapsverband van hun *nationaliteit*. Toch zijn deze afscheidingen niet waterdicht. Net zoals er zo nu en dan een strook niemandsland tussen twee landen bestaat, zijn er ook personen die bij geen enkele staat horen. Zij zijn de *staatlozen* van deze wereld – ook wel omschreven als verschoppelingen, juridische spoken en onpersonen, gezien hun hachelijke positie als buitenstaanders in deze moderne, goedgeordende wereld. Hun abnormale situatie vormt het onderwerp van dit boek.

In de eerste hoofdstukken wordt het al spoedig duidelijk dat de staatloosheidsproblematiek noch theoretisch, noch verwaarloosbaar is: staatloosheid vormt een hoogst acuut en urgent probleem dat over de hele wereld zo'n 15 miljoen mensen direct aangaat. Er vallen verschillende redenen voor staatloosheid aan te wijzen en er is geen regio die er niet mee te maken heeft. Meestal blijkt staatloosheid een bijzonder hardnekkig probleem, waarbij mensen (tientallen) jaren of zelfs hun hele leven in dit juridische niemandsland doorbrengen. Staatloosheid heeft ook het vermogen zichzelf in stand te houden en machteloos van de ene op de andere generatie overgedragen te worden. Vluchtige lezing van rapporten over staatloze bevolkingsgroepen is al genoeg om aan te tonen dat, ofschoon het effect van het ontbreken van een nationaliteit op de levens van individuele personen verschilt, het algehele beeld zeer verontrustend is. Staatloosheid beperkt het vermogen van mensen om aanspraak te maken op een hele reeks rechten en maakt hen kwetsbaar voor misbruik in de publieke en private sfeer. De individuele onveiligheid en marginalisatie die door staatlozen ondervonden wordt kan ook een dramatische kettingreactie teweegbrengen in hun familie en de gemeenschap waartoe zij behoren. Verder kunnen geschillen over nationaliteit en staatloosheid in ernstige mate bijdragen aan gedwongen migratie, nationale of internationale instabiliteit en zelfs conflicten.

Rond de eeuwwisseling werd de internationale gemeenschap, als gevolg van een ontwikkeling naar een beter begrip van de ernst en mogelijke gevolgen van staatloosheid – en doordat zich enkele grote, nieuwe golven staatlozen voordeden – ertoe aangespoord om zijn pogingen de kwestie op te lossen te hervatten. Vijftig jaar daarvoor stond staatloosheid ook bij de internationale gemeenschap in de belangstelling. In de nasleep van de Tweede Wereldoorlog was er een gigantische humanitaire crisis ontstaan. Een van de vele uitdagingen waarvoor men zich gesteld zag betrof de enorme aantallen mensen die op de een of andere manier ontworteld geraakt waren en bescherming nodig hadden. Een hele reeks onderzoeken en debatten leidde uiteindelijk tot het aannemen van drie onafhankelijke verdragen die een antwoord moesten bieden op het probleem van de "onbeschermden": het Verdrag inzake de Status van Vluchtelingen van 1951, het Verdrag betreffende de Status van Staatlozen van 1954 en het Verdrag tot Beperking van Staatloosheid van 1961. Terwijl het Vluchtelingenverdrag van 1951 snel in brede kringen aanvaard werd en tot op vandaag de hoeksteen voor de internationale vluchtelingenbescherming vormt, raakten de staatloosheidsverdragen lange tijd in de vergetelheid. Over het algemeen kan gezegd worden dat de belangstelling voor staatloosheid snel afnam om, zoals hierboven al aangestipt, pas in de jaren negentig van de vorige eeuw weer toe te nemen.

Tegen die tijd waren er echter enkele tientallen jaren verstreken sinds de verdragen over staatloosheid gesloten waren - en sinds er enige diepgaande studie van het fenomeen gemaakt was. Toen staatloosheid bij de internationale gemeenschap opnieuw in de belangstelling kwam te staan, werden er nieuwe inzichten in dit complexe probleem ontwikkeld, waarbij de vraag rees of de staatloosheidsverdragen die destijds terzijde gelegd waren nog een passend antwoord op de problematiek boden, of ooit geboden hadden. Bovendien kwam met het bewustzijn dat de internationale juridische omstandigheden, met name door de opkomst en ontwikkeling van de mensenrechtenwetgeving, in het algemeen sterk gewijzigd waren, de vraag op naar de blijvende waarde van de verouderde verdragen over staatloosheid.

Op een meer fundamenteel niveau bestaat de zorg of de internationale gemeenschap beschikt over de noodzakelijke middelen om effectief op het staatloosheidsprobleem te kunnen reageren. De huidige, toenemende zorg over het lot van de staatlozen vormde een geschikt moment om deze kwestie te onderzoeken, de lacunes in de internationale juridische structuren aan te wijzen en voorstellen te doen over hoe deze lacunes gedicht zouden kunnen worden. Kort samengevat is de vraag:

> **Hoe kan de manier waarop internationaal recht met de kwestie van staatloosheid omgaat zodanig verbeterd worden dat het individu en zijn/haar rechten optimaal beschermd worden?**

Om dit onderzoek te vergemakkelijken en er structuur aan te geven, is gekozen voor de benadering die ook in de staatloosheidsverdragen wordt toegepast, waarbij *preventie* en *bescherming* apart behandeld worden. Deel 2 is derhalve gewijd aan een analyse van de internationale richtlijnen betreffende het voorkomen van staatloosheid (met speciale aandacht voor de het Verdrag tot Beperking van Staatloosheid van 1961) en deel 3 geeft een beschouwing over de richtlijnen met betrekking tot de bescherming van staatlozen (met bijzondere nadruk op het Verdrag betreffende de Status van Staatlozen van 1954). In Deel 4 worden vervolgens de overkoepelende resultaten van het onderzoek besproken, alsmede de toekomst van de staatloosheidsverdragen en enkele overige uitdagingen.

Om het internationale juridische stelsel voor de preventie van staatloosheid te beoordelen is iedere oorzaak voor staatloosheid afzonderlijk besproken: technische oorzaken (d.w.z. bestuurlijke praktijken en wetsconflicten), willekeurige ontneming van nationaliteit, staatloosheid in het verband van staatsopvolging en de "nieuwe" oorzaken van staatloosheid (oorzaken die *na* het opstellen van het staatloosheidsverdrag van 1961 erkend zijn). De uiteindelijk conclusie is dat het huidige internationaal recht een groeiend gebrek aan acceptatie van staatloosheid vertoont, waarbij twee centrale principes steeds meer terrein winnen: het vermijden van staatloosheid bij de geboorte en het vermijden van denationalisatie die leidt tot staatloosheid. Uiteindelijk vormen deze twee richtlijnen alles wat nodig is om te bewerkstelligen dat staatloosheid voorkomen wordt, aangezien zij erop gericht zijn te verzekeren dat ieder individu aan het begin van zijn/haar leven een nationaliteit verwerft en dat deze nationaliteit niet verloren gaat tenzij een andere nationaliteit verworven wordt. Beide principes zijn genoemd in het Verdrag tot Beperking van Staatloosheid van 1961 en talrijke verdragen aangaande mensenrechten. In het Verdrag tot Beperking van Staatloosheid van 1961 zijn de principes vertaald in zorgvuldig geformuleerde bepalingen waarin in detail uiteengezet wordt welke staat verantwoordelijk is voor het verlenen van nationaliteit of voor het afzien van het intrekken van burgerschap, alsmede onder welke omstandigheden. In de mensenrechtenverdragen zijn vooral algemeen geformuleerde normen te vinden, zoals het recht van ieder kind om een nationaliteit te verwerven en het verbod op willekeurige ontneming van de nationaliteit. Het staatloosheidsverdrag van 1961 beperkt zijn ambities echter duidelijk tot *het terugbrengen van* het aantal gevallen van staatloosheid, zonder te voorzien in bepalingen over de ondubbelzinnige verlening of het behoud van nationaliteit wanneer staatloosheid dreigt, en geeft op een aantal kwesties geen overtuigend antwoord of behandelt deze kwesties zelfs helemaal niet. Intussen worden in het algemene kader van de mensenrechten breed geformuleerde normen aangereikt die hier en daar de verfijning missen die noodzakelijk is om ze volledig, correct en uniform toe te passen – en de werkelijk interessante en innovatieve ontwikkelingen die opgemerkt zijn staan nog in de kinderschoenen. Zo blijkt geen van beide benaderingen onfeilbaar. Ook biedt het gecombineerde effect van de twee sets normen geen garantie dat alle oorzaken van staatloosheid bij de wortel aangepakt zullen worden.

Deze bevinding bevestigde opnieuw het belang van normen ter bescherming van staatlozen, en deze zijn vervolgens onder de loep genomen: allereerst civiele en politieke rechten, vervolgens economische, sociale en culturele rechten en tenslotte de 'bijzondere behoeften' van de staatlozen. De uitkomst hiervan was meerduidig, net als de resultaten die aan het licht kwamen bij de bespreking van het voorkomen van staatloosheid. De ontwikkeling van de mensenrechtenwetgeving heeft in feite geleid tot een steeds verdergaand afdrijven van staatsburgerschap als het recht om rechten te hebben (zoals door het Amerikaanse Hooggerechtshof in een beroemde uitspraak aan het licht is gebracht) in de richting van 'denationalisatie' van bescherming. De erkenning van het *recht op een nationaliteit* als mensenrecht bevestigt echter ook opnieuw het blijvend belang van nationaliteit: het mensenrechtensysteem kan zijn aspiratie universeel te zijn alleen handhaven door de garantie dat ieder mens ook een nationaliteit heeft. Ofschoon derhalve de noodzaak tot een verdrag specifiek voor staatlozen tegenwoordig wellicht geringer is dan voor de komst van de grote mensenrechtenverdragen, is dit niet overbodig geworden. Het Staatloosheidsverdrag van 1954 tracht aan deze noodzaak tegemoet te komen, maar schiet op op veel punten tekort. Het grootste manco aan het verdrag is de methode die het zelf voorschrijft, waarbij verschillende rechten worden toegekend op grond van verschillende "hechtingsniveaus" (bijvoorbeeld alleen aan staatlozen die wettig in het land aanwezig zijn, of er wettig verblijven) en vaak slechts op een laag, incidenteel niveau (bijvoorbeeld niet meer rechten dan aan niet-onderdanen in het algemeen toegekend worden). Intussen worden binnen de mensenrechtenstructuur zelf richtlijnen ontwikkeld die specifiek gericht zijn op de situatie van niet-onderdanen of zelfs staatlozen, maar welke behandeling deze groepen volgens de huidige mensenrechtennormen precies verschuldigd is is op vele gebieden, bijvoorbeeld ten aanzien van economische, sociale en culturele rechten, nog steeds onduidelijk, in het bijzonder in ontwikkelingslanden.

Het is derhalve onmiskenbaar dat een aantal uitdagingen blijft bestaan, niet in het minst de uitdaging om toe te zien op de volledige implementatie en handhaving van alle bestaande internationale normen. Er zijn echter ook talrijke lacunes in de normatieve kaders voor de preventie van staatloosheid en bescherming van staatlozen gevonden. Als gevolg daarvan worden verschillende voorstellen gedaan ter nadere verduidelijking en uitwerking van richtlijnen die de bedoeling hebben *de manier waarop internationaal recht met de kwestie van staatloosheid omgaat zodanig te verbeteren dat het individu en zijn/haar rechten optimaal beschermd worden*. In het kader van zowel preventie als bescherming is het mogelijk geweest bepaalde actuele en relevante ontwikkelingen op het spoor te komen die ertoe bijgedragen hebben de weg voorwaarts te wijzen.

Een van de meest wijdverbreide problemen waar op ingegaan dient te worden is de samenhang tussen in- en uitsluiting op basis van nationaliteit, alsmede in- en uitsluiting op basis van immigratiestatus. Een voortdurende, essentiële functie van nationaliteit is dat deze de bezitter van de nationaliteit een "thuisbasis" verschaft, een staat waarnaar hij/zij altijd terug kan keren en waar hij/zij een onbetwistbaar verblijfsrecht heeft. Aan de ene kant impliceert dit dat staatlozen geen onbetwistbaar recht hebben om ergens te wonen, en in de praktijk is inderdaad gebleken dat het verwerven en behouden van wettige toegang tot het territorium van een staat voor staatlozen ernstige moeilijkheden oplevert. Dit leidt weer tot problemen met hechtenis, gescheiden leven van familie en het ontbreken van toegang tot rechten en diensten, waaronder een groot aantal rechten en diensten die in het Staatloosheidsverdrag van 1954 beschreven zijn. Aan de andere kant is duidelijk geworden dat staatloosheid tot ontheemding leidt. Daarenboven kan een onwettige of onduidelijke immigratiestatus bijdragen aan de totstandkoming en voortzetting van staatloosheid. Deze feiten versterken de urgentie waarmee staatlozen verzekerd moeten worden van het recht om ergens te wonen. Aldus is dit van alle potentiële, aanvullende normatieve activiteiten die besproken zijn, een van de meest dwingende en tegelijkertijd meest complexe gebieden. Er wordt gesteld dat de meest geëigende weg voorwaarts in dit opzicht is om voort te bouwen op de inspanningen van de Mensenrechtencommissie van de VN om, onafhankelijk van de vraag naar staatsburgerschap, het *eigen land* van een individu vast te stellen met het doel het toegangs- en verblijfsrecht te genieten. Staatlozen vormen duidelijk bij uitstek de groep die baat zou hebben bij een nadere uitwerking van dit begrip, aangezien zij zonder deze constructie blijvend een *eigen land* en de basisveiligheid die daarmee gepaard gaat zullen ontberen. Er is ook opgemerkt dat verdere kristallisatie en verheldering van de richtlijnen die betrekking hebben op preventie van staatloosheid absoluut onontbeerlijk is voor de poging vast te stellen welke staat als het *eigen land* van een staatloze beschouwd moet worden, omdat dit gelijk staat aan het vaststellen welk land "verantwoordelijk" is voor de staatloosheid van dit individu en derhalve de internationale normen geschonden heeft.

Een tweede, nog fundamentelere uitdaging, waarop nog geen passende respons gevonden is, bestaat in de identificatie van staatlozen en personen die het risico lopen staatloos te worden. Dit is een noodzakelijke stap in voorbereiding op het toepassen van regels die betrekking hebben op preventie van staatloosheid, bescherming van staatlozen en, uiteindelijk, het oplossen van bestaande gevallen van staatloosheid. Toch wordt deze kwestie in de twee staatloosheidsverdragen volledig over het hoofd gezien en heeft hij tot nu toe bedroevend weinig aandacht gekregen van de internationale gemeenschap. Zelfs de meest recente, zeer vooruitstrevende voorbeelden van internationale verdragen betreffende vragen van nationaliteit en staatloosheid raken nauwelijks aan het identificatieprobleem. Waar op mensenrechtenorganen een beroep gedaan is om in een bepaalde zaak de nationaliteit of staatloosheid van een aanvrager vast te stellen, hebben zij dit op een ad hoc – en soms tamelijk onnaspeurlijke – wijze gedaan, zonder te trachten regels of procedures voor algemeen gebruik of gebruik in de toekomst op te stellen. Om niettemin een begin te maken met het samenstellen van dergelijke richtlijnen, wordt in het laatste hoofdstuk van dit onderzoek de zoektocht naar relevante internationale praktijken verruimd en wordt lering getrokken op het gebied van het vaststellen van de vluchtelingenstatus en de jurisprudentie betreffende internationale aanspraken. Om mensen een reële kans te geven om van internationale normen betreffende staatloosheid te profiteren, moet deze aanzet tot identificatierichtlijnen nader verhelderd worden en in een toepasselijk document vastgelegd worden: om te beginnen in een handboek voor identificatie, maar later mogelijk in een aanvullend internationaal verdrag dat daarnaast ook andere bestaande lacunes in het internationale rechtssysteem dicht.

Vooruitblikkend naar de toekomst wordt gesteld dat de twee staatloosheidsverdragen wel toekomst hebben. Pleiten voor verbeterde toegang tot deze verdragen zou ook aan één van hun gemeenschappelijke manco's tegemoetkomen, namelijk het armzalige aantal staten dat zich er tot op heden aan verbonden heeft. Een toenemende acceptatie van de staatloosheidsverdragen zal hand in hand gaan met hun toenemende reikwijdte en toepassing wereldwijd, en het bereiken van dit doel zou nog worden versneld door het opstellen van richtlijnen om de identificatiekwestie op te lossen. Verder zullen er met hernieuwde inspanningen om, in een groter aantal landen en met behulp van een identificatiehandboek, uitvoering te geven aan de staatloosheidsverdragen, meer mogelijkheden komen om de overblijvende normatieve lacunes te herzien en te overwegen welke aanvullende maatregelen nodig zijn om de tenuitvoerlegging van deze instrumenten te bevorderen. Geen van beide verdragen zou afzonderlijk als het definitieve antwoord op staatloosheid moeten worden beschouwd – op respectievelijk preventie en bescherming – en de andere wegen tot verbetering van de internationale respons op staatloosheid, die in de loop van dit onderzoek zijn geschetst, zouden ook moeten worden bewandeld. Intussen is het echter de moeite waard om te streven naar een toename van het aantal staten dat de staatloosheidsverdragen ratificeert; dit is nu beslist gemakkelijker dan een halve eeuw geleden, aangezien de inhoud van de verdragen in de huidige internationale juridische situatie niet meer als radicaal of laakbaar bestempeld kan worden. Dit streven is ook ontegenzeggelijk de moeite waard vanuit het oogpunt van het individu, de staat en de internationale gemeenschap, in het bijzonder met het oog op het besef dat kwesties omtrent staatloosheid en nationaliteit kunnen escaleren tot een zaak van nationale of zelfs internationale veiligheid wanneer men ze voort laat woekeren.

Bibliography

Articles, Books and Reports

A

Advisory Board on Human Security (prepared by Constantin Sokoloff), *Denial of Citizenship: A Challenge to Human Security,* February 2005

Aleinikoff, A., "Between Principles and Politics: U.S. Citizenship Policy", in A. Aleinikoff et. al. (eds.), *From Migrants to Citizens. Membership in a changing world,* Brookings Institution Press, Washington D.C. 2000

Aleinikoff, A. & Klusmeyer, D., *Citizenship Policies for an Age of Migration,* Carnegie Empowerment for International Peace, Washington D.C.: 2002

Amnesty International, *Bhutan: Nationality, expulsion, statelessness and the right to return,* September 2000

Amor, A., *Annual Report of the Special Rapporteur on Religious Intolerance,* E/CN.4/2000/65, 15 February 2000

Andreassen, B., "Human Rights for Non-Citizens. Migrant Workers and the Trespassing of National Borders", *Joint sessions of workshops for the European Consortium for Political Research,* Salzburg: 1984

Ansley, F., "Constructing Citizenship Without a Licence: The Struggle of Undocumented Immigrants in the USA for Livelihoods and Recognition" in N. Kabeer (ed.) *Inclusive Citizenship Meanings and Expressions,* Zed Books, London: 2005

Arendt, H., "The Decline of the Nation-State and the End of the Rights of Man" in *The origins of totalitarianism,* Harcourt Brace Jovanovich, New York: 1948

B

Banning, T., van, *The Human Right to Property,* Intersentia, Antwerp: 2002

Batchelor, C., "Stateless Persons: Some Gaps in International Protection", in *International Journal of Refugee Law,* Vol. 7, 1995

Batchelor C., "Statelessness and the Problem of Resolving Nationality Status", in *International Journal of Refugee Law,* Vol. 10, 1998

Batchelor, C., "Developments in International law: The Avoidance of Statelessness Through Positive Application of the Right to a Nationality" in *Council of Europe's First Conference on Nationality*, Strasbourg: 2001

Batchelor, C., "The International Legal Framework Concerning Statelessness and Access for Stateless Persons", *European Union Seminar on the Content and Scope of International Protection: Panel 1 - Legal basis of international protection,* Madrid: 2002

Batchelor, C., *The 1954 Convention relating to the Status of Stateless Persons: Implementation within the European Union Member States and Recommendations for Harmonisation*, 2004

Batchelor, C., "Transforming International Legal Principles into National Law: The Right to a Nationality and the Avoidance of Statelessness", in *Refugee Survey Quarterly,* Vol. 25, 2006

Bauböck, R., *Transnational Citizenship. Membership and Rights in International Migration*, Edward Elgar, Cheltenham: 2002

Benhabib, S., *Transformations of Citizenship - Dilemmas of the Nation State in the Era of Globalisation*, Koniklijke van Gorcum, Assen: 2001

Benito, E., *Elimination of All Forms of Intolerance and Discrimination Based on Religion or Belief,* UN Doc. E.89.XIV.3, 1989

Blackman, J., "State Succession and Statelessness: The Emerging Right to an Effective Nationality under International Law", in *Michigan Journal of International law,* Vol. 19, 1998

Blitz, B., "Statelessness and the Social (De)Construction of Citizenship: Political Restructuring and Ethnic Discrimination in Slovenia", in *Journal of Human Rights,* Vol. 5, 2006

Boeles, P., "What is the use of nationality?" Valedictory lecture, Leiden University, 29 June 2007

Brownlie, I., "The Relations of Nationality in Public International Law", in *British Yearbook of International Law,* Vol. 39, 1963

Brownlie, I., *Principles of Public International Law*, Oxford University Press, Oxford: 2003

Bueren, G., *The International Law on the Rights of the Child*, Martinus Nijhoff, Dordrecht: 1995

Bustamante, J., *Report of the Special Rapporteur on the human rights of migrants,* E/CN.4/2006/73, 30 December 2005

C

Camarota, S., *Immigrants at mid-decade. A snapshot of America's foreign-born population in 2005,* Centre for Immigration Studies, December 2005

Cassel, D., "Equal Labor Rights for Undocumented Migrant Workers" in A. Bayefsky (ed.) *Human Rights and Refugees, Internally Displaced Persons and Migrant Workers*, Martinus Nijhoff, Leiden: 2006

Castles, S. & Davidson, A., *Citizenship and Migration. Globalisation and the Politics of Belonging*, Macmillan Press, London: 2000

Castles, S. & Miller, M., *The Age of Migration*, The Guildford Press, London: 2003

Chan, J., "The Right to a Nationality as a Human Right - The Current Trend Towards Recognition", in *Human Rights Law Journal,* Vol. 12, 1991

Chen, L., "The Equal Protection of Women in Reference to Nationality and Freedom of Movement", in *American Society of International Law Proceedings,* Vol. 69, 1975

Council of Europe, *European Convention on Nationality: Explanatory report,* Strasbourg: 1997

Council of Europe, Committee of Experts on Nationality, *Report on Conditions for the Acquisition and Loss of Nationality,* Strasbourg: 14 January 2003

Council of Europe, Committee of Experts on Nationality, *Report on Misuse of Nationality Laws,* Strasbourg: 20 April 2004

Council of Europe, *Council of Europe Convention on the avoidance of statelessness in relation to State succession - Explanatory Report,* Strasbourg: 2006

Córdova, R., *Nationality, Including Statelessness. Third Report on the Elimination or Reduction of Statelessness by Roberto Córdova, Special Rapporteur,* A/CN.4/81, New York: 11 March 1954

Costa, R., *Rights of Refugees in the Context of Integration: Legal Standards and Recommendations,* Geneva: June 2006

Craven, M., *The International Covenant on Economic, Social and Cultural Rights. A Perspective on its Development*, Clarendon Press, Oxford: 1998

Crawford, J., *The International Law Commission's Articles on State Responsibility*, Cambridge University Press, Cambridge: 2002

Crisp, J., *No solutions in sight: the problem of protracted refugee situations in Africa,* UNHCR Working Paper No. 75, January 2003

D

Dahrendorf, R., "The changing quality of citizenship", in B. van Steenbergen (ed.), *The condition of citizenship*", Sage Publications, London: 1994

Dankwa, E., "Working Paper on Article 2(3) of the International Covenant on Economic, Social and Cultural Rights", in *Human Rights Quarterly,* Vol. 9, 1987

Deen-Racsmany, Z., "The Nationality of the Offender and the Jurisdiction of the International Criminal Court", in *The American Journal of International Law,* Vol. 95, No. 3, 2001

Dent, J., *Research Paper on the Social and Economic Rights of Non-Nationals in Europe,* Brussels: 1998

Detrick, S., *The United Nations Convention on the Rights of the Child*, Martinus Nijhoff, Dordrecht: 1992

Detrick, S., *A commentary on the United Nations Convention on the Rights of the Child*, Kluwer, The Hague: 1999

Diène, D., *Report by the Special Rapporteur on contemporary forms of racism, racial discrimination, xenophobia and related intolerance, Addendum – Mission to the Russian Federation,* A/HRC/4/19/Add.3, 30 May 2007

Diène, D., *Report by the Special Rapporteur on contemporary forms of racism, racial discrimination, xenophobia and related intolerance, Addendum – Summary of cases transmitted to Governments and replies received,* A/HRC/4/19/Add.1, 5 June 2007

Doebbler, C., "A Human Rights Approach to Statelessness in the Middle East", in *Leiden Journal of International Law,* Vol. 15, 2002

Doek, J., "The CRC and the Right to Acquire and to Preserve a Nationality", in *Refugee Survey Quarterly,* Vol. 25, 2006

Donders, Y., *Towards a Right to Cultural Identity?*, Intersentia, Oxford: 2002

Donner, R., *The Regulation of Nationality in International Law*, Transnational Publishers, New York: 1994

Drzewicki, K., "The Right to Work and Rights in Work" in A. Rosas (ed.) *Economic, Social and Cultural Rights*, Martinus Nijhoff Publishers, Dordrecht: 1995

Duncan, W., "Nationality and the Protection of Children Across Frontiers: The Case of Intercountry Adoption", *3rd European Conference on Nationality - Nationality and the Child,* Strasbourg: 2004

E

Eide, A., "Cultural Rights as Individual Human Rights" in A. Rosas (ed.) *Economic, Social and Cultural Rights*, Martinus Nijhoff Publishers, Dordrecht: 1995

Eide, A., "Economic, Social and Cultural Rights as Human Rights" in A. Rosas (ed.) *Economic, Social and Cultural Rights*, Martinus Nijhoff Publishers, Dordrecht: 1995

Eide, A., "The Right to an Adequate Standard of Living Including the Right to Food" in A. Rosas (ed.) *Economic, Social and Cultural Rights*, Martinus Nijhoff Publishers, Dordrecht: 1995

Eide, A., "Citizenship and the minority rights of non-citizens", Working Paper prepared for the UN Sub-Commission on Prevention of Discrimination and Protection of Minorities, E/CN.4/Sub.2/AC.5/1999/WP.3, 15 April 1999

Elles, D., *International Provisions Protecting the Human Rights of Non-Citizens: Study,* New York: 1980

European Commission for Democracy 1997: European Commission for Democracy through Law, *Consequences of state succession for nationality,* Strasbourg: 10 February 1997

F

Faulks, K., *Citizenship*, Routledge, London: 2003

Ferrari, V., "Citizenship: Problems, Concepts and Policies" in M.L. Torre (ed.) *European Citizenship - An Institutional Challenge*, Kluwer Law International, The Hague: 1998

Flournoy, R., "International Problems in Respect to Nationality by Birth", in *American Society of International Law Proceedings,* Vol. 20, 1926

Franco, L., "Protection of Refugees and Solutions to the Refugee Problem: A Human Rights Perspective" in A. Schmid (ed.) *Whither Refugee? The Refugee Crisis: Problems and Solutions*, PIOOM, Leiden: 1996

Frelick, B., *Statelessness: The Denial of a Fundamental Human Right*, 19 April 2005

G

Galicki, Z., "State Succession and Nationality" in *Council of Europe's First Conference on Nationality*, Strasbourg: 1999

Galloway, D., "Citizenship: A Jurisprudential Paradox" in M.L. Torre (ed.) *European Citizenship - An Institutional Challenge*, Kluwer Law International, The Hague: 1998

Gelazis, N., "The European Union and the Statelessness Problem in the Baltic States", in *European Journal of Migration and Law,* Vol. 6, 2004

Gelazis, N., "An Evaluation of International Instruments that Address the Condition of Statelessness: A Case Study of Estonia and Latvia" R. Cholewinski (ed.) *International Migration Law*, T.M.C. Asser Press, The Hague: 2007

Gettys, L., "The Effect of Changes of Sovereignty on Nationality", in *American Journal of International Law,* Vol. 21, 1927

Goldston, J., "Holes in the Rights Framework: Racial Discrimination, Citizenship, and the Rights of Noncitizens", in *Ethics and International Affairs,* Vol. 20, 2006

Goodwin-Gill, G., "International Law and Human Rights: Trends Concerning International Migrants and Refugees", in *International Migration Review,* Vol. 23, 1989

Goodwin Gill, G., "The rights of refugees and stateless persons" in K.P. Saksena (ed.) *Human rights perspectives & challenges (in 1900's and beyond)*, Lancers Books, New Delhi: 1994

Goodwin-Gill, G. & McAdam, J., *The refugee in international law*, Oxford University Press, Oxford: 2007

Gorlick, B., *Human Rights and Refugees: Enhancing Protection through International Human Rights Law*, Geneva: October 2000

Gorlick, B., "(Mis)perception of Refugees, State Sovereignty, and the Continuing Challenge of International Protection" in A. Bayefsky (ed.) *Human Rights and Refugees, Internally Displaced Persons and Migrant Workers*, Martinus Nijhoff, Leiden: 2006

Grant, S., "The Legal Protection of Stranded Migrants" in R. Cholewinski (ed.) *International Migration Law*, TMC Asser Press, The Hague: 2007

Groenendijk, K., “Nationality, Minorities and Statelessness. The Case of the Baltic States”, in *Helsinki Monitor,* Vol. 4, 1993

Grossman, A., “Birthright Citizenship as Nationality of Convenience”, *3rd European Conference on Nationality - Nationality and the Child,* Strasbourg: 2004

H

Hailbronner, K., "Free Movement of EU Nationals and Union Citizenship" in R. Cholewinski (ed.) *International Migration Law*, TMC Asser Press, The Hague: 2007

Hammarberg, T., “Children” in A. Rosas (ed.) *Economic, Social and Cultural Rights*, Martinus Nijhoff Publishers, Dordrecht: 1995

Hannum, H., *The Right to Leave and Return in International Law and Practice*, Martinus Nijhoff Publishers, Dordrecht: 1987

Hart, B. & Groenendijk, K., "Multiple Nationality: The Practice of Germany and the Netherlands" in R. Cholewinski (ed.) *International Migration Law*, TMC Asser Press, The Hague: 2007

Harvey, C. & Barnidge, R., 'Human Rights, Free Movement, and the Right to Leave in International Law', in *International Journal of Refugee Law,* Vol. 19, 2007

Hathaway, J., *The Rights of Refugees Under International Law*, Cambridge University Press, Cambridge: 2005

Helfer, L., *Human Rights and Intellectual Property: Conflict or Coexistence?* in Minnesota Journal of Law, Science & Technology, Vol. 5, 2003

Hudson, M., *Report on Nationality, including Statelessness,* A/CN.4/50, 21 February 1952

Human Rights Watch, *Syria – The silenced Kurds,* Vol. 8, No. 4, October 1996

Human Rights Watch, *Roma in the Czech Republic – Foreigners in Their Own Land,* 1 June 1996

Human Rights Watch, *“Illegal People”: Haitians and Dominico-Haitians in the Dominican Republic,* Vol. 14, Number 1, April 2002

Human Rights Watch, *The Horn of Africa: Mass Expulsions and the Nationality Issue,* 30 January 2003

Human Rights Watch, *We don’t want to be refugees again,* HRW Briefing Paper for the 14th Ministerial Joint Committee of Bhutan and Nepal, 19 May 2003

Hutt, M., *Unbecoming Citizens. Culture, Nationhood, and the Flight of Refugees from Bhutan.*, Oxford University Press, New Delhi: 2005

I

Inter-American Commission for Human Rights, *Third report on the situation of human rights in Chile,* OEA/Ser.L/V/II.40, doc. 10, 1977

Inter-American Commission on Human Rights, *Chapter V – Situation of Haitians in the Dominican Republic,* in “Annual Report 1991”, OAE/Ser.L/V/II.81, Doc. 6, Rev. 1, 14 February 1992

Inter-American Commission on Human Rights, "Chapter IX: Situation of Haitian migrant workers and their families in the Dominican Republic", in *Report on the situation of human rights in the Dominican Republic,* OEA/Ser.L/V/II.104, 7 October 1999

International Law Association, *Final Report on Women's Equality and Nationality in International Law,* Committee on Feminism and International Law, London Conference, 2000

International Law Commission, "Draft Articles on Nationality of Natural Persons in Relation to the Succession of States - With Commentaries", in *Yearbook of the International Law Commission,* Vol. II, 1999

International Law Commission, *Report on the work of its 52nd Session,* UN General Assembly Official Records, 56th Session, Supplement No. 10, A/55/10, New York 2000

International Law Commission, *Report of the 54th Session,* UN General Assembly Official Records, 57th Session, Supplement No. 10, A/57/10, New York 2002

International Law Commission, *Preliminary report on the expulsion of aliens,* prepared by Special Rapporteur Maurice Kamto, A/CN.4/554, 2 June 2005

International Law Commission, *Diplomatic Protection – Comments and observations received from governments,* UN Doc. A/CN.4/561, 26 January 2006

International Law Commission, *Second report on the expulsion of aliens*, prepared by Special Rapporteur Maurice Kamto, A/CN.4/573, 20 July 2006

International Law Commission, *Report of the work of its 58th Session,* UN General Assembly Official Records, 61st Session, Supplement No. 10, A/61/10, New York 2006

International Law Commission, *Third report on the expulsion of aliens,* prepared by Special Rapporteur Maurice Kamto, A/CN.4/581, 19 April 2007

International Organisation for Migration, *World Migration 2003: Managing Migration - Challenges and Responses for People on the Move,* Geneva: 2003

International Rescue Committee, *Basic Information on Rights of Migrant Workers in Thailand*, ICR Bangkok, 2006

International Union for Child Welfare, *Stateless Children - A Comparative Study of National Legislation and Suggested Solutions to the Problem of Statelessness of Children,* Geneva: 1947

Iselin B. & Adams, M., *Distinguishing between Human Trafficking and People Smuggling,* UN Office on Drugs and Crime, 2003

Ismail, Y., "Is Toleration Enough?" in *Refugees Magazine,* Number 148, Issue 4, 2007

J

Jacobsen, K., *The forgotten solution: local integration for refugees in developing countries,* No. 45, Geneva: July 2001

Jahangir, A., *Annual Report of the Special Rapporteur on freedom of religion or belief,* E/CN.4/2005/61, 20 December 2004

Jahangir, A., *Annual Report of the Special Rapporteur on freedom of religion or belief,* A/HRC/4/21, 26 December 2006

Jayawickrama, N.,"The Judicial Application of Human Rights Law", Cambridge University Press, Cambridge: 2002

Joseph, J. & Schultz, J. & Castan, M., *The International Covenant on Civil and Political Rights. Cases, Materials and Commentary*, Oxford University Press, Oxford: 2000

K

Kamminga, M., 'State Succession in Respect of Human Rights Treaties', in *European Journal of International Law,* Vol. 7, 1996

Kartashkin, V., *The rights of women married to foreigners,* E/CN.4/Sub.2/2003/34, 30 June 2003

Kerdel, K., *Stateless persons of Indian origin in Sri Lanka - an overview,* Colombo: 9 June 2004

Krause, C., "The right to property" in A. Rosas (ed) *Economic, Social and Cultural Rights*, Martinus Nijhoff Publishers, Dordrecht: 1995

Krieken, P., "Disintegration and statelessness", in *Netherlands Quarterly of Human Rights,* Vol. 12, 1994

Klusmeyer, D. & Aleinikoff, A. (eds.), *From Migrants to Citizens: Membership in a Changing World*, Carnegie Endowment for International Peace, Washington: 2000

L

Lauterpacht, H., *Human Rights, the charter of the United Nations and the International Bill of the Rights of Man*, prepared for the Human Rights Committee, May 1948

Leckie, S., "The Right to Housing" in A. Rosas (ed) *Economic, Social and Cultural Rights*, Martinus Nijhoff Publishers, Dordrecht: 1995

Leclerc, P. & Colville, R., "In the Shadows", in *Refugees Magazine,* No. 147, Issue 3, 2007

Lee, T., *Statelessness, human rights and gender: irregular migrant workers from Burma in Thailand*, Martinus Nijhoff Publishers, 2005

Letschert, R., *The Impact of Minority Rights Mechanisms. The OSCE High Commissioner on National Minorities, the UN Working Group on Minorities and the CoE Advisory Committee on Minorities*, T.M.C. Asser Press, The Hague: 2005

Lewinski, S., von, *Intellectual Property, Nationality and Non-Discrimination*, paper presented at the "Panel Discussion on Intellectual Property and Human Rights", Geneva, 9 November 1998

Lillich, R., *The human rights of aliens in contemporary international law*, Manchester University Press, Manchester: 1984

Lynch, M., *Lives on hold: The human cost of statelessness,* Washington: 2005

Lynch, M., "Syria: Follow Through on Commitment to Grant Citizenship to Stateless Kurds", *Refugees International Bulletin,* Washington: 2005

Lynch, M. & Cook, T., *Citizens of nowhere. The stateless Biharis of Bangladesh,* Washington: 2006

Lynch, M. & Ali, P., *Buried Alive. Stateless Kurds in Syria,* Report for Refugees International, Washington: 2006

Lyon, B., "New International Human Rights Standards on Unauthorized Immigrant Worker Rights: Seizing an Opportunity to Pull Governments Out of the Shadows" in A. Bayefsky (ed.) *Human Rights and Refugees, Internally Displaced Persons and Migrant Workers*, Martinus Nijhoff, Leiden: 2006

M

Manly, M., "Sorry, wrong gender" in *Refugees Magazine,* Number 147, Issue 3, 2007

Marks, S. & Clapham, A., *International Human Rights Lexicon,* Oxford University Press, Oxford: 2005

Martin, D., "Citizenship in countries of immigration – Introduction", in Alexander Aleinikoff; D. Klusmeyer et. al. (ed.), *From Migrants to Citizens. Membership in a changing world*, Brookings Institution Press, Washington D.C. 2000

Martin, V., *Myanmarese Refugees in Thailand: No Freedom, No Choices,* US Committee for Refugees, World Refugee Survey 2004

McDougall, G., *Promotion and Protection of all Human Rights, Civil, Political, Economic, Social and Cultural Rights, Including the Right to Development – Report of the Independent Expert on Minority Issues,* A/HRC/7/23, 28 February 2008

McKean, W., *Equality and discrimination under international law,* Clarendon Press, Oxford: 1983

McNeil, D., "Founder of Zambia is declared stateless in high court ruling" *New York Times,* New York: Date 1999

Meijknecht, A., *Towards International Personality: The Position of Minorities and Indigenous Peoples in International Law,* Intersentia, Antwerp: 2001

Mikulka, V., *Third report on Nationality in relation to the Succession of States,* A/CN.4/480, Geneva: 27 February 1997

Miller, M., "Birth Registration: Statelessness and other repercussions for unregistered children", *3rd European Conference on Nationality - Nationality and the Child,* Strasbourg: 2004

Movement of Haitian and Dominico-Haitian Women (MUDHA), *Solidarity. With the struggle of the Dominican minority of Haitian descent for citizenship and justice,* Santo Domingo, August 2001

N

Nowak, M., "The Right to Education" in A. Rosas (ed) *Economic, Social and Cultural Rights*, Martinus Nijhoff Publishers, Dordrecht: 1995

Nyo, N., "Burmese Children in Thailand: Legal Aspects", in *Legal Issues on Burma Journal,* Burma Lawyers Council, No. 10, December 2001

O

O'Connell, D., *State succession in municipal and international law*, Cambridge University Press, Cambridge: 1967

Open Society Justice Initiative, *Racial Discrimination and the Rights of Non-Citizens. Submission to the UN Committee on the Elimination of Racial Discrimination on the occasion of its 64th Session,* New York: 2004

Open Society Justice Initiative, *Africa Citizenship and Discrimination Audit,* New York: 2004

Open Society Justice Initiative, *Citizenship and Equality in Practice: Guaranteeing Non-Discriminatory Access to Nationality, Protecting the Right to be Free from Arbitrary Deprivation of Nationality, and Combating Statelessness,* New York: November 2005

Open Society Justice Initiative, *Written Comments on the Case of Dilcea Yean and Violeta Bosico v. Dominican Republic,* New York: April 2005

Open Society Justice Initiative, *The Face of Statelessness: A Call for African Norms on the Right to Citizenship,* February 2007

P

Panhuys, H., van, *The Role of Nationality in International Law*, A.W. Sijthoff's Uitgeversmaatschappij, Leiden: 1959

Paulsen, E., "The citizenship status of the Urdu-speakers / Biharis in Bangladesh", in *Refugee Survey Quarterly,* Vol. 25, 2006

Perera, S., "Sri Lankan Success Story", in *Refugees Magazine,* Number 147, Issue 3, 2007

Pinheiro, P., *Report of the Special Rapporteur on the situation of human rights in Myanmar,* E/CN.4/2006/34, 7 February 2006; A/HRC/4/14, 12 February 2007; A/HRC/7/24, 7 March 2008

Pinkerton, C. & McLaughlan, G. & Salt, J., *Sizing the illegally resident population in the UK,* United Kingdom Home Office Online Report 58/04, Migration Research Unit, University College London

Piotrowicz, R., "Victims of trafficking and de facto statelessness", in *Refugee Survey Quarterly,* Vol. 21, 2002

Pizarro, G., *Specific Groups and Individuals - Migrant Workers,* Geneva: 30 December 2002

Plan International, *Universal Birth Registration - A Universal Responsibility,* Woking: 2005

Pouilly, C., “Africa’s Hidden Problem” in *Refugees Magazine,* Number 147, Issue 3, 2007

R

Redden, J., “Suddenly, you are nobody” in *Refugees Magazine,* Number 147, Issue 3, 2007

Refugees International, *Stolen Futures: The Stateless Children of Burmese Asylum Seekers,* 25 June 2004

Refugees International, *Stateless Biharis in Bangladesh: A humanitarian nightmare,* RI Bulletin, 13 December 2004

Refugees International, “Refugee Voices: Detained Stateless People in Kuwait”, 24 September 2007

Robinson, W. C., *Thailand: Background paper on human rights, refugees and asylum seekers,* Writenet Report commissioned by UNHCR, July 2004

Robinson, N., *Convention relating to the status of stateless persons - Its history and interpretation*, UNHCR, Geneva: 1955

Robinson, N., *The Universal Declaration of Human Rights. Its Origin, Significance, Application and Interpretation*, Institute of Jewish Affairs, New York: 1958

Ruiz, H. & Berg, M., “Unending Limbo: Warehousing Bhutanese Refugees in Nepal” in UNHCR (ed) *World Refugee Survey 2004*, UNHCR, Geneva: 2004

S

Sabourin, N., “The relevance of the European Convention on Nationality for non-European states” in *Council of Europe's First Conference on Nationality*, Strasbourg: 1999

Samore, W., “Statelessness as a consequence of the conflict of nationality laws”, in *American Journal of International Law,* Vol. 45, 1951

Schärer, R., 'The Council of Europe and the Reduction of Statelessness', in *Refugee Survey Quarterly,* Vol. 25, 2006

Scheinin, M., “The Right to Social Security” in AECKA Rosas (ed) *Economic, Social and Cultural Rights*, Martinus Nijhoff Publishers, Dordrecht: 1995

Schmid, A., “Whither Refugee? The Refugee Crisis: Problems and Solutions”, PIOOM, Leiden: 1996

Schodder, H., “Assisting the integration of formerly deported people in Crimea: ten years of UNHCR experiences” in *Beyond Borders,* Bulletin of UNHCR in Ukraine, 2005

Schuck, P., *Immigration, refugee and citizenship law in the United States,* in Donald Horowitz and Gerard Noiriel (Eds.), “Immigrants in two democracies. French and American Experience”, New York University Press, New York 1992

Sepulveda, M. & Banning, T., van & Gudmundsdotter, G. & Chamoun, C., *Universal and Regional Human Rights Protection: Cases and Commentaries*, University for Peace, Ciudad Colon: 2004

Shaw, M., *International Law*, Cambridge University Press, Cambridge: 2003

Shevel, O., "Crimean Tatars and the Ukrainian state: the challenge of politics, the use of law, and the meaning of rhetoric", paper delivered the Association for the Study of the Nationalities (ASN) Fifth Annual World Convention "Identity and the State: Nationalism And Sovereignty in a Changing World," Columbia University, New York, NY, April 13-15, 2000

Shiblak, A., *Citizens, Sub-citizens and Non-citizens: Statelessness in the Arab Region,* unpublished paper

Snelders, P. & Kraus, S. & Wijers, M., *Commentaar inzake de specifieke effecten van de Koppelingswet op de situatie van vrouwen t.b.v. de Tussentijdse Evaluatie Koppelingswet* [A commentary on the specific effects of the Linkage Law on the situation of women in aid of the mid-term evaluation of the Linkage Law] Komitee Zelfstandig Verblijfsrecht Migrantenvrouwen, E-Quality and Clara Wichmann Instituut, Amsterdam, 7 February 2000

Soysal, Y., *Limits of citizenship - Migrants and postnational membership in Europe*, The University of Chicago Press, Chicago: 1994

Staples, H., *The Legal Status of Third Country Nationals Resident in the European Union*, Kluwer Law International, The Hague: 1999

Steele, S.,"Comments on Okuda, Statelessness and the Nationality Act of Japan: Baby Andrew Becomes a Teenager and other Changes?" *Journal of Japanese Law,* Volume 9, Number 18, 2004

Steiner, H. & Alston, P., *International Human Rights in Context. Law, Politics and Morals*, Oxford University Press, Oxford: 2000

Stolcke, V., "The 'Nature' of nationality" in V Bader (ed) *Citizenship and exclusion*, Macmillan Press, London: 1997

Stratton, L., "The Right to Have Rights: Gender Discrimination in Nationality Laws", in *Minnesota Law Review,* Vol. 77, 1992

T

Thijn, E., van, *Human rights of irregular migrants*, Committee on Migration, Refugees and Population of the Parliamentary Assembly of the Council of Europe, Document 10924, 4 May 2006

Tiburcio, C., *The human rights of aliens under international and comparative law*, Kluwer Law International, The Hague: 2001

Tomasevski, K., "Health Rights" in AECKA Rosas (ed) *Economic, Social and Cultural Rights*, Martinus Nijhoff Publishers, Dordrecht: 1995

Torpey, J., *The Invention of the Passport. Surveillance, Citizenship and the State*, Cambridge University Press, Cambridge: 2000

U

UN, *A Study of Statelessness,* E/1112, New York: August 1949

UN, *Our rights as human beings: A discussion guide on the Universal Declaration of Human Rights,* New York: 1949

UN, *International migration and development,* Report of the Secretary General, UN Doc. A/60/971, 18 May 2006
UN Division for the Advancement of Women, *Women, Nationality and Citizenship,* New York: 2003
UNDP Regional Bureau for Asia and the Pacific, *Common Country Assessment on Bangladesh,* 2000
UN General Assembly, *Note by the secretariat on Nationality of natural persons in relation to the succession of States,* A/59/180, 26 July 2004 and A/59/180/Add.1, 26 August 2004
UN General Assembly, *Report of the Sixth Committee on Nationality of natural persons in relation to the succession of States,* A/59/504, 19 November 2004
UNHCR, *Identity documents for refugees,* Note on International Protection, Geneva: 20 July 1984
UNHCR, *Stateless persons: a discussion note,* EC/1992/SCP/CRP.4, Geneva: 1 April 1992
UNHCR, *Handbook on Procedures and Criteria for Determining Refugee Status under the 1951 Convention and the 1967 Protocol relating to the Status of Refugees,* HCR/IP/Eng/Rev.1, Reedited January 1992
UNHCR, *Handbook on Voluntary Repatriation: International Protection*, Geneva: 1996
UNHCR, "Statelessness and Citizenship" in *The State of the World's Refugees - A Humanitarian Agenda*, Oxford University Press, Oxford: 1997
UNHCR, *What would life be like if you had no nationality?* Information booklet, Geneva, March 1999
UNHCR, *Information and accession package: the 1954 Convention relating to the status of stateless persons and the 1961 Convention on the reduction of statelessness,* Geneva: January 1999
UNHCR, *Progress report on UNHCR activities in the field of statelessness,* EC/49/SC/CRP.15, Geneva: 4 June 1999
UNHCR, *Overview of UNHCR's Citizenship Campaign in Crimea,* Simferopol: December 2000
UNHCR, *Statistical Yearbook 2001,* Geneva, October 2002
UNHCR, *Annual Global Appeal,* Geneva, 2002
UNHCR, *Statelessness in Canadian Context – A Discussion Paper,* Ottawa, July 2003
UNHCR, *Annual Global Appeal,* Geneva, 2003
UNHCR, *Final report concerning the Questionnaire on statelessness pursuant to the Agenda for Protection,* Geneva: March 2004
UNHCR, *Protracted refugee situations*, EC/54/SC/CRP.14, Geneva: 10 June 2004
UNHCR, *Unending Limbo: Warehousing Bhutanese Refugees in Nepal,* World Refugee Survey 2004
UNHCR, *The World's Stateless - Questions and Answers,* Geneva: 2004
UNHCR, *Annual Global Appeal,* Geneva, 2004

UNHCR, *Procedural Standards for Refugee Status Determination under UNHCR's Mandate,* Geneva: 2005
UNHCR, *Self-study module 2: Refugee Status Determination. Identifying who is a refugee,* September 2005
UNHCR, *Annual Global Appeal*, Geneva, 2005
UNHCR, *UNHCR's activities in the field of statelessness: Progress Report,* EC/55/SC/CRP.13/Rev.1, Geneva: 30 June 2005
UNHCR and IPU, *Nationality and statelessness. A handbook for parliamentarians,* 2005
UNHCR, *Global Trends 2006,* Table 14 – Stateless Persons, Geneva, 2006
UNHCR, *Statistical Yearbook 2006 – Trends in Displacement, Protection and Solutions,* Geneva, December 2007
UNHCR, "The World's Stateless People" in *Refugees Magazine,* Number 147, Issue 3, 2007
UNHCR, *UNHCR Handbook for the Protection of Women and Girls,* January 2008
UNICEF, *Birth Registration: Right from the Start,* Florence: March 2002
UNICEF, *The State of the World's Children. Excluded and Invisible,* New York: 2006
UN Office on Drugs and Crime (UNODC), *Trafficking in Persons: Global Patterns,* Vienna: April 2006
US Department of State, *Trafficking in persons report 2006,* Washington: 2006

V

Varennes, F., de, "Towards effective participation and representation of minorities", prepared for the Sub-Commission on Prevention of Discrimination and Protection of Minorities of the UN Commission on Human Rights, May 1998, E/CN.4/Sub.2/AC5/1998/WP4
Vel, G., de, *Closing speech to the 1st European Conference on Nationality,* Director General for Legal Affairs of the Council of Europe, Strasbourg: 1999
Verdoodt, A., *Naissance et Signification de la Déclaration Universelle des Droits de l'Homme*, E. Warny, Louvain: 1964
Vohra, S., "Detention of Irregular Migrants and Asylum Seekers" in R. Cholewinski (ed.) *International Migration Law*, TMC Asser Press, The Hague: 2007

W

Waas, L., van, *Is Permanent Illegality Inevitable? The Challenges to Ensuring Birth Registration and the Right to a Nationality for the Children of Irregular Migrants - Thailand and the Dominican Republic,* Woking: 2006
Waas, L., van, 'The Children of Irregular Migrants: A Stateless Generation?' in *Netherlands Quarterly of Human Rights,* Vol. 25, 2007
Walker, D.J., "Statelessness: Violation or Conduit for Violation of Human Rights?" in *Human Rights Quarterly,* Vol. 3, No. 1, 1981

Weis, P., *Nationality and Statelessness in International Law*, Kluwer Academic Publishers Group, Dordrecht: 1979

Weis, P., "Diplomatic protection of nationals and international protection of human rights" in *International Journal of Refugee Law,* 1991

Weis, P., *The Refugee Convention, 1951*, Cambridge University Press, Cambridge: 1995

Weissbrodt, D., *The Right to a Fair Trial*, Martinus Nijhoff Publishers, The Hague: 2001

Weissbrodt, D., *Preliminary Report on the Rights of Non-Citizens,* E/CN.4/Sub.2/2001/20, Geneva: 6 June 2001

Weissbrodt, D., *Final Report on Prevention of Discrimination - The Rights of Non-Citizens,* E/CN.4/Sub.2/2003/23, 26 May 2003

Weissbrodt, D. & Collins, C., "The Human Rights of Stateless Persons", in *Human Rights Quarterly,* Vol. 28, 2006

Weissbrodt, D., "The Protection of Non-Citizens in International Human Rights Law" in R. Cholewinski (ed.) *International Migration Law*, TMC Asser Press, The Hague: 2007

Wooding, B. & Mosely-Williams, R., *Needed but unwanted,* Catholic Institute for International Relations, London 2004

World Intellectual Property Organisation, *WIPO Intellectual Property Handbook: Policy, Laws and Use,* WIPO Publication No. 489(E), Geneva 2004

Y

Youth Advocate Program International, *Stateless Children - Youth Who are Without Citizenship,* Washington DC: 2002

Z

Zagar, M., "Citizenship - Nationality: A Proper Balance Between the Interests of States and those of Individuals" in *Council of Europe's First European Conference on Nationality*, Strasbourg: 1999

Ziemele, I., *State Continuity and Nationality: The Baltic States and Russia. Past, Present and Future as Defined by International Law*, Martinus Nijhoff Publishers, Leiden: 2005

Zilberschats, Y., *The Human Right to Citizenship*, Transnational Publishers, Ardsley, NY: 2002

Zolberg, A., "Modes of Incorporation: Toward a Comparative Framework" in V. Bader (ed.) *Citizenship and Exclusion*, Macmillan Press, London: 1997

CASE LAW

African Commission on Human and Peoples' Rights

African Commission on Human and Peoples' Rights, *John K. Modise v. Botswana,* Comm. No. 97/93, Benin, November 2000

African Commission on Human and Peoples' Rights, *People v. Côte d'Ivoire,* pending

African Commission on Human and Peoples' Rights, *Yusuf Ali and others v. Kenya,* pending

Committee on the Elimination of Racial Discrimination

Committee on the Elimination of Racial Discrimination, *F.A. v. Norway,* CERD/C/58/D/18/2000, 21 March 2001

European Court of Human Rights / European Commission of Human Rights

European Court of Human Rights, *X. v. Austria,* No. 5212/71, Decision on Admissability, 5 October 1972

European Commission on Human Rights, *Kalderas Gipsies v. the Federal Republic of Germany and the Netherlands,* No. 7823/77-7824/77, 6 July 1977

European Commission of Human Rights, *Caprino v. the United Kingdom,* Application No. 6871/75, 3 March 1978

European Court of Human Rights, *Marckx vs. Belgium*, No. 6833/74, 13 June 1979

European Court of Human Rights, *Family K and W v. The Netherlands,* No. 11278/84, 1 July 1985

European Commission of Human Rights, *Harabi v. The Netherlands,* No. 10798/84, 5 March 1986

European Court of Human Rights of *The Holy Monestaries v. Greece,* Nos. 13092/87 and 13984/88, 9 December 1994

European Court of Human Rights, *Gaygusuz v. Austria,* No. 17371/90, 16 September 1996

European Court of Human Rights, *Chahal v. the United Kingdom,* No. 22414/93, 15 November 1996

European Court of Human Rights, *Decision as to the admissibility of Karassev v. Finland,* No. 31414/96, 12 January 1999

European Court of Human Rights, *Slavov v. Sweden,* No. 44828/98, 29 June 1999

European Court of Human Rights, *Maaouia v. France,* No. 39652/98, 5 October 2000

European Court of Human Rights, *Cyprus v. Turkey,* No. 25781/94, 10 May 2001

European Court of Human Rights, *Okonkwo v. Austria,* No. 35117/97, 22 May 2001

European Court of Human Rights, *Al-Nashif v. Bulgaria,* No. 50963/99, 20 June 2002
European Court of Human Rights, *Mamatkulov and Abdurasulovic v. Turkey, N*os. 46827/99 and 46951/99, 6 February 2003
European Court of Human Rights, *Mogos and Krifka v. Germany,* Decision on admissibility, No. 78084/01, 27 March 2003
European Court of Human Rights, *Slivenko v. Latvia,* No. 48321/99, 9 October 2003
European Court of Human Rights, *Sisojeva and others v. Latvia,* No. 60654/00, 16 June 2005
European Court of Human Rights, *Kaftailova v. Latvia,* No. 59643/00, 22 June 2006
European Court of Human Rights, *Tatishvili v. Russia,* No. 1509/02, 22 February 2007
European Court of Human Rights, *Makuc and others v. Slovenia,* No. 26808/06, pending

Human Rights Committee

Human Rights Committee, *Shirin Aumeeruddy-Cziffra and 19 other Mautitian women v. Mauritius*, Comm. No. 35/1978, Geneva: 9 April 1981
Human Rights Committee, *Case of Martins v. Uruguay,* Comm. No. R.13/57 Geneva: 23 March 1982
Human Rights Committee, *Case of Lichtensziteijn v. Uruguay,* Comm. No. R.19/77, Geneva: 3 March 1983
Human Rights Committee, *Gueye et al. v. France,* Comm. No. 196/1983, Geneva: 3 April 1989
Human Rights Committee, *Van Alphen v. The Netherlands,* Comm. No. 305/1988, Geneva: 23 July 1990
Human Rights Committee, *Kulomin v. Hungary,* Comm. No. 521/1992, Geneva: 22 March 1996
Human Rights Committee, *Adam v. The Czech Republic,* Comm. No. 586/1994, Geneva: 23 July 1996
Human Rights Committee, *Stewart v. Canada,* Comm. No. 538/1993, Geneva: 1 November 1996
Human Rights Committee, *Capena v. Canada,* Comm. No. 558/1993, Geneva: 3 April 1997
Human Rights Committee, *A. v. Australia,* Comm. No. 560/1993, Geneva: 3 April 1997
Human Rights Committee, *Blazek v. Czech Republic,* Comm. No. 857/1999, Geneva: 12 July 2001
Human Rights Committee, *Winata and Lan Li v. Australia,* Comm. No. 930/2000, Geneva: 26 July 2001

Human Rights Committee, *Jalloh v. The Netherlands,* Comm. No. 794/1998, Geneva: 26 March 2002
Human Rights Committee, *C. v. Australia,* Comm. No. 900/1999, Geneva: 28 October 2002
Human Rights Committee, *Baban et. al. v. Australia,* Comm. No. 1014/2001, Geneva: 6 August 2003
Human Rights Committee, *Bakhtiyari v. Australia,* Comm. No. 1069/2002, Geneva: 29 October 2003
Human Rights Committee, *Derksen v. the Netherlands,* Comm. No. 976/2001,Geneva: 15 June 2004
Human Rights Committee, *Borzov v. Estonia,* Comm. No. 1136/2002, Geneva: 25 August 2004
Human Rights Committee, *El Ghar v. Libyan Arab Jamahiriya,* Comm. No. 1107/2002, Geneva: 2 November 2004
Human Rights Committee, *D and E. v. Australia,* Comm. No. 1050/2002, Geneva: 11 July 2006
Human Rights Committee, *Shams et. al. v. Australia,* Comm Nos. 1255, 1256, 1259, 1260, 1266, 1268, 1270, 1288/2004, Geneva: 20 July 2007
Human Rights Committee, *Zdenek v. Czech Republic,* Comm. No. 1533/2006, Geneva: 31 October 2007
Human Rights Committee, *Gratzinger v. Czech Republic,* Comm. No. 1463/2006, Geneva: 13 November 2007
Human Rights Committee, *Tsjarov v. Estonia,* Comm. No. 1223/2003, Geneva: 14 November 2007

Inter-American Court of Human Rights

Inter-American Court of Human Rights, *Advisory Opinion on the Proposed Amendments to the Naturalisation provision of the Constitution of Costa Rica,* OC-4/84, 19 January 1984
Inter-American Court of Human Rights, *Ivcher Bronstein v. Peru,* Series C, Case 74, 6 February 2001
Inter-American Court of Human Rights, *Advisory Opinion on Juridical Condition and the Rights of Undocumented Migrants,* OC-18/03, 17 September 2003
Inter-American Court on Human Rights, *Yean and Bosico v. Dominican Republic,* Series C, Case 130, 8 September 2005
Inter-American Court on Human Rights, *Case of the Girls Yean and Bosico v. Dominican Republic – Monitoring Compliance with the Judgement,* Order of 28 November 2007

Mexico / USA General Claims Commission

Dickson Car Wheel Co. (USA) v. United Mexican States, UNRIAA, vol. IV, (Sales No. 1951.V.1), July 1931

Permanent Court of International Justice / International Court of Justice

Permanent Court of International Justice, *Tunis and Morocco Nationality Decrees case*, 1923

Permanent Court of International Justice, *Panevezys-Saldutiskis Railway case,* P.C.I.J. Series A/B, No. 76, 28 February 1939

International Court of Justice, *"Nottebohm Case" (Liechtenstein v. Guatamala)*, 1953

US Supreme Court

US Supreme Court, *Trop v. Dulles, Secretary of State et. al.*, 356 US 86, 1958

RESOLUTIONS, DECLARATIONS, CONCLUSIONS AND DECISIONS

AALCO

Asian-African Legal Consultative Organisation, *Resolution on Legal Identity and Statelessness*, 8 April 2006

Council of Europe

Council of Europe, *Recommendation of the Committee of Ministers to Member States on the Avoidance and Reduction of Statelessness,* No. R (1999) 18, Strasbourg, 15 September 1999

Parliamentary Assembly of the Council of Europe, *Resolution 1509 on Human Rights of Irregular Migrants,* Strasbourg, 27 June 2006

CSCE / OSCE

Conference for Security and Cooperation in Europe, *Concluding Document of Helsinki*, 1992

OSCE, *Ottawa Declaration of the OSCE Parliamentary Assembly,* Ottawa, July 1995

Organisation for Security and Cooperation in Europe, *Charter for European Security*, 1999

United Nations

UN Economic and Social Council, *Refugees and stateless persons,* Resolution 319B III (XI), 11 August 1950

UN General Assembly, *Question of the establishment, in accordance with the Convention on the Reduction of Statelessness, of a body to which persons claiming the benefit of the Convention may apply,* A/Res/3274 (XXIX), 10 December 1974

UN General Assembly, *Question of the establishment, in accordance with the Convention on the Reduction of Statelessness, of a body to which persons claiming the benefit of the Convention may apply,* A/Res/31/36, 30 November 1976

UN General Assembly, *Resolution on UN Body of Principles for the Protection of All Persons under Any Form of Detention or Imprisonment*, A/Res/43/173, 9 December 1988

UN General Assembly, *Office of the United Nations High Commissioner for Refugees,* A/Res/49/169, 24 February 1995

UN General Assembly, *Office of the United Nations High Commissioner for Refugees,* A/RES/50/152, 9 February 1996

UN General Assembly, *A world fit for children*, Twenty-Seventh Special Session of the GA, 11 October 2002

UN General Assembly, *Resolution on Nationality of natural persons in relation to the succession of States,* A/RES/59/34, 16 December 2004

UN General Assembly, *Office of the United Nations High Commissioner for Refugees,* A/Res/61/137, 25 January 2007

UNHCR Executive Committee

UNHCR Executive Committee, *Conclusion on Expulsion,* No. 7, Geneva: 1977

UNHCR Executive Committee, *General Conclusion on International Protection,* No. 29, Geneva: 1983

UNHCR Executive Committee, *General Conclusion on International Protection,* No. 50, Geneva: 1988

UNHCR Executive Committee, *General Conclusion on International Protection,* No. 79 Geneva: 1996

UNHCR Executive Committee, *General Conclusion on International Protection,* No. 85, Geneva: 1998

UNHCR Executive Committee, *Conclusion on the Prevention and Reduction of Statelessness and the Protection of Stateless Persons,* No. 78, Geneva: 1995

UNHCR Executive Committee, *General Conclusion on International Protection, No. 90,* 52nd Session, Geneva: 2001

UNHCR Executive Committee, *Conclusion No. 95: General Conclusion on International Protection,* Geneva: 10 October 2003

UNHCR Executive Committee, *Conclusion on Local Integration,* No. 104, Geneva: 2005

UNHCR Executive Committee, *Conclusion No. 106: Conclusion on Identification, Prevention and Reduction of Statelessness and Protection of Stateless Persons,* Geneva: 6 October 2006

UN (Sub-)Commission on Human Rights

UN Human Rights Commission, *Resolution on Human rights and arbitrary deprivation of nationality,* 1997/36, Geneva: 11 April 1997

UN Human Rights Commission, *Resolution on Human rights and arbitrary deprivation of nationality,* 1998/48, Geneva: 17 April 1998

UN Human Rights Commission, *Resolution on Human rights and arbitrary deprivation of nationality,* 1999/28, Geneva: 26 April 1999

UN Sub-Commission on Human Rights, *Resolution on Intellectual Property and Human Rights,* 25th Meeting, Geneva, 17 August 2000

UN Human Rights Commission, *Resolution on Human rights and arbitrary deprivation of nationality,* 2005/45, Geneva: 19 April 2005

UN Treaty body documents

Human Rights Committee

Human Rights Committee, *General Comment No. 8: Right to liberty and security of persons,* Geneva: 30 June 1982

Human Rights Committee, *General Comment No. 15: The Position of Aliens under the Covenant,* Geneva: 11 April 1986

Human Rights Committee, *General Comment 16: The right to respect of privacy, family, home and correspondence, and protection of honour and reputation,* Geneva: 8 April 1988

Human Rights Committee, *General Comment No. 17: Rights of the Child (Art. 24),* Geneva: 7 April 1989

Human Rights Committee, *General Comment 18: Non-discrimination,* Geneva: 10 November 1989

Human Rights Committee, *General Comment No. 19: Protection of the family, the right to marriage and equality of the spouses,* Geneva: 27 July 1990

Human Rights Committee, *General Comment No. 21: Replaces general comment 9 concerning humane treatment of persons deprived of liberty,* Geneva: 10 April 1992

Human Rights Committee, *General Comment 22: The Right to Freedom of Thought, Conscience and Religion,* A/48/40 vol. I, Geneva: 1993
Human Rights Committee, *General Comment No. 23: The Rights of Minorities,* Geneva: 8 April 1994
Human Rights Committee, *General Comment 25: The Right to Participate in Public Affairs, Voting Rights and the Right of Equal Access to Public Service,* A/51/40 vol.1, Geneva: 1996
Human Rights Committee, *General Comment No. 27: Freedom of movement,* Geneva: 2 November 1999
Human Rights Committee, *General Comment 28: Equality of Rights between Men and Women,* CCPR/C/21/Rev.1/Add.10, Geneva: 29 March 2000
Human Rights Committee, *General Comment No. 31: Nature of the General Legal Obligations Imposed on States Parties to the covenant,* CCPR/C/21/Rev.1/Add.13, Geneva: 26 May 2004
Human Rights Committee, *General Comment 32 on Article 14: Right to equality before courts and tribunals and to a fair trial,* CCPR/C/GC/32, Geneva: 23 August 2007 (Replacing *General Comment 13 on Article 14: Equality before the courts and the Right to a Fair and Public Hearing by an Independent Court Established by Law,* A/39/40, 13 April 1984)

Committee on Economic, Social and Cultural Rights

ESC Committee, *General Comment 3: The Nature of States Parties Obligations,* 14 December 1990
ESC Committee, *Revised general guidelines regarding the form and contents of reports to be submitted by state parties under articles 16 and 17 of the International Covenant on Economic, Social and Cultural Rights,* E/C.12/1991/1, 17 June 1991
ESC Committee, *General Comment 4: The right to adequate housing*, 13 December 1991
ESC Committee, *General Comment 7: The right to adequate housing – forced evictions*, 20 May 1997
ESC Committee, *General Comment 11: Plans of action for primary education,* 10 May 1999
ESC Committee, *General Comment 12: The right to adequate food*, 12 May 1999
ESC Committee, *General Comment 13: The right to education,* 8 December 1999
ESC Committee, *General Comment No. 14: The right to the highest attainable standard of health,* 11 August 2000
ESC Committee, *General Comment 15: The right to water*, 20 January 2003
ESC Committee, *General Comment No. 14: The right to the highest attainable standard of health,* 11 August 2000
ESC Committee, *General Comment No. 17: The right of everyone to benefit from the protection of the moral and material interests resulting from any scientific,*

literary or artistic production of which he or she is the author, E/C.12/GC/17, 12 January 2006
ESC Committee, *General Comment No. 18: The Right to Work,* 6 February 2006
ESC Committee, *General Comment No. 19 - The Right to Social Security,* Advanced unedited version, 4 February 2008

Committee on the Elimination of Racial Discrimination

Committee on the Elimination of Racial Discrimination, *CERD General Recommendation XXI: Right to Self-Determination,* New York: 1996
Committee on the Elimination of Racial Discrimination, *General Recommendation 30: Discrimination against Non-Citizens*, New York: 1 October 2004

Committee on the Elimination of Discrimination Against Women

Committee on the Elimination of Discrimination Against Women, *General Recommendation 21: Equality in marriage and family relations*, A/49/38, New York: 1994

Committee on the Rights of the Child

Committee on the Rights of the Child, *General guidelines for periodic reports,* CRC/C/58, Geneva: 20 November 1996
Committee on the Rights of the Child, *General Comment 3: HIV/AIDS and the Rights of the Child,* CRC/GC/2003/3, Geneva: 17 March 2003
Committee on the Rights of the Child, *General Comment 5: General Measures of Implementation of the Convention on the Rights of the Child*, Geneva: 27 November 2003
Committee on the Rights of the Child, *General Comment No. 6: Treatment of unaccompanied and separated children outside their country of origin*, Geneva: 1 September 2005

WEB RESOURCES AND NEWS ITEMS

AVERT, *Aids Orphans,* 2006, accessible via http://www.avert.org/aidsorphans
BBC News, *LA feels migrant day of action,* 2 May 2006, accessible via http://news.bbc.co.uk
Één Vandaag, *IND wil baby uitzetten* [Immigration and Naturalisation Service wants to deport baby], news broadcast, 6 December 2004,

http://www.tweevandaag.nl/index.php?module=PX_Story&func=view&cid=2 &sid=28947

IOM, *Facts and Figures: Global estimates and trends,* accessible via http://www.iom.int

McNeil, D., "Founder of Zambia is declared stateless in high court ruling" *New York Times,* New York: Date 1999

UNHCR, *The Problem of Statelessness has Become a Live Issue Again,* 2001, accessible via http://www.unhcr.org

UNHCR, *Sri Lanka makes citizens out of stateless tea pickers,* 2004, accessible via http://www.unhcr.org

UNHCR, *Crimean Tatars Receive Help from UNHCR to Return Home*, 9 June 2005, accessible via http://www.unhcr.org

UNHCR, *Divorce leaves some Vietnamese women broken-hearted and stateless,* 14 February 2007, accessible via http://www.unhcr.org

UNHCR, *Nepal: large-scale resettlement of refugees from Bhutan,* Briefing Notes, 25 March 2008, accessible via http://www.unhcr.org

INDEX

Terms followed by chapter and section numbers

A
Abandoned children – *see* foundlings
Acquisition of nationality
- adoption, III.1
- fraud, IV.4
- *jus domicilli,*III.1, IV.4, VII.2.1
- *jus sanguinis,*III.1, IV.1, IV.5, VII.1.1, VII.2.1, VIII.1
- *jus soli,* III.1, IV.1, IV.5, VI.3, VII.1.1, VII.2.1, VII.2.2.1, VIII.1, VIII.2
- marriage, III.1, IV.3
- naturalisation, IV.4, V.1.2, VII.2.1, XII.1, XII.4
- option, VI.1, VI.3, VI.4, VIII.2, VIII.3, XII.1

Adequate standard of living, right to, XI.5
Administrative assistance, XII.2.1
Adoption, IV.3
Assembly, freedom of (political), X.7.2
Association, freedom of, XI.3

B
Baltic states – *see* Estonia, Latvia, Lithuania
Bangladesh, II.2, VI.1, XI.5
Banyarwanda – *see* Democratic Republic of Congo
Bhutan, II.2, V.1, X.2.1, X.2.2, X.8
Bidoon – *see* Kuwait
Bihari – *see* Bangladesh
Birth registration, VII.1, VII.2.1.1, VII.2.2.1, VII.3, VIII.1, VIII.2, XII.2
Burma – *see* Myanmar

C
Cautio judicatum solvi, X.4.1, X.4.2
Civil registration – *see* birth and/or marriage registration

Clothing, right to – *see* adequate standard of living
Colombia, IV.1.2
Conflict, statelessness resulting in, II.2, II.3, XIV.4
Core obligations (ICESCR), XI.1, XI.9
Court, right of access to, V.2.2, X.4
Cultural rights, XI.7

D
Decolonisation, VI.1
Definition of statelessness, II.2, II.4, III.3, IX.3, XIV.2
Democratic Republic of Congo, II.2
Deportation – *see* expulsion
Deprivation of nationality – *see* loss of nationality
(arbitrary) Detention, II.2, X.2.1, X.7.1, X.8
Developing countries, economic rights for non-nationals in, XI.1, XI.9
Diplomatic protection, IX.1, XII.3, XII.4
Discrimination
- between citizens and non-citizens
  - general, IX.2, XIII.2
  - civil and political rights, X.1
  - economic, social and cultural rights, XI.1, XI.9
- in access to citizenship, IV.1, IV.5, V.1, V.3, VI.3, VI.4, VIII.1, VIII.2, VIII.3
- in immigration policy, X.2.2.2

Displacement, statelessness resulting in, II.2, II.3
Divorce – *see* marriage, effect on nationality
Dominican Republic, IV.1, V.1, V.3, VII.1.1, VII.1.2, VII.2.1.2, VIII.1, VIII.4, XIII.4
Dual, or multiple, nationality, III.1, III.2, IV.1, VI.1, VI.3, VI.4
Due process in the context of nationality attribution – *see* procedural guarantees

E
Education, right to, XI.6
Effective remedy, right to, V.2.2, VI.3, X.4
Enter, right to, IX.1, X.2.2, X.8, XIII.1, XIII.2, XIII.3
Estonia, II.2, VI.1, X.7.4, XII.1
Expression, freedom of, X.5, X.7.2
Expulsion – *see also* right to enter *and non-refoulement*, X.2.2

F
Facilitated access to nationality – *see also* naturalisation, VI.3
Family life, right to, X.2.2.2, X.7
Foundlings, IV.2, IV.5, VIII.1, VIII.2

Food, right to – *see* adequate standard of living
Former Socialist Federal Republic of Yugoslavia, II.3
Former USSR, II.3, VI.1
Formerly Displaced Persons (Crimea) – *see* Ukraine
Fraudulently acquired nationality, IV.4

G
Genuine link, III.1, IV.1, IV.3, IX.1

H
Health, right to, XI.8
Housing, right to – *see* adequate standard of living

I
Identification of statelessness, II.2, II.4, III.3, VI.2, VII.3, VIII.1, VIII.4, IX.3, XIII.4, XIV.2, XIV.3
Identity documents, XII.2, XII.4, XIII.1
Intellectual property, right to, XI.7
International cooperation, duty in the context of nationality disputes, VI.3, VI.4, XIV.3
Ireland, IV.1

K
Kazakhstan, II.2
Kenya, II.2
Korea, IV.1, IV.1.2
Kurds – *see* Syrian Arab Republic
Kuwait, II.2, X.2.2, XI.2, XI.3

L
Labour-related rights, XI.2
Latvia, II.2, VI.1, VI.3, X.7.4, XII.1
Levels of attachment, 1954 Statelessness Convention and, IX.3, XIII.1, XIV.1, Annex 3
- durable residence, IX.3
- lawful presence, X.2.1.1, X.2.2.1, XI.3.1
- lawful stay, X.4.1, XI.2.1, XI.3.1, XI.4.1, XI.5.1, XI.7.1, XII.2.1
- physical presence, X.5.1, XI.5.1
- subject to jurisdiction, X.4.1, X.6.1, X.6.1, XII.1.1

Lhotshampa – *see* Bhutan
Life, right to – *see also non-refoulement*, X.7
Lithuania, VI.1, VI.3
Loss or deprivation of nationality, III.1, IV.4, VII.2.1.1, VIII.2, VIII.3

M
Marriage
- children born out of wedlock, IV.1, VIII.1, VIII.2
- effect on nationality, III.1, IV.3, VIII.2, VIII.4
- registration, VII.1, XII.2

Mauritania, X.2.2
Migration, leading to increased risk of statelessness, III.1, IV.3, IV.4, VI.1, VII.2, VII.3, VIII.3
Minority rights, X.7.4
Morocco, XII.1
Movement, freedom of
- internal, X.2.1
- international – *see* right to enter

Myanmar, II.2, V.1, V.3, VII.2.1.1, X.2.1, X.5

N
Nationality of the claim – *see* diplomatic protection
National treatment – *see* standards of protection
Naturalisation
- and denial of citizenship, V.1.2
- facilitated, VI.3, XII.1, XII.4, XIII.3
- unreasonable impediments, V.1.2, XII.1.2, XIII.2

Nepal, II.2, X.2.2, X.8
Netherlands, II.1, II.2, IV.1, X.2.2, X.4
Non-refoulement, VII.2.1, X.2.2.1, X.2.2.2, X.8

O
Opinion, freedom of
Option, right of, VI.1, VI.3, VI.4, VIII.2, VIII.3, XII.1
Orphans, IV.2
Own country, X.2.2, X.8, XIII.2, XIII.3, XIV.1

P
Passports – *see* travel documents
Person, right to recognition as, X.3
Political rights, IX.1, X.7.3, X.8, XIII.2, XIII.3
Private life, right to, X.2.2.2, X.7
Procedural guarantees in the context of nationality attribution, V.2, V.3, VI.3, VI.4, VIII.2
Property, right to, X.6
Public assistance, relief – *see* social security

R
Rationing, XI.5.1
Reciprocity, IX.3, XI.4
Reduction of statelessness, XII.1, XII.4, XIII.1, XIII.2, XIV.2
Refugees, exposure to statelessness of, IV.4, VII.2.2, VIII.2, VIII.3
Religion, freedom of, X.5
Renunciation of nationality, III.1, IV.4
Resettlement, XII.1.1
Reside, right to – *see* right to enter
'Right to have rights', IX.1, XIV.1
Rohingya – *see* Myanmar
Russian Federation, II.2, VI.1, VI.3, XI.4, XIII.4

S
Self-determination, relevance in nationality attribution, III.1
Slavery, prohibition of, X.7
Social security, right to, XI.4
Solution, 1954 Statelessness Convention and right of, XII.1.1
Sri Lanka, VI.1, XII.1
Standards of protection or treatment, 1954 Statelessness Convention and, IX.3, XIII.1, XIV.1, Annex 3
- absolute rights, X.3.1, X.4.1, XII.1.1, XII.2.1
- assimilation to non-nationals, X.2.1.1, X.6.1, XI.2.1, XI.3.1, XI.5.1
- national treatment, X.4.1, X.5.1, XI.4.1, XI.5.1, XI.6.1, XI.7.1

Status determination
- Refugee Status Determination (RSD), XIII.4, XIV.3
- Stateless Person Status Determination (SPSD) – *see also* identification of statelessness, IX.3, XIII.4, XIV.3

Syrian Arab Republic, II.2, IV.1.2, V.1, V.3, X.6, X.7.2, XII.1

T
Tamils, Estate – *see* Sri Lanka
Thailand, VII.2.1.1, X.2.1, X.7.4, XI.4
Torture, freedom from – *see also non-refoulement*, X.7
Trafficking in persons
- as a cause of statelessness, VII.2.2, VIII.2, VIII.3
- vulnerability of stateless persons to, II.2

Travel documents
- statelessness and opportunities for obtaining, II.2, XII.2, XII.4
- freedom of movement, and, X.2.2, XII.2
- 1951 Refugee Convention Travel Document, XII.2.1
- 1954 Statelessness Convention Travel Document, XII.2.1, XII.4, XIII.1

Trial, right to a (fair), V.2.2, X.4

U
Ukraine, II.2, VI.1, VI.3
United Kingdom, IV.1, VI.1

V
Vietnam, IV.3
Vote, right to – *see* political rights

W
Water, right to – *see* adequate standard of living
Work , right to, XI.2

Z
Zimbabwe, II.2, IV.1.2

Curriculum Vitae

Laura van Waas (1981) studied International and European Law at Tilburg University, where she obtained her Masters degree (*cum laude*) in 2004. From 2004 to 2008, she was employed as PhD researcher at the Department of European and International Public Law of Tilburg University. In 2006, she was also engaged as a consultant for Plan International to look into the link between irregular migration, birth registration and statelessness, including through conducting field work in Thailand and the Dominican Republic. In 2007, she worked as a consultant for the United Nations High Commissioner for Refugees in Geneva, for whom she developed a thematic learning programme on statelessness. In addition, since 2004, she has devoted much of her spare time to establishing and managing Books 4 Life, a shop that raises money for charity through the sale of second-hand books.

School of Human Rights Research Series

The School of Human Rights Research is a joint effort by human rights researchers in the Netherlands. Its central research theme is the nature and meaning of international standards in the field of human rights, their application and promotion in the national legal order, their interplay with national standards and the international supervision of such application. The School of Human Rights Research Series only includes English titles that contribute to a better understanding of the different aspects of human rights

Published titles within the Series:

1 Brigit C.A. Toebes, *The Right to Health as a Human Rights in International Law*
ISBN 90-5095-057-4

2 Ineke Boerefijn, *The Reporting Procedures under the Covenant on Civil and Political Rights. Practice and Procedures of the Human Rights Committee*
ISBN 90-5095-074-4

3 Kitty Arambulo, *Strengthening the Supervision of the International Covenant on Economic, Social and Cultural Rights. Theoretical and Procedural Aspects*
ISBN 90-5095-058-2

4 Marlies Glasius, *Foreign Policy on Human Rights. Its Influence on Indonesia under Soeharto*
ISBN 90-5095-089-2

5 Cornelius D. de Jong, *The Freedom of Thought, Conscience and Religion or Belief in the United Nations (1946-1992)*
ISBN 90-5095-137-6

6 Heleen Bosma, *Freedom of Expression in England and under the ECHR: in Search of a Common Ground. A Foundation for the Application of the Human Rights Act 1998 in English Law*
ISBN 90-5095-136-8

7 Mielle Bulterman, *Human Rights in the External Relations of the European Union*
ISBN 90-5095-164-3

8 Esther M. van den Berg, *The Influence of Domestic NGOs on Dutch Human Rights Policy. Case Studies on South Africa, Namibia, Indonesia and East Timor*
ISBN 90-5095-159-7

9 Ian Seiderman, *Hierarchy in International Law: the Human Rights Dimension*
ISBN 90-5095-165-1

10 Anna Meijknecht, *Towards International Personality: the Position of Minorities and Indigenous Peoples in International Law*
ISBN 90-5095-166-X

11 Mohamed Eltayeb, *A Human Rights Approach to Combating Religious Persecution. Cases from Pakistan, Saudi Arabia and Sudan*
ISBN 90-5095-170-8

12 Machteld Boot, *Genocide, Crimes Against Humanity, War Crimes: Nullum Crimen Sine Lege and the Subject Matter Jurisdiction of the International Criminal Court*
ISBN 90-5095-216-X

13 Corinne Packer, *Using Human Rights to Change Tradition. Traditional Practices Harmful to Women's Reproductive Health in sub-Saharan Africa*
ISBN 90-5095-226-7

14 Theo R.G. van Banning, *The Human Rights to Property*
ISBN 90-5095-203-8

15 Yvonne M. Donders, *Towards a Right to Cultural Identity?*

ISBN 90-5095-238-0

16 Göran K. Sluiter, *International Criminal Adjudication and the Collection of Evidence: Obligations of States*
ISBN 90-5095-227-5

17 Nicola Jägers, *Corporate Human Rights Obligations: in Search of Accountability*
ISBN 90-5095-240-2

18 Magdalena Sepúlveda, *The Nature of the Obligations under the International Covenant on Economic, Social and Cultural Rights*
ISBN 90-5095-260-7

19 Mitsue Inazumi, *Universal Jurisdiction in Modern International Law: Expansion of National Jurisdiction for Prosecuting Serious Crimes under International Law*
ISBN 90-5095-336-2

20 Anne-Marie L.M. de Brouwer, *Supranational Criminal Prosecution of Sexual Violence: The ICC and the Practice of the ICTY and the ICTR*
ISBN 90-5095-533-9

21 Jeroen Gutter, *Thematic Procedures of the United Nations Commission on Human Rights and International Law: in Search of a Sense of Community*
ISBN 90-5095-557-6

22 Hilde Reiding, *The Netherlands and the Development of International Human Rights Instruments*
ISBN 978-90-5095-654-3

23 Ingrid Westendorp, *Women and Housing: Gender Makes a Difference*
ISBN 978-90-5095-669-7

24 Quirine A.M. Eijkman, *We Are Here to Serve You! Public Security, Police Reform and Human Rights Implementation in Costa Rica*
ISBN 978-90-5095-704-5

25 Antoine Ch. Buyse, *Post-conflict Housing Restitution. The European Human Rights Perspective with a case study on Bosnia and Herzegovina*
ISBN 978-90-5095-770-0

26 Gentian Zyberi, *The Humanitarian Face of the International Court of Justice: Its Contribution to Interpreting and Developing International Human Rights and Humanitarian Law Rules and Principles*
ISBN 978-90-5095-792-2

27 Dragos Cucereanu, *Aspects of Regulating Freedom of Expression on the Internet*
ISBN 978-90-5095-842-4

28 Ton Liefaard, *Deprivation of Liberty of Children in Light of International Human Rights Law and Standards*
ISBN 978-90-5095-838-7

www.ingramcontent.com/pod-product-compliance
Ingram Content Group UK Ltd.
Pitfield, Milton Keynes, MK11 3LW, UK
UKHW051918100926
8556IPUK00021B/1244

9 789050 958547